D1548377

alive

alive
[ə'laɪv] *adj*
vivo, a

* *No! I know Chang is alive!* ¡No! Sé que Tchang está vivo! *Alive??...* ¿¿Vivo??... *

1
2
5
3

all

all
[ɔːl]
I. *adj & pron*

4

...all

todo, toda, todos, todas

is this for all of us? ¿es ésto para todos nosotros?

9
11

all the problems will be solved todos los problemas serán solucionados

* *They've been walking all day...* Han estado caminando todo el día... *

10

---

pegar

pegar, pegarse
[pe'ɣar, se]
I. *v t*
1. to stick, to glue

pegó el sello en el sobre he stuck the stamp on the envelope

2. to hit, to strike

II. *v pr*
to hit each other, to fight

*¡*Ya te tengo!...* ¡*Toma!...* ¡*Vas a*

1
2
6
4

Se pegan en la calle.

ver!... I've got you!... Take that!... You wait!...
Se pegan en la calle. They are fighting in the street. *

peinar

peinar, peinarse
[peĭ'nar, se]
I. *v t*
to comb/do someone's hair

...peinar

Carmen es la que me peina Carmen is the one who does my hair

9
11

II. *v pr*
to comb/do one's hair

me voy a peinar I'm going to comb my hair

10
8

▶ **peine**
['peĭne] *n m*
comb

3
5

III. Idiom

7

Merry Christmas Adam, 1994!
Hablar español ahora!
love Mom and Dad!
XXX OOO

Merry Christmas Adam, 1994!

TINTIN
ILLUSTRATED DICTIONARY
TINTÍN
EN EL PAÍS DE LAS PALABRAS

English-Spanish / Spanish-English
Inglés-Español / Español-Inglés

Brian MOTT • Rosanna RION
Based on an idea by / Basado sobre une idea de
BOOKMAKER

Cartoons by / Imágenes de
HERGÉ
Chosen by / Seleccionadas por
Patrick MICHEL-DANSAC

HARRAP

in co-operation with / en cooperación con
METHUEN CHILDREN'S BOOKS

PLANNED AND PRODUCED / CONCEBIDO Y REALIZADO POR
BOOKMAKER

EDITORIAL DIRECTION / DIRECCIÓN EDITORIAL
Marie Garagnoux • Patrick Michel-Dansac

WITH / ASISTIDOS DE
Régine Ferrandis • Hélène Tilliette

COMPILED BY / REDACTADO POR
Brian Mott, Profesor de la Universidad de Barcelona
Rosanna Rión
David Jones • Francisca Sol, Teacher of Spanish

ILLUSTRATIONS CHOSEN BY / ILUSTRACIONES SELECCIONADAS POR
Patrick Michel-Dansac

LETTERING / LETREROS DE
Anne Delobel

LAYOUT / MAQUETA
Design /Concepción :
Claire Forgeot • DOS CARRÉ
Produced by / Realización :
Michèle Andrault • Monique Michel-Dansac

PRODUCTION / FABRICACIÓN
Véronique Celton

DTP / REALIZACIÓN CON PROGRAMA ASISTIDO POR ORDENADOR
LES PETITS PAPIERS

OTHERS CONTRIBUTORS / OTROS COLABORADORES
Christine Bull • Franco Caprino

© HARRAP BOOKS LTD, 1991
ART COPYRIGHT HERGÉ, exclusivity CASTERMAN

First published by
HARRAP BOOKS Ltd, 43-45 Annandale Street, Edinburgh EH7 4AZ

«The adventures of Tintin» are published in Spanish by   «Las Aventuras de Tintín» son publicadas en espagnol por
EDITORIAL JUVENTUD

ISBN 0-245-60361-1 (English edition)
ISBN 0-245-50130-4 (Spanish edition)

ADVERTENCIA

TINTÍN EN EL PAÍS DE LAS PALABRAS se consulta como un diccionario bilingüe tradicional en donde figura un vocabulario de base. Las palabras han sido seleccionadas a partir de listas de vocabulario establecidas para los cuatro primeros años de enseñanza secundaria.

Hemos escogido los sentidos y las traducciones más corrientes, presentados según la frecuencia de su empleo. Los ejemplos muestran las utilizaciones típicas de la palabra.

Cuando es necesario, los diferentes sentidos están seguidos de las principales expresiones idiomáticas en las cuales aparece la palabra.

A veces, según hemos estimado conveniente, hemos añadido expresiones idiomáticas que completan los diferentes sentidos del vocablo. Cada vez que ha sido possible hemos illustrado estos ejemplos con viñetas extraídas de los albúmes de Tintín. El texto de los globos ha sido escrito a partir de los ejemplos imaginados por los autores. Así pues el idioma aparece de una manera viva y muchas veces divertida pero con la exactitud gramatical y lexicográfica necesarias.

Consultar este diccionario es pues un medio eficaz y divertido de enriquecer el conocimiento del idioma.

Hemos intentado respetar el mundo de Hergé y conservar a todos los personajes con sus característis-

FOREWORD

TINTIN ILLUSTRATED DICTIONARY works like a traditional bilingual dictionary. It contains the basic vocabulary of English and Spanish, covering most of the words that learners are likely to come across in the first few years of studying a foreign language.

The meanings treated and the translations given are the most common ones ; they are given in order of frequency of occurrence. Examples show how the words are used in context. The different meanings are followed, if necessary, by the most important idiomatic expressions in which the headword is found.

Wherever possible, we have illustrated our examples with drawings from Hergé's Adventures of Tintin. The text of the speech bubbles has been modified to adapt the drawings to the examples chosen by the authors. In this way, language is put into context in a striking and lively fashion, sometimes with very amusing results. Consulting this dictionary is a way to learn while having fun.

We have made every effort to remain faithful to Hergé's world, by keeping the personalities and mannerisms of his characters. Tintin fans will recognize their heroes, and for others, who have

ticas y sus "manias". Los aficionados de Tintín reconocerán a todos les héroes y para los que los hubieran olvidado o no los conocieran muy bien, este diccionario será la ocasión de descubrirlos de nuevo.

En esta parte presentamos el castellano. Cuando una palabra es diferente del castellano hablado en América Latina, indicamos la abreviatura *Am*.

Cada palabra es el objeto de un artículo delimitado por un rectángulo gris horizontal en donde se registra la palabra de entrada y por un rectángulo gris vertical ajustado a la izquierda sobre el texto. Cuando el artículo tiene más de una columna, el rectángulo gris horizontal reaparece y la palabra de entrada se repite, precedida por puntos suspensivos. En cuanto a la estructura de los artículos, véanse los ejemplos presentados en las páginas de guarda (y también las páginas de los cuadros de signos fonéticos y abreviaturas utilizados en este diccionario). Los plurales irregulares ingleses están presentados así como los comparativos y superlativos ingleses y españoles.

Este diccionario comporta dos partes : inglés-español y español-inglés. Estas dos partes están separadas, en la mitad del libro, por un apéndice gramatical en donde figuran las reglas de base del español, los verbos irregulares españoles así como un cuadro de conjugación de los verbos ingleses y un cuadro de los números. La gramática inglesa se encuentra al final del diccionario.

forgotten them or who never knew them well, this dictionary will be the opportunity to rediscover them.

The dictionary takes British English as its base. When a word or its spelling is different in American English, this is indicated by the abbreviation *Am*.

Each entry is marked off by a horizontal grey rectangle containing the headword and a vertical grey rectangle to the left of the text. When an entry is more than one column long, the horizontal rectangle is repeated and the headword preceded by suspension points. The structure of the entries is presented in diagram form on the endpapers (together with pronunciation tables and a list of abbreviations used in the dictionary).

Irregular Spanish and English plurals are shown as well as irregular English verb forms, comparatives and superlatives.

The dictionary is in two parts: English-Spanish and Spanish-English. These two parts are separated by an appendix giving the basic grammatical rules of Spanish, plus a list of English irregular verbs, a Spanish verb conjugation table and a numbers table. The English grammar section can be found at the end of the dictionary.

Hergé's style of lettering has been followed in the illustrations. Below is a table of the capital letters, to help our English-speaking users who might be unaccustomed to this style of handwriting.

•A 𝒜	•B ℬ	•C 𝒞	•D 𝒟	•E ℰ	•F ℱ
•G 𝒢	•H ℋ	•I 𝒥	•J 𝒥	•K 𝒦	•L ℒ
•M ℳ	•N 𝒩	•O 𝒪	•P 𝒫	•Q 𝒬	•R ℛ
•S 𝒮	•T 𝒯	•U 𝒰	•V 𝒱	•W 𝒲	•X 𝒳
•Y 𝒴	•Z 𝒵				

a

a
[ə] *art*
an
[æn] *delante de vocal*
1. un, una

he is a spy es un espía

2. el, la

3. por
eighty kilometres an hour ochenta kilómetros por hora

able

able
['eɪbl] *adj*
Idiom
to be able to poder, ser capaz de, saber hacer

* Don't be sad, Mrs Wang; we'll be able to cure him... I promise you!... He'll soon be better!... No esté triste, señora Wang; podremos curarlo... ¡Se lo prometo!... ¡Pronto estará mejor! *

about

about
[ə'baut]
I. *adv*
1. alrededor de, hacia

I finish at about three termino hacia las tres

2. por ahí
he was wandering about, lost in the big city estaba caminando por ahí, perdido en la gran ciudad

3. Idiom
to be about to do something estar a punto de hacer algo

* Rrrring Rrrring Captain! That's funny! I was about to call you! ¡Capitán! ¡Es curioso!, ¡estaba a punto de llamarle! *

II. *prep*
1. acerca de, sobre

it was a film about animals era una película

...about

sobre animales

2. Idiom
what about going to the cinema? ¿qué te parece si vamos al cine?

and what about him? ¿y qué hay de él?

above

above
[ə'bʌv] *prep*
1. encima de

...above

* They are flying above the clouds. Están volando por encima de las nubes. *

2. Idiom
above all sobre todo

abroad

abroad
[ə'brɔːd] *adv*
al/por el/en el extranjero

he is travelling abroad está viajando por el extranjero

absent

absent
['æbsənt] *adj*
ausente

...absent

I'd like to speak to the director.

The director is absent, Sir!

* *I'd like to speak to the director.* Quisiera hablar con el director.
The director is absent, Sir! ¡El director está ausente, señor! *****

accelerate

accelerate
[æk'seleɪt] *v i*
acelerar

* *Accelerate, or we'll never catch*

...accelerate

Accelerate, or we'll never catch them up!

them up! ¡Acelera, o nunca los cogeremos! *****

accent

accent
['æksənt] *n*
1. acento *m*

he speaks with a german accent habla con acento alemán

2. acento *m*

...accent

English words don't have accents las palabras inglesas no llevan acento

accept

accept
[ək'sept] *v t*
aceptar

he accepted the agreement aceptó el pacto

accident

accident
['æksɪdənt] *n*
accidente *m*

he had an accident and broke his leg tuvo un accidente y se rompió una pierna

according to

according to
[ə'kɔːdɪŋ tu] *prep*
según

...according to

Meanwhile...

According to the pendulum, it's this way...

* *Meanwhile...* Mientras tanto...
According to the pendulum, it's this way... Según el péndulo, es por aquí... *****

across

across
[ə'krɒs] *adv*
1. a través de

we made our way

...across

across the thicket nos hicimos camino a través de la maleza

2. al otro lado de
my love is across the sea mi amor está al otro lado del mar

3. Idiom
to go across atravesar

we have to go across the desert tenemos que atravesar el desierto

act

act
[ækt]
I. *n*
acto *m*

II. *v i*
1. actuar

* *We'll have to act fast!* ¡Tendremos que actuar rápido! *****

2. actuar
Marilyn Monroe is acting in the film Marilyn Monroe actúa en la película

We'll have to act fast!

▶ **actor**
['æktə'] *n*
actor *m*

▶ **actress**
['æktrɪs] *n*
actriz *f*

she is my favourite actress ella es mi actriz preferida

actual

actual
['æktjuəl] *adj*
verdadero, a, real

he said his name was James, but his actual name was John dijo que su nombre era James, pero su verdadero nombre era John

▶ **actually**
['æktjuəlɪ] *adv*
de hecho

...actual

did you want to see me? yes, actually I was waiting for you ¿querías verme? sí, de hecho te estaba esperando

add

add
[æd] v t
añadir

...add

add the secret document to your papers añade el documento secreto en tus papeles

▶ **add up**
sumar

I'm trying to add up all these figures intento sumar todas estas cifras

address

address
[ə'dres] n
dirección f

he gave me a false address me dio una dirección falsa

admire

admire
[əd'maɪəʳ] v t
admirar

...admire

Oh, Snowy, I admire your courage... But for you, that lion would have eaten me...

You know, that lion wasn't as nasty as he looked.

* Oh, Snowy, I admire your courage... But for you, that lion would have eaten me... Oh, Milú, admiro tu coraje... Si no hubiera sido por tí, ese león me habría comido... *You know, that lion wasn't as nasty as he looked.* Sabes, ese león no era tan peligroso como parecía. *

admit

admit
[əd'mɪt] vt
1. admitir, reconocer

you must admit you lied debes reconocer que mentiste

2. admitir
he was admitted into the club fue admitido en el club

adventure

adventure
[əd'ventʃəʳ] n
aventura f

Billions of blue blistering barnacles!... I've had enough of these adventures...

* Billions of blue blistering barnacles!... I've had enough of these adventures... ¡Mil millones de demonios! Ya he tenido suficiente de estas aventuras... *

advertise

advertise
['ædvətaɪz]
I. v t
anunciar

his new film is advertised in all the newspapers su nueva película está anunciada en todos los periódicos

II. v i
hacer publicidad

▶ **advertisement**
[əd'vɜːtɪsmənt] n

anuncio m

* Read the advertisement they've put in the newspaper! ¡Lee el anuncio que han puesto en el periódico! *

▶ **advertising**
['ædvətaɪzɪŋ] n
publicidad f,
propaganda f

...advertise

Read the advertisement they've put in the newspaper!

advice

advice
[əd'vaɪs] n
consejo m

* Take my advice and leave! ¡Siga mi consejo y márchese! *

aeroplane

aeroplane
['eərəpleɪn] n
(Am: **airplane**)
avión m

Take my advice and leave!

afford

afford
[ə'fɔːd] v t
poder permitirse

if we can afford it, we'll buy a new house si podemos permitírnoslo, compraremos una casa nueva

afraid

afraid
[ə'freɪd] *adj*

Idiom
to be afraid of
tener miedo de

ghosts don't exist, don't be afraid! ¡los fantasmas no existen, no tengas miedo!

* Later at the Bristol... Más tarde en el Bristol...

I'm afraid we have no rooms, Sir. Lo siento pero no tenemos habitaciones, señor. *

after

after
['ɑːftər] *prep*
1. tras, después de

after having read Bianca's letter, he was in a very bad

...after

mood después de haber leído la carta de Bianca, estaba de muy mal humor

2. Idiom
after all después de todo

to be after perseguir

I don't know what he's after, but it's nothing good no sé lo que persigue, pero no es nada bueno

the day after tomorrow pasado mañana

▶ **afternoon**
[ɑːftə'nuːn] *n*
tarde *f*

I study in the afternoon estudio por la tarde

▶ **afterwards**
['ɑːftəwədz] *adv*
después

what shall we do afterwards? ¿que haremos después?

again

again
[ə'geɪn] *adv*
1. otra vez, de nuevo

oh, he did it again! ¡oh, lo hizo de nuevo!

2. Idiom
he said it again and again lo dijo una y otra vez

against

against
[ə'geɪnst] *prep*
1. contra

* Hurry up! ¡Dese prisa! *The ladder's against the wall...* La escalera está contra la pared... *

all the evidence is against him todas las pruebas están contra él

2. Idiom
it's against the law va contra la ley

it's against the rules va contra las normas

age

age
[eɪdʒ] *n*
1. edad *f*

at what age can you learn to drive? ¿a qué edad puedes aprender a conducir?

...age

2. Idiom
it's ages since I saw him last hace muchísimo tiempo desde la última vez que lo vi

ago

ago
[ə'gəu] *adv*
1. hace

Calculus left Marlin-

...ago

spike three weeks ago Tornasol se marchó de Moulinsart hace tres semanas

2. Idiom
long ago hace mucho tiempo

agree

agree
[ə'griː] *v i*
estar de acuerdo

...agree

I agree with you estoy de acuerdo contigo

▶ **agreement**
[ə'griːmənt] *n*
acuerdo *m*

* I'm sure we can come to an agreement, dear Mr Tintin! ¡Estoy seguro de que podemos llegar a un acuerdo, querido señor Tintín! *

ahead

ahead
[ə'hed] *adv*
delante

he ran on ahead corrió hacia delante

air

air
[eər] *n*
aire *m*

...air

* Quick, some air, I'm stifling! ¡Rápido, un poco de aire, me ahogo! *

▶ **airport**
['eəpɔːt] *n*
aeropuerto *m*

▶ **airplane** (Am)
→ AEROPLANE

...air

Quick, some air, I'm stifling!

alive

alive
[ə'laɪv] adj
vivo, a

* **No! I know Chang is alive!** ¡No! Sé que Tchang está vivo! **Alive??...** ¿¿Vivo??... *

all

all
[ɔːl]
I. adj & pron

No! I know CHANG IS ALIVE!

Alive ??...

...all

todo, toda, todos todas

is this for all of us? ¿es ésto para todos nosotros?

all the problems will be solved todos los problemas serán solucionados

* **They've been walking all day...** Han estado caminando todo el día... *

...all

They've been walking all day...

II. adv
1. todo, del todo, completamente

I know all about it lo sé todo al respecto

2. Idiom
all the better tanto mejor

all of a sudden de repente

not at all en absoluto

allow

allow
[ə'lau] v t
permitir

she's not allowed to speak a ella no se le permite hablar

allow me to introduce myself permítame que me presente

all right

all right
[ɔːl'raɪt]
I. adj
bien

I'm all right, don't worry estoy bien, no te preocupes

II. adv
de acuerdo

* **Do you mind if I have a quick look?** ¿Me permite echar una mirada?

...all right

All right... De acuerdo... *

almost

almost
['ɔːlməust] adv
casi

it's almost finished está casi terminado

Do you mind if I have a quick look?

All right...

alone

alone
[ə'ləun] adj
solo, a

* **Don't go alone, Captain, I'm coming with you...** No vaya solo, capitán, voy con usted... *

Don't go alone, Captain, I'm coming with you...

along

along
[ə'lɒŋ]
I. prep
a lo largo de

they have planted trees all along the avenue where I live han plantado árboles a todo lo largo de la avenida donde vivo

* **He's walking along the**

...along

river. Camina a lo largo del río. *

II. *adv*
Idiom
take me along with you llévame contigo

come along! ¡ven!

I'll be along in a few minutes estaré aquí en unos minutos

he's getting along fine le va bien

He's walking along the river...

aloud

aloud
[ə'laud] *adv*
en voz alta

to read aloud leer en voz alta

alphabet

alphabet
['ælfəbet] *n*
alfabeto *m*

already

already
[ɔːl'redɪ] *adv*
ya

the policemen are already there los policías ya están allí

also

also
['ɔːlsəu] *adv*
también

...also

I'm going to bed: I'm very tired and it's also very late voy a dormir: estoy muy cansado y también es muy tarde

although

although, though
[ɔːl'ðəu] *conj*
aunque

...although

although he's tired, he can't sleep aunque está cansado, no puede dormir

always

always
[ɔːl'weɪz] *adv*
siempre

* *Why do you always repeat what I say?* ¿Por qué siempre repites lo que digo? *

...always

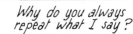

ambulance

ambulance
['æmbjuləns] *n*
ambulancia *f*

America

America
[ə'merɪkə] *n*
América *f*

► **American**
[ə'merɪk(ə)n]
I. *n*

...America

americano *m*, americana *f*

II. *adj*
americano, a

among

among
[ə'mʌŋ] *prep*
entre

there are flowers among the bushes hay flores entre las matas

and

and
[ænd]
I. *conj*
y

Snowy and Tintin are looking for Chang Milú y Tintín están buscando a Tchang

II. Idiom
one hundred and five ciento cinco

three thousand and twenty tres mil veinte

angry

angry
['æŋgrɪ] *adj*
angrier, angriest
enfadado, a

Calculus is very angry with Haddock Tornasol está muy enfadado con Haddock

animal

animal
['ænɪməl] *n*

...animal

animal *m*

* *Hurray!* ¡Hurra! *Llamas are very touchy animals...* Las llamas son unos animales muy susceptibles... *

ankle

ankle
['æŋk(ə)l] *n*
tobillo *m*

Llamas are very touchy animals...

announce

announce
[ə'naʊns] *v t*
anunciar

hurry up, our flight has been announced dese prisa, nuestro vuelo ha sido anunciado

another

another
[ə'nʌðəʳ] *adj & pron*
otro, otra, otro más,

...another

otra más

* *Would you like another cup of tea?* ¿Quieren otra taza de té? *

* *Several hours later...* Unas horas después...
Another one, that makes the seventh pair of tracks... Otro más, éste hace el séptimo par de huellas... *

answer

answer
['ɒːnsəʳ]
I. *v i*
responder, contestar

* *What about the skeleton, Wolff, was that you?* ¿Qué hay del esqueleto, Wolff, era usted?
Yes, skeleton, were you the Wolff? Come on, answer! Sí, esqueleto, era usted Wolff? ¡Vamos, conteste! *

...answer

II. *v t*
responder a

he answered my question él respondió a mi pregunta

III. *n*
respuesta *f*

he didn't know the answer no sabía la respuesta

any

any
['enɪ]
I. *adj*
1. cualquier, cualquiera, todo, toda

any excuse will do cualquier excusa servirá

2. alguno, a ninguno, a
is there any problem? no, there isn't any problem ¿hay algún problema? no, no hay ningún problema

3. *no traducible*
* *Great Snakes! I haven't got any money!* ¡Caramba! ¡No tengo dinero! *

II. *pron*
alguno, a ninguno, a

if there's any of you who want to go, just say it si hay alguno de vosotros que quiera ir, que lo diga

...any

III. *adv*
Idiom
are you feeling any better? ¿te encuentras algo mejor?

* *Accelerate or they'll catch up with us!* ¡Acelere o nos alcanzaran!
Impossible! This car can't go any faster! ¡Imposible! ¡Este coche no puede ir más rápido! *

▶ **anybody, anyone**
['enɪbɒdɪ], ['enɪwʌn] *pron*
1. cualquiera, alguno, nadie *(en frases negativas)*

anyone would know that cualquiera lo sabría

2. alguien
did you tell anybody ¿se lo dijiste a alguien?

3. nadie
don't give it to anybody no se lo des a nadie

▶ **anything**
['enɪθɪŋ] *pron*
1. algo

is there anything to eat? ¿hay algo de comer?

2. nada
I can't do anything for you no puedo hacer nada por tí

3. cualquier cosa
anything you say can be held against you cualquier cosa que diga puede ser usada en su contra

▶ **anyway**
['enɪweɪ] *adv*
de cualquier modo, como fuese

anyway, he wouldn't believe me de cualquier modo, no me creería

...any

▶ **anywhere**
['enɪweəʳ] adv
1. algún sitio

* *Is there anywhere we can talk in private?* ¿Hay algún sitio donde podamos hablar en privado? *Certainly, over there, we won't be disturbed...* Ciertamente, por allí, no nos molestarán... *

2. ningún sitio

we don't have anywhere to go no tenemos ningún sitio a donde ir

3. cualquier sitio
he can be hidden anywhere puede estar escondido en cualquier sitio

apart

apart
[ə'pɑːt] adv
aparte, separado

they were pulled apart because they were fighting fueron separados porque estaban peleándose

▶ **apart from**
aparte de

apart from that, everything is alright aparte de esto, todo está bien

appear

appear
[ə'pɪəʳ] v i
1. aparecer

the ghost appeared and disappeared el fantasma apareció y desapareció

2. parecer
* *Tuesday* Martes
He appears to be busy. Parece estar ocupado. *

...appear

apple

apple
['æp(ə)l] n
manzana f

* *That's a big apple!...* ¡Ésta sí que es una manzana grande!... *

appointment

appointment
[ə'pɔɪntmənt] n
cita f (de negocios)

I must leave because I have an appointment with my lawer at five debo marcharme porque tengo una cita con mi abogado a las cinco

apricot

apricot
['eɪprɪkɒt] n
albaricoque m

April

April
['eɪprəl] n
abril m

the first/second of April (Am: April first/second) el primero/dos de abril

area

area
['eərɪə] n
1. área f, región f, zona f

* *The research centre (Am: center) is in the Klow area...* El centro de investigación está en el área de Klow... *

the Liverpool area la región de Liverpool

2. barrio m

residential area barrio residencial

3. área f, superficie f
measure the area of this circle mide el área de este círculo

arm

arm
[ɑːm] n
brazo m

he hurt his arm se hizo daño en el brazo

▶ **armchair**
[ɑːm'tʃeəʳ] n
sillón m

arm

arm
[ɑːm] v t
armar

* *Look out, they're armed!* ¡Cuidado! ¡Están armados! *

▶ **arms** n pl
armas f pl

they've got new secret arms tienen nuevas armas secretas

army

army
['ɑːmɪ] n
pl armies
ejército m

around

around
[ə'raʊnd]
I. prep
1. alrededor, cerca de

...around

we walked around the building caminamos alrededor del edificio

2. hacia
he arrived around 1960 llegó hacia 1960

II. adv
all around por todos lados

there were soldiers all around había soldados por todos lados

arrange

arrange
[ə'reɪndʒ] v t
1. organizar

* *It was such a good idea to arrange this party!... I love dressing up!* ¡Fue una idea estupenda organizar esta fiesta!... ¡Me encanta disfrazarme!
So do I!... ¡A mí también!... *

2. ordenar

...arrange

he arranged the records on the shelves ordenó los discos en las estanterías

▶ **arrangement**
[ə'reɪndʒmənt] n
1. preparativo m

she made all the arrangements for the wedding hizo todos los preparativos para la boda

2. disposición

I don't like the arrangement of the pictures no me gusta la disposición de los cuadros

arrive

arrive
[ə'raɪv] v i
llegar

* *What time does the plane arrive in New York?* ¿A qué

...arrive

hora llega el avión a Nueva York?
At six o'clock. A las seis. *

▶ **arrival**
[ə'raɪv(ə)l] n
llegada f

art

art
[ɑːt] n
arte m

...art

he is a specialist on medieval art él es un especialista en arte medieval

article

article
['ɑːtɪk(ə)l] n
1. artículo m

we bought new articles for the shop

...article

compramos nuevos artículos para la tienda

2. artículo m
* *Look! There's an article about Red Rackham's treasure in the paper!* ¡Mire! ¡hay un artículo sobre el tesoro de Rackham el Rojo en el periódico! *

3. artículo m
"the" is the definite article "the" es el artículo definido

artist

artist
['ɑːtɪst] n
artista m f

as

as
[æz]
I. conj
1. puesto que

...as

as I'm sure you lied, I'm not going to believe you now puesto que estoy seguro de que mentiste, no voy a creerte ahora

2. mientras
he came towards me as I was standing up vino hacia mí mientras yo me levantaba

3. como
leave it as it is déjalo como está

...as

4. Idiom
* *As for me, I'm going for a walk in the park...* En cuanto a mí, voy a dar un paseo por el parque... *

as if como si

he talked as if he were mad hablaba como si estuviera loco

II. *adv*
as....as tan....como

* *When you go in, mind...* Cuando entren, tengan cuidado con...
The step?... ¿El escalón?...
No, the door... No, la puerta...
Thomson is as absent-minded... as Thompson. Hernández es tan despistado... como Fernández. *

...as

ashamed

ashamed
[əˈʃeɪmd] *adj*
Idiom
to be ashamed of tener verguenza de

you should be ashamed of yourself debería darte vergüenza

ask

ask
[ɑːsk] *v t*
1. preguntar

* *I'll ask a passer-by the way to the station. Provided there is a station, of course!* Preguntaré a un transeunte el camino a la estación.¡En caso de que haya estación, claro! *

2. invitar
you haven't been asked to attend this

...ask

meeting no has sido invitado a asistir a esta reunión

3. Idiom
to ask for pedir, preguntar por

she asked for you when she came around preguntó por tí cuando recobró la conciencia

asleep

asleep
[əˈsliːp] *adj*
Idiom
to be asleep estar dormido

to fall asleep dormirse

assign

assign *(Am)*
→ SET

astonish

astonish
[əˈstɒnɪʃ] *v t*
sorprender

to be astonished estar sorprendido

she was really astonished at his reaction estaba realmente sorprendida de su reacción

▶**astonishing**
[əˈstɒnɪʃɪŋ] *adj*
sorprendente

at

at
[æt] *prep*
1. en

I will be at the club this evening estaré en el club esta noche

2. a
at six o'clock a las seis

3. Idiom
I don't like being laughed at no me gusta que se rían de mí

I'm not very good at guessing no soy muy bueno en adivinar

attack

attack
[əˈtæk] *v t*
atacar

* *Who's he attacking?* ¿A quién está atacando? *

...attack

Who's he attacking?

attend

attend
[ə'tend] *v t*
asistir

* *Come on, Captain, you must attend the meeting. It's very important...* Vamos capitán, debe asistir a la reunión. Es muy importante... *

Come on, Captain, you must attend the meeting. It's very important...

attention

attention
[ə'tenʃ(ə)n] *n*
atención *f*

he never pays attention to what you say nunca presta atención a lo que dices

August

August
['ɔːgəst] *n*
agosto *m*

Australia

Australia
[ɒ'streɪlɪə] *n*
Australia *f*

► **Australian**
[ɒ'streɪlɪən]
I. *n*
australiano *m*
australiana *f*

II. *adj*
australiano, a

author

author
['ɔːθə'] *n*
autor, ra

the author of this book is Mexican la autora de este libro es mejicana

automatic

automatic
[ɔːtə'mætɪk] *adj*
automático, a

autumn

autumn
['ɔtəm] *n*
(*Am:* **fall**)
otoño *m*

average

average
['ævərɪdʒ]
I. *n*
media *f*,
promedio *m*

the average of the students' results is

...average

good la media de las notas de los estudiantes es buena

II. *adj*
medio, a, normal

the average temperature la temperatura media

avoid

avoid
[ə'vɔɪd] *v t*
evitar

...avoid

* *I would have liked to come with you, but the doctor told me to avoid going out.* Me hubiera gustado ir con usted, pero el doctor me dijo que evitara salir. *

awake

awake
[ə'weɪk] *adj*
despierto, a

I would have liked to come with you, but the doctor told me to avoid going out.

...awake

What's the matter, Captain? Are you awake?

* *What's the matter, Captain? Are you awake?* ¿Qué ocurre capitán?¿Está despierto? *

away

away
[ə'weɪ] *adv*
1. ausente

he's been away for a week ha estado ausente durante una semana

...away

2. Idiom
far away lejos

to go away irse

put the books away recoge los libros

to run away escapar

to throw away tirar

it's a long way away está lejos de aquí

it's two kilometres (Am: kilometers) away está a dos kilómetros

awful

awful
['ɔːful] *adj*
horrible

it's awful to think of it es horrible pensar en ello

► **awfully**
['ɔːfulɪ] *adv*
terriblemente, muy, muchísimo

she was awfully worried ella estaba muy preocupada

baby

baby
['beɪbɪ] *n*
pl babies
bebé *m*

she is expecting a baby está esperando un bebé

* Why is this baby crying? ¿Por qué está llorando este bebé?
Wooaaah! ¡Ouaaah! *

WOOAAAAAAAAH!

Why is this baby crying?

?

back

back
[bæk]
I. *n*
1. espalda *f*

2. parte posterior

II. *adj*
de atrás, trasero, a

the burglers went in through the back window los ladrones entraron por la ventana de atrás

III. *adv*
1. detrás, atrás

2. Idiom
to come back volver

to give back devolver

to pay back reembolsar

▶ **background**
['bækgraund] *n*
1. fondo *f*

in his painting there were mountains in

...back

the background en su cuadro había montañas en el fondo

2. antecedentes *m pl* pasado *m*

▶ **backwards**
['bækwədz] *adv*
1. para atrás

to walk backwards caminar para atrás

2. al revés

* Thundering typhoons! What a lovely ship! ¡Rayos y centellas! ¡Que barco tan bonito!
The Captain has put his pullover on backwards. El capitán se ha puesto el jersey al revés. *

Thundering typhoons! What a lovely ship!

The Captain has put his pullover on backwards.

bacon

bacon
['beɪk(ə)n] *n*
tocino *m*, beicon *m*

they have bacon and eggs for breakfast toman huevos con beicon para desayunar

bad

bad
[bæd] *adj*
worse [wɜːs],

...bad

worst [wɜːst]
1. malo, mal, mala

* I hope this bad weather won't last! ¡Espero que este mal tiempo no dure! *

he's not a bad man no es un hombre malo

...bad

I hope this bad weather won't last!

2. Idiom
I've got a bad headache tengo un dolor de cabeza muy fuerte

▶ **badly**
['bædlɪ] *adv*
mal, de forma descuidada

his house was very badly done su casa estaba muy mal hecha

bag

bag
[bæg] *n*
saco *m*, bolsa *f*

* *They've put Snowy into a bag!* ¡Han puesto a Milú en un saco! *

They've put Snowy into a bag!

baker

baker
['beɪkə'] *n*
1. panadero, a

2. Idiom
at the baker's en la panadería

balance

balance
['bæləns] *n*
equilibrio *m*

...balance

Tintin can't keep his balance. He's going to fall!

* *Tintin can't keep his balance. He's going to fall!* Tintín no puede mantener el equilibrio. ¡Va a caerse! *

ball

ball
[bɔːl] *n*
pelota *f*

ban

ban
[bæn] *v tr*
prohibir

banana

banana
[bə'nɑːnə] *n*
plátano *f*

band

band
[bænd] *n*
1. orquesta *f*

the band plays on Sundays la banda toca los domingos

2. cinta, tira
she tied her hair with a white band ató su pelo con una cinta blanca

3. Idiom
a rubber band una goma

▶ **band-aid** *(Am)*
→ STICKING PLASTER

bank

bank
[bæŋk] *n*
1. banco *m*

I have my money in the bank tengo el dinero en el banco

...bank

2. orilla, ribera *f*
the castle is on the north bank of the river el castillo está en la ribera norte del río

bar

bar
[bɑːʳ] *n*
1. barra *f*

* *I've got nothing to saw through the*

...bar

I've got nothing to saw through the bars with...

bars with... No tengo nada con que serrar las barras... *

2. bar *m*
we met in the bar nos encontramos en el bar

3. Idiom
a bar of soap una pastilla de jabón

a bar of chocolate una barra de chocolate

bargain

bargain
['bɑːgɪn] *n*
trato *m*, ganga *f*

bark

bark
[bɑːk] *v i*
ladrar

* *Why is Snowy barking like that?* ¿Por qué está ladrando así Milú?

...bark

Why is Snowy barking like that?

Woof! Woof!

...bark

Woof! Woof! ¡Guau! ¡Guau! *

basket

basket
['bɑːskɪt] *n*
cesta *f*, cesto *m*

* *Oh dear!... These baskets are quite heavy...* ¡Vaya!... Estas cestas son bastante pesadas... *

...basket

Oh dear!...These baskets are quite heavy...

bath

bath
[bɑːθ] *n*
1. baño *m*

I'd like to have (Am: take) a bath me gustaría tomar un baño

2. bañera *f*
this room has a bath (Am: bathtub) esta habitación tiene baño

▶ **bathroom**
['bɑːθruːm] *n*
cuarto de baño *m*

be

be
[biː]
I. *v i*
1. ser

the Castafiore is a singer la Castafiore es una cantante

are they good sailors? ¿son buenos marineros?

2. estar
how are you? ¿cómo estás?

she is in the park está en el parque

3. tener
he is eleven tiene once años

I'm very hungry tengo mucha hambre

I'm cold tengo frío

* *This tower is twenty metres (Am: meters) high!* Esta torre tiene veinte metros de alto *

...be

This tower is twenty metres high!

II. *v aux*
1. estar
Nota: para formar el presente y pasado continuo

what are you reading? ¿qué estás leyendo?

2. ser
Nota: para formar la voz pasiva
it was built two years ago fue construido hace dos años

beach

beach
[biːtʃ] *n*
playa *f*

* *They're landing on the beach.* Están desembarcando en la playa. *

They're landing on the beach.

bean

bean
[biːn] *n*
haba *f*

bear

bear
[beəʳ] *n*
oso *m*

a polar bear un oso polar

bear

bear
[beəʳ] *v t*
bore [bɔːʳ] borne [bɔːn]
soportar

I can't bear waiting no puedo soportar esperar

beard

beard
[bɪəd] *n*
barba *f*

beat

beat
[biːt]
beat [biːt]
beaten ['biːt(ə)n]

I. *v t*
1. pegar, golpear

* *He beat Snowy with a stick!* ¡Pegó a Milú con un palo! *

2. vencer, derrotar
our team was beaten last week nuestro equipo fue derrotado la semana pasada

He beat Snowy with a stick!

II. *v i*
latir

my heart was beating fast mi corazón latía de prisa

beautiful

beautiful
['bjuːtiful] *adj*
bello, a, hermoso, a

...beautiful

she's very beautiful
es muy hermosa

because

because
[bɪˈkɒz] *conj*
porque

he lied because he was afraid mintió porque tenía miedo

...because

► **because of**
prep
a causa de

he is ill because of the bad weather está enfermo a causa del mal tiempo

become

become
[bɪˈkʌm] *v i*
became [bɪˈkeɪm],

...become

The sea's becoming very rough! I don't know whether our boat will hold out...

become [bɪˈkʌm]
convertirse, hacerse, volverse, ponerse

* *The sea's becoming very rough! I don't know whether our boat will hold out...* ¡El mar se está poniendo muy agitado! No sé si nuestro bote resistirá... *

he became a very important man se convirtió en un hombre muy importante

bed

bed
[bed] *n*
cama *f*

* *You should go to bed...* Debería ir a la cama... *

► **bedroom**
[ˈbedruːm] *n*
habitación *f*, dormitorio *m*

...bed

You should go to bed...

beef

beef
[biːf] *n*
carne de vaca *f*

► **beefsteak**
[ˈbiːfstek] *n*
bistec *m*

beer

beer
[bɪəʳ] *n*
cerveza *f*

before

before
[bɪˈfɔːʳ]
I. *prep*
1. antes

before the war antes de la guerra

the day before yesterday antes de ayer

2. enfrente de, ante
he was before the king estaba ante el rey

II. *adv*
antes

...before

I've been here before...
Thundering typhoons'!

* *I've been here before...* Ya he estado aquí antes...
Thundering typhoons! ¡Rayos y centellas! *

III. *conj*
antes que, antes de que

do it now before you forget hazlo ahora antes de que te olvides

beg

beg
[beg]
begged, begged

I. *v i*
mendigar

he's begging in front of the church está mendigando frente a la iglesia

II. *v t*
1. rogar

he begged her to forgive him le rogó que

lo perdonara

2. Idiom
I beg your pardon le pido perdón

begin

begin
[bɪˈgɪn]
I. *v i*
began [bɪˈgæn]
begun [bɪˈgʌn]
empezar

...begin

he began crying
empezó a llorar

II. *v t*
the meeting begins now la reunión empieza ahora

▶ **beginner**
[brˈgɪnəʳ] *n*
principiante *m f*

▶ **beginning**
[brˈgɪnɪŋ] *n*
comienzo *m*,
principio *m*

behind

behind
[brˈhaɪnd]
I. *prep*
tras, detrás de

* *Stay here... I'll go and see what's behind that door...*
Quédate aquí... Yo iré a ver lo que hay tras aquella puerta... *

II. *adv*
atrás

I'll stay behind yo me quedaré atrás

Stay here... I'll go and see what's behind that door...

OK.

Belgium

Belgium
[ˈbeldʒɪəm] *n*
Bélgica *f*

▶ **Belgian**
[ˈbeldʒɪən]
I. *n*
belga *m f*

II. *adj*
belga

believe

believe
[brˈliːv]
I. *v t*
creer

nobody will believe it nadie lo creerá

II. *v i*
I believe in God yo creo en Dios

bell

bell
[bel] *n*
campana *f*

▶ **door bell**
[dɔːʳ bel] *n*
timbre *m*

belong

belong
[brˈlɒŋ] *v i*
pertenecer

...belong

who does the car belong to? ¿a quién pertenece el coche?

* *That scarf belongs to Chang!* ¡Aquella bufanda pertenece a Tchang! *

▶ **belongings**
[brˈlɒŋɪŋz] *n*
pertenencias *f pl*

are these your belongings? ¿son éstas tus pertenencias?

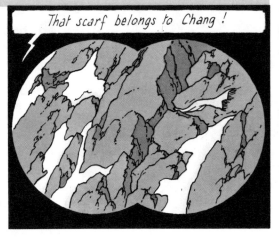

That scarf belongs to Chang !

below

below
[brˈləu]
I. *prep*
debajo (de), bajo

the temperature was five below zero la temperatura era de cinco bajo cero

II. *adv*
abajo, debajo

where are you? I'm here below! ¿dónde estás? ¡estoy aquí abajo!

belt

belt
[belt] *n*
cinturón *m*

fasten your safety belts abróchense los cinturones de seguridad

bend

bend
[bend]
I. *n*
curva *f*

...bend

There are a lot of bends in this road !

* *There are a lot of bends in this road!* ¡Hay muchas curvas en esta carretera! *

II. *v t*
bent, bent [bent]
doblar, torcer

he can't bend his knee no puede doblar la rodilla

III. *v i*
1. inclinarse

he bent forward to hear better se inclinó hacia adelante para oír mejor

2. cambiar de dirección, torcer

beside

beside
[brˈsaɪd] *prep*
al lado de, junto

they were standing beside one another estaban de pie uno al lado del otro

▶ **besides**
[brˈsaɪdz]
I. *prep*
aparte (de),
excepto

we were all there

...beside

besides his brother estábamos todos allí aparte de su hermano

II. adv
además

I must study Latin and French besides tengo que estudiar latín y además francés

* Come on, get up, Captain! We're off!...
¡Vamos, levántese, capitán! ¡Nos vamos!...

It's too far... besides I'm tired... ZZZ... ZZZ... Está demasiado lejos... además estoy muy cansado... ZZZ... ZZZ... *

best

best
[best]
I. adj
(el) mejor,
(la) mejor

...best

It's the best idea I've heard so far es la mejor idea que he oído hasta ahora

II. n
1. (el) mejor,
(la) mejor

she is the best ella es la mejor

2. lo mejor
do your best hazlo lo mejor que puedas

3. Idiom
they are the best of friends son los mejores amigos del mundo

III. adv
mejor

do what you think best haz lo que creas mejor

bet

bet
[bet] v t
bet, bet [bet]
apostar,
apostarse

I will bet all my money apostaré todo mi dinero

▶ **bet**
n.
apuesta f

better

better
['betəʳ]
I. adj
1. mejor

she's better at English than at geography se le da mejor el inglés que la geografía

2. Idiom
* Take this medicine, it will make you better... I promise you, with this you'll

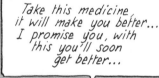

soon get better...Toma esta medicina, te hará sentir mejor... Te lo prometo, con esto pronto estarás mejor...*

II. adv
mejor

don't worry, I drive much better now no te preocupes, ahora conduzco mucho mejor

between

between
[br'twi:n] prep
1. entre

the relation between father and son is sometimes difficult la relación entre padre e hijo es a veces difícil

2. Idiom
between you and me entre tú y yo (en confidencia)

beyond

beyond
[br'jɒnd] prep
más allá de

there's a desert beyond those mountains hay un desierto más allá de aquellas montañas

bicycle

bicycle
['baɪsɪk(ə)l] n
bicicleta f

he rides his bicycle every morning va en bicicleta todas las mañanas

big

big
[bɪg] adj
bigger, biggest
grande

* Oh! What a big elephant! ¡Oh! ¡Qué elefante tan grande! *

bike

bike
[baɪk] n
bici (bicicleta) f

bill

bill
[bɪl] n
1. factura f

you must keep the bill debes guardar la factura

2. cuenta f
they left the restaurant without paying the bill (Am: check) se fueron del restaurante sin pagar la cuenta

3. *Am:* billete m

a ten-dollar bill un billete de diez dólares

bird

bird
[bɜːd] n
pájaro m

* *Wooaaah!* ¡Guau!
The bird's carrying Snowy away. El pájaro se lleva a Milú. *

...bird

Wooaaah!

The bird's carrying Snowy away.

birth

birth
[bɜːθ] n
nacimiento m

what's your date of birth? ¿cuál es tu fecha de nacimiento?

▶ **birthday**
['bɜːθdeɪ] n
cumpleaños m

happy birthday! ¡feliz cumpleaños!

bit

bit
[bɪt] n
1. trozo m, pedazo m

a bit of bread un trozo de pan

2. poco m
* *I feel a bit better today!* ¡Hoy me encuentro un poco mejor! *

bit by bit poco a poco

I feel a bit better today!

bite

bite
[baɪt] v t
bit [bɪt] bitten ['bɪtn]
morder

* *Ouch!* ¡Ay!
Snowy got angry and bit him! ¡Milú se enfadó y lo mordió! *

bitter

bitter
['bɪtə'] adj

OUCH!

Snowy got angry and bit him!

...bitter

amargo, a

it tastes bitter sabe amargo

black

black
[blæk]
I. adj
negro, a

...black

BAR

Haddock is dressed in black.

he likes black cats le gustan los gatos negros

II. n
negro m

* *Haddock is dressed in black.* Haddock viste de negro. *

▶ **blackboard**
['blækbɔːd] n
pizarra f

blame

blame
[bleɪm]
I. n
culpa f

put the blame on me, boys echarme la culpa a mí, chicos

II. v t
acusar, culpar, echar la culpa

don't blame her, there was nothing she could do no le eches la culpa, no había nada que pudiera hacer

blanket

blanket
['blæŋkɪt] n
manta f

I covered myself with a blanket me tapé con una manta

blazer

blazer
['bleɪzə'] n
chaqueta f

bleed

bleed
[bliːd] vi
bled, bled [bled]
sangrar

the wound is bleeding badly la herida está sangrando mucho

blind

blind
[blaɪnd] *adj*
ciego, a

love is blind el amor es ciego

blood

blood
[blʌd] *n*
sangre *f*

blow

blow
[bləu]
I. *n*
golpe *m*

she struck a blow on his jaw ella le pegó un golpe en la mandíbula

II. *v i*
blew [bluː]
blown [bləun]
soplar

blow harder! ¡sopla más fuerte!

▶ **blow out**
apagar (soplando)

* *Ah!... At last!...* ¡Ah!... ¡Al fin!... *We can't see anything, the wind has blown out the candle!...* No podemos ver nada, el viento ha apagado la vela!... *

▶ **blow up**
1. inflar

we have to blow up

...blow

this tyre tenemos que inflar este neumático

2. explotar
be careful, it's going to blow up! ¡ten cuidado, va a explotar!

blue

blue
[bluː]
I. *adj*

...blue

1. azul

the blue sea el mar azul

2. Idiom
he was feeling blue estaba triste

II. *n*
azul *m*

she dressed in blue ella vestía de azul

board

board
[bɔːd] *n*
1. tabla *f*

ironing board tabla de planchar

2. pizarra *f*
draw it on the board dibújalo en la pizarra

▶ **notice**
(*Am:* **bulletin) board**
tablero de anuncios

3. bordo *m*

* *Come on, Captain, you must come on board.* Vamos, capitán, debe subir a bordo. *I'm coming, I'm coming...* Ya vengo, ya vengo... *

4. junta *f*
the board is in a meeting la junta está reunida

5. pensión *f*
a room with full board una habitación con pensión completa

...board

▶ **boarding school**
['bɔːdɪŋskuːl] *n*
internado *m*

* *Stop it or I'll tell your father to send you to boarding school!...* ¡Para o le diré a tu padre que te envíe a un internado!... *No!...* ¡No!... *

boat

boat
[bəut] *n*
bote *m*, barca *f*

* *Good grief! A boat is chasing me!* ¡Rayos! ¡Una barca me está persiguiendo! *

body

body
['bɒdɪ] *n*
pl bodies ['bɒdɪz]

...body

1. cuerpo *m*

body and soul cuerpo y alma

2. cadáver *m*
the police found the body lying on the floor la policía encontró el cadaver tendido en el suelo

boil

boil
[bɔɪl]
I. v i
hervir

the milk is boiling la leche está hirviendo

II. v t
1. hervir

don't let it boil too much no dejes que hierva demasiado

2. Idiom
a boiled egg un huevo pasado por agua (o hervido)

bone

bone
[bəun] n
1. hueso m

* *Where did you find that bone?* ¿Dónde encontraste ese hueso? *

2. espina f
I've taken out the fish bones he quitado las espinas del pescado

book

book
[buk]
I. n
libro m

the professor is

...book

reading the book carefully el profesor está leyendo el libro atentamente

▶ **book-keeper**
[ˈbukkiːpəˈ] n
contable m f

▶ **exercise-book**
(*Am:* **notebook**)
[ˈeksəsaɪz-buk] n
cuaderno m

II. v t
reservar

...book

I've booked a room in this hotel he reservado una habitación en este hotel

▶ **bookcase**
[ˈbukkeɪs] n
estante para libros, biblioteca

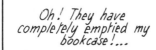

* *Oh! They have completely emptied my bookcase!...* ¡Oh! ¡Han vaciado completamente mi biblioteca!... *

boot

boot
[buːt] n
bota f

* *Let me put my boots on and I'll come!* ¡Deja que me ponga las botas y vendré! *OK!* ¡De acuerdo! *Quick... Hurry up, Tintin!* ¡Rápido... Date prisa Tintín! *

wellington/rubber boots botas de goma

border

border
[ˈbɔːdəˈ] n
frontera f

* *Tintin is going to cross the border.* Tintín va a cruzar la frontera. *

bored

bored
[bɔːd] adj

Tintin is going to cross the border.

...bored

Idiom
to be bored estar aburrido

put the television off, you look bored apaga el televisor, pareces aburrido

▶ **boring**
[ˈbɔːrɪŋ] adj
aburrido, a

this film is very boring esta película es muy aburrida

born

born
[bɔːn] adj
1. nacido, a

to be born nacer

2. Idiom
I was born in June nací en junio

borrow

borrow
[ˈbɒrəu] v t
tomar prestado

...borrow

she borrowed a fancy dress for the carnival tomó prestado un disfraz para el carnaval

both

both
[bəuθ]
I. *adj*
ambos, ambas, los dos, las dos

...both

I read both books leí ambos libros

II. *pron*
ambos, as, los dos, las dos

* *The Thompsons are both sick.* Hernández y Fernández, los dos están mareados. *

III. *adv*
a la vez

he's both intelligent and absent minded

The Thompsons are both sick.

él es a la vez inteligente y despistado

bother

bother
['bɒðəʳ]
I. *n*
molestia *f*

it's no bother to me no me es ninguna molestia

II. *v t*

...bother

molestar

don't bother the professor while he's working no molestes al profesor mientras está trabajando

III. *v i*
Idiom
don't bother to read it, I'll tell you no te molestes en leerlo, yo te lo contaré

IV. *interj*
¡caramba!, ¡caray!

bottle

bottle
['bɒt(ə)l] *n*
botella *f*

a bottle of wine una botella de vino

bottom

bottom
['bɒtəm] *n*
1. fondo *m*

...bottom

* *The wreck was at the bottom of the sea.* Los restos del naufragio estaban en el fondo del mar. *

2. trasero *m*
Snowy bit his bottom Milú le mordió el trasero

The wreck was at the bottom of the sea.

bound

bound
[baund]
I. *n*
límite *m*
II. *adj*
destinado, a

box

box
[bɒks] *n*
caja *f*

boy

boy
[bɔɪ] *n*
chico *m*

brain

brain
[breɪn] *n*
cerebro *m*

branch

branch
[brɑːntʃ] *n*
1. rama *f*

* *Tintin's hanging from a branch.* Tintín está colgando de una rama. *

2. sección *f*, sucursal *f*
the bank has branches all over the country el banco tiene sucursales por todo el país

Tintin's hanging from a branch.

brave

brave
[breɪv] *adj*
valiente

* *I was sure I'd find you in the end, Chang!...* ¡Estaba seguro de que al final te encontraría, Tchang!...
You've saved my life! You're very brave! ¡Me has salvado la vida! ¡Eres muy valiente! *

I was sure I'd find you in the end, Chang!...

You've saved my life! You are very brave!

bread

bread
[bred] *n*
pan *m*

a loaf of bread una barra de pan

break

break
[breɪk]
I. *n*
1. descanso *m*

...break

I need a break necesito un descanso

2. recreo *m*
the break is at ten thirty el recreo es a las diez treinta

II. *v t*
broke [brəuk]
broken ['brəuk(ə)n]
romper

he broke the glass rompió el vaso

III. *v i*
romper, romperse

mind, Tintin!, the rope is going to break ¡cuidado Tintín!, la cuerda va a romperse

▶ **break down**
['breɪkdaun]
averiarse, estropearse

* *The car's broken down. Let's get closer, without making any noise!* El coche se ha averiado. ¡Acerquémonos, sin hacer ruido! *

The car's broken down. Let's get closer, without making any noise!

▶ **break out**
1. estallar

the war has broken out! ¡ha estallado la guerra!

2. escaparse
the prisoners have broken out los prisioneros se han escapado

▶ **break up**
Idiom
school breaks up (Am: lets out) tomor-

...break

row la escuela se acaba mañana

▶ **break down**
['breɪkdaun] *n*
avería *f*

breakfast

breakfast
['brekfəst] *n*
desayuno *m*

I have breakfast

...breakfast

every morning at eight tomo el desayuno cada mañana a las ocho

bridge

bridge
[brɪdʒ] *n*
puente *m*

* *Quick, let's dive off the bridge!...* ¡Rápido, saltemos del puente!... *

...bridge

Quick, let's dive off the bridge!...

briefcase

briefcase
['briːfkeɪs] *n*
maletín *m*

the documents are in the briefcase los documentos están en el maletín

bright

bright
[braɪt] *adj*
1. brillante

...bright

this is very bright silver ésta es plata muy brillante

2. inteligente, listo, a
he thinks he is very bright él se cree muy inteligente

bring

bring
[brɪŋ] *v t*
brought, brought [brɔːt]
traer

...bring

* *It's a good thing I remembered to bring a picnic!* ¡Qué bien que me acordé de traer merienda!
Oh yes! ¡Oh si! *

▶ **bring up**
criar, educar

he has brought up his son to be respectful ha educado a su hijo para ser respetuoso

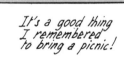

It's a good thing I remembered to bring a picnic!

Oh yes!

Britain

Britain
['brɪt(ə)n] *n*
Great Britain Gran Bretaña

▶ **British**
['brɪtɪʃ] *n & adj*
británico, a

brother

brother
['brʌðə'] n
hermano

my elder brother is a lawyer mi hermano mayor es abogado

brown

brown
[braun]
I. adj

...brown

1. marrón

I'd like a brown hat quisiera un sombrero marrón

2. moreno, a
she is brown and has beautiful black eyes es morena y tiene unos hermosos ojos negros

II. n
marrón m
he always dresses in brown siempre viste de marrón

brush

brush
[brʌʃ]
I. n
1. cepillo m

clean your coat with this brush limpia tu abrigo con este cepillo

2. pincel m

II. v t
1. cepillar

you have to brush your teeth now ahora tienes que lavarte los dientes

my mother brushes my hair mi madre me cepilla el pelo

2. barrer
please brush the floor por favor barre el suelo

build

build
[bɪld] vt
built, built [bɪlt]
construir

bullet

bullet
['bulɪt] n
bala f

* *He's been hit in the shoulder by a bullet...* Ha sido herido en el hombro por una bala... *

bulletin

bulletin (Am)
→ BOARD

He's been hit in the shoulder by a bullet...

bump

bump
[bʌmp]
I. n
1. golpe m

I got this bump while I was playing recibí este golpe mientras jugaba

2. bache m
careful with that bump on the road! ¡cuidado con aquel bache en la carretera!

II. v t
golpear, golpearse

she bumped her head on the cupboard door se golpeó la cabeza con la puerta del armario

▶ **bump into**
1. chocar, tropezar

I bumped against a chair because the room was very dark tropezé contra una silla

...bump

porque la habitación estaba muy oscura

2. Idiom
to bump into somebody tropezarse con alguien

burgle

burgle
['bɜːg(ə)l] v t
robar

Good grief!... I've been burgled!...

...burgle

* *Good grief!... I've been burgled!...* ¡Caramba!... ¡Me han robado!... *

▶ **burglar**
['bɜːglə']
ladrón m

▶ **burglary**
['bɜːglərɪ] n
pl burglaries
['bɜːglərɪz]
robo m, con fractura

burn

burn
[bɜːn] v t & v i
burned, burned, o burnt, burnt [bɜːnt]
quemar, arder

if you get near there you'll burn yourself si te acercas allí te quemarás

* *The prairie is burning!* ¡La pradera está ardiendo! *

The prairie is burning!

burst

burst
[bɜːst] *v i*
burst, burst [bɜːst]
1. estallar, reventar

the tyre has burst la rueda se ha reventado

2. Idiom
he burst out crying de repente empezó a llorar

the door burst open la puerta se abrió de repente

bus

bus
[bʌs] *n*
1. autobús

the bus never comes on time el autobús nunca llega a su hora

2. *Am:*
→ COACH

▶ **bus stop** *n*
['bʌsstop]
parada *f* de autobús

bush

bush
[buʃ]
arbusto *m*, mata *f*

it's covered with bushes está cubierto de arbustos

business

business
['bɪznɪs] *n*
1. negocios *m pl*

...business

he is on a business trip está en viaje de negocios

2. comercio *m*
he runs a small business lleva un pequeño negocio

busy

busy
['bɪzɪ] *adj*
busier, busiest
ocupado, a

...busy

He's very busy.

...busy

* *Saturday* Sábado
He's very busy. Está muy ocupado. *

▶ **busy** (*Am*)
→ ENGAGED

but

but
[bʌt]
I. *conj*
pero

...but

he's coming but he's not giving the signal ya viene pero no está haciendo la señal

II. *prep*
sin, excepto, menos, salvo

* *Everybody's here but Snowy.* Todos están aquí menos Milú. *

Everybody's here but Snowy.

butcher

butcher
['butʃər] *n*
carnicero, a

at the butcher's en la carnicería

butter

butter
['bʌtər] *n*
mantequilla *f*

button

button
['bʌt(ə)n]
I. *n*
botón *m*

II. *v t*
abrochar

buy

buy
[baɪ] *v t*
bought, bought [bɔːt]

...buy

comprar, comprarse

I bought this car last week me compré este coche la semana pasada

by

by
[baɪ]
I. *prep*
1. por

...by

this was discovered by the Professor esto fue descubierto por el profesor

2. en
* *Tintin came by train.* Tintín vino en tren. *

3. cerca de, al lado de, junto a
she's reading by the fire está leyendo al lado del fuego

4. antes
this will be finished by eight esto estará terminado antes de las ocho

II. *adv*
Idiom
time goes by el tiempo pasa

by myself yo solo (por mí mismo, a solas)

by and large en general

Tintin came by train.

cabbage

cabbage
['kæbɪdʒ] n
col f

cabin

cabin
['kæbɪn] n
1. camarote m

* *Police: we must search your cabin.* Policía: tenemos que

...cabin

> *Police: we must search your cabin.*

registrar su camarote. *

2. cabaña f

café

café
['kæfeɪ] n
café m

he's waiting for us in the café round the corner nos espera en el café de la esquina

cage

cage
[keɪdʒ] n
jaula f

the tiger doesn't like being in the cage al tigre no le gusta estar en la jaula

cake

cake
[keɪk] n
pastel m

...cake

on Sundays we have chocolate cake los domingos tomamos pastel de chocolate

call

call
[kɔːl]
I. n
1. llamada f

give him a telephone call hazle una llamada telefónica

2. visita f
I'll pay you a call next week te haré una visita la semana que viene

II. v t
1. llamar

* *Quick, call a doctor! I'm in pain!* ¡Rápido, llamen a un doctor! ¡Tengo dolor! *

2. llamar, nombrar
you should call him by his name deberías llamarle por su nombre

3. Idiom
to be called llamarse

III. v i
1. llamar, gritar

> *Quick, call a doctor! I'm in pain!*

he called me from the top of the mountain me llamó desde lo alto de la montaña

2. llamar
(por teléfono)
she called from a booth llamó desde una cabina

► **call off**
anular, cancelar

the meeting was called off la reunión fue anulada

► **call for**
pasar a buscar

I'll call for you in half an hour pasaré a buscarte dentro de media hora

► **call up**
llamar, telefonear

...call

▶ **call on**
visitar

I called on him last week le hice una visita la semana pasada

calm

calm
[kɑːm]
I. *adj*
tranquilo, a

...calm

the sea is very calm today el mar está muy tranquilo hoy

II. *n*
to keep calm mantener/ no perder la calma

▶ **calm down**
calmarse

* *So! I play the fool!...* ¡Así que hago el tonto, eh!... *Now, now, calm down...* Venga, venga, cálmese... *

camera

camera
['kæmrə] *n*
cámara/máquina fotográfica *f*

I can take very good pictures with this camera puedo tomar fotos muy buenas con esta cámara fotográfica

▶ **(movie) camera**
cámara *f*

television camera cámara de televisión

camp

camp
[kæmp]
I. *n*
campamento *m*

II. *v i*
acampar

* *The next evening...* La noche siguiente... *We'll camp here.* Acamparemos aquí. *There is where the snow starts.* Allí es donde empieza la nieve. *

▶ **camping**
[kæmpɪŋ] *n*
campamento *m*, camping *m*

▶ **go camping**
ir de campamento, ir de camping

can

can
[kæn] *v aux*
Nota: forma negativa **cannot**; *forma negativa abreviada* **can't**
1. poder

* *I'm too tired, Snowy. I can't go any further!* ¡Estoy muy cansado, Milú. ¡No puedo seguir! *

can you see what he's doing? ¿puedes ver lo que está haciendo?

...can

2. saber (hacer)
I can play the piano yo sé tocar el piano

3. Idiom
she can't hear you no te oye

can

can
[kæn] *n*
1. bidón *m*

* *A can of petrol (Am: gas)!...* ¡Un bidón de gasolina!... *

2. lata *f*
a can of beer una lata de cerveza

Canada

Canada
['kænədə] n
Canadá m

▶ **Canadian**
[kə'neɪdɪən]
I. n
canadiense m f

II. adj
canadiense

candle

candle
['kænd(ə)l] n
vela f, candela f

blow out the candle!
¡apaga la vela!

▶ **candy** (Am)
→ SWEET

cap

cap
[kæp]
1. gorro m

the soldier put his cap on and left el soldado se puso el gorro y se fue

2. gorra f
he put on his peaked cap se puso su gorra de visera

capital

Here we are in Sanaa, the capital of North Yemen!

...capital

capital
['kæpɪt(ə)l] n
1. capital f

* *Here we are, in Sanaa, the capital of North Yemen!* ¡Ya estamos aquí, en Sanaa, la capital de Yemen del Norte! *

2. mayúscula f
the message was written in capital letters el mensaje estaba escrito en letras mayúsculas

captain

captain
['kæptɪn] n
capitán m

the captain ordered his soldiers to keep on fighting el capitán ordenó a sus soldados que siguieran luchando

the captain of the football team was angry el capitán del equipo de fútbol estaba enfadado

car

Another car has caught fire!

car
[kɑːʳ] n
coche m

* *Another car has caught fire!* ¡Otro coche se ha incendiado! *

caravan

caravan
['kærəvæn] n
caravana f

...caravan

In the desert...

the caravan of camels is leaving the fort...

* *In the desert...* En el desierto...
The caravan of camels is leaving the fort... La caravana de camellos sale del fuerte... *

card

card
[kɑːd] n
1. naipe m, carta f

...card

this card game is too difficult for me este juego de cartas es demasiado difícil para mí

2. tarjeta
here you have my visiting card aquí tiene mi tarjeta de visita

cardigan

cardigan
['kɑːdɪgən] n
chaqueta f (de lana), rebeca f

care

care
[keəʳ]
I. n
1. cuidado m

please, use it with

...care

more care por favor, úsalo con más cuidado

2. preocupación f *his own cares stopped him from thinking clearly* sus propias preocupaciones le impedían pensar con claridad

3. Idiom *to take care of oneself* cuidarse

* *Goodbye, Tintin, and take care of yourself! If there's the slightest pro-*

blem, just use your radio... ¡Adiós, Tintín, y cuídese! Si hay el más mínimo problema, use su radio... *

II. *v i*
1. preocuparse, importarle a uno

we don't care what you say no nos importa lo que digas

2. Idiom *I couldn't care less!* ¡me tiene sin cuidado!

► **care for**
1. cuidar

they care for the sick cuidan a los enfermos

2. querer, apetecer
* *Would you care for a cup of tea, Tintin?* ¿Le apetece una taza de té, Tintín? *Certainly.* Con mucho gusto. *

► **careful** [ˈkeəf(ə)l] *adj*

1. cuidadoso, a, atento, a

he proceeded to a careful examination of the facts procedió a un cuidadoso examen de los hechos

2. Idiom *be careful, the Yeti might be dangerous* ten cuidado, el yeti podría ser peligroso

...care

► **careless** [ˈkeəlɪs] *adj* descuidado, a

don't be so careless no seas tan descuidado

► **caretaker** [ˈkeəteɪkəʳ] *n* vigilante m, portero, a

carpet

carpet [ˈkɑːpɪt] *n* alfombra f

I have to hoover the carpet tengo que pasar el aspirador por la alfombra

* *Ah, bliss! I'll be able to sleep comfortably on this carpet!* ¡Ah, qué felicidad! Podré dormir comodamente en esta alfombra! *

carriage

carriage [ˈkærɪdʒ] *n* vagón m, carruaje m

* *Crash Crack* Boum Crac *Over there, the carriage is falling... We jumped just in time...* Por allí, el vagón se cae... Hemos saltado justo a tiempo... *

* *It's funny... All the compartments in this carriage are*

empty... Es curioso... Todos los compartimientos en este vagón están vacíos... *

carrot

carrot [ˈkærət] *n* zanahoria f

carry

carry
['kærɪ] v t
carried, carried ['kærɪd]
1. llevar

* *Would you like some help?* ¿Quieren ayuda?
Certainly not. This crate is heavy but we can carry it ourselves!... Por supuesto que no. ¡Esta caja es muy pesada pero ya podemos llevarla nosotros mismos!... *

2. transportar
this train is carrying the secret material that we've ordered este tren transporta el material secreto que hemos pedido

▶ **carry** (*Am*: **go**) **on** continuar, seguir

carry on reading siga leyendo

▶ **carry out**
llevar a cabo, ejecutar

our plan has been carried out nuestro plan ha sido llevado a cabo

cartoon

cartoon
[kɑː'tuːn] n
1. dibujos animados *m pl*

I like cartoons, particulaly the Walt Disney ones me gustan los dibujos animados, en particular los de Walt Disney

2. cómic *m*, **caricatura** *f*
* *It's a cartoon of General Alcazar...* Es una caricatura del general Alcázar... *

case

case
[keɪs] n
1. maleta *f*, **equipaje** *m*

pack your cases haz tus maletas

2. funda *f*, **estuche** *m*
a jewel case un estuche para joyas

case

case
[keɪs] n
1. caso *m*

in that case we'll wait here en ese caso esperaremos aquí

2. Idiom
in case en caso de que, por si

in any case en cualquier caso, de todos modos, a fin de cuentas

castle

castle
['kɑːs(ə)l] n
castillo *m*

he lives in a castle vive en un castillo

cat

cat
[kæt] n
gato, a

catch

catch
[kætʃ] v t
caught, caught [kɔːt]
1. atrapar, capturar, coger

you throw the ball and I'll catch it tú tiras la pelota y yo la atraparé

2. sorprender, pillar, coger
* *If I catch that dog stealing food again!...* ¡Si pillo a ese pe-

rro robando comida otra vez!...
That's what happens when you leave doors open! ¡Eso es lo que pasa cuando se dejan las puertas abiertas! *

3. tomar, coger
if you hurry up you can still catch the plane si te das prisa aún puedes coger el avión

4. Idiom
* *I can't stop sneezing, I've caught a cold!* ¡No puedo parar de estornudar, he cogido un resfriado! *

5. entender
can you repeat it, please, I couldn't catch what you said puede repetirlo, por favor, no pude entender lo que ha dicho

...catch

▶ **catch up**
alcanzar, ponerse
al nivel, recuperar

*if you don't work
now, you'll have to
catch up later* si no
trabajas ahora, tendrás
que recuperar después

cause

cause
[kɔːz]

...cause

I. *n*
causa *f*

*the cause of the
accident was a very
clear matter* la causa
del accidente era un
asunto muy claro

II. *v t*
causar, provocar

* *Don't drive so fast,
you might cause an
accident!* ¡No conduzca
tan deprisa, puede pro-
vocar un accidente! *

ceiling

ceiling
['siːlɪŋ] *n*
techo *m*

cellar

cellar
['sələ^r] *n*
bodega *f*, sótano *m*

* *Professor Topolino
has been locked in
the cellar...* El profesor

...cellar

Professor Topolino has been locked in the cellar...

Topolino ha sido encer-
rado en el sótano... *

cent

cent
(*Am*)
[sent] *n*
centavo *m*

*I don't owe you a
cent more* no te debo
ni un centavo más

centimetre

centimetre
['sentɪmiːtə^r] *n*
(*Am:* **centimeter**)
centímetro *m*

centre

centre
['sentə^r] *n*
(*Am:* **center**)
centro *m*

* *Could you tell me*

...centre

...centre

*how to get to the
town centre (Am:
center of town)?*
¿Puede decirme cómo se
llega al centro de la
ciudad?
I certainly could, Sir.
Sin duda, señor. *

cereal

cereal
['sɪərɪəl] *n*
cereal *m*

certain

certain
['sɜːtən] *adj*
1. cierto, a,
seguro, a

* *It's Sakharine who
did it! I'm absolutely
certain!* ¡Fue Sakharine
quien lo hizo! Estoy
completamente seguro!...
It's very likely!... ¡Es
muy probable!... *

2. cierto, a
I have a certain

respect for him tengo
un cierto respeto hacia él

▶ **certainly**
['sɜːtənlɪ] *adv*
1. seguramente,
ciertamente,
sin duda

*he was certainly
there when I arrived*
él sin duda estaba allí
cuando yo llegué

2. por supuesto,
ciertamente

*have you carried
out the orders?
– certainly, sir!* ¿has
cumplido las órdenes?
– ¡ciertamente, señor!

chair

chair
[tʃeəʳ] *n*
silla *f*

* *I'm sorry, Mr Baxter... That chair wasn't very strong... I'll give you another one...* Lo siento, señor Baxter...Esa silla no era muy fuerte... Le daré otra... *

chalk

chalk
[tʃɔːk] *n*
tiza *f*

champion

champion
['tʃæmpɪən] *n*
campeón *m*, campeona *f*

chance

chance
[tʃɑːns] *n*
1. casualidad *f*

by chance por casualidad

I found the letter by chance encontré la carta por casualidad

2. posibilidad *f*
we still have got one chance if we keep together todavía tenemos una posibilidad si nos mantenemos juntos

3. ocasión *f*, oportunidad *f*
if you have the chance to talk to him, tell him about our plan si tienes la oportunidad de hablar con él, cuéntale nuestro plan

4. Idiom
to take one's chances correr el riesgo

change

change
[tʃeɪndʒ]
I. *n*
1. cambio *m*

* *The forecast announced a change in the weather. The storm will soon be over...* El pronóstico anunció un cambio de tiempo. La tormenta pronto pasará... *

can you give me change? ¿puede darme cambio?

2. Idiom
he could arrive on time, for a change podría llegar a tiempo, para variar

II. *v i*
1. cambiar

there's no direct train, we have to change in London no hay tren directo, tenemos que cambiar en Londres

2. cambiarse
I'm going to change for dinner voy a cambiarme para cenar

3. convertirse
she had changed into a beautiful young lady se había convertido en una joven y bella dama

III. *v t*
1. cambiar
he changed the bulb of my lamp cambió la bombilla de mi lámpara

I must change money tengo que cambiar dinero

2. cambiar de
I have changed my mind he cambiado de idea

3. Idiom
to change hands cambiar de dueño

channel

channel
['tʃæn(ə)l] *n*
1. canal, *m*

on channel 4 they have very good programmes (Am: programs) en el canal 4 tienen programas muy buenos

2. brazo *m* de mar, canal *m*

3. Idiom
the English Channel el canal de la Mancha

* *Tintin crossed the Channel by boat.* Tintín cruzó el canal de la Mancha en barco.
Way out Salida *

Tintin crossed the Channel by boat.

chapter

chapter
['tʃæptəʳ] *n*
capítulo *m*

character

character
['kærəktəʳ] *n*
1. carácter *m*

he has a charming character tiene un carácter encantador

...character

2. personaje m
the main character in the novel is a sailor el personaje principal de la novela es un marinero

charge

charge
[tʃɑːdʒ]
I. n
1. acusación f

...charge

the charge against him was theft la acusación contra él era de robo

2. Idiom
delivery charge gastos de envío

she is in charge of this section ella está a cargo de esta sección

I'll take charge of this, you just go me encargaré de esto, tú vete

II. v t
1. hacer pagar

how much does he charge? ¿cuanto hace pagar?

2. acusar
* **You are charged with murder!...** ¡Está acusado de asesinato!... *

III. v i
cargar, atacar
the cavalry charged la caballería atacó

You are charged with murder!...

charming

charming
['tʃɑːmɪŋ] adj
encantador, ora

your sister is really charming tu hermana es verdaderamente encantadora

chase

chase
[tʃeɪs] v t
perseguir

* **Wooah! Wooah!** ¡Guau! ¡Guau!
Snowy is chasing the cat... Milú está persiguiendo al gato... *

cheap

cheap
[tʃiːp] adj
barato, a

WOOAH ! WOOAH !

Snowy is chasing the cat...

...cheap

as they were so cheap I bought many of them como eran tan baratos compré muchos

cheat

cheat
[tʃiːt] v i
hacer trampas, engañar

he cheats at cards hace trampas jugando a las cartas

check

check
[tʃek] v t
comprobar, examinar

* **A trifling correction, I think... But we'd better just check my figures once more, we musn't make a mistake.** Una corrección mínima, creo... Pero mejor será que comprobemos los cálculos una vez más, no podemos equivocarnos. *

...check

A trifling correction, I think... But we'd better just check my figures once more, we musn't make a mistake.

▶ check in
registrarse, fichar

I'm checked in room number 402 estoy registrado en la habitación 402

▶ check (Am)
→ BILL

cheek

cheek
[tʃiːk] n
1. mejilla f

turn the other cheek pon la otra mejilla

2. Idiom
* **He called me a fool! What a cheek! He won't get away with it!** ¡Me ha llamado tonto¡ ¡Qué cara más dura! ¡No se saldrá con la suya! *

He called me a fool! What a cheek! He won't get away with it!

cheer

cheer
[tʃɪəʳ] v t
animar

cheer up! ¡anímate!

▶ cheers (para brindis)

cheers! ¡salud!

▶ cheerful
['tʃɪəful] adj
de buen humor, alegre

...cheer

* Too-ra... Loo-ra...Loor-ra-lay!... ¡La...lara...laralá!... *Tintin looks very cheerful.* Tintín parece muy alegre. *

Tintin looks very cheerful.

cheese

cheese
[tʃiːz] n
queso m

do you like cream cheese? ¿te gusta el queso fresco?

chemist

chemist
['kemist] n
(*Am:* **druggist**)
1. farmacéutico, a

2. químico, a
* *Who were we talking about?* ¿De quién estábamos hablando? *We were talking about that famous chemist, Professor Smith.* Estábamos hablando de aquel famoso químico, el profesor Smith. *

▶**chemistry**
['kemistri] n
química f

▶**chemist's**
['kemists] n
farmacia f

...chemist

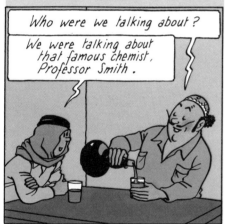

cherry

cherry
['tʃeri] n
pl cherries
cereza f

chest

chest
[tʃest] n
1. pecho m

* *Slap-bang, a punch in the chest!*

...chest

Slap-bang, a punch in the chest!

¡Y bam, un puñetazo en el pecho! *

2. cofre m, baúl m
quick, hide in that chest! ¡rápido, escóndete en ese baúl!

chicken

chicken
['tʃikin] n
pollo m

chief

chief
[tʃiːf]
I. n
jefe m

he is the Indian chief él es el jefe indio

II. adj
principal
the chief reason la razón principal

child

child
['tʃaild] n
pl children
['tʃildrən]
niño, niña

when I was a child cuando era niño

chimney

chimney
['tʃimni] n
chimenea

chin

chin
[tʃin] n
barbilla f

* *He hit Haddock on the chin!* ¡Golpeó a Haddock en la barbilla! *

He hit Haddock on the chin!

chip

chip
[tʃɪp] *n*
(*Am:* **french fry**)
patata frita *f*

fish and chips pescado con patatas fritas

chocolate

chocolate
['tʃɒklɪt] *n*
chocolate *m*

...chocolate

a bar of chocolate
una barra de chocolate

choice

choice
[tʃɔːs] *n*
1. elección *f*

2. Idiom
* *We have no choice...* No tenemos otro remedio...
We must kill him!...
¡Debemos matarle!... *

...choice

choose

choose
[tʃuːz] *vt & vi*
chose [tʃəuz]
chosen [tʃəuzn]
escoger, elegir

he chose very well
escogió muy bien

choose a card
escoge una carta

chop

chop
[tʃɒp]
I. *n*
tajada, costilla, chuleta

a pork chop una costilla de cerdo

II. *v t*
chopped, chopped
cortar, separar, picar

► **chop down**
derribar, abatir

Christmas

Christmas
['krɪsməs] *n*
Navidad *f*

we always go there for Christmas siempre vamos allí por Navidad

Father Christmas
papá Noel

Happy Christmas!
¡feliz Navidad!

church

church
[tʃɜːtʃ] *n*
iglesia *f*

this is a 12ᵗʰ century church es una iglesia del siglo XII

cigarette

cigarette
[sɪgəˈret] *n*
cigarrillo *m*

...cigarette

► **cigar**
[sɪˈgɑːʳ] *n*
cigarro, puro *m*

cinema

cinema
['sɪnəmə] *n*
cine *m*

what about going to the cinema (Am: movies)? ¿qué tal si vamos al cine?

circle

circle
['sɜːk(ə)l] *n*
círculo *m*

a vicious circle un círculo vicioso

circus

circus
['sɜːkəs] *n*
circo *m*

...circus

* *So you didn't know that there was a circus on the Moon, did you? I even heard that they needed two clowns... You two would do nicely!* ¡Así que no sabíais que había un circo en la Luna, eh? Pues hasta he oído que necesitaban dos payasos... Ustedes dos serían perfectos! *

...circus

city

city
['sɪtɪ] *n*
ciudad *f*
pl cities

I like driving in the city at night me gusta conducir por la ciudad de noche

class

class
[klɑːs] *n*
clase *f*

now I have my English class ahora tengo clase de inglés

I have a first class ticket tengo un billete de primera clase

► **classroom**
['klɑːsruːm] *n*
clase *f*, aula *f*

clean

clean
[kliːn]
I. *adj*
limpio, a

the house is very clean la casa está muy limpia

II. *vt & vi*
limpiar

* *I'm going to clean the furniture...* Voy a limpiar los muebles... *

clear

clear
[klɪəʳ]
I. adj
1. claro, a, transparente

a clear sky un cielo claro

2. evidente, claro, a
it's clear that we must think a way of getting out of here está claro que debemos pensar una manera de salir de aquí

II. v t & v i
disipar, limpiar

I'll clear your doubts yo disiparé tus dudas

▶ **clear off**
irse, largarse

clear off! I don't want to see you round here any more! ¡Lárgate! No quiero verte por aquí nunca más!

▶ **clear up**
1. esclarecer, resolver

* *We'll clear up this mystery*... Vamos a resolver este misterio... *

2. arreglar, ordenar
clear up this mess! ¡arregla este desorden!

▶ **clearly**
['klɪəlɪ] adv
1. con claridad

2. evidentemente, claramente, abiertamente,
he was clearly mistaken estaba claramente equivocado

3. Idiom
* *I can't hear you, could you speak more clearly?* No puedo oírle, puede hablar más

clerk

clerk
[klɑːk] n
oficinista m f

he works as a clerk in the bank trabaja de oficinista en el banco

clever

clever
['klevəʳ] adj
1. listo, a, inteligente

he thinks he is very clever se cree muy listo

2. hábil, astuto, a
* *He's not very clever!* ¡No es muy astuto! *

He's not very clever!

climb

climb
[klaɪm] v t & v i
trepar, subir, escalar

they are climbing the highest mountain están escalando la montaña más alta

clinic

clinic
['klɪnɪk] n
clínica f

* *What are you doing?* ¿Qué está haciendo?
I'm better: I'm leaving the clinic... Estoy mejor: voy a irme de la clínica... *

...clinic

clock

clock
[klɒk] n
reloj m

▶ **alarm clock**
[ə'lɑːmklɒk]
despertador

close

close
[kləus]
I. adj
cercano, a,
íntimo, a

a close friend un amigo íntimo

II. adv
cerca

come closer ven más cerca

close

close
[kləuz] v t & v i
cerrar

* *And now, Mrs Yamilah, close your eyes...* Y ahora, señora Yamilah, cierre los ojos... *

the shops (Am: stores) close at eight las tiendas cierran a las ocho

▶ **close down**
cerrar

the factory has closed down la fábrica ha cerrado

cloud

cloud
[klaud] *n*
nube *f*

▶ **cloudy**
['klaudı] *adj*
cloudier, cloudiest
nublado, a

that day the sky was cloudy aquel día el cielo estaba nublado

club

club
[klʌb]
I. *n*
1. club *m*

you can't come in the club no puedes entrar en el club

2. bastón, porra
* *He hit Tintin with a club...* Pegó a Tintín con un bastón... *

II. *n pl*
the ace of clubs el as de trébol

He hit Tintin with a club...

coach

coach
[kəutʃ] (*Am:* **bus**)
1. autocar *m*

* *Do you see that? They're taking the coach... There can't have been any seats left in the train...* ¿Ves eso? Cogen el autocar...No habría sitio en el tren... *

2. vagón

3. carruaje

...coach

4. entrenador
football coach entrenador de fútbol

coal

coal
[kəul] *n*
carbón *m*

a coal mine una mina de carbón

coast

In Kiltoch, the coast is rocky.

coast
[kəust] *n*
1. costa *f*

* *In Kiltoch the coast is rocky.* En Kiltoch la costa es rocosa. *

2. Idiom
the coast is clear no hay moros en la costa

coat

coat
[kəut] *n*
1. abrigo *m*

don't forget your coat no te olvides el abrigo

2. capa
a coat of paint una capa de pintura

cocoa

cocoa
['kəukəu] *n*
cacao *m*

coffee

coffee
['kɒfı] *n*
café *m*

black coffee un café solo

white coffee café con leche

coin

coin
[kɔın] *n*
moneda *f*

this is a false coin! ¡es una moneda falsa!

cold

cold
[kəuld]
I. *adj*
1. frio, a

the water is too cold el agua está demasiado fría

2. Idiom
I'm cold tengo frío

* *Hurry up, Snowy, it's terribly cold!* ¡Date prisa, Milú; hace mucho frío! *

II. *n*
resfriado *m*, constipado *m*

you'll catch a cold vas a coger un resfriado

* *Tchooo!* Achuuus! *The Captain's caught a cold.* El capitán ha cogido un resfriado. *

...cold

TCHOOO

The Captain's caught a cold.

collect

collect
[kə'lekt] v t
1. coleccionar

Mary collects perfumes María colecciona perfumes

2. recoger
I'll collect you at the school te recogeré en la escuela

▶ **collection**
[kə'lekʃ(ə)n] n
colección f

what a beautiful collection! ¡qué colección tan bonita!

colour

colour
['kʌləʳ] n
(*Am:* **color**)
color m

his eyes were a strange colour sus ojos eran de un color extraño

...colour

the colour has come out very well in these photos el color ha salido muy bien en estas fotos

come

come
[kʌm] v i
came [keɪm],
come [kʌm]

...come

venir

he came with his brother vino con su hermano

* *These cigarettes come from Borduria look at the pack Captain...* Estos cigarrillos vienen de Borduria mire el paquete, capitán... *Good grief!* ¡Dios mío! *

is he coming with us? ¿viene con nosotros?

...come

These cigarettes come from Borduria, look at the pack, Captain...

Good grief!...

▶ **come across**
encontrarse con (por casualidad)

▶ **come along**
venir, ir

* *Come along, we're going to be late!* ¡Venga, vamos a llegar tarde!
I'm coming... Ya voy... *

▶ **come back**
volver

Come along, we're going to be late!
I'm coming...

* *No, Sir, the Captain hasn't come back from his trip!* ¡No, señor, el capitán no ha vuelto de su viaje!
I'm telling you that nobody's in. The Captain hasn't come back from his trip! ¡Le digo que no hay nadie en casa. El capitán no ha vuelto de su viaje! *

▶ **come in**
entrar, llegar

No, Sir, the Captain hasn't come back from his trip!

I'm telling you that nobody's in. The Captain hasn't come back from his trip!

...come

please, do come in por favor, entre

he's just come in acaba de llegar

▶ **come on**
venir, ir

come on, don't stay behind! ¡vamos, no te quedes atrás!

Idiom
come on, don't get angry venga hombre, no te enfades

comfortable

comfortable
['kʌmftəbl] adj
comfortable, cómodo, a

this bed is very comfortable esta cama es muy comfortable

sit down and make yourself comfortable siéntese y póngase cómodo

comic

comic
['kɒmɪk]
I. n
1. cómico, a
(*comedian*)

2. comic m, tebeo m

▶ **comic strip** f
['kɒmɪk'strip]
tira f de comic

* *For goodness' sake Tintin, do you take me for a character out of a comic strip*

For goodness' sake Tintin, do you take me for a character out of a comic strip or what?

Wait for me!

...comic

or what? Por Dios Tintín, ¿me toma por un personaje en una tira de comic o qué?
Wait for me! ¡Espéreme! *

II. *adj*
cómico, a, gracioso, a

command

command
[kə'mɑːnd]

...command

I. *n*
1. orden *m*

at your command a sus órdenes

2. Idiom
* *Billions of blue blistering barnacles! I'm in command of this ship!* ¡Mil millones de demonios! ¡Yo estoy al mando de este barco! *

II. *vi & vt*
mandar, ordenar, tener el poder

Billions of blue blistering barnacles! I'm in command of this ship!

common

common
['kɒmən] *adj*
1. común, corriente

2. frecuente
don't be surprised, these kind of occurrences are very common here no se sorprenda, esta clase de cosas son muy frecuentes aquí

▶ **common sense** *n*
['kɒmən'sens]
sentido común *m*

* *If you had any common sense, you wouldn't have got the time wrong!... Do you hear?* Si tuviera algo de sentido común, no se habría equivocado en la hora!... ¿Me oye? *

...common

If you had any common sense, you wouldn't have got the time wrong!... Do you hear?

company

company
['kʌmpənɪ] *n*
pl companies
1. compañía *f*, sociedad *f*

limited company sociedad limitada

2. compañía *f*
I'll keep you company te haré compañía

compare

compare
[kəm'peəʳ] *vt & vi*
comparar

* *If I compare these two statues, I can see that one is a forgery!* ¡Si comparo estas dos estatuas, puedo ver que una es una falsificación! *

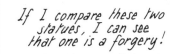

If I compare these two statues, I can see that one is a forgery!

competition

competition
[kɒmpɪ'tɪʃ(ə)n] *n*
1. competición *f*, concurso *m*

2. competencia

complain

complain
[kəm'pleɪn] *vi*
quejarse

...complain

he's always complaining siempre se está quejando

▶ **complaint** *n*
queja *f*

complete

complete
[kəm'pliːt]
I. *adj*
completo, a

...complete

Come on, stand up, Captain!

I can't go on, I'm completely exhausted!

that was a complete disaster aquello fue un completo desastre

II. *vt*
terminar

I've completed my project he terminado mi proyecto

▶ **completely**
[kəm'pliːtlɪ] *adv*
completamente

* *Come on, stand up, Captain!* ¡Vamos, levántese, capitán!
I can't go on, I'm completely exhausted! ¡No puedo seguir, estoy completamente agotado! *

compulsory

compulsory
[kəm'pʌlsərɪ] *adj*
obligatorio, a

computer

computer
[kəm'pjuːtə^r] n
computadora f,
ordenador m

* *There are several computers in the rocket to assist with the piloting...* Hay varias computadoras en el cohete para auxiliar el pilotaje... *

concern

concern
[kən'sɜːn] v t
afectar,
concernir

▶ **concerning**
[kən'sɜːnɪŋ] prep
acuerda de,
con respecto a

* *I have a question to ask you concerning Snowy.* Tengo que hacerles una pregunta acerca de Milú. *

concert

concert
['kɒnsət] n
concierto m

conclusion

conclusion
[kən'kluːʒ(ə)n] n
1. conclusión f,
final m

2. conclusión m,
deducción f

condition

condition
[kən'dɪʃ(ə)n] n
1. condición f

I'll do it on one condition lo haré con una condición

2. estado m
* *This boat doesn't seem to be in very good condition!* Este barco no parece estar en muy buen estado! *

conductor

conductor
[kən'dʌktə^r] n
1. director m de orquesta

the conductor bowed to the audience el director de la orquesta saludó al público

2. cobrador m (de autobús)

▶ **conductress**
[kən'dʌktrɪs] n
cobradora f (de autobús)

confidence

confidence
['kɒnfɪdəns] n
confianza f

I have no confidence in him no tengo confianza en él

confuse

confuse
[kən'fjuːz] v t
confundir

...confuse

▶ **confused**
[kən'fjuːzd] adj
1. perplejo, a,
desconcertado, a

she seemed very confused parecía muy desconcertada

2. confuso, a
it was all very confused todo era muy confuso

▶ **confusing**
[kən'fjuːzɪŋ] adj
lioso, a

▶ **confusion**
[kən'fjuːʒ(ə)n] n
confusión f

congratulate

congratulate
[kən'grætjuleɪt] v t
felicitar

▶ **congratulations**
[kən'grætjuˈleɪʃ(ə)nz] n pl
felicidades f pl

* *Let me shake your hand, Tintin... Congratulations!... Well done!... Thanks to you, we've arrested the culprits...* Permítame que le dé la mano,

Tintín... ¡Felicidades!... ¡Bien hecho!... Gracias a usted, hemos arrestado a los culpables... *

consider

consider
[kən'sɪdə^r] v t
1. examinar

we must consider the facts debemos examinar los hechos

...consider

2. considerar
he is considered a very tough opponent se le considera un rival muy duro

▶ **considerable**
[kən'sɪdərəbl] *adj*
considerable

* *All this has cost a considerable sum of money and called for an awful lot of work...* Todo esto ha costado una considerable

suma de dinero y ha necesitado una enorme cantidad de trabajo... *

consist

consist
[kən'sɪst] *v i*
1. consistir

her job consists of helping the teacher su trabajo consiste en ayudar al profesor

...consist

2. estar compuesto, constar de
the house consists of eight rooms la casa consta de ocho habitaciones

contain

contain
[kən'teɪn] *v t*
contener

...contain

* *The casket only contains old documents!...* ¡El cofre sólo contiene viejos documentos!...
Old documents?... It was a waste of time to go to all that trouble! ¿Viejos documentos?... ¡Fue una pérdida de tiempo tomarnos todo esa molestia! *

continent

continent
['kɒntɪnənt] *n*
continente *m*

the African continent el continente africano

he has just arrived from the continent acaba de llegar del continente (*Europa*)

continue

continue
[kən'tɪnjuː] *v i & v t*
continuar, seguir

we will continue working together continuaremos trabajando juntos

control

control
[kən'trəul]
I. *n*

...control

...control

1. control *m*

* *Heavens! The plane is out of control!* ¡Cielos! ¡He perdido el control del avión! *

2. mando *m*
* *I must reach the controls...* Tengo que alcanzar los mandos... *

3. autoridad *f*, **control** *m*
he has no control

over his pupils no tiene autoridad sobre sus alumnos

II. *v t*
1. dominar, controlar

she can't control his temper no puede dominar su genio

2. controlar
they control the quality of the goods controlan la calidad de las mercancías

convenient

convenient
[kən'viːnɪənt] *adj*
1. conveniente, cómodo, a, oportuno, a

we'll talk at a more convenient time hablaremos en un momento más oportuno

2. bien situado, a
his flat is convenient for his office su piso ésta bien situado para ir a su oficina

conversation

conversation
[kɒnvə'seɪʃ(ə)n] *n*
conversación *f*

he was listening to our conversation estaba escuchando nuestra conversación

convince

convince
[kən'vɪns] *v t*
convencer, persuadir

...convince

* Captain, we must convince them that we are innocent...
Capitán, debemos convencerles de que somos inocentes... *

cook

cook
[kuk]
I. n

...cook

* Ah, here's the cook...! What nice little dish have you made us for lunch?
¡Ah, aquí está el cocinero...! ¿Qué delicioso plato nos ha preparado para el almuerzo?
Spaghetti, Captain.
Espaguetis, capitán. *

cocinero m
cocinera f

II. v t
guisar

...cook

she cooks the meal every morning guisa la comida cada mañana

III. v i
1. cocinar

he cooks very well cocina muy bien

2. Idiom
these potatoes don't cook well estas patatas no se cuecen bien

▶ **cooker**
['kukə'] n

(*Am:* **stove**)
cocina f

we have bought a new cooker hemos comprado una cocina nueva

▶ **cooking**
['kukɪŋ] n
cocina f

Indian cooking is hot la comida india es picante

cool

cool
[ku:l] adj
1. fresco, a, frío, a

it's a nice cool evening hace una noche fresca y agradable

2. Idiom
to play it cool/to keep one's cool mantener la calma

▶ **cool down**
1. calmarse

he cooled down and began to speak se calmó y empezó a hablar

2. enfriar(se)

* Well, now we must let the engine cool down! ¡Bien, ahora debemos dejar que el motor se enfríe!
To be precise, we must let the engine cool down! ¡Yo aún diría más, debemos dejar que el motor se enfríe! *

copy

copy
['kɒpɪ]
copied, copied ['kɒpɪd]
I. v i & v t
copiar

II. n
copia f

corn

corn
[kɔ:n] n

...corn

1. trigo m, cereal m
2. (*Am*) maíz m

▶ **cornflakes**
['kɔ:nfleɪks] n pl
cornflakes m pl, copos m pl de maíz

corner

He's not going to pop up on the street corner like that...

corner
['kɔːnəʳ] n
1. esquina f

* *He's not going to pop up on the corner of the street like that...* No va a aparecer a la vuelta de la esquina así por las buenas... *

2. rincón

correct
[kə'rekt]
I. adj
correcto, a, exacto, a

this is the correct answer ésta es la respuesta correcta

* *Eight o'clock sharp! But that is not the correct time... This clock is definitely slow...* ¡Las ocho en punto! Pero ésta

Eight o'clock sharp! But that is not the correct time... This clock is definitely slow...

no es la hora exacta... Desde luego este reloj va atrasado... *

II. v t
corregir

correct me if I'm wrong corríjame si me equivoco

▶ **correction**
[kə'rekʃ(ə)n] n
corrección f

he didn't like the

corrections to the *script* no le gustaron las correcciones al guión

corridor
['kɒrɪdəʳ] n
pasillo m

the palace had long corridors el palacio tenía largos pasillos

cost
[kɒst]
I. v t
costar

* *How much does this boat cost?* ¿Cuánto cuesta este barco? *

II. n
coste m

the cost of living el coste de la vida

How much does that boat cost?

cottage
['kɒtɪdʒ] n
1. casa f de campo

Arnold has a cottage in Nunney Arnold tiene una casa de campo en Nunney

2. Idiom
thatched cottage casa de campo con tejado de paja

cotton
['kɒt(ə)n] n
algodón m

this skirt is 100% cotton esta falda es 100% algodón

cough
[kɒf]
I. n
tos f

this is a good cough syrup este jarabe es bueno para la tos

II. v i
toser

could
[kud] v aux
poder

could you tell me why? ¿podrías decirme por qué?

he couldn't help making a noise no podía evitar hacer ruido

* *Tintin still hasn't come back, he could have warned me...* Tintín todavía no ha vuelto. Hubiera podido avisarme... *

Tintin still hasn't come back, he could have warned me...

count
[kaunt] v i & v t
contar, numerar

he still has to count how many people will come aún tiene que contar cuántas personas vendrán

▶ **count on**
contar con

you can count on me puedes contar conmigo

counter
['kauntəʳ] n
1. mostrador m

she talked to us from behind the counter habló con nosotros desde detrás del mostrador

2. ficha f
I need counters to play necesito fichas para jugar

country

country
['kʌntrɪ] n
pl countries
1. país m

he is away from his country no está en su país

2. campo m
* Do you prefer to live in a town or in the country? ¿Prefiere vivir en la ciudad o en el campo? *

Do you prefer to live in a town or in the country?

couple

couple
['kʌpl] n
1. pareja f, matrimonio m

a young couple una pareja joven

2. Idiom
a couple of un par de, unos cuantos

a couple of days later... unos cuantos días más tarde...

course

course
[kɔːs] n
1. curso m

he has enrolled for the course se ha matriculado para el curso

2. transcurso m
in the course of these last days en el transcurso de estos últimos días

...course

3. rumbo m
I'm trying to hold my course! ¡intento mantener el rumbo!

4. Idiom
of course por supuesto, desde luego, naturalmente

* Well, of course, it's them over there, hiding behind their newspapers... Pues, desde luego que son ellos los de allí, escondiéndose

detrás de sus periódicos...
Thomson and Thompson! ¡Hernández y Fernández! *

of course not por supuesto que no

Well, of course, it's them over there, hiding behind their newspapers...

Thomson and Thompson!

cousin

cousin
['kʌzən] n
primo m
prima f

Angelica is my cousin Angélica es mi prima

cover

cover
['kʌvəʳ]
I. v t

...cover

cubrir, tapar

it's all covered with dust! ¡todo está cubierto de polvo!

II. n
1. cubierta f, tapa f

he put his signature on the cover of the book puso su firma en la cubierta del libro

2. Idiom
* Take cover! ¡Póngase a cubierto!
Bang Bang Pam pam *

...cover

Take cover!

BANG BANG

cow

cow
[kau] n
vaca f

* Where on earth is this cow taking me?... ¿Adónde diablos me está llevando esta vaca?...
Woof! Woof! ¡Guau! ¡Guau! *

Where on earth is this cow taking me?...

WOOF! WOOF!

crash

crash
[kræʃ]
I. *v i*
chocar

II. *n*
1. accidente *m*

the car crash occurred on the motorway el accidente de coche ocurrió en la autopista

2. estruendo *m*
there was a loud crash in the street hubo un gran estruendo

en la calle

▶ **crash into**
chocar contra

the lorry crashed into the wall el camión chocó contra la pared

crate

crate
[kreɪt] *n*
caja *f*

crazy

crazy
['kreɪzɪ] *adj*
crazier, craziest
loco, a

* *What are you doing, Captain? Have you gone crazy?* ¿Qué está haciendo, capitán? ¿Se ha vuelto loco? *

cream

cream
[kriːm] *n*
1. crema *f*

2. nata *f*
whipped cream nata batida

creep

creep
[kriːp] *v i*
crept, crept [krept]
arrastrarse,

deslizarse

* *Let's try to creep up behind the guards and surprise them...* Intentemos deslizarnos por detrás de los guardias y sorprenderlos... *

crew

crew
[kruː] *n*
tripulación *f*

cricket

cricket
['krɪkɪt] *n*
crícquet *m*

they are playing cricket están jugando al crícquet

crime

crime
[kraɪm] *n*
crimen *m*, delito *m*

...crime

he didn't commit the crime él no cometió el crimen

cross

cross
[krɒs]
I. *v i & v t*
1. cruzar

we'll cross the bridge now vamos a cruzar el puente ahora

...cross

2. Idiom
to cross over atravesar

II. *n*
cruz *f*, crucifijo *m*

* *It's a cross, isn't it?* Es una cruz, ¿verdad? *

III. *adj*
enfadado, a

don't be cross with me no te enfades conmigo

▶ **cross out**
tachar, borrar

cross out that letter tacha esa letra

▶ **crossroads**
['krɒsrəʊdz] *n*
cruce *m*

turn right at the crossroads gira a la derecha en el cruce

crowd

crowd
[kraʊd] *n*
muchedumbre *f*,
multitud *f*

I couldn't see him among the crowd no podía verlo entre la muchedumbre

cry

cry
[kraɪ]
I. *n*
grito *m*

* *Aaaaaah!* Aaaaaah! *They heard a cry...* Oyeron un grito... *

II. *v i*
1. llorar

he began crying empezó a llorar

2. gritar

...cry

They heard a cry...

she cried for help
gritó pidiendo ayuda

▶ **cry out**
pegar un grito

he cried out in pain
pegó un grito de dolor

cup

cup
[kʌp] *n*
1. taza *f*

I'd like a cup of coffee, please quisiera una taza de café, por favor

2. copa *f*
the team won the cup el equipo ganó la copa

cupboard

cupboard
['kʌbəd] *n*
armario *m*

the glasses are in the cupboard los vasos están en el armario

curious

curious
['kjuərɪəs] *adj*
1. curioso, a

* *Is that it?* ¿Ya está? *Yes, that's it! That will teach you to be curious, Snowy!* ¡Sí, ya está! ¡Esto te enseñará a no ser curioso, Milú! *

2. extraño, a
he looks very curious tiene un aspecto muy extraño

...curious

curtain

curtain
['kɜːt(ə)n] *n*
(*Am:* **drape**)
cortina *f*

could you please draw the curtains? ¿podría correr las cortinas, por favor?

cushion

cushion
['kuʃ(ə)n] *n*
cojín *m*

customer

customer
['kʌstəmə'] *n*
cliente *m*
clienta *f*

customs

customs
['kʌstəmz] *n pl*
aduana *f*

...customs

the dealer was caught at the customs cogieron al traficante en la aduana

cut

cut
[kʌt]
I. *n*
corte *m*
II. *v t*
cut, cut [kʌt]

...cut

1. cortar

be careful or you'll cut yourself ten cuidado o te cortarás

yesterday I had my hair cut ayer me cortaron el pelo

2. reducir, disminuir
they have cut our wages nos han reducido el salario

▶ **cut down**
1. derribar, talar

the tree was cut down el árbol fue derribado

2. reducir
they've cut down their expenses han reducido sus gastos

▶ **cut off**
1. cortar, amputar

the surgeon had to cut her leg off el cirujano tuvo que cortarle la pierna

2. desconectar, cortar
the telephone is cut off el teléfono está cortado

▶ **cut out**
1. recortar

the children are cutting out pieces of paper los niños recortan trozos de papel

2. Idiom
to cut out drinking/ smoking dejar de beber/fumar

cycle

cycle
['saɪk(ə)l]
I. *n*
1. bicicleta *f*, bici *f*

2. ciclo *m*

II. *v i*
ir en bicicleta

he cycles to work every morning va a trabajar en bicicleta cada mañana

D

dad

dad, daddy
[dæd, 'dædɪ] *n*
papá *m*

* *My daddy will be very cross with you!... And he'll cut your head off!...* ¡Mi padre se enfadará mucho contigo!...¡Y te cortará la cabeza!... *

My daddy will be very cross with you! And he'll cut you head off!...

daily

daily
['deɪlɪ] *adj*
diario, a
cotidiano, a

dairy

dairy
['deərɪ] *n*
pl dairies
lechería *f*

damage

damage
['dæmɪdʒ]
I. *n*
daño *m*
daños *m pl*

now the damage is done ahora el daño ya está hecho

II. *v t*
sufrir daño

thank God the book is not damaged menos mal que el libro no ha sufrido daño alguno

dance

dance
[dɑːns]
I. *n*
baile *m*, danza *f*

we'll give a dance in your honour ofreceremos un baile en tu honor

II. *v i & v t*
bailar

* *Let's dance! Let's dance!* ¡Bailemos! ¡Bailemos¡
Hurray! ¡Hurra! *

...dance

Let's dance! Let's dance!
Hurray!
Let's dance!
Look! That's the way white men dance!

Let's dance! ¡Bailemos!
Look! That's the way white men dance! ¡Mira! ¡Así es como bailan los blancos! *

danger

danger
['deɪndʒəʳ] *n*
peligro *m*

quick! Tintin is in danger ¡rápido! Tintín está en peligro

▶ **dangerous**
['deɪndʒərəs] *adj*
peligroso, a

this is a dangerous mission es una misión peligrosa

dare

dare
[deəʳ]
I. v i
1. atreverse

* *Who's there?*
¿Quién está ahí?
He daren't move. No
se atreve a moverse. *

*don't you dare tell
him* no te atrevas a
decírselo

2. Idiom
I dare say she's all

right supongo que está
bien

II. v t
desafiar

*I dare you to do it
faster* te desafío a que
lo hagas más rápido

▶ **daring**
['deərɪŋ] adj
atrevido, a

He daren't move.

dark

dark
[dɑːk]
I. adj
1. oscuro, a

*put the light on; it's
very dark* enciende la
luz; está muy oscuro

2. moreno, a
is she fair or dark?
¿es rubia o morena?

II. n
oscuridad f

*he was watching
from the dark* estaba
mirando desde la oscu-
ridad

▶ **darkness**
['dɑːknɪs] n
1. oscuridad f

2. Idiom
*the room was in
darkness* la habitación
estaba a oscuras

darling

darling
['dɑːlɪŋ] n
cariño m, querido, a

*we are together at
last, darling* estamos
juntos al fin, cariño

date

date
[deɪt]
I. n
1. fecha f

...date

*what's the date to-
day?* ¿qué fecha es hoy?

2. cita
*I've got a date
tonight* tengo una cita
esta noche

3. Idiom
it's up to date está al
día

out of date caducado,
pasado de moda

II. v i & v t
fechar, datar

daughter

daughter
['dɔːtəʳ] n
hija f

*we have a son and
a daughter* tenemos un
hijo y una hija

day

day
[deɪ] n
1. día m

*he studies four
hours a day* estudia
cuatro horas al día

* *Forward, Snowy!
We'll have to walk
all day!...* ¡Adelante,
Milú! Tenemos que
caminar todo el día!... *

2. Idiom
*the day before
yesterday* anteayer

...day

*the day after
tomorrow* pa-
sado mañana

dead

dead
[ded]
I. adj
muerto, a

* *Dead?* ¿Muerto?
*No, he's breathing,
he's not dead!* No,
respira, no está muerto! *

II. n
muerto, a

the dead los muertos

deaf

deaf
[def] adj
sordo, a

*don't shout!, I'm not
deaf* ¡no grites!, no estoy
sordo

deal

deal
[diːl]
I. n
1. negocio m,
trato m

it's a deal es un trato

2. Idiom
a great deal una gran
cantidad, mucho

*he has a great deal
of money* tiene mucho
dinero

...deal

II. *v t*
1. negociar

2. dar (las cartas)
deal the cards da las cartas

▶ **deal with**
tratar con, encargarse de

he is difficult to deal with es difícil tratar con él

dear

dear
[dɪəʳ] *adj*
1. querido, a

my dear friend mi querido amigo

2. caro, a
he sells his articles very dear vende sus artículos muy caros

3. Idiom
oh dear! ¡vaya por Dios!

death

Tintin and the Captain have been sentenced to death...

...death

death
[deθ] *n*
muerte *f*

* *Tintin and the Captain have been sentenced to death...* Tintín y el capitán han sido condenados a muerte... *

December

December
[dɪ'sembəʳ] *n*
diciembre *m*

...December

the first of December (Am: December first) el uno de diciembre

the 5th of December (Am: December 5) el cinco de diciembre

decide

decide
[dɪ'saɪd] *v i & v t*
decidir, decidirse

...decide

they decided to leave decidieron partir

▶ **decision**
[dɪ'sɪʒən] *n*
decisión *f*

you must make a decision debes tomar una decisión

deck

deck
[dek] *n*
cubierta *f*

* *The waves are covering the deck...* Las olas cubren la cubierta.. *

declare

declare
[dɪ'kleəʳ] *v t*
declarar

The waves are covering the deck...

...declare

War has been declared!... War has been declared!

* *War has been declared!... War has been declared!* ¡Ha sido declarada la guerra!... ¡Ha sido declarada la guerra! *

deep

deep
[di:p] *adj*
profundo, a
hondo, a

* *The river is really*

...deep

deep!... ¡El río es realmente profundo!... *Splash* Pluf *

defend

defend
[dɪ'fend] *v t*
defender

I will defend this place against all enemies defenderé este lugar contra todos los enemigos

The river is really deep !...

definite

definite
['defɪnɪt] *adj*
1. preciso, a
determinado, a

we must agree on a definite time debemos ponernos de acuerdo en una hora precisa

2. seguro, a
definitivo, a
their return is definite su vuelta es segura

...definite

▶ **definitely**
['defɪnɪtlɪ] adv
1. definitivamente, sin duda

she's definitely wrong ella está sin duda equivocada

2. absolutamente, por supuesto
are you coming? – definitely ¿vienes? — por supuesto

degree

degree
[dɪ'griː] n
1. grado m

two degrees below zero dos grados bajo cero

2. Idiom
up to a certain degree hasta cierto punto

3. licenciatura f, título m
he has a degree in

Arts tiene un título en Filosofía y Letras

delay

delay
[dɪ'leɪ]
I. n
retraso m, demora f

there will be a two hours delay habrá un retraso de dos horas

II. vi & vt
retrasar, demorar

I was delayed by a traffic jam me ha retrasado un atasco de tráfico

delicious

delicious
[dɪ'lɪʃəs] adj
delicioso, a

what a delicious

...delicious

meal! ¡qué comida tan deliciosa!

delight

delight
[dɪ'laɪt] n
1. deleite m, placer m

2. Idiom
he takes great delight in reading se deleita en la lectura

...delight

▶ **delighted**
[dɪ'laɪtɪd] adj
encantado, a

* *Tintin!... Captain!... I am delighted to see you again!...* ¡Tintín!... ¡capitán!... Estoy encantado de verles de nuevo!... *

▶ **delightful**
[dɪ'laɪtful] adj
encantador, ora, grato, a

it's a delightful village es una aldea encantadora

deliver

deliver
[dɪ'lɪvəʳ] v t
entregar

the message has been delivered el mensaje ha sido entregado

dentist

dentist
['dentɪst] n
dentista m f

to go to the dentist's ir al dentista

department

department
[dɪ'pɑːtmənt] n
departamento m, sección f

she works in the perfume department trabaja en la sección de perfumes

---

departure

departure
[dɪ'pɑːtʃəʳ] n
salida f, marcha f

the board shows the departures of the trains el tablero anuncia la salida de los trenes

depend

depend
[dɪ'pend] v i

...depend

depender

* *Tharkey, will we be able to leave tomorrow?* Tharkey, ¿podremos irnos mañana?
It depends on the weather; we'll decide tomorrow morning... Depende del tiempo; lo decidiremos mañana por la mañana... *

depth

depth
[depθ] n
profundidad f

describe

describe
[dɪs'kraɪb] v t
describir

* *Can you describe the car?* ¿Puede describir el coche?
Yes, it's a beige car

...describe

...describe

with a sunroof. Sí, es un coche beig con capota. *

▶ **description**
[dɪsˈkrɪpʃ(ə)n] *n*
descripción *f*

desert

desert
[ˈdezət]
I. *n*

...desert

desierto *m*

* *We're lost in the middle of the desert...* Estamos perdidos en medio del desierto... *

II. *adj*
1. desértico, a

a desert region una región desértica

2. Idiom
a desert island una isla desierta

▶ **deserted**
[deˈzɜːtɪd] *adj*
desierto, a

a deserted street una calle desierta

deserve

deserve
[dɪˈzɜːv] *v t*
merecer

he deserves a good rest se merece un buen descanso

design

design
[dɪˈzaɪn] *v i & v t*
1. idear, proyectar

this computer is designed for children este ordenador está ideado para niños

2. diseñar, dibujar
she designs beautiful vases diseña hermosos jarrones

desk

desk
[desk] *n*
1. pupitre *m*

2. escritorio *m*
* *These are the plans...* Estos son los planos...
Thank you, Professor. Put them on my desk. Gracias, profesor. Póngalos en mi escritorio. *

dessert

dessert
[dɪˈzɜːt] *n*
postre *m*

we have cake for dessert tenemos pastel de postre

destroy

destroy
[dɪˈstrɔɪ] *v t*
destruir

...destroy

* *The fire has destroyed everything!...* ¡El fuego lo ha destruido todo!... *

detail

detail
[ˈdiːteɪl] *n*
detalle *m*

you don't need to go into detail no es necesario que entres en detalles

detective

detective
[dɪˈtektɪv] *n*
detective *m f*

* *We've asked two famous detectives to investigate this case.* Hemos pedido a dos famosos detectives que investiguen el caso. *

develop

develop
[dɪˈveləp] *v t*
1. desarrollar

* *Very interesting, Professor, could you develop your idea?... I'm listening to you...* Muy interesante, profesor, ¿podría desarrollar su idea?... Le escucho... *

2. revelar
(*photographs, films*)
I must have my

...develop

Very interesting, Professor, could you develop your idea?... I'm listening to you...

photos developed tengo que revelar mis fotos

dial

dial
['daɪəl]
I. n
esfera f de reloj

II. v t
marcar (un número de teléfono)

...dial

* No, it's not Mr Cutts the butcher. You **dialled** (Am: **dialed**) the wrong **number!**... No, no es la carnicería Sanzot. Ha marcado un número equivocado!... *

No, it's not Mr Cutts the butcher, you dialled the wrong number!...

diamond

diamond
['daɪəmənd] n
diamante m

a diamond ring un anillo de diamantes

dictate

dictate
[dɪk'teɪt] v i & v t
dictar

he's dictating a

...dictate

letter to his secretary está dictando una carta a su secretaria

▶ **dictation**
[dɪk'teɪʃ(ə)n] n
dictado m

dictionary

dictionary
['dɪkʃənrɪ] n
diccionario m

...dictionary

look it up in the **dictionary** búscalo en el diccionario

die

die
[daɪ]
I. v i
morir

* *Don't miss him!... He must die!...* ¡No falles!...¡ Debe morir! *

...die

Don't miss him!... He must die!...

II. n
pl dice [daɪs]
dado m

difference

difference
['dɪfərəns] n
diferencia f

* *What's the difference between Thompson and*

...difference

What's the difference between Thompson and Thomson?

Thomson? ¿Cuál es la diferencia entre Fernández y Hernández? *

▶ **different**
['dɪfərənt] adj
diferente

difficult

difficult
['dɪfɪkəlt] adj
difícil

...difficult

it's a difficult problem es un problema difícil

* *The cave is difficult to reach: shall we try all the same?* La cueva es de difícil acceso: ¿lo intentamos igualmente? *Of course!* ¡Por supuesto! *

▶ **difficulty**
['dɪfɪkəltɪ] n
pl difficulties
dificultad f

The cave is difficult to reach shall we try all the same? *Of course!*

dig

dig
[dɪg] v i & v t
dug, dug [dʌg]
cavar

they were digging a tunnel estaban cavando un túnel

dining room

dining room
['daɪnɪŋruːm] n
comedor m

dinner

dinner
['dɪnə'] *n*
cena *f*, comida *f*

we must dress for dinner debemos vestirnos para la cena

dinner's ready! ¡la comida está lista!

direct

direct
[daɪ'rekt]
I. *adj*
directo, a

he took a direct route tomó una ruta directa

* *Zorrino, what is the most direct route to get to the Temple of the Sun?* Zorrino, ¿cuál es la ruta más directa para llegar al Templo del Sol?

Zorrino, what is the most direct route to get to the Temple of the Sun?

We must cross over the mountain.

We must cross over the mountain. Debemos cruzar al otro lado de la montaña. *

II. *vi & vt*
dirigir

he directs a small company dirige una pequeña empresa

▶ **direction**
[daɪ'rekʃ(ə)n] *n*
dirección *f*

* *Let's follow him! He*

went in that direction! ¡Sigámosle! ¡Se fue en esa dirección! *

▶ **directly**
[daɪ'rektlɪ] *adv*
1. directamente

go directly to the station vaya directamente a la estación

2. inmediatamente, enseguida
come home directly ven enseguida a casa

...direct

Let's follow him! He wen't in that direction!

dirty

dirty
['dɜːtɪ] *adj*
dirtier, dirtiest
sucio, a

* *Really, Snowy, you haven't only been drinking but you're dirty too!...* ¡Ya está bien, Milú, no sólo has estado bebiendo sino que además estás sucio!... *Dirty... You think... hic... that... hic... I'm dirty... hic...* Sucio... Tú crees... hip... que... hip... estoy sucio... hip...* .

Really, Snowy, you haven't only been drinking but you're dirty too!...

Dirty... You think... hic... that... hic... I'm dirty... hic...

disagree

disagree
[dɪsə'griː] *vi*
1. no estar de acuerdo, discrepar

* *I completely disagree with you!...* ¡No estoy nada de acuerdo contigo!.... *For goodness' sake, Captain, let me explain to you...* Por amor de Dios, capitán, déjeme que le explique... *

...disagree

I completely disagree with you!...

For goodness' sake, Captain, let me explain to you...

2. Idiom
salmon disagrees with me el salmón me sienta mal

disappear

disappear
[dɪsə'pɪə'] *vi*
desaparecer

the document has disappeared el documento ha desaparecido

disappoint

disappoint
[dɪsə'pɔɪnt] *vt*
decepcionar, defraudar, contrariar

the film disappointed us la película nos decepcionó

▶ **disappointment**
[dɪsə'pɔɪntmənt] *n*
decepción *f*

disaster

disaster
[dɪ'zɑːstə'] *n*
desastre *m*, catástrofe *f*

* *This is where the air disaster took place...* Aquí es donde la catástrofe aérea ocurrió... *Let's go!* ¡Vamos! *

This is where the air disaster took place...

Let's go!

discover

discover
[dɪsˈkʌvəʳ] v t
descubrir

we've discovered the treasure hemos descubierto el tesoro

▶ **discovery**
[dɪsˈkʌvərɪ] n
pl discoveries
descubrimiento m, hallazgo m

discuss

discuss
[dɪsˈkʌs] v t
discutir, hablar de

* *I'd like to discuss something with you!* ¡Me gustaría discutir algo con usted! *

▶ **discussion**
[dɪsˈkʌʃ(ə)n] n
discusión f

I'd like to discuss something with you!

disgusting

disgusting
[dɪsˈgʌstɪŋ] adj
asqueroso, a
repugnante

take that disgusting thing away llévate de aquí esa cosa asquerosa

dish

dish
[dɪʃ] n
plato m

...dish

I bought this dish in China compré este plato en China

▶ **dishes**
[ˈdɪʃɪz] n pl
platos m, vajilla f

I have to wash the dishes tengo que lavar los platos

---

distance

distance
[ˈdɪstəns] n
1. distancia f

* *The distance between us is narrowing.* La distancia entre nosotros se acorta. *

2. lejanía
he was lost in the distance se perdió en la lejanía

▶ **distant**
[ˈdɪstənt] adj

The distance between us is narrowing.

distante, lejano, a

she is a distant relative es una parienta lejana

district

district
[ˈdɪstrɪkt] n
1. región f

this is a desert region esta es una

...district

región desértica

2. barrio m
they were born in a poor district ellos nacieron en un barrio pobre

* *Profesor Fan-Hsi-Ying's house is in this district...* La casa del profesor Fan-Hsi-Ying está en este barrio... *

...district

Professor Fan-Hsi-Ying's house is in this district...

disturb

disturb
[dɪsˈtɜːb] v t
molestar

do not disturb no molestar

dive

dive
[daɪv] v i
sumergirse,
tirarse al agua

...dive

I must dive in and rescue Snowy!...

Careful Tintin! Careful! There are lots of sharks!...

...dive

* *I must dive in and rescue Snowy!...* ¡Tengo que tirarme al agua y rescatar a Milú!...
Careful, Tintin! Careful! There are lots of sharks!... ¡Cuidado, Tintín! ¡Cuidado! ¡Hay muchos tiburones!... *

divide

divide
[dɪ'vaɪd] *v i & v t*
1. partir, repartir

we divided the work between us nos repartimos el trabajo

2. dividir
this book is divided into two parts este libro está dividido en dos partes

56 divided by 8 is 7 56 dividido por 8 son 7

do

do
[duː]
did [dɪd] done [dʌn]
I. *v i & v t*
1. hacer

* *Tintin, stop! What are you doing?* ¡Tintín, deténgase! ¿Qué está haciendo? *

he did it yesterday lo hizo ayer

I have done my homework he hecho mis deberes

...do

Tintin, stop! What are you doing?

I'll do my best haré lo mejor que pueda

2. Idiom
how are you doing in your new job? ¿cómo te va en tu nuevo trabajo?

how do you do! ¡encantado de conocerle!

* *This is Tintin, Sir...* Le presento a Tintín, señor...
Fine! How do you do! I hope everything

This is Tintin, Sir...

Fine! How do you do! I hope everything went off all right...

...do

went off all right... ¡Bien, encantado de conocerle! Espero que todo le haya ido bien... *

that will do! ¡ya está bien!/¡basta ya!

that's got nothing to do with it esto no tiene nada que ver

II. *v aux*

do you work here? – yes, I do ¿trabajas aquí? – sí

what did he say? ¿qué dijo?

I don't like spinach no me gustan las espinacas

you like novels, don't you? te gustan las novelas, ¿verdad?

don't do it! ¡no lo hagas!

do your buttons up abróchate los botones

▶ **do without**
prescindir de, pasar sin

he can do without eating meat puede prescindir de comer carne

▶ **do up**
abrochar

dock

dock
[dɒk] *n*
dique *m*

the ship is being repaired in the dry dock el barco está siendo reparado en el dique seco

doctor

doctor
['dɒktər] *n*
doctor *m*, médico *m*

she needs a doctor necesita un médico

document

document
['dɒkjumənt] n
documento m

* *This document is of vital importance...* Este documento es de vital importancia... *

dog

dog
[dɒg] n
perro m

* *Well done, Snowy!... You are a very clever dog!...* ¡Bien hecho, Milú!... ¡Eres un perro muy listo!... *

dollar

dollar
['dɒləʳ] n
dólar m

...dollar

he changed dollars into pounds cambió dólares por libras

door

door
[dɔːʳ] n
puerta f

* *Blistering barnacles!!... The door's locked!... They've locked us in!...* ¡¡Mil

...door

millones de demonios!!... ¡La puerta está cerrada!... ¡Nos han encerrado dentro!... *

doubt

doubt
[daut]
I. v t
dudar

I doubt if he will come dudo que venga

...doubt

II. n
duda f

down

down
[daun]
I. prep
1. al pie de, al final de

* *The monastery is just down the*

...down

The monastery is just down the mountain...

mountain... El monasterio está justo al pie de la montaña... *

2. Idiom
to go down the stairs/the hill bajar las escaleras/la colina

to fall down the stairs caerse por las escaleras

to live down the street from someone vivir cerca de alguien

II. adv
1. abajo

walk up and down andar arriba y abajo

2. Idiom
to go down bajar, desdender

the lift (Am:elevator) is going down el ascensor está bajando

put your bags down deje sus maletas en el suelo

sit down siéntese

write it down escríbelo, anótalo, apúntalo

▶ **downstairs**
['daun'steəz] adv
abajo, en la planta de abajo/baja

they live downstairs viven abajo

come downstairs to the kitchen ven abajo a la cocina

dozen

dozen
['dʌz(ə)n] n
docena f

I would like a dozen eggs quisiera una docena de huevos

they cost 5 pounds a dozen cuestan 5 libras la docena

draw

draw
[drɔː]
I. n
empate m

the game ended in a draw el partido acabó en empate

II. v t
drew [druː],
drawn [drɔːn]
1. dibujar

he drew the house dibujó la casa

...draw

He's quite a big man with dark hair... I'll try and draw him for you...

* **He's quite a big man with dark hair... I'll try and draw him for you...**
Es un hombre bastante gordo de pelo oscuro... Se lo intentaré dibujar... *

2. correr
please could you draw the curtains? por favor, ¿puede correr las cortinas?

III. *v i*
1. dibujar

she draws very well dibuja muy bien

2. empatar
the two teams drew los dos equipos empataron

▶ **draw up**
1. pararse, detenerse

the car drew up near the corner el coche se paró cerca de la esquina

2. preparar
he drew up a contract preparó un contrato

▶ **drawer**
[drɔːʳ] *n*
cajón *m*

the letters are in the drawer las cartas están en el cajón

▶ **drawing**
['drɔːɪŋ] *n*
dibujo *m*

the background of the drawing was white el fondo del dibujo era blanco

dreadful

dreadful
['dredful] *adj*
horrible, espantoso, a

what happened to him was dreadful lo que le ocurrió fue horrible

dream

dream
[driːm]
I. *n*
sueño *m*

she always remembers her dreams siempre recuerda sus sueños

* **They are definitely Incan flowers...** Decididamente son flores incas...
Tintin is having a strange dream...

They are definitely Incan flowers...

Tintin is having a strange dream.

Tintín tiene un sueño extraño... *

II. *v i & v t*
dreamt, dreamt [dremt] *or* dreamed, dreamed
1. soñar

I dreamt I was in Venice soñé que estaba en Venecia

2. Idiom
I wouldn't dream of hurting you nunca se me ocurriría herirte

dress

dress
[dres]
I. *n*
vestido *m*

she was wearing a pink dress llevaba un vestido rosa

II. *v i & v t*
vestir, vestirse

the little girl was dressing her doll la niña estaba vistiendo a su muñeca

have you finished dressing? ¿has terminado de vestirte?

drill

drill
[drɪl]
I. *n*
1. taladro *m*

he made a hole in the wall with the drill hizo un agujero en la pared con el taladro

2. ejercicio *m*, **práctica** *f*
a grammar drill un ejercicio de gramática

II. *v i & v t*
ejercitar(se), instruir(se)

drink

drink
[drɪŋk]
I. *n*
1. bebida *f*

I'll bring the drinks for the party yo traeré las bebidas para la fiesta

2. Idiom
would you like a drink? ¿quieres tomar algo?

II. *v i & v t*

drank [dræŋk], drunk [drʌŋk]
beber

the Captain drinks whisky el capitán bebe whisky

drive

drive
[draɪv] *v i & v t*
drove [drəuv]
driven ['drɪv(ə)n]

...drive

1. conducir

* **I can't drive this vehicle!...** ¡No sé conducir este vehículo!... *

2. Idiom
her attitude is driving me mad su actitud está volviéndome loco

▶ **driver**
['draɪvəʳ] *n*
conductor *m*, **conductora** *f*

I can't drive this vehicle!...

drop

drop
[drɒp]
I. n
1. gota f

he drank to the last drop bebió hasta la última gota

raindrops gotas de lluvia

2. caída f, bajada f
there was a sudden drop in the price of oil hubo una bajada repentina en el precio del petróleo

II. vi & vt
dropped, dropped
[drɔpt]
1. dejar caer, caer(se)

the coins dropped out of her hands las monedas se le cayeron de las manos

2. Idiom
he drops his r's no pronuncia las erres

▶ **drop in**
pasar a visitar

drop in whenever you want pasa a visitarnos cuando quieras

▶ **drop off**
1. adormecerse, quedarse dormido

* *He dropped off in front of the fire.* Se quedó dormido frente al fuego. *

2. dejar *(a alguien en un sitio)*
drop me off here déjeme aquí

drown

drown
[draun]
vi & vt
ahogar(se)

* *Oh, no, Snowy, we're going to drown! Help!* ¡Oh, no, Milú, vamos a ahogarnos! ¡Socorro! *

...drown

drunk

drunk
[drʌŋk] adj
borracho, a

druggist

druggist *(Am)*
→ CHEMIST

dry

dry
[drai]
I. adj
drier, driest
seco, a

I need a dry towel necesito una toalla seca

II. vi & vt
secar(se)

* *How can we dry our clothes!* ¡Cómo podemos secarnos la ropa! *

duck

duck
[dʌk] n
pato m

dull

dull
[dʌl] adj
1. opaco, a, oscuro, a, cubierto, a

...dull

the sky is dull el cielo está cubierto

2. soso, a, aburrido, a
the film (Am: movie) was very dull la película era muy aburrida

3. torpe

during

during
['djuərɪŋ] prep
durante

she studied during the winter estudió durante el invierno

dust

dust
[dʌst] n
polvo m

there's a lot of dust in this room hay mucho polvo en esta habitación

▶ **dustbin**
['dʌstbɪn] n
(Am: **garbage can**)
cubo de basura m

▶ **dustman**
['dʌstmən] n
pl dustmen [dʌstmɪn]
(Am: **garbage collector**)
basurero m

▶ **dusty**
['dʌstɪ] adj
dustier, dustiest
polvoriento, a

we went along a dusty road fuimos por una carretera polvorienta

duty

duty
['djuːtɪ] n
pl duties
1. deber m

duty is duty el deber es el deber

2. Idiom
duty-free libre de impuestos

on duty de guardia

each

each
[iːtʃ]
I. *adj*
cada

each car has its own disadvantages cada coche tiene sus propias desventajas

II. *pron*
cada uno, a

they will each find their way cada uno encontrará su camino

Easy does it! Each of you will get one!...

* *Easy does it! Each of you will get one!...* ¡Con calma! ¡Cada uno tendrá uno!... *

they cost one pound each cuestan una libra cada uno

▶ **each other**
pron
el uno al otro

they listen to each other se escuchan el uno al otro

eager

eager
[ˈiːgəʳ] *adj*
1. deseoso, a
ansioso, a

she is eager to go to Venice está ansiosa por ir a Venecia

2. impaciente
she is eager to finish her work está impaciente por terminar su trabajo

ear

ear
[ɪəʳ] *n*
oreja *f*

* *Snowy pricks up his ears...* Milú aguza las orejas... *

...ear

Snowy pricks up his ears!

early

early
[ˈɜːlɪ]
earlier, earliest
I. *adj*
1. pronto *adv*

you're early for work today! ¡llegas pronto a trabajar hoy!

2. Idiom
early in the afternoon/evening a primera hora de la tarde/de la noche

II. *adv*
1. temprano, pronto

he goes to work very early va a trabajar muy temprano

2. Idiom
* *Early in the morning.* Por la mañana temprano. *

Early in the morning.

earn

earn
[ɜ:n] v t
1. ganar (*dinero por el trabajo*)

2. Idiom
to earn one's living ganarse la vida

earth

earth
[ɜ:θ] n
tierra f

...earth

he described the beauty of the sky and the earth describió la belleza del cielo y de la tierra

* *Hello... Hello... This is Tintin... We're moving away from the earth!...* Hola... Hola... Aquí Tintín... ¡Nos estamos alejando de la tierra!... *

Hello... Hello...This is Tintin... We're moving away from the Earth !...

east

east
[i:st]
I. n
este m

II. adj
este, del este

the east coast is dangerous la costa este es peligrosa

III. adv
al este, hacia el este

they went to the east fueron hacia el este

▶ **eastern**
['i:st(ə)n] adj
del este

▶ **eastward(s)**
['i:stwəd(z)] adj
hacia el este

Easter

Easter
['i:stəʳ] n
Pascua, Semana Santa

they went to Paris for Easter fueron a París en Semana Santa

Easter egg huevo de Pascua

easy

... but I can't drive this vehicle ...

Yes you can, it's very easy!...

easy
['i:zɪ] adj
easier, easiest
fácil

* *...but I can't drive this vehicle...* ...pero no sé conducir este vehículo... *Yes, you can; it's very easy!...* Sí que sabe; ¡es muy fácil!... *

eat

Come and have a look, I've found something to eat...

...eat

eat
[i:t] v i & v t
ate [eɪt]
eaten ['i:t(ə)n]
comer

* *Come and have a look, I've found something to eat...* Ven y echa una mirada, he encontrado algo para comer... *

educate

educate
['edjukeɪt] v t
educar

you must educate your children to be honest debes educar a tus hijos para que sean honestos

▶ **education**
[edju'keɪʃ(ə)n] n
educación f

effect

effect
[ɪ'fekt] n
efecto m

* *Has the medicine had any effect on you? Are you feeling better?...* ¿Le ha hecho algún efecto la medicina? ¿Se encuentra mejor?... *

Has the medicine had any effect on you ? Are you feeling better?...

effort

effort
['efət] n
esfuerzo m

you must make an effort if you want to win debes hacer un esfuerzo si quieres ganar

egg

egg
[eg] n
huevo m

...egg

I bought a dozen eggs compré una docena de huevos

eight

eight
['eɪt]
I. *adj*
1. ocho

2. Idiom
she is eight tiene ocho años

...eight

II. *n*
ocho *m*

▶ **eighteen**
[eɪ'tiːn]
I. *adj*
dieciocho

II. *n*
dieciocho *m*

▶ **eighty**
['eɪtɪ]
I. *adj*
ochenta

her grandfather is eighty su abuelo tiene ochenta años

eighty-two ochenta y dos

II. *n*
pl eighties

in the eighties en los (años) ochenta

Eire

Eire
['eərə] *n*
Eire *f*, la República de Irlanda

either

either
['aɪðər]
I. *adj & pron*
1. uno u otro, cualquiera de los dos

...either

You can take either road, they both lead to the village...
Thank you, I'll take the shortest...

...either

* *You can take either road, they both lead to the village...* Puede tomar uno u otro camino, ambos conducen al pueblo... *Thank you, I'll take the shortest...* Gracias, tomaré el más corto... *

2. ambos
on either side of the road a ambos lados de la calle

II. *adv*

tampoco

he doesn't like milk, and he doesn't like cheese either no le gusta la leche, y no le gusta el queso tampoco

▶ **either... or...**
conj
o... o...

you either come with us or go now o vienes con nosotros o te vas ahora

elbow

elbow
['elbəu] *n*
codo *m*

he was hurt in the elbow fue herido en el codo

elder

elder
['eldər] *adj*
mayor

...elder

this is her elder sister ésta es su hermana mayor

▶ **eldest**
['eldɪst] *adj*
el/la mayor (de todos)

Mary is the eldest of us María es la mayor de nosotros

▶ **elders**
['eldəz] *n*
ancianos *m pl*

electric

electric
[ɪ'lektrɪk] *adj*
eléctrico, a

▶ **electrician**
[ɪlek'trɪʃ(ə)n] *n*
electricista *m f*

▶ **electricity**
[ɪlek'trɪsɪtɪ] *n*
electricidad *f*

electricity can be dangerous la electricidad puede ser peligrosa

elephant

elephant
['elɪfənt] *n*
elefante *m*

eleven

eleven
[ɪlevn]
I. *adj*
1. once

2. Idiom
my best friend is

...eleven

eleven mi mejor amigo tiene once años

II. *n*
once *m*

else

else
[els] *adv*
1. más

* *Is there anybody*

...else

Is there anybody else?... No?... Let's go then!...

else?... No?... Let's go then!... ¿Hay alguien más?... ¿No?... ¡Vámonos entonces!... *

would you like anything else? ¿desea alguna cosa más?

2. Idiom
somewhere else (or elsewhere) algún otro sitio

or else sino, o bien

emergency

emergency
[ɪ'mɜːdʒənsɪ] *n*
pl emergencies
emergencia *f*

in an emergency en caso de emergencia

* *Hurry up! Don't you understand that this is an emergency?* ¡Dense prisa! ¿No comprenden que esto es una emergencia? *

an emergency lan-

...emergency

ding un aterrizaje de emergencia

emergency exit salida de emergencia

empty

empty
['emptɪ]
I. *adj*
emptier, emptiest
vacío, a

...empty

* *It's a good thing it's empty!...* ¡Menos mal que está vacío!... *

II. *v t*
emptied, emptied
['emptɪd]
vaciar

empty your case vacía tu maleta

It's a good thing it's empty!...

encourage

encourage
[ɪn'kʌrɪdʒ] *v t*
animar,
dar confianza

▶ **encouraging**
[ɪn'kʌrɪdʒɪŋ] *adj*
alentador, ora

end

end
[end]
I. *n*

...end

fin *m*, final *m*

this is the end of our worries éste es el final de nuestras preocupaciones

II. *v i & v t*
terminar, acabar

* *Everything ended well, as usual, didn't it, Snowy?* Todo acabó bien, como de costumbre, ¿no és así Milú?

Everything ended well, as usual, didn't it, Snowy?

It certainly did!

It certainly did! ¡Sí, ciertamente! *

he ended his book at last finalmente terminó su libro

enemy

enemy
['enəmɪ]
I. *n*
pl enemies

...enemy

enemigo *m*,
enemiga *f*

* *It's Tintin, our old enemy!...* Es Tintín, nuestro viejo enemigo!... *

II. *adj*
enemigo, a

the enemy army el ejército enemigo

...enemy

It's Tintin, our old enemy !...

engaged

engaged
[ɪn'geɪdʒd] *adj*
1. ocupado, a

I tried to call him, but the line's engaged (Am: busy) intenté llamarlo, pero la línea estaba ocupada

2. prometido, a
he is engaged to our neighbour está prometido con nuestra vecina

engine

engine
['endʒɪn] *n*
motor *m*

* *When we've blown up the tyres we'll check the engine.* Cuando acabemos de inflar los neumáticos, revisaremos el motor. *

▶ **engineer**
[endʒɪ'nɪəʳ] *n*
ingeniero *m*

When we've blown up the tyres we'll check the engine.

England

England
['ɪŋglənd] *n*
Inglaterra *f*

he was born in England nació en Inglaterra

Sussex is in the south of England Sussex está en el sur de Inglaterra

▶ **English**
['ɪŋglɪʃ]
I. *adj*

inglés, esa

English humour el humor inglés

II. *n*
1. inglés, esa

the English los ingleses

2. inglés *m*
does he speak English? ¿habla él inglés?

▶ **Englishman, Englishmen**
['ɪŋglɪʃmən, mɪn] *n*
inglés, ingleses *m*

the book was written by an Englishman el libro fue escrito por un inglés

▶ **Englishwoman, Englishwomen**
['ɪŋglɪʃwumən, wɪmɪn] *n*
inglesa, inglesas *f*

enjoy

enjoy
[ɪn'dʒɔɪ] *v t*
1. disfrutar de

I enjoyed my holidays disfruté de mis vacaciones

2. Idiom
to enjoy oneself divertirse/pasarlo bien

did you enjoy yourself at the party? ¿te divertiste en la fiesta?

enough

...enough

enough
[ɪ'nʌf]
I. *adv*
suficientemente, bastante

* *I can't go fast enough!* ¡No puedo ir lo suficientemente rápido! *

II. *adj*
1. suficiente, bastante

you've eaten enough cakes has comido bastantes pasteles

2. Idiom
I've had enough ya estoy harto

enquire

enquire
→ INQUIRE

enter

enter
['entə'] *v i & v t*

...enter

entrar, pasar

* *You may enter now...* Pueden pasar ahora... *

we entered the house entramos en la casa

entertain

entertain
[entə'teɪn] *v t*
divertir, distraer

he's very good at entertaining children sabe muy bien divertir a los niños

▶ **entertainment**
[entə'teɪnmənt] *n*
diversión, distracción

there were many entertainments in

...entertain

London había muchas diversiones en Londres

entire

entire
[ɪn'taɪə'] *adj*
entero, a

the entire world knew it el mundo entero lo sabía

...entire

▶ **entirely**
[ɪn'taɪəlɪ] *adv*
completamente, por entero

* *I entirely agree with you!* ¡Estoy completamente de acuerdo con usted!
Just as well!!! ¡¡¡Menos mal!!! *

envelope

envelope
['envələup] *n*
sobre *m*

she put the letter inside a blue envelope puso la carta dentro de un sobre azul

escape

escape
[ɪs'keɪp]
I. *v t & vi*
escapar, escaparse

...escape

you can't escape justice no puedes escapar a la justicia

II. *n*
1. escapada *f*, evasión *f*, huida *f*

after their escape from prison después de su evasión de la cárcel

2. Idiom
we had a narrow escape! ¡escapamos por los pelos!

especially

especially
[ɪˈspeʃ(ə)lɪ] *adv*
especialmente,
particularmente

* *It's especially hot today!* ¡Hoy hace un día particularmente caluroso! *

Europe

Europe
[ˈjuərəp] *n*
Europa *f*

It's especially hot today!

...Europe

there was war in Europe había guerra en Europa

▶ **European**
[juərəˈpɪən]
I. *n*
europeo *m*
europea *f*

II. *adj*
europeo, a

European culture la cultura europea

even

even
[ˈiːv(ə)n]
I. *adv*
aún, incluso

* *It's the end of the world!...* Es el fin del mundo!...
Everybody was frightened, even Tintin... Todos tenían miedo, incluso Tintín... *

II. *adj*
1. par

4 is an even number el 4 es un número par

2. llano, a, uniforme, plano, a
the table must be completely even la mesa debe ser completamente plana

3. Idiom
to get even with someone ajustar cuentas con alguien

...even

It's the end of the world !...

Everybody was frightened, even Tintin...

evening

evening
[ˈiːvnɪŋ] *n*
1. tarde *f*,
anochecer *m*,
noche *f*

come and see me in the evening ven a verme por la tarde

2. Idiom
yesterday evening anoche

event

event
[ɪˈvent] *n*
acontecimiento *m*

ever

ever
[ˈevəʳ] *adv*
1. jamás, nunca (*in negative and interrogative sentences*),
alguna vez

no one ever knew nadie lo supo nunca

...ever

Have you ever seen such a storm?

* *Have you ever seen such a storm?* ¿Ha visto alguna vez una tormenta así? *

2. Idiom
for ever para siempre

ever since desde entonces

every

every
[ˈevrɪ] *adj*

...every

todo, a, cada, todos los, todas las

I go swimming every day voy a nadar todos los días/cada día

▶ **everybody**
[ˈevrɪbɒdɪ]
everyone
[ˈevrɪwʌn] *pron*
todo el mundo, todos, as

she knew everybody at the party conocía a

todos en la fiesta

▶ **everything**
[ˈevrɪθɪŋ] *pron*
todo

everything is ready for our departure todo está listo para nuestra marcha

▶ **everywhere**
[ˈevrɪweəʳ] *adv*
en/por todas partes

...every

* *Snowy, Snowy!... Where on earth is he?* ¡Milú, Milú!... ¿Dónde diablos está?
I've looked everywhere... He mirado en todas partes...
Snowy!... ¡Milú!...
Snowy!... ¡Milú!... *

exact

exact
[ɪgˈzækt] *adj*
exacto, a, correcto, a

these were his exact words estas fueron sus palabras exactas

▶ **exactly**
[ɪgˈzæktlɪ] *adv*
exactamente, justamente

this is exactly what I thought es justamente lo que pensaba

exam

**exam,
examination**
[ɪgˈzæm]
[ɪgzæmɪˈneɪʃ(ə)n] *n*
examen *m*

he passed his exam aprobó el examen

▶ **examine**
[ɪgˈzæmɪn] *v t*
examinar

let's examine the facts examinemos los hechos

example

example
[ɪgˈzɑːmpl] *n*
ejemplo *m*

you should follow my example deberías tomar ejemplo de mí

for example por ejemplo

excellent

That's an excellent idea, Calculus!

excellent
[ˈeksələnt] *adj*
excelente

* *That's an excellent idea, Calculus!* Es una idea excelente, Tornasol! *

except

except
[ɪkˈsept] *prep*
excepto, menos

...except

Everybody's here except Tintin...
Yes, he hasn't come...

* *Everybody's here except Tintin...* Todo el mundo está aquí menos Tintín...
Yes, he hasn't come... Sí, no ha venido... *

exchange

exchange
[ɪksˈtʃeɪndʒ]
I. *v t*
cambiar, canjear, intercambiar

...exchange

we exchanged the documents for the prisoner intercambiamos los documentos por el prisionero

* *Let's exchange our hats!...* ¡Cambiémonos los sombreros!...
Let's try... Probemos... *

II. *n*
cambio *m*

I'll give you my badges in exchange for your stamps te

Let's exchange our hats!...
Let's try...

...exchange

doy mis cromos a cambio de tus sellos

▶ **stock exchange**
[stɒk ɪks'tʃeɪndʒ] *n*
bolsa (de valores)

excited

excited
[ɪk'saɪtɪd] *adj*
1. animado, a
excitado, a

...excited

2. alterado, a

▶ **exciting**
[ɪk'saɪtɪŋ] *adj*
emocionante, excitante

* *What an exciting story!* ¡Qué historia tan emocionante! *

excuse

excuse
[ɪk'skjuːs]
I. *n*
excusa *f*

this is not a good excuse no es una buena excusa

II. *v t*
excusar, disculpar, perdonar

excuse me for being so late discúlpame por llegar tan tarde

exercise

exercise
['eksəsaɪz] *n*
ejercicio *m*

this is a difficult exercise éste es un ejercicio difícil

* *So I don't get enough exercise, do I!... You'll see!* Así que no hago bastante ejercicio, he!... ¡Ahora verá!
Hup! ¡Hop!
Great! ¡Estupendo! *

...exercise

▶ **exercise book (Am: notebook)** *n*
cuaderno

▶ **exercise**
v i & v t
ejercitar, ejercer

to exercise one's rights ejercitar uno sus derechos

exit

exit
['egzɪt] *n*
salida *f*

emergency exit salida de emergencia

* *The exit must be this way...* La salida debe de estar por aquí... *

expect

expect
[ɪks'pekt] *v t*
suponer, esperar

* *General Alcazar! What a surprise, I didn't expect to meet you here!...* ¡General Alcázar! ¡Qué sorpresa! ¡No esperaba encontrarle aquí!...
Why not?... ¿Por qué no?... *

I expect so eso supongo/supongo que sí

expensive

expensive
[ɪk'spensɪv] adj
caro

* The equipment for the expedition to the Moon was very expensive, but everything is ready now... El material para la expedición a la Luna era muy caro, pero ahora todo está preparado... *

experiment

experiment
[ɪk'sperɪmənt] n
experimento m

* Come, Captain, come and have a look!... Venga, Capitán, venga y eche una mirada!...
Broken glass!... Calculus must have carried out an experiment!... ¡Cristales rotos!... ¡Tornasól debe de haber realizado un experimento!...*

explain

explain
[ɪk'spleɪn] v t
explicar

he will explain everything tonight lo explicará todo esta noche

► **explanation**
[ɪksplə'neɪʃ(ə)n] n
explicación f

extra

extra
['ekstrə] adj
1. suplementario, a extra

2. Idiom
there is no extra charge no hay que pagar suplemento

extraordinary

extraordinary
[ekstrə'ɔːdɪnərɪ] adj

...extraordinary

extraordinario, a

* The Thompsons! What an extraordinary coincidence! ¡Hernández y Fernández! ¡Qué coincidencia tan extraordinaria! *

extremely

extremely
[ɪk'striːmlɪ] adv
extremadamente

...extremely

* It's extremely hot tonight, don't you think, Snowy?... Hace una noche extremadamente calurosa, ¿no crees, Milú?... *

eye

eye
[aɪ] n
1. ojo m

green eyes ojos verdes

...eye

2. Idiom
* Keep your eye on him! ¡Vigílalo!
All right! ¡De acuerdo! *

► **eyebrow**
['aɪbrau] n
ceja f

► **eyelash**
['aɪlæʃ] n
pestaña f

► **eyelid**
['aɪlɪd] n
párpado m

face

face
[feɪs] *n*
1. cara *f*

* *His face is dirty.* Su cara está sucia. *

2. Idiom
to make (funny) faces hacer muecas

3. esfera *f*
the clock face la esfera del reloj

His face is dirty.

fact

fact
[fækt] *n*
1. hecho *m*

that's a fact esto es un hecho

2. Idiom
in fact de hecho, en realidad

in fact, I was about to leave de hecho, estaba a punto de irme

factory

factory
['fækt(ə)rɪ] *n*
pl factories
fábrica *f*

the factory was closed down la fábrica fue cerrada

fail

fail
[feɪl] *v i & v t*
1. fallar,
no ser capaz

...fail

she failed to understand us no fue capaz de entendernos

2. suspender
he failed the exam suspendió el examen

fair

fair
[feəʳ] *adj*
1. rubio, a

he's tall and fair es

...fair

alto y rubio

2. justo, a
that's not fair! ¡esto no es justo!

3. Idiom
fair game juego limpio

► **fairly**
['feəlɪ] *adv*
bastante, un poco

how was the film? — it was fairly good ¿cómo estuvo la película? — estuvo bastante bien

fall

fall
[fɔːl]
I. *n*
caída *f*

the fall of the Roman Empire la caída del imperio romano

II. *v i*
fell [fel]
fallen ['fɔːl(ə)n]
1. caer(se)

the rain keeps falling la lluvia sigue cayendo

* *Captain Haddock fell off his chair.* El capitán Haddock se cayó de la silla. *

2. bajar
the temperature has fallen la temperatura ha bajado

► **fall over/down**
caerse (al suelo)

he fell over and broke his leg se cayó al suelo y se rompió una pierna

Captain Haddock fell off his chair.

family

family
['fæmɪlɪ] n
pl families
familia f

* Here's my nice little family! ¡Esta es mi encantadora familia! *

famous

famous
['feɪməs] adj

...famous

famoso, a

he didn't like being famous no le gustaba ser famoso

far

far
[fɑːʳ] adv
farther, farthest/
further, furthest
1. lejos

...far

* Cheer up, Snowy, the village can't be very far... Ánimo, Milú, el pueblo no puede estar muy lejos... *

2. demasiado
this film is far too long esta película es demasiado larga

3. Idiom
how far is it? ¿a qué distancia está?

so far, so good hasta ahora todo bien

fare

fare
[feəʳ] n
1. billete m, precio m de un billete

all fares, please! ¡billetes, por favor!

2. Idiom
the return (Am: round-trip) fare is cheaper el billete de ida y vuelta es más barato

farm

farm
[fɑːm] n
granja f

▶ **farmer**
['fɑːməʳ] n
granjero m, granjera f, agricultor m, agricultora f

fashion

fashion
['fæʃ(ə)n] n
moda f

she always follows the fashion siempre sigue la moda

in fashion de moda

fast

fast
[fɑːst]
I. adj
rápido, a

a fast train un tren rápido

II. adv
1. deprisa, de prisa

* Ten thousand thundering typhoons! Don't drive so fast! ¡Mil millones de demonios! ¡No conduzcas tan de prisa! *

2. Idiom
fast asleep profundamente dormido

fat

fat
[fæt] adj
fatter, fattest
gordo, a

he is on a diet because he's fat está a dieta porque está gordo

father

father
['fɑːðəʳ] n
padre m

favour

favour
['feɪvəʳ] n
(Am: **favor**)
servicio m, favor m

* Will you do me a favour? Keep an eye

...favour

Will you do me a favour? Keep an eye on the car while I go hunting.

Yes Tintin.

on the car while I go hunting. ¿Me haces un favor? Vigílame el coche mientras voy a cazar. *Yes Tintin.* Sí Tintín. *

favourite

favourite
['feɪvərɪt] *adj*
(*Am*: **favorite**)
favorito, a,
preferido, a

...favourite

my favourite things
mis cosas preferidas

fear

fear
[fɪəʳ]
I. *n*
miedo *m*

he hid for fear of being discovered se escondió por miedo a ser descubierto

...fear

II. *vi & vt*
temer,
tener miedo de

she feared to speak
tenía miedo de hablar

▶ **fearful**
['fɪəful] *adj*
1. miedoso, a,
temeroso, a

* *Mice, mice!... It's crawling with mice in here!...* ¡Ratones!... ¡Esto está infestado de ratones!...

Thompson and Thomson are fearful... Fernández y Hernández son miedosos... *

2. horrendo, a,
espantoso, a
what a fearful affair!
¡qué asunto tan espantoso!

feather

feather
['feðəʳ] *n*
pluma *f*

Mice, mice!... It's crawling with mice in here!...

Thompson and Thomson are fearful ...

February

February
['februərɪ] *n*
febrero *m*

the first/second of February (Am: February first/second) el primero/dos de febrero

we'll meet on the 5th of February (Am: on February 5) nos veremos el 5 de febrero

fed up

fed up
['fedʌp] *adj*
harto, a

* *I'm fed up with waiting!* ¡Estoy harto de esperar!
Yes, I'm getting bored! ¡Sí, me aburro! *

I'm fed up with waiting!

Yes, I'm getting bored!

feed

feed
[fi:d] *vi & vt*
alimentar,
dar de comer

* *Come on, Snowy, I'm going to feed you!...* ¡Vamos, Milú, voy a darte de comer!...
Good idea!... ¡Buena idea!... *

Come on, Snowy, I'm going to feed you!...

Good idea!...

feel

feel
[fi:l]
I. *vt*
felt, felt [felt]
1. sentir

...feel

I felt a pain in my arm... I hope it's not serious...

Let me see, Tintin, don't move...

* **I felt a pain in my arm... I hope it's not serious...** Sentí dolor en el brazo... Espero que no sea serio...
Let me see, Tintín, don't move... Déjame ver, Tintín, no te muevas... *

2. tocar
feel my hand; it's cold toca mi mano; está fría

3. tener la sensación, presentir

I could feel something was about to happen presentía que algo estaba a punto de ocurrir

II. *v i*
1. sentirse, encontrarse

* *She doesn't feel very well...* No se encuentra muy bien... *

2. Idiom
I feel hungry/cold Tengo hambre/frío

She doesn't feel very well...

I feel like going for a walk me apetece dar un paseo

▶ **feeling**
['fi:lɪŋ] *n*
1. sentimiento *m*

she hurt his feelings hirió sus sentimientos

2. sensación *f*
a feeling of happiness una sensación de felicidad

...feel

3. Idiom
no hard feelings? ¿sin rencor?

feet

feet
[fi:t] → FOOT

fellow

fellow
['feləʊ] *n*
1. individuo *m*

he was a funny fellow era un individuo extraño

2. Idiom
fellow being prójimo

▶ **fellowship**
['feləʊʃɪp] *n*
camaradería *f*

fence

fence
[fens] *n*
valla *f*, **cerca** *f*

fetch

fetch
[fetʃ] *v t*
ir a buscar, traer

* *Go and fetch that bone, Snowy!...* ¡Ve a buscar ese hueso, Milú!... *

...fetch

Go and fetch that bone, Snowy!...

---

fever

fever
['fi:və'] *n*
fiebre *f*

he has a high fever tiene mucha fiebre

few

few
[fju:] *adj & pron*
poco(s), poca(s)

...few

* *I have very few clues in this case...* Tengo muy pocas claves en este caso... *

I have very few clues in this case...

▶ **a few**
unos pocos, unas pocas, algunos, algunas

a few people unas pocas personas

field

field
[fi:ld] *n*
1. campo *m*

a field of wheat un campo de trigo

2. terreno (*de juego*), **campo**
football/rugby field campo de fútbol/rugby

fifteen

fifteen
[fif'ti:n]
I. *adj*
quince

II. *n*
quince *m*

▶ **fifth**
[fɪfθ] *adj & n*
un quinto, la quinta parte

▶ **fifty**
['fɪftɪ]

I. *adj*
cincuenta

II. *n*
pl fifties
cincuenta *m*

in the fifties en los (años) cincuenta

fight

fight
[faɪt]
I. v i & v t
fought, fought [fɔːt]
luchar

II. n
lucha f

▶ **fighter**
['faɪtəʳ] n
luchador, ora,
boxeador, ora

figure

figure
['fɪgəʳ]
1. n
cifra f

*these figures are
wrong* estas cifras son
erróneas

2. imagen f

3. figura f, tipo m
*she has a nice
figure* tiene buen tipo

fill

fill
[fɪl] v i & v t
llenar, rellenar

* *Don't fill my glass!*
¡No llene mi vaso! *

film

film
[fɪlm]
(*Am:* **movie**)

...film

-1. película f

*the film was directed
by him* la película fue
dirigida por él

2. carrete, película
*the film in the
camera is finished* el
carrete de la máquina se
ha terminado

finally

finally
['faɪnəlɪ] adv
finalmente, al fin

find

find
[faɪnd] v t
found, found [faund]
encontrar

*we must find her
soon* debemos encon-

...find

trarla pronto

* *How did you find
the film (Am: movie)?*
¿Qué le pareció la
película?
Most interesting!...
¡De lo más interesante!... *

fine

fine
[faɪn]
I. adj

...fine

...fine

hermoso, a, bello, a

* *What a fine day!*
¡Qué día tan hermoso! *

2. Idiom
the weather is fine
hace buen tiempo

3. bien
*how are you? – I'm
fine, thank you* ¿cómo
estás? – estoy bien,
gracias

4. fino, a
cut the meat up fine,

please corte la carne
fina

II. n
multa f

* *I'm sorry, you'll
have to pay a fine.*
Lo siento, tendrá que
pagar una multa. *

finger

finger
['fɪŋgəʳ] n
dedo m

▶ **fingerprint**
['fɪŋgə,prɪnt] n
huella f, dactilar

*keep your fingers
crossed!* ¡mantén los
dedos cruzados!

finish

finish
['fɪnɪʃ]
I. v t
terminar, acabar

*he finished his
painting yesterday*
terminó su pintura ayer

II. v i
terminar, acabar

*I haven't finished
with you yet; stay
and listen* aún no he
terminado contigo; quéda-
te y escucha

...finish

Snowy's finished up nearly all the sausages...

▶ **finish up**
Idiom

* *Snowy's finished up nearly all the sausages...* Milú se ha terminado casi todas las salchichas... *

fire

fire
['faɪəʳ] *n*
1. fuego *m*

...fire

she was reading by the fire estaba leyendo junto al fuego

2. incendio *m*
fire alarm alarma de incendios

3. Idiom
* *The house is on fire.* La casa está ardiendo. *

fire! ¡disparen!

The house is on fire.

▶ **fire engine** *n*
['faɪəʳendʒən]
coche de bomberos

▶ **fireman**
['faɪəmæn] *n*
pl firemen
bombero *m*

▶ **fireplace**
['faɪəpleɪs] *n*
hogar *m*

firm

firm
[fɜ:m]
I. *n*
firma *f*, empresa *f*

the firm was growing la empresa estaba creciendo

II. *adj*
firme, sólido, a, fuerte

firm as a rock fuerte como una roca

first

first
[fɜ:st]
I. *adj & n*
primero, a

this is my first visit ésta es mi primera visita

Elizabeth the first Isabel primera

the first of May el primero de mayo

II. *adv*
1. primero,

al principio, antes

women and children first! ¡las mujeres y los niños primero!

2. por primera vez
I first saw her in Venice la vi por primera vez en Venecia

fish

fish
[fɪʃ]
I. *n*
pez *m*, pescado *m*

II. *vi & vt*
pescar

he likes fishing le gusta pescar

▶ **fisherman**
['fɪʃəmæn] *n*
pl fishermen
pescador

fit

fit
[fɪt]
fit, fit
I. *vi & vt*
1. ir bien, encajar

this doesn't fit into my plans esto no encaja en mis planes

2. caber
we don't fit in the car no cabemos en el coche

...fit

II. *adj*
fitter, fittest
en forma

to keep fit mantenerse en forma

III. *n*
ataque *m*

he had a fit le dió un ataque

five

five
[faɪv]
I. *adj*
cinco

II. *n*
cinco *m*

fix

fix
[fɪks] *vi & vt*
1. arreglar, reparar

* *Well?* ¿Y bien?
That's it!... The engine's fixed... ¡Ya está!... El motor está reparado... *

2. fijar, clavar
fix the picture to the wall clava el cuadro en la pared

Well? That's it!... The engine's fixed...

flag

flag
[flæg] *n*
bandera *f*

they saw the pirate flag vieron la bandera pirata

flame

flame
[fleɪm] *n*
llama *f*

flash

flash
[flæʃ]
I. *n*
1. flash *m*

the photographer used a flash el fotógrafo usó el flash

2. Idiom
a flash of lightning un relámpago

II. *v i*
emitir luz, brillar, centellear

* *Look over there, Captain!...* ¡Mire hacia allí, capitán!...
Yes, there's a light flashing... Sí, hay una luz brillando... *

flat

flat
[flæt]
I. *adj*
flatter, flattest
1. plano, a

he has flat feet tiene los pies planos

2. Idiom
a flat tyre una rueda deshinchada

...flat

II. *n*
(*Am:* **apartment**)
apartamento *m*

flavour

flavour
['fleɪvəʳ] *n*
(*Am:* **flavor**)
sabor *m*, gusto *m*

...flavour

this cake has a good flavour este pastel tiene buen sabor

my sweet is orange flavour mi caramelo es de sabor naranja

flight

flight
[flaɪt] *n*
1. vuelo *m*

...flight

run or you'll miss the flight corre o perderás el vuelo

2. Idiom
a flight of stairs un tramo, una escalera

float

float
[fləʊt] *v i*
flotar

...float

The raft is floating on the sea.

...float

The raft is floating on the sea. La balsa flota en el mar. *

floor

floor
[flɔːʳ] *n*
1. suelo *m*

I swept the floor barrí el suelo

...floor

2. piso *m*
* *Mr Tintín?* ¿El señor Tintín?
First floor (Am: second floor). Primer piso. *

flour

flour
['flaʊəʳ] *n*
harina *f*

...flour

she made bread with the flour hizo pan con la harina

flower

flower
['flaʊəʳ] *n*
flor *f*

she picked up a flower recogió una flor

flu

flu
[fluː] *n*
gripe *f*

he's got the flu tiene la gripe

fly

fly
[flaɪ]
I. *v i*
flew [fluː] flown [fləʊn]
1. volar

...fly

* We're flying too low!... ¡Estamos volando demasiado bajo!...
It's true, wait, we're going to land... Es verdad, espera, vamos a aterrizar... *

2. Idiom
are you flying or going by train? ¿vas en avión o en tren?

II. n
pl flies
mosca f

fog

fog
[fɒg] n
niebla f

there was fog in London... había niebla en Londres...

▶ **foggy**
['fɒgɪ] adj
foggier, foggiest
1. brumoso, a, de niebla

a foggy day un día de niebla

2. Idiom
he only had a foggy idea of what had happened sólo tenía una idea confusa de lo que había ocurrido

follow

follow
['fɒləu] v i & v t
seguir, perseguir

* I have a feeling we're being followed... Tengo la impresión de que nos siguen...
That's for sure, somebody's following us... Eso es seguro, alguien nos está siguiendo... *

...follow

fond

fond
[fɒnd] adj
Idiom

Captain Haddock is fond of whisky al capitán Haddock le gusta el whisky

we are fond of animals nos gustan los animales

food

food
[fuːd] n
1. comida f

* It's dog food. Es comida para perros. *

2. cocina f, comida f
I like Polish food me gusta la comida polaca

It's dog food.

fool

fool
[fuːl]
I. n
1. tonto, a

2. bufón

II. v t
tomar el pelo a

III. v i
bromear

foot

foot
[fut] n
pl feet [fiːt]
1. pie m

* Ouch, my foot! ¡Ay, mi pie! *

my feet hurt me duelen los pies

2. Idiom
we'll go on foot iremos a pie

3. pie (12 pulgadas, equivalente a 30.5 cm)

OUCH, my foot!

he's six feet tall mide 1, 83 m

football

football
['futbɔːl] n
(Am: **soccer**)
1. fútbol m

we play football at school jugamos a fútbol en el colegio

...football

a football match un partido de fútbol

2. balón m (de fútbol)

▶ **football ground** n
campo m de fútbol

for

for
[fɒr]
I. prep
1. para, por

but for you I would have left si no fuera por tí me habría ido

...for

* *A present for Snowy.* Un regalo para Milú. *

2. durante
we studied medicine for six years estudiamos medicina durante seis años

3. Idiom
he's gone for good se fue para siempre

what is this for? ¿para qué es esto?

II. *conj*
porque, pues

the old man sat in his armchair, for he was tired el anciano se sentó en su sillón, pues estaba cansado

forbidden

forbidden
[fə'bɪdən] *adj*
prohibido, a

it is forbidden to park here está prohibido aparcar aquí

shouting is forbidden está prohibido gritar

forecast

forecast
['fɔːkɑːst]
I. *n*
1. previsión *f*, pronóstico *m*

2. Idiom
* *The weather forecast, Captain!* ¡La previsión meteorológica, capitán! *

II. *v t*
predecir

...forecast

foreground

foreground
['fɔːgraund] *n*
primer plano *m*

* *Tintin is in the foreground.* Tintín está en primer plano. *

foreign

foreign
['fɒrən] *adj*
extranjero, a

Tintin is in the foreground.

...foreign

foreign languages lenguas extranjeras

▶ **foreigner**
['fɒrənə'] *n*
extranjero *m*
extranjera *f*

forest

forest
['fɒrɪst] *n*
bosque *m*

forget

forget
[fə'get] *v i & v t*
forgot [fə'gɒt]
forgotten [fə'gɒt(ə)n]
olvidar(se)

* *I've forgotten Snowy!* ¡Me he olvidado a Milú! *

forgive

forgive
[fə'gɪv] *v i & v t*

...forgive

forgave [fə'geɪv]
forgiven [fə'gɪv(ə)n]
perdonar

* *I'm sorry, Tintin, would you forgive me? Please, forgive me!* Lo siento, Tintín, ¿me perdona? ¡Por favor, perdóneme!
That's all right! ¡Está bien! *

forgive me for being late perdóname por llegar tarde

fork

fork
[fɔːk] *n*
tenedor *m*

fortnight

fortnight
['fɔːtnaɪt] *n*
dos semanas *f pl*, una quincena *f*

she'll be away for a fortnight estará fuera dos semanas

fortunately

fortunately
['fɔːtʃənɪtlɪ] adv
afortunadamente

fortunately we're back home afortunadamente ya estamos de vuelta a casa

fortune

fortune
['fɔːtʃuːn] n
fortuna f, suerte f

he happily spent all his fortune gastó felizmente toda su fortuna

I'll try my fortune probaré suerte

▶**fortune teller**
['fɔːtʃuːn 'teləʳ]
adivinador/ora

forty

forty
[ˈfɔːtɪ]
I. adj
cuarenta

II. n
pl forties
cuarenta m

the forties los años cuarenta

forward(s)

forward(s)
['fɔːwəd(z)] adv
1. adelante, hacia adelante

go forward, I'll follow you ve hacia adelante, yo te seguiré

2. Idiom
they walked backwards and forwards caminaban de acá para allá

four

four
[fɔːʳ]
I. adj
cuatro

II. n
cuatro m

* *Tintín is walking on all fours...* Tintín camina a cuatro patas.../a gatas... *

▶**fourteen**
[fɔːˈtiːn] adj & n
catorce

...four

Tintin is walking on all fours...

▶**fourth**
[fɔːθ] adj & n
cuarto

frame

frame
[freɪm] n
marco m

* *The frame was too heavy and the*

...frame

The frame was too heavy and the picture fell down.

picture fell down. El marco era demasiado pesado y el cuadro cayó. *

France

France
[frɑːns] n
Francia f

he was born in France nació en Francia

...France

I went to France and I learned French fui a Francia y aprendí francés

the Republic of France la República francesa

free

free
[friː] adj
1. libre

...free

he's free to come and go es libre de ir y venir

* *Never do that again!...* ¡No hagas esto nunca más!...
You're free, Snowy... Are you better? Eres libre, Milú... ¿Estás mejor? *

is that seat free? ¿está libre ese asiento?

2. gratuito, a

Never do that again!...
You're free, Snowy... Are you better?

the drinks are free! ¡las bebidas son gratuitas!

admission free entrada libre

▶**freedom**
['friːdəm] n
libertad f

* *Stranger! If you value your freedom... Make the sun shine again!* ¡Extranjero! ¡Si valoras tu libertad... Haz que el sol brille de nuevo! *

Stranger! If you value your freedom... Make the sun shine again!

freeze

freeze
[fri:z] *v i & v t*
froze [frəuz]
frozen ['frəuz(ə)n]
helar, congelar

I'm freezing! ¡me estoy helando!

yesterday it froze ayer heló

French

French
[frentʃ]
I. *adj*
francés, esa

Marie is French Marie es francesa

he likes French food le gusta la comida francesa

II. *n*
francés

he speaks French él habla francés

▶**Frenchman**
['frentʃmən] *n*
pl Frenchmen
francés *m*

the French los franceses

▶**Frenchwoman**
['frentʃwumən]
pl Frenchwomen
francesa *f*

▶**French fry**
(Am) → CHIP

frequent

frequent
['fri:kwənt] *adj*
frecuente

his visits are becoming less and less frequent sus visitas son cada vez menos frecuentes

▶**frequently**
['fri:kwəntlɪ] *adv*
frequentemente

it frequently snows here aquí nieva frecuentemente

fresh

fresh
[freʃ] *adj*
1. fresco, a

* Look! ¡Mire!
This crab isn't fresh! ¡Este cangrejo no es fresco!
But my crab is fresh, I promise you... Pero mi cangrejo es fresco, se lo prometo... *

I need some fresh air necesito un poco de aire fresco

...fresh

2. nuevo, a
a fresh start un nuevo comienzo

Friday

Friday
['fraɪdɪ] *n*
viernes *m*

I can see you on Friday podré verte el viernes

...Friday

I bought it last Friday lo compré el viernes pasado

fridge

fridge
[frɪdʒ]
(*Am:* refrigerator)
nevera *f*,
frigorífico *m*

the butter is in the fridge la mantequilla está en la nevera

friend

...friend

friend
[frend] *n*
amigo, a

* My dear Hercules, let me introduce you to two old friends of mine... Mi querido Hipólito, déjeme que le presente a dos viejos amigos míos...
Pleased to meet you, gentlemen... Encantado de conocerles, caballeros... *

we are good friends somos buenos amigos

he made friends with him se hizo amigo de él

▶**friendly**
['frendlɪ] *adj*
simpático, a
amistoso, a

he's very friendly es muy simpático

▶**friendship**
['frendʃɪp] *n*
amistad *f*

frighten

frighten
['fraɪt(ə)n] *v t*
asustar

don't frighten her no la asustes

Snowy is frightened Milú está asustado

▶**fright**
[fraɪt] *n*
susto *m*

from

from
[frɒm] *prep*
de

* A telegram for you, Sir... Un telegrama para usted, señor...
For me? Who can this telegram be from? ¿Para mí? ¿De quién puede ser este telegrama? *

from London to New York de Londres a Nueva York

...from

where do you come from? ¿de dónde eres?

this one is different from the others éste es diferente de los otros

front

front
[frʌnt]
I. *n*
1. frente *m*
2. fachada *f*

...front

the front of the building la fachada del edificio

3. Idiom
in front of delante de

in front delante

II. *adj*
1. delantero, a

Meanwhile ...

Your front leg is broken, Snowy...

* Meanwhile... Mientras tanto...
Your front leg is broken, Snowy... Tu pata delantera está rota, Milú... *

2. primero, a
the article was on the front page el artículo estaba en primera página

frost

frost
[frɒst] *n*
1. escarcha *f*, hielo *m*

there was a lot of frost on the ground

...frost

había mucha escarcha en el suelo

2. helada *f*

▶ **frosty**
['frɒstɪ] *adj*
frostier, frostiest
helado, a

fruit

fruit
[fruːt] *n*
fruta(s) *f (pl)*

...fruit

we need some fruit necesitamos un poco de fruta

he always drinks fruit juice siempre bebe zumo de frutas

fry

fry
[fraɪ] *v i & v t*
fried, fried
freir

...fry

she's frying the eggs está friendo los huevos

fried potatoes (Am: French fries) patatas fritas

fuel

fuel
[fjuəl] *n*
carburante *m*

full

full
[ful] *adj*
lleno, a

the bottle of whisky was full la botella de whisky estaba llena

* At full moon... En la luna llena... *

At full moon ...

fun

fun
[fʌn] *n*
1. diversión *f*

we did it for fun lo hicimos por diversión

2. Idiom
that's great fun esto es muy divertido

he makes fun of me se burla de mí

...fun

That's funny, there's nobody here ...

▶ **funny**
['fʌnɪ] *adj*
funnier, funniest
1. divertido, a

he's always telling funny stories siempre está contando historias divertidas

2. extraño
* That's funny, there's nobody here... Es extraño, aquí no hay nadie... *

fur

fur
[fɜːʳ] *n*
piel *f*

a fur coat un abrigo de piel

furious

furious
['fjuərɪəs] *adj*
furioso, a

furniture

furniture
['fɜːnɪtʃəʳ] *n*
muebles *m pl*

further

further, furthest
→ FAR

future

future
['fjuːtʃəʳ] *n*
1. futuro *m*, porvenir *m*

who knows what the future will bring quién sabe lo que el futuro nos traerá

2. Idiom
in future be more careful de ahora en adelante ten más cuidado

G G G G G

game

game
[geɪm] *n*
1. juego *m*

the game's up, go and work now el juego se ha terminado, vete a trabajar ahora

2. partida *f*, partido *m*
a game of chess una partida de ajedrez

a game of football un partido de fútbol

garage

garage
['gærɑː(d)ʒ] *n*
garaje *m*

garden

What a lovely day!

In the garden...

garden
['gɑːd(ə)n] *n*
jardín *m*

* *What a lovely day!* ¡Qué día tan bonito!
In the garden... En el jardín... *

...garden

▶ **gardening**
['gɑːdnɪŋ] *n*
horticultura *f*, jardinería *f*

gas

gas
[gæs] *n*
1. gas *m*

2. *Am:* → PETROL

3. Idiom

...gas

a gas station (Am) una gasolinera

gate

gate
[geɪt] *n*
puerta *f*, verja *f*, entrada *f*

* *The car has gone through the gate.* El coche ha entrado por la puerta. *

...gate

The car has gone through the gate.

gather

gather
['gæðəʳ]
I. *v t*
1. reunir, recoger

we're gathering information estamos recogiendo información

2. entender, deducir
I gather he is in danger deduzco que está en peligro

3. coger, tomar

Calculus has gathered roses for Bianca Tornasol ha cogido rosas para Bianca

II. *v i*
1. reunirse, juntarse

* *Why have all those people gathered around that cow?...* ¿Por qué toda esa gente se ha reunido alrededor de esa vaca?... *

2. Idiom

Why have all those people gathered around that cow?...

...gather

gather round, ladies and gentlemen! ¡acérquense, señoras y señores!

general

general
['dʒenərəl]
I. *adj*
general

the general opinion

...general

is against him la opinión general está contra él

II. *n*
general *m*

General Alcazar el general Alcázar

▶ **generally**
['dʒenrəlı] *adv*
generalmente

gentle

gentle
['dʒent(ə)l] *adj*
1. amable, bondadoso, a, cortés

he's very gentle with everybody es muy cortés con todo el mundo

2. suave
a gentle breeze una brisa suave

▶ **gently**
['dʒentlı] *adv*

suavemente, amablemente

gentleman

gentleman
['dʒent(ə)lmæn] *n*
pl gentlemen
1. señor *m*

that gentleman over there will tell you aquel señor de allí se lo dirá

...gentleman

2. caballero *m*
he's a real gentleman es un verdadero caballero

geography

geography
[dʒɪ'ɒgrəfı] *n*
geografía *f*

geography is a beautiful science la geografía es una bella ciencia

---

...geography

a geography book un libro de geografía

get

get
[get]
got, got [gɒt]
I. *v t*
1. recibir

I didn't get any news from her no recibí noticias suyas

...get

2. ir a buscar
go and get some help! ¡ve a buscar ayuda!

3. coger
* *A-tishoo!... I'm getting the flu!* ¡Atchús!... ¡Estoy cogiendo la gripe! *

4. hacer
Tintin got Haddock to come with him Tintín hizo que Haddock viniera con él

...get

5. Idiom
I got my house painted me pintaron la casa

6. conseguir
* *On the ocean...* En el oceano...
Have you got the radio repaired? ¿Ha conseguido arreglar la radio?
No! ¡No! *

I can't get it to work no consigo que funcione

7. entender, enterarse
O.K, I've got it. I have to leave, don't I? Vale, ya entiendo. Tengo que marcharme, ¿no es eso?

II. *v i*
1. ir

excuse me, how can I get to the station? disculpe, ¿cómo se va a la estación?

2. llegar
* *I hope I'll get there in time...* Espero llegar allí a tiempo... *

3. hacerse, volverse
it's getting late se está haciendo tarde

4. Idiom
* *Oh! The weather's getting stormy!...* ¡Oh! ¡El tiempo está empeorando!... *

G

...get

she's getting better every day está mejorando cada día

get ready! ¡prepárate!

get dressed vístete

get going! ¡andando!

▶ **to have got** → HAVE

▶ **get in**
1. subir

get in the car sube al coche

2. llegar
the train got in 5 minutes late el tren llegó 5 minutos tarde

▶ **get off**
bajar

I get off at the next stop bajo en la próxima parada

▶ **get on**
1. montarse

get on the horse móntate en el caballo

2. ir
how is she getting on? ¿cómo le va?

3. llevarse bien
they get on very well se llevan muy bien

4. continuar, seguir

* Get on with your work!... Blistering barnacles... Don't stop! ¡Sigan con su trabajo!.... ¡Millones de demonios!... ¡No paren! *

5. Idiom
he's getting on my nerves me está poniendo nerviosa

...get

▶ **get over**
1. cruzar

2. terminar con
I'd like to get it over with at once me gustaría terminar con esto de una vez

3. superar (un obstáculo)

▶ **get out**
1. salir

* Get out of here at once! ¡Salgan de aquí enseguida! *

2. sacar
the policeman could get nothing out of him el policía no pudo sacarle nada

▶ **get up**
levantarse

she gets up at eight in the morning se levanta a las ocho de la mañana

he got up and asked me to dance se levantó y me sacó a bailar

ghost

ghost
[gəust] n
fantasma m

gift

gift
[gɪft] n
1. regalo m

that's my gift for you este es my regalo para ti

2. don
he has a gift for getting into trouble tiene un don para meterse en problemas

▶ **gifted**
adj
dotado, a de talento

girl

girl
[gɜːl] n
chica f

the girls got together to devise a plan las chicas se reunieron para idear un plan

give

give
[gɪv]
v i & v t
gave [geɪv]
given ['gɪv(ə)n]
dar

* We're going to give this Tintin a good hiding... Vamos a darle a ese Tintín una buena paliza...
Shh! Silence! ¡Shh! ¡Silencio! *

81

...give

▶ **give up**

1. rendirse

don't give up no te rindas

2. renunciar a, dejar de
* *Er... No thank you, Lieutenant... I've given up drinking whisky...* Eh... No, gracias, teniente... He dejado de tomar whisky...
All right, I won't

Er... No thank you, Lieutenant... I've given up drinking whisky...

All right, I won't insist, then...

insist, then... Bien, entonces no insistiré... *

glad

glad
[glæd] *adj*
gladder, gladdest
contento, a

I'm very glad you've come estoy muy contento de que hayas venido

glass

glass
[glɑːs] *n*
1. vaso *m*

I need a glass of water necesito un vaso de agua

2. cristal *m*, vidrio *m*
this is made of glass esto está hecho de cristal

▶ **glasses**
n pl
gafas *f pl*

...glass

I can't find my glasses no encuentro mis gafas

glove

glove
[glʌv] *n*
guante *m*

she wore long gloves llevaba guantes largos

go

go
[gəu]
I. *v i*
1. ir

he's going to the station now ahora va a la estación

I hope everything goes well espero que todo vaya bien

2. Idiom
I must be going tengo que irme

* *Hello gentlemen, how did your trip go?* Hola señores, ¿cómo fue el viaje?
Very well, thank you. Muy bien, gracias. *

* *Tintin is going upstairs...* Tintín sube la escalera... *

3. volverse
he's gone nuts se ha vuelto majareta

4. ir a (*forma de futuro*)

Hello gentlemen, how did your trip go?

Very well, thank you.

...go

I'm going to learn French voy a aprender francés

are you going to go? ¿vas a ir?

II. *n*
Idiom

I'll have a go lo voy a probar

it's my go me toca a mí

▶ **go across**
atravesar

Tintin is going upstairs...

▶ **go away**
irse

▶ **go back**
volver

▶ **go down**
descender, bajar

▶ **go on**
1. continuar

go on studying, I'm leaving continua estudiando, yo me voy

2. Idiom
* *What's going on here?* ¿Qué pasa aquí?
I wonder!... ¡Me lo pregunto!... *

▶ **go out**
salir

we're going out for dinner vamos a salir a cenar

▶ **go over**
revisar

...go

What's going on here?

I wonder!...

▶ **go without**
pasar sin,
arreglárselas

*camels can go
without water for a
long time* los camellos
pueden pasar sin agua
durante mucho tiempo

goal

goal
[gəul] *n*
1. gol *m*

2. meta *f*

god

god
[gɒd] *n*
dios *m*

my God! ¡Dios mío!

the Greek gods los
dioses griegos

gold

gold
[gəuld] *n*
oro *m*

*it was all made of
gold* todo estaba hecho
de oro

▶ **goldfish**
['gəuldfɪʃ] *n*
pez *m* de colores

good

good
[gud]
I. *adj*
better, best
1. buen, bueno, a

he is a good man es
un buen hombre

good morning buenos
días

*good afternoon/
evening* buenas tardes

good night buenas
noches

* *Be good, Snowy!*
¡Sea bueno, Milú!
Woof! Woof! ¡Guau!
¡Guau! *

*he's very good at
geography* es muy
bueno en geografía

a good while un buen
rato

2. Idiom
it's good for nothing
no vale para nada

II. *n*
1. bien

Be good, Snowy!

Woof!
Woof!

* *This tea is going to
do me a lot of
good...* Este té me va a
hacer mucho bien... *

2. Idiom
*the danger is fin-
ished for good* el
peligro ha terminado para
siempre

▶ **good(s)**
n pl
mercancía(s) *f*

* *Have the goods
been delivered?* ¿Ha

This tea's going
to do me a lot
of good...

...good

Have the goods been delivered?

I don't know.
Ask the Captain...

sido entregada la mer-
cancía?
*I don't know. Ask
the Captain...* No lo sé.
Pregunte al capitán... *

*a goods (Am: freight)
train* un tren de mercan-
cías

▶ **goodbye**
[gud'baɪ] *interj*
adiós

*goodbye; come back
soon* adiós; vuelve
pronto

govern

govern
['gʌvən] *v i & v t*
gobernar

*Alcazar now governs
the country* Alcázar
ahora gobierna el país

▶ **government**
['gʌvənmənt] *n*
gobierno *m*

grandchildren

grandchildren
['græntʃɪldrən] *n pl*
nietos, nietas

▶ **granddaughter**
['grændɔːtəʳ] *n*
nieta *f*

▶ **grandfather**
['grænfɑːðəʳ] *n*
abuelo *m*

▶ **grandmother**
['grænmʌðəʳ] *n*
abuela *f*

...grandchildren

▶ **grandparents**
['grænpeərənts] *n pl*
abuelos *m/f*

▶ **grandson**
['grænsʌn] *n*
nieto *m*

grape

grape
[greɪp] *n*
uva *f*

...grape

a bunch of grapes un racimo de uva

grapefruit

grapefruit
['greɪpfruːt] *n*
pomelo *m*, toronja *f*

grass

grass
[graːs] *n*
1. hierba *f*

cows eat grass las vacas comen hierba

2. césped *m*
keep off the grass no pisen el césped

grateful

grateful
['greɪtful] *adj*
agradecido, a

* *Ah, Tintin! I'm very grateful to you for coming...* ¡Ah,Tintín! Te estoy muy agradecido por haber venido... *

great

great
[greɪt] *adj*
1. grande, enorme

a great castle un enorme castillo

2. grande, importante
he's a great actor es un gran actor

3. Idiom
great! ¡estupendo!

▶ **Great Britain** *n*
Gran Bretaña *f*

green

green
[griːn]
I. *adj*
verde

he had green eyes tenía ojos verdes

II. *n*
verde

* *He's dressed in green.* Viste de verde. *

He's dressed in green.

greengrocer

greengrocer
['griːngrəusəʳ]
(*Am:* **fruit-and-vegetable dealer**) *n*
1. verdulero, a

I asked the greengrocer if he had any lettuces le pregunté al verdulero si tenía lechugas

2. Idiom
at the greengrocer's en la verdulería

greeting

greeting
['griːtɪŋ] *n*
1. saludo *m*

«good morning» is a greeting «buenos días» es un saludo

2. Idiom
a greetings telegram un telegrama de saludo

grey

grey
[greɪ]
(*Am:* **gray**)
I. *adj*
gris

the sky is grey el cielo está gris

II. *n*
gris *m*

he was dressed in grey iba vestido de gris

grocer

grocer
['grəusəʳ] *n*
1. tendero, a

2. Idiom
at the grocer's en la tienda de ultramarinos/de comestibles

ground

ground
[graund] *n*
1. suelo *m*, tierra *f*

...ground

* *The milk has spilt on the ground...* La leche se ha derramado por el suelo... *

2. campo, terreno de juego
a football ground (*Am:* **field**) un campo de fútbol

▶ **ground floor**
(*Am:* **first floor**) *n*
planta baja *f*

The milk has spilt on the ground...

group

group
[gruːp] *n*
1. grupo *m*

a group of men were looking for him un grupo de hombres lo estaban buscando

2. grupo, conjunto
the Beatles were a great group los Beatles eran un grupo estupendo

grow

grow
[grəu]
grew [gruː]
grown [grəun]
I. *v i*
1. crecer

* *Nothing grows in this desert!* ¡No crece nada en este desierto! *

2. aumentar
their numbers are growing su número aumenta

3. volverse, hacerse
it began to grow dark empezó a hacerse oscuro

II. *v t*
cultivar

they grow vegetables cultivan verduras

▶ **grow up**
crecer (*children and animals*)

your son has grown up su hijo ha crecido

* *What do you want to be when you grow up?* ¿Qué quieres ser cuando seas mayor? *Reporter, Sir.* Reportero, señor. *

...grow

grown-up

grown-up
['grəunʌp]
I. *n*
adulto *m*

the grown-ups think they are always right los adultos piensan que siempre tienen razón

II. *adj*
adulto, a,
maduro, a

guess

guess
[ges] *v t*
1. adivinar

* *And guess who I've invited? Signora Castafiore! Isn't that funny?...* ¿Y adivinen a quién he invitado? ¡A la señora Castafiore! ¿No es curioso?... *

2. Idiom
have a guess! ¡adivina!

guest

guest
[gest] *n*
invitado, a

we're expecting guests tonight esperamos invitados esta noche

guilty

guilty
['gɪltɪ] *adj*
guiltier, guiltiest
culpable

he was found guilty fue declarado culpable

gun

gun
[gʌn] *n*
pistola *f*
revólver *m*, fusil *m*

* *Look out, Captain, he's got a gun!* ¡Cuidado, capitán, tiene una pistola! *Blistering barnacles!* ¡Millones de demonios! *

habit

habit
['hæbɪt] *n*
costumbre *f*,
hábito *m*

he's got a bad habit
tiene una mala costumbre

hair

hair
[heə^r] *n*
1. pelo *m*, cabello *m*

** Well, we'll have to
cut their hair then!...*
¡Bien, entonces les ten-
dremos que cortar el
pelo!... **

*the police found a
blond hair on his
coat* la policía encontró
un pelo rubio en su abrigo

2. Idiom
*I'm going to get
my hair cut* voy a
cortarme el pelo

▶ **hairdresser**
peluquero *m*
peluquera *f*

half

half
[hɑːf]
I. *n*
pl halves [hɑːvz]
mitad *f*

*I read half of the
story* leí la mitad de la
historia

cut the bread in half
corta el pan por la mitad

II. *adj*
medio, a

*he weighs 70 and a
half kilos* pesa 70 kilos
y medio

** Now watch... First
I take half a glass of
water... I say: half a
glass...* Ahora mire...
Primero cojo medio vaso
de agua... Como digo:
medio vaso... **

half an hour media
hora

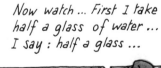

III. *adv*
1. medio

I'm half asleep estoy
medio dormido

2. Idiom
it's half past five son
las cinco y media

▶ **half term** *n*
vacaciones *f pl* a
mediados de tri-
mestre

hall

hall
[hɔːl] *n*
1. vestíbulo *m*

*he's waiting in the
hall* está esperando en el
vestíbulo

2. sala *f*
a concert hall una sala
de conciertos

hallo

hallo
[həˈləu]
hallo → HELLO

ham

ham
[hæm] n
jamón m

a slice of ham una
lonja de jamón

hand

hand
[hænd] n
1. mano f

* *Hands up!* ¡Manos
arriba! *

2. aguja f
*the hands of the
clock* las agujas del reloj

3. Idiom
we shook hands nos
dimos la mano

on the other hand...

por otra parte.../en cam-
bio...

second hand de se-
gunda mano

handkerchief

handkerchief
[ˈhæŋkətʃɪf] n
pl handkerchiefs
[ˈhæŋkətʃɪvz]
pañuelo m

hang

hang
[hæŋ]
hung, hung [hʌŋ]
I. v i & v t
colgar

hang your coat up
cuelga tu abrigo

*the lamp hung from
the ceiling* la lámpara
colgaba del techo

II. v t
ahorcar

happen

happen
[ˈhæpən] v i
1. ocurrir, suceder,
pasar

*what's happening
here?* ¿qué ocurre aquí?

2. Idiom
*I happened to be
there* resulta que yo
estaba allí

*would you happen
to know where she
is?* ¿sabrías por casua-
lidad dónde está?

happy

happy
[ˈhæpɪ] adj
happier, happiest
contento, a, feliz

* *Hurray! I'm happy!
Tintin has succeed-
ed!* ¡Hurra! ¡Estoy
contento! ¡Tintín lo ha
conseguido! *

happy birthday feliz
cumpleaños

▶ **happiness**
[ˈhæpɪnɪs] n
felicidad f

harbour

harbour
[ˈhɑːbər] n
(*Am*: **harbor**)
puerto m

hard

hard
[hɑːd]
I. adj
1. duro, a

as hard as a stone
duro como una piedra

2. difícil
it's hard to accept es
difícil de aceptar

II. adv
1. fuerte

knock hard! ¡llama
fuerte!

2. Idiom
to work hard trabajar
mucho

to rain hard llover
mucho

to try hard esforzarse

hard of hearing duro
de oído

▶ **hardly**
[ˈhɑːdlɪ] adv
apenas

* *Speak up, I can

hardly hear you...
Hable fuerte; apenas
puedo oírle... *

harm

harm
[hɑːm] n
daño m

*some fresh air won't
do you any harm* un
poco de aire fresco no te
hará daño

hat

hat
[hæt] n
sombrero m

hate

hate
[heɪt] v t
odiar

*I hate having to
wash up* odio tener que
lavar los platos

have

have
[hæv]
had, had [hæd]
I. v t
1. tener

I haven't the faintest idea no tengo ni la menor idea

***I haven't any money...** No tengo dinero... *

2. tomar
have some tea toma un poco de té

I'm going to have a bath voy a tomar un baño

II. v aux
1. haber

have you seen Ernesto? ¿has visto a Ernesto?

he said he had not been here before dijo que no había estado aquí antes

2. Idiom
I must have my

house painted tengo que hacer pintar la casa

▶ **have got**
1. tener

I've got a lot of geography books tengo muchos libros de geografía

2. Idiom
I've got it! ¡Ya lo tengo!

▶ **have to,**
have got to tener que

...have

* *It's late, I have (got) to go.* Es tarde, tengo que irme. *Goodbye.* Adiós. *

he

he
[hiː] pron
él

he is the man that I saw yesterday él es el hombre que vi ayer

head

head
[hed] n
1. cabeza f

* *Have you hurt your head?* ¿Se han hecho daño en la cabeza? *Yes, a little...* Sí, un poco... *Just a little...* Sólo un poco... *

2. jefe m
head of government jefe de gobierno

3. director m

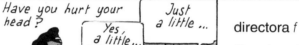

directora f

the head of the sales department el director del departamento de ventas

▶ **headache**
['hedeɪk] n
dolor m de cabeza

I've got a headache tengo dolor de cabeza

▶ **headmaster,**
headmistress

[hed'mɑːstə', mɪstrɪs] n
director m/ directora f de colegio

health

health
[helθ] n
salud f

...health

▶ **healthy**
['helθɪ] adj
healthier, healthiest
sano, a

**Snowy doesn't look very healthy, Doctor, what do you think?* Milú no parece muy sano, doctor. ¿Qué cree usted? *Quite right, let's see...* Cierto, veamos... *

heap

heap
[hiːp] n
montón m

a heap of books un montón de libros

hear

hear
[hɪə'] v i & v t
heard, heard [hɜːd]
1. oír

...hear

* *Speak up, I can't hear you!...* ¡Hable más fuerte; no le oigo!... *

2. tener entendido, enterarse de
I hear that he got away with it tengo entendido que se salió con la suya

heart

heart
[hɑːt] *n*
1. corazón *m*

her heart was beating fast su corazón latía deprisa

he has a good heart tiene buen corazón

2. corazón *m*, centro *m*
this is the heart of the matter este es el centro del asunto

3. Idiom
to learn by heart aprenderse de memoria

have a heart! ¡ten compasión!

heat

heat
[hiːt]
I. *n*
calor *m*

...heat

* *Poor old Snowy, you can't stand this heat... The flower is thirsty too...* Pobrecito Milú, no puedes soportar este calor... La flor también tiene sed... *

II. *vi & vt*
calentar, hacer calor

will you heat up my lunch? ¿quieres calentarme la comida?

▶ **heating**
['hiːtɪŋ] *n*
calefacción *f*

central heating calefacción central

heavy

heavy
['hevɪ] *adj*
heavier, heaviest
1. pesado, a

it's too heavy for me to lift no puedo levantarlo; es demasiado pesado

2. fuerte
a heavy rain una lluvia fuerte

3. Idiom
he's a heavy drinker es un bebedor empedernido

hello

hello
[hə'ləu] *interj*
1. hola

hello, I'm back again hola, ya estoy de vuelta

2. ¡oiga!, ¡oye!
(*to phone*)

3. ¡diga!
(*to answer the telephone*)

help

help
[help]
I. *vi & vt*
1. ayudar

* *Help me open this box...* Ayúdenme a abrir esta caja... *

2. Idiom
he is like that, he can't help it él es así, no puede evitarlo

to help oneself servirse

could I have some more? – help yourself ¿puedo tomar un poco más? – sírvase usted mismo

II. *interj*
socorro

help! ¡socorro!

III. *n*
ayuda *f*

this will be of

...help

great help esto será de gran ayuda

▶ **helpless**
['helplɪs] *adj*
1. desvalido, a desamparado, a inútil

2. Idiom
* *Chuff Chuff Chuff Chuff* Chu chu chu chu *They've tied Tintin up: he's helpless.* Han atado a Tintín: no puede hacer nada. *

he's helpless! ¡es un desastre!

her

her
[hɜːʳ]
I. *pron*
1. la

look for her! ¡búsquenla!

...her

2. le
give her the number denle el número

II. *adj*
1. su, sus (*de ella*)

this is her car éste es su coche

2. el, la, los, las
she opened her eyes abrió los ojos

▶ **hers**
[hɜːz] *pron*

1. suyo, suya, suyos, suyas

my house is hers, too mi casa es también suya

our worries are greater than hers nuestras preocupaciones son mayores que las suyas

2. Idiom
a friend of hers un amigo suyo

...her

► **herself**
[hɜː'self] pron
1. se

she is looking at herself in the mirror se está mirando en el espejo

2. ella misma
she told me herself me lo contó ella misma

3. Idiom
(all) by herself por sí misma, sola

here

here
[hɪə'] adv
1. aquí

* *Oh! I thought I'd put the pen down here...* ¡Oh! Creía que había dejado el bolígrafo aquí... *

2. Idiom
here is/are he aquí

here you are! ¡aquí tienes!

Oh! I thought I'd put my pen down here...

I've brought my papers; here you are he traído mis papeles; aquí los tienes

hero

hero
['hɪərəʊ] n
pl heroes
héroe m

hi

hi
[haɪ] interj
hola

hi, what's new? hola, ¿qué hay de nuevo?

hide

hide
[haɪd]
hid [hɪd]
hidden['hɪd(ə)n]

...hide

I. v t
esconder

I must hide this secret document tengo que esconder este documento secreto

II. v i
1. esconderse

* *Quick, hide behind the trees...* Rápido, escóndase detrás de los árboles... *

2. Idiom
they are playing at

Quick, hide behind the trees.

hide-and-seek están jugando al escondite

high

high
[haɪ]
I. adj
alto, a, elevado, a

a high mountain una montaña alta

high prices precios altos

...high

II. adv
alto, en lo alto

the Yeti lives high up in the mountains el yeti vive en lo alto de las montañas

hill

hill
[hɪl] n
colina f

she ran down the hill bajó corriendo por la colina

---

him

Where's Tintin? I can't see him!

him
[hɪm] pron
le, lo

* *Where is Tintín? I can't see him!* ¿Dónde está Tintín? ¡No lo veo! *

please, let me speak to him por favor, déjame hablarle

► **himself**
[hɪm'self] pron
1. se

* *The professor must have hurt himself!...* ¡El profesor debe de haberse hecho daño!... *

2. él mismo
he went to Paris himself fue a París él mismo

3. Idiom
(all) by himself por sí mismo, solo

The Professor must have hurt himself!...

hire

hire
['haɪə']
(*Am*: **rent**)
I. *v t*
alquilar

Tintin has hired a boat Tintín ha alquilado una barca

II. *n*
1. alquiler

car-hire (*Am*: *car-rental*) alquiler de coches

2. Idiom
for hire de alquiler/se alquila

his

his
[hɪz]
I. *adj*
1. su, sus *(de él)*

we saw his paintings vimos sus pinturas

...his

2. el, la, los, las
* *A few moments later...* Unos momentos después...
Hurray! He's opening his eyes!... ¡Hurra! ¡Está abriendo los ojos!... *

II. *pron*
1. suyo, suya, suyas, suyos

this hat is not mine, it's his este sombrero no es mío, es suyo

...his

2. Idiom
a friend of his un amigo suyo

history

history
['hɪstərɪ] *n*
historia *f*

history is my favourite subject la historia es mi asignatura preferida

hit

hit
[hɪt] *v i & v t*
1. pegar, golpear

don't hit him no le pegues

2. chocar
the car hit a tree el coche chocó contra un árbol

3. herir, tocar
I've been hit by a bullet he sido herido por una bala

hobby

hobby
['hɒbɪ] *n*
pl hobbies ['hɒbɪz]
pasatiempo *m*, hobby *m*, entretenimiento *m*

hold

hold
[həʊld] *v i & v t*
held, held [held]
1. tener, sujetar(se),

...hold

agarrar(se)

hold the bag a moment ten la bolsa un momento

* *Hold tight, Captain, hold tight!* ¡Sujétese fuerte, capitán, sujétese fuerte! *

2. contener
this tank holds fifty litres (Am: liters) este tanque contiene cincuenta litros

...hold

3. celebrar, mantener
they're holding a meeting están celebrando una reunión

► **hold on**
1. aguantar

hold on, we'll get you out of here aguante, le sacaremos de aquí

2. esperar
hold on while I write

this down espera mientras anoto esto

* *Meanwhile...* Mientras tanto...
Hello! Mr Tintin?... Hold on, I'll fetch him... ¡Hola! ¿el señor Tintín?... Espere un momento, voy a buscarlo... *

hole

hole
[həʊl] *n*
agujero *m*

a hole in the road un agujero en la carretera

holiday

holiday
['hɒlɪdeɪ]
(*Am*: **vacation**)
vacaciones *f pl*,

...holiday

fiesta *f*

Tintin and Haddock are on holiday Tintín y Haddock están de vacaciones

the school holidays las vacaciones del colegio

I have a holiday tomorrow mañana tengo fiesta

home

home
[həum]
I. n
1. casa f

he isn't at home no está en casa

2. residencia f
an old people's home una residencia de ancianos

3. Idiom
make yourself at home póngase cómodo

II. adv
a casa, en casa

come home right now vuelve a casa ahora mismo

▶ **homework**
['həumwɜːk] n
deberes m pl

honest

honest
['ɒnɪst] adj
honesto, a

honey

honey
['hʌnɪ] n
miel f

hope

hope
[həup] v i & v t
esperar

* *I hope that with this disguise I won't be recognized...* Espero que con este disfraz no seré reconocido... *

everything will be all right, won't it? – I hope so todo irá bien, ¿verdad? – eso espero

horrible

horrible
['hɒrɪbl] adj
horrible

horrid

horrid
['hɒrɪd] adj
horrible, espantoso, a

it was a horrid story fue una historia espantosa

horse

horse
[hɔːs] n
caballo m

she's riding a horse monta a caballo

hospital

hospital
['hɒspɪt(ə)l] n
hospital m

John works in a hospital Juan trabaja en un hospital

hot

hot
[hɒt] adj
hotter, hottest
1. caliente

this tea is very hot el té está muy caliente

2. Idiom
* *It's ever so hot today!...* ¡Sí que hace calor hoy!... *

I'm hot tengo calor

he has a hot temper tiene mal genio

hotel

hotel
[həu'tel] n
hotel m

hour

hour
['auə'] n
hora f

* *Tintin's been waiting for hours...* Tintín lleva horas esperando... *

...hour

Tintin's been waiting for hours...

house

house
[haus] n
casa f

* *Look what's happened to my house...* Mire lo que le ha ocurrido a mi casa... *

how

how
[hau] adv
1. cómo

...how

how are you? ¿cómo estás?

how can I get to the station? ¿cómo se va a la estación?

2. qué, lo
how terrible! ¡qué horrible!

I didn't know how much she suffered ignoraba lo mucho que sufría

...how

3. Idiom
how do you do? encantado, a, ¿qué tal?

how far is the village? ¿a qué distancia está el pueblo?

how long have you lived here? ¿cuánto tiempo has vivido aquí?

how many days do we have to wait? ¿cuántos días tenemos que esperar?

how much time is left? ¿cuánto tiempo queda?

how many people have been invited? ¿cuántas personas han sido invitadas?

2. Idiom
however difficult it is, I'll make it por más difícil que sea, lo conseguiré

II. *conj*
sin embargo

the Captain does not want to leave Marlinspike; however he'll go with Tintin el capitán no quiere irse de Moulinsart; sin embargo va a acompañar a Tintín

▶ **however**
[hau'evə']
I. *adv*
1. como sea, de cualquier modo

huge

huge
[hju:dʒ] *adj*
enorme

* *Oh dear, what a huge shark!... It's going to catch me!...* ¡Vaya, qué tiburón más enorme!... ¡Va a alcanzarme!... *

hullo

hullo
[hə'ləu]
hullo → HELLO

Oh dear, what a huge shark!... It's going to catch me!...

human

human
['hju:mən] *adj*
humano, a

a human being un ser humano

the human race el género humano

humour

humour
['hju:mə'] *n*
(*Am:* **humor**)

...humour

humor *m*

thank God he has a sense of humour! ¡menos mal que tiene sentido del humor!

hundred

hundred
['hʌndrəd]
I. *adj*
cien, ciento

a hundred roses cien rosas

...hundred

II. *n*
centenar *m*, cientos, centenares *m pl*

hundreds of fish cientos de peces

hungry

hungry
['hʌŋgrɪ] *adj*
hungrier, hungriest
Idiom

...hungry

Snowy is hungry.

* *Snowy is hungry.* Milú tiene hambre. *

hunt

hunt
[hʌnt] *v t*
cazar

he is hunting ducks está cazando patos

▶ **hunt down** perseguir

...hunt

they're hunting down the criminal están persiguiendo al criminal

hurry

hurry
['hʌrɪ]
I. *vi & v t*
hurried, hurried
darse prisa, ir deprisa,

...hurry

apresurarse

don't hurry; we've got time no te apresures; tenemos tiempo

▶ **hurry up** darse prisa

* *Hurry up!* ¡Dese prisa! *

II. *n*
prisa *f*

he's in a hurry tiene prisa

Hurry up!

hurt

hurt
[hɜ:t]
hurt, hurt
I. *v t*
herir, hacer daño, doler

she hurt him le hizo daño

he has hurt his finger with the knife se hirió el dedo con el cuchillo

II. *v i*
doler

don't touch my ankle; it hurts no toques mi tobillo; me duele

husband

husband
['hʌzbənd] *n*
marido *m*

I

I
[aɪ] *pron*
yo

I am an artist yo soy artista

I used to live in London (yo) solía vivir en Londres

ice

ice
[aɪs] *n*
hielo *m*

...ice

* Oh, dear!... I must be careful not to slip on the ice. It's very... ¡Dios mío!... Debo tener cuidado en no resbalar en el hielo. Es muy... *...dangerous!...* ¡...peligroso!... **

▶ **ice cream**
[ˈaɪskriːm] *n*
helado *m*

I like chocolate ice cream me gusta el helado de chocolate

idea

idea
[aɪˈdɪə] *n*
idea *f*

* Great snakes! A leopard!... Oh, I've got an idea!... ¡Caracoles! ¡Un leopardo!... ¡Ah, tengo una idea!... *What a horrible animal!...* ¡Qué animal más horrible!... **

...idea

if

if
[ɪf] *conj*
si

if Professor Calculus is there, we must go si el professor Tornasol está allí, debemos ir

ill

ill
[ɪl] *adj*
1. enfermo, a

he's ill in bed está en la cama enfermo

2. Idiom
I feel ill me encuentro mal

▶ **illness**
[ˈɪlnɪs] *n*
enfermedad *f*

illustrated

illustrated
['ɪləstreɪtəd] adj
ilustrado, a

* *This illustrated dictionary is really remarkable!...* ¡Este diccionario ilustrado es realmente extraordinario!... *

imagine

imagine
[ɪ'mædʒɪn] v t
imaginar

can you imagine my surprise? ¿puedes imaginar mi sorpresa?

▶ **imagination**
[ɪmædʒɪ'neɪʃ(ə)n] n
imaginación f

imitate

...imitate

imitate
['ɪmɪteit] v t
imitar

* *Stop imitating me, you wretched creature.* Deja de imitarme, miserable criatura.
Stop imitating me, you wretched creature. Deja de imitarme, miserable criatura. *

immediate

immediate
[ɪ'miːdɪət] adj
inmediato, a

▶ **immediately**
[ɪ'miːdɪətlɪ] adv
inmediatamente

* *Captain, you must come immediately!... yes... yes... immediately...* ¡Capitán, debe venir inmediatamente!... sí... sí... inmediatamente... *

immigrant

immigrant
['ɪmɪgrənt] n
inmigrante m f

impatient

impatient
[ɪm'peɪʃ(ə)nt] adj
impaciente

I'm impatient to see the drawing estoy

...impatient

impaciente por ver el dibujo

important

important
[ɪm'pɔːtənt] adj
importante

Professor Calculus has something important to tell us el profesor Tornasol tiene algo importante que decirnos

impossible

impossible
[ɪm'pɒsəb(ə)l] adj
imposible

* *It's impossible to go any futher... We are stuck in the seaweed...* Es imposible seguir adelante... Estamos atrapados en las algas... *

impressive

impressive
[ɪm'presɪv] adj
impresionante

* *Oh!... What an impressive sight!* Oh!... ¡Qué vista tan impresionante! *

improve

improve
[ɪm'pruːv] v i & v t
mejorar

...improve

* *I hope the weather will improve, otherwise...* Espero que el tiempo mejore, si no.. *

I have to improve my memory tengo que mejorar mi memoria

▶ **improvement**
[ɪmˈpruːvmənt] *n*
mejora *f*

I hope the weather will improve, otherwise...

in

in
[ɪn]
I. *prep*
1. en, dentro de

she lives in London vive en Londres

she went in that direction! ¡fue en aquella dirección!

it's in the box está dentro de/en la caja

he has it all in his mind lo tiene todo dentro de/en su cabeza

in March, in 1980 en marzo, en 1980

2. por
in the morning/ afternoon, evening por la mañana/tarde

3. Idiom
in time a tiempo

in writing por escrito

II. *adv*
1. en el interior,

dentro

* *He opened the door and looked in.* Abrió la puerta y miró dentro. *

2. en casa
I'm sorry, the Professor is not in now lo siento, el profesor no está en casa ahora

3. durante
in the night durante la noche

...in

He opened the door and looked in.

inch

inch
[ɪntʃ] *n*
pl inches [ˈɪnʃɪz]
pulgada *f (2, 54 cm)*

it's about six inches long tiene aproximadamente quince centímetros

twelve inches make one foot doce pulgadas son un pie

increase

increase
[ɪnˈkriːs]
I. *v t & v i*
aumentar

the driver increased speed el conductor aumentó la velocidad

* *The temperature's increasing!... I can't stand it any more...* ¡La temperatura está aumentando!... No puedo soportarlo más... *

The temperature's increasing!... I can't stand it any more...

II. *n*
[ˈɪnkriːs]
1. aumento *m*

there's been an increase in sales ha habido un aumento en las ventas

2. Idiom
on the increase aumentando/creciendo

indeed

indeed
[ɪnˈdiːd] *adv*
1. verdaderamente, realmente

* *I'm very tired indeed!... I just can't get up!...* ¡Estoy realmente muy cansado!... ¡No puedo levantarme!... *

2. Idiom
yes, indeed! ¡claro está!

indeed? ¿de veras?

I'm very tired indeed!... I just can't get up!...

independent

independent
[ɪndɪˈpendənt] *adj*
independiente

Indian

Indian
[ˈɪndɪən]
I. *n*
indio *m*, india *f*

II. *adj*
indio *m*, india *f*

industry

industry
[ˈɪndəstrɪ] *n*
pl industries
[ˈɪndəstrɪz]
industria *f*

influence

influence
[ˈɪnfluəns] *n*
influencia *f*

...influence

▶ **influential**
[ɪnfluˈənʃ(ə)l] *adj*
influyente

inform

inform
[ɪnˈfɔːm] *v i & v t*
informar

he has been well informed ha sido bien informado

...inform

▶ **information**
[ɪnfəˈmeɪʃ(ə)n] *n*
información *f*

we need more information about this matter necesitamos más información sobre este asunto

inhabitant

inhabitant
[ɪnˈhæbɪtənt] *n*
habitante *m f*

injure

injure
[ˈɪndʒəʳ] *v t*
dañar, herir

* *Captain, are you injured?* Capitán, ¿está herido? *

...injure

inn

inn
[ɪn] *n*
posada *f*, hostal *m*

▶ **innkeeper**
[ˈɪnkiːpəʳ] *n*
posadero, a

inquire

inquire
[ɪnˈkwaɪəʳ] *v i & v t*
1. averiguar, informarse

we must inquire about the dates debemos informarnos de las fechas

2. preguntar
we inquired after her health preguntamos por su salud

▶ **inquiry**
[ɪnˈkwaɪrɪ] *n*
pl inquiries
1. pregunta, investigación

2. Idiom
Tintin is making inquiries Tintín está investigando

inside

inside
[ɪnˈsaɪd]
I. *adv*
1. en el interior, dentro

* *Come inside; it's cold out there!* ¡Vengan dentro; hace frío ahí fuera!
We're coming.. Ya venimos... *

2. Idiom
inside out al revés

II. *prep*
dentro de, en el interior de

he is waiting inside the house está esperando dentro de la casa

III. *n*
interior *m*

the inside of the monastery el interior del monasterio

insist

insist
[ɪnˈsɪst] *v i*
insistir

I insist on seeing the prisoner insisto en ver al prisionero

instead

instead
[ɪnˈsted] *adv*
en vez de, en lugar de

...instead

there aren't any tickets for the theatre; shall we go to the cinema instead? no hay entradas de teatro; ¿vamos al cine en vez de ir al teatro?

he's not feeling well; shall I come instead of him? no se encuentra bien, ¿vengo yo en vez de él?

* *Thundering typhoons! What are you doing there, instead of pumping?* ¡Rayos y centellas! ¿Qué están haciendo aquí, en lugar de estar bombeando?
Us? We're resting... it's tiring work, you know... ¿Nosotros? Estamos descansando, es un trabajo cansado, sabe... *

intelligent

intelligent
[ɪn'telɪdʒənt] *adj*
inteligente

it wasn't very intelligent of you to skate on that ice no fuiste muy inteligente al patinar sobre ese hielo

intend

intend
[ɪn'tend] *v i*
proponerse

* *What do you intend to do now, Captain?* ¿Qué se propone hacer ahora, capitán?
I don't know... No lo sé... *

interest

interest
['ɪnt(ə)rɪst]
I. *v t*
interesar

football doesn't interest him el fútbol no le interesa

II. *n*
1. interés *m*

he shows great interest in biology muestra un gran interés por la biología

2. Idiom
to take an interest in interesarse por

she's taking a great interest in music cada vez se interesa más por la música

▶ **interested**
['ɪnt(ə)restɪd] *adj*
interesado, a

a friend of mine is very interested in old maps a un amigo mío le

...interest

interesan mucho los mapas antiguos

▶ **interesting**
['ɪnt(ə)rɪstɪŋ] *adj*
interesante

* *This is an interesting case...* Este es un caso interesante ...
To be precise: very interesting... Yo aún diría más: muy interesante... *

into

into
['ɪntuː] *prep*
1. en

* *Follow me. Let's go into the Professor's laboratory...* Sígame. Entremos en el laboratorio del profesor... *

in his dream Tintin turned into a bottle en su sueño Tintín se convirtió en botella

2. a
he dived into the water se lanzó al agua

introduce

introduce
[ɪntrə'djuːs] *v t*
presentar

* *Let me introduce you to Captain Haddock.* Permítame que le presente al capitán Haddock.
How do you do, Captain. Encantado, capitán. *

invent

invent
[ɪn'vent] *v t*
inventar

▶ **invention**
[ɪn'venʃ(ə)n] *n*
invención *f*

* *And this is my latest invention.* Y ésta es mi última invención. *

invisible

invisible
[ɪn'vɪzəb(ə)l] *adj*
invisible

invite

invite
[ɪn'vaɪt] *v t*
invitar

* *Thank you for inviting us to dinner!*
¡Gracias por invitarnos a cenar!

... *Cheers!* ¡... Salud!
... *Cheers!* ¡... Salud! *

Ireland

Ireland
['aɪələnd] *n*
Irlanda *f*

▶**Irish**
['aɪrɪʃ]
I. *n*
irlandés *m*

...Ireland

he's a teacher of Irish
es profesor de irlandés

the Irish los irlandeses

II. *adj*
irlandés, esa

▶**Irishman,
Irishwoman**
['aɪərɪʃmæn,
'aɪərɪʃwumən] *n*
pl Irishmen, Irishwomen
['aɪərɪʃmen,
'aɪərɪʃwɪmɪn]
irlandés *m*,
irlandesa *f*

iron

iron
['aɪən]
I. *n*
1. hierro *m*

iron is a metal el hierro es un metal

* *Take this iron bar to open the chest...*
Tome esta barra de hierro para abrir el cofre... *

2. plancha *f*
is the iron hot? ¿está caliente la plancha?

II. *v t*
planchar

island

island
['aɪlənd] *n*
isla *f*

* *There's Black Island ...* Allí está la Isla Negra ... *

...island

it

it
[ɪt] *pron*
1. él, ella, ello
Se aplica a cosas inanimadas, y a bebés y animales cuyo sexo se desconoce.

where's the cat? - it's under the table ¿dónde está el gato? – (él) está debajo de la mesa

2. lo, la, le
give it to me, please! ¡dámelo, por favor!

you don't need it tú no lo necesitas

3. *Se usa como sujeto en frases impersonales y no se traduce.*
it's warm hace calor

* *It's eleven o'clock.* Son las once. *

look! it's John! ¡mira! ¡es Juan!

▶**its**
[ɪts]
su, sus *(de él, de ella, de ello)*

the dog is helping its master el perro está ayudando a su dueño

▶**itself**
[ɪt'self] *pron*
1. se

my dog knows how to look after itself mi perro sabe como cuidarse

2. en sí, mismo, misma
the film itself is good, but it's too long la película en sí es buena, pero es demasiado larga

3. Idiom
(all) by itself solo, por sí mismo

jacket

jacket
['dʒækɪt] n
chaqueta f,
americana f

jam

jam
[dʒæm] n
1. mermelada f
confitura f

2. Idiom
traffic jam atasco de
tránsito, embotellamiento

January

January
['dʒænjuərɪ] n
enero m

*the first/second of
January (Am: Janua-
ry first/second)* el
primero/dos de enero

*he was born on the
20th of January (Am:
on January 20th)*
nació el 20 de enero

jar

jar
[dʒɑːˈ] n
tarro m, pote m,
jarra f

jet

jet, jet plane
[dʒet], ['dʒetpleɪn] n
avión m de reacción,
reactor m, jet m

he is a jet pilot es
piloto de jet

jewel

jewel
['dʒuːəl] n
joya f

► **jewellery**
(Am: jewelry)
['dʒuːəlrɪ] n
joyas f pl, alhaja,
joyería f,
piedra f preciosa

job

job
[dʒɒb] n
1. trabajo m

I've got a job for you
tengo un trabajo para ti

2. empleo m
he has a good job
tiene un buen empleo

3. Idiom
* *I had a job finding
the house.* Me costó
trabajo encontrar la casa. *

it's a good job we

...job

knew beforehand es
una suerte que lo supié-
ramos de antemano

join

join
[dʒɔɪn] v i & v t
1. juntar, unir

* *Once I've joined
these two wires, the
radio will work...* Una
vez haya unido estos dos

...join

cables, la radio funcio-
nará... *

2. juntarse, unirse
*I hope one day
you'll join us* espero
que un día te unirás a
nosotros

3. alistarse
*he didn't join the
army* no se alistó en el
ejército

4. entrar, afiliarse
she joined the club
se afilió al club

joke

joke
[dʒəuk]
I. n
1. chiste m,
broma f

* *Ha! Ha! Ha!
Ha!... Really,
Calculus, your
jokes are as
funny as ever...
Ha! Ha! Ha! Ha!
They are!... Ha!
Ha! Ha! Ha!...*
¡Ja! ¡Ja! ¡Ja! ¡Ja!...
Realmente, Tornasol,

...joke

Ha! Ha! Ha! Ha!... Really, Calculus, your jokes are as funny as ever... Ha! Ha! Ha! Ha! They are! Ha! Ha! Ha! Ha!...

sus chistes son tan divertidos como siempre... ¡Ja! ¡Ja! ¡Ja! ¡Ja! ¡De verdad! ... ¡Ja! ¡Ja! ¡Ja! ¡Ja! *

it must be a joke!
¡debe ser una broma!, ¿no?

2. Idiom
let's play a joke on her gastémosle una broma

II. *v i*
bromear

journalist

journalist
['dʒɜːnəlɪst] *n*
periodista *m f*

journey

journey
['dʒɜːnɪ] *n*
viaje *m*

* *Well, Cuthbert, are you going on a journey?* Entonces, Silvestre, ¿se va de viaje?

...journey

Well, Cuthbert, are you going on a journey?

No, I'm not, I'm going on a journey.

...journey

No, I'm not, I'm going on a journey. No, me voy de viaje. *

judge

judge
[dʒʌdʒ]
I. *n*
juez *m f*

II. *v i & v t*
juzgar

...judge

you can't judge from his words no puedes juzgar por sus palabras

July

July
[dʒuːˈlaɪ] *n*
julio *m*

the first/second of July (Am: July first/second) el primero/dos de julio

...July

he was born on the 5th of July (Am: on July 5) nació el 5 de julio

...jump

Woooah!

That's it, he's jumped out of the aeroplane. I hope his parachute will open!...

jump

jump
[dʒʌmp]
I. *v i & v t*
1. saltar

* *Woooah!* ¡Uaaaah! *That's it; he's jumped*

...jump

out of the aeroplane (Am: airplane). I hope his parachute will open!... Ya está; ha saltado del avión. ¡Espero que su paracaídas se abra! *

2. sobresaltar
when he came in, he made me jump cuando entró, me sobresaltó

3. Idiom

to jump the queue (Am: line) colarse, saltarse la cola

II. *n*
salto *m*

long/high jump salto de longitud/de altura

► **jumper (Am: sweater)**
['dʒʌmpəʳ] *n*
jersey *m*

June

June
[dʒuːn] *n*
junio *m*

the first/second of June (Am: June first/second) el primero/dos de junio

he was born the 4th of June (Am: on June 4) nació el 4 de junio

Junior

junior
['dʒuːnɪəʳ]
I. *adj*
1. más nuevo, a, más joven, menor

2. Idiom
junior school escuela primaria

II. *n*
hijo *m*

John Cross, Junior John Cross, hijo

just

just
[dʒʌst]
I. *adv*
1. justamente, exactamente

this is just what I said esto es exactamente lo que dije

2. solamente, sólo
we're just joking solamente estamos bromeando

3. Idiom

...just

to have just done something acabar de hacer algo

* Look, the helicopter has just landed... Mire, el helicóptero acaba de aterrizar... *

just a minute! ¡espere un momento!

II. adj
justo, a

he is a just man es un hombre justo

keen

keen
[kiːn] adj
1. entusiasta, ansioso, a

they are keen to find the treasure están ansiosos por encontrar el tesoro

2. agudo, a
* Fortunately you have a keen sense of smell, Snowy. You'll be able to follow their trail... Afortunadamente tienes

...keen

un sentido agudo del olfato, Milú. Podrás seguir su pista... *

3. Idiom
he's not very keen on work no le gusta mucho trabajar

keep

keep
[kiːp]
kept, kept [kept]

...keep

I. v t
1. guardar

* You can keep it; it might be useful... Puedes guardarlo; puede resultar útil... *

to keep a secret guardar un secreto

2. retener
you are late; what has kept you? llegas tarde; ¿qué te ha retenido?

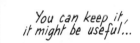

3. Idiom
keep an eye on him vigílalo

II. v i
1. continuar, seguir

* Hurry up; they're coming! ¡Dense prisa; ya vienen!
Keep running... Quick!... Sigan corriendo... ¡Rápido!... *

2. mantener
this will keep you awake esto te manten-

drá despierto

keep calm! ¡mantén la calma!

3. Idiom
how are you keeping? ¿cómo estás?

keep (to the) left circular por la izquierda

keep still! ¡estate quieto!

keep quiet! ¡cállate!

...keep

kettle

kettle
['ket(ə)l] n
hervidor m

I bought a new kettle compré un nuevo hervidor

key

key
[kiː] n
1. llave f

turn the key gira la llave

2. clave f
this is the key to the matter esta es la clave del asunto

3. tecla f
a piano key una tecla de piano

kick

kick
[kɪk] v i & v t
I. dar patadas, cocear

II. n
patada f

▶ kick out
echar (a patadas)

he was kicked out of the house fue echado de la casa

kill

kill
[kɪl] v t
matar

kind

kind
[kaɪnd]
I. *adj*
amable

* *Take this, it's for you, it's a present.* Toma esto; es para ti; es un regalo.
It's very kind of you! ¡Es muy amable de tu parte! *

II. *n*
clase *f*, tipo *m*

all kinds of fish toda clase de peces

she doesn't like this kind of food no le gusta este tipo de comida

▶ **kindness**
['kaɪndnɪs] *n*
amabilidad *f*

king

king
[kɪŋ] *n*
rey *m*

kiss

...kiss

kiss
[kɪs]
I. *n*
beso *m*

she gave me a kiss me dió un beso

II. *vi & vt*
besar(se)

* *Let me kiss you!* ¡Déjeme besarle! *

kitchen

kitchen
['kɪtʃɪn] *n*
cocina *f*

knee

knee
[niː] *n*
rodilla *f*

▶ **kneel**
[niːl] *vi*
knelt, knelt [nelt]
arrodillarse

knife

knife
[naɪf] *n*
pl knives [naɪvz]
cuchillo *m*

* *Heavens! my knife!* ¡Cielos! ¡Mi cuchillo! *

knock

knock
[nɒk]
I. *n*
golpe *m*

...knock

II. *vt*
golpear

somebody knocked him on the head alguien le golpeó en la cabeza

III. *vi*
1. golpear(se)

he knocked against the cupboard se golpeó contra el armario

2. Idiom
to knock at the door llamar a la puerta

...knock

▶ **knock down**
derribar, tirar por el suelo, atropellar

he was knocked down by a car fue atropellado por un coche

▶ **knock out**
noquear, dejar fuera de combate

* *The blow must have knocked him out...* El golpe debe de haberlo dejado fuera de combate... *

▶ **knock over**
tirar, derramar

be careful not to knock the glass over ten cuidado de no tirar el vaso

know

know
[nəʊ]
knew [njuː]
known [nəʊn] *vi & vt*
1. saber

he doesn't know anything about it no sabe nada de esto

what are their plans? – I don't know ¿cuáles son sus planes? – No lo sé

2. conocer
I don't know her very well no la conozco muy bien

▶ **knowledge**
['nɒlɪdʒ] *n*
conocimiento *m*, saber *m*

lack

lack
[læk]
I. n
falta f,
carencia f

II. v t
faltarle a uno,
carecer de

he lacks patience le falta paciencia

ladder

ladder
['lædə'] n
1. escalera f

* *Woooah!* ¡Guaaaah!
He's climbing the ladder... Está subiendo por la escalera... *

2. Idiom
you've got a ladder (Am: run) in your tights tienes una carrera en la medias

He's climbing the ladder...

lady

lady
['leɪdɪ] n
pl ladies
dama f, señora f

this lady is my friend esta señora es mi amiga

ladies and gentlemen señoras y señores

lake

lake
[leɪk] n
lago m

lamp

lamp
[læmp] n
lámpara f

land

land
[lænd]
I. n
1. tierra f

he works the land trabaja la tierra

2. país m, tierra f
he comes from a very far away land viene de un país muy lejano

II. v i
1. aterrizar

the plane landed at last el avión aterrizó finalmente

2. desembarcar
we'll land on this island desembarcaremos en esta isla

lane

lane
[leɪn] n
1. sendero m, camino m

* *In Tibet...* En el Tibet...
...Yes, definitely, this lane is too narrow, a lorry (Am: truck) couldn't get through... Sí, realmente, este sendero es demasiado estrecho, un camión no podría pasar... *

2. calle

3. carril

language

language
['læŋgwɪdʒ] n
1. lengua f, idioma m

how many languages does he speak? ¿cuántas lenguas habla?

2. lenguaje m
the legal language el lenguaje jurídico

large

large
[lɑːdʒ] *adj*
grande

last

last
[lɑːst]
I. *adj*
1. último, a

today is the last day of school hoy es el último día de colegio

...last

2. pasado, a
last Sunday el domingo pasado

last week la semana pasada

last year el año pasado

3. Idiom
the week before last hace dos semanas

II. *adv*
1. finalmente, por último

he spoke last at the meeting habló el último en la reunión

2. por última vez
* *When did you last see him?* ¿Cuándo lo vio por última vez? *Yesterday evening, I think...* Ayer por la noche, creo... *

3. Idiom
at last! ¡al fin!

III. *v i*
durar

...last

* *How long will this storm last?* ¿Cuánto tiempo durará esta tormenta? *

this can't last esto no puede durar

late

late
[leɪt]
I. *adj*
1. tarde, con retraso

* *Hurry up, we're late!* ¡Date prisa, llegamos tarde! *

the plane was late el avión llegó con retraso

it's getting late se hace tarde

2. Idiom
in the late afternoon a última hora de la tarde

II. *adv*
tarde, con retraso

▶ **lately**
['leɪtlɪ] *adv*
últimamente

have you seen Nick lately? ¿has visto a Nick últimamente?

▶ **later**
['leɪtə'] *adv*
1. más tarde

Tintin will arrive later Tintín llegará más tarde

2. Idiom
see you later! ¡hasta luego!

▶ **latest**
['leɪtɪst] *adj*
último, a

* *Have you heard the latest news?... A plane has crashed in Nepal...* ¿Ha oído las últimas noticias?... Un avión se ha estrellado en Nepal... *

...late

laugh

laugh
[lɑːf]
I. *v i*
1. reír

you make me laugh me haces reír

2. burlarse de, reírse de
don't laugh at her no te burles de ella

II. *n*
1. risa *f*

he has a loud laugh tiene una risa fuerte

2. Idiom
to do something for a laugh hacer algo por broma

law

law
[lɔː] *n*
1. ley *f*

...law

2. Idiom
to take the law into one's own hands tomarse la justicia por su mano

▶ **lawyer**
['lɔːjə'] *n*
abogado *m*, abogada *f*

lawn

lawn
[lɔːn] *n*
césped *m*

lay

lay
[leɪ] *v t*
laid, laid [leɪd]
1. poner

they laid the carpet pusieron la alfombra

...lay

2. Idiom
to lay the table poner la mesa

the hen has laid an egg la gallina ha puesto un huevo

lazy

lazy
['leɪzɪ] *adj*
lazier, laziest
perezoso, a

lead

lead
[liːd]
led, led [led]
I. *v t*
1. conducir

he led us to the door nos condujo hasta la puerta

2. dirigir
he leads a large company dirige una gran compañía

II. *v i*

1. ir a la cabeza

my horse is leading mi caballo va a la cabeza

2. conducir, llevar
this road leads to the city esta carretera lleva a la ciudad

III. *n*
1. correa *f*

* *Dogs must be kept on a lead (Am: leash) so that they don't run away...* Los

...lead

perros deben llevarse con correa para que no se escapen... *

2. Idiom
to take the lead tomar la delantera

▶ **leader**
['liːdəʳ] *n*
líder *m,* **jefe** *m*

we don't want any leader no queremos ningún jefe

leaf

leaf
[liːf] *n*
pl leaves
1. hoja *f*

the leaves are green las hojas están verdes

2. Idiom
turn over a new leaf borrón y cuenta nueva

lean

lean
[liːn] *v i & v t*
leaned, leaned/leant, leant [lent]
1. apoyar(se)

he was leaning against the wall estaba apoyado contra la pared

lean the ladder against the wall apoya la escalera contra el muro

2. inclinarse, asomarse

* *Tintin, don't lean out!...* ¡Tintín, no te asomes!... *

learn

learn
[lɜːn] *v i & v t*
learned, learned/learnt, learnt [lɜːnt]
aprender

he's learning to

...learn

drive está aprendiendo a conducir

they learn fast aprenden rápido

leather

leather
['leðəʳ] *n*
cuero *m*

a leather jacket una chaqueta de cuero

leave

leave
[liːv]
left, left [left]
I. *v i*
partir

we must leave right now debemos partir ahora mismo

II. *v t*
1. dejar

I must leave you now ahora debo dejarle

leave some for the

children deja algo para los niños

he left the money at home dejó el dinero en casa

2. Idiom
* *Leave me alone!...* ¡Déjeme en paz!... *

there's not much water left no queda mucha agua

this is left over from the party esto ha sobrado de la fiesta

...leave

▶ **leave out**
omitir, dejarse

he left out a number
omitió un número

left

left
[left]
I. *n*
izquierda *f*

...left

in England they drive on the left en Inglaterra conducen por la izquierda

* *Captain Haddock is sitting on Tintin's left...* El capitán Haddock está sentado a la izquierda de Tintín... *

II. *adj*
izquierdo, a

he writes with his left hand escribe con la mano izquierda

CHEEEP CHEEEP CHEEEP

Ssh!

Captain Haddock is sitting on Tintin's left...

III. *adv*
a la izquierda

your room is on the left, sir su habitación está a la izquierda, señor

▶ **left-hand**
[left'hænd] *adj*
izquierdo, a

on the left-hand side en el lado izquierdo, a la izquierda

leg

leg
[leg] *n*
1. pierna *f*

he broke his leg se rompió una pierna

2. pata *f*
* *Come on, Snowy, show me your leg... I must see whether it's broken!...* ¡Vamos, Milú, enséñame la pata... Tengo que mirar si está rota!... *

Come on, Snowy, show me your leg... I must see whether it's broken!...

lemon

lemon
['lemən] *n*
limón *m*

▶ **lemonade**
[lemə'neɪd] *n*
gaseosa *f*

lend

lend
[lend] *v t*
lent, lent [lent]

...lend

1. prestar

* *Can you lend me your car?* ¿Puede prestarme su coche? *Yes, of course!...* ¡Sí, por supuesto!... *

2. Idiom
to lend a hand echar una mano

I'm lending him a hand with his work le estoy echando una mano en su trabajo

Can you lend me your car?

Yes, of course!...

less

less
[les]
I. *adj*
menos

I have less worries than you tengo menos preocupaciones que tú

II. *adv*
1. menos

he travels less now
viaja menos ahora

2. Idiom

* *I'm getting used to walking on the moon... It's less and less difficult...* Me estoy acostumbrando a andar por la luna... Es cada vez menos difícil... *

I'm getting used to walking on the moon... It's less and less difficult...

lesson

lesson
['les(ə)n] *n*
lección *f*

let

let
[let]
let, let
I. *v t*
1. dejar, permitir

...let

let me explain déjeme explicar

they won't let her sing no la dejarán cantar

2. alquilar
rooms to let se alquilan habitaciones

3. Idiom
to let go of something soltar una cosa

I will let you know te avisaré

...let

II. *v aux* (en frases imperativas)

let's see veamos, vamos a ver

* *Let's go!... I hope you aren't too heavy!...* ¡Vamos!... ¡Espero que no peses mucho!... *

let's go for a walk vayamos a dar un paseo

▶ **let in**
hacer pasar, dejar pasar

Let's go!... I hope you aren't too heavy!...

who let you in? ¿quién le ha dejado pasar?

▶ **let off**
1. disparar, lanzar

the boys were letting off fireworks los niños lanzaban fuegos artificiales

2. perdonar, excusar, no castigar
her mother let him off but she scolded

him su madre no lo castigó pero lo regañó

▶ **let out**
dejar salir

* *Let me out!... Let me out!... Blistering barnacles!...* ¡Déjenme salir!... ¡Déjenme salir!... ¡Mil demonios!... *

Let me out!... Let me out!... Blistering barnacles!...

---

letter

letter
['letər] *n*
1. letra *f*

to write in small/capital letters escribir en minúsculas/mayúsculas

2. carta *f*
* *A few days later...* Unos pocos días después...
Tintin, you've got a letter from Cuthbert Calculus!... ¡Tintín, tiene una carta de Silvestre Tornasol!... *

A few days later...
Tintin, you've got a letter from Cuthbert Calculus!...

level

level
['lev(ə)l] *n*
nivel *m*

library

library
['laɪbrərɪ] *n*
pl libraries ['laɪbrərɪz]
bibliotéca *f*

lending library biblioteca de préstamo

lie

lie
[laɪ] *v i*
lay [leɪ], lain [leɪn]
tumbarse, tenderse

Tintin is lying on the floor Tintín está tendido en el suelo

you'd better lie on the bed for a while sería mejor que te tumbaras en la cama un rato

▶ **lie down**
acostarse, tumbarse

lie

lie
[laɪ]
lay, lain [leɪ, leɪn]
I. *v i*
mentir

don't lie to me no me mientas

...lie

II. *n*
mentira *f*

to tell lies decir mentiras

life

life
[laɪf] *n*
pl lives [laɪvz]
1. vida *f*

...life

it's a matter of life or death es un asunto de vida o muerte

doctors save many lives los médicos salvan muchas vidas

2. Idiom
I never saw such a thing in my whole life! ¡nunca he visto nada parecido en toda my vida!

once in a lifetime una vez en la vida

lift

lift
[lɪft]
I. *n*
(*Am:* elevator)
1. ascensor *m*
(*Am:* elevador)

2. Idiom
to give somebody a lift llevar a alguien (en coche)

* *Hello, Mr Calculus... would you like a lift to the village?* Hola, señor Tornasol... ¿quiere que lo lleve hasta el pueblo? *

Hello, Mr Calculus... would you like a lift to the village?

II. *v t*
alzar, levantar

it's too heavy for me to lift! ¡no puedo levantarlo; es demasiado pesado!

light

light
[laɪt] *adj*
ligero, a

...light

a light meal una comida ligera

this case is light esta maleta es ligera

light

light
[laɪt]
I. *n*
1. luz *f*

...light

* *Blistering barnacles!... The power has been cut off: there's no light...* ¡Mil demonios!... Se ha cortado la corriente: no hay luz... *

turn the lights on/off enciende/apaga la luz

2. fuego *m*
can you give me a light? ¿puede darme fuego?

Blistering barnacles!... The power has been cut off: there's no light...

II. *v t*
lit, lit [lɪt]
alumbrar, encender

the streets are lit las calles están alumbradas

III. *adj*
claro, a

her dress was light green su vestido era de color verde claro

►**lightning**
[ˈlaɪtnɪŋ] *n*
relámpago *m*

like

like
[laɪk] *v t*
gustar, querer

do you like to travel by train? ¿te gusta viajar en tren?

...like

Captain Haddock likes whisky al capitán Haddock le gusta el whisky

would you like to visit Moscow? ¿te gustaría visitar Moscú?

would you like more coffee? ¿quiere más café?

take as many as you like coge tantos como quieras

like

like
[laɪk] *prep*
1. como

he's not like his brother no es como su hermano

he's running like mad corre como un loco

2. Idiom
to look like parecerse a

* *Thomson looks like Thompson...* Hernández se parece a Fernández... *

it looks like it's going to be a fine day parece que va a hacer un buen día

►**likely**
[ˈlaɪklɪ] *adj*
1. probable

it's not very likely that you'll see him no es muy probable que lo veas

2. Idiom
she is likely to go to Italy es probable que vaya a Italia

Thomson looks like Thompson...

limit

limit
[ˈlɪmɪt]
I. *n*
límite *m*

speed limit límite de velocidad

II. *v t*
limitar

line

line
[laɪn] *n*
1. línea *f*

draw a straight line traza una línea recta

* *The first lines are illegible...* Las primeras líneas son ilegibles... *

2. vía *f*, línea *f*
the railway (Am: railroad) line vía, línea de tren

The first lines are illegible...

lip

lip
[lɪp] *n*
labio *m*

list

list
[lɪst] *n*
lista *f*

listen

listen
[ˈlɪs(ə)n] *v i*
escuchar

he's listening to the radio está escuchando la radio

litre

litre
[ˈliːtəʳ] *n*
(*Am:* **liter**)
litro *m*

little

little
[ˈlɪtl] *adj*
pequeño, a

little

little
[lɪtl]
less [les]
least [liːst]
I. *adj*
poco, a

...little

Later, in the rocket...

Hello, hello, this is Tintin... hello... we have very little oxygen left... hello... hello... we're stifling... hello... hello...

* *Later, in the rocket...* Más tarde, en el cohete...
Hello, hello, this is Tintin... Hello... we have very little oxigen left... hello... hello... we're stifling... hello... hello... Hola, hola, aquí Tintín... Hola... nos queda muy poco oxígeno... hola... hola... nos ahogamos... hola... hola... *

II. *n*
poco

he did very little for us hizo muy poco por nosotros

III. *adv*
poco

he is little known es poco conocido

live

live
[lɪv] *v i*
vivir

Chang lives in China Tchang vive en China

my parents lived through the war mis padres vivieron la guerra

live

live
[laɪv] *adj*
1. en directo

a live concert un concierto en directo

2. electrizado, a
a live rail un raíl electrizado

lively

lively
[ˈlaɪvlɪ] *adj*
1. vivaz

Snowy is a very lively dog Milú es un perro muy vivaz

2. animado, a
the meeting was very lively la reunión fue muy animada

living

llving
[ˈlɪvɪŋ] *n*
vida *f*

to earn a living ganarse la vida

▶ **living room**
[ˈlɪvɪŋruːm] *n*
sala *f* de estar, salón *m*

load

load
[ləud]
I. *v i & v t*
cargar

* *Are these the last ones?* ¿Son éstas las últimas?
No, we still have to load these two crates. No, todavía tenemos que cargar estas dos cajas. *

II. *n*
carga *f*

Are these the last ones?

No, we still have to load these two crates.

loaf

loaf
[ləuf] *n*
pl loaves [ləuvz]

a loaf of bread una barra de pan

local

local
[ˈləuk(ə)l] *adj*
local

local customs costumbres locales

lock

lock
[lɒk]
I. *n*
1. cerradura *f*

2. mechón *m*
a lock of hair un mechón de pelo

II. *v i & v t*
cerrar(se) con llave

* *Heavens!... He's locked the door!...* ¡Cielos!... ¡Ha cerrado la puerta con llave!... *

Heavens!... He's locked the door!...

London

London
[ˈlʌndən] *n*
Londres

▶ **Londoner**
[ˈlʌndənəʳ] *n*
londinense *m f*

lonely

lonely
[ˈləunlɪ] *adj*
lonelier, loneliest

...lonely

solo, a, solitario, a

she is a lonely traveller es una viajera solitaria

long

long
[lɒŋ]
I. *adj*
1. largo, a

...long

she has long hair tiene el pelo largo

2. Idiom
it's a long way está muy lejos

in the long run a la larga

II. adv
1. mucho tiempo

have you been waiting long? ¿has esperado mucho tiempo?

I saw the film long *ago* vi la película hace mucho tiempo

2. Idiom
he won't be long no tardará

I can't stand it any longer no puedo soportarlo más

all day/night long durante todo el día/toda la noche

* *Goodbye, Tintin...* Adiós, Tintín... *So long!* ¡Hasta luego! *

as long as mientras

I'll remember this party as long as I live recordaré esta fiesta mientras viva

look

look
[luk]
I. n
1. mirada f

a friendly look una mirada amigable

2. aire m, aspecto m *this teacher has a severe look* este profesor tiene un aire severo

3. Idiom
to have a look echar una mirada

...look

he has good looks es guapo

II. v i
1. mirar

look, it's Chang's scarf! mire, ¡es la bufanda de Tchang

* *I can't find my pipe. I've looked everywhere!* ¡No puedo encontrar mi pipa. He mirado en todas partes! *

2. Idiom
you look well tienes buen aspecto

she looks happy parece contenta

► **look after** cuidar

he looked after her during her illness la cuidó durante su enfermedad

► **look at** mirar

Captain Haddock is looking at the sea el capitán Haddock está mirando el mar

► **look for** buscar

they are looking for the treasure están buscando el tesoro

► **look into** investigar

Tintin is looking into

the matter Tintín está investigando el asunto

► **look forward to** esperar con ilusión

we look forward to seeing you soon esperamos con ilusión verle pronto

► **look out** tener cuidado

* *Look out, Tintin; he's got a gun! Stay*

...look

hidden! ¡Tenga cuidado, Tintín; tiene una pistola! ¡Manténgase escondido! *

► **look up**
1. mirar hacia arriba

2. buscar, comprobar
look it up in the dictionary búscalo en el diccionario

3. mejorar, ponerse mejor
things are looking up las cosas están mejorando

loose

loose
[luːs] adj
1. suelto, a, desatado, a

* *Oh! my shoelace is loose.* ¡Oh! el cordón de mi zapato está desatado. *

2. Idiom
to let loose liberar

lord

lord
[lɔːd] *n*
1. señor *m*

2. lord *m* (*pl:* lores)
the House of Lords
la Cámara de los Lores

lorry

lorry
['lɒrɪ] *n*
pl lorries
(*Am:* **truck**)
camión *m*

lose

lose
[luːz] *v i & v t*
lost, lost [lɒst]
1. perder

* *Thompson, I've lost my wallet!* ¡Fernández, he perdido mi cartera! *

he lost his job perdió su trabajo

2. Idiom
to lose one's way perder el camino/ perderse

lot

lot
[lɒt] *n*
Idiom
a lot of/lots of mucho/ muchos

there were lots of cars había muchos coches

loud

loud
[laud]
I. *adj*
ruidoso, a,
alto, a,
fuerte

the music is too loud la música está demasiado fuerte

II. *adv*
alto, fuerte

speak louder habla más fuerte

love

love
[lʌv]
I. *n*
1. amor *m*

a mother's love un amor materno

my love mi amor

2. Idiom
to fall in love enamorarse

lots of love, Nick besos, Nick

give my love to your mother dale recuerdos a tu madre de mi parte

II. *v t*
1. amar, querer

I love you te amo/te quiero

2. adorar, encantar
* *Is that you, Tintin? I just love these bones the birds left behind!* ¿Eres tú, Tintín? Me encantan estos huesos que los pájaros han dejado! *

▶**lovely**
['lʌvlɪ] *adj*
lovelier, loveliest
adorable,
encantador, ora,
precioso, a

low

low
[ləu]
I. *adj*
bajo, a

...low

in a low voice en voz baja

a low ceiling un techo bajo

II. *adv*
bajo

the plane is flying low el avión está volando bajo

luck

luck
[lʌk] *n*
suerte *f*

* *Goodbye, and good luck! I hope everything goes well for you!* ¡Adiós, y buena suerte! ¡Espero que todo les vaya bien! *

▶**luckily**
['lʌkɪlɪ] *adv*
por suerte

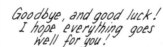

▶**lucky**
['lʌkɪ] *adj*
1. afortunado, a

2. Idiom
to be lucky tener suerte

luggage

luggage
['lʌgɪdʒ] *n*
equipaje *m*

lump

lump
[lʌmp] *n*
terrón *m*

a lump of sugar un terrón de azúcar

lunch

lunch
[lʌntʃ] *n*
almuerzo *m*

M M M M

machine

machine
[məˈʃiːn] n
1. máquina f

* *Cuthbert Calculus has invented an amazing machine...* Silvestre Tornasol ha inventado una máquina increíble... *

sewing machine máquina de coser

2. Idiom
washing machine lavadora

Cuthbert Calculus has invented an amazing machine...

►**machinery**
[məˈʃiːnərɪ] n
maquinaria f

we'll need new machinery necesitaremos maquinaria nueva

mad

mad
[mæd] adj
madder, maddest
1. loco, a

...mad

he's gone mad se ha vuelto loco

2. furioso, a, enfadado, a
the teacher is mad at him el profesor está furioso con él

3. apasionado, a, loco, a
she's mad about music está loca por la música

mail

mail
[meɪl] n
correo m

I'll send it by mail lo enviaré por correo

* *Some mail for me? My word, how can anyone know that I'm here?...* ¿Correo para mi? Dios mío, ¿quién puede saber que estoy aquí?... *

Some mail for me? My word, how can anyone know that I'm here? ...

main

main
[meɪn] adj
principal

go to the main door ve a la puerta principal

make

make
[meɪk]
I. n
marca f

...make

this make is new esta marca es nueva

II. v t
made, made [meɪd]
1. hacer, fabricar, construir

he made a new machine construyó una nueva máquina

he made some tea hizo té

2. hacer, obligar

...make

his answer made me think su respuesta me hizo reflexionar

they made him go le hicieron ir

3. hacer, poner
this noise makes me nervous este ruido me pone nervioso

4. Idiom
two and six make eight dos y seis hacen ocho

you have to make your bed tienes que hacerte la cama

make yourself at home póngase cómodo

make sure he understood asegúrate de que te entendió

it doesn't make sense no tiene sentido

I can't make it out no puedo entenderlo

▶ **make up**
1. inventar

* *Hello!... Come quick! I've just arrested a young boy who's making up a whole story...* ¡Hola!... ¡Venga rápido! Acabo de arrestar a un joven que está inventando toda una historia... *

2. maquillar(se)
he's making up to go on stage se está

maquillando para salir al escenario

3. Idiom
make up your mind decídete

▶ **make-up** *n*
maquillaje *m*

---

man

man
[mæn] *n*
pl men [mɛn]
hombre *m*

* *Tintin is following a man.* Tintín está siguiendo a un hombre. *

manage

manage
['mænɪdʒ]
I. *v i*

Tintin is following a man.

...manage

1. conseguir
he managed to convince him consiguió convencerle

2. apañarse
she can manage without this tool puede apañarse sin esta herramienta

II. *v t*
dirigir

she manages a large company dirige una gran compañía

▶ **manager**
['mænɪdʒəʳ] *n*
director, ora, administrador, ora

manner

manner
['mænəʳ] *n*
manera *f*

...manner

▶ **manners, good manners**
educación *f*

* *Thundering typhoons!... I'll teach you good manners, Abdullah!...* ¡Rayos y centellas!... Yo te enseñaré educación, Abdallah!... *Waaah! Waaah!...* ¡Buaaa! ¡Buaaa!... *

it's bad manners to shout gritar es de mala educación

...manner

many

many
['mɛnɪ]
more [mɔːʳ],
most [məust]
I. *adj*
1. muchos, as

she has many books tiene muchos libros

2. Idiom
as many as tantos como

he has as many

subjects as you tiene tantas asignaturas como tú

how many cuántos, as

how many keys has he got? ¿cuántas llaves tiene?

too many demasiados, as

she wants too many things quiere demasiadas cosas

II. *pron*
1. muchos, as

I haven't got many no tengo muchos

2. Idiom
as many tantos, as

I've got as many as you tengo tantos como tú

how many cuántos, as

too many demasiados, as

map

map
[mæp] *n*
mapa *m*, plano *m*

the treasure was marked on the map el tesoro estaba marcado en el mapa

city map plano de la ciudad

March

March
[mɑːtʃ] *n*
marzo *m*

the first/second of March el primero/dos de marzo

her birthday is on the 6th of March su cumpleaños es el 6 de marzo

mark

mark
[mɑːk]
I. *n*
1. nota *f*

he gets very good marks (Am: grades) saca muy buenas notas

2. marca *f*
* I thought as much!...He's got a mark on his neck... The poor man's been hit by a dart... ¡Lo que pensaba!... Tiene una marca en el cuello... El pobre hombre ha sido alcanzado por un dardo... *

3. mancha *f*
I have a blue mark on my skirt tengo una mancha azul en la falda

II. *v t*
marcar

this experience marked his life esta experiencia marcó su vida

I thought as much!... He's got a mark on his neck... The poor man's been hit by a dart...

market

market
['mɑːkɪt] *n*
mercado *m*

to go to market ir al mercado

* They are at the flea market... Están en el mercado de las baratijas... *

...market

They are at the flea market...

marmalade

marmalade
['mɑːməleɪd] *n*
mermelada *f* (de naranja)

marry

marry
['mærɪ] *v i & v t*
married, married ['mærɪd]
1. casarse

...marry

she married Gary se casó con Gary

he never married nunca se casó

2. Idiom
to get married casarse

▶ **marriage**
['mærɪdʒ] *n*
matrimonio *n*

mass

mass
[mæs] *n*
1. masa *f*

there's a mass of papers on his desk hay una masa de papeles en su escritorio

2. cantidad *f*
he's got masses of work tiene cantidad de trabajo

3. misa *f*
he goes to mass va a misa

match

match
[mætʃ]
I. *n*
1. partido *m*, encuentro *m*

a football match un partido de fútbol

2. cerilla *f*
give me a match dame una cerilla

II. *v i & v t*
hacer juego con

her shoes matched her belt sus zapatos hacían juego con su cinturón

III. *v t*
1. emparejar

2. igualar
no one can match her nadie puede igualarla

material

material
[mə'tɪərɪəl] *n*
1. tela *f*

I need some material for a skirt necesito tela para una falda

2. materia *f*
raw material materia prima

3. material *m*
building materials material de construcción

mathematics

mathematics
[mæθ'mætɪks] *n pl*
matemáticas *f pl*

do you like mathematics? ¿te gustan las matemáticas?

▶ **maths**
[mæθs] *n pl*
(*Am:* **math**)
matemáticas *f pl*

she is our maths teacher es nuestra profesora de matemáticas

matter

matter
['mætər] *n*
1. asunto *m*, cuestión *f*

it's an important matter es un asunto importante

2. Idiom
what's the matter? ¿qué ocurre?, ¿qué pasa?

* Hurray!... Hurray!... Come here, Tintin, and rejoice with me!.. ¡Hurra!... ¡Hurra!...

...matter

Hurray!... Hurray!... Come here, Tintin, and rejoice with me!...

For goodness' sake, Captain, what is the matter?

¡Venga aquí, Tintín, y alégrese conmigo!... **For goodness sake, Captain, what's the matter?** Por amor de Dios, capitán, ¿qué ocurre? *

what's the matter with him? ¿qué le pasa?

there's something the matter with the radio algo le pasa a la radio

as a matter of fact de hecho, en realidad

mattress

mattress
['mætrɪs] *n*
colchón *m*

* *Everyone is lying on his mattress...* Cada uno está tumbado en su colchón... *

Everyone is lying on his mattress...

May

May
[meɪ] *n*
mayo *m*

the first/second of May el primero/dos de mayo

her birthday is on the 12th of May su cumpleaños es el 12 de mayo

may

may
[meɪ] *v aux*
might [maɪt]
1. poder

he may stay puede quedarse

may I come in? ¿puedo entrar?

2. Idiom
she may come puede que venga

it might be possible podría ser

they may have lost their way puede que se hayan perdido

▶ **maybe**
['meɪbɪ] *adv*
quizás

* *Maybe he isn't at home, he's not answering the door!...* ¡Quizás no esté en casa; no contesta a la puerta!... *

Maybe he isn't at home, he's not answering the door!...

THUM THUMP

me

me
[miː] *pron*
me

tell me dime

read it to me léemelo

meal

meal
[miːl] *n*
comida *f*

mean

mean
[miːn] *adj*
1. tacaño, a

he's mean; he never pays for anything es tacaño; nunca paga nada

...mean

2. malo, a, mezquino, a
what a mean trick! ¡qué mala jugada!

mean

mean
[miːn] *v t*
meant, meant [ment]
1. querer decir, significar

...mean

I don't know what this means no sé lo que esto significa

do you know what I mean? ¿sabes lo que quiero decir?

2. Idiom
he didn't mean to do it no era su intención hacerlo

meanwhile

meanwhile
['miːnwaɪl] *adv*
mientras tanto

measure

measure
['meʒəʳ]
I. *v i & v t*
medir

measure the window mide la ventana

...measure

this room measures five metres (Am: meters) by three esta habitación mide cinco metros por tres

II. *n*
medida *f*

the gramme (Am: gram) is a measure of weight el gramo es una medida de peso

meat

...medicine

meat
[miːt] n
carne f

medicine

medicine
['medsɪn] n
1. medicina f,
medicamento m

* *Well, gentlemen,
do you have any*

*medicine to cure
him quickly?* Y bien,
señores, ¿tienen alguna
medicina para curarlo
rápidamente? *

2. medicina f
*she is studying medi-
cine* estudia medicina

*Well, gentlemen, do you have any medicine
to cure him quickly?*

? ? ? ? ? ? ? ?

meet

meet
[miːt]
met, met [met] v i & v t
1. encontrar,
encontrarse (con)

*I met Helen at the
party* me encontré con
Helen en la fiesta

*we'll meet on Labra-
dor Road* nos encontra-
remos en la calle Labrador

2. ir a buscar
meet me at the

...meet

station ven a buscarme
a la estación

3. conocer
*we first met in
Venice* nos conocimos
en Venecia

4. Idiom
*have you met Mr
Brett?* ¿conoce al señor
Brett?

▶ **meeting**
['miːtɪŋ] n
1. encuentro m

*Ah, my dear Captain Padlock, I'll never forget our first
meeting!*

*Haddock, Madam,
Captain Haddock.*

* *Ah, my dear Cap-
tain Padlock, I'll nev-
er forget our first
meeting!* ¡Ah, mi que-
rido capitán Padlock,
nunca olvidaré nuestro
primer encuentro!
*Haddock, Madam,
Captain Haddock.*
Haddock, señora, capitán
Haddock. *

2. reunión f
*they have a meeting
at four* tienen una
reunión a las cuatro

memory

memory
['meməri] n
pl memories
1. memoria f

*he has a good
memory* tiene buena
memoria

2. recuerdo
childhood memories
recuerdos de infancia

men

men
[men]
→ MAN

mend

mend
[mend] v i & v t
1. reparar

2. Idiom
*my radio needs
mending* mi radio
necesita una reparación

mention

mention
['menʃ(ə)n] v t
1. mencionar

*he mentioned it
without giving it
importance* lo mencio-
nó sin darle importancia

*he was mentioned
for the prize* fue men-
cionado para el premio

2. Idiom
* *I don't know what
would have become*

*of me without you.
Thank you ever so
much...* No sé que ha-
bría sido de mí sin usted.
Muchísimas gracias...
Don't mention it! ¡No
hay de que! *

*I don't know what would
have become of me without
you. Thank you ever so much...*

Don't mention it!

menu

menu
['menjuː] n
menú m

*what's on the
menu?* ¿qué hay en el
menú?

merry

merry
['meri] adj
merrier, merriest
alegre, feliz

...merry

Merry Christmas!
¡Feliz Navidad!

mess

mess
[mes] n
1. desorden m

2. Idiom
*he made a mess of
the whole matter* lió
todo el asunto

message

message
['mesɪdʒ] *n*
mensaje *m*

metal

metal
['metl] *n*
metal *m*

midday

midday
[mɪd'deɪ] *n*

...midday

mediodía *m*

middle

middle
['mɪdl] *n*
medio *m*, centro *m*

midnight

midnight
['mɪdnaɪt] *n*
medianoche *f*

might

might
[maɪt] *v aux*
poder *(condicional, pasado de MAY)*

it might be true pudiera ser cierto

* *Well! You are lucky!* ¡Bien! ¡Tiene suerte!
You might have broken your neck!... ¡Podría haberse roto el cuello!...
Be quiet! Thundering Typhoons!...

...might

¡Silencio! ¡Rayos y centellas!... *

mile

mile
[maɪl] *n*
milla *f* (=1,6 km)

it's 50 miles from here está a 80 kilómetros de aquí

milk

milk
[mɪlk] *n*
leche *f*

would you like some milk? ¿quiere un poco de leche?

▶ **milkman**
['mɪlkmən] *n*
pl milkmen
lechero *m*

million

million
['mɪlɪən] *n*
millón *m*

it cost a million dollars costó un millón de dólares

two million people dos millones de personas

mind

mind
[maɪnd]
I. *n*
1. mente *f*

2. Idiom
what do you have in mind? ¿qué piensas hacer?

* *What's on your mind, Tintin?* ¿Qué le preocupa, Tintín?
I wonder how we're going to find Zorrino... Me pregunto

cómo vamos a encontrar a Zorrino... *

he's out of his mind se ha vuelto loco

to make up one's mind decidirse

to change one's mind cambiar de idea

II. *v i & v t*
1. tener cuidado

mind the dog! ¡ten cuidado con el perro!

...mind

What's on your mind, Tintin?

I wonder how we're going to find Zorrino ...

2. Idiom
do you mind if I open the window? – I don't mind ¿le molesta si abro la ventana? – no me molesta

never mind! ¡no importa!

mind your own business ocúpese de sus asuntos, no se meta en esto

▶ **mind out**
(*Am:* **watch out**)
tener cuidado

mind out! ¡ten cuidado!

mine

mine
[maɪn] *pron*
1. mío, mía, míos, mías

his hair is longer than mine su pelo es más largo que el mío

2. Idiom
a friend of mine un amigo mío

minute

minute
['mɪnɪt] *n*
1. minuto *m*

* *Hello, Nestor, is the Captain in?* Hola, Néstor, ¿está el capitán en casa?
Yes, Mr Tintin, he'll see you in a few minutes... Sí, señor Tintín, lo verá dentro de unos minutos... *

2. momento *m*
just a minute! ¡un momento!

...minute

Hello, Nestor, is the Captain in?

Yes, Mr Tintin, he'll see you in a few minutes...

3. Idiom
it's ten minutes to four son las cuatro menos diez

mirror

mirror
['mɪrə'] *n*
espejo *m*

* *Would you like a comb as well?* ¿Quiere un peine también?

...mirror

No, thank you, just the mirror. No, gracias, sólo el espejo.
Yes, just the mirror, thank you... Sí, sólo el espejo, gracias... *

miserable

miserable
['mɪzərəbl] *adj*
1. triste, desgraciado, a

Would you like a comb as well?

No, thank you, just the mirror.

Yes, just the mirror, thank you...

...miserable

he looks miserable parece triste

2. miserable

miss

miss
[mɪs] *n*
señorita *f*

let me introduce you to Miss Holloway

...miss

permítame presentarle a la señorita Holloway

miss

miss
[mɪs] *v i & v t*
1. perder

* *Thomson has missed the train...* Hernández ha perdido el tren... *

...miss

2. echar de menos
he misses you te echa de menos

3. errar (el tiro, el golpe)

▶ **miss out** omitir

you missed out a word omitiste una palabra

Thomson has missed the train...

mistake

mistake
[mɪs'teɪk] *n*
error *m*

model

model
['mɒdl] *n*
1. modelo *m*, maqueta *f*

he makes models for architects hace maquetas para arquitectos

...model

2. modelo *m*
this car is the latest model este coche es el último modelo

3. modelo *m f*
my neighbour works as a model mi vecina trabaja de modelo

modern

modern
['mɒdən] *adj*
moderno, a

moment

moment
['məumənt] *n*
momento *m*, instante *m*

she's studying at the moment está estudiando de momento

* *Wait for me, I'll be back in a moment.* Espéreme, estaré de vuelta en un momento.
OK. OK. *

Wait for me, I'll be back in a moment.

O.K.

Monday

Monday
['mʌndɪ] *n*
lunes *m*

they work on Mondays trabajan los lunes

I'll leave on Monday me iré el lunes

money

money
['mʌnɪ] *n*
dinero *m*

she's making a lot of money hace/gana mucho dinero

monkey

monkey
['mʌŋkɪ] *n*
mono *m*

* *The monkeys have taken the Captain's gun...* Los monos han cogido la pistola del capitán... *

month

month
[mʌnθ] *n*
mes *m*

The monkeys have taken the Captain's gun...

...month

last/next month el mes pasado/próximo

monument

monument
['mɒnjumənt] *n*
monumento *m*

they went to visit the monument fueron a visitar el monumento

mood

mood
[muːd] *n*
humor *m*

* *Blistering barnacles!!!* ¡¡¡Millones de demonios!!!
The Captain is in a bad mood... El capitán está de mal humor... *

...mood

Blistering barnacles!!!

BANG

BANG

The Captain's in a bad mood...

moon

moon
[muːn] *n*
luna *f*

full/new moon luna llena/nueva

▶ **moonlight**
['muːnlaɪt] *n*
luz *f* de luna

* *The "Unicorn" in the moonlight...* El "Unicornio" a la luz de la luna... *

The "Unicorn" in the moonlight...

more

more
[mɔːr]
I. *adj*
más

we have more time tenemos más tiempo

there's no more water no hay más agua

would you like some more cheese? ¿quieres un poco más de queso?

...more

II. *pron*
más

do you need any more? ¿necesitas más?

III. *adv*
1. más

the Professor is more intelligent than him el profesor es más inteligente que él

we read more every day leemos más cada día

2. Idiom
she doesn't work any more ella ya no trabaja

he understood, more or less lo entendió, más o menos

this is getting more and more complicated esto se está volviendo más y más complicado

morning

morning
['mɔːnɪŋ] *n*
mañana *f*

* *Let's start with a few exercises as we do every morning...* Empezemos con unos cuantos ejercicios como hacemos cada mañana... *

the morning papers los periódicos de la mañana

early in the morning por la mañana temprano

Let's start with a few exercises as we do every morning...

he's been waiting the whole morning ha estado esperando toda la mañana

most

most
[məust]
I. *adj*
1. más

who has brought (the) most books? ¿quién ha traído más libros?

2. la mayoría
most days she goes to work la mayoría de los días va a trabajar

II. *pron*

1. la mayoría

do you need many? – I need most of them ¿necesitas muchos? – necesito la mayoría

most of my books are novels la mayoría de mis libros son novelas

2. Idiom
at the most a lo más, como más, como máximo

III. *adv*
1. más, el/la más

she had the most beautiful house of the village tenía la casa más bonita del pueblo

2. muy
you are most kind eres muy amable

mother

mother
['mʌðəʳ] *n*
madre *f*

motor

motor
['məutəʳ] *n*
motor *m*

an electric motor un motor eléctrico

...motor

▶**motorbike, motorcycle**
['məutəbaɪk]
['məutəsaɪkl] *n*
motocicleta *f*,
moto *f*

* *I'll go faster on this motorbike!...* ¡Iré más rápido en esta motocicleta!... *

▶**motorway**
['məutəweɪ] *n*
(*Am*: **freeway**)
autopista *f*

...motor

I'll go faster on this motorbike!...

mountain

mountain
['mauntɪn] *n*
montaña *f*

* *In the mountains...* En la montaña... *

moustache

moustache
[mə'staːʃ] *n*
(*Am*: **mustache**)
bigote *m*

In the mountains ...

mouth

mouth
[mauθ] *n*
boca *f*

move

move
[muːv]
I. *v t*
1. mover

move the table towards me mueve la mesa hacia mí

...move

2. Idiom
to move (house) mudarse de (casa)

II. *v i*
1. moverse

* *Don't move or I'll fire! I'll count up to ten!* ¡No se muevan o disparo! ¡Contaré hasta diez! *

2. mudarse

Don't move or I'll fire! I'll count up to ten!

▶**movement**
['muːvmənt] *n*
movimiento *m*

Mr

Mr
['mɪstəʳ] *n*
señor *m*

could I speak to Mr Brett, please? ¿podría hablar con el señor Brett, por favor?

Mrs

Mrs
['mɪsɪz] *n*
señora *f*

Mrs Lewis is our teacher la señora Lewis es nuestra profesora

much

much
[mʌtʃ]
I. *adj*
1. mucho, a

there's not much food no hay mucha comida

2. Idiom
how much time have we got? ¿cuánto tiempo tenemos?

there's too much sugar in my coffee

...much

hay demasiado azúcar en mi café

she's got so much work that she can't go with us tiene tanto trabajo que no puede venir con nosotros

so much the better! ¡tanto mejor!

II. *pron*
1. mucho, a

have you got any money on you? – not

much ¿llevas dinero? – no mucho

2. Idiom
drink as much as you like bebe tanto como quieras

how much is it? ¿cuánto es?

don't eat too much no comas demasiado

III. *adv*
mucho

he feels much better se siente mucho mejor

Mum

Mum, Mummy
[mʌm], ['mʌmɪ]
(*Am:* **Mom, Mommy**)
mamá *f*

murder

murder
['mɜːdə']
I. *v t*
asesinar

...murder

II. *n*
asesinato *m*

▶ **murderer**
['mɜːdərə'] *n*
asesino, a

museum

museum
[mjuː'zɪəm] *n*
museo *m*

...museum

* *The museum is closing!* ¡El museo se cierra!
It's already five o'clock... Ya son las cinco... *

...museum

The museum is closing! It's already five o'clock...

music

music
['mjuːzɪk] *n*
música *f*

▶ **musician**
[mjuː'zɪʃ(ə)n] *n*
músico, a

* *Boom Boom Boom Boom* Bum bum bum bum
The musicians are coming... Vienen los músicos... *

BOOM BOOM BOOM BOOM

The musicians are coming ...

must

must
[mʌst] *v aux*
1. deber, tener que

you must hide debes esconderte

* *They musn't see us!* ¡No deben vernos! *

2. deber de
he must have escaped through the window debe de haber escapado por la ventana

...must

They mustn't see us!

mutton

mutton
['mʌt(ə)n] *n*
carnero *m*, cordero *m*

mutton chop chuleta de cordero

my

my
[maɪ] *adj*
mi

Tintin is my friend Tintín es mi amigo

it's my turn es mi turno

my parents live in Scotland mis padres viven en Escocia

▶ **myself**
[maɪ'self] *pron*
1. me

I've cut myself me he cortado

2. yo mismo
I'll do it myself lo haré yo mismo

3. Idiom
(all) by myself por mí mismo, solo

mystery

mystery
['mɪstərɪ] *n*
pl mysteries
misterio *m*

▶ **mysterious**
[mɪs'tɪərɪəs] *adj*
misterioso, a

nail

nail
[neɪl]
I. n
1. clavo m

a hammer and nails
un martillo y clavos

2. uña f
she had long nails
tenías las uñas largas

II. v t
clavar

name

name
[neɪm] n
1. nombre m

*Calculus has lost his memory... Tornasol ha perdido la memoria...
But, Professor, you remember your name... your name... Calculus... Pero, profesór, recuerda su nombre... su nombre... Tornasol... *

.**2.** Idiom

Calculus has lost his memory...

But, Professor, you remember your name... your name ... Calculus ...

what's your name?
¿cómo te llamas?

my name is Tintin
me llamo Tintin

first/Christian name
nombre de pila

narrow

narrow
['næreʊ] adj
estrecho, a

...narrow

he lived in a narrow street vivía en una calle estrecha

nasty

nasty
['nɑːstɪ] adj
1. malo, a

he was a nasty man
era un hombre malo

...nasty

2. desagradable
what a nasty smell! ¡qué olor tan desagradable!

nationality

nationality
[næʃəˈnælɪtɪ] n
pl nationalities
nacionalidad f

natural

natural
['nætʃ(ə)rəl] adj
natural

▶ **naturally**
['nætʃ(ə)rəlɪ] adv
1. naturalmente, claro, por supuesto

did you understand him? - naturally! ¿lo entendiste? - ¡naturalmente!

can you do me a favour? - naturally! ¿me puede hacer un favor? - por supuesto

2. naturalmente, de forma natural

nature

nature
['neɪtʃəʳ] n
naturaleza f

* Nature in Scotland is very beautiful... La naturaleza en Escocia es muy bella... *

...nature

Nature in Scotland is very beautiful...

naughty

naughty
['nɔːtɪ] *adj*
naughtier, naughtiest
travieso, a

* *I bet it's Abdullah being naughty again!* ¡Apuesto a que Abdallah ha sido travieso de nuevo! *

I bet it's Abdullah being naughty again!

navy

navy
['neɪvɪ]
pl navies
['neɪvɪz]
marina *f*

near

near
[nɪə^r]
I. *adj*

...near

1. cercano, a

this is the nearest chemist ésta es la farmacia más cercana

2. Idiom
that was a near thing! ¡se salvó por los pelos!

II. *adv*
cerca

she lives quite near vive bastante cerca

III. *prep*
cerca de

she works near the University trabaja cerca de la Universidad

▶ **nearly**
['nɪəlɪ] *adv*
casi

Tintin nearly fell Tintín casi se cayó

necessary

necessary
['nesɪs(ə)rɪ] *adj*
1. necesario, a

* *We can go, Snowy, I have the necessary equipment now!...* ¡Podemos irnos, Milú; ahora ya tengo el equipo necesario... *

2. Idiom
a necessary evil un mal necesario

We can go, Snowy, I have the necessary equipment now!...

neck

neck
[nek] *n*
cuello *m*

need

need
[niːd]
I. *v t*
1. necesitar

* *I need your help, Chang, do you*

...need

I need your help, Chang, do you understand?

Yes, yes, Tintin, I do...

understand? Necesito tu ayuda, Tchang, ¿entiendes?
Yes, yes, Tintin, I do... Sí, sí, Tintín, entiendo... *

2. Idiom
you needn't have done it no era necesario que lo hiciese

II. *n*
necesidad *f*

there's no need for you to do it no hay necesidad de que lo hagas

neighbour

neighbour
['neɪbə^r] *n*
(*Am*: **neighbor**)
vecino *m*, vecina *f*

our nextdoor neighbour nuestro vecino de al lado

neither

neither
['naɪðə^r]
I. *pron & adj*

...neither

Neither you nor I can make it across this gap!...

ninguno, a, ninguno de los dos, ninguna de las dos

neither of them is here ninguno de ellos está aquí

II. *adv*
ni

* *Neither you nor I can make it across this gap!...* Ni tú ni yo podemos conseguir cruzar este hoyo!... *

III. *conj*

tampoco

I can't see the Captain – neither can I no veo al capitán – yo tampoco

nervous

nervous
['nɜːvəs] *adj*
nervioso, a

the nervous system el sistema nervioso

nest

nest
[nest] *n*
nido *m*

never

never
['nevə^r] *adv*
1. nunca, jamás

* *I've no more strength... I'll never manage*

...never

I've no more strength... I'll never manage it...

it... No me quedan más fuerzas... Nunca lo conseguiré... *

2. Idiom
never mind no importa

new

new
[njuː] *adj*
1. nuevo, a

...new

Calculus wants to show us his new invention Tornasol quiere enseñarnos su nuevo invento

2. Idiom
what's new? ¿qué hay de nuevo?

news

news
[njuːz] *n pl*

...news

noticia(s) *f pl*

good news buenas noticias

a piece of news una noticia

* *Tintin's listening to the news...* Tintín está escuchando las noticias... *

▶**newspaper**
['njuːzpeɪpəʳ] *n*
periódico *m*

CLIC

Tintin's listening to the news...

New Zealand

New Zealand
[njuːˈziːlənd] *n*
Nueva Zelanda *f*

next

next
[nekst]
I. *adj*
1. próximo, a

we're going to the cinema next week

...next

vamos al cine la semana próxima

take the next street on the left coge la próxima calle a la izquierda

2. Idiom
* *The next day...* Al día siguiente... *

II. *adv* .
1. después

what shall we do next? ¿qué haremos después?

The next day...

2. al lado
sit next to me siéntate a mi lado

▶**next door**
[nekst dɔːʳ] *adv*
(en) la casa de al lado

they live next door to us viven en la casa de al lado

nice

nice
[naɪs] *adj*
1. simpático, a, agradable

Nick is very nice Nick es muy simpático

2. bonito, a
what a nice dress! ¡qué vestido tan bonito!

3. bueno, a
what a nice day it is! ¡que día tan bueno hace!

...nice

a nice cup of tea una buena taza de té

4. Idiom
we had a nice time nos lo pasamos bien

it's nice and warm in here se está bien caliente aquí

night

night
[naɪt] *n*

...night

noche *f*

on Sunday night el domingo por la noche

* *Good night, Zorrino!* ¡Buenas noches, Zorrino!
Good night, señor Tintín! ¡Buenas noches, señor Tintín! *

last night ayer por la noche

Good night, Zorrino!

Good night, señor Tintin!

nine

nine
[naɪn]
I. *adj*
nueve

II. *n*
nueve *m*

nineteen

nineteen
[naɪnˈtiːn]
I. *adj*
diecinueve

...nineteen

II. *n*
diecinueve *m*

ninety

ninety
['naɪntɪ]
I. *adj*
noventa

she is ninety-five tiene noventa y cinco años

...ninety

in nineteen ninety en mil novecientos noventa

II. *n*
pl nineties
noventa *m*

in the nineties en los años noventa

no

no
[nəu]
I. *adv*

...no

no

is it cold? - no, it isn't ¿hace frío? - no

your idea is no better than mine tu idea no es mejor que la mía

II. *adj*
1. no

he has no patience no tiene paciencia

2. Idiom

nobody

nobody
['nəubɒdɪ] *pron*
nadie

* *It says: "no entry"...* Dice "prohibida la entrada"...
Let's go in anyway! ¡Entremos igualmente!
No entry Prohibida la entrada *

...nobody

nobody understood her nadie la entendió

noise

noise
[nɔɪz] *n*
ruido *m*

* *I heard a noise!* ¡He oído un ruido!
So did I... Yo también... *

...noise

▶ **noisy**
['nɔɪzɪ] *adj*
noisier, noisiest
ruidoso, a

none

none
[nʌn] *pron*
ninguno, a

none of the prisoners could

...none

escape ninguno de los prisioneros podía escapar

how many cars will be needed? – none ¿cuántos coches se necesitarán? – ninguno

nonsense

nonsense
['nɒnsəns] *n*
disparate *m*,

...nonsense

absurdidad *f*,
tontería *f*

don't talk nonsense! ¡no digas disparates!

no one

no one
['nəuwʌn] *pron*
nadie

no one saw the

...no one

Captain nadie vio al capitán

nor

nor
[nɔːʳ] *conj*
1. ni

he's neither worried nor frightened no está preocupado ni tiene miedo

...nor

2. tampoco
she won't come – nor will I no vendrá – yo tampoco

normal

normal
['nɔːm(ə)l] *adj*
normal

* *Don't worry; the situation is perfectly*

...normal

normal! ¡No se preocupen; la situación es perfectamente normal! *

north

north
[nɔːθ]
I. *n*
norte *m*

the north of Italy el norte de Italia

...north

II. *adj*
norte

North America América del norte

III. *adv*
**al norte,
hacia el norte**

▶ **Northern**
['nɔːθən] *adj*
del norte

Northen Ireland Irlanda del norte

nose

nose
[nəuz] *n*
nariz *f*

...nose

* *What have I got on my nose?* ¿Qué tengo en la nariz? *

not

not
[nɒt] *adv*
forma abreviada: **n't**
no

Tintin is not (isn't) here today Tintín no está aquí hoy

note

note
[nəʊt] *n*
1. nota *f*, apunte *m*

to take notes tomar apuntes

2. billete
a pound note (Am: bill) un billete de una libra

3. nota *f*
a high/low note una nota alta/baja

nothing

nothing
['nʌθɪŋ] *pron*
nada

* *But... there's nothing in this box!... Nothing at all!...* Pero... ¡no hay nada en esta caja!... ¡Nada de nada!...*

there's nothing like a nice cup of tea no hay nada como una buena taza de té

notice

notice
['nəʊtɪs] *n*
1. aviso *m*

2. anuncio *m*, cartel *m*
she put up a notice colgó un anuncio

3. Idiom
don't take any notice of him no le hagas ningún caso

noun

noun
[naʊn] *n*
nombre *m*, sustantivo *m*

common noun nombre común

proper noun nombre propio

November

November
[nəʊ'vembəʳ] *n*
noviembre *m*

now

now
[naʊ]
I. *adv*
1. ahora

2. Idiom
now and then de vez en cuando

by now ya

in a month from now dentro de un mes

up till now hasta ahora

II. *interj*

¡vamos!, ¡venga!

* *I am playing the fool, am I?* Estoy haciendo el tonto ¿no es eso? *Now, now! Don't get angry!* ¡Venga, venga! ¡No se enfade! *

►**nowadays**
['naʊədeɪz] *adv*
hoy en día

nowhere

nowhere
['nəʊweəʳ] *adv*
por/en/a ninguna parte/ningún sitio
I can find Snowy nowhere no encuentro a Milú por ninguna parte

nuisance

nuisance
['njuːs(ə)ns] *n*
1. fastidio *m*, lata *f*

...nuisance

what a nuisance! ¡qué fastidio!/¡qué lata!

* *These mosquitoes are a nuisance!* ¡Estos mosquitos son un fastidio! *

2. Idiom
she's a little nuisance! ¡es una pesada!

number

number
['nʌmbəʳ] *n*
1. número *m*

number 10, Downing street el número 10 de la calle Downing

2. número *m*, cantidad *f*
a large number of people were willing to help una gran cantidad de personas estaban dispuestas a ayudar

nurse

nurse
[nɜːs] *n*
1. enfermera *f*

she's studying to be a nurse estudia para ser enfermera

2. Idiom
male nurse enfermero *m*

►**nursery school**
['nɜːsərɪˈskuːl] *n*
parvulario *m*

O

obey

obey
[ə'beɪ] *v t*
obedecer

you must obey the doctor tienes que obedecer al médico

object

object
['ɒbʒekt] *n*
1. objeto *m*

...object

he bought all kinds of old objects compró toda clase de objetos viejos

2. propósito *m*, fin *m*
with the object of con el propósito de

obvious

obvious
['ɒbvɪəs] *adj*
evidente, obvio, a

...obvious

it's obvious we're in trouble es evidente que estamos en apuros

occur

occur
[ə'kɛːʳ] *v i*
occurred, occurred
1. ocurrir, suceder, pasar

the fire occurred

...occur

yesterday el incendio ocurrió ayer

2. ocurrírsele a alguien
it occurred to me to go and see her se me ocurrió ir a verla

ocean

ocean
['əuʃ(ə)n] *n*
océano *m*

o'clock

o'clock
[ə'klɒk] *adv*

*Let's see, what time is it? It's ten o'clock, I have some time left before I go. Veamos, ¿qué hora es? Son las diez en punto; aún me queda un poco de tiempo antes de irme. *

...o'clock

October

October
[ɒk'təubəʳ] *n*
octubre *m*

the first/second of October (Am: October first/ second) el uno/dos de Octubre

her birthday is on the 10th of October (Am: on October 10) su cumpleaños es el 10 de octubre

odd

odd
[ɒd] *adj*
1. extraño, a
raro, a

* That's odd... I heard a noise... Let's go in carefully. Es extraño... He oído un ruido... Entremos con cuidado. *

2. impar
7 is an odd number el 7 es un número impar

of

of
[əv] *prep*
de

look, there's a photo of Tintin mira, hay una foto de Tintín

it's a question of honour es una cuestión de honor

at the top of the hill en la cima de la colina

off

off
[ɒf]
I. *prep*
1. de

he fell off a tree se cayó de un árbol

2. Idiom
there's a chemist just off the main street hay una farmacia a dos pasos de la calle principal

II. *adv*
Idiom

we're off to Barcelona tomorrow vamos a Barcelona mañana

he asked for a day off pidió un día libre

take your coat/shoes off quítate el abrigo/los zapatos

to switch the light/television off apagar la luz/la televisión

turn the tap (Am: faucet) off cierra el grifo

special offer: $20 off oferta especial: 20 dólares menos

offer

offer
['ɒfəʳ]
I. *v t*
ofrecer

* *Can I offer you something to drink?* ¿Puedo ofrecerle algo de beber? *

II. *n*
proposición *m*, oferta *f*

they made me an offer me hicieron una proposición

Can I offer you something to drink?

office

office
['ɒfɪs] *n*
oficina *f*

officer

officer
['ɒfɪsəʳ] *n*
oficial *m*

often

often
['ɒfən] *adv*
a menudo, frecuentemente

oil

oil
[ɒɪl] *n·*
1. petróleo *m*

they are searching for oil están buscando petróleo

...oil

2. aceite *m*
olive oil aceite de oliva

3. óleo
an oil painting una pintura al óleo

OK, okay

OK, okay
[əu'keɪ]
I. *interj*
de acuerdo, vale

...OK

Are you OK, Captain?
Yes.

let's go - OK vámonos - de acuerdo

II. *adj*
Idiom

* *Are you OK, Captain?* ¿Está usted bien, capitán? *Yes.* Sí. *

is it OK if I leave it here? ¿va bien si lo dejo aquí?/¿puedo dejarlo aquí?

old

old
[əuld] *adj*
1. viejo, a

this house is very old esta casa es muy vieja

an old friend un viejo amigo

2. Idiom
she's ten years old tiene diez años

how old are you? ¿cuántos años tienes?

▶ **old-fashioned**
adj
pasado, a de moda

this dress is old-fashioned este vestido está pasado de moda

on

on
[ɒn]
I. *prep*
1. sobre, en

on the wall en la pared

it's on the table está sobre la mesa

2. sobre, acerca de
* *Look, there's an article on Signora Castafiore in the newspaper!* ¡Mira, hay un artículo sobre la

Look, there's an article on Signora Castafiore in the newspaper!

Signora Castafiore en el periódico! *

3. Idiom
on foot a pie

she's on holiday(Am: vacation) está de vacaciones

on the left a la izquierda

come on Monday ven el lunes

II. *adv*
Idiom

...on

put your coat on ponte el abrigo

he had nothing on estaba desnudo

and so on etc.

switch the light/television on enciende la luz/el televisor

* My word! The radio's on!... ¡Cáspita! ¡La radio está encendida!... *That's certainly surprising!* ¡Es verdade-

ramente sorprendente! *

the tap (Am: faucet) is on el grifo está abierto

from now on de ahora en adelante

go straight on siga recto

once

once
[wʌns]
I. *adv*
1. una vez

I go to London once a year/month/day voy a Londres una vez al año/mes/día

I once saw something like that una vez vi algo parecido

2. Idiom
once upon a time érase una vez

stop at once! ¡detente ahora mismo!

they were all speaking at once todos hablaban a la vez

II. *conj*
una vez que, cuando

where shall we go once you finish? ¿dónde iremos cuando termines?

one

one
[wʌn]
I. *adj*
1. uno, a

how many bottles? – just one ¿cuántas botellas? – sólo una

2. Idiom
her baby is one su bebé tiene un año

II. *n*
uno, a

one and one are two uno y uno son dos

III. *pron*
1. uno, a

* One must take one's shoes off in the mosque. Uno tiene que quitarse los zapatos en la mezquita. *

2. Idiom
this one éste, ésta

that one ése, ésa/ aquél, aquélla

these ones éstos, éstas

which one? ¿cuál?

which ones? ¿cuáles?

▶ **one another**
pron
se, el uno al otro

they don't talk to one another no se hablan

we must help one another debemos ayudarnos los unos a los otros

...one

▶ **one's**
[wʌnz] *adj*
su, el, la

to keep one's word cumplir con su palabra

▶ **oneself**
[wʌn'self]
oneselves *pl*
[wʌn'selvz]
1. se

* Quick! Quick! I must unjam this mechanism... ¡Rápido! ¡Rápido! Tengo que desatascar este mecanismo... *One can easily hurt oneself doing that...* Uno puede dañarse fácilmente haciendo eso... *

2. uno, a, mismo, a, sí mismo, a

One can easily hurt oneself doing that...

...one

it's best to do it oneself es mejor que lo haga uno mismo

3. Idiom
(all) by oneself por sí solo, a, solo, a

only

only
['əʊnlɪ]
I. *adv*
1. solamente, sólo

I will only say it once sólo lo diré una vez

2. Idiom
* *Two weeks later...* Dos semanas más tarde...
If only we could stop pumping... Ojalá pudiésemos dejar de bombear...
If only... Ojalá... *

Signora Castafiore only just arrived Castafiore acaba de llegar

II. *adj*
único, a

it was the only problem he had era el único problema que tenía

he's an only child es hijo único

onto

onto
['ɒntu] *prep*
sobre, en

climb onto my shoulders súbete sobre mis hombros

open

open
['əʊpən]
I. *v t*
abrir

...open

he opened the bottle abrió la botella

II. *v i*
abrir(se)

the door won't open la puerta no se abre

do they open on Sundays? ¿abren los domingos?

III. *adj*
abierto, a

* *In Marlinspike...* En Moulinsart...

Nestor has left the door open... Néstor ha dejado la puerta abierta... *

...operation

they'll operate on her for appendicitis la van a operar de apendicitis

operation

operation
[ɒpə'reɪʃn] *n*
operación *f*

▶ **operate**
[ɒpə'reɪt] *v t*
operar

opportunity

opportunity
[ɒpə'tjuːnɪtɪ] *n*
pl opportunities
ocasión *f*
oportunidad *f*

now you have the opportunity of going back there ahora tienes la oportunidad de volver allí

opposite

opposite
['ɒpəzɪt]
I. *prep*
enfrente de

the shop is opposite the bank la tienda está enfrente del banco

II. *adj*
1. de enfrente

the door opposite la puerta de enfrente

2. opuesto, a,

contrario, a
we have opposite views tenemos opiniones contrarias

III. *n*
lo contrario *m*,
lo opuesto *m*

whatever I say, you always say the opposite diga lo que diga, tú siempre dices lo contrario

or

or
[ɔːʳ] *conj*
o

* *Shall I put my beard on top...* ¿Pongo la barba encima...
or... underneath?... Blistering barnacles! That's no better!... o... debajo?... ¡Millones de demonios! !Así no es mejor!... *

orange

orange
['ɒrɪndʒ]
I. n
naranja f

orange juice zumo de naranja

II. adj
naranja inv

he has orange socks tiene calcetines naranja

order

order
['ɔːdə']
I. n
1. orden f

it's an order! ¡es una orden!

2. pedido
to put in an order hacer un pedido

3. orden m
in alphabetical order en orden alfabético

4. Idiom
out of order averiado

he only did it in order to help you sólo lo hizo para ayudarte

II. v t
1. ordenar

he ordered them to run les ordenó que corrieran

2. pedir
we ordered wine pedimos vino

ordinary

ordinary
['ɔːdɪn(ə)rɪ] adj
normal, corriente

organize

organize
['ɔːgənaɪz] v t
organizar

...organize

she organized the meeting organizó la reunión

original

original
[ə'rɪdʒɪn(ə)l] adj
1. original

he has very original ideas tiene ideas muy originales

...original

2. original, primitivo, a
* *We have had to alter our original plan; now everything's settled.* Hemos tenido que cambiar nuestro plan original; ahora todo está en orden. *Very well, Wolf; thank you very much...* Muy bien, Wolf; muchas gracias... *

other

other
['ʌðə']
I. adj
otro, a

the other book is better el otro libro es mejor

the other day el otro día

II. pron
otro, a

we have forgotten about the others nos hemos olvidado de los otros

ought

ought
[ɔːt] v aux
deber

* *You ought to go to the dentist's, my dear Haddock...* Debería ir al dentista, mi querido Haddock... *

...ought

...ought

he ought to have told me debería habérmelo dicho

our

our
[auə'] adj
nuestro, a
nuestros, as

our cars are very fast nuestros coches son muy rápidos

...our

this is our friend, Tintin éste es nuestro amigo, Tintín

▶**ours**
[auəz] pron
1. nuestro,a
nuestros, as

this dog is ours este perro es nuestro

2. Idiom
a friend of ours un amigo nuestro

▶**ourselves**
[auə'selvz] pron
1. nos

we have enjoyed ourselves nos hemos divertido

2. nosotros mismos
we saw it ourselves lo vimos nosotros mismos

3. Idiom
(all) by ourselves por nosotros mismos, nosotros solos

out

out
[aut] adv
1. fuera

he locked us out nos dejó fuera

2. Idiom
to be out no estar (en casa, en la oficina, etc)

Mr Brett is out, but he'll soon be back el señor Brett no está, pero no tardará

he ran out salió corr-

iendo

the fire is out el fuego está apagado

we're out of tea se nos ha terminado el té

▶**out of**
prep
1. fuera de

have no fear; you're out of danger no tengas miedo; estás fuera de peligro

...out

2. por
he did it out of kindness lo hizo por amabilidad

▶ **outdoor**
[aut'dɔːʳ] *adj*
al aire libre

an outdoor swimming pool una piscina al aire libre

▶ **outdoors**
[aut'dɔːz] *adv*
fuera

let's play outdoors juguemos fuera

▶ **outside**
[aut'saɪd]
I. *adv*
fuera

the car is waiting outside el coche está esperando fuera

II. *prep*
delante de

we'll meet outside the church nos encontraremos delante de la iglesia

III. *n*
exterior *m*

the outside of the house el exterior de la casa

oven

oven
['ʌvən] *n*
horno *m*

over

over
['əuvəʳ]
I. *adv*
1. acabado, a terminado, a

...over

our troubles are over, Tintin nuestros problemas han terminado, Tintín

2. una vez más
count them over cuéntalos una vez más

3. Idiom
all over por todas partes

over here por aquí

over there por allí

* *Over there!...*

...over

Look... Water!... Water!... ¡Por allí!... ¡Mire...Agua!.. ¡Agua!... *

over and over again una y otra vez

II. *prep*
1. (por) encima de, sobre

there was a sign over the door había un letrero por encima de la puerta

look over the hedge mira por encima del seto

2. al otro lado de
the shop is over the street la tienda está al otro lado de la calle

3. más de
he is over thirty tiene más de treinta años

4. durante
we'll talk about it over lunch hablaremos de ello durante la comida

▶ **overcoat**
['əuvəkəut] *n*
abrigo *m*

▶ **overtake**
[əuvə'teɪk] *v t*
(*Am:* **pass**)
overtook [əuvə'tuk]
overtaken
[əuvə'teɪk(ə)n]
adelantar

* *I'll try to overtake that car!...* ¡Voy a tratar de adelantar a ese coche!... *

owe

owe
[əu] *v t*
deber

I owe you 5 pounds te debo 5 libras

she owes you nothing no te debe nada

own

own
[əun]
I. *adj*
propio, a

* *The Yeti!... Up there!... I saw it!... I saw it with my own eyes!...* ¡El yeti!... ¡Allí arriba!... ¡Lo vi!... ¡Lo vi con mis propios ojos!... *

II. *n*
Idiom

I have a car of my

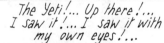

own tengo un coche propio/mío

III. *v t*
poseer

I own a horse poseo un caballo

▶ **own up**
confessar, reconocer

▶ **owner**
['əunəʳ] *n*
propietario, a

P O P Q O P

pack

pack
[pæk]
I. v t
1. embalar, empaquetar

we must pack the furniture tenemos que embalar los muebles

2. poner en la maleta
did you pack your pyjamas? ¿has puesto tu pijama en la maleta?

> Have you packed your bags?
>
> Not yet, I've got to finish this letter!...

II. v i & v t
hacer la maleta

* *Have you packed your bags?* ¿Ha hecho la maleta?
Not yet. I've got to finish this letter!... Aún no. ¡Tengo que terminar esta carta!... *

I haven't packed yet aún no he hecho la maleta.

▶ **package** (Am)
→ PARCEL

page

page
[peɪdʒ] n
página f

open your books at page 12 abran los libros en la página 12

* *There are only a few pages left of this newspaper...* Sólo quedan unas pocas páginas de este periódico... *

> There are only a few pages left of this newspaper...

pain

pain
[peɪn] n
dolor m

to be in pain tener dolor

paint

paint
[peɪnt]
I. n
pintura f

...paint

* *Caution! Wet paint!* ¡Atención! ¡Pintura fresca! *

a coat of paint una capa de pintura

II. v t
pintar

she's painting her car está pintando su coche

▶ **painter**
['peɪntə'] n
pintor, ora

> CAUTION! WET PAINT!

▶ **painting**
['peɪntɪŋ] n
pintura f, cuadro m

this is a painting by Turner éste es un cuadro de Turner

pair

pair
[peə'] n
1. par m

a pair of socks un par de calcetines

...pair

2. pareja f (people, animals)

3. Idiom
a pair of trousers (Am: pants) pantalones, pantalón

in pairs de dos en dos

pajamas

pajamas (Am)
→ PYJAMAS

pale

pale
[peɪl] adj
pálido, a

* *You look very pale, are you all right?... What's the matter?... Answer me!...* Se te ve muy pálido; ¿te encuentras bien?... ¿Qué ocurre?... ¡Contéstame!... *

he turned pale se puso pálido

pan

pan
[pæn] n
cacerola f

► **frying pan**
sartén f

► **pancake**
['pænkeɪk] n
crêpe f

pants

pants (Am)
→ TROUSERS

paper

paper
['peɪpəʳ] n
1. papel m

a sheet of paper una hoja de papel

2. periódico m
the morning paper el periódico de la mañana

3. documentación f, papeles m pl
your papers, please su documentación, por favor

parcel

parcel
['pɑːs(ə)l] n
(Am: **package**)
paquete m

* *Where does this parcel come from?* ¿De dónde viene este paquete?
Why don't you open it? ¿Por qué no lo abres? *

...parcel

pardon

pardon
['pɑːd(ə)n] n
I. n
1. perdón m

2. Idiom
I beg your pardon? ¿cómo dice?

II. v t
dispensar, perdonar, disculpar

pardon me dispénseme

parents

parents
['peərənts] n pl
padres m pl

* *I'll tell my parents and they'll punish you!...* ¡Se lo diré a mis padres y te castigarán!...
Good idea!... ¡Buena idea!... *

park

park
[pɑːk]
I. n
1. parque m

* *He couldn't possibly have left the park...* Es imposible que haya abandonado el parque... *

2. Idiom
car park (Am: parking lot) aparcamiento m

II. v i & v t
aparcar

...park

* *Can we park our car in front of the gates?* ¿Podemos aparcar el coche delante de la verja?
Yes, of course... Sí, por supuesto... *

you can park there puede aparcar allí

► **parking**
['pɑːkɪŋ] n
1. aparcamiento m

2. Idiom

no parking prohibido aparcar

part

part
[pɑːt] n
1. parte f

part of the story was false parte de la historia era falsa

...part

2. pieza *f*
spare parts piezas de recambio

3. papel *m*
the actor learned his part el actor aprendió su papel

4. Idiom
to take part in something tomar parte/ participar en algo

to work part time trabajar a horas (*ej:* media jornada)

particular

particular
[pə'tɪkjuləʳ]
I. *adj*
(en) particular, (en) especial

nothing particular nada especial

for no particular reason por ninguna razón en particular

II. *adv*
in particular especialmente, particularmente

▶ **particularly**
[pə'tɪkjuləlɪ] *adv*
particularmente

* *... and there's one point I'd particularly like to stress...* ... y hay un punto que me gustaría remarcar particularmente... *

party

party
['pɑːtɪ] *n*

...: and there's one point I'd particularly like to stress...

...party

pl parties
1. fiesta *f*

they are giving a party dan una fiesta

2. grupo *m*
a party of soldiers un grupo de soldados

3. partido *m*
the Labour/Conservative Party el Partido laborista/ conservador

pass

pass
[pɑːs]
I. *n*
1. paso *(in the mountain) m*

2. pase
a pass to the goalkeeper un pase al portero

3. permiso *m*, pase *m*
* *Your passes are perfectly in order... I'll take you there...*

Your passes are perfectly in order... I'll take you there...

Sus pases están en perfecto orden... Los llevaré allí... *

4. Idiom
to get a pass aprobar

II. *v t*
1. pasar

could you pass me the salt, please? ¿puede pasarme la sal, por favor?

he passed the ball pasó la pelota

2. pasar por delante
we passed an old house on our way to the village pasamos por delante de una vieja casa camino del pueblo

3. pasar, aprobar
did you pass the exam? ¿pasaste el examen?

III. *v i*
1. pasar

let me pass! ¡déjeme pasar!

time passes for everyone el tiempo pasa para todos

2. Idiom
to pass out desmayarse

passenger

passenger
['pæsɪndʒəʳ] *n*
pasajero *m*, pasajera *f*

passengers for Brighton go to platform 2 los pasajeros para Brighton diríjanse al andén numero 2

passer-by

passer-by
['pɑːsə'baɪ] *n*
pl passers-by
transeúnte *m*

* *What are the passers-by looking at?* ¿Qué están mirando los transeúntes? *

What are the passers-by looking at ?...

passport

passport
['pɑːspɔːt] *n*
pasaporte *m*

past

past
[pɑːst]
I. *prep*
1. pasado, a

...past

it's past midnight es pasada la media noche

* **The hospital is past the mosque, a little further along to your left...** El hospital está pasada la mezquita, un poco más adelante a su izquierda...
Alright, thank you... De acuerdo, gracias... *

2. por delante de
to go past something or somebody

pasar por delante de algo o alguien

3. más allá de
she lives past the station vive más allá de la estación

4. Idiom
it's half past one es la una y media

II. *adj*
1. pasado, a

the past generation la generación pasada

2. último, a pasado, a
these past days estos últimos días/estos días pasados

III. *n*
1. pasado *m*

he had a mysterious past tenía un pasado misterioso

2. pretérito *m*
the past of a verb el pretérito de un verbo

pastime

pastime
['pɑːstaɪm] *n*
pasatiempo *m*

playing chess is her favourite pastime jugar al ajedrez es su pasatiempo favorito

path

path
[pɑːθ] *n*
sendero *m*,
camino *m*

* **I'm sure he went along this path...** Estoy seguro de que fue por este camino... *

patience

patience
['peɪʃ(ə)ns] *n*

...patience

paciencia *f*

* **I'm beginning to run out of patience!...** ¡Estoy empezando a perder la paciencia!... *

▶ **patient**
['peɪʃ(ə)nt]
I. *adj*
paciente

he is a patient teacher es un profesor paciente

II. *n*
paciente *m f*,
enfermo, a

the doctor is examining a patient el doctor está examinando a un paciente

pavement

pavement
['peɪvmənt] *n*
(*Am*: **sidewalk**)
acera *f*

we must walk on the pavement debemos caminar por la acera

pay

pay
[peɪ]
paid, paid [peɪd]

...pay

I. *v t*
1. pagar

we'll pay you at the end of the month te pagaremos al final de mes

2. Idiom
to pay a visit hacer una visita

II. *v i*
pagar

* **Well then, do you think it'll be alright?**

Entonces, ¿cree que todo irá bien?
Yes, it's perfect. How much did you pay for this diving suit?... Sí, es perfecto. ¿Cuánto pagó usted por este traje de buzo?... *

blistering barnacles, they'll pay for this! ¡millones de demonios, pagarán por esto!

pea

pea
[piː] *n*
guisante *m*

peace

peace
[piːs] *n*
paz *f*

peach

peach
[piːtʃ] *n*
melocotón *m*

pear

pear
[peəʳ] *n*
pera *f*

pedestrian

pedestrian
[pəˈdestrɪən] *n*
1. peatón *m*

2. Idiom
pedestrian crossing (Am: crosswalk) paso de peatones

* *It's lucky there is a pedestrian crossing!...* ¡Qué suerte que haya un paso de peatones!... *

pen

pen
[pen] *n*
bolígrafo *m*

he lent me his pen me prestó su bolígrafo

pence

pence
[pens] *n pl*
peniques *m pl*

...pence

it costs 99 pence cuesta 99 peniques

pencil

pencil
[ˈpens(ə)l] *n*
lápiz *m*

I've lost my pencil he perdido mi lápiz

penny

penny
[ˈpenɪ] *n*
pl pennies & pence
penique *m*

how many pennies have you got? ¿cuántos peniques tienes?

one penny won't be enough un penique no será suficiente

people

people
[ˈpiːp(ə)l] *n*
1. personas *f pl*

many people were waiting muchas personas estaban esperando

2. gente *f*
* *It's lucky there are a lot of people... In this crowd we'll pass unnoticed...* Es una suerte que haya mucha gente... Entre esta muchedumbre pasaremos inadvertidos... *

3. pueblo *m*
the peoples of Asia los pueblos de Asia

4. Idiom
English people los ingleses

Spanish people los españoles

pepper

pepper
[ˈpepəʳ] *n*
pimienta *f*

performance

performance
[pəˈfɔːməns] *n*
representación *f*

the performance was a success la representación fue un éxito

perhaps

perhaps
[pəˈhæps] *adv*
quizás, tal vez

do you believe it? – perhaps it is true ¿lo crees? – quizás sea verdad

period

period
[ˈpɪərɪəd] *n*
1. período *m*,

...period

época *f*

he's the best painter of this period es el mejor pintor de este período

2. punto *m* final

3. clase *f*
the English period la clase de Inglés

person

person
[ˈpɜːs(ə)n] *n*
1. persona *f*

John is a nice person Juan es una persona simpática

I've never seen her in person nunca la he visto en persona

2. Idiom
a young person un/una joven

▶ **personal**
[ˈpɜːsən(ə)l] *adj*
personal

* *A personal message for you, Tintin!* ¡Un mensaje/recado personal para usted, Tintín! *

pet

pet
[pet] *n*
animal *m* doméstico

* *Two pets...* Dos animales domésticos... *

petrol

petrol
['petrəl] *n*
(*Am*: **gas(oline)**)
gasolina *f*

Two pets...

...petrol

we need petrol necesitamos gasolina

phone

phone
[fəun]
I. *n*
teléfono *m*

he's on the phone now ahora está al teléfono

...phone

we're not on the phone (*Am*: *we have no phone*) no tenemos teléfono

II. *vi & vt*
telefonear, llamar por teléfono

* *Great, a telephone box, I'll phone the Captain straight away!* ¡Estupendo - ¡Una cabina telefónica! ¡Voy a telefonear al capitán ahora mismo! *

Great, a telephone box, I'll phone the Captain straight away!

...phone

don't phone now no telefonees ahora

▶ **phone box** *n*
(*Am*: **phonebooth**)
cabina *f* telefónica

photo

photo
['fəutəu] *n*
foto *f*

take a photo of the

...photo

house toma/saca una foto de la casa

▶ **photograph**
['fəutəgrɑːf] *n*
fotografía *f*

this photograph has come out perfect esta fotografía ha salido perfecta

▶ **photographer**
[fə'tɒgrəfəʳ] *n*
fotógrafo *m*,
fotógrafa *f*

piano

piano
[pɪ'ænəu] *n*
piano *m*

she plays the piano every day toca el piano cada día

pick

pick
[pɪk] *vt*
1. escoger

...pick

pick the one you like best escoge él que te guste más

2. coger
she's picking flowers está cogiendo flores

▶ **pick up**
1. recoger

pick up the paper from the floor, please recoge el papel del suelo, por favor

2. pasar a recoger
he picked me up at the theatre me pasó a recoger en el teatro

picnic

picnic
['pɪknɪk] *n*
1. excursión *f* al campo, merienda *f* (campestre)

...picnic

2. Idiom
we'll have a picnic on Sunday iremos a merendar al campo el domingo

picture

picture
['pɪktʃəʳ] *n*
1. cuadro *m*, pintura *f*

* *Look... a globe!...*

...picture

Look... a globe!...
Yes, it was hidden by the picture!...

¡Mira... un globo terráqueo!...
Yes, it was hidden by the picture!... ¡Sí, estaba escondido por el cuadro!... *

2. fotografía *f*
Bianca Castafiore's picture is in the paper la fotografía de Bianca Castafiore está en el periódico

▶ **pictures**
(*Am*: **movies**) *n pl*
cine *m*

they went to the pictures fueron al cine

pie

pie
[paɪ] *n*
pastel *m*, tarta *f*

a meat pie un pastel de carne

piece

piece
[piːs] *n*
1. trozo *m*, pedazo *m*

...piece

I need a piece of paper necesito un trozo de papel

2. Idiom
a piece of advice un consejo

a piece of furniture un mueble

a piece of news una noticia

to fall to pieces deshacerse

pig

pig
[pɪg] *n*
cerdo *m*

pile

pile
[paɪl] *n*
pila *f*

* *Calculus knocked a pile of plates over and lots of other*

...pile

Calculus knocked a pile of plates over and lots of other things...

...pile

things... Tornasol hizo caer una pila de platos y muchas otras cosas... *

pillar-box

pillar-box
['pɪləbɒks] *n*
(*Am:* **mailbox**)
buzón *m*

pilot

pilot
['paɪlət] *n*
piloto *m*

pink

pink
[pɪŋk]
I. *adj*
rosa

Bianca is wearing a pink dress Bianca lleva un vestido rosa

...pink

II. *n*
rosa *m*

pink suits you el rosa te sienta/queda bien

pipe

pipe
[paɪp] *n*
1. tubería *f*, tubo *m*, cañería *f*

these pipes need mending estas tuberías

...pipe

necesitan ser reparadas

2. pipa *f*
* *There. I've managed to repair my pipe...* Ya está. He conseguido reparar mi pipa... *

pity

pity
['pɪtɪ]
I. *n*

...pity

1. pena *f*, lástima *f*

what's a pity! ¡qué lástima!

it's a pity you didn't come es una pena que no vinieras

2. compasión *f*

II. *v t*
compadecer

don't pity her no la compadezcas

place

place
[pleɪs] *n*
lugar *m*, sitio *m*

Captain Haddock said he had been in that place before el capitán Haddock dijo que había estado en aquel sitio antes

I've lost my place in the queue me lugar en la cola

plain

plain
[pleɪn]
I. *adj*
1. sencillo, a, simple

she is wearing a plain dress lleva un vestido sencillo

2. claro, a, evidente
it's plain to me that we must leave para mí está claro que debemos irnos

II. *n*
llano *m*, llanura *f*

the plain was very dry la llanura era muy seca

plan

plan
[plæn]
I. *n*
1. plan *m*, proyecto *m*

...plan

* *What can we do?* ¿Qué podemos hacer? *Wait!... I've got a plan... Listen carefully...* ¡Esperen!... Tengo un plan... Escuchen con atención... *Yes, we're listening. You always have good ideas!...* ¡Sí, le escuchamos!... ¡Usted siempre tiene buenas ideas!... *

2. plano *m*
the thieves had a

...plan

What can we do?

Wait!... I've got a plan... Listen carefully...

Yes, we're listening. You always have good ideas!...

plan of the bank los ladrones tenían un plano del banco

II. v t
planear, proyectar

they are planning their revenge están planeando su venganza

plane

plane
[pleɪn] n
avión m

the plane will be delayed el avión será retrasado

plant

plant
[plɑːnt] n
planta f

plastic

plastic
['plæstɪk]
I. n
plástico m

it's made of plastic está hecho de plástico

II. adj
plástico, a,
de plástico

a plastic cup una taza de plástico

plate

plate
[pleɪt] n
1. plato m

a soup plate un plato sopero

2. placa f
* *His name is on the plate...* Su nombre está en la placa *

3. Idiom
number plate matrícula

...plate

DʳJ.W.MÜLLER

His name is on the plate...

platform

platform
['plætfɔːm] n
andén m

passengers for Blackpool go to platform 1 los pasajeros para Blackpool vayan al andén número 1

play

play
[pleɪ]
I. v t

...play

1. jugar

they played chess jugaron al ajedrez

2. tocar *(an instrument)*
can you play the piano? ¿sabes tocar el piano?

3. Idiom
to play the part of hacer el papel de

II. v i
jugar

Abdullah is playing in the garden Abdallah está jugando en el jardín

III. n
obra f (de teatro)

he saw a play by Pinter vio una obra de Pinter

▶ **player**
['pleɪəʳ] n
jugador m,
jugadora f

▶ **playground**
['pleɪgraund] n
1. patio m *(of a school)*

the playground is very big el patio (de la escuela) es muy grande

2. patio m de juegos
the children are in the playground los niños están en el campo de juegos

pleasant

pleasant
['plez(ə)nt] adj
agradable

I had a pleasant surprise tuve una sorpresa agradable

please

please
[pliːz]
I. interj
por favor

...please

* *Pass me the binoculars, please!* ¡Páseme los prismáticos, por favor! *

II. v t
contentar, agradar

▶ **pleased**
[pliːzd] adj
1. contento, a,
satisfecho, a

2. Idiom
pleased to meet you encantado (de conocerle)

Pass me the binoculars please!

plenty

plenty
['plentɪ] n
1. abundancia f

2. Idiom
he's got plenty of friends tiene muchos amigos

* *There's no need to hurry, we've got plenty of time.* No hay necesidad de apresurarse; tenemos mucho tiempo. *

There's no need to hurry, we've got plenty of time.

plum

plum
[plʌm] *n*
ciruela *f*

plural

plural
['pluərəl]
n & adj
plural *m*

pocket

pocket
['pɒkɪt] *n*
bolsillo *m*

* *Wait, I've got a gun in my pocket...* Espere; tengo una pistola en mi bolsillo...
Quick, give it to me... Rápido, démela... *

▶ **pocket money**
(*Am:* **allowance**) *n*
dinero *m* de bolsillo

poem

poem
['pəʊɪm] *n*
poema *m*

▶ **poetry**
['pəʊtrɪ] *n*
poesía *f*

point

point
[pɔɪnt]
I. *n*
1. punta *f*

the tool has a sharp point el utensilio tiene la punta afilada

2. punto *m*
* *We're back to the point we started from, what shall we do?* Estamos otra vez en el punto donde empezamos. ¿Qué vamos a hacer?

...point

I don't know. No lo sé. *

the answer gave him ten points la respuesta le dio diez puntos

3. Idiom
that's not the point esa no es la cuestión

there's no point in worrying no tiene sentido preocuparse

II. *v i*
1. apuntar

she's pointing at them ella los está apuntando

2. señalar
he was pointing to the door estaba señalando hacia la puerta

III. *v t*
apuntar

* *Don't point that gun at him!* ¡No apunte esa escopeta hacia él! *

▶ **point out**
señalar

I'd like to point out that he was wrong me gustaría señalar que él estaba equivocado

poison

poison
['pɔɪz(ə)n]
I. *n*
veneno *m*

II. *v t*
envenenar

* *Somebody's tried to poison Snowy!* ¡Alguien ha intentado envenenar a Milú! *

police

police
[pə'liːs] *n inv*
policía *f*

* *We've been sent by the French police to help you... We've put on disguise, so we won't be noticed.* Hemos sido enviados por la policía francesa para ayudarle... Nos hemos disfrazado, así que no seremos reconocidos.
To be precise, so we won't be noticed...

Yo aún diría más, así que no seremos reconocidos... *

▶ **policeman policewoman**
[pə'liːsmən, wumən] *n*
pl policemen, policewomen
policía *m f*, agente *m f* de policía

polite

polite
[po'laɪt] adj
(bien) educado, a, cortés

be polite sé educado

political

political
[pə'lɪtɪk(ə)l] adj
político, a

---

a political party un partido político

▶ **politician**
[pə'lɪtɪʃ(ə)n] n
político m

▶ **politics**
['pɒlɪtɪks] n
política f

we are interested in politics nos interesa la política

pollute

pollute
[pə'luːt] v t
contaminar

the factory polluted the water la fábrica contaminaba el agua

▶ **pollution**
[pə'luːʃ(ə)n] n
contaminación f

pool

pool
[puːl] n
1. charco m

2. piscina f
an indoor (swimming) pool una piscina cubierta

poor

poor
[puəʳ] adj
1. pobre

...poor

a poor district un barrio pobre

2. malo, a
* *This knife is really poor quality!...* ¡Este cuchillo es de muy mala calidad!... *

3. pobre
poor man, he had an accident! ¡pobre hombre, tuvo un accidente!

...poor

popular

popular
['pɒpjuləʳ] adj
1. popular

popular music música popular

2. frecuentado, a
it's a very popular place es un sitio muy frecuentado

3. popular, querido, a, de éxito
he's a popular actor es un actor popular/de éxito

4. de moda
red is very popular this year el rojo está muy de moda este año

pork

pork
[pɔːk] n
cerdo m

a pork chop una chuleta de cerdo

port

port
[pɔːt] n
puerto m

* *The boat is leaving port...* El barco está abandonando el puerto... *

possible

possible
['pɒsɪb(ə)l] adj
posible

the boat is leaving port...

...possible

* *I'll do everything possible to help you...* Haré todo lo posible para ayudarles... *

do it as soon as possible hazlo tan pronto como sea posible

▶ **possibly**
['pɒsɪblɪ] adv
1. posiblemente

he is possibly the best worker we've ever had es posible-

I'll do everything possible to help you...

mente el mejor trabajador que hemos tenido

2. Idiom
I'll do it as quickly as I possibly can lo haré tan rápido como pueda/me sea posible

can you possibly be here at three? ¿sería posible que estuvieses aquí a las tres?

post

post
[pəust]
I. n
1. poste m

Tintin is tied to a post Tintín está atado a un poste

2. correo m
I'll send it by post (Am: mail) lo enviaré por correo

3. puesto m
the soldiers must

watch from their posts los soldados deben vigilar desde sus puestos

II. v t
enviar (por correo)

I have to post (Am: mail) this letter tengo que enviar esta carta

▶ **postcard**
[pəustkɑːd] n
postal f

...post

I'll send you a postcard te enviaré una postal

▶ **postman**
['pəustmən] *n*
(Am: **mailman**)
pl postmen
cartero *m*

* *Look what the postman's just brought!...*
¡Mira lo que el cartero acaba de traer!... *

Look what the postman's just brought!...

▶ **post office**
['pəustɔfɪs] *n*
estafeta *f*,
oficina *f* de correos

he works at the post office trabaja en correos

poster

poster
['pəustə'] *n*
póster *m*, cartel *m*

the man on this poster looks like General Alcazar este hombre en el cartel se parece al general Alcázar

potato

potato
[pə'teɪtəu] *n*
pl potatoes
patata *f*

she hates boiled potatoes no le gustan las patatas hervidas

pound

pound
[paund] *n*
1. libra *f*

* *How much is this boat?* ¿Cuánto vale esta barca?
I'll let you have it for ten pounds!... ¡Se lo dejo en diez libras!... *

2. libra *f* (= 453 gramos)
I'd like a pound of flour, please quisiera una libra de harina, por favor

How much is this boat?

I'll let you have it for ten pounds!...

pour

pour
[pɔː']
I. *v t*
1. echar, verter

pour the water here vierta el agua aquí

2. servir
shall I pour you some more coffee? ¿le sirvo más café?

II. *v i*
Idiom

* *After the ˙show...*

After the show...

The audience comes pouring out of the theatre...

...pour

Después del espectáculo...
The audience comes pouring out of the theatre (Am: theater)... El público sale en tropel del teatro... *

it's pouring (with rain) llueve a cántaros

▶ **pour down**
llover mucho/ fuerte/a cántaros

we can't go out, it's

pouring down no podemos salir, está lloviendo a cántaros

power

power
['pauə'] *n*
1. poder *m*

* *Hurray for Alcazar!*
¡Hurra por Alcázar!
Hurray! ¡Hurra!

...power

Hurray for Alcazar!

Hurray!

What enthusiasm!

General Alcazar has just seized power...

What enthusiasm!
¡Qué entusiasmo!
General Alcazar has just seized power...
El general Alcázar acaba de tomar el poder... *

2. fuerza *f*,
energía *f*
electric power energía eléctrica

practice

practice
['præktɪs] n
1. práctica f

one needs a lot of practice to sing well se necesita mucha práctica para cantar bien

put it into practice ponlo en práctica

2. ejercicios m pl
have you done your piano practice? ¿has hecho tus ejercicios de piano?

3. Idiom
she's out of practice está desentrenada

▶ **practise**
(*Am*: **practice**)
['præktɪs] v t
practicar, ejercitarse, entrenarse

she practises playing chess for three hours a day se ejercita en jugar al ajedrez durante tres horas diarias

precious

precious
['preʃəs] adj
1. precioso, a

* *Thundering typhoons! Precious stones! Diamonds! Oh my word!...* ¡Rayos y centellas! ¡Piedras preciosas! ¡Diamantes! ¡Dios mío!... *

2. Idiom
this book is very precious to me este libro es de gran valor para mí

prefer

prefer
[prɪ'fɜːr] v t
preferir

prepare

prepare
[prɪ'peər]
I. v t
1. preparar

* *And the next*

morning... Y a la mañana siguiente... *We have prepared a room for you...* Hemos preparado una habitación para ustedes... *

2. Idiom
be prepared to help estate preparado para ayudar

II. v i
prepararse

we are preparing for an attack nos estamos preparando para un ataque

prescription

prescription
[prɪ'skrɪpʃn] n
receta f (médica)

the doctor made out a prescription el médico hizo una receta

present

present
['prez(ə)nt]
I. n
1. regalo m

what a nice present! ¡qué regalo más bonito!

2. presente m
the present of a verb el presente de un verbo

3. Idiom
the Captain is away at present el capitán está ausente actualmente

II. adj
1. actual

the present situation is difficult la situación actual es difícil

2. presente
he was not present at the meeting no estuvo presente en la reunión

3. Idiom
the present tense el presente

president

president
['prezɪdənt] n
presidente m, presidenta f

the president is arriving at five el presidente llegará a las cinco

press

press
[pres]
I. v t
1. apretar

* *What happens if I press these buttons?... I wonder!... Never mind, I'll try! I'll see then!...* ¿Qué pasa si aprieto estos botones?... ¡Me lo pregunto!... No importa, ¡lo probaré! ¡Y entonces lo veré!... *

...press

2. planchar

II. *n*
prensa *f*

the English press la prensa inglesa

Nick works for the press Nick trabaja para la prensa

pretend

pretend
[prɪˈtend] *v t*
1. fingir

he is pretending to be asleep finge estar dormido

2. pretender

3. dárselas de, hacerse pasar por
he pretended to be a policeman se hizo pasar por policía

pretty

pretty
[ˈprɪtɪ]
I. *adj*
prettier, prettiest
bonito, a

* *Their costumes are really pretty, aren't they?* Sus trajes son realmente bonitos, ¿verdad? *

II. *adv*
bastante

she's pretty tall es bastante alta

prevent

prevent
[prɪˈvent] *v t*
impedir

the wall prevented us from seeing la pared nos impedía ver

price

price
[praɪs] *n*
precio *m*

low prices precios bajos

prime minister

prime minister
[praɪmˈmɪnɪstəʳ] *n*
primer ministro *m*, primera ministra *f*

prison

prison
[ˈprɪzn] *n*
prisión *f*, cárcel *f*

* *How am I possibly going to escape from this prison?* ¿Cómo voy a poder escapar de esta prisión? *

he was sent to prison lo metieron en la cárcel

private

private
[ˈpraɪvət] *adj*
1. privado, a

they held a private meeting mantuvieron una reunión privada

2. particular
private lesson clase particular

3. Idiom
they spoke in private hablaron en privado

probable

probable
[ˈprɒbəbl] *adj*
probable

the probable result el resultado probable

▶ **probably**
[ˈprɒbəblɪ] *adv*
probablemente

* *Tintin has probably got lost! We must look for him!...* ¡Probablemente Tintín se ha

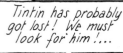

perdido! ¡Tenemos que buscarle!... *

problem

problem
[ˈprɒbləm] *n*
problema *m*

we must find a solution to the problem debemos encontrar una solución al problema

produce

produce
[prəˈdjuːs] *v t*
producir

the factory produces glass la fábrica produce cristal

▶ **product**
[ˈprɒdʌkt] *n*
producto *m*

▶ **production**
[prəˈdʌkʃ(ə)n] *n*
producción *f*

professor

professor
[prəˈfesəʳ] *n*
profesor *m*, profesora *f*

the professor gave a lecture on literature el profesor dio una conferencia sobre literatura

programme

programme
['prəugræm] n
(Am: **program**)
programa m

a television programme un programa de televisión

progress

progress
['prəugres] n
progreso(s) m

she's making progress está haciendo progresos

promise

promise
['prɒmɪs]
I. n

...promise

promesa f

II. v t
prometer

* *Foreigners, you must promise me that you will say nothing!...* ¡Extranjeros; deben prometerme que no dirán nada!...
Son of the Sun, I promise you that we'll keep the secret!... ¡Hijo del Sol, te prometo que guardaremos el secreto!... *

protect

protect
[prə'tekt] v t
proteger

we must protect him from his enemies debemos protegerle de sus enemigos

protest

protest
[prə'test] v i
protestar

...protest

we protested against the war protestamos contra la guerra

proud

proud
[praud] adj
orgulloso, a

* *Well done, Tintin! You've made it! I'm proud of you!* ¡Bien hecho, Tintín! ¡Lo conseguiste! ¡Estoy orgulloso de ti! *

...proud

prove

prove
[pruːv]
I. v t
probar

* *Can you prove what you claim?... I need proof, you know!* ¿Puede probar lo que pretende?... ¡Necesito pruebas, sabe! *

II. v i
resultar

...prove

the document proved to be false el documento resultó ser falso

provide

provide
[prə'vaɪd] v t
proveer

I will provide them with food los proveeré de comida

...provide

▶ **provided that**
conj
a condición de que

I will tell you provided that you'll keep the secret te lo contaré a condición de que guardes el secreto

pub

pub
[pʌb] n
bar m

...pub

let's go to the nearest pub vamos al bar más cercano

public

public
['pʌblɪk]
I. adj
público, a

a public library una biblioteca pública

...public

II. n
público m

the public liked the play al público le gustó la obra

she doesn't want to kiss him in public no quiere besarle en público

▶ **publicity**
[pʌb'lɪsɪtɪ] n
publicidad f

pudding

pudding
['pudɪŋ] n
1. pudín m, pastel m

Christmas pudding pastel de Navidad

2. postre m

pull

pull
[pul]
I. *v t*
1. estirar de, tirar de

pull the rope estira de la cuerda

2. Idiom
don't pull my leg no me tomes el pelo

II. *v i*
estirar, tirar

when I say so, all pull! ¡cuando lo diga, estiren todos!

▶ **pull down**
derribar, demoler

the house was pulled down la casa fue derribada

▶ **pull up**
1. parar(se), detener(se)

pull up at the traffic-lights detente en el semáforo

2. subir, levantar

3. acercar, acercarse
pull your chair up acerque su silla

▶ **pullover**
['puləuvə'] *n*
(*Am*: **sweater**)
jersey *m*, suéter *m*

she's wearing a white pullover lleva un jersey blanco

punish

punish
['pʌnɪʃ] *v t*
castigar

pupil

pupil
['pjuːp(ə)l] *n*
alumno *m*, alumna *f*

the pupils were writing los alumnos estaban escribiendo

purple

purple
['pɜːp(ə)l]
I. *adj*
púrpura, morado, a

II. *n*
púrpura, morado

dressed in purple vestido de morado

purpose

purpose
['pɜːpəs] *n*
1. propósito *m*, intención *f*

the purpose of the film is to entertain la intención de la película es divertir

2. Idiom
she did it on purpose lo hizo adrede

purse

purse
[pɜːs] *n*
monedero *m*

push

push
[puʃ]
I. *v t*
1. empujar

push the door empuja la puerta

...push

Quick, push the red button!

2. apretar
* *Quick, push the red button!* ¡Rápido, apriete el botón rojo! *

II. *v i*
empujar

don't push, please no empuje, por favor

put

put
[put] *v t*
put, put
1. poner

put your gun on the table ponga la pistola sobre la mesa

2. explicar, poner
let me put it in other words déjeme explicarlo con otras palabras

▶ **put away**
guardar

...put

put the toys away guarda los juguetes

▶ **put back**
colocar de nuevo, volver a poner

put the glass back in the cupboard coloca el vaso de nuevo en el armario

▶ **put off**
1. aplazar, posponer

The launch has been put off until tomorrow.

* *The launch has been put off until tomorrow.* El lanzamiento ha sido aplazado hasta mañana. *

2. Idiom
he puts me off no puedo ni verle

▶ **put on**
1. poner

put your coat on póngase el abrigo

2. encender

put the lights on enciende las luces

▶ **put out**
apagar

* *Oh! They've put the lights out!...* ¡Oh! ¡Han apagado las luces!... *

▶ **put up**
alojar

I'll put you up for the night puedo alojarte por la noche

Oh! They've put the lights out!...

???

...put

▶ **put up with**
soportar,
aguantar(se)

*you'll have to put up
with it* tendrás que
aguantarte

pyjamas

pyjamas
[pɪ'dʒɑːməz] *n pl*
(*Am:* **pajamas**)
pijama *m*

a pair of pyjamas un
pijama

*   *Tintin is in pyja-
mas...* Tintín está en
pijama...
*Come on, Snowy,
let's go to bed now...*
Vamos, Milú, vámonos a la
cama ahora...
That's a good idea!
¡Es una buena idea! *

quarrel

quarrel
['kwɒrəl]
I. *n*
disputa *f*,
discusión *f*, pelea *f*

*they were having a
quarrel* tenían una
discusión

II. *v i*
quarrelled, quarrelled
(*Am:* quarreled)
discutir, pelearse

stop   quarrelling

...quarrel

about that dejad de
pelearos por eso

quarter

quarter
['kwɔːtəʳ] *n*
1. cuarto *m*

2. Idiom
*it's a quarter past
eight* son las ocho y
cuarto

queen

queen
[kwiːn] *n*
reina *f*

question

question
['kwestʃ(ə)n] *n*
1. pregunta *f*

*   *Can I ask you a
question, Professor?*
¿Puedo hacerle una pre-

...question

gunta, profesor?
*Do you have some-
thing to ask me?...*
¿Tiene algo que pregun-
tarme?... *

2. cuestión *f*,
asunto *m*
*the question is... if
he will accept it* la
cuestión es... si lo acep-
tará

queue

queue
[kjuː]
(*Am:* **line**)
I. *n*
fila *f*, cola *f*

a queue of people
una cola de gente

II. *v i*
hacer cola

we must queue (up)
(*Am: line up*) debemos
hacer cola

quick

quick
[kwɪk]
I. *adj*
rápido, a

*I'll have a quick
shower* tomaré una
ducha rápida

II. *adv*
rápido, deprisa

*   *Quick, Tintin!...
Come and have a
look, it's extraor-
dinary!* ¡Deprisa, Tintín!...

¡Venga y eche un vistazo,
es extraordinario! *

▶ **quickly**
['kwɪklɪ] *adv*
rápidamente

quiet

quiet
['kwaɪət] *adj*
1. silencioso, a,
tranquilo, a,

...quiet

callado, a

a very quiet life una
vida muy tranquila

2. Idiom
be quiet! ¡cállense!

quite

quite
[kwaɪt] *adv*
1. bastante

...quite

she's quite tall
es bastante alta

2. totalmente,
completamente
he's quite wrong
está completamente
equivocado

3. Idiom
quite a lot of un
buen número de

R R R R R R

rabbit

rabbit
['ræbɪt] n
conejo m

race

race
[reɪs] n
1. carrera f

* *I wonder who's going to win this race!...* ¡Me pregunto

quién va a ganar esta carrera!... *

2. raza f

3. Idiom
the human race el género humano

radio

radio
['reɪdɪəu] n
radio f

railway

...railway

railway
['reɪlweɪ] n
(Am: **railroad**)
ferrocarril m, vía f
del tren, vía f férrea

* *Ah! There's the railway!... Let's follow the track and we'll get to the station...*
¡Ah! ¡Allí está la vía del tren!... Sigámosla y llegaremos a la estación...
Great! You've found the solution again.
¡Estupendo! Has encon-

trado la solución de nuevo. *

▶ **railway** (Am: **railroad**) **station** n
estación f (de ferrocaril

rain

rain
[reɪn]
I. n

...rain

lluvia f

I like the rain me gusta la lluvia

II. v i
llover

* *That's it! It's raining! Let's put the hood (Am: top) up!...*
¡Ya está! ¡Llueve! ¡Vamos a poner la capota!... *

▶ **raincoat**
['reɪnkəut] n

impermeable m, gabardina f

▶ **raindrop**
['reɪndrɒp] n
gota f de lluvia

▶ **rainy**
['reɪnɪ] adj
rainier, rainiest
lluvioso, a

rapid

rapid
['ræpɪd] adj
rápido, a

there was a rapid rise in prices hubo una rápida subida de los precios

rare

rare
[reəʳ] adj
1. raro, a, escaso, a

...rare

I hope we'll be able to film some rare species...

* *I hope we'll be able to film some rare species...* Espero que podamos filmar algunas especies raras... *

2. poco hecho, a
how would you like your steak? – rare, please ¿cómo desea el filete? – poco hecho, por favor

▶ **rarely**
['reəlɪ] adv
raramente,
muy pocas veces

rat

rat
[ræt] n
rata f

rather

rather
['rɑːðəʳ] adv
1. bastante

it's rather boring es bastante aburrido

...rather

2. más bien
he is rather fat than thin es más bien gordo que delgado

3. Idiom
I'd rather study now preferiría estudiar ahora

I'd rather you came tomorrow preferiría que viniese mañana

would you rather go now or later? ¿preferiría ir ahora o más tarde?

raw

raw
[rɔː] adj
1. crudo, a

raw meat carne cruda

2. Idiom
raw materials materias primas

reach

reach
[riːtʃ] v t
alcanzar, llegar a

can you reach the bulb? ¿puedes alcanzar la bombilla?

* *I wonder whether we'll reach the island today...* Me pregunto si llegaremos a la isla hoy...
I'm begining to doubt it... Empiezo a dudarlo... *

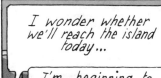

I wonder whether we'll reach the island today...

I'm beginning to doubt it...

read

read
[riːd] v i & v t
read, read [red]
leer

we read the letter leímos la carta

she's learning to read está aprendiendo a leer

▶ **reading**
['riːdɪŋ] n
lectura f

* *I love reading, I need these peaceful moments to rest after my adventures!* ¡Me encanta la lectura, necesito estos momentos tranquilos para descansar después de mis aventuras! *

...read

I love reading, I need these peaceful moments to rest after my adventures!

ready

ready
['redɪ] adj
preparado, a
listo, a

she says that dinner is ready dice que la cena está preparada

Captain, we must go now. Is your luggage ready? Capitán, ya tenemos que irnos. ¿Está listo su equipaje?

* *Are you ready? I'll throw you the rope...*

...ready

¿Está preparado? Voy a tirarle la cuerda...
Go ahead!... ¡Adelante!... *

real

real
[rɪəl] adj
real, verdadero, a

this is a film and not real life esto es una película y no la vida real

Are you ready? I'll throw you the rope...

Go ahead!...

...real

► **really**
['rɪəlɪ] adv
1. realmente, verdaderamente

2. Idiom
I liked the play – really? me gustó la obra – ¿de veras?

realize

realize
['rɪəlaɪz] v t

You don't realize the difficulties; Captain!...

darse cuenta

* *You don't realize the difficulties, Captain!...* ¡No se da cuenta de las dificultades, capitán!... *

reason

reason
['riːz(ə)n] n
razón f

...reason

that's not a good reason esa no es una buena razón

receive

receive
[rɪ'siːv] v t
recibir

did you receive my message? ¿recibiste mi mensaje?

recent

recent
['riːs(ə)nt] adj
reciente

it's a recent design es un diseño reciente

► **recently**
['riːs(ə)ntlɪ] adv
recientemente

the document was recently discovered el

...recent

documento fue descubierto recientemente

recess

recess (*Am*)
→ BREAK

recognize

recognize
['rekəgnaɪz] v t

...recognize

reconocer

* *Cuthbert, don't you recognize me? It's me, Haddock!* Silvestre, ¿no me reconoce? ¡Soy yo, Haddock! *

record

record
['rɪkɔːd]
I. n
1. disco m

Cuthbert, don't you recognize me? It's me, Haddock!

...record

they were listening to records estaban escuchando discos

2. record m
she's broken the record! ¡ha batido el record!

II. v t
[rɪ'kɔːd]
grabar, registrar

I recorded the concert grabé el concierto

► **record player** n
tocadiscos m

red

red
[red]
I. adj
rojo, a

* *He's red with anger.* Está rojo de cólera. *

a red rose una rosa roja

II. n
1. rojo m

she dressed in red vestía de rojo

He's red with anger.

2. Idiom
to see red ponerse rojo de cólera/ furioso

reduce

reduce
[rɪ'djuːs] v t
reducir

reduce speed reduzca la velocidad

refuse

refuse
[rɪ'fjuːz] v t
rehusar, negarse a

* *It's no good, he refuses to talk, we must find some other way!* ¡No sirve de nada, rehusa hablar, debemos encontrar otra manera! *

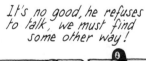

It's no good, he refuses to talk, we must find some other way!

relation

relation
[rɪˈleɪʃ(ə)n] *n*
1. pariente *m*,
parienta *f*

*he's a distant rela-
tion* es un pariente lejano

2. relación *f*
*the relation between
the two documents
wasn't clear* la relación
entre los dos documentos
no estaba clara

relative

relative
[ˈrelətɪv] *n*
pariente *m*,
parienta *f*

* *But... where are
we going?...* Pero...
¿adónde vamos?...
*Come in, I'd like you
to meet a relative of
mine...* Entren, me gus-
taría que conociesen a un
pariente mío... *

relax

relax
[rɪˈlæks] *v i*
descansar,
relajarse

*relax and don't
worry* relájese y no se
preocupe

religion

religion
[rɪˈlɪdʒən] *n*
religión *f*

remain

remain
[rɪˈmeɪn] *v i*
permanecer,
quedar

it remains untouched
permanece intacto

*what remains to be
done?* ¿qué falta por
hacer?

remember

remember
[rɪˈmembəʳ] *v i & v t*
recordar,
acordarse de

*do you remember
her name?* ¿recuerdas
su nombre?

I can't remember no
puedo acordarme

remind

remind
[rɪˈmaɪnd] *v t*
recordar

remind me to do it
recuérdame que lo haga

* *You'll see. He's a
great chap (Am:
guy)!* Ya verá. ¡Es un
tipo estupendo!
*He reminds me of
somebody, but I
can't remember who
it is...* Me recuerda a
alguien, pero no consigo
acordarme de quien... *

rent

rent
[rent]
I. *n*
alquiler

*she can't pay the
rent* no puede pagar el
alquiler

II. *v t*
alquilar

*they rent the house
during the summer*
alquilan la casa durante el
verano

repair

repair
[rɪˈpeəʳ] *v t*
reparar,
arreglar

repeat

repeat
[rɪˈpiːt] *v t*
repetir

...repeat

* *Careful, it's a
secret, don't repeat
it to anybody.* Cui-
dado, es un secreto, no lo
repita a nadie. *

replace

replace
[rɪˈpleɪs] *v t*
1. remplazar,
reemplazar

...replace

...replace

* *We'll have to replace this broken mirror...* Tendremos que reemplazar este espejo roto...
Yes... I'll do it myself... Si... Lo haré yo mismo... *

2. **reponer, colocar de nuevo**
he replaced the book on the shelf colocó el libro de nuevo en la estantería

reply

reply
[rɪ'plaɪ]
I. *v i & v t*
replied, replied [rɪ'plaɪd]
responder, contestar

he hasn't replied (to) my letter no ha contestado mi carta

II. *n*
pl replies
respuesta *f*

his reply arrived late su respuesta llegó tarde

reporter

reporter
[rɪ'pɔːtəʳ] *n*
reportero, a periodista, *m f*

republic

republic
[rɪ'pʌblɪk] *n*
república *f*

rescue

rescue
['reskjuː] *v t*
rescatar, salvar

* *Wooaaah!* ¡Guaaauh!
Let's hope I'll get there in time to rescue Snowy! ¡Ojalá llegue a tiempo para rescatar a Milú! *

reserve

reserve
[rɪ'zɜːv] *v t*
reservar

this table has been reserved esta mesa ha sido reservada

▶ **reservation**
[rɪzə'veɪʃ(ə)n] *n*
1. reserva *f*

he has a reservation for this train tiene una reserva para este tren

2. reserva *f*
he accepted it without reservation lo aceptó sin reserva(s)

responsible

responsible
[rɪs'pɒnsɪb(ə)l] *adj*
responsable

* *Well, I'm waiting for an explanation. What do you have*

...responsible

to say? Bien, estoy esperando una explicación. ¿Qué tiene que decir?
Yes, I'm responsible for what has happened. Sí, soy responsable de lo que ha pasado. *

rest

rest
[rest]
I. *v i*

...rest

descansar

* *Let's rest here for a moment.* Descansemos aquí un momento. *

II. *v t*
dejar, apoyar

rest the ladder against the wall apoye la escalera contra la pared

III. *n*
1. reposo *m*

...rest

she has worked hard and deserves a rest ha trabajado mucho y merece un descanso

2. resto *m*
you already know the rest of the story ya sabes el resto de la historia

3. los/las demás, los/las otros, as *pl*
the rest of them will wait there los otros esperarán allí

restaurant

restaurant
['rest(ə)rɒnt] *n*
restaurante *m*

result

result
[rɪ'zʌlt] *n*
resultado *m*

the final result el resultado final

return

return
[rɪ'tɜːn]
I. *v i*
volver

* *He wonders whether he'll ever return to America.* Se pregunta si volverá alguna vez a América. *

II. *v t*
devolver

I have to return the book to the library tengo que devolver el libro a la biblioteca

III. *n*
1. vuelta *f*, **regreso** *m*

we are waiting for her return esperamos su vuelta

2. Idiom
in return a cambio

a return (ticket) un billete de ida y vuelta

...return

He wonders whether he'll ever return to America

many happy returns (of the day)! ¡feliz cumpleaños!

revolution

revolution
[revə'lu:ʃ(ə)n] *n*
revolución *f*

the French Revolution la revolución francesa

rice

rice
[raɪs] *n*
arroz *m*

rice pudding arroz con leche

rich

rich
[rɪtʃ] *adj*
rico, a

...rich

she doesn't want to be rich no quiere ser rica

rid

rid
[rɪd] *v t*
1. librar

2. Idiom
to get rid of something librarse/deshacerse de algo

ride

ride
[raɪd]
rode [rəʊd],
ridden ['rɪdn]

I. *vi & vt*
montar (en, a)

* *The Captain is riding a horse... well... the Captain is trying to ride a horse...* El capitán está montando a caballo... bueno... está intentando montar a caballo... *

can you ride a bicycle? ¿sabes montar en bicicleta?

II. *n*
1. paseo *m*

let's go for a ride on our bicycles/in the car vamos a dar un paseo en bicicleta/en coche

2. Idiom
can you give me a ride to Edinburgh? ¿puedes llevarme a Edimburgo?

The Captain is riding a horse... well... the Captain is trying to ride a horse...

right

right
[raɪt]
I. *adj*
1. derecho, a

he writes with his right hand escribe con la mano derecha

2. correcto, a, acertado, a, justo, a
that's the right attitude ésta es la actitud correcta

is this the right way? ¿es éste el camino correcto?/¿es ésta la manera correcta?

3. Idiom
you're right tienes razón

II. *n*
1. derecha *f*

the door is on the right la puerta está a la derecha

...right

2. derecho *m*
* *You have no right to keep me here!* ¡No tienen derecho a retenerme aquí!
You should have minded your own business! ¡Deberías haberte ocupado de tus asuntos! *

3. Idiom
the ambulance has the right of way la ambulancia tiene preferencia

You have no right to keep me here!
You should have minded your own business!

III. *adv*
1. a la derecha

turn right at the next corner gire a la derecha en la siguiente esquina

2. bien, correctamente
nothing seems to go right nada parece ir bien

3. exactamente, justo

it's right at the end of the corridor está exactamente al final del pasillo

4. Idiom
right away en seguida

right in the middle en pleno centro

right now ahora mismo

▶ **right-hand**
['raɪt'hænd] *adj*
1. derecho, a

...right

the right-hand side of the road el lado derecho de la calle

2. Idiom
he is my right-hand man él es mi brazo derecho

ring

ring
[rɪŋ]
I. n
1. anillo m

he gave her a diamond ring le dio un anillo de diamantes

2. círculo m
let's form a ring formemos un círculo

3. llamada f
give him a ring tomorrow hazle una llamada mañana

4. Idiom
there was a ring at the door sonó el timbre de la puerta

II. vi & vt
rang [ræŋ], rung [rʌŋ]
1. sonar

the telephone is ringing el teléfono está sonando

2. tocar
* Rrrring Rrrring
Someone's ringing the door bell!... ¡Al-

guien está tocando el timbre de la puerta!... *

3. llamar
* Quick, ring (Am: call) the police! Hurry up! ¡Rápido, llame a la policía! ¡Dese prisa!
No! You go and I'll wait for you here! ¡No! ¡Vaya Usted y yo le esperaré aquí! *

4. Idiom
his name rings a bell su nombre me suena

...ring

▶ **ring up (Am: call)** llamar (por teléfono), telefonear

ring me up if you have news llámame si tienes noticias

ripe

ripe
[raɪp] adj
maduro, a

...ripe

ripe cherries cerezas maduras

rise

rise
[raɪz]
I. vi
rose [rəuz], risen ['rɪz(ə)n]
1. subir

the smoke rose to the ceiling el humo

...rise

the sun is rising...

subió hasta el techo

2. levantarse
he rose to close the door se levantó para cerrar la puerta

3. salir (the sun)
* The sun is rising...
Sale el sol... *

II. n
aumento m, subida f

she asked her boss for a rise (Am: raise) pidió un aumento a su jefe

risk

risk
[rɪsk]
I. n
riesgo m

Tintin is running a great risk Tintín está corriendo un gran riesgo

II. vt
arriesgar

he risked his fortune for her arriesgó su fortuna por ella

river

river
['rɪvəʳ] n
río m

* There now, we can get across the river... Ya está, podemos cruzar el río... *

▶ **riverside**
['rɪvəsaɪd] n
1. orilla f del río

2. Idiom
down by the riverside a orillas del río

There now, we can get across the river ...

road

road
[rəud] n
carretera f, calle f, camino m

rob

rob
[rɒb] vt
robbed, robbed
robar, asaltar

he robbed the bank asaltó el banco

...rob

▶ **robbery**
['rɒbərɪ] n
pl robberies ['rɒbərɪz]
robo m

the robbery was committed yesterday el robo se cometió ayer

rocket

rocket
['rɒkɪt] n
cohete m

roof

roof
[ru:f] n
tejado m

there was a cat on the roof había un gato en el tejado

room

room
[ru:m] n
1. habitación f, cuarto m

...room

this room is very big esta habitación es muy grande

2. dormitorio m she was sleeping in her room estaba durmiendo en su dormitorio

3. sitio m there's no room here for the two of us aquí no hay sitio para los dos

rope

the rope has broken!...

...rope

rope
[rəup] n
cuerda f

* The rope has broken!... ¡Se ha roto la cuerda!... *

rose

rose
[rəuz] n
rosa f

rough

rough
[rʌf] adj
1. áspero, a

this cloth is rough esta tela es áspera

2. agitado, a (the sea) a rough sea un mar agitado

3. aproximado, a it's a rough translation es una traducción aproximada

4. Idiom a rough copy un borrador

round

round
[raund]
I. adj
redondo, a

the Knights of the Round Table los Caballeros de la Mesa Redonda

II. adv
Idiom

all the year round durante todo el año

▶ go round
1. dar la vuelta, girar

2. Idiom a merry-go-round un tiovivo

...round

▶ **look round**
mirar alrededor

▶ **turn round**
dar(se) la vuelta

▶ **round** (Am: **around**)
prep
1. alrededor de

* There's a wall all round the garden... Hay un muro alrededor del jardín... *

...round

There's a wall round the garden ...

2. Idiom it's just round the corner está a la vuelta de la esquina

I'll show you round the house le enseñaré la casa

▶ **round trip** (Am)
→ RETURN

row

row
[rəu] n
fila f, hilera f

my ticket is for the first row mi entrada es para la primera fila

row

row
[rau] n

...row

1. alboroto m, escándalo m

* Stop that row, I'm trying to sleep!... Blistering barnacles!... Stop it!... ¡Basta de alboroto, estoy intentando dormir!... ¡Mil diablos!... ¡Basta!... *

2. Idiom to have a row with somebody tener una riña con alguien

royal

royal
['rɔɪəl] adj
real

the Royal Family la familia real

rubber

rubber
['rʌbəʳ] n
1. goma f

...rubber

tyres (Am: tires) are made of rubber los neumáticos están hechos de goma

2. goma f de borrar
can you lend me your rubber (Am: eraser), please? ¿puedes dejarme tu goma de borrar, por favor?

ruin

ruin
['ruːn]
I. n
ruina f

the ruins of the castle las ruinas del castillo

II. v t
arruinar

he's ruining his life está arruinando su vida

rule

rule
[ruːl]
I. n
1. regla f, norma f

* *That dog can't come in here with that protective suit on... That's the rule!* ¡Ese perro no puede entrar aquí con ese traje de protección puesto... ¡Es la norma!
Oh, I didn't know!... ¡Oh, no lo sabía!... *

2. Idiom
as a rule por norma

II. v t
mandar

▶ **ruler**
['ruːləʳ] n
1. regla f

draw a straight line with a ruler dibuja una línea recta con una regla

2. soberano, a, jefe m de Estado

...rule

run

run
[rʌn]
ran [ræn], run [rʌn]
I. v i
1. correr

he runs faster than you corre más rápido que tú

the water is running; turn the tap off está corriendo el agua; cierra el grifo

2. circular

that bus runs on Sundays ese autobús circula los domingos

3. funcionar
the engine is running el motor está funcionando

4. Idiom
to run up/down the stairs bajar/subir corriendo por las escaleras

to run out of somewhere salir corriendo de un sitio

in the long run a la larga

II. v t
dirigir, llevar

she runs this shop ella dirige esta tienda

▶ **runabout**
['rʌnəbaut] n
vagabundo, a

▶ **runaway**
['rʌnəweɪ] n
fugitivo, a

▶ **run away**
v i
escapar, huir

▶ **run over**
v t
atropellar

rush

rush
[rʌʃ]
I. n
1. avalancha f, afluencia f

2. prisa f
I'm in a rush tengo prisa

3. Idiom
there was a rush for the exit corrieron en tropel hacia la salida

II. v i
abalanzarse, precipitarse, darse prisa

* *The shark rushed towards our heroes...* El tiburón se precipitó hacia nuestros héroes... *

the shark rushed towards our heroes...

sad

sad
[sæd] *adj*
sadder, saddest
triste

* What's wrong with this dog? He's been here all day!... ¿Qué le pasa a este perro? ¡Ha estado aquí todo el día!... *He looks so sad!... I don't know why!...* ¡Parece tan triste!... ¡No sé por qué!... *

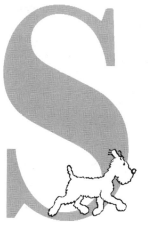

safe

safe
[seɪf]
1. seguro, a, a salvo

it's safer to talk inside es más seguro hablar dentro

you'll be safe there estarás a salvo allí

2. Idiom
safe and sound sano y salvo

▶ **safety**
['seɪftɪ] *n*
seguridad *f*

safety belt cinturón de seguridad

...sail

vela *f*

* Up sails! I said up sails!... Do you hear?... Up sails! ¡Icen las velas! ¡Dije que icen las velas!... ¿Me oyen?... ¡Icen las velas!... *

II. *v i*
1. navegar

Captain, we have to sail west capitán, debemos navegar hacia el oeste

sail

sail
[seɪl]
I. *n*

...sail

2. Idiom
to go sailing salir a navegar

III. *v t*
gobernar (una embarcación)

▶ **sailor**
['seɪlə'] *n*
marinero *m*

my father was a sailor mi padre era marinero

salad

salad
['sæləd] *n*
ensalada *f*

to dress a salad aderezar/aliñar una ensalada

sale

sale
[seɪl] *n*
1. venta *f*

...sale

sales department departamento de ventas

2. rebajas *f pl*
the January sales las rebajas de enero

3. Idiom
* Castle for sale Castillo en venta *

salt

salt
[sɒlt] n
sal f

same

same
[seɪm]
I. adj
mismo, a

* *They're both wearing the same clothes.* Ambos llevan la misma ropa. *

They're both wearing the same clothes.

II. pron
el mismo, la misma, los mismos, las mismas

their car is the same as ours su coche es el mismo que el nuestro

sand

sand
[sænd] n
arena f

...sand

* *In the desert...* En el desierto...
There's nothing but miles and miles of sand. No hay más que kilómetros y kilómetros de arena. *

In the desert...

There's nothing but miles and miles of sand.

sandwich

sandwich
['sændwɪtʃ] n
bocadillo m

Saturday

Saturday
['sætədɪ] n
sábado m

the meeting is on Saturday la reunión es el sábado

saucepan

saucepan
['sɔːspən] n
cacerola f

saucer

saucer
['sɔːsəʳ] n
platillo m

a flying saucer un platillo volante

sausage

sausage
['sɒsɪdʒ] n
salchicha f, longaniza f

save

save
[seɪv] v t
1. salvar

Tintin has saved my life Tintín me ha salvado la vida

2. ahorrar
she's saving money to travel está ahorrando dinero para viajar

to save time/space ahorrar tiempo/espacio

say

say
[seɪ] v t
said, said [sed]
1. decir

* *What did you say?* ¿Qué has dicho?
I said that I can't hear what you're saying. He dicho que no puedo oír lo que dices. *

it is said that he is very brave se dice que es muy valiente

What did you say?

I said that I can't hear what you're saying.

2. Idiom
I say! (Am: say!) ¡Vaya!

scared

scared
[skeəd] adj
asustado, a

I'm not scared no estoy asustado

school

school
[skuːl] n

scarf

scarf
[skɑːf] n
pl scarves [skɑːvz]
bufanda f

put your scarf on; it's cold ponte la bufanda; hace frío

...school

1. colegio m, escuela f

she is at school now está en la escuela ahora

* *There's the school... And over there is the hospital...* Allí está la escuela... Y por allí está el hospital... *

2. Idiom
secondary school (Am: high school) instituto, escuela secundaria

...school

There's the school... And over there is the hospital...

▶ **schoolboy**
['skuːlbɔɪ] n
colegial m

▶ **schoolchildren**
['skuːltʃɪldrən] n pl
colegiales m pl

▶ **schoolgirl**
['skuːlgɜːl]
colegiala f

▶ **schoolmaster**
['skuːlmɑːstəʳ]
maestro m de escuela

science

science
['saɪəns] n
ciencia f

▶ **scientist**
['saɪəntɪst] n
científico, a

Professor Topolino is an important scientist el profesor Topolino es un importante científico

score

score
[skɔːʳ]
I. n
tantos m pl,
puntos m pl,
resultado n

the final score was 5 to 1 el resultado final fue de 5 a 1

II. v t
marcar

she scored two points marcó dos puntos

Scotland

Scotland
['skɒtlənd] n
Escocia f

▶ **Scot**
[skɒt] n
escocés m,
escocesa f

▶ **Scottish**
['skɒtɪʃ] adj
escocés,
escocesa

scratch

scratch
[skrætʃ]
I. v t
rascar, arañar
II. n
rasguño m,
arañazo m

sea

sea
[siː] n
mar m

...sea

the sea is very rough el mar está muy agitado

▶ **seasick**
['siːsɪk] adj
mareado, a

* *They are seasick...* Están mareados... *

▶ **seaside**
['siːsaɪd] n
costa f, orillas f pl
del mar

They are seasick...

we went to the seaside fuimos a la costa

search

search
[sɜːtʃ]
I. v i
buscar

...search

Military police: we're going to search your cabin.

???

they are searching for gold están buscando oro

II. v t
registrar

* *Military police: we're going to search your cabin.* Policía militar: vamos a registrar su camarote. *

season

season
['siːz(ə)n] n
estación f

the four seasons las cuatro estaciones

seat

seat
[siːt] n
asiento m

...seat

front/back seat of the car el asiento delantero/trasero del coche

is this seat free? ¿está libre este asiento?

take a seat tome asiento

second

second
['sekənd]
I. n
1. segundo m

ten seconds diez segundos

2. momento m
just a second, please! ¡un momento, por favor!

II. adj
segundo, a

...second

The mummy's second victim!...

* *The mummy's second victim!...* ¡La segunda víctima de la momia!... *

a second-class ticket un billete de segunda clase

...secret

this is a secret affair éste es un asunto secreto

II. *n*
secreto *m*

can you keep a secret? ¿puedes guardar un secreto?

secret

secret
['si:krɪt]
I. *adj*
secreto, a

...see

see
[si:] *v i & v t*
saw [sɔ:], seen [si:n]

1. ver

can you see the Captain? ¿puede ver al capitán?

2. ver, comprender
do you see what I mean? ¿ve lo que quiero decir?

3. acompañar, conducir
I'll see you home voy a acompañarle a casa

4. vigilar

see that nobody is following us vigila que nadie nos siga

5. Idiom
(I'll) see you tomorrow! ¡hasta mañana!

see you later! ¡hasta luego!

▶ **see off**
despedirse

I'll see you off at the airport me despediré de ti en el aeropuerto

...see

▶ **see to**
1. ocuparse de

she's seeing to the arrangements se está ocupando de los preparativos

2. reparar, arreglar
I've brought you this radio; can you see to it? le traigo esta radio; ¿puede arreglarla?

seem

seem
[si:m] *v i*
parecer

so it seems eso parece

he doesn't seem to agree no parece estar de acuerdo

selfish

selfish
['selfiʃ] *adj*
egoista

sell

sell
[sel] *v t*
sold, sold [səuld]
vender

* *Do you want to sell me your boat?...*

...sell

Do you want to sell me your boat?

¿Quiere venderme su barca?... *

send

send
[send] *v t*
sent, sent [sent]
enviar, mandar

send it by post envíalo por correo

...send

▶ **send back**
devolver,
mandar de vuelta

send these books back; we don't need them devuelve estos libros; no los necesitamos

▶ **send for**
mandar a buscar,
ir a buscar

* *He's not well, we must send for the doctor.* No está bien,

He's not well, we must send for the doctor.

debemos mandar a buscar al médico. *

sense

sense
[sens] *n*
1. sentido *m*

* *Snowy has a very keen sense of smell!* ¡Milú tiene un sentido del olfato muy agudo! *

...sense

Snowy has a very keen sense of smell!

...sense

he's got no sense of humour (Am: humor) no tiene sentido del humor

common sense sentido común

2. Idiom
it doesn't make sense no tiene sentido

sentence

sentence
['sentəns]
I. n
frase f

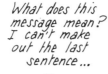

* What does this message mean? I can't make out the last sentence... ¿Qué significa este mensaje? No entiendo la última frase... *

II. v t
condenar

separate

separate
['sepərət]
I. adj
separado, a

they work in separate laboratories

...separate

they have sentenced him to prison lo han condenado a la cárcel

trabajan en laboratorios separados

II. v t
separar

* I've lost the Professor, we were separated in the crowd. Come with me, we'll try to find him... He perdido al profesor. La muchedumbre nos ha separado. Venga conmigo. Intentaremos encontrarlo... *

...separate

I've lost the Professor, we were separated in the crowd. Come with me, we'll try to find him...

September

September
[sep'tembə'] n
septiembre m

serious

serious
['sɪərɪəs] adj
1. serio, a

he had a serious appearance tenía un aspecto serio

...serious

2. grave
it's not a serious illness no es una enfermedad grave

serve

serve
[sɜːv] v t
servir

dinner is served la cena está servida

...serve

▶ **service**
['sɜːvɪs] n
servicio m

set

set
[set]
I. n
1. juego m

a tea set un juego de té

...set

2. aparato m
a TV set un aparato de televisión

II. v t
set, set [set]
1. poner

set the table, please pon la mesa, por favor

I'm going to set the alarm-clock voy a poner el despertador

...set

the teacher didn't set (Am: assign) us any homework el maestro no nos puso deberes

2. Idiom
to set free dejar libre

to set fire to a house pegarle fuego a una casa

III. v i
1. ponerse

* We must hurry, Snowy, the sun will

be setting soon... Tenemos que darnos prisa, Milú. El sol se pondrá pronto... *

2. fijarse, cuajarse
wait for the glue to set espera que se fije el pegamento

▶ **set about**
ponerse a

they set about repairing the car se pusieron a reparar el coche

We must hurry, Snowy, the sun will be setting soon...

▶ **set off**
partir

we'll set off tomorrow morning partiremos mañana por la mañana

▶ **set up**
1. organizar

it's all set up todo está organizado

2. establecer(se)

3. edificar, levantar
they set up a statue levantaron una estatua

settle

settle
['set(ə)l]
I. v t
1. instalar

she settled the baby in the car instaló el niño en el coche

S

...settle

2. poner en orden, arreglar
let's settle all these matters vamos a poner en orden todos estos asuntos

3. zanjar, resolver
that settles the problem esto zanja el problema

4. calmar
this will settle your nerves esto te calmará los nervios

II. *v i*
1. instalarse
they settled in London se instalaron en Londres

2. posarse
the bird settled on a branch el pájaro se posó en una rama

3. caer, depositarse
dust settled on the shelves el polvo se depositó en los estantes

▶ **settle down**
1. acomodarse
* *Let me settle down in my armchair and read me Abdullah's letter...* Déjeme acomodarme en mi sillón y léame la carta de Abdallah... *

2. instalarse, establecerse

seven

seven
['sevn]
I. *adj*
siete

II. *n*
siete *m*

▶ **seventeen**
[sev(ə)n'ti:n]
I. *adj*
diecisiete

II. *n*
diecisiete *m*

▶ **seventy**
['sev(ə)ntɪ]
I. *adj*
setenta

seventy-one setenta y uno

II. *n*
pl seventies
setenta *m*

the seventies los años setenta

several

several
['sev(ə)rəl] *adj & pron*
varios, as

* *Abdullah, I've told you several times not to do that!...* ¡Abdallah, te he dicho varias veces que no hagas eso!...
Waaah! Waaah! ¡Uaaah! ¡Uaaah! *

severe

severe
[sɪ'vɪəʳ] *adj*
1. severo, a

a severe punishment un severo castigo

2. grave
* *I must have a very severe illness.* Debo de tener una enfermedad muy grave.
No, you are seasick... No, estás mareado... *

...severe

sew

sew
[səu] *v t*
sewed, sewn [səun]
coser

shadow

shadow
['ʃædəu] *n*
sombra *f*

I saw his shadow on the wall vi su sombra en la pared

shake

shake
[ʃeɪk]
shook [ʃuk],
shaken [ʃeɪkn]
I. *v t*
1. sacudir, agitar

shake well before use agítese bien antes de usar

2. Idiom
to shake hands darse la mano

* *Let's forget it and shake hands!* ¡Olvidémoslo y démonos la mano!

...shake

Okay! ¡De acuerdo! *

II. *v i*
temblar

he was shaking with cold estaba temblando de frío

shall

shall
[ʃæl] *v aux*
forma negativa **shan't**

...shall

[ʃɑːnt]
1. *(para formar el futuro)*

I shall tell you tomorrow te lo diré mañana

we shan't go with you no iremos con ustedes

2. *(para hacer sugerencias)*
shall we play chess? ¿jugamos al ajedrez?

shame

shame
[ʃeɪm] *n*
1. verguenza *f*

2. Idiom
* *Shame on you!... I wonder whether you'll ever be sensible...* ¡Debería darte verguenza!... Me pregunto si alguna vez serás razonable... *

3. pena *f*
what a shame! ¡qué pena!

shan't

shan't → SHALL

shape

shape
[ʃeɪp]
I. *n*
forma *f*

II. *v t*
dar forma, moldear

share

share
[ʃeəʳ]
I. *v t*
compartir

▶ **share (out)**
repartir, distribuir

share the sweets between you repartid los caramelos entre vosotros

II. *n*
parte *f*

sharp

sharp
[ʃɑːp] *adj*
1. afilado, a

the knife was very sharp el cuchillo estaba muy afilado

2. brusco, a, repentino, a
a sharp turn to the left un giro repentino hacia la izquierda

3. agudo, a
a sharp pain un dolor agudo

4. Idiom
* *Look sharp, Snowy...* Date prisa, Milú... *

she

she
[ʃiː] *pron*
1. ella

2. *not translated*
she works as a translator trabaja de traductora

sheep ...sheet

sheep
[ʃiːp] *n inv*
oveja *f*

sheet

sheet
[ʃiːt] *n*
1. sábana *f*

2. hoja *f*
* *What's written on this sheet of paper?* ¿Qué hay escrito en esta hoja de papel? *

shelf

shelf
[ʃelf] *n*
pl shelves [ʃelvz]
estantería *f*

shell

shell
[ʃel] *n*
1. cáscara *f*

egg shell cáscara de huevo

2. concha *f*
* *Let's go and gather shells on the beach...* Vamos a recoger conchas en la playa... *

▶ **shellfish** *n*
[ˈʃelfɪʃ]
marisco *m*

shelter

shelter
[ˈʃeltəʳ]
I. n
resguardo m

to take shelter poner-se a resguardo

II. v i & v t
resguardar, proteger

the trees sheltered the house from the wind los arboles protegian la casa del viento

shine

shine
[ʃaɪn] v i
shone, shone [ʃɒn]
brillar

* *Look, something's shining over there! Can't you see? It's straight ahead of us.* ¡Mire, algo está brillando por allí! ¿No lo ve? Está justo delante de nosotros. *

ship

ship
[ʃɪp] n
barco m

a merchant ship un barco mercante

shirt

shirt
[ʃɜːt] n
camisa f

shock

shock
[ʃɒk] n
1. susto m

2. choque m

3. sacudida f (eléctrica), calambre m
* *Look out! An electric ray!* ¡Vigila! ¡Un torpedo!
Oh! He's got an electric shock from the fish!... ¡Oh! ¡Ha recibido una sacudida eléctrica del pez!... *

...shock

shoe

shoe
[ʃuː] n
zapato m

these shoes are not my size estos zapatos no son de mi talla

shoot

shoot
[ʃuːt]
shot, shot [ʃɒt]
I. v i
disparar

* *Hands up!... Don't move!... Don't try to escape or I'll shoot!...* ¡Manos arriba!... ¡No se muevan!... ¡No traten de escapar o dispararé! *

II. v t
1. disparar

...shoot

he shot three rabbits disparó a tres conejos

he was shot in the arm le dispararon en el brazo

2. lanzar
the rocket was shot to the moon el cohete fue lanzado a la luna

shop

shop
[ʃɒp] n
1. tienda f, almacén m

2. Idiom
baker's shop panadería

▶ **shopkeeper**
[ˈʃɒpkiːpəʳ] n
tendero, a

* *Good gracious, that shopkeeper (Am: storekeeper) is*

...shop

Senhor Oliveira da Figueira! ¡Caramba, ese tendero es el Señor de Oliveira! *

▶ **shopping**
['ʃɒpɪŋ] *n*
compra *f*

to go shopping ir de compras

shore

shore
[ʃɔːʳ] *n*
1. costa *f*

2. playa *f*

3. orilla *f*
the ship went on shore el barco atracó en la orilla

short

short
[ʃɔːt] *adj*
1. corto, a

a short letter una carta corta

2. bajo, a
he's rather short es bastante bajo

3. Idiom
a short cut un atajo

she's short of money le falta dinero

Bill is short for William Bill es el diminutivo de William

▶ **shorts**
[ʃɔːts] *n pl*
pantalón *m* corto

he always wears shorts siempre lleva pantalón corto

shot

shot
[ʃɒt] *n*
1. disparo *m*

* *I heard shots!...* ¡He oído disparos!... *

2. fotografía *f*
all these shots are very good todas estas fotografías son muy buenas

...shot

should

should
[ʃud] *v aux*
1. deber
(condicional)

* *You shouldn't drink so much, Captain!* ¡No debería beber tanto, capitán! *Boohoo... Boo... hoo... hoo... Booh... hoo... Boo.. hoo...* Buaaa... Buu.. aa... aa... Buu... aa... Buu... aa... *

2. *(para formar el condicional)*

I should like to go to Venice me gustaría ir a Venecia

shoulder

shoulder
['ʃəuldəʳ] *n*
hombro *m*

shout

shout
[ʃaut]
I. *v i*
gritar

don't shout, I'm not deaf no grite, no estoy sordo

II. *n*
grito *m*

show

show
[ʃəu]
I. *n*
1. espectáculo *m*

the show will be on until Sunday el espectáculo se representará hasta el domingo

2. exposición *f*
a car show una exposición de coches

II. *v t*
showed, shown [ʃəun]
enseñar, mostrar

* *Again! This is the third check! We have to show our passports again...* ¡Otra vez! ¡Éste es el tercer control! Tenemos que enseñar nuestros pasaportes de nuevo... *

I'll show you the way voy a enseñarles el camino

▶ **show off**
presumir

...show

▶ **show up**
1. presentarse, aparecer, venir

she didn't show up at the party no se presentó a la fiesta

2. verse, destacarse
the cat's eyes showed up in the dark los ojos del gato se veían en la oscuridad

shower

shower
[ˈʃauər] *n*
1. chubasco *m*, chaparrón *m*

* *Ugh, there's going to be a shower! We must take cover... Come along...* ¡Uf, va a caer un chubasco! Debemos refugiarnos... Venga conmigo... *You're right, Chang...* Tienes razón, Tchang... *

2. ducha *f*

to have a shower tomar/darse una ducha

shut

shut
[ʃʌt]
I. *adj*
cerrado, a

the shops are shut las tiendas están cerradas

...shut

II. *v t*
shut, shut
cerrar

* *And don't forget to shut the doors!* ¡Y no se olviden de cerrar las puertas! *

III. *v i*
cerrarse

the chemist doesn't shut today la farmacia no cierra hoy

...shut

this case won't shut no se puede cerrar esta maleta

▶ **shut up**
callarse

shut up, we can't hear Tintin! ¡cállense, no podemos oír a Tintín!

sick

sick
[sɪk] *adj*
1. enfermo, a

he's sick in bed está enfermo en la cama

2. mareado, a
to be sick estar mareado

3. harto, a
I'm sick of Abdullah's tricks estoy harto de las bromas de Abdallah

side

...side

side
[saɪd] *n*
1. lado *m*

* *There!... I'm on the other side of the river!...* ¡Ya está!... ¡Estoy al otro lado del río!... *

whose side are you on? ¿de qué lado estás?

lie on your side estírate de lado

the other side of the street el otro lado de la calle

2. equipo *m*
our side has won nuestro equipo ha ganado

▶ **side road** *n*
calle *f* secundaria

▶ **sidewalk** (*Am*)
→ PAVEMENT

sight

sight
[saɪt] *n*
1. vista *f*

she has good (eye) sight tiene buena vista

2. espectáculo *m*
it was a sad sight era un triste espectáculo

3. Idiom
to see the sights/to go sightseeing visitar los monumentos

he disappeared

from sight desapareció de la vista

sign

sign
[saɪn]
I. *n*
1. señal *f*, seña *f*

* *Why are they making signs? What's happening?* ¿Por qué

...sign

...sign

están haciendo señales? ¿Qué ocurre? *

2. indicación *f*, señal *f*, cartel *m*
follow the sign siga la señal

* *The Thompsons didn't see the sign!...* ¡Hernández y Fernández no vieron el cartel!... *

3. signo *m*, indicio *m*
his words were a sign of good will sus

The Thompsons didn't see the sign!...

palabras fueron un signo de buena voluntad

II. *v i & v t*
firmar

sign here, please firme aquí, por favor

silence

silence
['saɪləns] *n*
silencio *m*

...silence

What a strange place... No trees, no life... Nothing that might disturb the silence...

...silence

* *What a strange place... No trees, no life... Nothing that might disturb the silence...* Qué lugar más extraño... No hay árboles, no hay vida... Nada que pueda romper el silencio... *

▶**silent**
['saɪlənt] *adj*
1. silencioso, a

he's a silent man es un hombre silencioso

2. Idiom
keep silent about this matter guarda silencio respecto a este asunto

silly

silly
['sɪlɪ] *adj*
sillier, silliest
tonto, a

don't be silly! ¡no seas tonto!

similar

similar
['sɪmɪləʳ] *adj*
parecido, a, similar

simple

simple
['sɪmp(ə)l] *adj*
1. fácil, simple

* *Come on, Thompson, you can do it, it's simple!* ¡Va-

...simple

Come on, Thompson, you can do it, it's simple!

mos, Fernández, puede hacerlo, es fácil! *

2. sencillo, a
they lead a very simple life llevan una vida muy sencilla

▶**simply**
['sɪmplɪ] *adv*
1. simplemente, sencillamente

2. absolutamente
the food was simply delicious la comida fue absolutamente deliciosa

since

since
[sɪns]
I. *prep*
desde

she has been living in Venice since 1985 vive en Venecia desde 1985

II. *conj*
1. desde que

we have missed her since she left la hemos echado de menos desde que se fue

2. puesto que
since you are tired, I'll do the work puesto que estás cansado, yo haré el trabajo

sing

sing
[sɪŋ] *v i & v t*
sang [sæŋ], sung [sʌŋ]
cantar

...sing

WOW-OW

wow-ow - wow-ow - ow-wowww!

Snowy is singing with Signora Castafiore...

S

...sing

* Wow - ow - wow - ow - ow - wowww! ¡Gua - uu - gua - uu - uu - guauuu!
Snowy is singing with Signora Castafiore... Milú está cantando con la Castafiore... *

▶ **singer**
['sɪŋəʳ] *n*
cantante *m f*

a rock singer un cantante de rock

single

single
['sɪŋg(ə)l] *adj*
1. solo, a

there wasn't a single mistake no había ni un solo error

2. de ida
a single (Am: one way) ticket un billete de ida

3. individual
a single room/bed una habitación/cama individual

4. soltero, a
are you married or single? ¿es usted casado o soltero?

sink

sink
[sɪŋk]
I. *n*
1. fregadero *m (in the kitchen)*

...sink

put the dish in the sink pon el plato en el fregadero

2. lavabo *m (in the bathroom)*

II. *vi & vt*
sank [sæŋk],
sunk [sʌŋk]
hundir(se)

* *The boat is sinking!...* ¡El barco se está hundiendo!... *

The boat is sinking!...

sir

sir
[sɜːʳ] *n*
1. señor *m*

what would you like, sir? ¿qué desea, señor?

2. sir *m*
Sir John White sir John White

3. Idiom
Dear Sir... Muy Señor mío...

sister

sister
['sɪstəʳ] *n*
hermana *f*

my sister's name is Carolina el nombre de mi hermana es Carolina

sit

sit
[sɪt] *vi & vt*
sat, sat [sæt]
1. sentar(se)

she was sitting by the fire estaba sentada al lado del fuego

2. Idiom
to sit (for) an examination hacer un examen

▶ **sit down**
sentarse

Please sit down, Colonel!

* *Please sit down, Colonel!* ¡Por favor, siéntese, coronel! *

▶ **sitting room**
['sɪtɪŋ'ruːm] *n*
(*Am:* **living room**)
sala *f* de estar, salón *m*

six

six
[sɪks]
I. *adj*
seis

he is six tiene seis años

II. *n*
seis *m*

▶ **sixteen**
[sɪks'tiːn]
I. *adj*
dieciséis

II. *n*
dieciséis *m*

▶ **sixty**
['sɪkstɪ]
I. *adj*
sesenta

II. *n*
pl sixties
sesenta

in the sixties en los años sesenta

size

size
[saɪz] *n*
1. tamaño *m*

it's the size of an elephant es del tamaño de un elefante

2. talla *f*
* *You're dressed now!...* ¡Ya está vestido!...
I've got a space suit too, but I don't think it's my size... Yo también tengo un traje

You're dressed now!...
I've got a space suit too, but I don't think it's my size ...

espacial, pero no creo que sea de mi talla... *

3. número *m*
I take size nine uso el número nueve

skate

skate
[skeɪt] n
patín m

ice/roller skate patín
de cuchilla/ruedas

ski

ski
[ski:]
I. n
esquí m

...ski

II. v i
1. esquiar

she's learning to ski
está aprendiendo a es-
quiar

water skiing esquí
acuático

2. Idiom
to go skiing ir a esquiar

:

skin

skin
[skɪn] n
piel f

* Tintin is coming
on that boat... You'll
see, his skin isn't
black like ours...
Tintín viene en ese
barco... Ya verás, su piel
no es negra como la
nuestra... *

skirt

skirt
[skɜːt] n
falda f

sky

sky
[skaɪ] n
pl skies
cielo m

* The sky is lovely.
El cielo es hermoso. *

sky

sleep

sleep
[sli:p]
I. n
1. sueño m

I was woken from a
deep sleep me desper-
taron de un profundo sueño

...sleep

2. Idiom
* Captain! ¡Capitán!
I think I'll have a
little sleep! ¡Creo que
voy a echar una cabe-
zadita! *

II. v i
slept, slept [slept]
dormir

he sleeps like a log
duerme como un tronco

slice

slice
[slaɪs] n
rebanada f (of bread),
tajada f (of meat),
lonja f (of ham)

slide

slide
[slaɪd]
I. n
1. tobogán m

...slide

he fell off the slide se
cayó del tobogán

2. diapositiva f
I have slides of our
trip tengo diapositivas de
nuestro viaje

II. v i
slid, slid [slɪd]
resbalar,
deslizarse,
escurrirse

the sledge slid on
the snow el trineo se
escurrió en la nieve

slight

slight
[slaɪt] adj
pequeño, a,
ligero, a, leve

we have a slight
problem tenemos un
pequeño problema

slip

slip
[slɪp] v i
slipped, slipped
1. resbalar

I slipped on the ice
resbalé en el hielo

2. Idiom
* The vase slipped
out of my hands!...
¡El jarro se me ha esca-
pado de las manos!... *

slope

slope
[sləʊp] n
inclinación f,
pendiente f

a mountain slope
la pendiente de una
montaña

slow

slow
[sləʊ] *adj*
1. lento, a

this car is very slow este coche es muy lento

2. Idiom
my watch is five minutes slow mi reloj va cinco minutos atrasado

▶ **slowly**
['sləʊlɪ] *adv*
lentamente, despacio

* *Drive more slowly, Tintin, you're going to kill us!...* ¡Conduce más despacio, Tintín, vas a matarnos!... *

small

small
[smɔːl] *adj*
pequeño, a

* *The submarine is really small!...* ¡El submarino es realmente pequeño!... *

...small

The submarine is really small!...

smell

smell
[smel]
I. *n*
1. olor *m*

a nice smell un olor agradable

2. Idiom
there's a smell of burning huele a quemado

II. *v t*
smelt, smelt [smelt]
oler

* *Captain, can you smell anything?* Capitán, ¿no huele nada? *Sniff... Sniff...* Sniff... Sniff...
Yes... there's a smell of burning in here... Sí... aquí huele a quemado...
Where is it coming from? ¿De dónde viene? *

III. *v i*
oler
how good you smell! ¡qué bien hueles!

it smells of fish huele a pescado

smile

smile
[smaɪl]
I. *v i*
sonreír

she smiled at me me sonrió

...smile

I'm so happy to see a smile on your face again...

II. *n*
sonrisa *f*

* *I'm so happy to see a smile on your face again...* Estoy tan contento de ver de nuevo una sonrisa en tu cara... *

smoke

smoke
[sməʊk]
I. *v i & v t*
fumar

the Captain smokes a pipe el capitán fuma en pipa

II. *n*
humo *m*

* *What's that smoke over there?* ¿Qué es ese humo de ahí?
It's a fire! ¡Es un incendio! *

What's that smoke over there?
It's a fire!

smooth

smooth
[smuːð] *adj*
liso, a, suave

▶ **smoothly**
['smuːðlɪ] *adv*
sin problema

snack

snack
[snæk] *n*
merienda *f*, bocado *m*

...snack

I had a snack five minutes ago tomé un bocado hace cinco minutos

snake

What's this snake doing ?

snake
[sneɪk] *n*
culebra *f*,
serpiente *f*

* *What's this snake doing?* ¿Qué está haciendo esta culebra? *

sneeze

sneeze
[sniːz] *v i*
estornudar

* *Atchooo!* ¡Atchuuus!
He's sneezing! ¡Está
estornudando! *

snow

snow
[snəu]
I. *v i*
nevar

...snow

ATCHOOO

He's sneezing !

* *Oh! It's snowing again!* ¡Oh! ¡Está nevando otra vez! *

II. *n*
nieve *f*

► **snowball**
['snəubɔːl] *n*
bola *f* de nieve

► **snowman**
['snəumæn] *n*
pl snowmen ['snəumen]
muñeco *m* de nieve

...snow

Oh! It's snowing again !

so

so
[səu] *adv*
1. tan

it's so funny I can't stop laughing es tan divertido que no puedo parar de reír

2. también
I love the theatre – so do I me encanta el teatro – a mí también

3. eso, que sí
has the Captain arrived? – I think so
¿ha llegado el capitán? – eso creo/creo que sí

* *Do you think it's this way?* ¿Crees que es por ahí?
I hope so!... ¡Espero que sí!... *

4. así
the so called... el así llamado...

5. Idiom
so far hasta ahora

so long! ¡hasta la vista!

Do you think it's this way?

I hope so !...

and so forth/and so on etcétera...

► **so that**
conj
para que,
de modo que

soap

soap
[səup] *n*
jabón *m*

soccer

soccer
[sɒkəʳ] *n*
fútbol *m*

► **soccer field**
campo *m* de fútbol

► **soccer ball**
balón *m* de fútbol

sock

sock
[sɒk] *n*
calcetín *m*

soft

soft
[sɒft] *adj*
blando, a, suave

► **softly**
['sɒftlɪ] *adv*
suavemente

soldier

soldier
['səuldʒeʳ] *n*
soldado *m*,
militar *m*

...soldier

a lead soldier un soldado de plomo

some

some
[sʌm]
I. *adj*
1. algún, alguna, algunos, algunas, unos, unas

I need some chairs

...some

necesito algunas sillas

2. un poco de
do you want some wine? ¿quiere un poco de vino?

II. *pron*
algunos, algunas, unos, unas

I have a lot of sweets – give me some tengo muchos caramelos – dame algunos

some of you already

know the plan algunos de ustedes ya conocen el plan

► **somebody, someone**
['sʌmbɒdɪ],
['sʌmwʌn] *pron*
alguien

somebody has to do it alguien tiene que hacerlo

* *Listen, the noise is getting nearer...*

...some

Listen, the noise is getting nearer... Somebody's coming!...

Somebody's coming!... Escuche, el ruido se acerca... ¡Alguien viene!... *

▶ **something**
['sʌmθɪŋ]
alguna cosa, algo

there's something strange hay algo raro

▶ **sometimes**
['sʌmtaɪmz]
algunas veces,

It's true, I'm sometimes absent-minded, but it's rare!

a veces

* *It's true, I'm sometimes absent-minded, but it's rare!* ¡Es verdad, a veces estoy despistado, pero es raro! *

▶ **somewhere**
['sʌmweəʳ]
1. algún sitio, alguna parte

* *I've seen that face somewhere before... It's Müller!...* ¡Esta cara

I've seen that face somewhere before... It's Müller!...

...some

la he visto antes en alguna parte... Es Müller!... *

2. Idiom
somewhere else (alguna) otra parte

son

son
[sʌn] *n*
hijo *m*

...son

And this is my son Chang Lin-Yi...

* *And this is my son Chang Lin-Yi...* Y éste es mi hijo Tchang Lin-Yi... *

song

song
[sɒŋ] *n*
canción *f*

soon

soon
[suːn] *adv*
1. pronto

* *Goodbye, Tintin!* ¡Adiós, Tintín!
Goodbye, I'll see you soon! ¡Adiós, hasta pronto! *

2. Idiom
as soon as tan pronto como, en cuanto

...soon

Goodbye, Tintin!

Goodbye, I'll see you soon!

sorry

sorry
['sɒrɪ]
I. *adj*
sorrier, sorriest
Idiom

I'm sorry to be late siento llegar tarde

I feel sorry for him siento pena por él/ me da pena

II. *interj*
1. perdón, lo siento

* *Oh! Sorry!* ¡Oh! ¡Perdón!
Wooah! ¡Guauh! *

2. Idiom
say sorry to the little boy pídele perdón al niño

Oh! Sorry!

Wooah!...

sort

sort
[sɔːt] *n*
clase *f*, tipo *m*

this sort of fish is rare esta clase de pez es poco frecuente

soul

soul
[səul] *n*
alma *f*

sound

sound
[saund]
I. *n*
1. ruido *m*

I heard a sound he oído un ruido

2. sonido *m*
the sound of a violin el sonido de un violín

II. *v t*
tocar,
hacer sonar

sound the horn! ¡toca el claxon!

* *Blistering barnacles!... A periscope!... Sound the alarm...* ¡Millones de demonios!... ¡Un periscopio!... Haga sonar la alarma... *

III. *v i*
1. sonar

2. Idiom
it sounds like a good idea parece buena idea

Blistering barnacles !... A periscope !... Sound the alarm...

soup

soup
[su:p] *n*
sopa *f*

fish soup sopa de pescado

sour

sour
[sauəʳ] *adj*
amargo, a

it tastes sour sabe amargo

south

south
[sau:θ]
I. *n*
sur *m*

the south of England el sur de Inglaterra

II. *adj*
1. del sur

the south seas los mares del sur

2. Idiom
South America Sudamérica, América del Sur

the South Pole el Polo Sur

III. *adv*
al sur, hacia el sur

* *There's an oasis 50 kilometres (Am: kilometers) south of here, in this direction...* Hay un oasis a 50 kilómetros al sur de aquí, en esta dirección... *

▶ **southern**
['sʌðən] *adj*
del sur

There's an oasis 50 kilometres south of here, in this direction...

the southern hemisphere el hemisferio del sur

souvenir

souvenir
[su:və'nɪəʳ] *n*
recuerdo *m*,
souvenir *m*

I bought a souvenir for you te he comprado un recuerdo

space

space
['speɪs] *n*
1. espacio *m*

there's too much space between the lines hay demasiado espacio entre las líneas

2. espacio *m*
* *We're floating in space... It's a good thing I'm tied!* ¡Estamos flotando en el espacio... Menos mal que estoy atado! *

We're floating in space... It's a good thing I'm tied!

spade

spade
[speɪd] *n*
pala *f*

I need a spade to dig in the garden necesito una pala para cavar en el jardín

Spain

Spain
[speɪn] *n*
España *f*

...Spain

▶ **Spanish**
['spænɪʃ] *adj & n*
español, a

spare

spare
[speəʳ]
I. *adj*
1. de recambio, de repuesto

a spare wheel

...spare

una rueda de recambio

2. sobrante

3. Idiom
spare time tiempo libre

II. *v t*
Idiom

have you got any sugar you can spare me? ¿tiene algo de azúcar que me pueda dejar?

speak

speak
[spi:k] *v i*
spoke [spəuk],
spoken [spəuk(ə)n]
hablar

he speaks Italian
habla italiano

▶ **speak up**
hablar más fuerte

* *I'm asking your name...* Le estoy preguntando su nombre...
Speak up, I can't

hear you...! ¡Hable más fuerte, no le oigo! *

special

special
['speʃ(ə)l] *adj*
especial

* *You need a special permit to enter here. Have you got one?* Necesita un permiso especial para entrar aquí. ¿Tiene uno? *

...special

spectacles

spectacles
['spektək(ə)lz] *n pl*
gafas *f pl*

I can't see very well without my spectacles (Am: eyeglasses) no veo muy bien sin mis gafas

speech

speech
[spi:tʃ] *n*
discurso *m*

...speech

* *Attention, please!... Mr Baxter is about to make a short speech!...* ¡Atención, por favor!... ¡El señor Baxter va a pronunciar un breve discurso!... *

speed

speed
[spi:d] *n*
velocidad *f*

...speed

...speed

* *The train is gathering speed, why doesn't Tintin jump out now?* El tren está cogiendo velocidad. ¿Por qué no salta ahora Tintín? *

spell

spell
[spel] *v t*
spelt, spelt [spelt]
1. deletrear

...spell

can you spell your name, please? ¿puede deletrearme su nombre, por favor?

2. escribir
how do you spell that name? ¿cómo se escribe ese nombre?

▶ **spelling**
['spelɪŋ]
ortografía *f*

spelling mistakes
faltas de ortografía

spend

spend
[spend] *v t*
spent, spent [spent]
1. gastar

she spends a lot of money gasta mucho dinero

2. pasar
I've spent a lot of time preparing this plan he pasado mucho tiempo preparando este plan

spider

spider
['spaɪdə'] *n*
araña *f*

* *It's a spider...* Es una araña... *

It's a spider...

spill

spill
[spɪl] v t
spilt, spilt [spɪlt]
tirar, derramar

don't spill the tea no tires el té

spite

spite
[spaɪt] n
Idiom

...spite

in spite of a pesar de

* *We must go on in spite of the snow...* Debemos seguir a pesar de la nieve... *

We must go on in spite of the snow...

spoil

spoil
[spɔɪl] v t
spoilt, spoilt [spɔɪlt]
1. estropear, echar a perder

don't spoil our plans no estropees nuestros planes

she has spoilt her dress ha echado a perder su vestido

2. mimar
a spoilt child un niño mimado

sponge

sponge
[spʌndʒ] n
esponja f

spoon

spoon
[spuːn] n
cuchara f

a silver spoon una cuchara de plata

sport

sport
[spɔːt] n
deporte m

* *The Captain has always done a lot of sport, that's why he can walk so fast!* ¡El capitán siempre ha hecho mucho deporte, por eso puede caminar tan rápido! *

▶ **sports car** n
coche m deportivo

The Captain has always done a lot of sport, that's why he can walk so fast!

▶ **sportsman**
['spɔːtsmən] n
pl sportsmen
deportista m

▶ **sportswoman**
['spɔːtswumən] n
pl sportswomen
deportista f

spot

This is the spot where the plane crashed...

...spot

spot
[spɒt] n
1. sitio m, lugar m

* *This is the spot where the plane crashed...* Este es el lugar donde el avión se estrelló... *

2. gota f
a spot of rain una gota de lluvia

3. mancha f
you've got a spot of

ink on your shirt tienes una mancha de tinta en la camisa

4. lunar m
a dress with blue spots un vestido con lunares azules

5. grano (on the body)

spread

spread
[spred]
spread, spread
I. v t
1. extender

the eagle spread its wings el águila extendió las alas

2. poner
spread some butter on the toast pon mantequilla en la tostada

II. v i
difundirse

the news spread fast las noticias se difundieron rápidamente

spring

spring
[sprɪŋ] n
1. primavera f

we're going on holiday in spring vamos de vacaciones en la primavera

...spring

2. muelle m, resorte m
a spring broke se rompió un muelle

3. manantial m, fuente f (of water)

square

square
[skweəʳ]
I. adj
cuadrado, a

...square

a square table una mesa cuadrada

II. *n*

1. cuadro *m (figure)*

2. plaza *f*
Leicester square la plaza Leicester

staff

staff
[stɑːf] *n*
personal *m*

...staff

our company needs more staff nuestra compañía necesita más personal

stage

stage
[steɪdʒ] *n*
escenario *m*

a wooden stage un escenario de madera

stairs

Here are your keys, your room is up the stairs...

stairs
[steəz] *n*
1. escalera(s) *f (pl)*

2. Idiom
* *Here are your keys, your room is up the stairs...* Aquí están sus llaves. Su habitación está arriba... *

▶ **staircase**
['steəkeɪs] *n*
escalera *f*

stamp

stamp
[stæmp] *n*
sello *m*

I bought stamps at the post office compré sellos en Correos

stand

stand
[stænd]
stood, stood [stud]
I. *v i*

...stand

estar de pie, tenerse de pie

he was standing by the door estaba de pie al lado de la puerta

II. *v t*

1. colocar, poner

stand the book on the shelf coloca el libro en la estantería

2. soportar

he's always shouting; I can't stand him siempre está gritando; no puedo soportarlo

▶ **stand up**
1. levantarse

stand up, please levántese, por favor

2. Idiom
stand up straight! ¡ponte derecho!

star

star
[stɑːʳ] *n*
1. estrella *f*

* *There are no clouds, you can see the stars! How lovely!...* ¡No hay nubes; se pueden ver las estrellas! ¡Qué hermoso!... *

2. estrella *f*
he's a film (Am: movie) star es una estrella de cine

There are no clouds, you can see the stars! How lovely!...

stare

stare
[steəʳ] *v i*
mirar fijamente

don't stare at me like that! ¡no me mires así fijamente!

start

start
[stɑːt]
I. *n*

...start

1. comienzo *m*, principio *m*

that's a good start es un buen comienzo

2. susto *m*, sobresalto *m*

II. *v i*
1. empezar, comenzar

the play has already started la obra ya ha comenzado

2. arrancar, ponerse en marcha
the car won't start el coche no arranca

III. *v t*
1. empezar, comenzar

to start a new life empezar una nueva vida

2. poner en marcha
start the engines! ¡ponga en marcha los motores!

▶ **start out**
partir, salir

they started out on a journey two days ago salieron de viaje hace dos días

state

state
[steɪt]
I. *n*

...state

1. estado *m*

the house was in a very good state la casa estaba en muy buen estado

2. Estado *m*
the United States of America los Estados Unidos de América

head of state jefe de Estado

II. *v t*
decir, declarar,

...state

afirmar

he stated that he hadn't seen anything declaró que no había visto nada

station

station

['steɪʃ(ə)n] *n*
estación *f*

we'll meet at the station nos encon-

...station

traremos en la estación

bus station estación de autobuses

stay

stay

[steɪ]
I. *n*
estancia *f*

she enjoyed her stay in London disfrutó de su estancia en Londres

...stay

II. *v i*
1. quedarse, permanecer

* How long are you staying in this country? ¿Cuánto tiempo se quedarán en este país? *Only a few days, why?* Sólo unos días. ¿Por qué? *

2. alojarse
I'm staying at the Hotel Royal me alojo en el Hotel Royal

▶ **stay in**
quedarse en casa

he's staying in, but we can go out él se queda en casa, pero nosotros podemos salir

▶ **stay out**
quedarse fuera, no entrar

you go in; I'll stay out entra tú; yo me quedaré fuera

steak

steak

[steɪk] *n*
bistec *m*

I'd like my steak rare, please querría el bistec poco hecho, por favor

steal

steal

[stiːl] *v t*
stole [stəʊl], stolen [stəʊl(ə)n]
robar

he stole her jewels robó sus joyas

* The magpie... ¡La urraca...
...it has... ...ha...
...stolen the key!... ...robado la llave!... *

steam

steam

[stiːm] *n*
vapor *m*

* A steam engine... Una máquina de vapor... *

steel

steel

[stiːl] *n*
acero *m*

A steam engine ...

steep

steep

[stiːp]
I. *adj*
empinado, a

* It's a steep climb! ¡Es una subida empinada! *

II. *v i & v t*
empapar, remojar

steep the onions in vinegar remoja las cebollas en vinagre

step

step
[step]
I. n
1. escalón m

the step is broken el escalón está roto

2. paso m
don't move, one step and I'll fire! ¡no se mueva, un paso y disparo!

step by step paso a paso

3. medida f
what steps have to be taken? ¿qué medidas deben tomarse?

II. v i
stepped, stepped
dar un paso, pisar

▶ **step back**
retroceder

stick

stick
[stɪk]
I. n
1. palo m

get that stick, Snowy! ¡coge ese palo, Milú!

2. bastón m
he walked with a stick caminaba con bastón

II. v t
stuck, stuck [stʌk]
1. pegar

stick the stamp on the envelope pega el sello en el sobre

2. clavar, hundir
the animal stuck its claws in its prey el animal clavó las uñas en su presa

3. meter
stick it in the cupboard métele en el armario

III. v i
atrancarse, bloquearse

the door has (got) stuck la puerta se ha atrancado

▶ **sticking plaster**
[stɪkɪŋ'plaːtər] n
(*Am*: **band-aid**)
tirita f,
esparadrapo m

▶ **stuck**
[stʌk] adj
atascado, a,
atrancado, a,
bloqueado, a

still

still
[stɪl]
I. adv
1. aún, todavía

she's still working todavía está trabajando

I'll phone the Captain, or better still I'll go and see him telefonearé al capitán, o mejor aún lo iré a ver

2. aún así,
a pesar de ello

It might be dangerous, but I'll still do it!

* *It might be dangerous, but I'll still do it!* ¡Puede ser peligroso, pero aún así lo haré! *

II. adj
tranquilo, a,
quieto, a

the night was very still la noche era muy tranquila

stir

stir
[stɜːʳ] v t
stirred, stirred
remover

stir the soup remueve la sopa

stocking

stocking
['stɒkɪŋ] n
media f

a pair of stockings un par de medias

stomach

stomach
['stʌmək] n
estómago m

I've got stomach ache tengo dolor de estómago

stone

stone
[stəun] n
piedra f

...stone

The Captain is throwing stones into the water!...
Hello!
SPLASH

* *The Captain is throwing stones into the water!...* ¡El capitán está tirando piedras al agua!...
Hello! ¡Hola! *

the Stone Age la edad de piedra

▶ **stone** n inv
6, 35 kg

he weighs 11 stone pesa 70 kilos

stop

stop
[stɒp]
I. n
1. parada f

a bus stop una parada de autobús

2. Idiom
full stop punto final

to put a stop to something poner término a algo

II. v i
stopped, stopped
parar(se),
detener(se)

stop at the traffic lights para en el semáforo

my watch has stopped mi reloj se ha parado

III. v t
1. parar, detener

* *Hey you!...* ¡Eh usted!...
Stop that man! ¡Detengan a ese hombre!

...stop

Hey you!...

Stop that man!

What's happening?

What's happening?
¿Qué ocurre? *

2. dejar de
he should stop smoking debería dejar de fumar

store

store
[stɔːʳ] *n*
1. reserva *f*, provisión *m*

...store

we'll need a good store of food necesitaremos una buena provisión de comida

2. tienda *f*, almacén *m*

▶ **storehouse**
['stɔːhaus] *n*
almacén *m*, depósito *m*

storm

storm
[stɔːm] *n*
tormenta *f*, tempestad *f*

a sand storm! ¡una tormenta de arena!

* *They're going back to avoid the storm...* Vuelven para escapar de la tormenta... *

a storm lashed down on our ship una tormenta/tempestad azotó nuestro barco

...storm

They're going back to avoid the storm...

story

story
['stɔːrɪ] *n*
pl stories
historia *f*

he's always telling funny stories siempre cuenta historias divertidas

stove

stove
[stəuv] (*Am*)
→ COOKER

straight

straight
[streɪt]
I. *adj*
derecho, a, recto, a

draw a straight line dibuja una línea recta

II. *adv*
1. directamente

he went straight to school fue directamente al colegio

2. Idiom
straight on todo recto

Where shall I go?

Go straight on until you come to the village!

...straight

* *Where shall I go?*
¿Adónde voy?
Go straight on until you come to the village! ¡Vaya todo recto hasta llegar al pueblo! *

straight away ahora mismo

strange

strange
[streɪndʒ] *adj*
1. extraño, a

* *What strange people!* ¡Qué gente tan extraña! *

2. desconocido, a
we are lost in a strange country estamos perdidos en un país desconocido

▶ **stranger**
['streɪndʒəʳ] *n*

What strange people!

desconocido, a

she told him not to talk to strangers le dijo que no hablara con desconocidos

S

strawberry

strawberry
['strɔːbərɪ] n
pl strawberries
fresa f

a strawberry ice-cream un helado de fresa

street

street
[striːt] n
calle f

strenght

strength
[streŋθ] n
fuerza f

* *Here they come. Tintin seems to have no strength left. The Captain is having to carry him...* Ahí llegan. A Tintín parece que no le quedan fuerzas. El capitán tiene que llevarlo... *

Here they come. Tintin seems to have no strength left. The Captain is having to carry him...

strike

strike
[straɪk]
I. v t
struck, struck [strʌk]
1. golpear

they struck him on the head le golpearon en la cabeza

2. encender
strike a match enciende una cerilla

3. dar (la hora)
* *The clock has just struck 8, I'm late!...*

The clock has just struck 8, I'm late!...

...strike

¡El reloj acaba de dar las ocho, llego tarde! *

II. v i
hacer huelga

the workmen are threatening to strike los trabajadores amenazan con hacer huelga

III. n
huelga f

to go on strike declararse en huelga, ir a la huelga

string

string
[strɪŋ] n
1. cordel m, cuerda f

she tied up the box with a string ató la caja con un cordel

2. cuerda f
(of an instrument)
a guitar string una cuerda de guitarra

strong

strong
[strɒŋ] adj
fuerte

the Captain is strong el capitán es fuerte

the coffee is too strong el café está demasiado fuerte

stubborn

stubborn
['stʌbən] adj
tozudo, a,
terco, a

study

study
['stʌdɪ] v t
studied, studied ['stʌdid]
estudiar

she's studying Italian estudia italiano

...study

► **student**
['stjuːd(ə)nt] n
estudiante m f

he's a biology student es un estudiante de biología

stupid

stupid
['stjuːpɪd] adj
estúpido, a

...stupid

Don't be stupid, Thompson, maybe it's not a mirage!...

* *Don't be stupid, Thompson, maybe it's not a mirage!...* ¡No seas estúpido, Fernández, quizás no sea un espejismo!... *

subject

subject
['sʌbdʒekt] n
1. sujeto m

...subject

the subject of the sentence el sujeto de la frase

2. asignatura f
how many subjects have you got? ¿cuántas asignaturas tienes?

3. tema m
let's change the subject cambiemos de tema

4. súbdito, a
he's a British subject es un súbdito británico

suburb

suburb(s)
['sʌbɜːb(s)] n
afueras f pl

in the suburbs en las afueras

subway

subway *(Am)*
→ UNDERGROUND

succeed

succeed
[sək'siːd] *v i*
1. triunfar, tener éxito

he succeeded in his enterprise tuvo éxito en su empresa

2. Idiom
* *We've succeeded!... The "Unicorn" is here!...* ¡Lo hemos conseguido!... ¡El "Unicornio" está aquí!... *

▶ **success**
[sək'ses] *n*
éxito *m*

the play was a great success la obra fue un gran éxito

such

such
[sʌtʃ] *adj*
1. tan

...such

I've never seen such a big fish before nunca había visto un pez tan grande

2. tal
I've never said such a thing nunca dije tal cosa

3. Idiom
such as como

she has visited many countries, such as Italy and Holland ha visitado muchos paises, como Italia y Holanda

sudden

sudden
['sʌd(ə)n] *adj*
1. repentino, a

a sudden blow un golpe repentino

2. Idiom
all of a sudden de repente

▶ **suddenly**
['sʌd(ə)nlɪ] *adv*
repentinamente, de repente

...sudden

suddenly I saw you there de repente te vi allí

suffer

suffer
['sʌfəʳ] *v i & v t*
sufrir

you'll have to suffer the consequences tendrás que sufrir las consecuencias

sugar

sugar
['ʃugəʳ] *n*
azúcar *m*

a lump of sugar un terrón de azúcar

suggest

suggest
[sə'dʒest] *v t*
sugerir, proponer

...suggest

* *I suggest that we stop here for a short rest...* Propongo que nos paremos aquí para tomarnos un pequeño descanso... *Excellent idea!...* ¡Excelente idea!... *

▶ **suggestion**
[sə'dʒestʃ(ə)n] *n*
sugerencia *f*, proposición *m*

suit

suit
[suːt]
I. *n*
1. traje *m*

he was wearing a white suit llevaba un traje blanco

2. pleito *m* (law)

3. palo *m* (cards)

II. *v t*
1. sentarle a uno

* *Does this coat suit me?* ¿Me sienta bien este abrigo? *

2. convenir, ir bien
does this plan suit you? ¿le va bien este plan?

▶ **suitcase**
['suːtkeɪs] *n*
maleta *f*

a leather suitcase una maleta de piel

sum

sum
[sʌm]
I. *n*
1. suma *f*

this sum is wrong esta suma está mal

2. cantidad *f*, suma *f* (of money)
this will cost a large sum of money esto costará una gran cantidad de dinero

II. *v t*
1. sumar

2. Idiom
to sum up resumir

summer

summer
['sʌməʳ] *n*
verano *m*

next summer el verano que viene

summer holidays (Am: vacation) vacaciones de verano

sun

sun
[sʌn] *n*
sol *m*

▶ **sunny**
['sʌnɪ] *adj*
sunnier, sunniest
1. soleado, a

a sunny day un día soleado

2. Idiom
it's sunny hace sol

▶ **sunrise**
['sʌnraɪz] *n*
amanecer *m*

▶ **sunset**
['sʌnset] *n*
ocaso *m*, anochecer *m*, puesta *f* del sol

▶ **sunstroke**
['sʌnstrəuk] *n*
insolación *f*

Sunday

Sunday
['sʌndɪ] *n*
domingo *m*

last Sunday el domingo pasado

I'll see you on Sunday lo veré el domingo

supermarket

supermarket
['suːpəmɑːkɪt] *n*
supermercado *m*

supper

supper
['sʌpəʳ] *n*
cena *f*

supply

supply
[sə'plaɪ]
I. *n*
pl supplies
suministro *m*, provisión *f*

* *Our supply of oxygen is running low...* Nuestra provisión de oxígeno está agotándose... *

II. *v t*
supplied, supplied

proveer, abastecer, suministrar

he supplied us with food nos abasteció de comida

suppose

suppose
[sə'pəuz] *v t*
1. suponer

...suppose

* *I suppose you are Tintin...* Supongo que usted es Tintín...
Yes, I am. Sí, soy yo. *

2. Idiom
you're supposed to know this se supone que lo sabes

supposing it rains? ¿Y si llueve?

sure

sure
[ʃuəʳ] *adj*
1. seguro, a

* *I'm sure the treasure is there!* ¡Estoy seguro de que el tesoro está allí! *

2. Idiom
I feel sure about it no tengo ninguna duda

to make sure asegurarse

▶ **surely**
['ʃuəlɪ] *adv*
Idiom

surely you don't expect me to believe that? ¿no esperarás que me crea eso?

surname

surname
['sɜːneɪm] *n*
apellido *m*

how do you spell your surname? ¿cómo se escribe su apellido?

surprise

surprise
[sə'praɪz]
I. *n*
sorpresa *f*

* *Hurray! Here he is!...* ¡Hurra! ¡Aquí está!...
Captain, what a nice surprise!... ¡Capitán, qué agradable sorpresa!... *

II. *v t*
sorprender

the letter surprised him la carta lo sorprendió

...surprise

surround

surround
[sə'raund] v t
rodear

suspect

suspect
[səs'pekt] v t
sospechar

he suspected an ambush sospechaba una emboscada

...suspect

▶ **suspicious**
[səs'pɪʃəs] adj
1. sospechoso, a

he looks very suspicious su apariencia es muy sospechosa

2. desconfiado, a
* *You seem suspicious, Tintin, don't you trust him?* Parece desconfiado, Tintín. ¿No se fía de él? *I don't know!* ¡No sé! *

swallow

swallow
['swɒləu] v t
tragar

sweep

sweep
[swiːp] v t
swept, swept [swept]
barrer

I have to sweep the floor tengo que barrer el suelo

sweet

sweet
[swiːt]
I. adj
dulce

the cake was very sweet el pastel era muy dulce

II. n
caramelo m

she gave me a sweet (Am: candy) me dió un caramelo

swim

swim
[swɪm]
I. v i
swam [swæm]
swum [swʌm]
1. nadar

* *They have to swim across to the other bank.* Tienen que nadar a la otra orilla. *

2. Idiom
to go swimming ir a nadar

II. n
Idiom

to go for a swim ir a nadar

I had a swim before breakfast fui a nadar antes de desayunar

▶ **swimming pool** n
['swɪmɪŋ'puːl]
piscina f

They have to swim across to the other bank.

swing

swing
[swɪŋ]
I. v i
swung, swung
[swʌŋ]
balancearse, columpiarse

the monkey was swinging from a branch el mono se balanceaba de una rama

...swing

II. v t
mover, balancear, columpiar

he was swinging his arms to call us movía los brazos para llamarnos

III. n
columpio m

the children are playing on the swings los niños están jugando en los columpios

switch

switch
[swɪtʃ] n
interruptor m

where is the light switch? ¿dónde está el interruptor?

▶ **switch on**
encender

* *I'll switch on the radio and listen to the news...* Voy a encender la radio y escuchar las noticias... *

...switch

▶ **switch off**
apagar

switch the light off before you leave apaga la luz antes de marchar

Switzerland

Switzerland
['swɪtsələnd] n
Suiza f

▶ **Swiss**
[swɪs]
I. adj
suizo, a

II. n
the Swiss los suizos

T

table

table
['teɪb(ə)l] n
1. mesa f

please set the table
por favor, pon la mesa

2. tabla f
multiplication tables
tablas de multiplicar

tail

tail
[teɪl] n

Wooah!
Wooah!

Snowy is wagging his tail...

...tail

cola f, rabo m

Wooah! Wooah!
¡Guau! ¡Guau!
Snowy is wagging his tail... Milú está meneando la cola... *

take

take
[teɪk] v t
took [tuk],
taken ['teɪk(ə)n]

...take

1. tomar, coger

I'll take a taxi cogeré un taxi

take an aspirin toma una aspirina

2. llevar(se)
take me to the station lléveme a la estación

she took my car se llevó mi coche

3. Idiom
to take an exam

examinarse

take it as it is acéptalo como es

it took me two hours to get there tardé dos horas en llegar allí

he took a photo of the children sacó una foto de los niños

to take place ocurrir, pasar

to take advantage aprovecharse

...take

to take care cuidar

don't take any notice no hagas caso

to take for granted dar por supuesto/ sentado

▶ **take after**
parecerse a

▶ **take away**
llevar(se)

pizzas to take away (Am: to take out) pizzas para llevar

▶ **take off**
1. quitarse

take your coat off quítese el abrigo

2. despegar
* *The plane is taking off...* El avión está despegando... *

▶ **take over**
1. encargarse de

take over the busi-

The plane is taking off...

ness encárgate de los negocios

2. reemplazar, sustituir
do you want me to take over from you? ¿quieres que te reemplace/sustituya?

talk

talk
[tɔːk] *v i*
hablar

* *I'd like to talk to you in private... Is it possible?...* Me gustaría hablar con usted en privado... ¿Es posible?... *

tall

tall
[tɔːl] *adj*

...tall

1. alto, a

he's quite tall es bastante alto

* *The gorilla is taller than Tintin...* El gorila es más alto que Tintín... *

2. Idiom
how tall are you?
¿cuánto mides?

he's 6 feet tall mide 1,83 m

The gorilla is taller than Tintin...

tap

tap
[tæp] *n*
(*Am:* **faucet**)
grifo *m*

turn the tap off
cierra el grifo

tape

tape
[teɪp] *n*
1. cinta *f*

2. cinta *f* magnetofónica, cassette *f*
this song is on record and on tape esta canción está en disco y en cassete

▶ **tape recorder**
[teɪprɪˈkɔːdəʳ] *n*
magnetofón *m*,
magnetófono *m*,
(*Am:* grabadora *f*)

taste

taste
[teɪst]
I. *n*
gusto *m*, sabor *m*

a sweet taste un gusto dulce

...taste

II. *v t*
probar

taste the soup prueba la sopa

III. *v i*
tener gusto a, saber a

it tastes of apple sabe/tiene gusto a manzana

taxi

...taxi

taxi
[ˈtæksɪ] *n*
taxi *m*

* *Taxi, to the station!...* ¡Taxi, a la estación!...
Taxi! Follow that car! ¡Taxi! ¡Siga ese coche! *

tea

tea
[tiː] *n*
1. té *m*

* *Tintin is drinking tea...* Tintín está bebiendo té... *

2. merienda *f*
we have tea at half past four tomamos la merienda a las cuatro y media

Tintin is drinking tea...

▶ **teapot**
[ˈtiːpɒt] *n*
tetera *f*

▶ **teaspoon**
[ˈtiːspuːn] *n*
cucharilla *f*

▶ **teatime**
[ˈtiːtaɪm] *n*
la hora *f* del té

teach

teach
[tiːtʃ] *v t*
taught, taught [tɔːt]
enseñar

she teaches music
enseña música

I'll teach you how to drive te enseñaré a conducir

▶ **teacher**
[ˈtiːtʃəʳ] *n*
maestro, a

...teach

profesor, ora

he's a maths teacher es profesor de matemáticas

team

team
[tiːm] *n*
equipo *m*

tear

tear
[teəʳ]
tore [tɔːʳ],
torn [tɔːn]
romper, desgarrar, rasgar

he tore his shirt se rompió la camisa

▶ **tear out**
arrancar

the calendar page had been torn out la

hoja del calendario había sido arrancada

▶ **tear up**
romper (en pedazos)

* *This piece of paper has been torn up...* Esta hoja de papel ha sido rota en pedazos... *

tear

tear
[tɪəʳ] *n*
lágrima *f*

dry your tears enjúgate las lágrimas

teeth

teeth
→ TOOTH

telegram

telegram
['telɪgræm] *n*
telegrama *m*

telephone

telephone
['telɪfəun]
I. *n*
teléfono *m*

the telephone's ring-

...telephone

ing el teléfono está sonando

she's on the phone now ahora está al teléfono

are you on the telephone? ¿tiene teléfono?

II. *vi & vt*
telefonear, llamar (por teléfono)

we must telephone the police debemos llamar a la policía

* *Thank you.* Gracias. *Who's telephoning at this time?* ¿Quién llama a estas horas? *

▶ **telephone box** (*Am:* **telephone booth**)
['telɪfəun'bɒks] *n*
cabina *f* (telefónica)

▶ **telephone number**
['telɪfəun'nʌmbəʳ] *n*
número *m* de teléfono

television

television
[telɪ'vɪʒ(ə)n] *n*
1. televisión *f*

Spanish television la televisión española

2. televisor *m*
* *Oh, the television is on!...* ¡Oh, el televisor está encendido!...
The plane is taking off... El avión está despegando... *

tell

tell
[tel] *v t*
told, told [təuld]
1. decir

tell him to be careful dile que tenga cuidado

she told me the truth me dijo la verdad

2. contar
the story she told us was incredible la historia que nos contó era increíble

3. ver
you could tell by his looks that he was frightened se podía ver por su apariencia que tenía miedo

▶ **tell off**
reñir

* *Abdullah, your father will tell you off, come here!...* ¡Abdallah, tu padre te reñirá, ven aquí!...
No!!!!!... ¡¡¡¡¡No!!!!!... *

...tell

Abdullah, your father will tell you off, come here !...

No !!!!!...

temper

temper
['tempə'] *n*
1. humor *m*,
genio *m*

*to be in a good/bad
temper* estar de buen/
mal humor

2. Idiom
he's in a temper está
muy enfadado

*don't lose your
temper* no te enfades

temperature

temperature
['temp(ə)rətʃə'] *n*
1. temperatura *f*

* *It's so hot! The
temperature is so
high that everything
is melting...* ¡Hace
mucho calor! La tempe-
ratura es tan alta que todo
se está derritiendo... *

2. fiebre *f*
*he's got a tempe-
rature* tiene fiebre

It's so hot! The temperature is so high that everything's melting...

ten

ten
[ten]
I. *adj*
diez

II. *n*
diez *m*

tennis

tennis
['tenɪs] *n*
tenis *m*

tense

tense
[tens]
I. *adj*
tenso, a

*there was a tense
atmosphere* había una
atmósfera tensa

II. *n*
1. tiempo *m*

2. Idiom
the future tense el
tiempo futuro del verbo

tent

tent
[tent] *n*
tienda *f* de cam-
paña

term

term
[tɜːm] *n*
1. trimestre *m*

*this term (Am:
quarter) we'll study
literature* este trimestre
estudiaremos literatura

2. Idiom
*to be on good/bad
terms with some-
body* tener buenas/malas
relaciones con alguien

terrible

terrible
['terɪb(ə)l] *adj*
terrible

a terrible accident un
accidente terrible

test

test
[test] *n*
1. examen *m*,
prueba *f*

*he got good results
in his maths test* sacó
buena nota en el examen
de matemáticas

2. ensayo *m*,
prueba *f*
*Tintin passed the
first test* Tintín pasó la
primera prueba

textbook

textbook
['tekstbuk] *n*
libro *m* de texto

*a geography text-
book* un libro de texto de
geografía

than

than
[ðən] *conj*
que

...than

* *Their motorcycles
are faster than our
car!...* ¡Sus motocicletas
son más rápidas que
nuestro coche!... *

thank

thank
[θæŋk] *v t*
agradecer,
dar las gracias

Their motorcycles are faster than our car!

...thank

*I'd like to thank you
for your kindness*
quisiera agradecerle su
amabilidad

▶**thanks**
[θæŋks]
I. *n pl*
gracias *f pl*

*thanks for helping
me* gracias por ayudarme

II. *interj*
gracias

...thank

thanks very much muchas gracias

another cup of tea? – no, thanks ¿otra taza de té? – no, gracias

▶ **thanks to**
prep
gracias a

we escaped thanks to our friends escapamos gracias a nuestros amigos

▶ **thank you**
interj
gracias

* Thank you! ¡Gracias! *

thank you very much muchas gracias

thank you for your help gracias por tu ayuda

another cup of tea? – no thank you ¿otra taza de té? – no, gracias

that

...that

that
[ðæt]
I. *adj*
pl those [ðəuz]
ese, esa, esos, esas
aquel, aquella, aquellos, aquellas

that country is dangerous Tintín aquel país es peligroso, Tintín

those records are very expensive esos discos son muy caros

II. *pron dem*
pl those
ése, ésa, eso, ésos, ésas
aquél, aquélla, aquello, aquéllos, aquéllas

that was the best film I've seen aquélla fue la mejor película que he visto

* Haaaah! ¡Aaaaah!

What's that? ¿Qué es eso? *

do you prefer these or those? ¿prefieres éstos o aquéllos?

III. *pron rel*
que, el que, la que, los que, las que, el cual, la cual, los cuales, las cuales, quien, quienes

the girl that I loved la chica a quien quería

I want the treasure that you found quiero el tesoro que encontraste

IV. *conj*
que

he says that he's hungry dice que tiene hambre

he liked the play so much that he saw it twice le gustó tanto la obra que la vio dos veces

V. *adv*
tan, así de

I couldn't imagine it was that expensive no podía imaginar que fuese tan caro

the

the
[ðe] *art def*
1. el, la, los, las

...the

he was watering the roses estaba regando las rosas

2. Idiom
* Quick, get in the plane... Rápido, suba al avión... *

the sooner the better cuanto antes mejor

theatre

theatre
['θɪətəʳ] *n*
(*Am*: **theater**)
teatro *m*

their

their
[ðeəʳ] *adj*
su, sus (*de ellos, de ellas*)

...their

that's their house ésa es su casa

▶ **theirs**
[ðeəz] *pron*
1. suyo, suya, suyos, suyas (*de ellos, de ellas*)

the house is theirs la casa es suya/de ellos

2. Idiom
a friend of theirs un amigo suyo

them

them
[ðem] *pron*
los, las, ellos, ellas

these presents are for them estos regalos son para ellos

take them to the station llévalos a la estación

▶ **themselves**
[ðem'selvz] *pron*
1. se

...them

have they hurt them-selves? ¿se han hecho daño?

2. ellos mismos, ellas mismas
they'll do it them-selves lo harán ellos mismos

3. Idiom
(all) by themselves solos, por sí solos

then

then
[ðen]
I. *adv*
1. entonces

he was very young then era muy joven entonces

2. después, luego, a continuación
we visited Paris and then Rome visitamos París y después Roma

II. *conj*
entonces

what's the matter then? ¿qué ocurre entonces?

there

there
[ðeəʳ]
I. *adv*
1. allí

...there

we were there while you waited estábamos allí mientras esperabas

over there por allí

there is our friend allí está nuestro amigo

2. Idiom
there is/are hay

there's a car on the corner hay un coche en la esquina

* *There are five men*

in the car... Hay cinco hombres en el coche... *

please lend me your book - there you are por favor, déjeme su libro - aquí tiene

II. *interj*
venga

there, there, don't cry venga, venga, no llore

...there

There are five men in the car...

these

these
→ THIS

they

they
[ðeɪ] *pron*
1. ellos, ellas

they bought the house ellos compraron la casa

...they

2. *not translated*
the girls said they would study las chicas dijeron que estudiarían

3. se
they say you're a very intelligent thief se dice que usted es un ladrón muy inteligente

thick

thick
[θɪk] *adj*
1. grueso, a

2. espeso, a

3. denso, a
a thick fog una densa niebla

thief

thief
[θiːf] *n*
pl thieves [θiːvz]
ladrón, ona

* *You thief! My wa-llet!!!... I've got you this time!...*¡Ladrón! ¡¡¡Mi cartera!!!... ¡Esta vez te he cogido!... *

thin

thin
[θɪn] *adj*
thinner, thinnest
1. delgado, a

he's tall and thin es alto y delgado

2. fino, a
a thin slice una rebanada fina

thing

thing
[θɪŋ] *n*
1. cosa *f*

my favourite things mis cosas favoritas

2. Idiom
that's the best thing you could do eso es lo mejor que podías hacer

I won't say a thing no diré ni palabra

▶**things**
[θɪŋz] *n pl*
1. ropa *f*

2. cosas *f pl*

think

think
[θɪŋk]
thought, thought [θɔːt]
I. *v i*
pensar

...think

I'm trying to think estoy intentando pensar

she doesn't think of him any more ya no piensa en él

think about it piénsalo

II. *v t*
pensar, creer

do you think he will come? – no, I don't think so ¿crees que va a venir? – no, no lo creo

I think you're right creo que tiene razón

that's what I think eso es lo que yo pienso

third

third
[θɜːd]
I. *adj*
tercero, a

...third

II. *n*
tercero, a

thirsty

thirsty
['θɜːstɪ] *adj*
thirstier, thirstiest
Idiom

to be thirsty tener sed

* Be brave, Captain, we must go on...

...thirsty

Tenga valor, capitán, debemos continuar...
I'm so thirsty!... ¡Tengo tanta sed!... *

thirteen

thirteen
[θɜːˈtiːn]
I. *adj*
trece

II. *n*
trece *m*

thirty

thirty
['θɜːtɪ]
I. *adj*
treinta

II. *n*
pl thirties ['θɜːtɪz]
treinta *m*

this

this
[ðɪs]
pl these [ðiːz]

...this

I. *adj*
este, esta, estos, estas

this car isn't ours este coche no es nuestro

these horses are tired estos caballos están cansados

II. *pron*
éste, ésta, esto, éstos, éstas

what's this? ¿qué es esto?

...this

this is my book éste es mi libro

do you prefer these or those? ¿prefieres éstos o aquéllos?

those

those
→ THAT

though

though
[ðəu]
I. *conj*
1. aunque

* I'll try to catch up with them though they're almost there!... ¡Voy a tratar de alcanzarlos aunque ya casi han llegado!... *

2. Idiom
as though como si

it looks as though it's going to rain

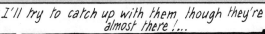

parece como si fuera a llover

even though aunque, a pesar de que

I'll help you even though I'm tired te ayudaré a pesar de que estoy cansado

II. *adv*
pero, sin embargo

he will probably agree; you never know, though proba-

...though

blemente estará de acuerdo; pero nunca se sabe

thousand

thousand
['θauzənd]
I. adj
mil

it costs two thousand dollars cuesta dos mil dólares

...thousand

II. n
mil m, millar m

how many do you need? – two thousand ¿cuántos necesitas? – dos mil

there were thousands of people había miles/millares de personas

threaten

threaten
['θret(ə)n] v t
amenazar

three

three
[θri:]
I. adj
tres

II. n
tres m

throat

throat
[θrəut] n
garganta f

I've got a sore throat me duele la garganta

through

through
[θru:]
I. prep
1. a través de

...through

* *They went through the wall!...* ¡Pasaron a través de la pared!... *

2. por
she looked through the window miró por la ventana

to send through the post enviar por correo

3. durante
all through my life durante toda mi vida

II. adv

...through

They went through the wall!...

Idiom

to be through with something/someone terminar con algo/ romper con alguien

to go through atravesar

to be through an exam aprobar un examen

Monday through Friday (Am) de lunes a viernes

throw

throw
[θrəu] v t
threw [θru:],
thrown [θrəun]
tirar, lanzar, arrojar

* *Quick, let's throw him a rope!* ¡Rápido, tirémosle una cuerda! *

▶ **throw away**
tirar (a la basura)

throw these pieces of paper away tira estos papeles

...throw

Quick, let's throw him a rope!

thumb

thumb
[θʌm] n
pulgar m

he sucked his thumb se chupaba el pulgar

thunder

thunder
['θʌndəʳ] n
trueno m

* *Bom Brom Bobom* Bom Brom Bobom
The thunder's rumbling. El trueno retumba. *

▶ **thunderstorm**
['θʌndəstɔ:m] n
tormenta f, tempestad f

BOM BROM BOBOM

The thunder's rumbling.

Thursday

Thursday
['θɜ:zdɪ] n
jueves m

his birthday is next Thursday su cumpleaños es el próximo jueves

we have an exam on Thursday tenemos un examen el jueves

ticket

ticket
['tɪkɪt] *n*
1. billete *m*

a bus ticket un billete de autobús

2. entrada *f*
a theatre (Am: theater) ticket una entrada de teatro

tide

tide
[taɪd] *n*
marea *f*

the tide is coming in/going out la marea está subiendo/bajando

tidy

tidy
[taɪdɪ]
I. *adj*

...tidy

tidier, tidiest
ordenado, a

the house was very tidy la casa estaba muy ordenada

II. *v t*
tidied, tidied
ordenar, arreglar

let's tidy the room arreglemos la habitación

tie

tie
[taɪ]
I. *n*
corbata *f*

II. *v t*
1. atar

they tied his hands le ataron las manos

2. Idiom
to tie a knot hacer un nudo

▶ **tie up**
atar

tie up your shoes átate los zapatos

* *Tied up as they are, they'll keep still!* ¡Atados como están, se estarán quietos! *

...tie

tight

tight
[taɪt]
I. *adj*
apretado, a, ajustado, a

II. *adv*
1. bien

the bottle is shut tight la botella está bien cerrada

2. Idiom
hold tight! ¡agárrate fuerte!

till

till
[tɪl]
I. *prep*
hasta

I'll wait until tomorrow esperaré hasta mañana

II. *conj*
hasta que

the child cried till his mother came back el niño lloró hasta que regresó su madre

time

time
[taɪm] *n*
1. tiempo *m*

* *Hurry up, we haven't got much time!* ¡Dese prisa, no tenemos mucho tiempo! *

you can't do two things at the same time no puedes hacer dos cosas al mismo tiempo

she left a short time

...time

ago se fue hace poco tiempo

it's a long time since I last saw her hace mucho tiempo que no la veo

have you been waiting for a long time? ¿hace mucho tiempo que estás esperando?

2. hora *f*
what time is it? ¿qué hora es?

it's time to go to bed es hora de irse a la cama

the train arrived on time el tren llegó a la hora

3. vez *f*
this is the first time that she has visited Venice es la primera vez que visita Venecia

how many times have I told you that? ¿cuántas veces te he dicho eso?

4. Idiom
to have a good time pasarlo bien

we had a good time at the circus nos lo pasamos bien en el circo

▶ **timetable**
['taɪmteɪb(ə)l] *n*
horario *m*

the plane timetable el horario de los aviones

tin

tin
[tɪn] *n*
(*Am:* **can**)
lata *f*

* *Let's open a tin of crab...* Abramos una lata de cangrejo... *

▶ **tinned**
[tɪnd] *adj*
(*Am:* **canned**)
enlatado, a

...tin

tinned peas guisantes enlatados

tiny

tiny
['taɪnɪ] *adj*
tinier, tiniest
minúsculo, a

Let's open a tin of crab...

tip

tip
[tɪp] *n*
propina *f*

tire

tire (Am)
→ TYRE

tired

tired
[taɪəd] *adj*
1. cansado, a

she was tired estaba cansada

2. Idiom
to be tired of estar harto, a de

▶**tiring**
['taɪərɪŋ] *adj*
cansado, a

a tiring job un trabajo cansado

title

title
['taɪt(ə)l] *n*
1. título *m*

I forgot the title of the film se me olvidó el título de la película

2. título *m*
he has the title of Sir tiene el título de Sir

to

to
[tuː] *prep*
1. a

* *We're going to Brest!* ¡Nos vamos a Brest! *

I'll give this record to my sister le daré este disco a mi hermana

from Monday to Friday de lunes a viernes

2. menos
it's ten to eight son las

We're going to Brest!

ocho menos diez

3. para
I'm here to help you estoy aquí para ayudarte

4. de
it's difficult to understand es difícil de entender

something to eat algo de comer

5. (indica el infinitivo)
I'd like to read that book me gustaría leer ese libro

toast

toast
[təust] *n*
1. tostada *f*

spread butter on the toast pon mantequilla en la tostada

2. brindis *m*
I propose a toast to the Captain propongo un brindis por el capitán

3. Idiom
to drink a toast to someone brindar por alguien

tobacco

tobacco
[tə'bækəu] *n*
tabaco *m*

today

today
[tə'deɪ] *adv & n*
hoy

today is her birthday hoy es su cumpleaños

toe

toe
[təu] *n*
dedo *m* del pie

together

together
[tə'geðəʳ] *adv*
juntos, as

we'll go together iremos juntos

toilet

toilet
['tɔɪlɪt] *n*
cuarto *m* de baño, lavabo *m*, servicios *m pl*

tomato

tomato
[tə'mɑːtəu] *n*
tomate *m*

tomato sauce salsa de tomate

tomorrow

tomorrow
[tə'mɒrəu] *adv & n*
mañana *adv & n f*

tomorrow we'll be safe mañana estaremos a salvo

the day after tomorrow pasado mañana

tongue

tongue
[tʌŋ] *n*
lengua *f*

put out your tongue, please saque la lengua, por favor

tonight

tonight
[tə'naɪt] *adv*
esta noche *f*

...tonight

I will see the Captain tonight veré al capitán esta noche

too

too
[tu:] *adv*
1. también

he speaks French and Italian too habla francés y también italiano

...too

2. demasiado
it's never too late nunca es demasiado tarde

he works too hard trabaja demasiado

tool

tool
[tu:l] *n*
herramienta *f*

tooth

tooth
[tu:θ] *n*
pl teeth [ti:θ]
1. diente *m*

I had a tooth out me sacaron un diente

2. Idiom
wisdom tooth muela del juicio

▶ **toothache**
['tu:θeɪk] *n*
dolor *m* de muelas

* *Blistering barnacles!... I have a toothache!...* ¡Millones de demonios!... ¡Tengo dolor de muelas!... *

▶ **toothbrush**
['tu:θbrʌʃ] *n*
cepillo *m* de dientes

▶ **toothpaste**
['tu:θpeɪst] *n*
dentífrico *m*, pasta *f* de dientes

top

top
[tɒp] *n*
1. cima *f*, cumbre *f*

the top of the mountain la cima de la montaña

2. copa *f*
the top of the tree la copa del árbol

3. parte *f* de arriba
the top of the page la parte de arriba de la página

4. tapa *f*
the top of the saucepan la tapa de la cacerola

5. Idiom
on top of the cupboard encima del armario

from top to bottom de arriba abajo

torch

torch
[tɔ:tʃ] *n*
(*Am:* **flashlight**)
linterna *f*, antorcha *f*

total

total
['təʊt(ə)l]
I. *n*
total *m*

in total, we spent

...total

20 dollars en total, gastamos 20 dólares

II. *adj*
total, completo, a

total silence silencio total/completo

touch

touch
[tʌtʃ] *v t*
tocar

...touch

...touch

dont' touch the sculpture no toques la escultura

▶ **touch down**
aterrizar

* *Hallo, this is the moon rocket... In a few minutes, we'll be touching down on the moon...* Hola, aquí el cohete lunar... Dentro de unos minutos aterrizaremos en la luna... *

tour

tour
[tuəʳ] *n*
excursión *f*, viaje *m*, visita *f*

we went on a coach (Am: bus) tour fuimos de excursión en autocar

▶ **tourist**
['tuərɪst] *n*
turista *m f*

towards

toward(s)
[tə'wɔ:dz] *prep*
(*Am:* **toward**)
1. hacia

* *They're heading towards the east...* Se encaminan hacia el este... *

2. hacia, por
her feelings towards us sus sentimientos hacia nosotros

...towards

3. hacia, cerca de
*towards the end of
the month* hacia finales
de mes

towel

towel
['tauəl] *n*
toalla *f*

tower

tower
['tauəʳ] *n*
torre *f*

the control tower la
torre de control

town

town
[taun] *n*
ciudad *f*,
población *f*

toy

toy
[tɔɪ] *n*
juguete *m*

track

track
[træk] *n*
1. huella *f*, pista *f*

*Snowy, follow the
track!* ¡Milú, sigue la
pista!

...track

2. sendero *m*,
camino *m*

3. vía *f*
*railway (Am: rail-
road) track* vía del tren

traffic

traffic
['træfɪk] *n*
circulación *f*,
tráfico *m*

...traffic

▶ **traffic jam**
['træfɪk'dʒæm] *n*
atasco *m* (de cir-
culación),
embotellamiento *m*

▶ **traffic lights** (*Am:*
traffic light)
['træfɪk'laɪts] *n pl*
semáforo *m*

*stop at the next
traffic lights* para en el
siguiente semáforo

train

train
[treɪn]
I. *n*
tren *m*

*** The train has been
running for several
hours.** El tren está
corriendo desde hace
varias horas. ***

II. *v t*
1. entrenar

he trains the players
entrena a los jugadores

2. amaestrar,
domar
*this horse is well
trained* este caballo está
bien domado

III. *v i*
entrenarse,
formarse

*this tennis player
trains every day* este
tenista se entrena cada
día

translate

translate
[træns'leɪt] *v t*
traducir

*he translates from
English into Spanish*
traduce del inglés al
español

▶ **translation**
[træns'leɪʃ(ə)n] *n*
traducción *f*

trap

trap
[træp] *n*
trampa *f*

travel

travel
['trævəl]
I. *v i*
travelled, travelled
(*Am:* traveled)
viajar

...travel

*he always travels by
train* siempre viaja en
tren

II. *n*
viaje *m*

travel agency agencia
de viajes

▶ **traveller**
['trævləʳ] *n*
(*Am:* **traveler**)
viajero, a

▶ **traveller's cheque**
(*Am:* **traveler's
check**)
cheque *m* de viaje

tray

tray
[treɪ] *n*
bandeja *f*

*the waiter is carrying
a tray* el camarero lleva
una bandeja

treasure

treasure
['treʒəʳ] *n*
tesoro *m*

*** The treasure may
be here!** ¡El tesoro
podría estar aquí! ***

tree

tree
[triː] n
1. árbol m

2. Idiom
pine tree pino

apple tree manzano

trick

trick
[trɪk] n
1. truco m

...trick

a magic trick un truco de magia

2. Idiom
to play a trick on someone gastarle una broma a alguien

trip

trip
[trɪp] n
viaje m

...trip

have a good trip! ¡qué tenga un buen viaje!

trouble

trouble
['trʌb(ə)l] n
1. problema m, dificultad f, lío m

* *Your going to get into trouble! You'd better hide!* ¡Va a meterse en líos! ¡Será

...trouble

You're going to get into trouble! You'd better hide!

mejor que se esconda! *

2. molestia f
you've taken a lot of trouble to come here se ha tomado muchas molestias al venir aquí

trousers

trousers
['trauzəz] n
(*Am*: **pants**)
pantalones m pl,

...trousers

pantalón m

a pair of trousers unos pantalones, un pantalón

truck

truck
[trʌk] n
camión m

true

true
[truː] adj
1. verdadero, a

2. Idiom
is it true that Müller is behind all this? ¿es verdad que Müller está detrás de todo esto?

trunk

trunk
[trʌŋk] n

...trunk

1. baúl m

open this trunk abre este baúl

2. *Am:* maletero m
the trunk of the car el maletero del coche

3. tronco m
a tree trunk un tronco de árbol

4. trompa f
an elephant's trunk la trompa de un elefante

truth

truth
[truːθ] n
verdad f

he always says the truth siempre dice la verdad

try

try
[traɪ]
I. n
pl tries [traɪz]

...try

1. intento m

* *Let's go!* ¡Vamos! *Hurray! That's it!* ¡Hurra! ¡Ya está! *He succeeded at the first try...* Lo consiguió al primer intento... *

2. Idiom
let me have a try déjame intentarlo

II. v t
tried, tried [traɪd]
1. intentar

I'll try to do it better intentaré hacerlo mejor

2. probar
try this soup prueba esta sopa

▶ **try on** probarse (*clothes*)

try this dress on pruébate este vestido

...try

Let's go!

Hurray! That's it!

He succeeded at the first try...

Tuesday

Tuesday
['tjuːzdɪ] n
martes m

tune

tune
[tʃuːn] n
melodía f, tonada f, aire m

I can't remember the tune no recuerdo la melodía

turn

turn
[tɜːn]
I. n
1. giro m

there's a sharp turn to the left hay un giro brusco a la izquierda

2. turno m
wait your turn espera tu turno

we'll keep watch by turns vigilaremos por turnos

3. Idiom
* *Now, Thompson, it's my turn to drive...* Ahora, Fernández, me toca conducir... *

whose turn is it to play? ¿a quién le toca jugar?

II. v i & v t
1. girar(se)

turn right at the next corner gira a la derecha en la siguiente esquina

...turn

turn the page gira la página

2. dar(se) la vuelta
he turned to listen to us se dio la vuelta para escucharnos

3. volverse, ponerse
it turned red se volvió rojo

▶ **turn back**
dar la vuelta

we have to turn back, the path ends here tenemos que dar la vuelta, el camino termina aquí

▶ **turn down**
1. rehusar, rechazar

he turned down the plan rehusó/ rechazó el plan

2. bajar
turn the radio down, it's too loud baja la radio, está demasiado fuerte

▶ **turn into**
convertir(se)

the frog turned into a prince la rana se convirtió en un príncipe

▶ **turn off**
apagar

turn the radio off apaga la radio

▶ **turn on**
encender

turn the television on enciende el televisor

▶ **turn over**
1. volcar

* *The car turned over!...* ¡El coche volcó!... *

2. Idiom
turn over the page pase la página

to turn over an idea in one's mind dar vueltas a una idea en la cabeza

---

...turn

The car turned over!...

twelve

twelve
[twelv]
I. *adj*
1. doce

2. Idiom
at twelve o'clock a las doce

II. *n*
doce *m*

twenty

twenty
['twentı]
I. *adj*
veinte

II. *n*
pl twenties ['twentız]
veinte *m*

in the twenties en los años veinte

twice

twice
[twaıs] *adv*
dos veces

we saw the play twice vimos la obra dos veces

---

twin

twin
[twın] *n*
gemelo, a

* *Thomson and Thompson look alike but they are not twins.* Hernández y Fernández se parecen pero no son gemelos. *

Thomson and Thompson look alike but they are not twins.

two

two
[tuː] *adj*
I. dos

II. *n*
dos *m*

tyre

tyre
[taıəʳ] *n*
(*Am*: **tire**)
neumático *m*

U V U V U

ugly

ugly
['ʌglɪ] adj
uglier, ugliest
feo, a

the ugly duckling el patito feo

umbrella

umbrella
[ʌm'brelə] n
paraguas m

...umbrella

My umbrella!... My umbrella!... My dear old umbrella! I've found it at last!

* *My umbrella!... My dear old umbrella! I've found it at last!* ¡Mi paraguas!... ¡Mi queridísimo paraguas! ¡Al fin lo he encontrado! *

uncle

uncle
['ʌŋk(ə)l] n
tío m

under

under
['ʌndəʳ] prep
1. bajo, debajo de

* *Tintin is swimming under water...* Tintín está nadando bajo el agua... *

2. menor de *children under 8 travel free* los niños menores de 8 años viajan gratis

▶ **underground**
['ʌndəgraund]
I. adj
subterráneo, a

an underground passage un pasadizo subterráneo

II. n
metro m

she goes to work by underground (Am: subway) va a trabajar en metro

...under

Tintin is swimming under water.

understand

understand
[ʌndə'stænd] v t
understood, understood
[ʌndə'stud]
entender, comprender

* *I don't understand what you're saying!...* ¡No entiendo lo que dice!... *

क्या? फिर वही?

I don't understand what you're saying!...

unhappy

unhappy
[ʌn'hæpɪ]
unhappier, unhappiest
triste, infeliz

he was no longer unhappy ya no estaba triste

united

united
[ju'naɪtɪd] adj
unido, a

...united

▶ **United Kingdom** n
Reino m Unido

▶ **United States** n pl
Estados m pl Uni-
dos

university

university
[juːnɪˈvɜːsɪtɪ] n
pl universities
universidad f

...university

she goes to (Am: to
the) university va a la
universidad

unless

unless
[ʌnˈles] conj
a menos (de) que

* *Don't move from
here unless I tell
you to!* ¡No se mueva
de aquí a menos que se
lo diga! *

...unless

Don't move from here,
unless I tell you to!

until

until
[ʌnˈtɪl]
I. prep
hasta

*we'll wait until
tomorrow* esperaremos
hasta mañana

II. conj
hasta que

*wait here until the
Captain arrives* es-
pere aquí hasta que llegue
el capitán

unusual

unusual
[ʌnˈjuːʒuəl] adj
1. raro, a
poco frecuente

2. extraño, a, raro, a,
fuera de lo normal
* *Call me if anything
unusual happens.*
LLámeme si ocurre algo
fuera de lo normal.
*Alright, chief, I'll stay
here!* ¡Bien, jefe, me
quedaré aquí! *

...unusual

Call me if anything
unusual happens.

Alright, chief,
I'll stay here!

up

up
[ʌp]
I. adv
1. arriba, en lo alto

*she's imprisoned up
in the tower* está
encarcelada arriba en la
torre

2. en el/al aire
*Tintin threw the
bone up* Tintín lanzó el
hueso al aire

3. Idiom
to be up estar levantado

to get up levantarse

*she got up very
early this morning* se
levantó muy pronto esta
mañana

to go up subir

*the temperature is
going up* la temperatura
está subiendo

to jump up levantarse
de un salto

II. prep
1. en lo alto de

*he lives up the
mountains* vive en lo
alto de la montaña

2. Idiom
*he climbed up the
cliff* escaló el acantilado

* *Whoooaah!* ¡Guaaauh!
*It's climbing up the
tree.* Está trepando al
árbol. *

▶ **up to**
prep
1. hasta

*Mr Wagner will play
the piano up to the
evening* el señor
Wagner tocará el piano
hasta la noche

2. Idiom
it's up to you es cosa
tuya/allá tú

what are they up to?
¿qué se traen entre
manos?

up to date al día, al
corriente

...up

Woooaah!

It's climbing up the tree.

upset

upset
[ʌpˈset]
I. adj
1. triste,
preocupado, a

*he's upset because
he wasn't allowed
to go* está triste porque
no le permitieron ir

2. contrariado, a
* *The Captain looks
upset. What did you
say to him?* El capitán
parece contrariado. ¿Qué
le ha dicho? *

The Captain looks upset,
what did you say to
him?

3. revuelto, a
*I've got an upset
stomach* tengo el estó-
mago revuelto

II. v t
upset, upset
1. entristecer,
acongojar,
trastornar

*it upsets me to know
he's ill* me entristece
saber que está enfermo

2. contrariar, alterar

...upset

don't upset him now, he's got enough problems no lo contraries ahora, ya tiene suficientes problemas

3. tirar, volcar
she upset the vase with her elbow tiró el jarrón con el codo

upstairs

upstairs
[ʌp'steəz] *adv*

...upstairs

Tintin is coming upstairs.

1. arriba (de las escaleras)

he lives upstairs vive arriba

2. Idiom
* *Tintin is coming upstairs.* Tintín está subiendo (las escaleras). *

urgent

urgent
['ɜːdʒənt] *adj*
urgente

us

us
[ʌs] *pron*
nosotros, as

the present was for us el regalo era para nosotros

use

use
[juːs]
I. *n*
1. uso *m*

...use

now I know the use of this tool ahora sé el uso de esta herramienta

2. Idiom
it's no use shouting no sirve de nada gritar

what's the use of waiting here? ¿de qué sirve esperar aquí?

this map is (of) no use este mapa no sirve

II. *v t*
1. usar, utilizar

...use

I'll use this rope to tie myself to the ladder...

* *I'll use this rope to tie myself to the ladder...* Voy a usar esta cuerda para atarme a la escalera... *

2. consumir
this car uses too much petrol este coche consume demasiada gasolina

▶ **use up**
terminar(se), agotar, acabar

the coal is used up se ha terminado el carbón

▶ **used**
[juːzd] *adj*
1. usado, a, de secunda mano

a used car un coche usado/de secunda mano

2. acostumbrado, a
she's used to working hard está acostumbrada a trabajar mucho

3. Idiom
to get used to something acostumbrarse a algo

▶ **used to**
['juːstuː] *v aux*
Idiom

when she was young she used to work hard cuando era joven, solía trabajar mucho

he used to be a singer había sido cantante

he's not so funny as he used to no es tan divertido como acostumbraba a ser

▶ **useful**
['juːsful] *adj*
útil

* *These binoculars are very useful!* ¡Estos prismáticos son muy útiles! *

...use

These binoculars are very useful!

useless

useless
['juːslɪs] *adj*
1. inútil

it's useless to try to convince them es inútil intentar convencerles

2. Idiom
he's useless at business es un inepto para los negocios

usual

usual
['juːʒuəl] *adj*
1. habitual, normal

he arrived later than usual llegó más tarde de lo habitual

2. Idiom
Snowy is not his usual self Milú no parece él mismo

as usual como de costumbre

▶ **usually**
['juːʒuəlɪ] *adv*
normalmente

she's usually very punctual normalmente es muy puntual

vacant

vacant
['veɪkənt] *adj*
libre, vacante

...vacant

excuse me, is this seat vacant? disculpe, ¿está libre este asiento?

vacation

vacation (*Am*)
→ HOLIDAY

valley

valley
['vælɪ] n
valle m

the valley is behind those mountains el valle está detrás de esas montañas

van

van
[væn] n
1. camioneta f

Hurry up! Follow that van!... Hurry up!...

...van

* *Hurry up! Follow that van!... Hurry up!...* ¡Dese prisa! ¡Siga a esa camioneta!... ¡Dese prisa!... *

2. Idiom
removal (Am: moving) van camión de mudanzas

vegetable

vegetable
['vedʒtəb(ə)l] n
legumbre f,

...vegetable

verdura f

vehicle

vehicle
['viːɪk(ə)l] n
vehículo m

verb

verb
[vɜːb] n
verbo m

very

very
['verɪ] adv
1. muy

she's very nice es muy agradable·

2. mucho
* *It's very hot!* ¡Hace mucho calor! *

3. Idiom
very much mucho/muchísimo

I liked the film very much me gustó mucho la película

...very

It's very hot!

victory

victory
['vɪktərɪ] n
victoria f

view

view
[vjuː] n
1. vista f

* *The next morning.* A la mañana siguiente.
There's a nice view

...view

The next morning.

There's a nice view from the summit!

from the summit! ¡Hay una vista muy bella desde la cima! *

2. punto m de vista, opinión f
in my view, we should wait a bit longer en mi opinión, deberíamos esperar un poco más

from my point of view desde mi punto de vista

village

village
['vɪlɪdʒ] n
pueblo m, aldea f

violence

violence
['vaɪələns] adj
violencia f

acts of violence actos de violencia

...violence

▶**violent**
['vaɪələnt] adj
violento, a

visit

visit
['vɪzɪt]
I. n
visita f

we'll pay you a visit some day algún día te haremos una visita

...visit

II. v t
visitar

we'll visit our cousin next month visitaremos a nuestro primo el mes próximo

I'd like to visit this church me gustaría visitar esta iglesia

▶**visitor**
['vɪzɪtəʳ] n
visitante m f, visita f

voice

voice
[vɔɪs] n
voz f

vote

vote
[vəut]
I. n
1. voto m

a secret vote un voto secreto

...vote

2. voto m
the motion was adopted by 25 votes to 17 la moción fue adoptada por 25 votos a favor y 17 en contra

II. v i & v t
votar

vote (for) Mr Brett! ¡vote al señor Brett!

wage

wage
[weɪdʒ] *n*
salario *m*, sueldo *m*

he asked for a rise in his wages pidió un aumento de salario

wait

wait
[weɪt] *v i*
1. esperar

...wait

* *I've been waiting here for over an hour! Why doesn't the boat come back?* ¡He estado esperando aquí desde más de una hora! ¿Por qué no vuelve el barco? *

hurry up, they're waiting for us! ¡date prisa, nos están esperando!

2. servir
to wait on someone atenderle/servirle a alguien

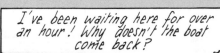

I've been waiting here for over an hour! Why doesn't the boat come back?

▶ **waiter**
[weɪtəʳ] *n*
camarero *m*

▶ **waiting room**
['weɪtɪŋ'ruːm] *n*
sala *f* de espera

▶ **waitress**
['weɪtrɪs] *n*
camarera *f*

wake

wake
[weɪk] *v t*
woke [wəuk],
woken ['wəuk(ə)n]
despertar

* *A loud noise woke me!... It came from there!...* ¡Me ha despertado un ruido fuerte!... ¡Vino de allí!... *

▶ **wake up**
1. despertar

wake me up at seven despiérteme a las siete

...wake

A loud noise woke me!... It came from there!...

2. despertarse
wake up, it's late! ¡despiértate, es tarde!

Wales

Wales
[weɪlz] *n*
País *m* de Gales

▶ **Welsh**
[welʃ]
I. *adj*
galés, galesa

...Wales

II. *n*
1. galés *m*

do you speak Welsh? ¿habla galés?

2. *the Welsh* los Galeses

▶ **Welshman, Welshwoman**
['welʃmən]
['welʃwumən]
galés *m*
galesa *f*

walk

walk
[wɔːk]
I. *n*
1. paseo *m*

2. Idiom
let's go for a walk! ¡vayamos a dar un paseo!

I'll take the dog for a walk sacaré el perro a pasear

it's a ten minute walk from here está a diez minutos andando desde aquí

II. *v i*
1. caminar, andar

he's learning to walk está aprendiendo a caminar

I walked here he venido andando hasta aquí

2. pasear(se)
* *I like walking in the park!* ¡Me gusta pasear por el parque! *

...walk

I like walking in the park!

wall

wall
[wɔːl] *n*
muro *m*, pared *f*,
tapia *f*

*there was a picture
on the wall* había un
cuadro en la pared

wallet

wallet
['wɒlɪt]
cartera *f*

* *Let's have a
look!... ¡Veamos!...
And now nobody
can steal my wallet!*
¡Y ahora nadie puede
robarme la cartera! *

Let's have a look!...

And now nobody can steal my wallet!

want

want
[wɒnt] *v t*
1. querer

* *Snowy wants to
show me some-
thing!* ¡Milú quiere
enseñarme algo!
Woof! Woof! ¡Guau!
¡Guau! *

2. buscar, requerir
*he's wanted by the
police* es buscado por la
policía

Snowy wants to show me something!

Woof! Woof!

war

war
[wɔːʳ] *n*
guerra *f*

*the country was no
longer at war* el país
ya no estaba en guerra

warder

warder
['wɔːdə]] *n*
(*Am*: **guard**)
guardián *m*

warm

warm
[wɔːm]
I. *adj*
1. caliente

*the soup is still
warm* la sopa está
todavía caliente

2. cálido, a
today is a warm day
hoy es un día cálido

II. *v t*
calentar

...warm

*warm your hands by
the fire* caliéntate las
manos cerca del fuego

warn

warn
[wɔːn] *v t*
advertir

*I warned him of the
danger* le advertí del
peligro

wash

wash
[wɒʃ]
I. *n*
Idiom

to have a wash
lavarse

II. *v t*
lavar(se)

*I have to wash the
clothes* tengo que lavar
la ropa

wash your hands
lávate las manos

III. *v i*
lavarse

*I'd rather wash in
hot water* prefiero
lavarme con agua caliente

▶ **wash up**
lavar los platos,
fregar

*I'll wash up (Am: do
the dishes)* yo lavaré
los platos/fregaré

▶ **washing**
['wɒʃɪŋ] *n*
1. colada *f*

2. Idiom
to do the washing
hacer la colada, lavar la
ropa

waste

waste
[weɪst]
I. *n*
1. pérdida *f*

it's a waste of time
es una pérdida de tiempo

2. despilfarro *m*,
derroche *m*

II. *v t*
1. perder

*don't waste more
time* no pierdas más
tiempo

...waste

2. derrochar, despilfarrar, desperdiciar
he likes wasting money le gusta derrochar dinero

don't waste your talent no desperdicies tu talento

watch

watch
[wɒtʃ]
I. *n*
1. reloj *m* (de pulsera)

my watch is slow mi reloj va retrasado

2. Idiom
* *And that night...* Y aquella noche...
Keep watch here, I'll try to get into the building... Vigila aquí, voy a intentar entrar en el edificio...

OK!... ¡De acuerdo!... *

II. *v t*
1. mirar, ver

the cat is watching the birds el gato está mirando a los pájaros

he's watching television está viendo la televisión

2. vigilar
* *The police are watching the house!* ¡La policía vigila la casa! *

...watch

▶ **watch out** tener cuidado

watch out, there's a car coming! ¡ten cuidado, viene un coche!

water

water
['wɔːtər] *n*
agua *f*

...water

soda water agua gaseosa

wave

wave
[weɪv]
I. *n*
ola *f*

there were high waves había olas altas

...wave

II. *v t*
agitar

look, they're waving a white flag! ¡mira, agitan una bandera blanca!

III. *v i*
hacer señas con la mano

he waved to us from the ship nos hacía señas con la mano desde el barco

way

way
[weɪ] *n*
1. camino *m*

a passerby told me the way un transeúnte me explicó el camino

what way shall we go? ¿qué camino tomamos?

2. dirección *f*
* *Are you sure we're going the right way, Captain?* ¿Está seguro de que vamos en la

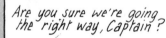

dirección correcta, capitán? *

3. manera *f*, forma *f*
do it (in) this way hazlo de esta manera

* *We must find a way out of here...* Tenemos que encontrar una forma de salir de aquí... *

4. Idiom
it's a long way está lejos

the way in la entrada

the way out la salida

come this way, please venga por aquí, por favor

by the way... por cierto...

we

we
[wiː] *pron*
1. nosotros

we didn't do it nosotros no lo hicimos

2. *not translated*
we live here vivimos aquí

weak

weak
[wiːk] *adj*
1. débil

he's still weak aún se encuentra débil

2. ligero, a
this coffee is weak este café es ligero

3. flojo, a
a weak argument un argumento flojo

weapon

weapon
['wep(ə)n] *n*
arma *f*

a defense weapon un arma de defensa

wear

wear
[weəʳ] *v t*
wore [wɔː],
worn [wɔːn]

...wear

Tintin is wearing a cowboy hat...

...wear

llevar (puesto)

* *Tintin is wearing a cowboy hat...* Tintín lleva un sombrero vaquero... *

▶ **wear out**
usar, (des)gastar

your shoes are worn out tus zapatos están desgastados

weather

weather
['weðəʳ] *n*
1. tiempo *m*

what's the weather like? ¿qué tiempo hace?

2. Idiom
the weather is hot/cold hace calor/frío

▶ **weather forecast**
['weðəʳˈfɔːkaːst] *n*
previsión *f* meteorológica

wedding

wedding
['wedɪŋ] *n*
boda *f*

Wednesday

Wednesday
['wenzdɪ] *n*
miércoles *m*

week

week
[wiːk] *n*
semana *f*

we'll finish next week acabaremos la semana próxima

▶ **weekend**
[wiːˈkend] *n*
fin *m* de semana

weigh

weigh
[weɪ] *v t*
pesar

he weighed the parcels pesó los paquetes

▶ **weight**
[weɪt] *n*
peso *m*

* *Snowy, you're eating too much, you're going to put on weight!* ¡Milú, estás comiendo demasiado, vas a ganar peso! *

...weigh

Snowy, you're eating too much, you're going to put on weight!

welcome

welcome
['welkəm]
I. *adj*
bienvenido, a

you're always welcome here siempre eres bienvenido aquí

welcome to England bienvenido a Inglaterra

II. *n*
bienvenida *f*

they gave us a warm welcome nos dieron una cálida bienvenida

III. *v t*
dar la bienvenida, acoger

they welcomed us with a party nos dieron la bienvenida con una fiesta

well

well
[wel]
I. *adv*
1. bien

Signora Castafiore sings very well la Castafiore canta muy bien

2. bastante
she's well above forty tiene bastante más de cuarenta años

3. Idiom
as well también

did you go as well? ¿fuiste tú también?

as well as así como

II. *adj*
bien

how are you? – very well, thank you ¿cómo estás? – muy bien, gracias

III. *interj*
vaya

...well

* *Drat! I've given myself away!...* ¡Caramba! ¡Me han descubierto!...
Well! What a surprise! ¡Vaya! ¡Qué sorpresa! *

IV. n
pozo m

there's no more water in this well ya no hay agua en este pozo

west

west
[west]
I. n
oeste m

* *It keeps pointing towards the west...* Sigue señalando al oeste... *

II. adj
oeste

the west coast la costa oeste

III. adv
al oeste,
hacia el oeste

the palace is a few miles west of here el palacio está a unos kilómetros al oeste de aquí

▶ **western**
['westən]
I. adj
del oeste,
occidental

...west

Western Europe Europa del oeste/occidental

II. n
novela f,
película f del oeste

there's a good western on television tonight hay una buena película del oeste en la televisión esta noche

wet

wet
[wet] adj
wetter, wettest
1. mojado, a

your clothes are still wet tu ropa está aún mojada

2. húmedo, a
the weather is very wet el tiempo es muy húmedo

3. Idiom
wet paint pintura fresca/recién pintado

what

what
[wɒt]
I. adj
qué

what time is it? ¿qué hora es?

what a pity! ¡qué lástima/pena!

what a charming girl! ¡qué chica más encantadora!

II. pron
1. qué, lo que

what would you like? ¿qué desea?

I wonder what Tintin is planning me pregunto qué planea Tintín

did you hear what he said? ¿oíste lo que dijo?

2. Idiom
what about me? ¿y yo qué?

what about the Captain? ¿qué hay del capitán?

what's this for? ¿para qué es/sirve esto?

III. interj
qué

what! are you sure? ¡qué! ¿estás seguro?

▶ **whatever**
[wɒt'evəʳ]
I. adj
el/la que sea,
los/ las que sean,
cualquiera...que,
cualquiera que sea

...what

choose whatever book you like elige el libro que sea/cualquier libro que quieras

II. pron
1. lo que,
todo lo que

you can ask whatever you want puedes pedir lo que sea/lo que quieras

2. Idiom
whatever it is, it must be a good surprise sea lo que sea, debe ser una buena sorpresa

whatever do you mean? ¿qué diablos quiere decir?

* *Whatever are you doing, Captain?* ¿Pero qué está haciendo, capitán?/¿Pero qué es lo qué está haciendo, capitán? *

wheel

wheel
[wiːl] n
1. rueda f

2. Idiom
steering wheel volante m

when

when
[wen]
I. adv
cuándo

...when

when did Tintin arrive? ¿cuándo llegó Tintín?

* *Mind my beard!* ¡Cuidado con mi barba!
Tell me when you're ready. Dígame cuándo esté listo. *

II. conj
cuando

she was reading a book when I arrived estaba leyendo un libro cuando llegué

III. rel
cuando,
en que

the moment when I arrived el momento en que llegué

▶ **whenever**
[wen'evəʳ]
I. conj
1. cuando

...when

do it whenever you can hazlo cuando puedas

2. sea cuando sea
whenever I try, I get mixed up sea cuando sea que lo intento, me hago un lío

II. *adv*
cuándo

whenever did he arrive? ¿cuándo diablos ha llegado?

Mind my beard!

Tell me when you're ready...

where

where
[weəʳ]
I. *adv*
(a)dónde

where are you going? ¿adónde vais?

I don't know where she is no sé dónde está

II. *pron rel*
donde, en que

we went to the place where I found it

fuimos al lugar donde lo encontré

▶ **wherever**
[weərˈevəʳ]
I. *conj*
donde,
donde sea que/
dondequiera que

you can go wherever you like puedes ir donde quieras

I'll find Snowy wherever he is encontraré a Milú donde sea que esté/dondequiera que esté

II. *adv*
dónde

wherever have you been? ¿dónde diablos has estado?

whether

whether
[ˈweðəʳ] *conj*
si

* *I don't know whether I'll make it...* No sé si lo conseguiré... *

which

which
[wɪtʃ]
I. *adj*
qué

I don't know whether I'll make it...

...which

which way did they go? ¿qué camino tomaron?

II. *pron*
cuál, cuáles

I wonder which (one) is the real map me pregunto cuál es el mapa verdadero

III. *pron rel*
que, el cual/que,
la cual/que,
los cuales/que,
las cuales/que

take the book which has a blue cover coge el libro que tiene las tapas azules

* *There's the car which I saw in the street!* ¡Allí está el coche que vi en la calle! *Yes, that's it!* ¡Sí, es ése! *

this is the house which I told you about ésta es la casa de la cual te hablé

There's the car which I saw in the street!

Yes, that's it!

while

while
[waɪl]
I. *conj*
1. mientras

she studied French while she was in Paris estudió francés mientras estuvo en París

2. mientras que
I like tea, while he hates it a mí me gusta el té, mientras que él lo odia

II. *n*
1. rato *m*

2. Idiom
a long while ago hace mucho tiempo

it's worth while vale la pena

whisper

whisper
[ˈwɪspəʳ] *vi & vt*
cuchichear,
susurrar

whistle

whistle
[ˈwɪsl]
I. *n*
1. silbido *m*,
pitido *m (act, sound)*

2. silbato *m*, pito *m*
(instrument)

II. *vi & vt*
silbar

* *Are you coming Snowy?* ¿Vienes Milú? *Tintin is whistling to Snowy.* Tintín está silbando a Milú. *

Are you coming, Snowy?

Tintin is whistling to Snowy.

white

white
[waɪt]
I. *adj*
blanco, a

a white rose una rosa blanca

II. *n*
blanco *m*

white suits you el blanco te sienta bien

who

who
[huː]
I. *pron interr*
quién

who are you? ¿quién
eres tú?

II. *pron rel*
quien, que

*this is the man who
followed us* es el
hombre que nos siguió

*the woman who(m) I
met in London* la
mujer que/a quien conocí en
Londres

▶ **whoever**
[huːˈevəʳ] *pron*
1. quien

*give it to whoever you
want* dáselo a quien quieras

2. Idiom
whoever told you that?
¿quién diablos te dijo eso?

whole

whole
[həul] *adj*
completo, a,
entero, a

*I'll tell the whole
world* se lo diré al mundo
entero

whose

whose
[huːz]
I. *pron interr*

...whose

de quién

* *But Snowy, whose
umbrella is that?*
Pero Milú, ¿de quién es
ese paraguas? *

II. *pron rel*
cuyo, os, as,
del cual, de la cual,
de los cuales, de
las cuales

*the man whose hat
was black* el hombre
cuyo sombrero era negro

why

why
[waɪ] *adv*
por qué

why are you sad?
¿por qué estás triste?

why not? ¿por qué no?

wide

wide
[waɪd] *adj*
ancho, a

wife

wife
[waɪf] *n*
pl wives [waɪvz]
esposa *f*

wild

wild
[waɪld] *adj*
1. salvaje

* *All the wild animals
are running away...
Let's do the same!...*

...wild

Todos los animales salva-
jes están huyendo... ¡Haga-
mos lo mismo!... *

2. silvestre
wild flower flor silvestre

3. furioso, a

will

will
[wɪl]
I. *v aux*
1. *(se utiliza para formar
el futuro)*

...will

*will you be
here tomor-
row?* ¿estarás
aquí mañana?

2. *(se utiliza
como forma de
cortesía)*
*will you open
the window,
please?* ¿querrá
abrir la ventana,
por favor?

II. *n*
voluntad *f*

willing

willing
['wɪlɪŋ] *adj*
1. dispuesto, a

*she's always willing
to help* siempre está
dispuesta a ayudar

2. servicial,
complaciente
he's very willing es
muy servicial

win

win
[wɪn] *v i & v t*
won, won [wʌn]
ganar

who won the match?
¿quién ganó el partido?

wind

wind
[wɪnd] *n*
viento *m*

...wind

* *There's a very
strong wind blow-
ing...* Sopla un viento
muy fuerte... *

▶ **windy**
['wɪndɪ] *adj*
windier, windiest
Idiom

it's windy hace viento

window

window
['wɪndəu]
1. ventana *f*

she's looking through the window está mirando por la ventana

2. escaparate *m*
there were vases in the shop (Am: store) window había jarros en el escaparate

wine

wine
[waɪn] *n*
vino *m*

red/white wine vino tinto/blanco

wing

wing
[wɪŋ] *n*
ala *f*

the bird spread its wings el pájaro abrió las alas

winter

winter
['wɪntəʳ] *n*
invierno *m*

wipe

wipe
[waɪp] *v t*
limpiar, enjugar, secar

wipe the dishes seca los platos

wish

wish
[wɪʃ]
I. *n*
deseo *m*

she was granted a wish le concedieron un deseo

best wishes! ¡mis mejores deseos!

II. *v t*
1. desear

I wish you the best of luck te deseo la mejor suerte

I wish I were in China desearía estar en China

2. Idiom
I wish I had known! ¡Ojalá lo hubiera sabido!

she has all she can wish for tiene todo lo que puede desear

what more can you wish for? ¿qué más puedes pedir?

with

with
[wɪð] *prep*
1. con

I agree with you estoy de acuerdo con usted

2. de
the boy with long hair el chico de pelo largo

he's shaking with cold está temblando de frío

without

without
[wɪ'ðaut] *prep*
sin

you shouldn't go out without your umbrella no deberías salir sin tu paraguas

woman

woman
['wumən] *n*
pl women ['wɪmɪn]
mujer *f*

wonder

wonder
['wʌndəʳ] *v t*
preguntarse

* I wonder what they're doing... Me pregunto qué están haciendo... *

▶ **wonderful**
['wʌndəful] *adj*
maravilloso, a

wood

wood
[wud] *n*
1. bosque *m*

let's go for a walk in the wood(s) demos un paseo por el bosque

2. madera *f*

wool

wool
[wul] *n*
lana *f*

word

word
[wɜːd] *n*
1. palabra *f*

words are not enough to thank you las palabras no bastan para darte las gracias

I'll keep my word cumpliré mi palabra

2. letra *f*
I don't know the words of this song no sé la letra de esta canción

work

work
[wɜːk]
I. *n*
1. trabajo *m*

he doesn't like hard work no le gusta el trabajo duro

2. obra *f*
the complete works of Shakespeare las obras completas de Shakespeare

roadworks obras (en la carretera)

3. Idiom
to be out of work estar sin trabajo/parado

II. *v i*
1. trabajar

she works in the mornings trabaja por las mañanas

2. funcionar
* Heck!... Nothing works in this plane!... ¡Caramba!... ¡No funciona nada en este avión!... *

...work

I hope my plan works espero que mi plan funcione

III. *v t*
trabajar, cultivar, explotar

▶ **work out**
1. calcular

2. salir bien

▶ **worker**
[wɜːkəʳ] *n*
trabajador, ora obrero, a

world

world
[wɜːld] *n*
mundo *m*

worry

worry
[wʌrɪ] *v i*
worried, worried
preocuparse

don't worry, I'll look for her no te preocupes, yo la buscaré

worse

worse
[wɜːs]
I. *adj*
peor

the weather is worse than yesterday el tiempo está peor que ayer

II. *adv*
peor

he's behaving worse than ever se porta peor que nunca

▶ **worst**

[wɜːst]
I. *adj*
el/la peor, los/las peores

* *This is the worst sandstorm I've ever seen!* ¡Esta es la peor tormenta de arena que he visto!
What wind! ¡Qué viento! *

II. *adv*
peor

he does it worst él lo hace peor

worth

worth
[wɜːθ] *adj*
Idiom

to be worth valer la pena

it's worth a lot of money vale mucho dinero

it's not worth it no vale la pena

would

would
[wud] *v aux*
1. *(se usa para formar el condicional)*

I would come if you asked me vendría si me lo pidieras

I wouldn't say she was wrong yo no diría que ella estuviese equivocada

2. *(se usa como forma de cortesía)*

would you close the door, please? ¿querría cerrar la puerta, por favor?

3. *(describe una acción repetida en el pasado)*
we would often have long talks solíamos tener largas conversaciones

4. Idiom
I'd (I would) rather you didn't go preferiría que no fueses

he'd rather stay in Marlinspike preferiría quedarse en Moulinsart

wrap

wrap (up)
[ræp] *v t*
wrapped, wrapped
1. tapar(se)

wrap him (up) in this

...wrap

blanket tápale con esta manta

2. envolver
wrap these presents (up) envuelve estos regalos

wrist

wrist
[rɪst] *n*
muñeca *f*

write

write
[raɪt] *v i & v t*
wrote [rəut], written ['rɪt(ə)n]
escribir

she wrote poems escribía poemas

...write

▶ **write down**
anotar, escribir

write down his telephone number anota su número de teléfono

▶ **writer**
['raɪtəʳ] *n*
escritor, ora

▶ **writing**
['raɪtɪŋ] *n*
escrito *m*, escritura *f*, letra *f*

wrong

wrong
[rɒŋ]
I. *adj*
1. falso, a, erróneo, a, incorrecto, a

the answer is wrong la respuesta es incorrecta

2. Idiom
to be wrong estar equivocado

* *No, this is not Mr*

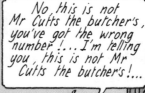

Cutts the butcher's, you've got the wrong number!... I'm telling you, this is not Mr Cutts the butcher's!... ¡No, no es la carnicería Sanzot, se ha equivocado de número!... ¡Le digo que no es la carnicería Sanzot!... *

II. *adv*
mal

they did it wrong lo hicieron mal

yard

yard
[jɑːd] *n*
1. yarda *f*
(0, 91 metros)

it's about a hundred yards away está a unos cien metros

2. patio *m*
the children are playing in the yard los niños están jugando en el patio

year

year
[jɪəʳ] *n*
año *m*

he's ten years old tiene diez años

* *Is he a general?* ¿Es un general?
Yes, General Alcazar... He is an old friend of mine, we've known each other for years... I met him in South America... Sí, el general Alcázar... Es un viejo

amigo mío. Nos conocemos desde hace años... Lo conocí en Sudamérica... *

happy New Year! ¡Feliz año nuevo!

yellow

yellow
['jeləu]
I. *adj*

...yellow

amarillo, a

* *The Captain's car is yellow.* El coche del capitán es amarillo. *

II. *n*
amarillo *m*

yellow suits you el amarillo te sienta bien

...yellow

The Captain's car is yellow.

yes

yes
[jes] *adv*
sí

are you a friend of Tintin's? – yes, I am ¿eres amigo de Tintín? – sí

I didn't do it – yes you did no lo hice – sí, lo hiciste

yesterday

yesterday
['jestədeɪ] *adv*
ayer

the Captain arrived yesterday el capitán llegó ayer

the day before yesterday anteayer

you

you
[juː] *pron*

...you

1. tú, vosotros, usted, ustedes

where are you from? ¿de dónde son ustedes/sois vosotros?

2. *not translated*
* *Good morning, Professor Calculus!* ¡Buenos días, profesor Tornasol!
Tintin, are you all right? Tintín, ¿estás bien? *

...you

3. te, os, lo, la, los, las, le, les
I'll give you a present voy a darte un regalo

4. uno
you must be careful nowadays uno tiene que ser prudente hoy día

young

young
[jʌŋ] *adj*
joven

* *Let's go...* Vamos ...
The young reporter Tintin at work!... ¡El joven reportero Tintín trabajando!... *

your

your
[jɔː] *adj*
tu, tus,
vuestro, a, os, as,
su (*de usted(es)*),
sus (*de usted(es)*)

is this your coat? ¿es éste tu abrigo?

open your books at page 10 abran sus libros en la página 10

...your

▶ **yours**
[jɔːz] *pron*
1. tuyo, a, os, as, vuestro, a, os, as, suyo, a (*de usted (es)*), os, as (*de usted(es)*)

is this book yours? ¿es tuyo este libro?

these presents are yours estos regalos son vuestros

these jewels are yours estas joyas son

suyas/de usted

2. Idiom
a friend of yours un amigo tuyo

▶ **yourself**
[jɔː'self] *pron*
1. te, os, se

* *How awful!... Look at yourself in the mirror, Tintin!...* ¡Qué horrible!... Mírese en el espejo, Tintín!... *

2. tú mismo, a,

usted mismo, a
you should do it yourself deberías hacerlo tú misma

3. Idiom
(all) by yourself (tú, usted) solo, a,
por ti mismo, a,
por usted mismo, a

▶ **yourselves**
[jɔː'selvz] *pron*
1. os, se

have you hurt your-

selves? ¿os habéis hecho daño?

2. vosotros, as, mismos, as, ustedes mismos, as
can you do it yourselves? ¿lo podéis hacer vosotros mismos?

3. Idiom
(all) by yourselves (vosotros, as, ustedes) solos, as,
por vosotros, as, mismos, as,
por sí mismos, as

youth

youth
[juːθ] *n*
pl youths [juːðz]
1. joven *m*

some youths were singing algunos jóvenes estaban cantando

2. juventud *f*
in my youth en mi juventud

▶ **youth club**
['juːθˈklʌb] *n*
club *m* juvenil

▶ **youth hostel**
['juːθˈhɒstl] *n*
albergue *m* juvenil

zero

zero
['zɪərəʊ] *n*
cero *m*

* *Later...* Más tarde...
It's cold... The temperature is well

...zero

below zero... Hace frío... La temperatura está muy por debajo de cero... *

zoo

zoo
[zuː] *n*
zoo *m*, parque *m* zoológico

SPANISH GRAMMAR

ABBREVIATIONS

DO	= direct object		Part	= participle
IO	= indirect object		Subj	= subjunctive
Ind	= indicative		S	= subject
Inf	= infinitive			

STRESS

• Words that end in a vowel, *n* or *s* are stressed on the syllable before last: *perro*, *detectives*.
• Words that end in a consonant other than *n* or *s* are stressed on the last syllable: *profesor*, *pared*.
• Words that are exceptions to these two rules have a written accent on the stressed vowel: *Milú, Tintín, capitán*.
• Notes:
– Sometimes, the plural forms has a written accent when the singular does not: *un joven → dos jóvenes*.
Exceptions: *carácter → caracteres, régimen → regímenes*.
– The written accent is used to distinguish words with the same form but different meanings or grammatical uses: *mi* (poss adj); *mí* (pers pron).

GENDER AND NUMBER

Gender: masculine/feminine

• Adjectives and participles that end in *o* form the feminine by changing *o* to *a*: *un perro travieso, una niña traviesa*.
• Other adjectives and participles have the same form for masculine and feminine: *un jersey verde, una falda verde*.
• Exceptions:

– Nationality adjectives: *francés → francesa, español → española*.
– Adjectives that end in *-án, -ín, -ón, -ete, -ote*: *burlón → burlona*.
– Most adjectives that end in *-or*: *trabajador → trabajadora*.
(Invariable adjectives: *peor, mejor, menor, mayor, superior, inferior, exterior, interior, anterior, posterior, ulterior*.)

Number: singular/plural

• Words that end in a vowel take *s* to form the plural: *detective → detectives*.
• Words that end in a consonant add *-es* to form the plural: *ciudad → ciudades, país → países*.
• Note: words that end in *z* form the plural in *-ces*: *voz → voces*.

SUFFIXES

Diminutive suffixes

• *-ito, -illo* are added to words that end in *a* or *o* or a consonant other than *n* or *r*: *perro → perrito, Isabel → Isabelita, árbol → arbolillo, chica → chiquilla*.
• *-cito, -cillo* are added to words that end in *e, n* or *r*: *calle → callecita, comedor → comedorcillo*.
• *-ecito, -ecillo* are added to words of one syllable or words that contain a diphthong:
luz → lucecita, viento → vientecillo.

Augmentative suffixes

The commonest augmentative suffixes are *-ón, -ona* and *-azo, -aza*:
hombre → hombrón, ojos → ojazos.

Other suffixes

• The suffixes *-al* and *-ar* are often used to designate places where certain plants abound: *trigal (campo de trigo), pinar (bosque de pinos)*.
• The suffixes *-ada* and *-azo* may refer to a blow given with a certain instrument: *pico → picotazo* (peck); *cuchillo → cuchillada* (slash, knife wound)

THE ARTICLE

The definite article
el, la, los, las

• The masculine singular article contracts with the prepositions *a* and *de*: *a + el = al, de + el = del*.
• The feminine singular article *la* is replaced by *el* before nouns that begin with stressed *(h)a*: *el agua, el hambre*.
But: *la alta montaña, la alcachofa*.
• The plural article can be used to express age and time:
a los dos años, Milú era muy travieso; el capitán llegó a las tres de la tarde
• Omission:
– Before *casa* (meaning *(at)* home), *misa, caza, pesca* when these words are used in a general sense and not modified:
está en casa del capitán; fue a misa/de caza/de pesca.
– Before a superlative that follows a noun that already has the article:

Tornasol es el hombre más atolondrado que conozco.
– Before most names of countries: *Francia, España.*

The indefinite article
un, una, unos, unas

The plural forms are not as common as the singular ones: *son detectives.*
They are used as follows:
• To express approximation:
*Abdallah tiene **unos** seis años* Abdullah is about six years old.
• To express the idea of *algunos*, as some, a few:
*esperemos a Tintín **unos** minutos más* let's wait for Tintin for just a few more minutes.
• Before a plural noun as the subject at the beginning of a sentence:
***unos** campesinos preguntaron por ti* some peasants asked for you.
• No indefinite article is used before otro and cierto: ***otro** día* another day, ***cierta** planta* a certain plant.

The neuter article *lo*

It is used as follows:
• *Lo* + Adj or Past Part:
***lo difícil** va a ser encontrar a los bandidos* the difficult part is going to be finding the bandits;
***lo bueno** de esto es que...* the good thing about this is that...
• *Lo* + Adj or Past Part + *que* + V:
*no te puedes imaginar **lo contento** que estoy, Tintín* you can't imagine how happy I am, Tintín.
• *Lo de* the business/the question of:
*solucionaremos **lo del** robo más tarde* we'll solve the question of the robbery later.
• *Lo que* = what:
*no entiendo **lo que** dices* I don't understand what you are saying.

POSSESSIVES

Possessive adjectives

There are two series of possessive adjectives in Spanish:
• The weak forms:
mi, mis = my

tu, tus = your
su, sus = his, her, their, your (polite form)
nuestro, a, os, as = our
vuestro, a, os, as = your
Example:
*este es **su** coche* this is his/her/their/your car (depending on context).
• The strong forms, which go after the noun:
mío, a, os, as = my, of mine
tuyo, a, os, as = your, of yours
suyo, a, os, as = his, of his, her, of hers, their, of theirs, your, of yours (polite form)
nuestro, a, os, as = our, of ours
vuestro, a, os, as = your, of yours
Example:
*un amigo **suyo*** a friend of his/hers/theirs/yours (according to context);
*el coche **mío*** my car/this car of mine.
• Note: the article with the reflexive form of the verb is often preferred in Spanish to the possessive:
***se** puso **el** abrigo* he put his coat on.

Possessive pronouns

The possessive pronouns are the strong form of the possessive with the article:
el mío, la mía, los míos, las mías; el tuyo...; el suyo...; el nuestro...; el vuestro...
Example: *mi casa y **la suya*** my house and his/hers/theirs/yours.

DEMONSTRATIVES

Demonstrative adjectives

There are three series of demonstratives in Spanish, which refer to three degrees of proximity (spatial, temporal or affective).

Este, a, os, as
These forms mean this, these, i. e. near me, (the speaker) in space or time:
***esta** pipa es mía, Tintín.*

Ese, a, os, as
These forms mean that, those, i. e. near you (the second person), in space or time:
*¿**ese** libro es tuyo?*

The affective use (near you in thoughts or feelings) can be seen in:
*me gusta **esa** idea.*
In such sentences the value may be pejorative:
*no me gusta nada **ese** hombre.*

Aquel, aquella, aquellos, aquellas
These forms refer to things and ideas which are away from the speaker and the second person:
*en **aquel** tiempo, vivíamos felices.*
The affective value is often positive:
***aquel** hombre era un santo;*
***aquellas** casas eran sólidas.*

Demonstrative pronouns

• The demonstrative pronouns have the same form as the adjectives, but the masculine and feminine forms bear a written accent:
***éste** es el detective de quien te hablé.*
• The neuter forms *esto, eso, aquello* have no accent and are invariable:
***eso** no me interesa.*

PERSONAL PRONOUNS

Subject pronouns: *yo, tú, él, ella, usted, nosotros, as, vosotros, as, ellos, as, ustedes*

They are used emphatically or to clarify: ***yo** te comprendo, Milú; **él** no sabe nada* (without the pronoun, this latter sentence could mean he/she knows nothing or you know nothing).

Object pronouns (not used with prepositions)

DO: *me, te, lo, le, la, nos, os, los, les, las*
• For people, *lo, le, los, les* are used with masculine objects, and *la, las* with feminine objects.
• For things, *lo, los* are used with masculine objects, and *la, las* with feminine objects.
Examples:
*no **lo/le** he visto* I didn't see him;
*no **lo** veo* I can't see it;
*no **la** veo (tu casa/a tu hermana)* I can't see it/her.

IO: *me, te, le, nos, os, les*
le voy a escribir I'm going to write to him/her/you.

Reflexive pronouns:
me, te, se, nos, os, se

se está lavando he/she/it is washing, you are washing.

Object pronouns after prepositions: *mí, tí, él, ella, usted, ustedes, sí* (reflexive)

me fío de tí I trust you
hablaron entre sí they talked among themselves.
• There are certain irregular forms with the preposition *con*:
conmigo (with me), *contigo* (with you), *consigo* (with himself/herself/itself/themselves/yourself/yourselves).

The polite form

To address adults with whom we are not familiar we use *usted* + a third person singular verb (if we are talking to only one person), or *ustedes* + a third person plural verb:
¿puede usted llevarme al aeropuerto?
ustedes pueden pasar ya.

Position of the personal pronoun

• Although the object and reflexive forms of the personal pronouns normally precede the verb in Spanish, they may follow:
The infinitive: *Milú no quiere lavarse /Milú no se quiere lavar.*
The gerund: *Milú está lavándose/Milú se está lavando.*
The imperative: *lávate, Milú/que te laves, Milú.*
Note the written accents!

• Note: *le(s) + lo(s) → se lo(s); le(s) + la(s) → se la(s).*
Example: *se los voy a dar /voy a dárselos* I'm going to give them to him/her/you.
• Pronouns may either precede the conjugated verb or follow an infinitive

or gerund: *no se lo puedo decir/no puedo decírselo.*
• The IO pronoun always precedes the DO one (*me lo* not *lo me* etc).

INDEFINITES

• *Mucho* (a lot of, much, many), *poco* (little, few), *demasiado* (too much, too many), *bastante* (quite a lot) are inflected when they are adjectives or pronouns (*veo pocas casas*), but not when they are adverbs (*Bianca Castafiore come demasiado*).
• *Otro, a, os, as* (see "The indefinite article")
• *Alguno, a, os, as* (some, a few); *ninguno, a* (no, neither, none, nobody); *algo* (something, anything, nothing); *nada* (nothing); *alguien* (somebody); *nadie* (nobody, anybody).
Spanish permits double-negative constructions:
no lo sabe nadie = nadie lo sabe.
Alguno and *ninguno* are shortened to *algún* and *ningún* before masculine singular nouns: *algún día le hablaré; no hay ningún coche.*
• *Todo, a, os, as* (all)
Lo is generally used before the verb when *todo* follows: *ya lo sé todo.*
• *Cualquiera* (any) shortens to cualquier before nouns: *cualquier persona* but *una persona cualquiera.*
• *Cada* (each, every) is invariable.
• *Ambos, as* (both):
ambos son detectives.

IMPERSONAL CONSTRUCTIONS

• Some verbs, such as *llover* and *nevar*, only exist in the third person singular. The accompanying pronoun in English will be it:
llueve it is raining; *nevaba* it was snowing.
• The passive construction with *se* (*pasiva refleja*) is common in Spanish where English has an indicative verb:
no se puede aprender una lengua en un

mes you/one/people can't learn a language in a month;
¿se puede? may we come in?
desde aquí se ve el mar you can see the sea from here.
Note the subject-verb agreement in sentences like:
por la noche se oyen ruidos raros.
• *Hace* and *hay* are common in expressions referring to the weather:
hace sol, hace viento, hay niebla (it is sunny, windy, foggy).
• *Hay que = se tiene que*:
Hay que creer en algo one has to believe in something.
• Spanish also uses the pronoun *uno* like English one, particularly when the person speaking feels involved or when the verb in question is already reflexive:
a veces, uno no sabe qué hacer.
uno se levanta muy temprano, y está cansado todo el día.
• The third person plural is also used impersonally in Spanish, especially when it is a question of one particular act on a particular occasion (*llaman a la puerta* there's someone at the door) or when the subject is collective and taken for granted (*cuentan que hay fantasmas en la casa* they say the house is haunted).

THE ADJECTIVE

The Spanish adjective agrees in gender and number.

The comparative

• Of superiority: *más ... que* (more ... than).
• Of equality: *tan ... como* (as ... as, not as/so ... as).
• Irregular comparatives: *pequeño → menor, grande → mayor, malo → peor.*

The superlative

Relative
El/la/los/las más..., el/la/los/las menos (the most..., the least): *tú eres el más inteligente.*

Absolute (very)
• *Muy*: *la Castafiore tiene una voz muy linda.*

- The suffix *-ísimo, a, os, as*: *tiene una voz lindísima.*

Apocope

Certain adjectives lose their final vowel or syllable when they are placed before a noun.
- *grande → gran*:
un gran hombre, una gran experiencia.
- *bueno → buen, malo → mal, alguno → algún, ninguno → ningún, primero → primer, tercero → tercer*,
before a masculine noun:
es su primer coche.
- *cualquiera → cualquier*:
cómprale cualquier cosa (but: *una cosa cualquiera*).
- *ciento → cien*, before a noun or an additional numeral:
cien pesetas, cien mil libras.
- *santo → san*, before a proper noun (except *Tomás* and *Domingo*):
San Francisco (but: *un santo varón*).
- *uno → un*:
sólo un libro.

THE ADVERB

Adverbs of manner

- Many of these are formed by adding *-mente* to the feminine form of the adjective or to the invariable adjectival form: *lento → lentamente, difícil → dificilmente.*
- When there are two or more adverbs in *-mente* together, only the last one takes the suffix:
le contestó fría y severamente.
- *Recientemente* reduces to *recién* before a past participle:
está recién llegado he has just arrived.

Adverbs of time

Position:
- *ya no* comes immediately before the verb:
ya no vendrá más he won't come any more.
- *nunca, jamás* (never), *tampoco* (neither, not ... either) are used in two different constructions:
no me lo dijo nunca/nunca me lo dijo;
no lo sé tampoco/tampoco lo sé.

PREPOSITIONS

A

Two important uses:
- Before a personal DO:
llamaré a Tchang; ¿has visto a Milú?
- Expressing motion towards (English: to):
vamos a España; fuimos a la cama en seguida.

Con

See object pronouns after prepositions.

De

Denotes:
- Material of which something is made:
esta estatua es de oro.
- Belonging:
este coche es del señor Latón.
- A special characteristic:
esta chica es de pelo rubio.
- Function (as):
trabaja de enfermera en este barco.

En

Denotes position or location:
vive en Madrid he lives in Madrid.

Para

Denotes:
- Purpose: *trabaja para ganarse la vida.*
- Destination:
tengo un regalo para Abdallah.
- Direction: *me voy para Lima.*
- Point of view:
para mí, no es una buena idea.

Por

Denotes:
- Cause: *ha mentido por ti* he lied for you.
- Movement through or around:
hace dos años, pasamos por Sildavia; Milú está paseando por el parque.
- Exchange:
le doy veinte mil pesetas por su perro, Tintín.
- The agent in the passive voice:
ha sido atropellado por un coche.

CO-ORDINATION

- *Y* becomes *e* before words that begin with *(h)i*:

Abdallah es caprichoso e insoportable.
- *O* becomes *u* before words that begin with *(h)o*:
tendrá siete u ocho años.
- When a contrast or a correction is expressed, Spanish does not use *pero*, but *sino* or *sino que*:
no es usted, sino él que lo ha hecho mal.
¡no sólo mientes, sino que robas!

RELATIVE PRONOUNS

Que (who(m), which, that)

It is used for both people and things, and can be the subject or the object:
el libro que lees the book (which/that) you are reading;
la señora que está hablando the lady who/that is talking.

Quien(es) (who(m))

It can only refer to people:
los detectives con quienes hablo se llaman Hernández y Fernández.

El/la/los/las que, el/la/los/las cuales (who(m), which, that)

These forms are used for both people and things: *los cuadros de los cuales te hablé están en el museo.*

Cuyo, a, os, as (whose, of which)

This possessive relative is used for people or things: *el libro cuyo título es...* the book whose title/the title of which is...

THE VERB

SER AND *ESTAR*

Ser describes essential characteristics, whether they be temporary or permanent. *Estar* describes temporary states or circumstances.

Before a noun, pronoun, numeral or infinitive: *ser*

ese hombre **es** *un ladrón; ¿***eres** *tú?; ***éramos** *tres en el barco; ¡qué agradable* **es** *descansar!*

Before an adjective:
• If we are describing an essential characteristic or a permanent condition: *ser*
Tintín **es** *muy inteligente.*
• If we are describing a temporary state: *estar*
el capitán **está** *enfermo.*
• Many adjectives change their meaning depending on whether they are used with *ser* or *estar*:
es *malo* he is bad/naughty **está** *malo* he is ill;
es *listo* he is clever **está** *listo* he is ready.

Before an expression of place or time: *estar*
Tintín **está** *en el Perú.*

To express origin: *ser*
Zorrino **es** *del Perú.*

Before a past participle:
• To describe the action: *ser*
Fue *herido por los bandidos.*
• To describe the result of the action or state: *estar*
Milú **está** *herido.*

In impersonal constructions (it is ... that ...): *ser*
es *aquí donde vive Tchang.*

To describe position: *estar*
Bianca Castafiore **está** *de pie; Milú* **está** *al lado de Tintín.*

To express belonging: *ser*
esta bufanda **es** *de Zorrino.*

To state the material of which something is made: *ser*
la estatua **es** *de oro.*

THE SUBJUNCTIVE

The subjunctive mood is used in Spanish:

• After certain conjunctions like: *para que* (so that), *a no ser que* (unless), *ojalá* (I wish), *con tal que* (on condition that), etc:
te lo digo para que lo **sepas.**
• In relative clauses that do not state known fact:
buscamos un hombre que **hable** *alemán* we haven't got anyone in mind yet.
Compare: *buscamos a un hombre que* **habla** *alemán* we know who we are looking for.
• After verbs expressing desire:
quiero que **vengas.**
• After words expressing uncertainty (*puede que, es posible que, quizás, no creo que, me temo que*):
es posible que **haya** *perdido el tren; quizá no* **venga;**
me temo que no **vaya** *a volver.*
• In third person imperatives and second person negative imperatives:
no **diga** *nada; no* **vengan** *hasta mañana; no* **compres** *tanto; no* **hagáis** *eso.*
• In clauses of concession:
lo compraré, aunque no **quieras** I'm going to buy it whether you like it or not.
• After verbs of ordering, advising, recommending, prohibiting:
te aconsejo que te **quedes** *en casa.*
• After time conjunctions in clauses referring to the future: *cuando* (when), *en cuanto, tan pronto como* (as soon as), *hasta que* (until, till):
cuando **llegue,** *iremos al cine.*
Compare: *no sé cuándo* **llegará** (indirect question).
• In hypothetical conditions:
si lo **supiera,** *te lo diría* if I knew, I'd tell you;
si lo **hubiera** *sabido, te lo habría dicho* if I'd known, I'd have told you.
• In comparisons after *como si*:
la trata como si **fuera** *su hija* he treats her as if she were his daughter.

THE PRESENT PERFECT AND THE SIMPLE PAST

• The Spanish present perfect tense is used, as in English, when there is no specific time reference or when the action has not been completed:
*¿***has estado** *alguna vez en Inglaterra?* have you ever been to England?
todavía no **he acabado** *este libro* I still haven't finished this book.
Compare the simple past tense in:
fuimos *a Inglaterra el año pasado* we went to England last year;

recibí su carta hace unos días I received his letter a few days ago.
• The main difference between the perfect tense in Spanish and in English is that in Spanish it is often used to refer to completed action in the recent past, whereas in English any kind of completed action is expressed in the simple past:
esta mañana **he recibido** *(or: recibí) una carta* this morning I received a letter;
ha entrado *(or entró) hace un momento* she came in a moment ago.
• Note that in English we very often use the present perfect with since and for to say how long something has been going on, whereas Spanish often has the present tense in constructions of this kind:
lo **conozco** *desde 1960* I've known him since 1960;
estoy *aquí desde hace dos horas/***llevo** *dos horas aquí* I've been here for two hours;
hace cinco años que **estudio** *francés* I've been studying French for five years.

TENSE AGREEMENT WITH THE INDICATIVE AND SUBJUNCTIVE MOODS

No quiero que él **venga,** *pero sí me* **gustaría** *que tú* **vinieses.**

Tense in main clause	Tense in subordinate clause
present indicative future indicative present perfect indicative imperative	present subjunctive
imperfect imperative simple past indicative pluperfect indicative conditional	imperfect or pluperfect subjunctive

ADJETIVOS NUMERALES — NUMERALS

Numerales cardinales — Cardinal numbers

cero	0	nought
uno	1	one
dos	2	two
tres	3	three
cuatro	4	four
cinco	5	five
seis	6	six
siete	7	seven
ocho	8	eight
nueve	9	nine
diez	10	ten
once	11	eleven
doce	12	twelve
trece	13	thirteen
catorce	14	fourteen
quince	15	fifteen
dieciséis	16	sixteen
diecisiete	17	seventeen
dieciocho	18	eighteen
diecinueve	19	nineteen
veinte	20	twenty
veintiuno	21	twenty-one
veintidós	22	twenty-two
treinta	30	thirty
treinta y uno	31	thirty-one
treinta y dos	32	thirty-two
cuarenta	40	forty
cincuenta	50	fifty
sesenta	60	sixty
setenta	70	seventy
ochenta	80	eighty
noventa	90	ninety
ciento, cien	100	a/one hundred
ciento uno	101	a hundred and one
ciento dos	102	a hundred and two
ciento cincuenta	150	a hundred and fifty
doscientos	200	two hundred
doscientos uno	201	two hundred and one
doscientos dos	202	two hundred and two
mil	1.000 (1000)	a/one thousand
mil uno	1.001 (1001)	a thousand and one
mil dos	1.002 (1002)	a thousand and two
dos mil	2.000 (2000)	two thousand
un millón	1.000.000	a/one million
dos millones	2.000.000	two millions

Numerales ordinales — Ordinal numbers

primero	1º	1st	first
segundo	2º	2nd	second
tercero	3º	3rd	third
cuarto	4º	4th	fourth
quinto	5º	5th	fifth
sexto	6º	6th	sixth
séptimo	7º	7th	seventh
octavo	8º	8th	eighth
noveno	9º	9th	ninth
décimo	10º	10th	tenth
undécimo, onceno	11º	11th	eleventh
duodécimo	12º	12th	twelfth
decimotercero	13º	13th	thirteenth
decimocuarto	14º	14th	fourteenth
decimoquinto	15º	15th	fifteenth
decimosexto	16º	16th	sixteenth
decimoséptimo	17º	17th	seventeenth
decimoctavo	18º	18th	eighteenth
decimonono	19º	19th	nineteenth
vigésimo	20º	20th	twentieth
vigésimo primero	21º	21st	twenty-first
vigésimo segundo	22º	22nd	twenty-second
trigésimo	30º	30th	thirtieth

CONJUGATION OF SPANISH VERBS

REGULAR SPANISH VERBS

	-ar verbs	-er verbs	-ir verbs
infinitive	cantar	comer	vivir
indicative present	canto	como	vivo
	cantas	comes	vives
	canta	come	vive
	cantamos	comemos	vivimos
	cantáis	coméis	vivís
	cantan	comen	viven
imperfect	cantaba	comía	vivía
	cantabas	comías	vivías
	cantaba	comía	vivía
	cantábamos	comíamos	vivíamos
	cantabais	comíais	vivíais
	cantaban	comían	vivían
simple past	canté	comí	viví
	cantaste	comiste	viviste
	cantó	comió	vivió
	cantamos	comimos	vivimos
	cantasteis	comisteis	vivisteis
	cantaron	comieron	vivieron
future	cantaré	comeré	viviré
	cantarás	comerás	vivirás
	cantará	comerá	vivirá
	cantaremos	comeremos	viviremos
	cantaréis	comeréis	viviréis
	cantarán	comerán	vivirán
conditional	cantaría	comería	viviría
	cantarías	comerías	vivirías
	cantaría	comería	viviría
	cantaríamos	comeríamos	viviríamos
	cantaríais	comeríais	viviríais
	cantarían	comerían	vivirían
subjunctive present	cante	coma	viva
	cantes	comas	vivas
	cante	coma	viva

	cantemos	comamos	vivamos
	cantéis	comáis	viváis
	canten	coman	vivan
imperfect	cantara	comiera	viviera
	cantaras	comieras	vivieras
	cantara	comiera	viviera
	cantáramos	comiéramos	viviéramos
	cantarais	comierais	vivierais
	cantaran	comieran	vivieran
	cantase	comiese	viviese
	cantases	comieses	vivieses
	cantase	comiese	viviese
	cantásemos	comiésemos	viviésemos
	cantaseis	comieseis	vivieseis
	cantasen	comiesen	viviesen
future	cantare	comiere	viviere
	cantares	comieres	vivieres
	cantare	comiere	viviere
	cantáremos	comiéremos	viviéremos
	cantareis	comiereis	viviereis
	cantaren	comieren	vivieren
imperative	canta	come	vive
	cante	coma	viva
	cantemos	comamos	vivamos
	canted	comed	vivid
	canten	coman	vivan
present participle	cantando	comiendo	viviendo
past participle	cantado	comido	vivido

IRREGULAR SPANISH VERBS

1. = Present 2. = Imperfect 3. = Simple past 4. = Future
5 = Conditional 6. = Imperative 7. = Present subjunctive
8. = Imperfect du subjunctive 9. = Future subjunctive
10. = Present participle 11. = Past participle

abrir 11. abierto
acentuar 1. acentúo..., acentuamos... - 7. acentúe ... acentuemos...
acordar 1. acuerdo..., acordamos, acordáis, acuerdan - 6. acuerda... - 7. acuerde,... acordemos, acordeis, acuerden
acostar like acordar
actuar like acentuar
adquirir 1. adquiero,... adquirimos, adquirís, adquieran - 6. adquiere, adquiramos, adquirid, adquieran - 7. adquiera,...adquiramos, adquiráis, adquieran
advertir 1. advierto,... advertimos, advertís, advierten - 3. advertí,... advertieron - 6. advierte, advierta, advirtamos, advertid, adviertan -7. advierta,... advirtamos, advirtáis, adviertan - 8. advirtiera *or* advirtiese, advirtieras *or* advirtieses, advirtiera *or* advirtiese... 9. advirtiere, advirtieres, advirtiere... - 10. advirtiendo
afluir 1. afluyo, afluyes... afluimos, afluís, afluyen - 3. afluí, afluiste, afluyó, afluimos, afluisteis, afluyerón - 6. afluye,... afluyamos, afluid, afluyan - 8. afluyera *or* afluyese... - 9. afluyere, afluyeres - 10. afluyendo
agradecer like crecer
ahogar, alargar takes u before e
alcanzar takes c before e
almorzar like acordar; takes c before e
alzar takes c before e
amanecer like crecer
amenazar takes c before e
andar 3. anduve, anduviste, anduvo, anduvimos, anduvisteis, anduvieron - 8. anduviera *or* anduviese... - 9. anduviere, anduvieres...
anochecer like crecer
apagar takes u before e
aparecer like crecer
apetecer like crecer
apretar like calentar
aprobar like acordar
arrancar c becomes qu before e
atacar c becomes qu before e
atraer like traer
autorizar takes c before e
avanzar takes c before e
buscar c becomes qu before e
caber 1. quepo, cabes, cabe, cabemos, cabeis, caben - 3. cupe, cupiste, cupo, cupimos, cupisteis, cupieron - 4. cabré, cabrás... - 5. cabría, ... - 7. quepa, quepas,... - 8. cupiera *or* cupiese... - 9. cupiere...
caer 1. caigo, caes, cae, caemos, caeis, caen - 3. caí, caíste, cayó, caímos, caísteis, cayeron - 6. cae, caiga, caigamos, caigáis, caigan - 7. cayera *or* cayese... - 8. cayere... - 10. cayendo - 11. caído
calentar 1. caliento,... calentamos, calentáis, calientan - 6. calienta, caliente, calentemos, calentad, calienten - 7. caliente, ... calentemos, calentéis, calienten
cargar takes u before e
cazar takes c before e
cerrar like calentar
coger takes j before a and o
colgar like acordar; takes u before e
colocar c becomes qu before e
comenzar like acordar; takes c before e
conducir 1. conduzco, conduces, conduce, ...- 3. conduje, condujiste, condujo, condujimos, condujisteis, condujeron - 6. conduce, conduzca, conduzcamos, conducid, conduzcan - 7. conduzca, conduzcas, ... - 8. condujera *or* condujese... - 9. condujere...
conseguir like pedir; loses its u before a and o
convertir like advertir
corregir 1. corrijo, corriges, corrige... - 3. corregí, corregiste, corrigió, corregimos, corregisteis, corregieron - 6. corrige, corrija, corrijamos,

	corrigid, corrijan - 7. corrija,... - 8. corrigiera *or* corrigiese… - 9. corrigiere… - 10. corrigiendo
costar	like acordar
crecer	1. crezco, creces,…- 6. crece, crezca, crezcamos, creced, crezcan - 7. crezca, crezcas …
creer	like leer
criticar	c becomes qu before e
cruzar	takes c before e
cubrir	11. cubierto
chocar	c becomes qu before e
dar	1. doy, das, da, … - 3. di, diste, dio, dimos, disteis, dieron 6. da, dé, demos, dad, den - 7. dé, des,… - 8. diera *or* diese,… - 9. diere, dieres, diere, diéremos, diereis, dieren
decir	1. digo, dices, dice, decimos, decís, dicen - 3. dije, dijiste, dijo, dijimos, dijisteis, dijeron - 4. diré, dirás, dirá, diremos, diréis, dirán - 5. diría, … - 6. di, diga, digamos, decid, digan - 7. diga, … - 8. dijera *or* dijese… - 9. dijere,… - 8. diciendo - 11. dicho
detener	like tener
devolver	like volver
distraer	like traer
doler	like mover
dormir	1. duermo,… dormimos, dormís, duermen - 3. dormí, dormiste, dormís, durmió, dormimos, dormisteis, durmieron - 6. duerme, duerma, durmamos, dormid, duerman - 7. duerma, … durmamos, durmáis, duerman - 8. durmiera *or* durmiese… - 9. durmiere,… - 10. durmiendo
edificar	c becomes qu before e
elegir	like corregir
embarcar	c becomes qu before e
encender	1. enciendo,… encendemos, encendéis, encienden - 6. enciende, encienda, encendamos, encended, enciendan - 7. encienda,… encendamos, encendáis, enciendan
encontrar	like acordar
envolver	like volver
equivocar	c becomes qu before e
escoger	takes j before a and o
escribir	11. escrito
estar	1. estoy, estás, está, estamos, estáis, están - 3. estuve, estuviste, estuvo, estuvimos, estuvisteis, estuvieron - 6. está *or* estate, esté, estemos, estad *or* estaos, estén - 7. esté, estés, esté, estemos, estéis, estén - 8. estuviera *or* estuviese,… estuviéramos *or* estuviésemos, estuvierais *or* estuvieseis, estuvieran *or* estuviesen - 9. estuviere, … estuviéremos, estuviereis, estuvieren
exigir	takes j before a and o
explicar	c becomes qu before e
guiar	1. guío,… guiamos, guiais, guían - 6. guía, guíe, guiemos, guiad, guíen - 7. guíe, guíes, guíe, guiemos, guiéis, guíen
haber	1. he, has, ha, hemos, habéis, han - 2. había, … - 3. hube, hubiste, hubo, hubimos, hubisteis, hubieron - 4. habré, habrás, habrá, habremos,

	habréis, habrán - 5. habría,… - 6. haya, … - 7 hubiera *or* hubiese, … - 8. hubiere,… - 10 habiendo - 11. habido
hacer	1. hago, haces, hace, hacemos, hacéis, hacen - 3 hice, hiciste, hizo, hicimos, hicisteis, hicieron - 4 haré, harás, hará, haremos, haréis, harán - 5. haría … - 6. haz, haga, hagamos, haced, hagan - 7 haga, … - 8. hiciera *or* hiciese… - 9. hiciere… - 10. haciendo - 11. hecho
helar	like calentar
indicar	c becomes qu before e
influir, instruir	like afluir
introducir	like conducir
ir	1. voy, vas, va, vamos, vais, van - 2. iba, … íbamos, ibais, iban -3. fui, fuiste, fue, fuimos, fuisteis, fueron - 6. ve, vaya, vayas, id, vayan - 7. vaya, … - 8. fuera *or* fuese… - 9. fuere… - 10. yendo - 11. ido
jugar	1. juego, juegas, juega, jugamos, jugáis, juegan - 3. jugué, jugaste, jugó, jugamos, jugasteis, jugaron - 6. juega, juegue, juguemos, jugad, jueguen - 7. juegue,… juguemos, juguéis, jueguen
justificar	c becomes qu before e
juzgar	takes u before e
leer	3. leí, leíste, leyó, leímos, leísteis, leyeron - 8. leyera *or* leyese… - 9. leyere… - 10. leyendo
llegar	takes u before e
llover	like mover
madrugar	takes u before e
manifestar	like calentar
mentir	like sentir
merendar	like calentar
morder	like mover
morir	1. muero, … morimos, morís, mueren - 3. morí, moriste, murió, morimos, moristeis, murieron - 6. muere, muera, muramos, morid, mueran - 7. muera,… muramos, muráis, mueran - 8. muriera *or* muriese… - 9. muriere… - 10. muriendo - 11. muerto
mover	1. muevo,… movemos, movéis, mueven - 6. mueve, mueva, movamos, moved, mueven - 7. mueva, … movamos, mováis, muevan
nacer	1. nazco, naces, … - 6. nace, nazca, nazcamos, naced, nazcan - 7. nazca, nazcas…
obedecer	like crecer
obtener	like tener
oír	oigo, oyes, oye, oímos, oís, oyen - 3. oí, oíste, oyó, oímos, oísteis, oyeron - 6. oye, oiga, oigamos, oíd, oigan - 7. oiga, oigas, … - 8. oyera *or* oyese… - 9. oyere… - 10. oyendo - 11. oído
oler	huelo, hueles, huele, olemos, oléis, huelen - 6. huele, huelas, olamos, oled, huelan - 7. huela, huelas, huela, olamos, oláis, huelan
oponer	like poner
padecer	like crecer
pagar	takes u before e
parecer	like crecer

pedir	1. pido, pides, pide, pedimos, pedís, piden - 3. pedí, pediste, pidió, pedimos, pedisteis, pidieron - 6. pide, pida, pidamos, pedis, pidan - 7. pida, pidas, pida, pidamos, pidáis, pidan - 8. pidiera *or* pidiese - 10. pidiere… 11. pidiendo	**segar**	like calentar; takes u before e
		seguir	like pedir ; u before a and o
pegar	takes u before e	**sembrar**	like sentar
pensar	1. pienso, … pensamos, pensáis, piensan - 6. piensa, piense, pensemos, pensad, piensen - 7. piense, … pensemos, penséis, piensen	**sentar**	1. siento, sientas, sienta, sentamos, sentáis, sientan - 6. sienta, siente, sentemos, sentad, sienten - 7. siente, … sentemos, sentéis, sienten
perder	like encender	**sentir**	1. siento, … sentimos, sentís, sienten - 6. siente, sienta, sintamos, sentid, sientan - 7. sienta, … sintamos, sintáis, sientan - 8. sintiera *or* sintiese… - 9. sintiere… -10. sintiendo
perjudicar	c becomes qu before e		
permanecer	like crecer		
pertenecer	like crecer		
poder	1. puedo, … podemos, podéis, pueden - 3. pude, pudiste, pudo, pudimos, pudisteis, pudieron - 4. podré, podrás,… - 5. podría, podrías, … - 6. puede, pueda, podamos, poded, puedan - 7. pueda, puedas, … - 8. pusiera *or* pusiese… - 9. pusiese… - 10. pudiendo	**ser**	1. soy, eres, es , somos, sois, son - 2. era,…éramos, erais, eran - 3. fui, fuiste, fue, fuimos, fuisteis, fueron - 4. seré, serás, será, seremos, seréis, serán - 5. sería… - 6. sé, sea, seamos, sed, sean - 7. sea, seas, sea, seamos, seáis, sean - 8. fuera *or* fuese… - 9. fuere… - 10. siendo - 11. sido
poner	1. pongo, pones, pone, ponemos, ponéis, ponen - 3. puse, pusiste, puso, pusimos, pusisteis, pusieron - 4. pondré, pondrás, pondrá, pondremos, pondréis, pondrán - 5. pondría… - 6. pon, ponga, pongamos, poned, pongan - 7. ponga… - 8. pusiera *or* pusiese… - 9. pusiere… 10. poniendo - 11. puesto	**servir**	like pedir
		significar	c becomes qu before e
		sobresalir	like salir
		soler	like mover
		soltar, sonar	like calentar
		sonreír	like reír
		soñar	like calentar
		suponer	like poner
poseer	like leer	**tener**	1. tengo, tienes, tiene, tenemos, tenéis, tienen - 3. tuve, tuviste, tuvo, tuvimos, tuvisteis, tuvieron - 4. tendré, tendrás,…- 5. tendría… - 6. ten, tenga, tengamos, tened, tengan - 7. tenga, tengas… - 8. tuviera *or* tuviese… - 9. tuviere…
probar	like acordar		
producir	like conducir		
proponer	like poner		
proteger	takes j before a and o	**tocar**	c becomes qu before e
querer	1. quiero, … queremos, queréis, quieren - 3. quise, quisiste, quiso, quisimos, quisisteis, quisieron - 4. querré, querrás, querrá, querremos, querréis, querrán… - 5. querría… - 6. quiere, quiera, queramos, quered, quieran - 7. quiera, … queramos, queráis, quieran - 8. quisiera *or* quisiese… - 9. quisiere… 11. querido	**traducir**	like conducir
		traer	1. traigo, traes, trae, traemos, traéis, traen - 3. traje, trajiste, trajo, trajimos, trajisteis, trajeron - 6. trae, traiga, traigamos, traed, traigan - 7. traiga, traigas… - 8. trajera *or* trajese… - 9. trajere… - 10. trayendo - 11. traído
recordar	like acordar	**tragar**	takes u before e
regar	like calentar ; takes u before e	**valer**	1. valgo, vales, vale, valemos, valéis, valen - 4. valdré, valdrás… - 5. valdrías… - 6. val *or* vale, valga, valgamos, valed, valgan - 7. valga…
reír	1. río, ríes, ríe, reímos, reís, ríen - 3. reí, reíste, rió, reímos, reísteis, rieron - 6. ríe, ría, riamos, reíd, rían - 7. ría, rías, ría, riamos, riáis, rían - 8. riera *or* riese… - 9. riere… - 10. riendo	**venir**	1. vengo, vienes, viene, venimos, venís, vienen - 3. vine, viniste, vino, vinimos, vinisteis, vinieron - 4. vendré, vendrás… - 5. vendría… - 6. ven, venga, vengamos, venid, vengan - 7. venga, vengas… - 8. viniera *or* viniese… - 9. viniere… - 10. viniendo
resolver	like mover		
rodar	like acordar		
romper	11. roto	**ver**	1. veo, ves, ve, vemos, veis, ven - 3. vi, viste, vio, vimos, visteis, vinieron - 4. veré, verás… - 5. vería… - 6. vea, vea, veamos, ved, ven - 7. vea, veas… - 8. viera *or* viese… - 9. viere… - 10. viendo - 11. visto
saber	1. sé, sabes, sabe, … - 3. supe, supiste, supo, supimos, supisteis, supieron - 4. sabré, sabrás, sabrá, sabremos, sabréis, sabrán - 5. sabría… - 6. sabe, sepa, sepamos, sabed, sepan - 7. sepa, sepas, …- 8. supiera *or* supiese…- 9. supiere…		
		verificar	c becomes qu before e
		volar, volcar	like acordar
sacar	c becomes qu before e	**volver**	1. vuelvo, vuelves, vuelve, volvemos, volvéis, vuelven - 6. vuelve, vuelva, volvamos, volved, vuelvan - 7. vuelva, vuelvas… - 11. vuelto
salir	1. salgo, sales, sale, salimos, salís, salen - 4. saldré, saldrás, saldrá, saldremos, saldréis, saldrán - 5. saldría… - 6. sal, salga, salgamos, salid, salgan - 7. salga, salgas, …		
		zambullir	3. zambullí… zambulleron - 8. zambullera *or* zambullese… - 9. zambullese… - 10. zambullendo
satisfacer	like hacer		

LOS VERBOS IRREGULARES EN INGLÉS

be	was, were	been
beat	beat	beaten
become	became	become
begin	began	begun
bet	bet (betted)	bet (betted)
bite	bit	bitten
blow	blew	blown
break	broke	broken
bring	brought	brought
build	built	built
burn	burnt (burned)	burnt (burned)
buy	bought	bought
catch	caught	caught
choose	chose	chosen
come	came	come
cost	cost	cost
cut	cut	cut
deal	dealt	dealt
dig	dug	dug
dive	dived (*Am* dove)	dived
do	did	done
draw	drew	drawn
dream	dreamed (dreamt)	dreamed (dreamt)
drink	drank	drunk
drive	drove	driven
eat	ate	eaten
fall	fell	fallen
feed	fed	fed
feel	felt	felt
fight	fought	fought
find	found	found
fly	flew	flown
forget	forgot	forgotten
forgive	forgave	forgiven
freeze	froze	frozen
get	got (*Am* gotten)	got
give	gave	given
go	went	gone
grow	grew	grown
have	had	had
hear	heard	heard
hide	hid	hidden
hold	held	held
hurt	hurt	hurt
keep	kept	kept
know	knew	known
lay	laid	laid
lead	led	led
lean	leant (leaned)	leant (leaned)
learn	learnt (learned)	learnt (learned)
leave	left	left
lend	lent	lent
lie	lay	lain
lose	lost	lost
make	made	made
mean	meant	meant
meet	met	met
pay	paid	paid
put	put	put
quit	quit (quitted)	quit (quitted)
read	read	read
ride	rode	ridden
ring	rang	run
rise	rose	risen
run	ran	run
say	said	said
see	saw	seen
sell	sold	sold
send	sent	sent
set	set	set
sew	sewed (sewed)	sewn
shake	shook	shaken
shine	shone	shone
shoot	shot	shot
show	showed (showed)	shown
shut	shut	shut
sing	sang	sung
sink	sank	sunk
sit	sat	sat
sleep	slept	slept
slide	slid	slid
smell	smelt (smelled)	smelt (smelled)
speak	spoke	spoken
speed	sped (speeded)	sped (speeded)
spell	spelt (spelled)	spelt (spelled)
spend	spent	spent
spill	spilt (spilled)	spilt (spilled)
spoil	spoilt (spoiled)	spoilt (spoiled)
spread	spread	spread
spring	sprang	sprung
stand	stood	stood
steal	stole	stolen
stick	stuck	stuck
strike	struck	struck
swim	swam	swum
swing	swung	swung
take	took	taken
teach	taught	taught
tear	tore	torn
tell	told	told
think	thought	thought
throw	threw	thrown
understand	understood	understood
upset	upset	upset
wake	woke	woken
wear	wore	worn
win	won	won
write	wrote	written

NUMERALS — ADJETIVOS NUMERALES

Cardinal numbers — Numerales cardinales

nought	0	cero
one	1	uno
two	2	dos
three	3	tres
four	4	cuatro
five	5	cinco
six	6	seis
seven	7	siete
eight	8	ocho
nine	9	nueve
ten	10	diez
eleven	11	once
twelve	12	doce
thirteen	13	trece
fourteen	14	catorce
fifteen	15	quince
sixteen	16	dieciséis
seventeen	17	diecisiete
eighteen	18	dieciocho
nineteen	19	diecinueve
twenty	20	veinte
twenty-one	21	veintiuno
twenty-two	22	veintidós
thirty	30	treinta
forty	40	cuarenta
fifty	50	cincuenta
sixty	60	sesenta
seventy	70	setenta
seventy-five	75	setenta y cinco
eighty	80	ochenta
eighty-one	81	ochenta y uno
ninety	90	noventa
ninety-one	91	noventa y uno
a *or* one hundred	100	ciento, cien
a hundred and one	101	ciento uno
a hundred and two	102	cento dos
a hundred and fifty	150	ciento cincuenta
two hundred	200	doscientos
two hundred and one	201	doscientos uno
two hundred and two	202	doscientos dos
a *or* one thousand	1 000	(1000)mil
a thousand and one	1.001	(1001)mil uno
a thousand and two	1.002	(1002)mil dos
two thousands	2.000	(2000)dos mil
a *or* one million	1.000.000	un millón

Ordinal numbers — Numerales ordinales

first	1st	1º	primero
second	2nd	2º	segundo
third	3rd	3º	tercero
fourth	4th	4º	cuarto
fifth	5th	5º	quinto
sixth	6th	6º	sexto
seventh	7th	7º	séptimo
eighth	8th	8º	octavo
ninth	9th	9º	noveno
tenth	10th	10º	décimo
eleventh	11th	11º	undécimo, onceno
twelfth	12th	12º	duodécimo
thirteenth	13th	13º	decimotercero
fourteenth	14th	14º	decimocuarto
fifteenth	15th	15º	decimoquinto
sixteenth	16th	16º	decimosexto
seventeenth	17th	17º	decimoséptimo
eighteenth	18th	18º	decimoctavo
nineteenth	19th	19º	decimonono
twentieth	20th	20º	vigésimo
twenty-first	21st	21º	vigésimo primero
twenty-second	22nd	22º	vigésimo segundo
thirtieth	30th	30º	trigésimo

Véase la gramática inglesa al final del diccionario, p. XI.

a

a
[a] *prep*
1. to

fuimos a Londres el año pasado we went to London last year

el niño escribe a su abuela the little boy is writing to his grandmother

voy a hacer mis deberes I'm going to do my homework

2. at
a las seis at six o'clock

a cien kilómetros por hora at a hundred kilometres an hour

3. *no traducible*
* *Perdone señora... ¿Conocía usted a Balthazar?* Excuse me, madam... Did you know Balthazar?
Sí señor, naturalmente. Yes, of course, sir. *

abajo

abajo
[a'βaxo] *adv*
1. (down) below

desde el avión veíamos los campos abajo from the plane we could see the fields (down) below

2. Idiom
la policía registró la casa de arriba abajo the police searched the house from top to bottom

abandonar

abandonar
[aβando'nar] *v t*
1. to leave,
to abandon

* *¡Debemos abandonar este lugar en el acto!* We must leave this place straight away! *

2. give up
abandona la idea si no da resultado give up the idea if it doesn't work

...abandonar

abanico

abanico
[aβa'niko] *n m*
fan

abogado

abogado, a
[aβo'ɣaðo, a] *n*
lawyer

su padre fue abogado his father was a lawyer

abrazar

abrazar
[aβra'θar] *v t*
to hug,
to embrace

* *El profesor abraza al capitán.* The Professor is hugging the Captain. *

El profesor abraza al capitán.

abrigar

abrigar, abrigarse
[aβriˈɣar, se]
I. v t
to shelter,
to keep warm

II. v pr
to wrap up, to keep
oneself warm

* *Hace frío fuera;
abríguese antes de
salir, Tintín.* It's cold
outside; wrap up well
before you go out, Tintin.

Hace frío fuera, abríguese antes de salir, Tintín.

Vale, vale, de acuerdo.

*Vale, vale, de acuer-
do.* All right, I will. *

▶ **abrigo**
[aˈβriɣo] n m
overcoat, coat

abril

abril
[aˈβril] n m
April

...abril

*el primero/dos de
abril* the first/second of
April (Am : April first/
second)

abrir

abrir, abrirse
[aˈβrir, se]
I. v t
to open

* *¡Tintín, Tintín!
¡Despiértate!* Tintin!

...abrir

Tintin! Wake up!
*¡Ah! ¡ ya abre los
ojos!* Ah! He's opening
his eyes! *

II. v pr
to open

*esta ventana no se
abre* this window won't
open

▶ **abierto, a**
[aˈβjerto,a] adj
open

la ventana está

...abrir

*¡Tintín, Tintín!
¡Despiér-
tate!*

¡Ah! ¡ya abre los ojos!

abierta de par en par
the window is wide open

abuelo

abuelo, a
[aˈβwelo, a] n
grandfather,
grandmother

▶ **abuelos**
[aˈβwelos] n m pl
grandparents

aburrir

aburrir, aburrirse
[aˈβuɾir, se]
I. v t
to bore

*las películas largas
me aburren* long films
bore me

II. v pr
to be bored

* *¡Mil millones de
demonios! ¡Real-
mente, con usted
uno no puede abu-*

*¡Mil millones de demonios!
¡Realmente con usted, uno
no puede aburrirse nunca!*

rrirse nunca! Billions
of blue blistering bar-
nacles! It's really impossible ever to be bored
with you ! *

acabar

acabar
[akaˈβar]
I. v t
to finish, to end

*acaba la leche y
vámonos* finish your
milk and let's go

II. v i
1. to finish, to end

*la clase acaba a las
doce* the class finishes at
twelve

*El cohete acaba
de salirse de
la órbita ...*

2. to end up,
to finish up
*acabaron en la
cárcel* they ended up in
prison

3. to have just
* *El cohete acaba
de salirse de la
órbita...*The rocket has
just left its orbit... *

acampar

acampar
[akamˈpar] v i
to camp

acaso

acaso
[aˈkaso] adv
1. perhaps

acaso venga perhaps
he'll come

2. by any chance

...acaso

¿acaso ha sido él?
was it him, by any chan-
ce?

3. Idiom
por si acaso just in
case

accidente

accidente
[akθiˈðente] n m
accident

acción

acción
[ak'θjon] n f
action

aceite

aceite
[a'θeĭte] n m
oil

▶ **aceituna**
[aθeĭ'tuna] n f
olive

acelerar

acelerar
[aθele'rar] v i & v t
to accelerate,
to go faster

* ¡El tren acelera
cada vez más! The
train is going faster and
faster! *

aceptar

aceptar
[aθep'tar] v t
to accept

acera

acera
[a'θera] n f
pavement

los niños juegan en
la acera the children are
playing on the pavement

acerca de

acerca de
[a'θerka de] prep
about

* ¿Qué sabe usted
acerca del general
Alcázar?... Lo vio
usted ayer ¿no?
What do you know about
General Alcázar?... You
saw him yesterday, didn't
you? *

...acerca de

acercar

acercar
[aθer'kar] v t
to bring near(er)

acercad las sillas
bring the chairs nearer

▶ **acercarse a**
[aθer'karse a] v pr
to approach,
to get near(er)

el cohete espacial
se acerca a la luna
the rocket is approaching
the moon

ácido

ácido, a
['aθiðo, a] adj
acid

acompañar

acompañar
[akompa'ɲar] v t
to accompany,
to go with,
to come with

* Voy a dar una

...acompañar

...acompañar

vuelta... Milú, ¿quie-
res acompañarme?
I'm going for a walk...
Snowy, do you want to
come with me?
¡Hombre, pues cla-
ro!... Well, of course!... *

la cantante será
acompañada por un
pianista the singer will
be accompanied by a
pianist

aconsejar

aconsejar
[akonse'xar] v t
to advise

le aconsejo que no
se acerque I advise
you not to approach

acordarse

acordarse
[akor'ðarse] v pr
to remember

...acordarse

* Pero, profesor ¿no
se acuerda del
cohete, del viaje a
la luna, del castillo
de Moulinsart?... But
Professor, don't you
remember the rocket, the
journey to the moon, the
Castle of Marlinspike?... *

acostar

acostar, acostarse
[akos'tar, se]
I. v t
to put to bed,
to lay down

* ¿Dónde estoy?...
No reconozco esta
habitación. ¿Por
qué me han acos-
tado aquí?... Where
am I?... I don't recognize
this room. Why have they
put me to bed here?... *

...acostar

II. *v pr*
to go to bed

¿a qué hora se acostó anoche? what time did he go to bed last night?

acostumbrar

acostumbrar, acostumbrarse
[akostum'brar, se]
I. *v i*
to be in the habit of

...acostumbrar

* *Las llamas acostumbran a hacer esto cuando están enfadadas.* Llamas are in the habit of doing this when they are angry.
Pero, ¿quién se cree que es? But who does he think he is? *

II. *v pr*
to get used to, to get accustomed to

actitud

actitud
[akti'tuð] *n f*
attitude

actor

actor, actriz
[ak'tor, ak'triθ] *n*
actor, actress

mi padre conoce a esta actriz de cine my father knows this film actress

actuar

actuar
[ak'twar] *v i*
to act

* *El actor que actúa en esta película es fantástico...* The actor who acts in this film is fantastic...
¿No encuentra que se parece mucho al general Alcázar? Don't you think he looks a lot like General Alcazar? *

acudir

acudir
[aku'ðir] *v i*
to come (along), to turn up

al oír los gritos, los chicos acudieron en su ayuda on hearing the shouting, the boys came to help

acuerdo

acuerdo
[a'kwerðo] *n m*
1. agreement

2. Idiom
¡de acuerdo¡ (all) right! O. K.!

de acuerdo con in accordance with

* *De acuerdo con lo previsto, el cohete debería despegar dentro de cinco minutos...* In accordance with plans, the rocket

should take off in five minutes... *

adelantar

adelantar, adelantarse
[aðelan'tar, se]
I. *v t*
1. to advance, to move forward

2. to overtake

...adelantar

adelantemos este coche let's overtake this car

II. *v i*
1. to be fast

este reloj siempre adelanta this watch is always fast

2. to improve, to make progress
ha adelantado con el inglés he's made progress in English

III. *v pr*
to step forward

▶ **adelante**
[aðe'lante]
I. *adv*
1. forward

2. Idiom
de aquí en adelante in future, from now on

II. *interj*

¡adelante! come in!

* *...¡Adelante!...* ...Charge!... *

...adelantar

...¡Adelante!...

▶ **adelanto**
[aðe'lanto] n m
progress, advancement, advance

además

además
[aðe'mas] adv
moreover, what's more

* Se lo diré a mi papá y mi papá te

...además

castigará y además te hará empalar... I'll tell my dad and my dad will punish you and, what's more, he'll have you impaled...
¡Cállate! Shut up! *

adiós

adiós
[a'ðjos]
I. n m
goodbye

Se lo diré a mi papá y mi papá te castigará y además te hará empalar...
¡Cállate!

...adiós

II. interj
goodbye

* ¡Adiós! Goodbye! *

adivinar

adivinar
[aðiβi'nar] v t
to guess

¿puedes adivinar la respuesta? can you guess the answer?

¡Adiós!

admirar

admirar
[aðmi'rar] v t
to admire

siempre he admirado tu valentía I've always admired your bravery

▶ **admiración**
[admira'θion] n f
admiration

admitir

admitir
[aðmi'tir] v t
to admit

si no entiendes, admítelo if you don't understand, admit it

sólo cien personas serán admitidas a la sala only one hundred people will be admitted into the hall

adonde

¿Adónde van? Al primero.

adonde
[a'ðonde] adv
where

te llevo adonde quieras I'll take you where you want

* ¿Adónde van? Where are you going?
Al primero. To the first floor. *

adoptar

adoptar
[aðop'tar] v t
to adopt

Hernández adoptó una actitud muy digna Thomson adopted a very dignified attitude

adrede

adrede
[a'ðreðe] adv
on purpose, deliberately

¡me has pisado adrede! you trod on my foot on purpose!

aduana

tenéis que pasar por la aduana you have to go through customs

aduana
[a'ðwana] n f
customs

advertir

advertir
[aðβer'tir] *v t*
1. to warn

* *¡Advierta la torre de control!* Warn the control tower!
Sí, hay que aterrizar... Yes, we must land... *

le advierto que se trata de una misión muy peligrosa I warn you that this is a very dangerous mission

2. to notice
nadie advirtió la presencia del ladrón en la casa nobody noticed the burglar in the building

aeropuerto

aeropuerto
[aero'pwerto] *n m*
airport

aficionado

aficionado, a
[afiθjo'naðo, a]
I. *adj*
fond

* *Así pues, como le decía, soy aficionado al arte primi-*

tivo y poco a poco he constituido una pequeña colección. Estas son mis últimas adquisiciones. Well, as I was telling you, I'm fond of primitive art and little by little I've built up a small collection. These are my latest acquisitions. *

II. *n*
1. fan

2. amateur

afín

afín
[a'fin] *adj*
similar

tenemos gustos afines we have similar tastes

afirmar

afirmar
[afir'mar] *v t*
to affirm

afuera

afuera
[a'fwera] *adv*
outside

* *Si no le importa, prefiero salir afuera...* If you don't mind, I'd prefer to go outside... *

▶ **afueras**
[a'fweras] *n f pl*
outskirts

queremos mudarnos a las afueras del pueblo we want to move to the outskirts of town

agarrar

agarrar, agarrarse
[aɣa'rar, se]
I. *v t*
to seize, to grab, to catch hold of

II. *v pr*
to hold on

* *¡Cuidado! ¡Agárrate fuerte!* Be careful! Hold on tight! *

agitar

agitar, agitarse
[axi'tar, se] *v t & pr*
to shake

agítese bien antes de usar shake well before use

agosto

agosto
[a'ɣosto] *n m*
August

agosto es un mes caluroso en España August is a hot month in Spain

agradable

agradable
[aɣra'ðaβle] *adj*
pleasant, nice

hemos pasado una tarde muy agradable we've had a very pleasant evening

agradar

agradar
[aɣra'ðar] *v t*
to please, to like

...agradar

a Milú le agrada estar en la compañía de Tintín Milú likes Tintin's company

agradecer

agradecer
[aɣraðe'θer] *v t*
to thank

* *¡Ya casi hemos llegado!* We're almost there!

...agradecer

¡Ya casi hemos llegado!

¡No sé cómo agradecerle su ayuda!.

No sé cómo agradecerle su ayuda! I don't know how to thank you for your help. *

agricultor

agricultor, a
[aɣrikul'tor, a] *n*
farmer

agua

Ha desaparecido en el agua...

agua
['aɣwa] *n f*
water

* *Ha desaparecido en el agua...* He's disappeared in the water... *

agudo

agudo, a
[a'ɣuðo, a] *adj*
high-pitched, shrill

...agudo

oímos un sonido agudo we heard a shrill noise

aguja

aguja
[a'ɣuxa] *n f*
needle

agujero

agujero
[aɣu'xero] *n m*
hole

ahí

ahí
[a'i] *adv*
there,
over there

ponlo ahí put it over there

ahogar

¡Me ahogo!...

-F.E.I.C.

ahogar, ahogarse
[ao'ɣar, se]
I. *v t*
1. to drown

2. to suffocate

II. *v pr*
1. to drown

* *¡Me ahogo!...* I'm drowning!... *

2. to suffocate
nos ahogamos de calor aquí it's so hot we're suffocating here

ahora

ahora
[a'ora] *adv*
1. now

2. Idiom
ahora mismo right now

ahora bien now, now then, however

pensaba ir al hotel; ahora bien si insistes iré a tu casa I was thinking of going to the hotel; however if you insist I'll stay at your place

ahorrar

ahorrar
[ao'rar] *v t*
to save

esta máquina te ahorrará mucho tiempo this machine will save you a lot of time

▶**ahorros**
[a'oros] *m pl*
savings

¿qué vas a hacer con todos tus ahorros? what are you going to do with all your savings?

aire

Han perdido... conocimiento... Apenas tenemos ... oxígeno... El aire... es...irrespirable... No ... puedo ... más ...

aire
[ˈaĭre] *n m*
air

* *Han perdido... conocimiento... Apenas tenemos...oxígeno... El aire... es... irrespirable... No... puedo... más...* They've lost... consciousness... We've hardly... any oxygen... The air... is... unbreathable... I can't... take... any more... *

ajedrez

Voy a ganar esta partida de ajedrez...

ajedrez
[axeˈðreθ] *n m*
chess

* *Voy a ganar esta partida de ajedrez...* I'm going to win this game of chess... *

al

al
[al] *art*
1. to the

...al

¡vamos al cine! let's go to the cinema!

2. Idiom
al llegar comimos on arriving we had lunch

albañil

albañil
[alβaˈŋil] *n m*
bricklayer, mason

alcalde

alcalde, esa
[alˈkalde, alkalˈdesa] *n*
mayor, mayoress

alegrar

alegrar, alegrarse
[aleˈɣrar, se]
I. *v t*
to please

II. *v pr*
to be pleased

...alegrar

* *¡Oh! mi querido capitán Kappock, ¡cuánto me alegra verle!* Oh! my dear Captain Kappock, I'm so pleased to see you!
¿¿Usted aquí?? ¿Cómo es posible? What are you doing here? I can't believe it! *

▶ **alegre**
[aˈleɣre] *adj*
happy, cheerful

¿cómo es que estás

¡Oh! mi querido capitán Kappock, ¡cuánto me alegra verle!
¿¿Usted aquí?? ¿Cómo es posible?

tan alegre hoy? how come you're so cheerful today?

Alemania

Alemania
[aleˈmanja] *n f*
Germany

▶ **alemán, ana**
[aleˈmana] *n & adj*
German

algo

algo
[ˈalɣo]
I. *pron indet*
something, anything

tiene algo que no me gusta there's something about him I don't like

II. *adv*
rather, a little

este puzzle es algo difícil this puzzle is rather difficult

algodón

algodón
[alɣoˈðon] *n m*
cotton

todas sus camisas son de algodón all his shirts are made of cotton

alguien

alguien
[ˈalɣjen] *pron indet*
somebody,

...alguien

Oye, Tintín, ¿todavía no podemos salir?
¡¡Chis!!, alguien viene...
CRAC

someone, anybody, anyone

* *Oye, Tintín, ¿todavía no podemos salir?* Hey, Tintin, can't we get out yet?
¡¡Chis!!, alguien viene... Shush! Someone's coming...
Crac Crack *

alguno

alguno, algún, a
[al'ɣuno, al'ɣun, a]
I. *adj indet*
1. some, any

algún día te arrepentirás some day you'll be sorry

* *¿Qué hago, capitán? Algunos barcos están ya muy cerca...* What shall I do, Captain? Some of the boats are very close now...

¿Qué hago, capitán? Algunos barcos están ya muy cerca...

¡Todo a estribor, grumete!

¡Todo a estribor, grumete! Hard to starboard, cabin boy! *

2. no
esta historia no tiene interés alguno this story is of no interest at all

3. Idiom
algún que otro the odd

leo algún que otro tebeo I read the odd comic

II. *pron indet*
1. some, any

2. one
alguno de ellos one of them

alimentar

alimentar
[alimen'tar] *v t*
to feed, to nourish

almacén

almacén
[alma'θen] *n m*
store, shop

* *¿Cántaros? Lo siento, no me queda ninguno en todo el almacén... Se me han roto todos.* Pitchers? Sorry, I haven't got a single one left in the whole store... They've all been broken. *

¿Cántaros? Lo siento, no me queda ninguno en todo el almacén... Se me han roto todos.

almendra

almendra
[al'mendra] *n f*
almond

almohada

almohada
[almo'aða] *n f*
pillow

mi hermano siempre duerme sin almohada my brother always sleeps without a pillow

almorzar

almorzar
[almor'θar] *v i*
to have lunch

* *¿Por qué no se queda a almorzar con nosotros?* Why don't you stay and have lunch with us? *

▶ **almuerzo**
[al'mwerθo] *n m*
lunch

este almuerzo es excesivo para mí this lunch is too much for me

...almorzar

¿Por qué no se queda a almorzar con nosotros?

alojarse

alojar, alojarse
[alo'xar, se]
I. *v t*
to put up,
to accommodate

¿nos puedes alojar? can you put us up ?

II. *v pr*
to stay

nos alojamos cada año en el mismo hotel we stay at the same hotel every year

alquilar

alquilar
[alki'lar] *v t*
to rent, to hire

vamos a alquilar un coche let's hire a car

▶ **alquiler**
[alki'ler] *n m*
rent, rental, hire
(charge)

alrededor

alrededor
[alreðe'ðor] *adv*
1. around, round

desfilaron alrededor de la iglesia they paraded round the church

2. about
alrededor de cien about a hundred

▶ **alrededores**
[alreðe'ðores] *n m pl*
surroundings,
outskirts

A

...alrededor

los alrededores de Madrid the outskirts of Madrid

altiplano

altiplano
[alti'plano] *n m*
high plateau

alto

alto, a
['alto, a]
I. *adj*
1. high

* *¡Uf! la cumbre está realmente muy alta... Si pudiera descansar...* Phew! the summit is really high... If only I could rest... *

2. tall
un chico alto, un edificio alto, un árbol alto a tall boy, a tall building, a tall tree

3. Idiom
en las altas horas in the small hours

II. *adv*
1. high (up)

el avión vuela alto the plane is flying high

2. loud
no hables tan alto don't speak so loud

III. *interj*

¡alto¡ halt!

altura

altura
[al'tura] *n f*
1. height

* *¡Qué altura! ¡Es impresionante!* What a height! It's impressive! *

2. Idiom
nuestros hombres están a la altura de la tarea our men are up to the task

aludir

aludir
[alu'ðir] *v i*
to allude

alumno

alumno, a
[a'lumno, a] *n*
pupil, student

alumnos universitarios university students

allá

allá
[a'ʎa] *adv*
1. there, over there

la isla del tesoro está allá the treasure island is over there

2. Idiom
más allá beyond

¡allá tú! that's up to you!

¡allá ellos! that's their funeral!

allí

allí
[a'ʎi] *adv*
there, over there

¿lo ves allí? can you see it over there?

amable

amable
[a'maβle] *adj*
nice, kind

...amable

* *¿Un regalo para mí? ¡Qué amable eres!* A present for me? How kind of you!
Mira, te voy a enseñar cómo funciona. Look, I'll show you how it works. *

amanecer

amanecer
[amane'θer]
I. *v impers*
to begin
to get light

saldremos cuando amanezca we'll leave when it begins to get light

II. *v i*
to wake up

amaneceremos en la isla when we wake up, we'll be on the island

...amanecer

III. *n m*
dawn, daybreak

* *Al amanecer...* At dawn...
¿Qué hay de nuevo? What's new? *

amar

amar
[a'mar] *v t*
to love

amargo

amargo
[a'margo, a] *adj*
bitter

¡qué gusto más amargo! what a bitter taste!

amarillo

amarillo
[ama'riλo, a] *adj*
yellow

...amarillo

* *A mí me gusta este traje amarillo...*
I like this yellow suit...
A mí también. So do I. *

ambiente

ambiente
[am'bjente]
I. *n m*
atmosphere, surroundings

...ambiente

II. *adj*
surrounding

ambos

ambos, as
['ambos, as] *adj pl*
both, the two

* *Ambos detectives son muy distraídos.*
Both detectives are very absent-minded. *

...ambos

Ambos detectives son muy distraídos.

ambulancia

ambulancia
[ambu'lanθja] *n f*
ambulance

¡deprisa! ¡llama a una ambulancia!
quick! Call an ambulance!

América

América
[a'merika] *n f*
America

...América

América del Norte/Sur (Norteamérica/Sudamérica)
North/South America

América Central (Centroamérica) Central America

amigo

amigo, a
[a'migo, a] *n & adj*
friend

...amigo

Milú es el mejor amigo de Tintín Snowy is Tintin's best friend

▶ **amistad**
[amis'tað] *n f*
friendship

amor

amor
[a'mor] *n m*
love

ancho

ancho, a
['antʃo, a] *adj*
wide, big

* *Este poncho le viene un poco ancho, pero así, parece usted un auténtico indio...* This poncho is a bit big for you but, dressed like that, you look like a real Indian...
Sí, por esto me lo he puesto... Yes, that's why I put it on... *

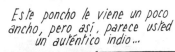

andar

andar
[an'dar]
I. *v i*
1. to walk

2. Idiom
los niños andan correteando arriba
the children are running around upstairs

andamos mal de dinero we haven't got much money

II. *interj*

¡anda ya! get away! come on!

andén

andén
[an'den] *n m*
platform

el tren entrará por el andén número 1
the train will come in on platform 1

anillo

anillo
[aˈniʎo] *n m*
ring

animal

animal
[aniˈmal] *n m*
1. animal

* *¡Ay! Menos mal que este animal no puede entrar, ¿no te*

...animal

parece, Milú? Oh! It's just as well this animal can't get in, isn't it, Snowy? *

2. beast, brute
¡qué animal eres! what a brute you are!

ánimo

ánimo
[ˈanimo] *n m*
1. courage

* *¡Socorro!* Help! *¡Ánimo, capitán, ya voy!* Take courage, Captain, I'm coming! *

2. Idiom
con ánimo de with the intention of

...ánimo

¡Ánimó, capitán, ya voy!

anoche

anoche
[aˈnotʃe] *adv*
last night

anochecer

anochecer
[anotʃeˈθer]
I. *v impers*
to get dark

* *Si vamos de prisa, llegaremos antes de*

...anochecer

Si vamos de prisa, llegaremos antes de que anochezca.

que anochezca. If we hurry, we'll arrive before it gets dark. *Sniff* Sniff. *

SNIFF SNIFF

II. *n m*
nightfall

anteayer

anteayer
[anteaˈʎer] *adv*
the day before yesterday

antes

antes
[ˈantes]
I. *adv*
1. before, beforehand

yo lo vi antes que tú I saw it before you did

2. rather
prefiero ir en tren antes que en avión I'd prefer to go by train rather than by plane

3. Idiom

...antes

cuanto antes, lo antes posible as soon as possible

II. *prep*
before

llame antes de entrar knock before entering

III. *conj*
before

antes de que te vayas before you go

antiguo

antiguo
[antiˈɣwo, a] *adj*
old, ancient

* *¡Miren! Esta máscara pertenece a una civilización antigua.* Look! This mask belongs to an ancient civilization. *

¡Miren! Esta máscara pertenece a una civilización antigua.

añadir

añadir
[aɲaˈðir] *v i & v t*
to add

año

año
[ˈaɲo] *n m*
1. year

2. Idiom
¿cuántos años tienes? how old are you?

...año

¡feliz año nuevo!
happy New Year!

apagar

apagar
[apa'ɣar] *v t*
to put out,
to switch off,
to turn off/out

* *¡Pronto! ¡Ayúdeme
a apagar el fuego!*

...apagar

¡Pronto! ¡Ayúdeme a apagar el fuego! El barco puede explotar...

El barco puede explotar... Quick! Help me to put out the fire! The boat might explode... *

aparato

aparato
[apa'rato] *n m*
machine,
piece of apparatus,
device

...aparato

¡Fíjese, capitán! Es el mismo aparato que el que vimos en casa del profesor.

¡Vaya! ¡Qué coincidencia!

* *¡Fíjese, capitán! Es el mismo apara-to que el que vimos en casa del pro-fesor.* Look, Captain! It's the same machine as we saw in the Professor's house.
¡Vaya! ¡Qué coinci-dencia! Well! What a coincidence! *

aparcar

aparcar
[apar'kar] *v t*
to park

aparecer

aparecer
[apare'θer] *v i*
to appear, to turn up, to come along

de repente apareció un fantasma suddenly a ghost appeared

apearse

apearse
[ape'arse] *v pr*
to get off, to alight

nos apeamos en la próxima parada we get off at the next stop

apellido

apellido
[ape'ʎido] *n m*
surname

apenas

Me pregunto cómo ha podido romperse, apenas si lo he tocado...

...apenas

apenas
[a'penas] *adv*
1. hardly

el anciano apenas sale de casa the old man hardly goes out

2. Idiom
apenas si... hardly

* *Me pregunto cómo ha podido romper-se, apenas si lo he tocado...* I can't un-derstand how it's got bro-ken; I've hardly touched it... *

apetecer

apetecer
[apete'θer] *v i*
to feel like,
to fancy

Milú, ¿te apetece un hueso? Snowy, do you fancy a bone?

▶ **apetito**
[ape'tito] *n m*
appetite

apreciar

apreciar
[apre'θjar] *v t*
to value,
to be fond of,
to appreciate

aprecia mucho a los niños she's very fond of children

aprender

Lo siento, pero sólo he aprendido la teoría... Es mi primera clase práctica...

...aprender

aprender
[apren'der] v t
to learn

* *Lo siento, pero sólo he aprendido la teoría... Es mi primera clase práctica...* I'm sorry, but I've only learnt the theory... It's my first practical class... *

apretar

apretar
[apre'tar]
I. v t
to squeeze,
to hug,
to be (too) tight

me aprietan estos zapatos these shoes are too tight for me

II. v i
Idiom

hoy el calor aprieta mucho the heat is oppressive today

aprovechar

aprovechar
[aproβe'tʃar]
I. v t
to make the most of, to take advantage of

¡aprovecha las vacaciones! make the most of your holiday!

II. v i
Idiom

¡que aproveche! enjoy your meal!

aquel

aquel, aquella, aquellos, as
[a'kel, a'keʎa, ɑ'keʎos, as] *adj*
1. that, those

aquella maleta es mía that case is mine

2. Idiom
en aquel entonces then, at that time

aquél

aquél, aquélla, aquéllos, as
[a'kel, a'keʎa, ɑ'keʎos, as] *pron*
that (one),
those (ones)

estos caramelos son más ricos que aquéllos these sweets are tastier than those (ones)

▶ **aquello**
[a'keʎo] *pron dem nt*
that, that business

...aquél

tenemos que hablar de aquello we have to talk about that business

aquí

aquí
[a'ki] *adv*
here

* *¡Milú, ven aquí!* Snowy, come here! *¡Guau!* Woof! *

...aquí

¡Milú ven aqui!
¡Guau! ¡Guau!

árbol

árbol
['arβol] *n m*
tree

arder

arder
[ar'ðer] *v i*
to burn

...arder

* *¡Oiga! ¡Llamando a la torre de control! El motor derecho está ardiendo... Repito: el motor derecho está ardiendo.* Hello! Calling control tower! The right-hand engine is on fire... Repeat: the right-hand engine is on fire. *

¡Oiga! ¡Llamando a la torre de control! El motor derecho está ardiendo... Repito: el motor derecho está ardiendo.

arena

arena
[a'rena] *n f*
sand

* *¡Vaya, Milú! ¡Sólo nos faltaba una tempestad de arena!* Blast, Snowy! That's all we needed, a sandstorm! *

¡Vaya Milú! ¡Sólo nos faltaba una tempestad de arena!

armario

armario
[ar'marjo] *n m*
cupboard

arrancar

arrancar
[aran'kar]
I. v t
to pull, to pull up,
to pull out,
to snatch

...arrancar

el dentista le arrancó el diente malo the dentist pulled his bad tooth out

el viento arrancó el periódico de sus manos the wind snatched the paper from his hands

II. v i
to start

* *¡Qué suerte! El coche ha arrancado a la primera.* What

...arrancar

¡Qué suerte! El coche ha arrancado a la primera.

luck! The car's started first time.

arreglar

arreglar
[aㄱe'ɣlar] v t
1. to put in order

tengo que arreglar estos papeles I must put these papers in order

...arreglar

2. to mend
papá está arreglando el coche dad is mending the car

3. to settle
hay que arreglar este asunto we must settle this business

4. to arrange
Liszt arregló varias obras para piano Liszt arranged a number of works for piano

arriba

arriba
[aㄱiβa] adv
1. up, up there, upwards

* *Mire allá arriba... en el árbol... hay... como manchas de sangre...* Look up there... in the tree... it looks like... bloodstains... *

¡Venga, arriba, levántate! Come on, get up!

Mire allá arriba...en el árbol... hay...como manchas de sangre...

...arriba

2. upstairs
me parece haber oído un chillido en el piso de arriba I thought I heard a scream from the flat upstairs

3. Idiom
de arriba abajo from top to bottom, from head to foot

¡arriba Tintín! up with Tintín!

* *¡Arriba las manos!* Hands up! *

¡Arriba las manos!

arroz

arroz
[a'ㄱoθ] n m
rice

arroz a la cubana rice with tomato and fried egg

artista

artista
[ar'tista] n
artist

asar

asar
[a'sar] v t
to roast

ascensor

ascensor,
(*Am*: **elevador**)
[asθen'sor, eleβa'ðor]
n m
lift

* *En este hotel hay*

...ascensor

En este hotel hay dos ascensores.

dos ascensores. In this hotel there are two lifts. *

así

así
[a'si] adv
1. like this,
in this way, so

hazlo así do it like this

...así

¿así que, no vas? so you're not going?

2. Idiom
así como both... and...,
as well as

asiento

asiento
[a'sjento] n m
seat

asistir

asistir
[asis'tir]
I. v t
1. to assist

* *¡Vaya, vaya! ¡Qué extraña coincidencia!* Well, well! What a strange coincidence!
Le presento a los detectives que le asistirán a usted en esta empresa. These are the detectives who will assist you in this venture. *

...asistir

2. to look after, to care for
los heridos fueron asistidos por la Cruz Roja the wounded were looked after by the Red Cross

II. *v i*
to attend

el rey asistió a la cena ofrecida en su honor the king attended the dinner organized in his honour

¡Vaya, vaya! ¡Qué extraña coincidencia!

Le presento a los detectives que le asistirán a usted en esta empresa.

asomar

asomar, asomarse
[aso'mar, se]
I. *v t*
to show

¡no asomes la cara nunca más por aquí! don't ever show your face round here again!

II. *v pr*
1. to show

se asomaba su cabeza por encima de la tapia his head showed above the wall

2. to lean out
es peligroso asomarse it is dangerous to lean out of the window

asombrar

asombrar, asombrarse
[asom'brar, se]
I. *v t*
to amaze

...asombrar

tu valor me asombra your bravery amazes me

II. *v pr*
to be amazed

astuto

astuto
[as'tuto, a] *adj*
clever, cunning

asunto

asunto
[a'sunto] *n m*
matter, affair, business

esto es un asunto muy delicado this is a very delicate matter

*** Bueno, hablemos de nuestro asunto, Tintín...** Now, let's discuss our business, Tintin. *

Bueno, hablemos de nuestro asunto, Tintín...

asustar

asustar, asustarse
[asus'tar, se]
I. *v t*
to frighten, to scare

Milú ha asustado al gato Snowy has frightened the cat

II. *v pr*
to be frightened

no te asustes del yeti : es muy amable don't be frightened by the Yeti : he's very kind

atar

atar, atarse
[a'tar, se] *v t & v pr*
to tie

*** Me han atado las manos a la espalda; me va a ser difícil comer en estas condiciones...**They've tied my hands behind my back; it's going to be difficult to eat like this. *

...atar

Me han atado las manos a la espalda, me va a ser difícil comer en estas condiciones...

atardecer

atardecer
[atarðe'θer]
I. *v impers*
to get dark

II. *n m*
late afternoon, evening, dusk

*** ¡Aaaaaah!... ¡Qué ganas tengo de dormir!...** Aaaaaah!... I'm so sleepy!
Al atardecer... At dusk... *

atención

atención
[aten'θjon] *n f*
1. attention

*** Bueno, ahora, debemos procurar no llamar la atención.** Right, now we must be careful not to attract attention. *

2. kindness, civility, courtesy
gracias por tantas atenciones thank you for your kindness

¡Aaaaaah!... ¡Qué ganas tengo de dormir!...

Al atardecer...

...atención

> Bueno, ahora, debemos procurar no llamar la atención.

3. Idiom
prestar/poner aten-ción to pay attention

aterrizar

> Un poco más tarde...

> Señoras y señores, vamos a aterrizar dentro de diez minutos...

aterrizar
[ateᵗri'θar] *v i*
to land

* *Un poco más tarde...* A little later... *Señoras y señores, vamos a aterrizar*

...aterrizar

dentro de diez minu-tos... Ladies and gentle-men, we will be landing in ten minutes' time... *

atraer

atraer
[atra'er] *v t*
to attract

Mallorca atrae a mucha gente Majorca attracts a lot of people

atrasar

atrasar, atrasarse
[atra'sar, se]
I. *v i*
to be slow

mi reloj siempre atrasa diez minutos my watch is always ten minutes slow

II. *v pr*
to be late/behind

siempre voy atrasa-do con el trabajo I'm always behind with my work

▶ **atrás**
[a'tras] *adv*
1. back, behind

¡no te quedes atrás! don't get left behind!

* *¡Capitán!... La puerta de atrás está abierta... Cuidado con el escalón...* Cap-tain!... The back door is open... Mind the step... *

2. Idiom
dos meses atrás two

> ¡Capitán!... La puerta de atrás estaba abierta... Cuidado con el escalón...

months earlier

¡atrás! get back!

atravesar

atravesar
[atraβe'sar] *v t*
to cross

está atravesando la calle he is crossing the street

atreverse

atreverse
[atre'βerse] *v pr*
to dare

no me atrevo a saltar I don't dare to jump

atropellar

atropellar
[atrope'ʎar] *v t*
to run over,

...atropellar

to knock down

por poco me atro-pelló un camión I was almost run over by a lorry

aun

aun
[a'un] *adv*
1. even

la quiero aun más

...aun

que él I love her even more than he does

2. Idiom
aun cuando even if, even though, although

aun cuando llegaras tarde, tendrías tiem-po para comer even if you were late, you woud have time for lunch

aún

aún
[a'un] *adv*
still

aún está en la cama he's still in bed

aunque

aunque
[a'unke] *conj*
although, though, even though

...aunque

aunque es algo bajita, es guapa although she is rather short, she is pretty

aunque haga sol, Tornasol llevará su paraguas even though the sun is shining, Calculus will take his umbrella

autobús

autobús
[aŭto'βus] *n m*
bus

* ... *Van a coger el autobús.* ... They are going to catch the bus. *

autopista

autopista
[aŭto'pista] *n f*
motorway

avanzar

avanzar
[aβan'θar] *v i & v t*
to go forward, to advance

* *¡Cuidado, capitán! ¡Avancemos sin hacer ruido!* Careful Captain! We must advance without making any noise ! *

avenida

avenida
[aβe'niða] *n f*
avenue

aventura

aventura
[aβen'tura] *n f*
adventure

a Tintín le atrae mucho la aventura
Tintin loves adventure

avería

avería
[aβe'ria] *n f*
breakdown, mechanical fault

* *Creo que no es una avería importante... ¡Ah! ¡Ya lo veo! Es solamente un cable... Enseguida termino...* I don't think it's a serious fault... Ah! There it is! It's just a wire... I'll soon be finished... *¡Date prisa! Ahí vienen...* Quick! They're coming... *

avión

avión
[a'βjon] *n m*
aeroplane, airplane, plane, aircraft

avisar

avisar
[aβi'sar] *v t*
to warn

...avisar

El capitán intenta avisar a Tintín.

* *El capitán intenta avisar a Tintín.* The Captain is trying to warn Tintin. *

avispa

avispa
[a'βispa] *n f*
wasp

* *¡Ay!* Ouch!
¡Ay! ¡Maldita avispa! ¡Me ha picado

...avispa

...avispa

en la nariz! Ouch!
Wretched wasp! It's stung
me on the nose! *

ayer

ayer
[aˈʎer] *adv*
yesterday

*les vi ayer por la
mañana* I saw them
yesterday morning

ayudar

ayudar
[aʎuˈðar] *v t*
to help

* *¡Espera, Milú! ¡Te
voy a ayudar!* Wait,
Snowy! I'll help you! *

ayuntamiento

ayuntamiento
[aʎuntaˈmjento] *n m*
town hall

azafata

azafata
[aθaˈfata] *n f*
air hostess,
stewardess

* *La azafata sirve la*

La azafata sirve la comida.

comida. The air hostess
is serving lunch. *

azotea

azotea
[aθoˈtea] *n f*
terrace roof

*están tomando el
sol en la azotea* they
are sunbathing on the
terrace roof

azteca

azteca
[aθˈteka] *adj & n*
Aztec

azúcar

azúcar
[aˈθukar] *n m*
sugar

un terrón de azúcar
a sugar-lump, a lump of
sugar

azul

azul
[aˈθul] *adj*
blue

* *El cielo es azul,
el calor... ago-
biante...* The sky is
blue, the heat...
oppressive... *

El cielo es azul, el calor... agobiante...

bacalao

bacalao
[baka'lao] *n m*
cod

bachillerato

bachillerato
[batʃiʎe'rato] *n m*
s c h o o l - l e a v i n g
examination

bailar

bailar
[baǐ'lar] *v i & v t*
to dance

no sé bailar el tango
I can't dance the tango

▶ **baile**
['baǐle] *n m*
dance, dancing

lo que más me gusta es el baile folklórico what I most enjoy is country dancing

bajar

bajar
[ba'xar]
I. *v t*
1. to get down,
to bring down,
to lower

¿me ayuda a bajar esta maleta? would you help me get this case down?

2. to go down,
to come down,
to descend

* *¡Nunca más bajaré la escalera de cuatro en cuatro!* I'll never again come down the stairs four at a time! *

II. *v i*
to go down,
to come down,
to descend

¿puedes bajar de ahí un momento? can you come down from there a moment?

▶ **bajo**
['baxo]
I. *adv*
quietly,
in a low voice

¡ más bajo, por favor! more quietly, please! (quieter please!)

II. *adj*
f baja ['baxa]
1. low

2. short, small

...bajar

III. *prep*
under, underneath,
beneath, below

balcón

balcón
[bal'kon] *n m*
balcony

balde

balde
['balde] *n m*
1. bucket

2. Idiom
de balde free (of charge)

en balde in vain, no use

* *Estoy intentando llamar, pero es en balde...* I'm trying to get through, but it's no use...
¡Insista! ¡Hay que conseguirlo! Keep trying! We have to do it! *

balón

balón
[ba'lon] n m
ball

el balón está fuera de juego the ball is offside

▶ baloncesto
[balon'θesto] n m
basket-ball

▶ balonmano
[balon'mano] n m
hand-ball

▶ balonvolea
[balonbo'lea] n m
volley-ball

banco

banco
['banko] n m
1. bench

están sentados en un banco they are sitting on a bench

2. bank

bandera

Tintín planta la bandera.

bandera
[ban'dera] n f
flag

* *Tintín planta la bandera.* Tintin raises the flag. *

bañar

bañar, bañarse
[ba'ɲar, se]
I. v t
to bath

...bañar

Tintín tiene que bañar a Milú Tintin has to bath Snowy

II. v pr
to bathe,
to go for a swim

* *¡Qué gusto bañarse en medio del desierto!* How wonderful to bathe in the middle of the desert!
¡Desde luego! Not half! *

▶ baño
['baɲo] n m
bath, swim, bathroom

tomó un buen baño she had a good swim

barato

barato, a
[ba'rato, a] adj
1. cheap,

...barato

...barato

inexpensive, economical

*¿*Barato? ¿Usted lo encuentra barato?* Cheap? You find it cheap? *El más barato de toda la isla.* The cheapest on the whole island. *

2. Idiom
sale barato it's not expensive

barba

barba
['barba] n f
1. beard

* *¡Ay!* Ouch!
¡Madre mía! ¡No es una barba postiza! Oh dear! It isn't a false beard!
¡Pues claro que no es una barba postiza! ¡En buen lío se ha metido usted! ¡Exijo explicaciones! Well, of course it isn't a false beard! You're in

trouble! I demand an explanation! *

2. Idiom
hacer la barba to shave

llevar a uno de la barba to lead somebody by the nose

barco

El barco zarpa del puerto.

barco
['barko] *n m*
ship, boat

* *El barco zarpa del puerto.* The ship is leaving the port. *

barrer

barrer
[ba'rer] *v i & v t*
to sweep (up)

...barrer

¡Ay, qué vida! Barrer tanto polvo con lo constipado que estoy...

* *¡Ay, qué vida! Barrer tanto polvo con lo constipado que estoy...* Oh, what a life! Sweeping up all this dust with the cold I've got... *

barrio

barrio
['barjo] *n m*
district, area, neighbourhood

bastante

bastante
[bas'tante]
I. *adj*
1. enough, sufficient

no tenemos bastante dinero we haven't enough money

2. quite a lot of

II. *adv*
1. enough

* *Me parece que han comido bas-* *tante...* I think they've eaten enough... *

2. quite, fairly, pretty, rather
¡ten cuidado! ¡es bastante peligroso! be careful! he's pretty dangerous!

bastar

bastar
[bas'tar] *v i*
to be enough

Me parece que han comido bastante ...

...bastar

¡*basta ya!* that's quite enough!

batalla

batalla
[ba'taʎa] *n f*
battle

* *Fue una batalla encarnizada.* It was a bloody battle. *

...batalla

Fue una batalla encarnizada.

beber

beber
[be'ββer] *v t & v i*
to drink

Bélgica

Bélgica
['belxika] *n f*
Belgium

...Bélgica

▶**belga**
['belɣa] *adj & n*
Belgian

beso

beso
['beso] *n m*
kiss

biblioteca

biblioteca
[biβlio'teka] *n f*
library

bicicleta

...bicicleta

bicicleta, bici
[biθik'leta] *n f*
bicycle

* *El señor Wagner ha cogido la bicicleta de Néstor...* Mr Wagner has taken Nestor's bicycle... *

bien

bien
[bien]
I. *n m*
good, benefit

II. *adv*
1. well, right

* *¡Muy bien! ¡Me parece que ya están todos!* Right! I think that's the lot! *

2. good
sabe muy bien it tastes very good

...bien

3. Idiom
es más bien bajo he's rather short

► **o bien**
[o bien] *conj*
or

se puede ir en avión o bien en tren you can go either by plane or by train

► **bienes**
[bienes] *n m pl*
goods, property, riches

billete

billete
[bi'ʎete] *n m*
1. ticket

un billete de ida y vuelta a return ticket

...billete

2. banknote, note, bill
un billete de diez libras a ten-pound note

blanco

blanco
['blaŋko]
I. *n m*
1. white, whiteness

...blanco

2. target
el tirador dio en el blanco the marksman hit the mark

3. Idiom
me quedé en blanco my mind went blank

II. *adj*
f blanca ['blaŋka]
white

una paloma blanca a white dove

blando

blando, a
['blando, a] *adj*
soft

es blando al tacto it's soft to touch

boca

boca
['boka] *n f*
1. mouth

...boca

2. Idiom
boca arriba face up

boca abajo face down

► **boca de metro**
underground entrance

bocadillo

bocadillo
[boka'ðiʎo] *n m*
sandwich

...bocadillo

* *Te doy mi bocadillo pero luego, déjame en paz...* I'll give you my sandwich, but then leave me alone... *

bochorno

bochorno
[bo'tʃorno] *n m*
1. close/thundery weather

...bochorno

hoy hay bochorno the weather is very close today

2. embarrassment
¡qué bochorno sufrí! it was so embarrassing!

boda

boda
['boða] *n f*
wedding, marriage

bolígrafo

bolígrafo
[bo'liɣrafo] n m
ball-point pen

bolsa

bolsa
['bolsa] n f
1. bag

toma la bolsa de la compra take the shopping bag

...bolsa

¡Alto, la bolsa o la vida!

2. Idiom
* *¡Alto, la bolsa o la vida!* Hold it there, your money or your life! *

▶ **bolsillo**
[bol'siʎo] n m
pocket

¿qué llevas en el bolsillo? what have you got in your pocket?

▶ **bolso**
['bolso] n m
bag, handbag

bomba

bomba
['bomba] n f
bomb

bombero

bombero
[bom'bero] n m
fireman

* *Los bomberos van a apagar un incendio.* The firemen are going to put out a fire. *

...bombero

DING DING DING

FIRE BRIGADE

Los bomberos van a apagar un incendio.

bombilla

bombilla
[bom'biʎa] n f
(light) bulb

hay que cambiar la bombilla we have to change the bulb

bonito

bonito, a
[bo'nito, a] adj
pretty

borde

borde
['borðe] n m
edge

¡cuidado! ¡la taza está al borde de la mesa! look out! the cup's on the edge of the table!

▶ **bordillo**
[bor'ðiʎo] n m
kerb

borrar

borrar
[bo'řar] v t
to rub out,
to wipe out,
to erase,
to cross off

¡borra este nombre de la lista! cross this name off the list!

bosque

bosque
['boske] n m
wood, woods

* *¡Qué silencio!... ¡Cuánta paz en este bosque!...* Isn't it quiet!... It's so peaceful in this wood!... *

bota

bota
['bota] n f

¡Qué silencio!... ¡Cuánta paz en este bosque!...

...bota

1. boot

botas de fútbol football boots

2. wineskin
llena esta bota fill up this wineskin

botella

botella
[bo'teʎa] n f
bottle

...botella

¡Una botella intacta!

...botella

* *¡Una botella intacta!* One bottle intact! *

botón

botón
[bo'ton] *n m*
button

se me ha caído un botón de la chaqueta I've lost a button off my jacket

brazo

brazo
['braθo] *n m*
1. arm

el agresor le sujetó torciéndole el brazo the attacker held him down by twisting his arm

2. Idiom
es mi brazo derecho he's my right-hand man

brillar

brillar
[bri'λar] *v i*
to shine

*¡Ya he encontrado la esmeralda! ¡Cómo brilla! I've found the emerald! Look how it shines! *

▶ **brillante**
[bri'λante]
I. *adj*
brilliant

un científico brillante a brilliant scientist

II. *n m*
diamond

los piratas han encontrado un arca llena de brillantes the pirates have found a chest full of diamonds

broma

broma
['broma] *n f*
1. joke

* *¡La típica broma! ¡Pobre capitán, sólo le faltaba eso!* A practical joke! The poor Captain, that's all he needed! *¡Aaaaay!* Ow! *

2. Idiom
no estoy para bromas I'm in no mood for jokes

bueno

bueno, buen, a
['bweno, 'bwen, a] *adj*
1. good

¡qué buena idea! what a good idea!

2. Idiom
por las buenas o por las malas by fair means or foul

buey

buey
['bwei] *n m*
ox

▶ **carro de bueyes**
oxcart

bufanda

bufanda
[bu'fanda] *n f*
scarf

burlar

burlar, burlarse
[bur'lar, se]
I. *v t*
to deceive,
to outwit

el ladrón ha burlado la policía the thief has outwitted the police

II. *v pr*
to mock,
to make fun of

no te burles de mí don't make fun of me

burro

burro
['buro] *n m*
1. donkey

2. idiot, ass
¡qué burro es! what an ass he is!

buscar

buscar
[bus'kar] *v t*
to look for

...buscar

* *Buscan el tesoro de Rackham el Rojo.* They are looking for Red Rackham's treasure. *

buzón

buzón
['bu'θon] *n m*
letter-box

el buzón está al final de esta calle the letter-box is at the end of this road

Buscan el tesoro de Rackham el Rojo.

C Ch C.C.

caballo

caballo
[ka'βaλo] *n m*
horse

* *El capitán Haddock tiene una curiosa manera de montar a caballo...* Captain Haddock has a strange way of riding his horse. *

El capitán Haddock tiene una curiosa manera de montar a caballo...

caber

caber
[ka'βer] *v i*
1. to fit

tanta gente no cabe en la sala so many people won't fit in the room

2. Idiom
cabe decir it must be said

no cabe duda there is no doubt

cabeza

cabeza
[ka'βeθa] *n f*
1. head

¡cuidado con la cabeza! mind your head!

2. Idiom
* *Se cayó de cabeza.* He fell headlong *

tirarse de cabeza al agua to dive into the water

...cabeza

Se cayó de cabeza.

cabina

cabina
[ka'βina] *n f*
1. telephone box, telephone kiosk, telephone booth

* *Oiga, soy el capitán Haddock; le llamo desde una cabina...* Hello, it's Captain Haddock; I'm in a telephone box... *

2. cabin, cockpit

Oiga, soy el capitán Haddock, le llamo desde una cabina...

cabo

cabo
['kaβo] *n m*
1. end, extremity

2. Idiom
llevar a cabo to carry out, to effect

al fin y al cabo after all

al cabo de tres meses after three months, three months later

de cabo a rabo from one end to the other, from

...cabo

beginning to end, from top to bottom, from cover to cover

3. cape
el Cabo de Buena Esperanza the Cape of Good Hope

cabra

cabra
[ˈkaβra] *n f*
goat

cacahuete

cacahuete
[kakaˈ(g)wete] *n m*
peanut

cada

cada
[ˈkaða]
I. *adj*
1. each, every

toma una de estas píldoras cada cuatro horas take one of these pills every four hours

* *Pero... ¿qué les ocurre?...* Hey... what's wrong with them?...
A cada segundo... hic... me sale una burbuja. Every second...

...cada

hic... I blow a bubble...
Yo aún diría... hic... más... hic... To be... hic... precise... hic...
¡Ole! Yo también quiero hacerlo... Great! I want to do it, too... *

2. Idiom
cada vez más, cada día más more and more

hay cada vez más tránsito por las *carreteras* there is more and more traffic on the roads

cada vez más pálido paler and paler

II. *pron*
cada uno, a, cada cual each one, every one

hay dos caramelos para cada uno de vosotros there are two sweets for each one of you

caer

caer, caerse
[kaˈer, se]
I. *v i*
1. to fall

2. to be (situated)
no sé por dónde cae el puente romano I don't know where the Roman bridge is

3. Idiom
¡ya caigo! I get it!

caer en la cuenta to realize

...caer

II. *v pr*
1. to fall

* *¡Capitán! ¿se ha caído?* Captain! Did you fall over?
¡Mil millones de demonios! ¿Quién ha roto el escalón? Billions of blue blistering barnacles! Who broke that step? *

2. Idiom
caerse de miedo to be terrified

café

café
[kaˈfe] *n m*
coffee, café

café solo black coffee

café con leche white coffee

caja

caja
[ˈkaxa] *n f*
1. box, crate

...caja

* *¡La caja!... ¡Se cae!* The crate!... It's falling! *

2. cash register, cashdesk

3. safe

▶ **cajón**
[kaˈxon] *n m*
drawer

calcetín

calcetín
[kalθet'in] n m
sock

calcetines de lana
woollen socks

calcular

calcular
[kalku'lar] v t
to calculate,
to work out

calendario

calendario
[kalen'darjo] n m
calendar

calentar

calentar
[kalen'tar] v t
to heat (up),
to warm (up)

*voy a calentar la
sopa* I'll heat the soup

...calentar

¡Ten cuidado!
¡Está demasiado
caliente...

▶ **caliente**
[ka'ljente] adj
hot, warm

* *¡Ten cuidado! Está
demasiado calien-
te...*Be careful! It's too
hot... *

calma

calma
['kalma] n f
calm, calmness

calor

calor
[ka'lor] n m
heat, warmth

calzada

calzada
[kal'θaða] n f
road, roadway

* *Hay charcos en
la calzada.* There
are puddles on the
road. *

...calzada

Hay charcos en la calzada.

calzado

calzado
[kal'θaðo] n m
shoes, footwear

callar

callar, callarse
[ka'ʎar, se]
I. v i & v pr
to be quiet,
to keep quiet,
to shut up

...callar

Lo que tengo que decirte
es un secreto... Pero
ahora prefiero callarme...
no estamos solos...

¡cállate ya de una
vez!shut up for once and
for all!

* *Lo que tengo que
decirte es un se-
creto... Pero ahora
prefiero callarme...
no estamos solos...*
What I have to tell you is a
secret... But now I prefer
to keep quiet... we're not
alone... *

II. v t
to keep secret

calle

calle
['kaʎe] n f
street, road

* *¡Taxi! ¡Calle
Labrador, veintiséis!*
Taxi! 26, Labrador Street!
Sí, señor. Right, sir. *

*calle de dirección
única* one-way street

¡Taxi! ¡Calle
Labrador, veintiséis!

Sí,
señor.

cama

cama
['kama] n f
bed

*¿aún está en la
cama?* is he still in bed?

cámara

cámara
['kamara] n f
1. room, chamber,
hall

...cámara

¡Es increíble! ¡Hay aquí
un periodista con una
cámara fotográfica y
usted ni siquiera
está peinado!

Esto...

...cámara

música de cámara
chamber music

2. camera
* *¡Es increíble! ¡Hay aquí un periodista con una cámara fotográfica y usted ni siquiera está peinado!* It's incredible! There's a journalist here with a camera and you haven't even combed your hair!
Esto... But... *

camarero

camarero, a
[kama'rero, a] *n*
waiter, waitress *f*

* *¡Camarero, por favor!* Waiter, would you mind! *

¡Camarero, por favor!

cambiar

cambiar, cambiarse
[kam'bjar, se]
I. *v t*
to change, to exchange

¿me quiere cambiar este cuchillo? se me ha caído could you change this knife for me? it fell on the floor

¿me puede cambiar estas libras en pesetas? can you change these pounds into pesetas for me?

II. *v pr*
to change one's clothes

me voy a cambiar I'm going to change my clothes

▶ **cambio**
['kambjo] *n m*
1. change

* *Se espera un*

...cambiar

Se espera un cambio climático. Mañana no podremos salir al mar.

cambio climático. Mañana no podremos salir al mar. They're expecting a change in the weather. We won't be able to go out to sea tomorrow. *

2. (small) change
lo siento; no tengo cambio I'm sorry; I've no change

3. Idiom
en cambio on the other hand

a cambio in exchange

si yo te doy este libro, ¿qué me puedes dar tú a cambio? if I give you this book, what can you give me in exchange?

caminar

caminar
[kami'nar] *v i*
to walk

...caminar

¡Rayos y truenos! ¡Ya estoy harto de caminar!

* *¡Rayos y truenos! ¡Ya estoy harto de caminar!* Ten thousand thundering typhoons! I'm fed up with walking! *

▶ **camino**
[ka'mino] *n m*
path, track

seguimos un camino de herradura por el bosque we followed a bridle path through the wood

camión

camión
[kam'jon] *n m*
lorry, truck

* *Ha chocado contra un camión.* He's crashed into a lorry. *

camisa

camisa
[ka'misa] *n f*
shirt

Ha chocado contra un camión.

campana

campana
[kam'pana] *n f*
1. bell

2. Idiom
hacer campana to play truant

campeón

campeón, a
[kampe'on, a] *n*
champion

campesino

campesino, a
[kampe'sino, a] *n*
peasant

campo

campo
['kampo] *n m*
1. field

las vacas están en el campo the cows are in the field

...campo

2. country, country side
viven en el campo they live in the country

3. field, pitch, ground
han ido al campo de fútbol they've gone to the football ground

4. Idiom
fueron (a) campo traviesa they went across country

...campo

Dormiremos a campo raso y montaremos la guardia por turnos.

Vale.

* *Dormiremos a campo raso y montaremos la guardia por turnos.* We'll sleep in the open and take turns at standing guard. *Vale.* O. K. *

cana

cana
['kana] n f
white/grey hair

cancelar

cancelar
[kanθe'lar] v t
to cancel

han cancelado mi vuelo my flight has been cancelled

canción

canción
[kanθj'on] n f
song

cansar

Esta excursión me ha cansado y además estoy sediento...¿ Tú, no, Milú?

HOTEL LAS CUMBRES

...cansar

cansar, cansarse
[kan'sar, se]
I. v i & v t
to tire (out)

* *Esta excursión me ha cansado y además estoy sediento... ¿Tú no, Milú?* This excursion has tired me out and, what's more, I'm thirsty... Aren't you, Snowy? *

II. v pr
to get tired

▶ **cansancio**
[kan'sanθjo] n m
tiredness, weariness

cantar

cantar
[kan'tar]
I. v t
to sing

...cantar

¡AAAH! ME RÍO DE VERME TAN BELLA EN ESTE ES...

y la Castafiore cantó...

* *¡Aaah! Me río de verme tan bella en este es...* Oh! I laugh to see myself so beautiful in this mi... *Y la Castafiore cantó...* And Castafiore sang... *

II. v i
1. to confess

2. Idiom
es cosa de coser y cantar it's as easy as pie

cantidad

cantidad
[kanti'ðað] n f
quantity, sum

le pagaremos la cantidad de diez libras we will pay you the sum of ten pounds

capa

capa
['kapa] n f
1. cloak, cape

...capa

al torero se le ha caído la capa the bullfighter has dropped his cape

2. layer
una capa de nieve a layer of snow

capaz

capaz
[ka'paθ] adj
capable, able

capital

capital
[kapi'tal]
I. n f
capital

* *Sanfación, capital de Nuevo Rico.* Sanfación, the capital of Nuevo Rico. *

II. adj
capital, supreme

un asunto de una importancia capital a matter of supreme importance

Sanfación, capital de Nuevo Rico...

caprichoso

caprichoso, a
[kapri'tʃoso, a] adj
capricious, whimsical, wilful

* *¡No eres más que un niño caprichoso!* You're just a wilful child! *¡Hiii!* Ow-ow! *

...caprichoso

¡No eres más que un niño caprichoso!

¡Hiii!

cara

¡Póngase de cara a la pared!

cara
['kara] *n f*
1. face

su cara me resulta conocida her face is familiar to me

2. look, appearance
tiene cara de payaso he looks like a clown

3. Idiom
¡qué cara! what a cheek!

plantar cara a uno to stand up to somebody

¿cara o cruz? heads or tails?

¡Póngase de cara a la pared! Face the wall!*

caracol

caracol
[kara'kol]
I. *n m*
snail

II. *interj*
¡caracoles! good heavens!

carácter

carácter
[ka'rakter] *n m*
character

caramba

¡caramba!
[ka'ramba] *interj*
good gracious!

caramelo

caramelo
[kara'melo] *n m*
sweet

¿puedo coger otro caramelo? can I take another sweet?

caravana

Me parece que están contentos de viajar en la caravana.

caravana
[kara'βana] *n f*
1. caravan

* *Me parece que están contentos de viajar en la caravana.* I think they are happy to ride in the caravan. *

2. stream, queue, tailback
una caravana de coches a stream of cars

cargar

cargar
[kar'ɣar] *v i & v t*
to load

* *He hecho cargar su equipaje sobre las llamas.* I've had your luggage loaded onto the llamas. *

He hecho cargar su equipaje sobre las llamas.

caricia

caricia
[ka'riθja] *n f*
stroke, caress, pat

cariño

cariño
[ka'riɲo] *n m*
affection, fondness, tenderness, liking

* *El lorito me ha tomado cariño; me sigue por todas partes...* The little parrot has taken a liking to me; he follows me everywhere... *

El lorito me ha tomado cariño, me sigue por todas partes...

carne

carne
['karne] n f
1. meat

no me gusta la carne de vaca I don't like meat

2. Idiom
en carne y hueso in the flesh

en carne viva in the raw

me pone la carne de gallina it gives me goose pimples

carnet

carnet
[kar'net] n m
1. notebook, bankbook, card

2. Idiom
el carnet de conducir driving licence

el carnet de identidad identity card, ID card

caro

caro, a
['karo, a] adj
dear, expensive

ese coche es carísimo that car is extremely expensive

carrera

carrera
[ka'rrera] n f
1. race

vamos a echar una carrera hasta el final de la calle I'll give you a race to the end of the street

2. studies pl
no he terminado la carrera I haven't finished my studies yet

carretera

carretera
[ka'rretera] n f
road

* ¡Mil rayos! ¡Vaya más despacio, la carretera es muy mala! Thundering typhoons! Drive more slowly! The road is very bad! Están haciendo obras, señor... There are roadworks, sir... *

...carretera

carro

carro
['karro] n m
1. cart

* ¡Alto! ¿Qué lleva en ese carro? Stop! What have you got on that cart? Arroz, mi capitán. Rice, Captain. *

2. Am: car

---

carta

carta
['karta] n f
1. letter

* ¿Se lo sirvo con hielo? Do you want ice with it?
Sí, gracias... ¡Mire, capitán! ¡una carta de su amiga Bianca Castafiore! Yes, thank you... Look, Captain! A letter from your friend Bianca Castafiore! *

2. card

voy a barajar las cartas I'm going to shuffle the cards

3. map

4. menu

▶ **cartero**
[kar'tero] n m
postman

cartera

...cartera

cartera
[kar'tera] *n f*
1. briefcase

2. wallet
* *¡Me han robado la cartera!* My wallet's been stolen! *

casa

casa
['kasa] *n f*
1. house

...casa

una casa de tres pisos a three-storey house

2. building

3. Idiom
casa de Correos Post Office

estar en casa to be at home

* *Nada...* No news
No está en casa... He's not at home... *

ir a casa to go home

casarse

casarse
[ka'sarse] *v pr*
to marry,
to get married

se van a casar en junio they're getting married in June

casco

casco
['kasko] *n m*
1. helmet

...casco

llevar casco to wear a helmet

2. district, area

casi

casi
['kasi] *adv*
almost, nearly

casi estamos we're almost there

caso

caso
['kaso] *n m*
1. case

* *Es realmente un caso curioso... Naturalmente todavía no podemos decir nada al respecto; habrá que esperar unos días...* It's really a strange case... Of course, we can't say anything about it yet; we'll have to wait for a few days...
Nunca habíamos

visto un caso parecido... We've never seen a case like it... *

2. Idiom
los niños no hacen caso al profesor the children aren't taking any notice of the teacher

¿qué haríamos en caso de guerra? what would we do in the event of war?

castañuela

castañuela
[kasta'ɲwela] *n f*
castanet

castellano

castellano
[kaste'ʎano]
I. *n m*
Castilian, Spanish

el castellano es la primera lengua oficial de España Cas-

...castellano

tilian is the first official language of Spain

II. *adj*
f castellana
[kaste'ʎana]
Castilian

castigo

castigo
[kas'tiɣo] *n m*
punishment

castillo

castillo
[kas'tiʎo] *n m*
1. castle

* *Milú, este castillo parece abandonado...* Snowy, this castle seems deserted... *

2. Idiom
hacer castillos en el aire to build castles in the air

casualidad

casualidad
[kaswali'ðað] *n f*
chance

fue pura casualidad it was purely a matter of chance

catarro

catarro
[ka'taro] *n m*
cold

...catarro

tengo un catarro muy fuerte I've got a very bad cold

causa

causa
['kausa] *n f*
1. cause, reason

la causa de la avería es desconocida the cause of the breakdown is unknown

...causa

2. Idiom
a causa de because of, on account of

cazar

cazar
[ka'θar] *v t*
to hunt

▶ **cazador, a**
[kaθa'ðor, a] *n*
hunter

...cazar

¡Qué suerte! Podremos comer carne durante varios días...

¡Somos unos cazadores excelentes!

* *¡Qué suerte! Podremos comer carne durante varios días...* What luck! We'll be able to eat meat for several days...
¡Somos unos cazadores excelentes! We're excellent hunters! *

cebolla

cebolla
[θe'βoλa] *n f*
onion

te voy a calentar una sopa de cebolla I'll heat up some onion soup for you

celebrar

celebrar
[θele'βrar] *v t*
to celebrate

vamos a celebrar el Año Nuevo we're going to celebrate New Year's Day

cementerio

cementerio
[θemen'terjo] *n m*
cemetery

cenar

cenar
[θe'nar]
I. *v i*
to have dinner

¿a qué hora cenáis normalmente? what time do you normally have dinner?

II. *v t*
to have for dinner

vamos a cenar un poco de pescado we're going to have some fish for dinner

▶ **cena**
['θena] *n f*
dinner

centro

centro
['θentro] *n m*
centre

el centro de la ciudad the city centre

...centro

centro comercial shopping centre

cerca

cerca
['θerka]
I. *adv*
near, nearby, close

II. *prep*
1. *cerca de* near (to), close to

...cerca

* *¡Uf! Menos mal que ha frenado a tiempo...* Phew! Thank goodness it braked in time...
El tren se ha parado cerca de Tintín. The train has stopped near Tintin. *

2. about, approximately
cerca de cien personas about a hundred people

...cerca

¡Uf! Menos mal que ha frenado a tiempo...

El tren se ha parado cerca de Tintín.

cerdo

cerdo
['θerðo] *n m*
pig, pork

cerilla

cerilla
[θe'riλa] *n f*
match

una caja de cerillas a box of matches

cerrar

cerrar
[θe'rar] *v i & v t*
to close, to shut

* *¡Qué viento! Menos mal que me he despertado... Voy a cerrar la ventana enseguida.* What a wind! It's just as well I woke up. I'm going to shut the window right away. *

...cerrar

¡Qué viento! Menos mal que me he despertado... Voy a cerrar la ventana enseguida.

cerveza

cerveza
[θerˈβeθa] n f
beer

césped

césped
[ˈθespeð] n m
lawn, grass

prohibido pisar el césped keep off the grass

cesto

cesto
[ˈθesto] n m
basket

el cesto de la colada the clothes basket

cielo

cielo
[ˈθjelo] n m
1. sky

* *¡Capitán, mire!*

...cielo

¡Vamos derecho a una tormenta!...
Look, Captain! We're heading straight into a storm!...
Sí,... el cielo está cada vez más oscuro... y ya caen las primeras gotas...
Yes,... the sky's getting blacker and blacker... and here come the first drops of rain... *

2. heaven
¡cielos! good heavens!

...cielo

¡Capitán, mire! ¡Vamos derecho a una tormenta!
Sí,... el cielo está cada vez más obscuro... y ya caen las primeras gotas...

ciencia

ciencia
[ˈθjenθia] n f
science

* *¿Es un casco nuevo?* Is it a new helmet?
Los progresos de la ciencia nos permiten trabajar con materiales modernos. The advances in science enable us to work with modern materials. *

¿Es un casco nuevo?
Los progresos de la ciencia nos permiten trabajar con materiales modernos.

cierto

cierto, a
[ˈθjerto, a] adj
1. a certain

cierta persona que conozco a certain person I know

2. positive, definite
una promesa cierta a definite promise

3. true
no es cierto it isn't true

4. Idiom
no se sabe a cien-

...cierto

cia cierta it isn't known for sure

por cierto by the way

* *Pero... por cierto... ¿por qué no voy...?* Hey... by the way... why don't I go...?
¿Ir... pero adónde? Go... where? *

Pero... por cierto...¿ por qué no voy...?
¿ Ir... pero adónde?

cigarrillo

cigarrillo
[θiɣaˈr̄iλo] n m
cigarette

un paquete de cigarrillos a packet of cigarettes

cigüeña

cigüeña
[θiˈɣweɲa] n f
stork

...cigüeña

la cigüeña tiene las patas muy largas the stork has very long legs

cine

cine
[ˈθine] n m
cinema, pictures

hace tiempo que no voy al cine I haven't been to the cinema for ages

circo

circo
[ˈθirko] n m
circus

podrían ser payasos en un circo you could be clowns in a circus

círculo

círculo
[ˈθirkulo] n m
circle

ciruela

ciruela
[θi'rwela] n f
plum

cita

cita
['θita] n f
1. engagement, appointment, date, rendez-vous

2. Idiom
* ¿Por qué me ha

¿Por qué me ha dado cita en este lugar?

...cita

dado cita en este lugar? Why did you arrange to meet me in this place? *

ciudad

ciudad
[θju'ðað] n f
city, town

* Visitan la ciudad. They are visiting the city. *

...ciudad

Visitan la ciudad.

claro

claro, a
['klaro, a]
I. adj
clear, light, bright

tienes una voz muy clara you have a very clear voice

II. n m
Idiom

no sacamos nada en claro we didn't come to any definite conclusions

III. interj
¡claro! of course!

clase

clase
['klase] n f
1. class, lesson

¿cuántas clases tienes a la semana? how many classes do you have a week?

...clase

No he tenido tiempo de verlo... Dígame... ¿qué clase de animal era? ¿Un jabalí?

No, aquí no hay jabalíes. Ha sido un tapir.

...clase

2. class, kind, type, sort
* No he tenido tiempo de verlo... Dígame... ¿qué clase de animal era? ¿Un jabalí? I didn't have time to see it... Tell me... what sort of animal was it? A wild boar?
No, aquí no hay jabalíes. Ha sido un tapir. No, there are no wild boar around here. It was a tapir. *

billete de primera clase first-class ticket

clavel

clavel
[kla'βel] n m
carnation

cliente

cliente
[klj'ente] n
customer, client

hoy he tenido pocos clientes I haven't had many customers today

clima

clima
['klima] n m
climate

...clima

Irlanda tiene un clima húmedo Ireland has a damp climate

cobrar

cobrar
[ko'βrar] v i & v t
1. to charge

¿sabes cuánto me cobraron por esto? do you know how much

...cobrar

they charged me for this?

2. to be paid, to collect one's salary

cobre

cobre
['koβre] n m
copper

cocina

cocina
[ko'θina] n f
1. kitchen

2. cooker
una cocina eléctrica
an electric cooker

3. cooking,
cookery, cuisine
un libro de cocina a
cookery book

*la cocina española
es muy buena* Spanish cooking is very good

coche

¿Hace tiempo
que tienes este
coche?

Una semana.

coche
['kotʃe] n m
1. car

* *¿Hace tiempo que
tienes este coche?*
Have you had this car
long?
Una semana. One
week. *

2. Idiom
coche de línea coach

coger

¡Milú, mira lo que he cogido
del suelo!... ¡Un cigarrillo
extranjero!...

...coger

coger
[ko'xer] v t
1. to take, to get

*cogió el paraguas y
salió fuera* she took her
umbrella and stepped
outside

2. to pick up
* *¡Milú, mira lo que
he cogido del suelo!... ¡Un cigarrillo
extranjero!...* Snowy!
Look what I've picked up
off the floor!... A foreign
cigarette!... *

3. to catch
vas a coger un resfriado you'll catch a cold

cohete

cohete
[ko'ete] n m
rocket

*el cohete está dando la vuelta a la
luna* the rocket is orbiting
the moon

cola

¡Oh! ¡Milú se ha
pillado la cola
en la puerta!

cola
['kola] n f
1. tail

* *¡Oh! ¡Milú se ha
pillado la cola en la
puerta!* Oh! Snowy
caught his tail in the door! *

2. queue

3. Idiom
*me temo que tendremos que hacer
cola* I'm afraid we'll have
to queue up

coleccionar

coleccionar
[kolekθjo'nar] v t
to collect

* *Y yo colecciono
carteras...* And I collect
wallets... *

▶ **colección**
[kolek'θjon] n f
collection

...coleccionar

Y yo colecciono carteras...

colegio

colegio
[ko'lexjo] n m
school, college

*salgo del colegio a
la una* I come out of
school at one o'clock

colgar

colgar
[kol'ɣar]
I. v t
to hang up

...colgar

cuelga tus pantalones en el armario
hang your trousers up in
the wardrobe

II. v i
1. to hang

2. to hang up
* *¡Oiga!... ¡Por favor,
no cuelgue! ¡Oiga!...
¡Ah! ¿Es usted, señor Cantonneau?...
Ahora le oigo mejor...*
Hello!... Don't hang up,
please! Hello!... Oh! Is it

...colgar

you, Mr Cantonneau?... Now I can hear you better... *

colina

colina
[ko'lina] n f
hill

colocar

colocar, colocarse
[kolo'kar, se]
I. v t
to put, to place

coloca los platos en la mesa put the plates on the table

han colocado un satélite en órbita they've put a satellite in orbit

II. v pr
to get a job

se ha colocado bien he's got a good job

color

color
[ko'lor] n m
colour

siempre saco fotos en color I always take colour photos

columna

columna
[ko'lumna] n f
column, pillar

* *¡Conque escondido detrás de la columna, ¿eh? Pero no te escaparás...* So you're hiding behind the pillar, are you? But you won't get away... *

...columna

comedia

comedia
[ko'medja] n f
1. comedy, play

2. Idiom
hacer comedia to play around

* *¡No hagas comedia y estate quieto! ¿Me oyes, especie de granuja?* Don't play around and just keep still! Do you hear me, you rascal?
¡Suéltame, Mil Rayos, me haces daño! Se lo diré a mi papá... Let

go of me, Blistering Barnacles, you're hurting me! I'll tell my father... *

comedor

comedor
[kome'ðor] n m
dining room

nos veremos luego en el comedor I'll see you in the dining room later

---

comentar

comentar
[komen'tar] v t
to comment on

▶ **comentario**
[komen'tarjo] n m
comment

comenzar

comenzar
[komen'θar] v t & v i
to begin, to start

comer

comer
[ko'mer]
I. v i
to eat,
to have lunch

* *Esto me preocupa. No sé si decírselo al capitán...* This is worrying. I don't know whether to tell the Captain...
¡Tintín! ¿No come? ¿En qué está pensando? ¡Tintín! Tintin! Aren't you eating?

What are you thinking about? Tintin! *

II. v t
to have for lunch

hemos comido pollo we had chicken for lunch

cómico

cómico, a
['komiko, a] adj
funny, comical, amusing

...cómico

comida

comida
[ko'miða] n f
1. food

me gusta la comida china I like Chinese food

2. meal
¿cuántas comidas tomas al día? how many meals do you have a day?

como

como
['komo]
I. prep
like, as

* *Hernández es como Fernández.* Thomson is like Thompson. *

me trata siempre como amigo he always treats me as a friend

II. adv
like, as

Hernández es como Fernández.

mi hermana canta como la Castafiore my sister sings like Castafiore

III. conj
1. as, since, if

tú tocas el piano tan bien como yo you play the piano as well as I do

como llueve, no podemos salir as it's raining, we can't go out

como no lo hagas, te voy a castigar if you don't do it, I'll punish you

2. Idiom
así como as soon as

como si nada as if nothing had happened

cómo

cómo
['komo] adv
1. how

¿cómo está tu madre? how's your mother?

2. Idiom
¡cómo corre tu perro! your dog can certainly run!

¿cómo es eso? how come?

¡cómo no! with pleasure!

cómodo

cómodo, a
['komoðo, a] adj
1. comfortable

este coche es muy cómodo this is a very comfortable car

2. convenient, handy
el coche es muy cómodo para desplazarse the car is very convenient for getting around

compañero

compañero, a
[kompa'ɲero, a] n
friend, companion

* *Milú es un fiel compañero.* Snowy is a faithful companion. *

compañía

compañía
[kompa'ɲia] n f
1. company

Milú es un fiel compañero.

...compañía

* *Ya verá, capitán, este loro le hará compañía; ya sabe algunas palabras...* Look, Captain, this parrot will keep you company; he already knows a few words...
Mil... ejem... A thousand... hem... *

2. company
una compañía de seguros an insurance company

comparar

comparar
[kompa'rar] v t
to compare

* *Compare estos tres documentos... Parecen exactamente iguales, pero hay una pequeña diferencia. ¡A ver si la descubre!...* Compare these three documents... They look exactly alike, but there's a slight difference. See if you can find it!... *

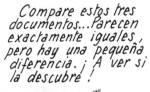

completo

completo, a
[kom'pleto, a] *adj*
complete, full (up)

el restaurante está completo the restaurant is full up

comprar

comprar
[kom'prar] *v t*
to buy

comprender

comprender
[kompren'der] *v t*
to understand

no comprendo tu pregunta I don't understand your question

comprobar

comprobar
[kompro'βar] *v i & v t*
1. to check

...comprobar

¿has comprobado los resultados? have you checked the results?

2. to establish, to see for oneself
* *Como pueden comprobar, esta playa les servía de pista de aterrizaje.* As you can see for youselves, this beach served them as a landing-strip. *

común

común
[ko'mun] *adj*
1. common

tenemos intereses comunes we have common interests

2. Idiom
por lo común generally

comunicar

comunicar
[komuni'kar] *v i & v t*
1. to communicate

no podemos comunicar con los indios; no hablan nuestra lengua we can't communicate with the Indians; they don't speak our language

2. Idiom
está comunicando (el teléfono) the line's engaged

con

con
[kon] *prep*
1. with

* *¿Por qué traes llamas, Zorrino?* Why have you brought llamas, Zorrino?
Vendrán con nosotros, capitán. Llevarán nuestras cosas. They're coming with us, Captain. They'll carry our things. *

...con

2. to
es amable con todo el mundo she's nice to everybody

3. Idiom
con que and so, so

llegamos todos muy cansados, y era muy tarde; con que fuimos a la cama we all arrived very tired and it was very late; so we went to bed

concierto

concierto
[kon'θjerto] *n m*
concert

cóndor

cóndor
['konðor] *n m*
condor

* *¡Dios mío! ¡El cóndor se lleva a Milú!* Good heavens! The condor is

...cóndor

carrying Snowy away!
¡Socorro! Help! *

conducir

conducir
[kondu'θir] *v i & v t*
to drive

* *¡Tengo que conducir más despacio!...* I must drive more slowly!... *

...conducir

¡Tengo que conducir más despacio!...

conmigo

conmigo
[kon'miɣo] *pron*
with me, on me,
to me

¡Milú! ¡Ven conmigo! Snowy! Come with me! (Come to me!)

conocer

conocer
[kono'θer] *v t*
1. to know

¿conoce usted al capitán? do you know the Captain?

2. to meet
la conocí en Paris
I met her in Paris

3. to get to know,
to learn about
me gusta conocer otros países I like getting to know other countries

conquista

conquista
[koŋ'kista] *n f*
conquest

* *Brindo a su salud, deseándoles de todo corazón el mayor éxito en su viaje... Gracias a ustedes, el hombre va a emprender la conquista del espacio...* I drink to your health, wishing you with all my heart the greatest success on your journey...

Thanks to you, man is going to undertake the conquest of space...*

▶ **conquistador, a**
[koŋkista'ðor, a] *n adj*
1. conquering

2. conqueror,
conquistador

...conquista

Brindo a su salud, deseándoles de todo corazón el mayor éxito en su viaje... Gracias a ustedes, el hombre va a emprender la conquista del espacio...

consciente

consciente
[ko(n)'sθjente] *adj*
conscious, aware

consecuencia

consecuencia
[konse'kwenθja] *n f*
consequence,
result

como consecuencia as a consequence, in consequence, as a result

conseguir

¡No conseguirán apagar el incendio! ¡Esto va a explotar!

...conseguir

conseguir
[konse'ɣir] *v t*
1. to manage to,
to succeed in

* *¡No conseguirán apagar el incendio! ¡Esto va a explotar!* They won't manage to put out the fire! This thing is going to explode! *

2. to get, to achieve
el pueblo consiguió la libertad the people achieved freedom

consigo

consigo
[kon'siɣo] *pron*
with (on, to) you/
one/him/her/it/them

no lleva nada consigo he isn't taking anything with him

no llevan dinero consigo they haven't any money on them

contar

contar
[kon'tar] *v i & v t*
1. to count (up)

el cajero está contando el dinero the cashier is counting the money

2. to recount, to tell
te voy a contar una historia I'm going to tell you a story

3. Idiom
contar con to count on

Cuento con usted para hacer este trabajo...

¡Bien, jefe!

* *Cuento con usted para hacer este trabajo...* I'm counting on you to do this work... *¡Bien, jefe!* OK, boss! *

▶ **cuento**
['kwento] *n m*
1. story, tale

2. Idiom
tiene mucho cuento he exaggerates everything

contento

contento, a
[kon'tento, a] *adj*
happy, glad

* *¡Tralala lala lala!*
Tralala lala lala!
Pues... no entiendo por qué están tan contentos... Well... I don't understand why they're so happy... *

contestar

contestar
[kontes'tar] *v i & v t*
to answer

tengo muchas cartas que contestar I have a lot of letters to answer

no sé contestar la pregunta I don't know how to answer the question

contigo

contigo
[kon'tiɣo] *pron*
with, on, to you

¡no hablo contigo! I'm not talking to you!

continuar

continuar
[konti'nwar] *v i & v t*
1. to continue,

...continuar

to go on, to carry on

continúa leyendo de momento go on reading for the moment

continuaremos esta conversación mañana we'll carry on this conversation tomorrow

2. Idiom
continuará to be continued

contra

contra
['kontra] *prep*
1. against

* *Puso la escalera contra el reloj.* He leant the ladder against the clock. *

2. Idiom
en contra de against, opposed to

estamos totalmente en contra de estos planes we are totally opposed to these plans

Puso la escalera contra el reloj.

contrario

contrario, a
[kon'trarjo, a] *adj*
1. opposed, opposite, contrary

este plan es contrario a los intereses de la mayoría de la gente this plan is contrary to most people's interests

2. Idiom
en sentido contrario the other way, in the other direction, in the opposite direction

todo lo contrario quite the reverse, quite the opposite

conversación

conversación
[kombersa'θjon] *n f*
conversation

* *Naturalmente, es una conversación confidencial...* Of

...conversación

Naturalmente es una conversación confidencial...

course, this is a confidential conversation... *

convertir

convertir, convertirse
[komber'tir, se]
I. *v t*
to convert,
to transform,
to change

...convertir

II. *v pr*
to change

* *La oruga se ha convertido en mariposa.* The caterpillar has changed into a butterfly. *

La oruga se ha convertido en mariposa.

copa

copa
['kopa] *n f*
1. glass

vamos a sacar las copas para el vino let's get the wine glasses out

2. cup
aquel club de fútbol ha ganado la Copa Mundial that football club has won the World Cup

corazón

corazón
[koraˈθon] *n m*
1. heart

2. Idiom
de buen corazón
kind-hearted

corregir

corregir
[koˈrexir] *v t*
to correct, to mark

...corregir

los profesores tienen que corregir muchos ejercicios teachers have to mark a lot of exercises

correo

correo
[koˈreo] *n m*
post, mail

* *Aquí tiene el correo*

...correo

de hoy. ¿Puede firmar el recibo del paquete? Here's today's post. Could you sign the receipt for the parcel? *

▶ **Correo(s)**
[koˈreos] *n (pl)*
Post Office

voy a pasar por Correos a echar estas postales I'm going to the Post Office to post these cards

Aquí tiene el correo de hoy ¿ Puede firmar el recibo del paquete?

correr

correr, correrse
[koˈrer, se]
I. *v i*
1. to run

* *¿Por qué corre el capitán?* Why is the Captain running? *

2. to hurry, to rush
siempre corre con el coche he is always rushing around in his car

II. *v t*
to travel over

...correr

¿ Por qué corre el capitán?

el capitán ha corrido medio mundo the Captain's travelled over half the world

III. *v pr*
to move up

¡córrete un poco! move up a bit!

corrida

¡ Se cree que está en una corrida!

corrida
[koˈriða] *n f*
bullfight

* *¡Se cree que está en una corrida!* He thinks he's in a bullfight. *

corriente

corriente
[koˈrjente]
I. *n f*

...corriente

1. current, stream

2. draught

3. Idiom
estar al corriente to be up-to-date

II. *adj*
1. normal, ordinary

2. common

3. running *(agua)*

cortar

¡Je! ¡Je! ¡Voy a cortar la cuerda!...

cortar
[korˈtar] *v i & v t*
to cut

* *¡Je! ¡Je! ¡Voy a cortar la cuerda!...* Hee! Hee! I'm going to cut the rope!... *

cortés

cortés
[korˈtes] *adj*
polite

...cortés

▶ **cortesía**
[kortesˈia] *n f*
politeness

corteza

corteza
[korˈteθa] *n f*
1. bark *(árbol)*

2. skin *(fruta)*
la corteza del melón

...corteza

es muy dura the skin of the melon is very hard

3. crust *(pan)*

corto

corto, a
['korto, a] *adj*
1. short

2. stupid
* *¡Pero qué corto eres! ¡Si todavía no me había parado!*
Oh! You're so stupid! I hadn't even stopped! *

3. Idiom
corto de vista, corto de oído short-sighted, hard of hearing

cosa

cosa
['kosa] *n f*
1. thing

¿qué es esa cosa?
what is that thing?

2. business, things, affair
¿cómo van las cosas? how are things?

ésa es cosa mía
that's my affair

3. strange idea
¡tienes cada cosa

...cosa

tú! you get such strange ideas!

4. Idiom
* *Vámonos ya, no sea cosa que alguien nos sorprenda...* Let's go now in case someone catches us...
¡Adiós!... ¡Y hasta pronto! Goodbye!... See you soon! *

costa

costa
['kosta] *n f*
coast

* *La costa no queda lejos... Ya casi llegamos...* The coast isn't far away... We're almost there... *

costa

costa
['kosta] *n f*
1. cost, price

2. Idiom
a toda costa at any price

a costa de at the expense of

▶ **costar**
[kos'tar] *v i & v t*
1. to cost

...costa

¿cuánto cuesta? how much does it cost?

2. to take
cuesta poco esfuerzo it doesn't take much effort

costumbre

costumbre
[kos'tumbre] *n f*
custom, habit

crecer

crecer
[kre'θer] *v i*
to grow, to increase

la ciudad ha crecido mucho the city has grown a lot

este año has crecido dos centímetros this year you've grown two centimetres

* *La hiedra ha crecido.* The ivy has grown. *

creer

creer
[kre'er] *v i & v t*
to think, to believe

¿qué crees que pasará? what do you think will happen?

¿crees en las fantasmas? do you believe in ghosts?

criado

criado, a
[krj'aðo, a]
I. *adj*
bred, reared, brought up

un joven bien criado
a well-bred young man

II. *n m*
servant

* *Néstor es el criado del capitán.* Nestor is the Captain's servant. *

...criado

Néstor es el criado del capitán.

cristiano

cristiano, a
[kris'tjano, a] *adj & n*
Christian

criticar

criticar
[kriti'kar] *v t*
to criticize

ése siempre critica a los demás he's always criticizing other people

cruce

cruce
['kruθe] *n m*
crossroads

para en el cruce stop at the crossroads

crudo

crudo, a
['kruðo, a] *adj*
raw, rare, underdone

...crudo

me gusta el bistec crudo I like my steak rare

cruel

cruel
[kru'el] *adj*
cruel

no seas cruel conmigo, por favor please don't be cruel to me

cruz

cruz
[cruθ] *n f*
cross

* *¡Aquí está la cruz que buscábamos!* Here's the cross we were looking for!
¿Ha visto? ¡Aquí está la cruz que buscábamos! Do you see that? Here's the cross we were looking for! *

¡Aquí está la cruz que buscábamos!

¿Ha visto? ¡Aquí está la cruz que buscábamos!

cruzar

cruzar, cruzarse
[kru'θar, se]
I. *v t*
to cross,
to go across

para llegar al mercado, cruzas el parque y ya está to get to the market, you go across the park and you're there

II. *v pr*
to cross (each other), to intersect

donde las carreteras se cruzan hay un hospital where the roads intersect there is a hospital

cuaderno

cuaderno
[kwa'ðerno] *n m*
exercise book, notebook

he perdido mi cua-

...cuaderno

derno I've lost my exercise book

cuadrado

cuadrado
[kwa'ðraðo]
I. *n m*
square

II. *adj*
f cuadrada [kwa'ðraða]
square

...cuadrado

una mesa cuadrada a square table

kilómetros cuadrados square kilometres

cuadro

cuadro
['kwadro] *n m*
picture, painting

* *El cuadro se ha caído...* The picture has fallen... *

...cuadro

El cuadro se ha caído...

cual

cual, cuales
[kwal, 'kwales]

► **el cual, la cual**
pron rel
which, who, whom

el castillo, el cual se construyó en el siglo once, es el más bello del país the castle, which was built in the eleventh century, is the most beautiful in the country

la mendiga, la cual era ciega, se situaba cada día en la misma esquina the beggar, who was blind, stood on the same corner every day

había diez policías, tres de los cuales estaban armados there were ten policemen, three of whom were armed

...cual

▶ **lo cual**
[lo kwal] *pron rel*
1. which

su tío le dio cinco libras, lo cual fue muy generoso por su parte his uncle gave him five pounds, which was very generous of him

2. Idiom
por lo cual so

no llevaba dinero encima, por lo cual tuve que ir al banco I had no money on me, so I had to go to the bank

con lo cual at which, whereupon

la cena acabó a las once, con lo cual todo el mundo empezó a despedirse the dinner ended at eleven o'clock, whereupon everybody began to say goodbye

cual si as if

cuál

cuál, cuáles
[kwal, 'kwales]
pron interr
1. what

¿cuál es su nombre? what's your name?

¿cuál es la fecha de hoy? what's today's date?

2. which
¿cuál de éstos pertenece a Tintín? which of these belongs to Tintín?

3. Idiom
tres chicos a cuál más gandul three boys each as lazy as the other

cualquiera

cualquier, cualquiera, cualesquier, cualesquiera
[kwal'kjer, kwal'kjera, kwales'kjer, kwales'kjera]
I. *adj indet*
any

cualquier autobús nos va bien any bus is all right for us

puede sentarse en cualquier sitio you can sit in any seat

...cualquiera

II. *pron indet*
any (one), anyone, anybody

puede elegir cualesquiera de estos discos de aquí you can choose any of these records here

¡eso lo sabe cualquiera! anybody knows that!

cuando

cuando
['kwando] *adv*
1. when

* *Cuando vuelva, dígale que me llame; es muy urgente. Gracias. Adiós.* When he comes back, tell him to phone me; it's very urgent. Thank you. Goodbye. *

2. Idiom
de cuando en cuando, de vez en cuando from time to time

Cuando vuelva, dígale que me llame, es muy urgente. Gracias. Adiós.

cuándo

cuándo
['kwando] *pron interr*
when

¿cuándo te vas? when are you leaving?

cuanto

cuanto
['kwanto]
I. *adj & pron rel*
all (that), everyone that, as much as, as many as

cuantos la conocen la quieren everyone that knows her loves her

le daré cuanto dinero necesite I'll give you all the money you need

...cuanto

coja cuantos quiera take as many as you want

II. *adv & conj*
Idiom

cuanto más... más... the more... the more...

cuanto más... menos... the more... the less

* *Cuanto más bebe, más ganas tiene de beber.* The more he drinks, the more he wants to drink. *

Cuanto más bebe, más ganas tiene de beber.

en cuanto a as for

en cuanto a ti as for you

en cuanto as soon as

* *En cuanto lleguen, avísame... Ya sabes, estoy en el sótano... y les espero con impaciencia.* As soon as they arrive, let me know... As you know, I'm in the basement... and I'm anxious to see them. *

En cuanto lleguen, avísame... Ya sabes, estoy en el sótano... y les espero con impaciencia.

cuanto antes as soon as possible

te lo diré cuanto antes I'll let you know as soon as possible

cuanto antes mejor the sooner the better

* *¡Así que Tintín se ha burlado de mí! Pues ahora verá cómo las gasto... ¡Ah, malvado! ¡Cuánto antes nos encon-*

...cuanto

¡Así que Tintín se ha burlado de mí! Pues ahora verá cómo las gasto... ¡Ah, malvado! ¡Cuanto antes nos encontremos mejor!...

tremos mejor!... So Tintin laughed at me! Well, I'll show him... Oh, the rascal! The sooner we meet the better!... *

unos cuantos, unas cuantas a few

► tanto... cuanto...
adj & pron correl
as much... as...,
as many... as...

había tantas muje-res cuantos hom-

bres there were as many women as men

► tanto más...
cuanto más/que...
adj & pron correl
all the more...
since/because

cuánto

cuánto, a
[kwˈanto, a]

...cuánto

I. adj & pron interr
how much,
how many

¿cuánto cuestan los sellos? how much are the stamps?

¿cuántas hojas ne-cesitas? how many sheets do you need?

II. adj & pron excl
how, how hard,
what a lot

¡cuánto trabaja! how

...cuánto

hard he works! (doesn't he work hard!)

¡cuántas moscas! what a lot of flies!

cuarto

cuarto
[ˈkwarto] n m
room

cuarto de estar
living-room

...cuarto

* En el cuarto de ba-ño... In the bathroom... *

cubrir

cubrir, cubrirse
[kuˈβrir, se]
I. v t
to cover

II. v pr
to be covered

En el cuarto de baño...

...cubrir

el suelo se cubrió de nieve en poco tiempo the ground was soon covered in snow

cuchara

cuchara
[kuˈtʃara] n f
spoon

cuchillo

cuchillo
[kuˈtʃiλo] n m
knife

* El lanzador de cuchillos ejecuta su número. The knife thro-wer is performing his act. *

cuello

cuello
[ˈkweλo] n m
neck

El lanzador de cuchillos ejecuta su número.

cuenta

cuenta
[ˈkwenta] n
1. account

no tengo cuenta bancaria I haven't got a bank account

2. bill
* ¡Camarero!... ¡La cuenta, por favor! Waiter... The bill, please! Enseguida. Right away. *

¡Camarero!... ¡La cuenta, por favor! Enseguida.

cuerda

cuerda
[k'werða] n f
1. rope

* *¿Puede alcanzar la cuerda?* Can you reach the rope? *

2. string

3. Idiom
dar cuerda al reloj to wind one's watch up

cuerno

cuerno
[k'werno] n m
1. horn, antler

2. Idiom
* *¡Cobarde! ¡Vete al cuerno!* Coward! Go to the devil!
No le oye, capitán... He can't hear you, Captain... *

cuero

cuero
[k'wero] n m
1. leather

2. Idiom
en cueros stark naked

el ladrón me dejó en cueros the robber left me penniless

cuerpo

cuerpo
[k'werpo] n m
1. body

2. Idiom
vivir a cuerpo de rey to live like a king

cuesta

cuesta
[k'westa] n f
1. slope, hill

* *¡Qué ligero sube la cuesta este coche!* Doesn't this car climb the hill easily! *

2. Idiom
llevar a cuestas to carry on one's back

cuestión

cuestión
[kwes'tjon] n f
question, matter

...cuestión

una cuestión candente a burning question

cuidar

cuidar, cuidarse
[kwi'ðar, se]
I. v t
to look after,
to take care of

* *La enfermera ha cuidado a los heridos.*

...cuidar

The nurse has been looking after the wounded. *

II. v pr
to look after,
to look after oneself

tus padres se cuidarán de ti your parents will look after you

¡cuídate! look after yourself!

La enfermera ha cuidado a los heridos.

▶ **cuidado**
[kwi'ðaðo] n m
1. care

2. Idiom
¡cuidado! look out! (be careful!)

tener cuidado, ir con cuidado to be careful

* *¡Ooooh!... ¡Tenga cuidado, Tintín!... ¡Ooooh!* Ooooh!... Be careful, Tintin!... Ooooh! *

...cuidar

¡Ooooh!...¡ Tenga cuidado, Tintín!... ¡Ooooh!...

culpa

culpa
['kulpa] *n f*
blame, fault

tú no tienes la culpa
it's not your fault (you're not to blame)

cultivar

Los campos están cultivados.

cultivar
[kulti'βar] *v t*
to cultivate, to till, to work

* *Los campos están cultivados.* The fields have been cultivated. *

cumpleaños

cumpleaños
[kumple'aɲos] *n m*
birthday

...cumpleaños   ...cumplir

¡feliz cumpleaños!
happy birthday!

cumplir

cumplir
[kum'plir] *v t*
1. to carry out, to follow, to keep

* *¿Por qué me detienen?* Why have you arrested me?

¿Por qué me detienen?

Cumplimos órdenes.

Cumplimos órde-nes. We're just following orders. *

siempre cumple las promesas he always keeps promises

2. to reach
cuando cumplas dieciocho años, podrás hacer lo que quieras when you reach the age of eighteen, you'll be able to do whatever you like

▶ **cumplido**
[kum'pliðo]
I. *n m*
1. courtesy, politeness

ésta es sólo una visita de cumplido this is just a courtesy visit

2. Idiom
¡no hagáis cumpli-dos, por favor! don't stand on ceremony, please!

II. *adj*
f cumplida [kum'pliða]
complete, perfect

misión cumplida
mission complete

curar

curar, curarse
[ku'rar, se]
I. *v t*
to cure

* *Estoy buscando el medicamento que cure a mi hijo. Espero encontrarlo pronto.* I'm looking for the medicine that will cure my son. I hope I'll find it soon. *

II. *v pr*
to get better,

Estoy buscando el medicamento que cure a mi hijo. Espero encontrarlo pronto.

to recover

se curó rápida-mente he recovered quickly

curioso

curioso, a
[kur'joso, a] *adj*
1. curious, strange

2. inquisitive

cuyo

cuyo, a
['kuʝo, a] *pron rel*
whose

tu amiga, cuyo nombre se me olvi-dó, es muy bonita your friend, whose name I've forgotten, is very pretty

la Castafiore, cuyas joyas han desapa-recido, esta deses-perada Castafiore, whose jewels have dis-appeared, is in despair

chabola

chabola
[tʃa'βola] *n f*
1. shack

¿quién habita esa chabola? who lives in that shack?

2. Idiom
chabolas f pl shanty town

chaqueta

chaqueta
[tʃaˈketa] n f
jacket

* *El capitán lleva una chaqueta de cuadros.* The Captain is wearing a checked jacket. *

charlar

charlar
[ˈtʃarlar] v i
to chat

El capitán lleva una chaqueta de cuadros.

...charlar

está charlando con la vecina she's chatting to her neighbour

chico

chico, a
[ˈtʃiko, a] n
boy, girl

aquellos señores tienen un chico y dos chicas those people have a boy and two girls

...chico

Dos chiquillos...

▶**chiquillo, a**
[tʃiˈkiʎo, a] n
kid, youngster

* *Dos chiquillos...* Two youngsters... *

chillar

chillar
[tʃiˈʎar] v i
to shout, to scream

chimenea

chimenea
[tʃimenˈea] n f
chimney

* *¡Tiene razón! ¡Se ha escapado por la chimenea!* You're right!

...chimenea

¡Tiene razón! ¡Se ha escapado por la chimenea!

He's got away up the chimney! *

chisme

chisme
[ˈtʃisme] n m
1. piece of gossip

no quiero oír esos chismes I don't want to hear your gossip

2. thing, gadget

chiste

¡Ja! ¡Ja! ¿Te cuento el último chiste? ¡Es divertidísimo!

chiste
[ˈtʃiste] n m
joke

* *¡Ja! ¡Ja! ¿Te cuento el último chiste? ¡Es divertidísimo!* Ha! Ha! Do

...chiste

you want to hear the latest joke? It's hilarious! *

chocar

chocar
[tʃoˈkar]
I. v i
to crash into, to hit

un coche ha chocado contra la valla a car has crashed into the fence

...chocar

II. v t
to shock

tu comportamiento ha chocado a tu padre your behaviour has shocked your father

chocolate

chocolate
[tʃokoˈlate] n m
chocolate

...chocolate

un pastel de chocolate a chocolate cake

chófer

chófer
[ˈtʃofer] n m
1. chauffeur
2. driver

chorizo

chorizo
[tʃoˈriθo] n m
1. sausage
2. thief

chulo

chulo, a
[ˈtʃulo, a] adj
1. smart

¡qué coche más

...chulo

chulo! what a smart car!

2. cocky
¡no te pongas chulo! don't get cocky!

churro

churro
[ˈtʃuˈro] n m
fritter

daño

daño
['daɲo] *n m*
hurt, harm, damage

* *¡Aaaay!* Ow!
¿Le hago daño, capitán?... Se ha hecho usted un esguince... Am I hurting you, Captain?... You've sprained your ankle... *

dar

dar
[dar] *v t*
1. to give

* *Zorrino, ¿no te acuerdas que un día te di una medalla?...* Zorrino, don't you remember that one day I gave you a medal?... *

2. Idiom
dar las gracias to thank

...dar

me da lo mismo it's all the same to me

dar un paseo to go for a walk

darse prisa to hurry up

* *¡Dése prisa!* Hurry up! *

darse cuenta to realize

el reloj dio la una the clock struck one

de

de
[de] *prep*
1. of

una taza de café a cup of coffee

2. in
el chico más inteligente de la clase the most intelligent boy in the class

vestido de azul dressed in blue

3. from
es de Madrid he's from Madrid

debajo

debajo
[de'βaxo]
I. *adv*
underneath, below

II. *prep*
debajo de under,

...debajo

underneath, beneath, below

el gato está debajo de la mesa the cat is under the table

deber

deber
[de'βer]
I. *v t*
to owe

...deber

me debes mil pesetas you owe me a thousand pesetas

II. *v i*
must, to have to

debo cumplir la misión I must accomplish the mission

III. *n m*
duty, obligation

▶ **deberes**
[de'βeres] *n pl*
homework

débil

débil
['deβil] *adj*
weak

* *Está muy débil... Es mejor llevarlo al hospital, allí le haremos otros análisis...* He's very weak... We'd better take him to hospital; there we can do some more tests on him... *

Está muy débil... Es mejor llevarlo al hospital, allí le haremos otros análisis...

decidir

decidir
[deθi'ðir] *v i & v t*
to decide

¿has decidido ya? have you decided yet?

▶ **decisión**
[deθi'sion] *n f*
decision

debemos tomar una decisión ahora we must make a decision now

decir

decir
[de'θir] *v t*
1. to say, to tell

¡di algo! say something!

dile que venga tell him to come

2. Idiom
* *¡Diga, sí, dígame! ¡Mil rayos! ¡Diga! ¡Hable más alto, no oigo nada!* Hello, yes, hello! Blistering barnacles! Speak up, I can't hear anything! *

¡Diga, sí, dígame! ¡Mil rayos! ¡Diga! ¡Hable más alto, no oigo nada!

¿qué quiere decir? what do you mean?

mejor dicho or rather

hace calor, mejor dicho, mucho calor it's hot, or rather, very hot

dedo

dedo
['deðo] *n m*
1. finger

...dedo

¡Rayos y centellas! ¡Loro de los demonios!... ¡Me has mordido el dedo, sí, especie de bicharraco!

¡Rayos y centellas!...

...dedo

* *¡Rayos y centellas! ¡Loro de los demonios!... ¡Me has mordido el dedo, sí, especie de bicharraco!* Thundering typhoons! You damned parrot!... You bit my finger, yes, you little beast! *¡Rayos y centellas!...* Thundering typhoons!... *

2. Idiom
dedo del pie toe

dejar

dejar
[de'xar] *v t*
1. to leave

* *¿Dónde quiere que les sirva el aperitivo, aquí o en el salón? Déjelo sobre la mesa; ya nos serviremos nosotros mismos.* Where do you want me to serve the aperitif, here or in the lounge? Leave it on the table; we'll help ourselves. *

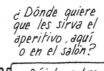

¿Dónde quiere que les sirva el aperitivo, aquí o en el salón?

Déjelo sobre la mesa, ya nos serviremos nosotros mismos.

2. to let, to allow
su padre no la deja salir por la noche her father does not let her go out at night

3. to lend
¿me puedes dejar el jersey? can you lend me your jersey?

4. Idiom
dejar de to stop

deja de morderte las uñas stop biting your nails

no dejar de not to forget to

no dejes de comprar pan don't forget to buy bread

del

del
[del] *art cont*
of the, in the, from the

bajó del coche he got out of the car

delante

delante
[de'lante]
I. *adv*
in front

...delante

Está delante de la puerta.

II. *prep*
delante de in front of

* *¡Clac!* Slam!
Está delante de la puerta. He is in front of the door. *

delgado

delgado, a
[del'γaðo, a] *adj*
thin

demás

demás
[de'mas] *adj & pron*
1. others, the others, the rest

los demás libros son tuyos the other books are yours

quédate lo demás keep the rest

2. Idiom
por lo demás moreover

los demás other people, others

hay que tener respeto por los demás one must have respect for others

demasiado

demasiado
[dema'sjaðo]
I. *adj*
f demasiada
[dema'sjaða]
too much, too many

hay demasiados coches en el parking there are too many cars in the car park

II. *adv*
too, too much

* *¡Esto es demasiado! ¡Piratas de agua*

*dulce!...¡ Iconoclastas!...*This is too much! Freshwater swabs!... Iconoclasts!... *

demostrar

demostrar
[demos'trar] *v t*
to demonstrate, to show, to prove

demuéstralo prove it

dentro

dentro
['dentro]
I. *adv*
inside

¿lo dejo dentro o fuera? shall I leave it inside or not?

II. *prep*
dentro de in, inside

* *¡Mira, Milú! ¡Los pergaminos que tanto hemos buscado! ¡Aquí están,*

dentro de la cartera! Look, Snowy! The parchments we've been looking so hard for! Here they are, inside the wallet! *

volveremos dentro de una semana we'll be back in a week's time

...dentro

¡Mira, Milú! ¡Los pergaminos que tanto hemos buscado! ¡Aquí están, dentro de la cartera!...

departamento

departamento
[departa'mento] *n m*
1. department

¿en qué departamento trabaja? what department does he work in?

2. compartment
éste es un departamento de no fumadores this is a non-smoking compartment

depender

depender
[depen'der] *v i*
to depend

depende de si llueve o no it depends on whether it rains or not

deporte

deporte
[de'porte] *n m*
sport

...deporte

Tintín hace deporte.

* *Tintín hace deporte.* Tintin practises sport. *

derecho

derecho
[de'retʃo]
I. *n m*
1. right

usted no tiene el derecho de hablarme así you have no right to talk to me like that

2. law
estudia derecho he studies law

3. Idiom
¡no hay derecho! it's not fair!

II. *adj*
f derecha [de'retʃa]
1. straight

2. right, right-hand
el pie derecho the right foot

3. Idiom
a mano derecha on the right

III. *adv*
straight (on)

siga derecho por esta calle go straight on down this road

▶ **derecha**
[de'retʃa] *n f*
right,
right-hand side

al final de la calle tuerza a la derecha at the end of the street turn right

derrochar

derrochar
[de'ro'tʃar] *v t*
to waste,

...derrochar

to squander

derrochó su fortuna he squandered his fortune

derrota

derrota
[de'rota] *n f*
defeat

el ejército sufrió una grave derrota the army suffered a serious defeat

desaparecer

desaparecer
[desapare'θer] *v i*
to disappear

* *¡Un eclipse! ¡Por eso ha desaparecido el sol!* An eclipse! That's why the sun's disappeared!
No se preocupe, capitán, se trata sólo de un eclipse. Don't worry, Captain; it's just an eclipse.
¡Guauuu! Bow-wow! *

...desaparecer

desarrollar

**desarrollar,
desarrollarse**
[desaro'λar, se]
I. *v t*
to develop

II. *v pr*
1. to develop,
to advance

la ciencia se ha desarrollado mucho en el siglo veinte science has advanced greatly in the twentieth century

2. to take place
la acción se desarrolla durante la Segunda Guerra Mundial the action takes place in the Second World War

▶ **desarrollo**
[desa'roλo] *n m*
development,
advancement

el desarrollo de la industria the development of industry

desayunar

desayunar
[desaju'nar]
I. *v i*
to have breakfast

* *Gauu..Au* Bow...wow
Mientras el capitán y Tintín desayunan... While the Captain and Tintin are having breakfast... *

II. *v t*
to have for breakfast

siempre desayuno café con leche y tostadas I always have white coffee and toast for breakfast

▶ **desayuno**
[desa'juno] *n m*
breakfast

descalzo

descalzo, a
[des'kalθo, a] *adj*
barefoot, without any shoes on

* *¡Oh! ¡Pobrecilla; va descalza!* Oh! Poor little thing; she hasn't any shoes on!
¡Uuh! ¡Uuh! Boo-hoo! *

...descalzo

descansar

descansar
[deskan'sar] *v i*
to rest

* *¡Cuánto pesa esta mochila!... ¡Si pudiera descansar...!* This rucksack is so heavy!... If only I could rest...! *

▶ **descanso**
[des'kanso] *n m*
1. rest

2. break, interval

describir

describir
[deskri'βir] *v t*
to describe

▶ **descripción**
[deskrip'θjon] *n f*
description

descubrir

descubrir
[desku'βrir] *v t*
1. to discover

* *¡Por fin hemos descubierto el tesoro! ¡Fíjese! Quién lo hubiera pensado...* At last we've discovered the treasure! Fancy that! Who would have thought it possible...*

2. to reveal,
to give away
nos descubrió sus

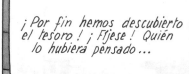

intenciones he revealed his intentions to us

▶ **descubrimiento**
[deskuβri'mjento] *n m*
discovery

desde

desde
['desðe] *prep*
1. from, since

...desde

se divisaba desde lejos it was visible from a long way off

desde su llegada since his arrival

2. Idiom
desde hace for

vivimos en Málaga desde hace un año we've been living in Malaga for a year

desde luego of course

desear

desear
[dese'ar] *v t*
to want, to desire,
to wish for

* *¿Desea usted una copa, profesor?* Do you want a drink, Professor? *

desempeñar

desempeñar
[desempe'ɲar] *v t*
to play, to hold,
to perform

desempeñar un papel to play a part

¿qué cargo desempeña en la empresa? what position does he hold in the firm?

desesperar

**desesperar,
desesperarse**
[desespe'rar, se]
I. *v i & v t*
to despair,
to give up hope

desespero de verle otra vez I've given up hope of seeing him again

II. *v pr*
to despair, to give up hope

D

desgracia

desgracia
[des'ɣraθja] n f
misfortune

▶ **desgraciado, a**
[desɣra'θjaðo, a] adj
wretched, unlucky

* *¡Vamos, vamos, capitán!... ¡Cálmese!* Come now, come now, Captain!... Calm down!
Qué desgraciado soy! ¡Uuh! What a wretched fellow I am! Boohoo! *

desierto

desierto
[de'sjerto] n m
desert

* *¡Animo, capitán! Pronto saldremos del desierto...* Don't despair, Captain! We'll soon be out of the desert...
¡Algo de beber! ¡Tengo sed! Give me something to drink! I'm thirsty! *

desnudar

desnudar, desnudarse
[desnu'dar, se] v t & v pr
to undress

desobedecer

desobedecer
[desoβeðe'θer] v i
to disobey

en el ejército no hay que desobe-

...desobedecer

decer nunca una orden in the army you must never disobey an order

▶ **desobediente**
[desoβe'ðjente] adj
disobedient

* *Milú, eres un perro muy desobediente. No me gusta nada esto.* Snowy, you're a very disobedient dog. I'm not pleased about that at all. *

desorden

desorden
[de'sorðen] n m
disorder, mess

* *¡Qué desorden! Todo está revuelto... No sé por dónde empezar...* What a mess! Everything's upside down... I don't know where to begin... *

despacio

despacio
[des'paθjo] adv
slowly

si hablas más despacio, te entenderé mejor if you speak more slowly, I'll understand you better

despedir

despedir, despedirse
[despe'ðir, se]
I. v t
to dismiss, to sack

lo han despedido del trabajo he's been sacked (from his job)

II. v pr
to say goodbye, to see off

* *¡Adiós!... ¡Hasta otro día!...* Goodbye!...

Nuestros amigos se despiden.

See you again some other time!...
¡Hasta pronto!... See you soon!...
¡Buen viaje!... Have a good journey!...
Nuestros amigos se despiden. Our friends are saying goodbye. *

fuimos a la estación a despedirnos de él we went to the station to see him off

▶ **despedida**
[despe'ðiða] n f
goodbye, farewell

despegar

**despegar,
despegarse**
[despe'ɣar, se]
I. v t
to unstick, to detach

II. v i
to take off

*el avión ha despega-
do* the plane has taken off

III. v pr
to come off,
to come unstuck

despertar

**despertar,
despertarse**
[desper'tar, se]
I. v t
to wake up,
to awaken, to rouse

*me despertó el
ruido del tráfico* I was
woken up by the sound of
the traffic

II. v pr
to wake up

suelo despertarme

a las siete I usually
wake up at seven

▶ **despertador**
[desperta'ðor] n m
alarm clock

* *¡Un despertador!*
An alarm clock!
Rrrr Rrrr *

después

después
[des'pwes]
I. adv
later, after,
afterwards

II. prep
after

*después de la guer-
ra reconstruyeron el
pueblo* after the war they
rebuilt the town

detalle

Tintín examina un detalle.

detalle
[de'taʎe] n m
1. detail

* *Tintín examina un
detalle.* Tintin is ex-
amining a detail. *

2. gesture
*¡qué detalle más
bonito!* what a nice
gesture!

detener

...detener

detener
[dete'ner] v t
to arrest

* *Pero... ¿por qué
me detienen?* But...
why are you arresting me?
*No te hagas el
inocente... Después
explicarás lo que ha
pasado en el
banco...* Don't pretend
to be innocent... After-
wards you can explain
what happened in the
bank... *

detrás

detrás
[de'tras]
I. adv
behind

II. prep
detrás de behind

* *Tintín y Milú se
han escondido de-
trás de la cortina.*
Tintin and Snowy have
hidden behind the curtain. *

*Tintín y Milú se han escondido
detrás de la cortina.*

devolver

devolver
[deβol'βer] v t
1. to return,
to give back

*por cierto, tengo que
devolverte esos
libros* by the way, I must
give you those books back

2. to throw up,
to vomit
*ha devuelto la comi-
da* he's thrown up his
lunch

día

día
['ðia] n m
1. day

* *Los restos del avión se encuentran allá. Nos quedan dos días de marcha.* The wreckage of the plane is over there. We still have two days' walk. *

2. Idiom
el día de hoy today

Los restos del avión se encuentran allá. Nos quedan dos días de marcha.

¿*qué día es?* what's the date?

el día menos pensado when you least expect it

al día siguiente the following day

un día sí y otro no every other day

ponerse al día to catch up

hoy (en) día nowadays

diálogo

diálogo
[dj'aloɣo] n m
dialogue

dibujar

dibujar
[diβu'xar] v t
to draw

* *¿Quién ha dibujado esto?* Who drew this? *

...dibujar

decidimos quedarnos. El sol y nos hizo verter abundantes

¿ *Quién ha dibujado esto?*

...dibujar

► **dibujo**
[di'βuxo] n m
drawing

diccionario

diccionario
[di(k)θjo'narjo] n m
dictionary

diciembre

diciembre
[di'θjembre] n m
December

el veinticinco de diciembre the twenty-fifth of December

dictado

dictado
[dik'taðo] n m
dictation

diente

diente
['djente] n m
1. tooth

* *El capitán se lava los dientes.* The Captain is cleaning his teeth. *

dientes postizos false teeth

2. Idiom
hablar entre dientes to mumble, to mutter

► **dentífrico**
[den'tifriko] n m
toothpaste

► **dentista**
[den'tista] n m
dentist

El capitán se lava los dientes.

---

diferencia

diferencia
[dife'renθja] n f
1. difference

¿cuál es la diferencia entre éste y aquél? what's the difference between this one and that one?

2. Idiom
a diferencia de unlike

► **diferente**
[dife'rente] adj
different

difícil

difícil
[di'fiθil] adj
difficult, hard

es difícil aprender ruso it's difficult to learn Russian

► **dificultad**
[difikul'tað] n f
difficulty, trouble

tuve dificultades para conseguir el pasaporte I had difficulty getting my passport

¡diga!

¡diga! → DECIR

dignidad

dignidad
[diɣni'ðað] n f
dignity

dinero

dinero
[di'nero] n m
money

* *Tintín no acepta el dinero...* Tintin hasn't accepted the money... *

Tintín no acepta el dinero...

Dios

Dios
[djos] n pr
1. God

2. Idiom
¡Dios mío! Good heavens!

¡vaya por Dios! well I never!

gracias a Dios thank heaven

como Dios manda properly

dirección

dirección
[direk'θjon] n f
1. address

ponga claramente su dirección write your address clearly

2. direction, way
* *¡Es por aquí!... Los pasos van en esta dirección!* It's this way!... The footsteps lead off in this direction. *

¡Es por aquí!... ¡Los pasos van en esta dirección!

disco

disco
['disko] n m
record, disc

es su último disco it's his latest record

discutir

discutir
[disku'tir] v i & v t
1. to discuss

...discutir

están discutiendo el asunto they're discussing the matter

2. to argue
¡deja de discutir! stop arguing!

▶ **discusión**
[disku'sjon] n f
1. discussion

2. argument
una discusión acalorada a heated argument

disfrazar

disfrazar, disfrazarse
[disfra'θar, se]
I. v t
to disguise

II. v pr
to disguise oneself

se disfrazó de policía he disguised himself as a policeman

▶ **disfraz**
[dis'fraθ] n m
disguise

disgustar

disgustar, disgustarse
[dizɣus'tar, se]
I. v t
to displease, to annoy

* *Me disgusta mucho que husmees en el cubo de la basura... Como lo vuelvas a hacer, te pongo bozal.* I'm very annoyed at your sniffing in the dustbin. If you do it again, I'll put a muzzle on you. *

Me disgusta mucho que husmees en el cubo de la basura... Como lo vuelvas a hacer, te pongo bozal.

II. v pr
to be displeased, to be annoyed

▶ **disgusto**
[diz'ɣusto] n m
1. displeasure, annoyance

2. Idiom
me causó un gran disgusto it was a great blow to me

llevarse un disgusto to be upset, to be annoyed

disimular

disimular
[disimu'lar] v i & v t
to hide

¿qué pretendes disimular? what are you trying to hide?

disparar

disparar
[dispa'rar] v i & v t
to fire, to shoot

...disparar

¡Alto o disparo!... ¡Muy bien!

* *¡Alto o disparo!... ¡Muy bien!* Stop or I'll shoot!... Right! *

distancia

distancia
[dis'tanθja] n f
distance

distinto

distinto, a
[dis'tinto, a] adj
1. clear, distinct

2. different

distraer

distraer
[distra'er]
I. v t
to distract, to relax

...distraer

II. v i
to relax

los hobbys distraen your hobbies relax you

▶ **distracción**
[distrak'θjon] n f
1. hobby

2. absent-mindedness, forgetfulness

divertirse

divertirse
[diβer'tirse] v pr
to amuse oneself,
to have a good time,
to have fun

* *Abdallah se divierte mucho en Moulinsart.* Abdullah has fun in Marlinspike. *

▶ **divertido, a**
[diβer'tiðo, a] adj
amusing, fun

Abdallah se divierte mucho en Moulinsart.

dividir

dividir
[diβi'ðir] v t
to divide

divisar

divisar
[diβi'sar] v t
to make out

doble

doble
['doβle] adj & n m
double

documentación

documentación
[dokumenta'θjon] n f
papers,
documents

si no llevamos la documentación en

...documentación

regla, tendremos problemas con la policía if our papers are not in order, we'll get into trouble with the police

doler

doler
[do'ler] v i
to hurt, to ache

* *Capitán, ¿cómo está Tintín?* Captain,

...doler

how's Tintin?
Mejor, pero todavía le duele la cabeza. Better, but his head still aches. *

dominar

dominar
[domi'nar]
I. v t
1. to dominate,
to rule (over)

Capitán, ¿cómo está Tintín?

Mejor, pero todavía le duele la cabeza.

...dominar

los moros dominaron a España durante casi ocho siglos the Moors ruled Spain for nearly eight centuries

2. to have a good command of
domina el inglés he has a good command of English

II. v i
to dominate,
to predominate

domingo

domingo
[do'minɣo] n m
Sunday

don

don, doña
[don, 'doɲa] n
don, doña

buenos días, don Felipe good morning, don Felipe

donde

donde
['donde] adv
where, in which

éste es el sitio donde encontré las llaves this is the place where I found the keys

dónde

dónde
['donde] adv interr
where

...dónde

¡¡¡Milú!!! Pero ¿por dónde has pasado? ¡Ale! ¡desátame y vámonos de aquí cuanto antes!

* *¡¡¡Milú!!! Pero ¿por dónde has pasado? ¡Ale! ¡desátame, y vámonos de aquí cuanto antes!* Snowy!!! Where did you come from? Come on! Untie me and let's get out of here as soon as possible! *

doña

doña → DON

dormir

dormir, dormirse
[dor'mir, se]
I. v i
to sleep

¿has dormido bien? did you sleep well?

...dormir

II. v pr
to fall asleep,
to go to sleep

* *¡Capitán! ¡Capitán! ¡No se duerma! ¡Despiértese!* Captain! Captain! Don't go to sleep! Wake up!
Rrr Rrr *

...dormir

¡Capitán! ¡Capitán! ¡No se duerma! ¡Despiértese!

RRR

ducha

ducha
[ˈdutʃa] n f
shower

▶ **ducharse**
[dutˈʃarse] v pr
to have a shower

duda

duda
[ˈduða] n f
doubt

...duda

* *No cabe la menor duda que Tintín se ha escapado, y eso que le habíamos puesto las esposas...* There's no doubt at all that Tintin has escaped, even after we put handcuffs on him...
Yo diría aún más: no cabe la menor duda que Tintín se ha escapado. To be precise: there's no doubt that Tintin has escaped. *

No cabe la menor duda que Tintín se ha escapado, y eso que le habíamos puesto las esposas

Yo diría aún más: no cabe la menor duda que Tintín se ha escapado.

dudar

dudar
[duˈðar]
I. v i & v t
to doubt

no lo dudo I don't doubt it

II. v i
to hesitate

si necesitan algo, no duden en comunicárnoslo if you need anything, don't hesitate to tell us

dueño

dueño, a
[ˈdweɲo, a] n
owner, landlord, employer

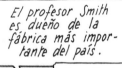

El profesor Smith es dueño de la fábrica más importante del país.

Ya entiendo...

* *El profesor Smith es dueño de la fábrica más importante del país.* Professor Smith is the owner of the most important factory in the country. *Ya entiendo...* I see... *

dulce

dulce
[ˈdulθe]
I. n m
sweet

II. adj
sweet

durante

durante
[duˈrante] prep
1. during

...durante

durante el desayuno
during breakfast

2. for
durante tres horas
for three hours

durar

durar
[duˈrar] v i
to last

* *El viaje ha durado*

...durar

El viaje ha durado dos horas largas.

VT-D

dos horas largas. The journey lasted a good two hours. *

duro

duro
[ˈduro] n m
1. five-peseta coin, five pesetas

cuesta cinco duros it costs twenty-five pesetas

...duro

2. Idiom
no tengo ni un duro
I'm broke

duro

duro, a
[ˈduro, a] adj
1. hard, tough, stale

este pan está duro
this bread is stale

2. Idiom

...duro

No soy sordo, sólo soy un poco duro de oído...

* *No soy sordo; sólo soy un poco duro de oído...* I'm not deaf; I'm just a bit hard of hearing... *

e

e
[e] *conj before i or hi*
and

echar

echar, echarse
[e'tʃar, se]
I. *v t*
1. to throw

echa leña al fuego throw some wood on the fire

...echar

2. to throw out
le echaron del bar he was thrown out of the bar

3. to post
voy a echar estas cartas I'm going to post these letters

4. Idiom
vamos a echar una partida de ajedrez let's play a game of chess

¿qué película echan hoy por la televi-

sión? what film is on the television today?

II. *v pr*
1. to lie down

siempre me echo un rato después de comer I always lie down for a while after lunch

2. Idiom
echarse a perder to go off, to go bad

edad

edad
[e'ðað] *n f*
1. age

2. Idiom
tiene dos años de edad she's two years old

cumplir la mayoría de edad to come of age

Edad de (la) Piedra Stone Age

edificio

edificio
[eði'fiθjo] *n m*
building

* *En este edificio está Tintín... ¿Lo ves?... Está con su perro, cerca de la ventana. Apunta bien y, sobre todo, no lo falles* Tintin is in that building... Can you see him?... He's with his dog, near the window. Aim carefully and, above all, don't miss him. *

...edificio

En ese edificio está Tintín... ¿Lo ves?... Está con su perro, cerca de la ventana. Apunta bien y, sobre todo, no lo falles.

educar

educar
[eðu'kar] *v t*
to educate, to bring up

se educó en el campo he was brought up in the country

▶ **educado, a**
[eðu'kaðo, a] *adj*
well-mannered, polite

efecto

efecto
[e'fekto] *n m*
1. effect, result

2. Idiom
a este efecto to this end

surtir efecto to have the desired effect

en efecto in fact, as a matter of fact

ejemplo

ejemplo
[e'xemplo] *n m*
1. example

2. Idiom
por ejemplo for example

dar ejemplo to set an example

sin ejemplo unprecedented, unparalleled

ejercicio

ejercicio
[exer'θiθjo] *n m*
exercise

* *Un poco de ejercicio físico es muy sano...* A little physical exercise is very healthy... *

Un poco de ejercicio físico es muy sano...

ejército

ejército
[e'xerθito] *n m*
army

el

el, la, los, las
[el, la, los, las] *art*
1. the

el hombre the man

la mujer the woman

los niños the children

...el

las familias the families

2. *no traducible*
me gustan los animales I like animals

el hombre y la sociedad man and society

▶ **el/la/los/las de**
[el, la, los, las de]
pron dem
that/those of,
the one(s) in/on

mi coche, el de usted y el de la

...el

izquierda my car, yours and the one on the left

▶ **el/la/los/las que**
[el, la, los, las ke] *pron rel*
he/those who,
the one(s) that

el que compramos no vale the one we bought is no good

los que no obedecen serán castigados those who do not obey will be punished

él

él, ella, ellos, ellas
[el, 'eλa, 'eλos, 'eλas] *pron pers*
1. he, she, they

ellos lo hicieron they did it

2. him, her, them
es ella it's her

me voy con él I'm going with him

electricidad

electricidad
[elektriθi'ðað] *n f*
electricity

▶ **eléctrico, a**
[e'lektriko, a] *adj*
electric(al)

* *¡Guaaauh!* Wooah!
Tintín ha enchufado el ventilador eléctrico. Tintin has plugged in the electric fan. *

¡GUAAAUH!

Tintín ha enchufado el ventilador eléctrico.

elegante

elegante
[ele'ɣante] *adj*
elegant, smart

* *...de verme tan bella en este espejo...* to see myself so beautiful in this mirror...
Va siempre muy elegante... She is always very elegant... *

ella

ella →ÉL

...DE VERME TAN BELLA EN ESTE ESPEJO...

Va siempre muy elegante...

ello

ello
['eλo] *pr nt*
it, this, that

a causa de ello because of it/this/that

ello me obligó a reconsiderar el problema this obliged me to reconsider the problem

embarcar

Los pasajeros embarcan...

...embarcar

embarcar
[embar'kar] *v i*
to embark,
to go on board

* *Los pasajeros em-
barcan...* The passen-
gers are going on board... *

▶ **embarque**
[em'barke] *n m*
embarkation

tarjeta de embarque
boarding pass

embargo

embargo
[em'barɣo] *n m*
Idiom

sin embargo however,
nevertheless

*teníamos que haber
comprado bocadi-
llos; sin embargo,
no tuvimos tiempo*
we should have bought
sandwiches; however, we
did not have time

emigrar

emigrar
[emi'ɣrar] *v i*
to emigrate

▶ **emigrante**
[emi'ɣrante] *adj & n*
emigrant

*los emigrantes no
siempre disfrutan de
buenas condiciones
laborales* emigrants do
not always have good
working conditions

empezar

...empezar

empezar
[empe'θar] *v i & v t*
to begin, to start

* *He empezado a
descifrar este per-
gamino... ¿Qué le
parece?* I've begun to
decipher this parchment...
What do you think?
¡Es fantástico! It's
fantastic! *

emplear

emplear
[emple'ar] *v t*
to use, to employ

* *Aquí tiene tres mil
dólares... y elimine
a Tintín, que para
eso lo empleo a
usted...* Here are three
thousand dollars... get rid
of Tintin; that's what
you're employed for...
¡Cuente conmigo!
Count on me! *

▶ **empleado, a**
[emple'aðo, a] *adj
& n*
employee,
worker, clerk

*empleado de
banco* bank clerk

▶ **empleo**
[em'pleo] *n m*
1. use

2. job,
employment

empresa

empresa
[em'presa] *n f*
firm, enterprise,
company

*una empresa par-
ticular* a private com-
pany

empujar

empujar
[empu'xar] *v t*
to push

...empujar

* *¡Va!... ¡Empujemos
fuerte! ¡Otra vez!...
¡Venga!... Un... Dos...*
Come on!... Push hard!
Again!... Come on!...
One...Two... *

¡no empujéis! don't
push!

en

en
[en] *prep*
1. in

...en

Néstor lleva las botellas en una bandeja.

está en el baño he's
in the bathroom

2. on
* *Néstor lleva las
botellas en una
bandeja.* Nestor is
carrying the bottles on a
tray. *

3. at
está en la puerta he's
standing at the door

*espérame en la
parada de autobús,
o bien en la esta-*

...en

ción wait for me at the bus stop, or at the station

4. to
Milú es el primero en llegar Snowy is the first to arrive

enamorarse

enamorarse
[enamo'rarse] *v pr*
to fall in love

me enamoré de ella casi enseguida I fell in love with her almost immediately

encantar

encantar
[enkan'tar] *v t*
1. to bewitch,

...encantar

to cast a spell on

2. to charm, to delight
* *¡Ah! Me río de verme tan bella en este espejo...* Oh! I laugh to see myself so beautiful in this mirror... *¡Me encanta la tele!* I love the telly! *

▶ **encantado, a**
[enkan'taðo] *adj*
1. delighted

2. Idiom
una casa encantada a haunted house

encender

encender
[enθen'der] *v t*
1. to light

2. to turn on, to switch on
* *Pom Pom Pom*

...encender

Knock Knock Knock
¡Llaman a la puerta! ¡Rápido, Tintín, encienda la luz! There's someone at the door! Quick, Tintin, turn the light on! *

encerrar

encerrar, encerrarse
[enθe'rrar, se]
I. *v t*

...encerrar

to lock up, to shut in

II. *v pr*
to lock oneself up, to shut oneself in

se encierra en su cuarto he shuts himself in his room

encima

encima
[en'θima] *adv*

...encima

1. above, over

viven en el piso de encima they live in the flat above

2. besides, on top of that
es informal y, si por eso fuera poco, encima mentiroso he's unreliable and, as if that weren't enough, a liar on top of that

3. Idiom
no llevaba dinero en-

cima I wasn't carrying any money

▶ **encima de**
[en'θima de] *prep*
1. on, on top of

los libros están encima de la mesa the books are on the table

2. Idiom
por encima de over

el avión pasó por encima de nuestras cabezas the plane passed over our heads

encina

encina
[en'θina] *n f*
holm oak, evergreen oak

encontrar

encontrar, encontrarse
[enkon'trar, se]
I. *v t*
to find, to meet

...encontrar

* *¡Oh!* Oh!
¡Guau! Bow wow!
¿Qué ha encontrado Milú? What has Snowy found? *

¿dónde nos encontramos? where shall we meet?

II. *v pr*
1. to be, to be situated, to stand

la iglesia se en-

cuenta en lo alto del pueblo the church stands in the upper part of the town

2. feel
¿se encuentra bien? do you feel all right?

▶ **encuentro**
[en'kwentro] *n m*
1. meeting, encounter

2. match, game

enchufar

...enchufar

enchufar
[entʃuˈfar] v t
to plug in

* *Tengo que enchufar la radio.* I must plug the radio in. *

enemigo

enemigo, a
[eneˈmiɣo, a] adj & n
enemy

* *¡Victoria!* Victory! *¡Nuestros enemigos han abandonado el país!* Our enemies have fled the country! *¡Hemos ganado!* We've won! *

energía

energía
[enerˈxia] n f
energy

la crisis de la energía the energy crisis

enero

enero
[eˈnero] n m
January

enfadarse

enfadarse
[enfaˈðarse]
I. v t
to make angry, to anger, to annoy

II. v pr
to get angry

* *¡Mil rayos!* Blistering barnacles! *Cuando el capitán se enfada, es terrible...* When the Captain gets angry, its terrible... *

enfermo

enfermo, a
[enˈfermo, a]
I. adj
1. ill, sick

está muy enfermo he's very ill

2. Idiom
caer enfermo, ponerse enfermo to fall ill

II. n
sick person, patient

enfrente

enfrente
[enˈfrente]
I. adv
opposite, facing

* *Estoy en el café de enfrente.* I'm in the bar opposite. *

II. prep
enfrente de opposite, facing

su casa está enfrente de la mía his house is opposite mine

...enfrente

engañar

engañar
[engaˈɲar] v t
to deceive

¡no me engañes! don't deceive me!

engordar

engordar
[engorˈðar]
I. v i
to get fat

...engordar

II. v t
to make fat, to fatten

el chocolate engorda chocolate makes you fat

enhorabuena

enhorabuena
[enoraˈβwena] n f
1. congratulations pl

...enhorabuena

2. Idiom
dar la enhorabuena to congratulate

ensalada

ensalada
[ensaˈlaða] n f
salad

enseguida

enseguida, en seguida
[enseˈɣiða] adv
immediately, straight away, right away, at once

* *Voy a buscar mi maleta y nos vamos enseguida...* I'll go and get my case and we'll be off straight away... *

...enseguida

Voy a buscar mi maleta y nos vamos enseguida...

enseñar

enseñar
[ense'ɲar] *v t*
1. to teach

mi hermano me enseñó a nadar my brother taught me to swim

2. to show
te voy a enseñar cómo se hace I'll show you how to do it

ensuciar

ensuciar, ensuciarse
[ensu'θjar, se]
I. *v t*
to (make) dirty, to soil

has ensuciado el suelo con las botas you've made the floor dirty with your boots

II. *v pr*
to get dirty

* *¡Cómo te has en-*

¡Cómo te has ensuciado, Tintín!

...ensuciar

suciado, Tintín! Look how dirty you've got, Tintín! *

entender

entender, entenderse
[enten'der, se]
I. *v i & v t*
to understand

¿entiendes lo que quiero decir? do you understand what I mean?

...entender

II. *v pr*
1. to understand each other

hablan lenguas muy distintas; no se entienden they speak very different languages; they don't understand each other

2. to get on
no se entiende en absoluto con su mujer he doesn't get on at all with his wife

enterarse

enterarse
[ente'rarse] *v pr*
to hear, to learn, to find out

* *Nos hemos enterado de que ha descubierto petróleo...* We've heard that you've discovered oil... *

Nos hemos enterado de que ha descubierto petróleo... ¡50.000!... ¡100.000!...

entero

entero, a
[en'tero, a] *adj*
whole, entire

usted tiene que pagarme la cantidad entera you have to pay me the whole sum

entonces

entonces
[en'tonθes] *adv*

...entonces

1. then

llegó todo el mundo, y entonces empezó la fiesta everyone arrived, and then the party began

2. Idiom
por/en aquel entonces at that time

por aquel entonces estaba en Nueva York at that time I was in New York

entrar

¿Puedo entrar, por favor?

entrar
[en'trar] *v i*
to come in, to enter

* *¿Puedo entrar, por favor?* Can I come in, please? *

▶ **entrada**
[en'traða] *n f*
1. entrance

2. entry
la entrada de España en el Mercado Común the entry of

...entrar

Spain into the Common Market

3. ticket
¿has comprado las entradas? did you get the tickets?

4. Idiom
de entrada to begin with, right from the start

me gustó de entrada I liked him right from the start

entre

entre
['entre] *prep*
1. between

* *Hay una cortina de agua entre ustedes y yo, pero la podrán atravesar gracias a la cuerda...* There's a barrier of water between you and me, but you'll be able to cross it thanks to the rope...
O.K. O.K. *

2. among
la casa estaba escondida entre los árboles the house was hidden among the trees

* *He decidido vivir entre los indios Arumbayas.* I've decided to live among the Arumbaya Indians.
¿Ah, sí? ¿Y va a dejar de ser explorador? Have you? And are you going to stop exploring? *

...entre

entregar

entregar
.[entre'ɣar] *v t*
to deliver, to hand in, to hand over

entusiasmar

entusiasmar, entusiasmarse
[entusjaz'mar, se]
I. *v t*
to fill with enthusiasm, to delight

...entusiasmar

II. *v pr*
to get enthusiastic, to be delighted

enviar

enviar
[em'bjar] *v t*
to send

te envié una carta hace dos semanas I sent you a letter two weeks ago

envidiar

envidiar
[embi'ðjar] *v t*
to envy

¡cuánto te envidio! how I envy you!

envolver

envolver
[embol'βer] *v t*
to wrap up

...envolver

un paquete envuelto en papel de embalar a parcel wrapped up in brown paper

época

época
['epoka] *n f*
period, time, age, epoch

en aquella época at that time

equipaje

equipaje
[eki'paxe] *n m*
luggage, baggage

* *Bueno, pues ya sólo me falta preparar el equipaje.* Right, now all I need to do is get the luggage ready. *

equipo

equipo
[e'kipo] *n m*
1. team

...equipo

un equipo de hockey a hockey team

2. equipment, gear
tengo que comprar un equipo de caza I must buy some hunting gear

equivocarse

equivocarse
[ekiβo'karse] *v pr*
to make a mistake,

...equivocarse

to be wrong

* *Me he equivocado de calle.* I've got the wrong street. *¿Dónde estamos?* Where are we? *

error

error
[e'ror] *n m*
mistake, error

escalera

Tintín baja la escalera.

...escalera

escalera
[eska'lera] *n f*
stairs, staircase

* *Tintín baja la escalera.* Tintin is running down the stairs. *

escapar

escapar, escaparse
[eska'par, se] *v i & v pr*
to escape,
to run away

...escapar

cinco prisioneros han escapado de la cárcel five prisoners have escaped from prison

escaparate

escaparate
[eskapa'rate] *n m*
shop window

* *Al ver el escaparate, se llevaron una sor-*

...escaparate

Al ver el escaparate, se llevaron una sorpresa.

presa. On looking in the shop window, they got a surprise. *

escena

escena
[es'θena] *n f*
scene

¡qué escena más conmovedora! what a touching scene!

esclavitud

esclavitud
[esklaβi'tuð] *n f*
slavery

escoger

escoger
[esko'xer] *v t*
to choose,
to select

hay tres platos a escoger there are three dishes to choose from

esconder

esconder, esconderse
[eskon'der, se]
v t & v pr
to hide

se escondió en el armario he hid in the cupboard

escopeta

escopeta
[esko'peta] *n f*
gun, rifle

* *¡Mi escopeta aún puede servir!* My gun still serves some purpose! *¡Dios mío!* Good heavens! *

escribir

escribir
[eskri'βir] *v i & v t*
to write

he estado dos horas escribiendo cartas I've spent two hours writing letters

escuchar

escuchar
[esku'tʃar] *v i & v t*
to listen

...escuchar

¡Escúchame bien, Abdallah, y esta vez no hagas tonterías!

* *¡Escúchame bien, Abdallah, y esta vez no hagas tonterías!* Listen to me carefully, Abdullah, and this time don't do anything stupid.
Zuit Whizz
Pam Thud *

ZUIT
PAM
PAM

escuela

escuela
[es'kwela] *n f*
school

escuela de baile dancing school

ese

ese, esa, esos, esas
['ese, a, os, as] *adj dem*
that, those

...ese

¡no toques esas cosas! don't touch those things!

ése

ése, ésa, ésos, ésas
['ese, a, os, as]
pron dem
that one, those ones

...ése

nuestra casa es ésa our house is that one

esencial

esencial
[esen'θjal] *adj*
essential

lo esencial es que cumplamos la misión the essential thing is that we accomplish the mission

esfuerzo

esfuerzo
[es'fwerθo] *n m*
effort

¡Ánimo, capitán, un último esfuerzo!
¡Ya estoy harto!

* *¡Ánimo, capitán, un último esfuerzo!* Come on, Captain, a last effort!
¡Ya estoy harto! I've had enough! *

eso

eso
['eso] *pron dem nt*
1. that, that business

no sé nada de eso I don't know anything about that

2. Idiom
a eso de about

llegaríamos a eso de las dos we must have arrived about two o'clock

espacio

espacio
[es'paθjo] *n m*
1. space, room

en las grandes ciudades falta espacio vital in big cities there is a lack of living space

2. space
* *¡Soy el primer perro conquistador del espacio!* I'm the first dog to conquer space! *

¡Soy el primer perro conquistador del espacio!

3. Idiom
un espacio publicitario an advertisement, a commercial

espalda

espalda
[es'palda] *n f*
1. back, shoulders

2. Idiom
caerse de espaldas to fall (flat) on one's back

* *Tintín se ha caído de espaldas.* Tintin has fallen flat on his back. *

volver la espalda turn one's back

Tintín se ha caído de espaldas.

España

España
[es'paɲa] n f
Spain

▶ **español, a**
[espa'ɲol, a]
I. adj
Spanish

II. n
Spaniard

una pareja de españoles a couple of Spaniards

especial

¡Compren el diario!
¡Edición especial!

especial
[espe'θjal] adj
1. special

* *¡Compren el diario! ¡Edición especial!* Get your paper! Special edition! *

2. particular, fussy
aquél es muy especial he's a very fussy person

3. Idiom
en especial in particular

espectador

espectador, a
[espekta'ðor, a] n
spectator, onlooker, audience

* *Tintín y los otros espectadores miran con atención el nodo.* Tintin and the rest of the audience are watching the news very attentively. *

Tintín y los otros espectadores miran con atención el nodo.

▶ **espectáculo**
[espek'takulo] n m
show, spectacle

...espectador

fue a ver un espectáculo de variedades he went to see a variety show

espejo

espejo
[es'pexo] n m
mirror

* *El espejo se ha roto...* The mirror's broken... *

...espejo

El espejo se ha roto...

esperanza

esperanza
[espe'ranθa] n f
hope

hay pocas esperanzas de que venga there's little hope of his coming

▶ **esperar**
[espe'rar] v i & v t
1. to wait

hace una hora que esperamos el autobús we've been waiting for the bus for an hour

2. to hope
espero que te encuentres bien I hope you are well

3. to expect
espero una llamada de John I'm expecting a call from John

4. to look forward to

▶ **espera**
[es'pera] n f
wait, waiting

sala de espera waiting-room

espeso

espeso, a
[es'peso, a] adj
thick, dense

nos metimos en un bosque muy espeso we entered a very dense wood

---

esposo

esposo, a
[es'poso, a] n
husband *m*, wife *f*

esquiar

esquiar
[es'kjar] v i
to ski

esquiador

esquiador, a
[eskja'ðor, a] n
skier

esquina

esquina
[es'kina] n f
1. corner

2. Idiom
* *A la vuelta de la esquina...* Round the corner... *

...esquina

A la vuelta de la esquina...

estación

estación
[esta'θjon] n f
1. station

estación espacial space station

2. season
de las cuatro estaciones prefiero el verano of the four seasons I prefer summer

estanco

estanco
[es'tanko] n m
tobacconist's shop

estar

estar
[es'tar] v i
1. to be

el profesor no está en casa en este momento the Professor

...estar

is not at home at the moment

2. Idiom
¡ya está! that's it! (it's done!)

estar de buenas to be in a good mood

¿estamos? agreed?

estoy por llamarle para decirle lo que pienso de él I'm in half a mind to call him and tell him what I think of him

estatua

estatua
[es'tatwa] *n f*
statue

* *¡La estatua!... ¡Ya está! ¡Ya la tengo!* The statue!... That's it! I've got it at last! *

este

este
['este] *n m*
east

Yugoslavia cae al este de Rumania y Bulgaria Yugoslavia lies to the east of Rumania and Bulgaria

este

este, esta, estos, estas
['este, a, os, as]
adj dem
this, these

este coche corre más que aquél this car goes faster than that one

este año hemos hecho muchas excursiones we've been on a lot of excursions this year

éste

éste, ésta, éstos, éstas
['este, a, os, as]
pron dem
this one, these ones

* *¡Eh! ¡mi maleta!* Hey! My case!
¡Ah, no! ¡Mi maleta es ésta! On, no! My case is this one! *

estilo

estilo
[es'tilo] *n m*
1. style

no me gusta el estilo de este escritor I don't like this writer's style

2. Idiom
por el estilo similar

no es igual, pero por el estilo it isn't the same, but it's similar

esto

esto
['esto] *pron dem nt*
this, this business

esto del robo this business of the robbery

estorbar

estorbar
[estor'βar] *v i & v t*
to be in the way, to obstruct

...estorbar

las maletas estorban aquí the cases are in the way here

estrecho

estrecho, a
[es'tretʃo, a]
I. *adj*
narrow, tight

pantalones estrechos tight trousers

...estrecho

II. *n m*
strait(s)

el Estrecho de Gibraltar the Straits of Gibraltar

estrella

estrella
[es'treλa] *n f*
star

...estrella

...estrella

* *¿Ve usted la estrella?* Can you see the star? *

estropear

estropear
[estrope'ar]
I. *v t*
to spoil,
to damage,
to ruin

las heladas han

...estropear

estropeado la cose-cha the frosts have ruined the harvest

II. *v pr*
to go bad, to spoil, to change for the worst

* *Además de que nos hemos aburrido, ¡el tiempo se ha estropeado!...* On top of our being bored, the weather has changed for the worst!... *

Además de que nos hemos aburrido, ¡el tiempo se ha estropeado!...

estudiar

estudiar
[estu'djar] *v i & v t*
to study

estudiamos inglés
we study English

estupendo

estupendo, a
[estu'penðo] *adj*
great

* *¡Estupendo!* Great! *

...estupendo

¡Estupendo!

...estupendo

▶**estupendamente**
[estupenda'mente] *adv*
wonderfully, great

me siento estupen-damente I feel great

Europa

Europa
[eǔ'ropa] *n f*
Europe

...Europa

una Europa unida a united Europe

▶**europeo, a**
[eǔro'peo, a] *adj & n*
European

evitar

evitar
[eβi'tar] *v t*
to avoid, to prevent

exagerar

exagerar
[eɣsaxe'rar] *v i & v t*
to exaggerate

examen

examen
[e'ɣsamen] *n m*
exam(ination)

excelente

excelente
[esθe'lente] *adj*
excellent

* *¡No sé qué le han puesto al agua, pero la encuentro excelente!...* I don't know what they've put in the water, but it's excellent!... *

¡No sé qué le han puesto al agua, pero la encuentro excelente!...

---

excepto

excepto
[es'θepto] *adv*
except (for)

excursión

excursión
[eskur'sjon] *n f*
excursion, trip

exigir

exigir
[eɣsi'xir] *v t*
to demand,
to require

* *¡Margarita! ¿Eres tú, Margarita?* Margaret! Is that you, Margaret? *¡Cierren inmediata-mente ese transistor! ¡Exijo silencio!* Turn that transistor off immediately. I demand silence! *

¡Margarita! ¿Eres tú, Margarita?

¡Cierren inmediata-mente ese transistor! ¡Exijo silencio!

▶**exigente**
[eɣsi'xente] *adj*
demanding

existir

existir
[eɣsis'tir] *v i*
to exist, to be

existe otro barco parecido a éste there's another boat like this one

éxito

éxito
['eɣsito] *n m*
1. success

2. Idiom
tener éxito to be successful

experimento

experimento
[esperi'mento] *n m*
experiment

...experimento

Es el laboratorio donde el profesor realiza sus experimentos.

* *Es el laboratorio donde el profesor realiza sus experimentos.* It's the laboratory where the Professor conducts his experiments. *

...explicar

¿Me pueden explicar ustedes por qué hacen tanto ruido?

Sí, claro...

explicar

explicar
[espli'kar] v t
to explain

* ¿Me pueden expli-

...explicar

car ustedes por qué hacen tanto ruido? Could you explain to me why you are making so much noise?
Sí, claro... Yes, of course... *

▶ **explicación**
[esplika'θjon] n f
explanation

no pude seguir las explicaciones del profesor I couldn't follow the Professor's explanations

explotar

Ha explotado una bomba.

explotar
[esplo'tar]
I. v t
to exploit

II. v i
to explode

* *Boum* Boom
Ha explotado una bomba. A bomb has exploded. *

expresar

**expresar,
expresarse**
[espre'sar, se]
I. v t
to express

II. v pr
to express oneself

se expresa muy bien she expresses herself very well

exterior

exterior
[este'rjor] adj & n m
exterior, outside

el exterior del edificio the outside of the building

---

extranjero

extranjero, a
[estraŋ'xero, a]
I. adj
foreign

II. n m
foreign country, abroad

¿has estado alguna vez en el extranjero? have you ever been abroad?

el año que viene

vamos al extranjero we're going abroad next year

extrañar

**extrañar,
extrañarse**
[estra'ɲar, se]
I. v t
to surprise

...extrañar

* *A Tintín le extraña esta pelea.* This fight surprises Tintin. *

II. v pr
to be surprised at

▶ **extraño, a**
[es'traɲo, a] adj
strange

A Tintín le extraña esta pelea.

fábrica

fábrica
['faβrika] *n f*
factory, works,
plant, mill

una fábrica de pa-pel a paper mill

fácil

fácil
['faθil] *adj*
easy, simple

...fácil

* *¿Ir a la luna? Nada más fácil, ¿verdad? ¡Ja, ja, ja! ¡Ay, profesor, usted siempre me hará reír!...* Go to the moon? There's nothing simpler, is there? Ha, ha, ha! Oh, Professor, you'll always make me laugh!... *

esto es fácil de hacer it's easy to do

► **facilidad**
[faθili'ðað] *n f*
ease, facility

fachada

fachada
[fa't∫aða] *n f*
front, façade

van a renovar la fachada de la cate-dral they are going to renovate the façade of the cathedral

faena

faena
[fa'ena] *n f*

...faena

task, job, work

tenemos mucha faena we've got a lot of work

falda

falda
['falda] *n f*
1. skirt

2. foot of a moun-tain

falso

falso, a
['falso, a] *adj*
1. false, untrue

2. false,
not genuine
una moneda falsa a false coin

3. two-faced
no te fíes de él; es muy falso don't trust him; he's very two-faced

falta

falta
['falta] *n f*
1. mistake

una falta de ortogra-fía a spelling mistake

2. lack
* *Exijo una explica-ción... Decirme que hago el indio... ¿Habráse visto mayor falta de cortesía?* I demand an explanation... You tell me I'm playing the fool... I've

never known of such a lack of courtesy!... *

3. Idiom
falta de educación bad manners

hacer falta to need

nos hace falta más agua we need more water

sin falta without fail

preséntese aquí ma-ñana a las nueve sin falta report here at nine tomorrow without fail

sacar faltas a al-guien to find fault with someone

a/por falta de for want of, for lack of

faltar

faltar
[fal'tar] *v i*
1. to be lacking, to lack

no le falta nada he lacks nothing

2. to be missing, to be absent
faltaron seis personas en la reunión six people were absent from the meeting

3. to be left
sólo falta una sema-

na para las Navidades there's only a week left till Christmas

4. Idiom
¡no faltaría más! of course!

* *¡Sólo faltaba esto! Han raptado a mi hijo!* That's all I needed! They've kidnapped my son! *

* *Poco faltó para que se ahogara.* He almost drowned. *

Poco faltó para que se ahogara.

fama

fama
['fama] *n f*
reputation

familia

familia
[fa'milja] *n f*
family

la familia política in-laws

farmacia

farmacia
[far'maθja] *n f*
pharmacy, chemist's

busco una farmacia de guardia I'm looking for an all-night chemist's

farol

farol
[fa'rol] *n m*
street lamp

el camión chocó contra el farol the lorry hit the street lamp

fastidiar

fastidiar
[fasti'ðjar] *v t*
1. to annoy,

...fastidiar

to bother

¡deja de fastidiar! stop bothering other people!

2. Idiom
¡no fastidies! you can't mean it!

► **fastidio**
[fas'tiðjo] *n m*
nuisance, chore

¡qué fastidio! what a nuisance!

* *¡Qué fastidio esta bomba!* What a chore this pump is!
Sí, tienes razón; yo aún diría más: ¡qué fastidio! Yes, you're right; to be precise: what a chore it is! *

...fastidiar

favor

favor
[fa'ßor] *n m*
1. favour

¿te puedo pedir un favor? could you do me a favour?

2. Idiom
por favor please

haga el favor de no fumar please do not smoke

en/a favor de in favour of

yo estoy en favor de pedir más ayuda I'm in favour of asking for more help

tenemos a Tintín a nuestro favor we have Tintin on our side

febrero

febrero
[fe'ßrero] *n m*
February

...febrero

en los años bisiestos febrero tiene veintinueve días en vez de veintiocho in leap years February has twenty-nine days instead of twenty-eight

fecha

fecha
['fetʃa] *n f*
1. date

...fecha

| 16 MIÉRCOLES | 17 JUEVES | 18 VIERNES | 19 SÁBADO | 20 DOMINGO | 21 LUNES | 22 MARTES |

El calendario indica las fechas.

* *Miércoles Jueves Viernes Sábado Domingo Lunes Martes* Wednesday Thursday Friday Saturday Sunday Monday Tuesday *El calendario indica las fechas.* The calendar shows the dates. *

2. Idiom
fecha tope deadline, closing date

con fecha uno de enero dated the first of January

felicitar

felicitar
[feliθi'tar] *v t*
1. to congratulate

le felicito por el éxito de su experimento I congratulate you on the success of your experiment

2. Idiom
felicitar a alguien (por) su cumpleaños to wish someone a Happy Birthday

...felicitar

▶ **felicitación**
[feliθita'θjon] *n f*
greeting(s), wish

▶ **felicidad**
[feliθi'ðað] *n f*
happiness

▶ **¡felicidades!**
[feliθi'ðaðes] *interj*
1. congratulations! best wishes!

* *¡Bravo! ¡Felicidades! Unas pa-*

labras para nuestros oyentes... Bravo! Congratulations! A few words for our listeners... *Pues... estoy emocionado...* Well... I'm touched... *

2. happy birthday! many happy returns!

▶ **feliz**
[fe'liθ] *adj*
happy

feo

feo, a
['feo, a] *adj*
ugly

feria

feria
['ferja] *n f*
1. fair, market

2. agricultural show

feroz

feroz
[fe'roθ] *adj*
ferocious

el león es un animal feroz the lion is a ferocious animal

fiera

fiera
['fjera] *n f*
wild animal

...fiera

* *¡No voy a dejarme impresionar por una fiera!* I'm not going to allow myself to be impressed by a wild animal! *

fiesta

fiesta
['fjesta] *n f*
1. party

¡vamos a dar una fiesta! let's have a party!

2. holiday, day off
el viernes tengo fiesta I have the day off on Friday

3. fun and games, festivities, merrymaking

figurar

figurar, figurarse
[fiɣu'rar, se]
I. *v i*
to appear

II. *v pr*
to imagine, to suppose

* *Pues qué, ¿te figuras que hay un esqueleto?* What, you think there's a skeleton? *

...figurar

fijar

fijar, fijarse
[fi'xar, se]
I. *v t*
to fix, to set,
to agree on

fijemos una hora let's
agree on a time

II. *v pr*
to notice,
to pay attention

*¿se ha fijado en el
color de su vestido?*
did you notice the colour
of her dress?

fila

fila
['fila] *n f*
1. row, tier, line

*vamos a sentarnos
en la primera fila* let's
sit in the front row

*una fila de coches
esperaba en el se-
máforo* there was a line
of cars waiting at the traffic
lights

2. Idiom
en fila india in single
file

fin

fin
[fin] *n m*
1. end

esto es el fin this is the
end

2. aim, purpose,
objective
el fin de la misión the
purpose of the mission

3. Idiom
en fin... well..., anyway...

al fin, en fin, por fin
finally, at last

* *A lo lejos aparece
un avión..* A plane
appears in the distance...
¡Por fin! Son ellos! At
last! It's them! *

a fines de siglo
towards the end of the
century

a fin de in order to

a fin de que in order
that, so that

...fin

final

final
[fi'nal]
I. *n m*
end

* *Fin* The end
*Al final todo se arr-
egla.* Everything works
out all right in the end. *

II. *n f*
final

III. *adj*
final, last

Al final todo se arregla.

finca

finca
['finka] *n f*
property, land,
country house,
estate

* *Esta es la finca
del capitán Had-
dock... ¡Mira! Hay
un coche delante de
la puerta.* This is
Captain Haddock's pro-
perty... Look! There's a car
outside the door. *

...finca

flaco

flaco, a
['flako, a] *adj*
1. thin, lean

2. Idiom
punto flaco weak point,
weak spot

flamenco

flamenco, a
[fla'menko, a]
I. *adj & n*
1. Flemish

...flamenco

el arte flamenco
Flemish art

2. flamenco
*canta y baila fla-
menco* she can sing and
dance flamenco

II. *n m*
flamingo

los flamencos rosas
(pink) flamingos

flauta

flauta
['flauta] *n f*
flute

flojo

flojo, a
['floxo, a] *adj*
1. loose

*este tornillo está
flojo* this screw is loose

...flojo

2. weak
*se quedó
muy flojo
después de
la enferme-
dad* he was
very weak after
the illness

flor

Capitán, le ofrezco este ramo de flores en nombre de todos sus amigos. Que tenga suerte y... ¡buen viaje!

flor
[flor] *n f*
1. flower

* *Capitán, le ofrezco este ramo de flores en nombre de todos sus amigos. Que tenga suerte y... ¡buen viaje!* Captain, I present you with this bunch of flowers on behalf of all your friends. Good luck and... have a good journey! *

2. Idiom

la flor y nata the cream, the pick

fonda

fonda
[ˈfonda] *n f*
boarding house

¿hay alguna fonda por aquí para pasar la noche? is there a boarding house near here to spend the night?

fondo

¡Ah! Todavía queda una gota en el fondo de la botella...

...fondo

fondo
[ˈfondo] *n m*
1. bottom, far end, background

* *¡Ah! Todavía queda una gota en el fondo de la botella...* Ah! There's still a drop at the bottom of the bottle... *

2. Idiom
en el fondo te quiere deep down he really loves you

forastero

forastero, a
[forasˈtero, a] *adj & n*
stranger

forma

forma
[ˈforma] *n f*
1. form, shape

en forma de U U-shaped

...forma

2. way, manner
no hay forma de convencerle there's no way of persuading him

3. Idiom
de todas formas anyway

en forma fit

de esta forma in this way

formal

formal
[formal] *adj*
1. formal

2. serious, reliable
llegará a la hora; es muy formal he'll be on time; he's very reliable

formalidad

formalidad
[formaliˈðað] *n f*
1. form, formality

rellenar este impreso es sólo una formalidad filling in this form is just a formality

2. seriousness, reliability

fotografía

fotografía, foto
[fotoɣraˈfia, foto] *n f*
photograph, photo

* *Saca una foto de Tintín y Tchang* He's taking a photo of Tintin and Tchang. *

▶ **fotógrafo, a**
[foˈtoɣrafo, a] *n*
photographer

es un fotógrafo excelente he's an excellent photographer

fracaso

fracaso
[fraˈkaso] *n m*
failure, disaster

es un fracaso total it's a complete disaster

Saca una foto de Tintín y Tchang.

Francia

Francia
[ˈfranθja] *n f*
France

▶ **francés, a**
[franˈθes, a]
I. *adj*
French

habla francés corrientemente he speaks French fluently

II. *n*
Frenchman *m*,
French woman *f*

franco

franco
['franko] n m
franc

franco

franco, a
['franko, a] adj
frank

seré franco contigo
I'll be frank with you

frase

frase
[frase] n f
1. phrase

2. sentence

3. Idiom
frase hecha stock phrase, set expression

frente

frente
['frente]
I. n f
forehead

II. n m
1. front

va a hacer más frío: se aproxima un frente frío it's going to get colder: a cold front is approaching

2. Idiom
chocaron de frente they crashed head-on

hay que hacer frente a la crisis we must face the crisis

hacer frente a grandes gastos to meet considerable expense

frente a, en frente de facing, opposite

su casa está en frente de la nuestra his house is opposite ours

fresa

fresa
['fresa] n f
strawberry

▶ **fresón**
[fre'son] n m
strawberry

fresco

fresco, a
['fresko, a]
I. adj
1. fresh, clean, new

necesito un poco de aire fresco I need a little fresh air

2. fresh, cool, cold
¿tienes un poco de agua fresca? have you got some cold water?

3. cheeky, saucy

¡no seas tan fresco! don't be so cheeky!

II. n m
fresh air

vamos a tomar el fresco let's get some fresh air

frío

Hace mucho frío...

frío, a
[fřio, a] adj & n m
cold

* *Hace mucho frío...* It's very cold... *

frito

frito, a
['frito, a] adj
1. fried

...frito

2. Idiom
patatas fritas chips

frontera

frontera
[fron'tera] n f
frontier, border

fruta

¡Vaya! He calculado mal...

La fruta cae sobre el capitán.

fruta
['fruta] n f
fruit

¿te gusta la fruta? do you like fruit?

* *¡Vaya! He calculado mal...* Drat! I've miscalculated...
La fruta cae sobre el capitán. The fruit is falling on the Captain. *

fuego

fuego
['fweɣo] n m
1. fire

* *¡Huy!* Ow!
El fuego arde en la chimenea. The fire is burning in the fireplace. *

2. Idiom
¿tienes fuego? have you got a light?

fuegos artificiales fireworks

...fuego

¡HUY!

El fuego arde en la chimenea.

fuente

fuente
['fwente] *n f*
1. fountain, spring

* *El capitán ha bebido agua de la fuente.* The Captain has drunk water from the fountain. *

2. source
viene de fuente desconocida it's from an unknown source

El capitán ha bebido agua de la fuente.

...fuente

3. dish, platter
una fuente de carne con patatas a dish of meat and potatoes

fuera

fuera
['fwera] *adv*
out, outside

* *¡Guau!* Bow-wow!
Milú está fuera. Snowy is outside. *

...fuera

¡Guau!

Milú está fuera.

▶ **fuera de**
['fwerade] *prep*
1. outside (of), out of

el periquito estaba fuera de su jaula the budgie was outside its cage

2. apart from
podemos ir cualquier día fuera del lunes we can go any day apart from Monday

3. Idiom
fuera de alcance out of reach

fuera de serie unheard of

fuerza

fuerza
['fwerθa] *n f*
1. strength, force

2. Idiom

...fuerza

¡Aaaúpa! ¡Lo he conseguido!

Tintín es muy fuerte.

...fuerza

a la fuerza, por fuerza by force

fuerza de gravedad force of gravity (gravitational pull)

▶ **fuerte**
['fwerte] *adj*
strong

* *¡Aaaúpa! ¡Lo he conseguido!* Uuup! I made it!
Tintín es muy fuerte. Tintin is very strong. *

fumar

fumar
[fu'mar] *v i & v t*
to smoke

fuma en pipa he smokes a pipe

funcionar

funcionar
[funθjo'nar] *v i*
1. to work, to function

...funcionar

¡Ya está! ¡Las máquinas vuelven a funcionar!

¡Estupendo! Esperemos que ahora todo vaya bien...

* *¡Ya está! ¡Las máquinas vuelven a funcionar!* That's it! The engines are working again!
¡Estupendo! Esperemos que ahora todo vaya bien... Great! Let's hope everything goes well now... *

2. Idiom
no funciona out of order

fútbol

fútbol
['fuðβol] *n m*
football

gafas

gafas
['gafas] *n f pl*
glasses

* *¡Estoy perdido! Sin gafas no veo nada... ¡Ah! ¡Aquí están!* I'm lost! I can't see a thing without glasses. Ah! Here they are! *

gallina

gallina
[ga'ʎina] *n f*
hen

▶ **gallo**
['gaʎo] *n m*
1. cock

2. Idiom
en menos que canta un gallo before you can say Jack Robinson

gana

gana
['gana] *n f*
1. desire, wish

2. Idiom
tengo ganas de verte I'm longing to see you

hace lo que le da la gana he does just as he likes

no me da la gana I don't feel like it

de buena gana willingly

de mala gana reluctantly

no tengo gana I'm not hungry

ganado

ganado
[ga'naðo] *n m*
cattle

garaje

garaje
[ga'raxe] *n m*
garage

* *Más tarde...* Later...
¡Vayan a buscar el coche y llévenlo al garaje! Go and get the car and take it to the garage!
Ahora vamos, jefe... Right away, boss... *

garbanzo

garbanzo
[gar'βanθo] *n m*
chickpea

de primero comeremos garbanzos for first course we'll have chickpeas

garra

Las garras del cóndor hieren a Tintín.

...garra

garra
['gaɾa] n f
1. claw, talon

* *Las garras del cóndor hieren a Tintín.* The claws of the condor hurt Tintin. *

2. Idiom
caer en las garras de alguien to fall into somebody's clutches

gas

gas
[gas] n m
1. gas

2. Idiom
gas hilarante laughing gas

gas lacrimógeno tear gas

aġua mineral con gas sparkling mineral water

gaseosa

gaseosa
[ga'seosa] n f
lemonade

* *¡Milú! ¡Pero qué haces!* Snowy! What are you doing?
Bebo la gaseosa... Estoy tan sediento que bebería un litro y más. I'm drinking the lemonade... I'm so thirsty I could drink a litre or more.
¡Si no lo veo, no lo creo! You have to see it to believe it! *

gasolina

gasolina
[gaso'lina] n f
petrol

gastar

gastar
[gas'tar] v i & v t
1. to spend,
to waste

gastas demasiado dinero en discos you spend too much money on records

2. to use up
su coche gasta mucha gasolina his car uses up a lot of petrol

3. to wear out
está muy gastado it's quite worn out

4. Idiom
¡no gastes saliva! don't waste your breath! (save your breath!)

gato

El gato encorva el lomo.

gato, a
['gato, a] n
cat

* *¡Pfff!* Pffft!
El gato encorva el lomo. The cat is arching its back. *

▶ **gatear**
[gate'ar] v i
to climb,
to clamber, to crawl

gaviota

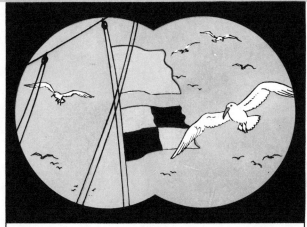

Las gaviotas vuelan...

...general

gaviota
[ga'βjota] n f
seagull

* *Las gaviotas vuelan...* The seagulls are flying around... *

general

general
[xene'ral]
I. n m
general

el general Alcázar General Alcazar

II. adj
1. general, common

ideas generales general ideas

2. Idiom
en general, por lo general generally, on the whole

▶ **generalmente**
[xeneral'mente] adv
generally

generoso

generoso, a
[xene'roso, a] adj
generous

genio

genio
['xenjo] n m
1. character, nature

2. genius
el profesor es un genio the Professor is a

...genio

genius

3. Idiom
tiene genio he can be quick-tempered

gente

gente
['xente] *n f*
people *pl*

gente bien upper-class people

...gente

había mucha gente en la fiesta there were a lot of people at the party

gesto

gesto
['xesto] *n m*
1. grimace, (expression on one's) face

...gesto

Hace gestos de dolor.

2. gesture
hizo un gesto para que lo siguiéramos he made a gesture for us to follow

3. Idiom
* *¡Aaay!* Ow!
¿Le duele mucho? Does it hurt a lot?
Hace gestos de dolor. He looks in pain. *

gimnasia

gimnasia
[xim'nasja] *n f*
gymnastics

gitano

gitano, a
[xi'tano, a] *n & adj*
gypsy

un carromato de gitanos a gypsy caravan

gobierno

gobierno
[go'βjerno] *n m*
government

golosina

golosina
[golo'sina] *n f*
sweet, delicacy

a los niños les gustan las golosinas children like sweet things

...golosina

▶ **goloso, a**
[go'loso, a] *adj*
sweet-toothed, fond of sweet things

golpe

golpe
['golpe] *n m*
1. blow, hit

* *Recibe un golpe sobre la cabeza.* He

...golpe

Recibe un golpe sobre la cabeza.

is hit on the head. *

2. Idiom
un golpe bien dado a well-aimed blow

cerrar de golpe to slam/to bang

a golpes intermittently, in fits and starts

de golpe y porrazo all of a sudden

goma

goma
['goma] *n f*
1. rubber

botas de goma rubber boots

2. rubber
una goma de borrar a rubber

3. elastic band

4. glue, gum

gordo

gordo, a
['gordo, a]
I. *adj*
1. fat

* *¡Es usted demasiado gordo!* You're too fat! *

2. Idiom
me cae gordo I can't stand him

II. *n m*
big, first prize

le tocó el gordo he won the big prize

gorra

gorra
['gořa] *n f*
cap

* *Bang* Bang
El capitán lleva una gorra. The Captain is wearing a cap. *

...gorra

El capitán lleva una gorra.

▶ **gorrón, ona**
[go'řon, ona] *n*
scrounger

gota

gota
['gota] *n f*
1. drop

han caído unas gotas de agua a few drops of rain fell

...gota

2. Idiom
sudar la gota gorda
to sweat blood

gracias

gracias
['graθjas]
I. *n f pl*
thank you, thanks

* *Muchas gracias por haberme defen-*

...gracias

dido, señor. Thank you very much for defending me, sir. *

II. *prep*
gracias a thanks to

gracias a ellos, pudimos escapar
thanks to them, we were able to escape

▶ **dar las gracias**
→ DAR

gracioso

gracioso, a
[gra'θjoso, a] *adj*
1. funny, amusing, witty

siempre hace comentarios graciosos
he always makes witty remarks

* *Pam* Bang
¡Oh!... no es nada... A mi dulce cordero le gusta poner petardos por todo el palacio... ¡Qué gra-

...gracioso

cioso es! ¿verdad?
Oh!... it's nothing... My sweet lamb likes to put fireworks all round the palace... Isn't he funny!
¡Ah!... sí... Oh!... yes... *

2. charming, graceful

3. Idiom
hacerse el gracioso
to clown around

Gran Bretaña

Gran Bretaña
[granbre'taɲa] *n f*
Great Britain

grande

gran, grande
[gran, 'grande]
I. *adj*
1. big, large

...grande

2. Idiom
a lo grande on a grand scale

II. *n m*
grande de España
grandee

granizo

granizo
[gra'niθo] *n m*
hail

grano

grano
['grano] *n m*
1. grain.

granos de arena
grains of sand

2. spot
tiene la cara llena de granos his face is covered in spots

3. Idiom
ir al grano to get to the point

grave

grave
['graβe] *adj*
1. serious, grave

2. seriously ill

3. grave, low, deep
tiene una voz muy grave he has a very deep voice

grifo

grifo
['grifo] *n m*
tap

no abras los grifos
don't turn the taps on

gris

gris
[gris] *adj & n m*
grey

la policía de aquel país lleva uniforme

...gris

gris the police of that country wear a grey uniform

gritar

gritar
[gri'tar] *v i & v t*
to shout, to cry

* *¿Pero qué dice? ¡Grite más fuerte, que no le oigo!* What

...gritar

did you say? Shout louder, I can't hear you. *

▶ **grito**
['grito] n m
shout, cry

grupo

grupo
['grupo] n m
1. group

...grupo

2. group, band
toca guitarra en un grupo he plays guitar in a group

guapo

guapo, a
['gwapo, a] adj
good-looking, attractive

guardar

guardar
[gwar'dar] v t
1. to guard, to watch over

2. to put away
guardó el dinero en el bolsillo he put the money away in his pocket

3. to keep
guardar un secreto to keep a secret

▶ **guardia**
['gwarðja] n m
1. guard, sentry

2. policeman

guerra

guerra
['geῙa] n f
war

guiar

guiar
['gjar] v t
to guide, to lead, to steer

un aldeano los guió hasta el otro pueblo a peasant guided them to

...guiar

the other village

▶ **guía**
['gja]
I. n
guide

II. n f
1. guide, guidebook

consulta la guía have a look in the guide(book)

2. Idiom
la guía telefónica the telephone directory

guisar

guisar
[gi'sar] v i & v t
to cook, to stew

patatas guisadas potato stew

guitarra

guitarra
[gi'taῙa] n f
guitar

...guitarra

Se oye el rasgueo de una guitarra...

...guitarra

* *Se oye el rasgueo de una guitarra...* The strumming of a guitar can be heard... *

gustar

gustar
[gus'tar]
I. v t
to taste, to try

gústalo a ver cómo

...gustar

está taste it and see what it's like

II. v i
to please, to like

me gustan los helados italianos I like Italian ice cream

▶ **gusto**
['gusto] n m
1. taste

¡qué gusto más raro! what a strange taste!

2. pleasure
* *¡Qué gusto da bañarse cuando se está sucio!* What a pleasure it is to have a swim when you're dirty! *

3. Idiom
mucho gusto/tanto gusto pleased to meet you

con mucho gusto certainly, with pleasure

estar a gusto to feel at ease, to feel comfortable

haber

haber
[a'βer]
I. *v aux*
1. to have

¿dónde habéis estado? where have you been?

2. Idiom
haber de to have to, must

he de hacerlo I have to do it

II. *v impers*

1. to be

¿cuántos niños hay en el club de natación? how many children are there in the swimming club?

2. Idiom
hay que hacerlo it has to be done

no hay que preocuparse you mustn't worry

¡hola! ¿qué hay? hello! how's it going?

habitación

habitación
[aβita'θjon] *n f*
room

* *Su habitación, señora...* Your room, madame...
Muchas gracias. Thank you very much. *

hay habitaciones dobles y habitaciones individuales en el hotel there are double and single rooms in the hotel

habitante

habitante
[aβi'tante] *n*
inhabitant

España tiene casi 39 millones de habitantes Spain has almost 39 million inhabitants

hablar

hablar
[a'βlar] *v i & v t*
to speak, to talk

hacer

hacer, hacerse
[a'θer, se]
I. *v t*
to do, to make

no sé qué hacer I don't know what to do

...hacer

voy a hacer las camas I'm going to make the beds

hace como que no quiere saber nada de ella he acts as if he doesn't want anything to do with her

II. *v i*
to act, to behave

III. *v pr*
1. to get, to become, to grow

se hace tarde it's getting late

2. to pretend
se hace el sordo he's pretending to be deaf

IV. *v impers*
1. to be

hace frío/calor it's cold/hot

2. ago
hace dos años fui a Francia I went to France two years ago

3. Idiom
(desde) hace since, for

estamos aquí desde hace dos horas/hace dos horas que estamos aquí we've been here for two hours

* *¿Cuánto tiempo hace que vamos en coche?* How long have we been on the road?
Mucho, pero no te duermas ahora. A long time, but don't go to sleep now.

...hacer

¿Cuánto tiempo hace que vamos en coche? Mucho, pero no te duermas ahora.

Rron. Rron. Zzzzzz. Zzzzzz. *

hacia

hacia
['aθja] prep
1. towards

caminó hacia las montañas he walked towards the mountains

2. Idiom
hacia arriba y hacia

...hacia

abajo up(wards) and down(wards)

3. about
llegarían hacia las cinco it must have been about five when they arrived

hallar

hallar, hallarse
[a'ʎar, se] v t
to find

hallaron el tesoro they found the treasure

hambre

hambre
['ambre] n f
1. hunger

2. Idiom
tener hambre to be hungry

morir de hambre to die of starvation

hasta

hasta
['asta]

...hasta

Pero Tintín... eso no es posible... ¡Adiós! ¡Hasta luego!

...hasta

I. prep
1. until, till, as far as

no podemos ir hasta las seis we can't go until six

te acompaño hasta la esquina I'll come with you as far as the corner

2. Idiom
* *Pero Tintín... eso no es posible...* But Tintin... that isn't possible...
¡Adiós! ¡Hasta lue-

go! Bye bye! See you later! *

¡hasta el sábado! See you on Saturday!

¡Hasta ahora! See you in a minute!

II. adv
even

III. conj
hasta que until, till

no hagas nada hasta que llegue el jefe don't do anything till the boss comes

helar

¡Está helado!... ¡Rápido, el whisky!

helar, helarse
[e'lar, se]
I. v t
to freeze

el intenso frío heló el lago the intense cold froze the lake

II. v i & v pr
to freeze

el agua hiela a una temperatura de 0 °C water freezes at 0 °C

▶ **helado**
[e'laðo]
I. adj
f helada [e'laða]
frozen

* *¡Está helado!... ¡Rápido, el whisky!* He's frozen!... Quick, get the whisky! *

II. n m
ice cream

un helado de vainilla a vanilla ice cream

hermano

hermano, a
[er'mano, a] n
brother m, sister f

¿tienes hermanos? have you any brothers or sisters?

hermoso

hermoso, a
[er'moso, a] adj
beautiful, fine, lovely

...hermoso

¡qué cuadro más hermoso! what a beautiful picture!

herramienta

herramienta
[eˈra'mjenta] n f
tool

hielo

hielo
['j(dz)elo] n m
ice

cubitos de hielo ice cubes

café con hielo iced coffee

hierba

hierba
['j(dz)erβa] n f
grass

se echaron sobre la hierba they lay down on the grass

hierro

hierro
['j(dz)ero] n m
iron

* *¡Mira! Esa gente viene aquí...* Look! Those people are coming over here...
Delante de la verja de hierro forjado. In front of the wrought-iron gate. *

...hierro

¡Mira! Esa gente viene aquí...

Delante de la verja de hierro forjado.

higuera

higuera
[i'ɣera] n f
fig tree

hijo

hijo, a
['ixo, a]
I. n
son m, daughter f

II. n m pl
children

...hijo

¿cuántos hijos tie-
nen? how many children
have they got?

hilo

hilo
['ilo] n m
1. thread, yarn

2. wire

...hilo

3. Idiom
he perdido el hilo I've
lost the thread (of the
conversation)

hinchar

hinchar, hincharse
[in'tʃar, se]
I. v t
to blow up,
to inflate

...hinchar

* *Cuando los mecá-
nicos hayan termi-
nado de hinchar los
neumáticos, me gus-
taría que controla-
ran el aceite...*When
the mechanics have
finished blowing up the
tyres, I'd like them to
check the oil... *

II. v pr
to swell (up)

Cuando los mecánicos hayan terminado de hinchar los neumáticos, me
gustaría que controlaran el aceite...

hispanoameri-cano

hispanoamericano, a
[ispanoameri'kano, a]
adj & n
South American,
Latin American

historia

historia
[is'toria] n f
1. history

la historia de la

...historia

humanidad the history
of mankind

2. story

3. Idiom
¡déjate de historias!
come to the point!

hogar

hogar
[o'ɣar] n m
1. fireplace

...hogar

* *Coge un leño del
hogar.* He is taking a
piece of wood from the
fire. *

2. home, household

hoja

hoja
['oxa] n f
1. leaf

Coge un leño del hogar.

...hoja

2. sheet, piece
una hoja de papel a
sheet of paper

3. blade
una hoja de afeitar a
razor blade

¡hola!

¡hola!
['ola] interj
hello!

...¡hola!

¡Hola!
¿Qué tal?

* *¡Hola! ¿qué tal?*
Hello! How are you? *

holgazán

holgazán, ana
[olɣa'θan, a]
I. *adj*
idle, lazy

II. *n*
idler, loafer

hombre

hombre
['ombre]

...hombre

I. *n m*
man

* **¡Hombre al agua!...
Vamos a salvarlo...**
Man overboard!... Let's
save him... *

II. *interj*
¡hombre!

**¡hombre! ¡qué sor-
presa!** my goodness!
what a surprise!

hombro

hombro
['ombro] *n m*
1. shoulder

**se lo cargó a los
hombros** he loaded it
on his shoulders

2. Idiom
**encogerse de hom-
bros** to shrug one's
shoulders

**mira a los demás
por encima del
hombro** he looks down
on others

hongo

hongo
['onɣo] *n m*
mushroom,
toadstool

* **Un hongo enor-
me...** An enormous toad-
stool... *

hora

hora
['ora] *n f*
1. hour, time

Un hongo enorme...

...hora

¿qué hora es? what's
the time?

**el avión vuela a
novecientos kiló-
metros por hora** the
plane flies at nine hundred
kilometres an hour

2. Idiom
¡ya era hora! about
time, too!

ya es hora de it's
(high) time to

en las altas horas in
the small hours

horchata

horchata
[or'tʃata] *n f*
horchata (*Spanish
cold drink made of
almonds and orgeat*)

hormiga

hormiga
[or'miɣa] *n f*
ant

* **Las hormigas le
molestan.** The ants are
annoying him. *

...hormiga

GRRRON GRRRON
GRRRON

Las hormigas le molestan.

hormigón

hormigón
[ormi'ɣon] *n m*
concrete

hormigón armado
reinforced concrete

hospital

hospital
[ospi'tal] *n m*
hospital

hotel

hotel
['otel] *n m*
hotel

**un hotel de cuatro
estrellas** a four-star
hotel

hoy

hoy
[oĭ]
1. *adv*
today, nowadays

la fecha de hoy to-
day's date

2. Idiom
de hoy en adelante
from now on

* **De hoy en adelan-
te te llamaré Mil
Rayos... ¡Ale! ¡Ven
conmigo!** From now on

De hoy en adelante te
llamaré Mil Rayos...
¡Ale! ¡Ven conmigo!

I'll call you Blistering
Barnacles... Come on!
Come with me! *

hoy día, hoy en día
nowadays

**hoy en día los viajes
son más rápidos**
nowadays journeys are
faster

huelga

huelga
['welɣa] *n f*
1. strike

2. Idiom
hacer huelga to go on strike

todos los taxistas han hecho huelga all the taxi-drivers have gone on/come out on strike

huella

huella
['welʎa] *n f*
1. footstep

* *¡Fíjense! Huellas de pasos en la tierra... ¿Habrá entrado alguien?...* Look! Footsteps in the earth... Can anyone have got in?... *

2. trace
sin dejar huella without leaving a trace

huerto

huerto
['werto] *n m*
kitchen garden

está en el huerto, arrancando las malas hierbas he's in the kitchen garden, pulling up the weeds

hueso

hueso
['weso] *n m*
bone

* *¡Vaya reserva de huesos, eh! ¿Qué me decís?* What a stock of bones, eh! What do you say? *

...hueso

humanidad

humanidad
[umani'ðað] *n f*
humanity, mankind

su gran cualidad es su humanidad his one great quality is his humanity

▶ **humano, a**
[u'mano, a] *adj*
human

seres humanos human beings, humans

húmedo

húmedo, a
['umeðo, a] *adj*
damp, humid

¿tienes otra toalla? Ésta está húmeda have you got another towel? This one's damp

Barcelona es una ciudad húmeda Barcelona is a humid city

humilde

humilde
[u'milde] *adj*
humble

son gente muy humilde they are very humble people

humo

humo
['umo] *n m*
smoke

* *Cada vez hay más humo.* There is more and more smoke. *

▶ **humear**
[ume'ɑr] *v i*
to smoke,
to give off smoke

Cada vez hay más humo.

humor

humor
[u'mor] *n m*
1. humour

tiene poco sentido del humor he hasn't much of a sense of humour

2. Idiom
estar de buen/mal humor to be in a good/bad mood

ida

ida
['iða] *n f*
1. going, departure

un billete de ida y vuelta a return ticket

2. Idiom
idas y venidas comings and goings

idea

idea
['iðea] *n f*
idea

* *¡Tengo una idea!*
I've got an idea! *

idioma

idioma
[i'ðjoma] *n m*
language

¡Tengo una idea!

...idioma

¿cuántos idiomas hablas? how many languages do you speak?

iglesia

iglesia
[i'ɣlesja] *n f*
church

se van a casar por la iglesia they are going to get married in church

igual

igual
[i'ɣwal]
I. *adj*
1. equal, (the) same, similar

* *Las dos maletas son iguales.* The two cases are the same. *

2. Idiom
me es/da igual it makes no difference to me

II. *adv*
perhaps

...igual

Las dos maletas son iguales.

igual no viene perhaps he isn't coming

III. *n m*
equal

ilusión

ilusión
[ilu'sjon] *n f*
1. hope, dream

es la ilusión de mi

...ilusión

vida it's the dream of a lifetime

2. excitement, thrill
* *Me hace mucha ilusión viajar con ustedes, pero preferiría dormir en un camarote...* I'm thrilled to travel with you, but I'd prefer to sleep in a cabin... *

3. Idiom
no te hagas ilusiones don't build up false hopes

Me hace mucha ilusión viajar con ustedes, pero preferiría dormir en un camarote...

imagen

imagen
[i'maxen] *n f*
1. image, picture

vio su imagen reflejada en el espejo he saw his image reflected in the mirror

2. Idiom
es la viva imagen de su madre she's the spitting image of her mother

3. statue
una imagen de bronce a bronze statue

imaginar

**imaginar,
imaginarse**
[imaxi'nar, se]
I. *v t*
to imagine

nunca imaginé que nos volveríamos a encontrar I never imagined we'd meet up again

II. *v i & v pr*
to imagine

me imagino que sí I imagine so

imitar

imitar
[imi'tar] *v t*
to imitate,
to mimic,
to follow suit

* *¡Qué suerte! Los monos me han visto lanzar nueces de coco y me han imitado...* What good luck! The monkeys saw me throwing coconuts and followed suit... *

impaciencia

impaciencia
[impa'θjenθja] *n f*
impatience

impedir

impedir
[impe'ðir] *v t*
to obstruct,
to prevent

impermeable

impermeable
[imperme'able]
I. *adj*
waterproof

II. *n m*
raincoat,
mackintosh

* *¡Cómo llueve!... ¡Y yo, sin impermeable!* What a downpour!... And here am I without a raincoat!
¡El paraguás!.. Claro, capitán... ¡Milú,

dame el paraguas! The umbrella!... Of course, Captain... Snowy, give me the umbrella! *

importancia

importancia
[impor'tanθja] *n f*
importance

* *Bien, ¿qué quiere decirme?* Right, what did you want?

...importancia

Señor, tengo que hablarle de un asunto de gran importancia... Preferiría verle a solas... Sir, I have to talk to you about a matter of great importance... I'd prefer to see you alone... *

▶ **importante**
[impor'tante] *adj*
1. important

2. large,
considerable

3. serious

importar

importar
[impor'tar]
I. *v i*
1. to be important,
to matter

no importa it doesn't matter

...importar

2. to mind
¿le importa si fumo? do you mind if I smoke?

II. *v t*
to import

Gran Bretaña importa coches japoneses Great Britain imports Japanese cars

imposible

imposible
[impo'siβle] *adj*
impossible

impresionar

impresionar
[impresjo'nar] *v i & v t*
1. to impress
2. to shock

imprudencia

imprudencia
[impru'ðenθja] *n f*
imprudence,
carelessness

▶ **imprudente**
[impru'ðente] *adj*
imprudent,
careless

es un conductor muy imprudente he's a very careless driver

inca

¡El templo de los incas!

inca
['iŋka] *n*
Inca

* *¡El templo de los incas!* The temple of the Incas! *

incendio

incendio
[in'θendjo] *n m*
fire

...incendio

¡Un incendio!

* *¡Un incendio!* A fire! *

▶ **incendiar, incendiarse**
[in'θendjar]
I. *v t*
to set on fire, to set fire to, to set alight

II. *v pr*
to catch fire

las cortinas se incendiaron the curtains caught fire

independencia

independencia
[indepen'denθja] *n f*
independence

▶ **independiente**
[indepen'djente] *adj*
independent

indicar

indicar
[indi'kar] *v t*
1. to indicate, to show
2. to tell
nos indicaron que estábamos a punto de aterrizar they told us we were about to land

indio

indio, a
['indjo, a] *adj & n*
Indian

* *Te he visto defender al muchacho indio... Eres muy generoso... Pero ten cuidado.* I saw you stand up for the Indian boy... You are very decent... But be careful. *¿Qué quiere decir?* What do you mean? *

...indio

Te he visto defender al muchacho indio... Eres muy generoso... Pero ten cuidado.

¿Qué quiere decir?

industrial

industrial
[industrj'al]
I. *adj*
industrial

II. *n*
industrialist, manufacturer

inferior

inferior
[imfe'rjor]
inferior, lower

la parte inferior the lower part/side, the underside

influir

influir
[imflw'ir] *v i*
to influence, to affect

...influir

¡Ya veréis! La estrella va a ejercer una influencia terrible sobre todos vosotros...

...influir

el cansancio puede influir en nuestras decisiones tiredness may influence our decisions

► **influencia**
[imflw'enθja] *n f*
influence

* *¡Ya veréis! La estrella va a ejercer una inflencia terrible sobre todos vosotros...* You'll see! The star will exert a terrible influence on all of you... *

informar

informar
[imfor'mar] *v t*
to inform, to tell, to report

ingenuo

ingenuo, a
[iɲ'xenwo, a] *adj*
ingenuous, naïve

inglés

inglés, esa
[iŋ'gles, a]
I. *adj*
English

el humor inglés
English humour

II. *n*
Englishman *m*,
English woman *f*

los ingleses the English

inmenso

inmenso, a
[immenso, a] *adj*
immense

inmóvil

inmóvil
[im'moβil] *adj*
immobile, motionless

inocencia

inocencia
[ino'θenθja] *n f*
innocence

► **inocente**
[ino'θente] *adj*
innocent

* *Es inocente, pero lo han condenado.* He is innocent, but they have convicted him. *

...inocencia

Es inocente, pero lo han condenado.

inquilino

inquilino, a
[inki'lino, a] *n*
tenant

allí no vive el dueño, sino unos inquilinos the owner doesn't live there, only some tenants

instituto

instituto
[insti'tuto] *n m*
1. institute

2. secondary school

instruir

instruir, instruirse
[instrw'ir, se]
I. *v t*
to instruct, to teach

...instruir

el sargento instruyó a los soldados en el manejo de las armas the sergeant taught the soldiers how to use their weapons

II. *v pr*
to learn,
to educate oneself

instrumento

instrumento
[instru'mento] *n m*
instrument

* *Ya estoy cansado de este instrumento... La Castafiore me obliga a tocar el piano día y noche... ¡Ya estoy harto!* I'm tired of this instrument... Castafiore makes me play the piano night and day... I've had enough! ¿Ah?... Oh?... *

Ya estoy cansado de este instrumento... La Castafiore me obliga a tocar el piano día y noche... ¡Ya estoy harto!

¿Ah?...

inteligencia

inteligencia
[inteli'xenθja] *n f*
intelligence

► **inteligente**
[inteli'xente] *adj*
intelligent

es mucho más inteligente de lo que parece she's much more intelligent than she seems

interesar

interesar, interesarse
[intere'sar, se]
I. *v i & v t*
1. to interest

2. Idiom
la geología me interesa I'm interested in geology

* *¡Oiga, joven!... Su pozo de petróleo me interesa. ¡Le doy cinco mil dólares!... ¡Firme aquí!*

...interesar

¡Oiga joven!... Su pozo de petróleo me interesa. ¡Le doy cinco mil dólares!...¡Firme aquí!

Listen, young man!... I'm interested in your oil well. I'll give you five thousand dollars!... Sign here! *

II. *v pr*
to be interested,
to take an interest

▶ **interés**
[inte'res] *n m*
interest

* *Vamos a marcharnos. El interés de este viaje es pura-*

Vamos a marcharnos. El interés de este viaje es puramente científico...

mente científico...
We're going to leave. The interest of this journey is purely scientific... *

▶ **interesante**
[intere'sante] *adj*
interesting

es un libro muy interesante it's a very interesting book

---

interior

interior
[inte'rjor] *adj & n m*
interior, inside

en la parte interior on the inside

interno

interno, a
[in'terno, a]
I. *adj*
internal, domestic

...interno

II. *n*
boarder, pupil at boarding school

intérprete

intérprete
[in'terprete] *n*
interpreter

trabaja de intérprete she works as interpreter

interviú

¡Silencio! ¡vamos a empezar la interviú!

¡Acción!

interviú, interview
[inter'βj'u] *n m/f*
interview

* *¡Silencio! ¡Vamos a empezar la interviú!* Quiet! We're going to begin the interview! *¡Acción!* Action! *

introducir

introducir
[introðu'θir]

...introducir

I. *v t*
to introduce, to insert, to put in

II. *v pr*
to get in, to slip in

inútil

inútil
[i'nutil] *adj*
useless

es inútil que llores it's useless for you to cry

---

invadir

invadir
[imba'ðir] *v t*
to invade

▶ **invasión**
[imba'sjon] *n f*
invasion

▶ **invasor**
[imba'sor, a] *adj & n m*
invader

* *¡Silencio! El general está a salvo... y el invasor ha sido*

¡Silencio! El general está a salvo...y el invasor ha sido rechazado.

rechazado. Silence! The General is safe... and the invader has been repelled. *

inventar

inventar
[imben'tar] *v t*
to invent, to make up

...inventar

He inventado una máquina que va a sorprenderle mucho...

...inventar

* *He inventado una máquina que va a sorprenderle mucho...* I've invented a machine that will surprise you no end... *

▶ **invento**
[im'bento] *n m*
invention

la última invención del profesor the Professor's latest invention

investigar

investigar
[imbesti'ɣar] *v i & v t*
to investigate,
to do research

* *Investigan el caso...* They are investigating the case... *

▶ **investigación**
[imbestiɣa'θjon] *n f*
1. investigation

* *Aquí termina nuestra investigación: ¡queda usted de-*

...investigar

tenido! Our investigation ends here: you're under arrest! *

2. research (work)
investigación científica Scientific research

invierno

invierno
[im'bjerno] *n m*
winter

invitar

invitar
[imbi'tar] *v t*
1. to invite

2. to treat
¿me dejas invitarte a esto? can I treat you to this?

▶ **invitación**
[imbita'θjon] *n f*
invitation

ir

ir, irse
[ir, se]
I. *v i*
1. to go, to come

¿Adónde vas? Where are you going?

voy a ir a Madrid I'm going to go to Madrid

¡voy! I'm coming!/Just coming!

iré esta noche a tu casa I'll come to your house tonight

2. to be
iba muy despistado he was very confused

3. to suit
ese pantalón te va muy bien those trousers suit you

4. Idiom
¿cómo te va todo? how are things?

voy por el médico I'll fetch the doctor

¡Vaya! Well, I'm blessed!/ What a surprise!

¡Vaya susto! What a fright!

ir de paseo to go for a walk

ir de compras go shopping

II. *v pr*
to go (away),
to leave, to be off

* *¡Adiós, nos vamos!* Goodbye, we're off! *

¡vete! go away!

...ir

ironía

ironía
[iro'nia] *n f*
1. irony

2. sarcasm

3. Idiom
salir con ironías to be sarcastic

▶ **irónico, a**
[i'roniko, a] *adj*
1. ironical

2. sarcastic

isla

isla
['isla] *n f*
island

* *Esta motora nos llevará a la Isla Negra en poco tiempo...* This motorboat will get us to Black Island in no time... *

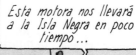

izquierdo

izquierdo, a
[iθ'kjerðo, a] *adj*
left

puso la mano en el bolsillo izquierdo he put his hand in his left pocket

▶ **izquierda**
[iθ'kjerða] *n f*
left, left (-hand) side

aparece en la foto a la izquierda she's on the left-hand side of the photo

jabón

jabón
[xa'βon] *n m*
soap

jamás

jamás
[xa'mas] *adv*
1. ever, never

es la mejor película que jamás haya visto it's the best film I've ever seen

2. Idiom
nunca jamás never again

para siempre jamás for ever and ever

jamón

jamón
[xa'mon] *n m*
ham

jardín

jardín
[xar'din] *n m*
garden

* *Vamos a preguntar a ese hombre que cultiva el jardín si sabe algo sobre la Castafiore...* Let's ask that man working in the garden if he has heard any news of Castafiore... *Bueno...* All right... *

jaula

jaula
[xa'ŭla] *n f*
cage

jefe

jefe
['xefe] *n*
chief

...jefe

* *¡Escuchad a vuestro jefe!... ¡Hemos de capturar a Tintín!...* Listen to your chief!... We must capture Tintin!... *

jersey

jersey
[xer'seĭ] *n m*
jersey, pullover, sweater

jinete

jinete
[xi'nete] *n m*
horseman, rider

* *Los jinetes se llevan a Tintín.* The horsemen are leading Tintín away. *

joven

joven
[xo'βen]
I. *adj*

...joven

young

II. *n*
young man *m*,
young woman *f*

judío

judío, a
[xud'ĩo, a]
I. *adj*
Jewish

II. *n*
Jew *m*, Jewess *f*

juego

juego
['xweɣo] *n m*
1. game

un juego de cartas a
card game

2. set
un juego de café a
coffee set

3. Idiom
un juego de pala-bras a play on words, a
pun

hacer juego to match

...juego

*la corbata hace
juego con la ameri-cana* the tie matches the
jacket

▶**juguete**
[xu'ɣete] *n m*
toy

* *¡Papa! ¡Hay un
hombre muy malo
que me rompe los
juguetes!...* Dad!
There's a bad man
breaking my toys!... *

jueves

jueves
['xweβes] *n m*
Thursday

juez

juez
['xweθ] *n m*
judge

jueces judges

jugar

jugar, jugarse
[xu'ɣar, se]
I. *v i*
to play

*los niños están
jugando al tenis* the
children are playing tennis

II. *v t*
to gamble, to stake,
to put

*voy a jugar diez
dólares a esta carta*
I'm going to put ten dollars
on this card

III. *v pr*
to risk, to stake

* *Tintín, recuerde
usted que en esta
expedición se juega
usted la vida...* Tintin,
remember that you're
risking your life on this
expedition...
*¡Bueno, bueno! No
se preocupe dema-siado... Ya sé que la
policía me busca,
de modo que seré
muy prudente...* All

...jugar

right, all right! Don't get so
worried.... I know the
police are looking for me,
so I'll be very careful... *

*¡me jugaría la
cabeza!* I'd stake my life
on it!

▶**jugador, a**
[xuɣa'dor, a] *n*
player

*es el mejor jugador
del equipo* he's the
best player in the team

No está en su sano
juicio.

juicio

juicio
['xwiθjo] *n m*
1. reason,
good sense

* *No está en su
sano juicio.* He's lost
his reason. *

2. opinion
*a mi juicio, no tiene
razón* in my opinion,
he's wrong

3. trial

4. judgement
el Juicio Final the Last
Judgement

julio

julio
['xuljo] *n m*
July

llegaremos el pri-mero de julio we'll
arrive on the first of July

junio

junio
['xunjo] *n m*
June

*estamos a quince
de junio* it's the 15th of
June

juntar

juntar, juntarse
[xun'tar, se]
I. v t
1. to join,
to put together

éramos muchos para comer, así que juntamos dos mesas there were a lot of us for lunch, so we put two tables together

2. to collect, to raise
juntamos dinero para la expedición

we raised money for the expedition

II. v pr
to join, to meet

se juntó con ellos en la esquina he met them on the corner

▶ **junto, a**
['xunto, a] adj
together

vivimos juntos we live together

* *¡Hola, capitán! ¡Qué sorpresa, eh! He venido con mi familia. Pensé que te gustaría vernos todos juntos...*Hello, Captain! What a surprise, eh! I've come with my family. I thought you'd like to see us all together... *

▶ **junto**
['xunto]
I. adv

se sentó junto he sat close by

II. prep
by

junto a la ventana by the window

jurar

jurar
[xu'rar] v t & v i
to swear

justicia

justicia
[xus'tiθja] n f
justice

* *¡Otra vez en la cárcel, Milú!... No sé qué hace la justicia*

...justicia

en este país... Here we are in prison again, Snowy!... I don't know what's wrong with justice in this country... *

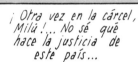

justificar

justificar
[xustifi'kar] v t
to justify

puedo justificar mi

...justificar

actitud I'm able to justify my attitude

justo

justo
['xusto]
I. adj
f justa ['xusta]
1. fair, just

el juicio fue justo it was a fair trial

...justo

2. exact
el precio justo the exact price

3. tight
este pantalón me viene muy justo these trousers are very tight on me

II. adv
just, exactly

llegó justo en el momento en que íbamos a salir he came just as we were about to leave

juventud

juventud
[xuβen'tud] n f
youth

juzgar

juzgar
[xuθ'ɣar] v i & v t
1. to judge

juzgue usted mismo judge for yourself

...juzgar

a juzgar por su aspecto, es detective to judge by his appearance, he's a detective

2. to consider, to think
juzgué imprescindible llamar al médico I thought it was imperative to phone the doctor

kilo

kilo(gramo)
['kilo('gramo)] n m
kilo(gramme)

déme dos kilos de manzanas give me two kilos of apples

kilómetro

kilómetro
[ki'lometro] n m
kilometre

* *Este coche nos viene siguiendo desde hace diez kilómetros... Es inquietante...* This car has been following us for the last ten kilometres... It's worrying... *

L l L.l L.l L

la

la → EL

labio

labio
[ˈlaβjo] *n m*
1. lip

2. Idiom
no se muerde los labios he's outspoken

labor

labor
[laˈβor] *n f*
work

labrador

labrador, a
[laβraˈðor, a] *n*
farmer *m*,
peasant (woman) *f*

ladera

ladera
[laˈðera] *n f*
slope, side, hillside

* *Suben por la ladera sur.* They are climbing up the south side of the mountain.*

Suben por la ladera sur.

lado

lado
[ˈlaðo]
I. *n m*
1. side

2. Idiom
por otro lado on the other hand, moreover

dejar a un lado/de lado to leave aside, to pass over

II. *prep*
al lado de next to, near

viven al lado de nosotros they live next to us

ladrar

ladrar
[laˈðrar] *v i*
to bark

ladrillo

ladrillo
[laˈðriλo] *n m*
brick

ladrón

ladrón, ona
[laˈðron, a] *n*
thief

* *¡Ladrones! ¡Ladrones!* Stop thief! *

...ladrón

¡ *Ladrones! ¡Ladrones!*

lago

lago
[ˈlaɣo] *n m*
lake

lámpara

lámpara
[ˈlampara] *n f*
lamp

una lámpara de mesa a table lamp

lana

lana
['lana] n f
1. wool

2. Idiom
jersey de lana woollen sweater

lápiz

lápiz
['lapiθ] n m
pencil

largo

largo
['larɣo]
I. adj
f larga ['larɣa]
1. long

tiene las piernas muy largas he has very long legs

2. Idiom
dar largas a un asunto to put off a decision

A lo largo de una cresta...

a la larga in the long run

pasar de largo to go by (without noticing or stopping)

II. prep

a lo largo de all along, throughout

* *A lo largo de una cresta...* All along a ridge... *

...largo

III. adv

¡largo! Get out!

IV. n m
length

lástima

lástima
['lastima] n f
1. pity, shame

¡qué lástima! what a pity!

...lástima

2. Idiom
me da lástima I feel sorry for him/her

lata

lata
['lata] n f
1. tin, can

una lata de cerveza a can of beer

* *Tintín echa la lata a la basura.* Tintin is

...lata

Tintín echa la lata a la basura.

throwing the can away. *

2. Idiom
dar la lata to be a nuisance, be a bore

¡qué lata! what a nuisance!

le

le, les
[le, les] pron pers
1. (to/for) him/her/it/them

...le

No quiero asustarle, capitán, pero temo por la vida de Tornasol... Así que me voy a Ginebra...

A ver si encuentro ese dichoso papel...

le vi ayer I saw him yesterday

dale el dinero give him the money/give the money to him

les di el regalo I gave them the money/I gave the money to them

les ayudaremos we'll help them

2. (to/for) you
* *No quiero asustarle, capitán, pero*

temo por la vida de Tornasol... Así que me voy a Ginebra... I don't want to alarm you, Captain, but I fear for Calculus's life... So I'm going to Geneva...
A ver si encuentro ese dichoso papel... Let's see if I can find that blessed paper... *

lección

lección
[lek'θjon] n f
lesson

lectura

lectura
[lek'tura] n f
1. reading, reading matter

2. Idiom
una persona de mucha lectura a well-read person

leche

leche
['letʃe] *n f*
milk

leche desnatada
skim(med) milk

leer

leer
[le'er] *v i & v t*
to read

¡Capitán, mire!...
¿Ha leído esto?... Un
avión se ha estre-
llado en el Nepal...
Captain, look!... Have you
read this?... A plane's
crashed in Nepal... *

legumbre

legumbre
[le'ɣumbre] *n f*
vegetable

lejos

lejos
['lexos]
I. *adv*
1. far (away),
a long way (away)

no está muy lejos it
isn't very far (away)

2. Idiom
a lo lejos in the distance

* *¡Se ven unos faros*
a lo lejos!... Rápido...
¡Escondámonos!
There are some headlights

...lejos

in the distance!... Quick!...
Let's hide! *

de/desde lejos from
a long way off, from a
distance

II. *prep*

lejos de far from, a long
way from

lengua

lengua
['leŋgwa] *n f*
1. tongue

morderse la lengua
to bite one's tongue

2. language,
tongue
lengua materna mo-
ther tongue

leña

leña
['leɲa] *n f*
wood

letra

letra
['letra] *n f*
1. letter

letras mayúsculas y
minúsculas capital and
small letters

...letra

2. (hand) writing
tienes una letra muy
clara you have very clear
handwriting

3. words *pl*
no sé la letra de esa
canción I don't know
the words to that song

4. Idiom
a la letra, al pie de
la letra literally, to the
letter

levantar

levantar
levantarse
[leβan'tar, se]
I. *v t*
to raise, to lift

si queréis preguntar
algo, levantad la
mano if you want to ask
anything, raise your hand

¡no me levantes la
voz! don't raise your
voice to me!

II. *v pr*
to get up, to rise

...levantar

El viento se levanta.

* *Wooouihhh*
Woosh
El viento se
levanta. The wind
is getting up. *

ley

ley
[leɪ] *n f*
1. law

2. Idiom
oro/plata de ley
pure gold/silver

liberar

¡Gracias por liberarme!

liberar
[liβe'rar] *v t*
to free, to set free,
to liberate

* *¡Gracias por libe-*
rarme! Thank you for
setting me free! *

► **libertad**
[liβer'tað] *n f*
1. liberty, freedom

la Estatua de la
Libertad the Statue of
Liberty

...liberar

2. Idiom
tomarse la libertad de to take the liberty of

me he tomado la libertad de servirme I've taken the liberty of serving myself

▶ **libre**
['liβre] *adj*
free

¿está libre este sitio? is this seat free?

librería

librería
[liβrer̃ia] *n f*
bookshop

▶ **libro**
['liβro] *n m*
book

ligero

ligero, a
[li'xero, a] *adj*
1. light

...ligero

es ligero; no pesa nada it's light; it hardly weighs anything at all

2. quick, swift
más ligero que una bala as quick as a flash

limón

limón
[li'mon] *n m*
lemon

limpiar

Va a hacer la limpieza.

limpiar
[lim'pjar] *v t*
to clean, to wipe

¿has limpiado el suelo? have you wiped the floor?

▶ **limpio, a**
['limpjo, a] *adj*
clean

el gato es un animal muy limpio the cat is a very clean animal

...limpiar

▶ **limpieza**
[lim'pjeθa] *n f*
1. cleaning

* *Va a hacer la limpieza.* He's going to do the cleaning. *

2. cleanness, cleanliness

línea

línea
['linea] *n f*
1. line

en línea recta in a straight line

2. Idiom
en líneas generales in broad terms

líneas aéreas airlines

3. figure
guardar la línea to keep one's figure (trim)

lío

lío
[l'io] *n m*
1. mess, fuss, row, problem

2. Idiom
meterse en un lío to get into trouble

se armó un lío tremendo there was a tremendous row

lista

lista
['lista] *n f*
1. list

2. register
el profesor está llamando la lista the teacher is calling the register

listo

listo, a
['listo, a] *adj*
1. ready

¡espera!; no estamos listos wait! we aren't ready

2. clever
¡qué listo eres! ¡what a clever thing you are!

3. Idiom
¡no te pases de listo! don't try to be too clever!

lo

lo
[lo] *art nt*
the, what

* *Lo increíble es que todavía no hayas entendido que no quiero que molestes al gato... ¡Ale! ¡Vuelve a casa!* What is incredible is that you still haven't understood that I don't want you to bother the cat... Go on! Go home! *

Lo increíble es que todavía no hayas entendido que no quiero que molestes al gato...   ¡Ale! ¡Vuelve a casa!

lo

lo, la, los, las
[lo, la, los, las]
pron pers
him, her, it, them

¿lo oyes? can you hear it?

¿los quiere comprar? – no, no los necesito do you want to buy them? – no, I don't need them

▶ **lo de**
[lo ðe] *pron dem*
the business of,
about

te llamaré por lo del viernes I'll ring you about Friday

los de → el de

▶ **lo que**
[lo ke] *pron rel*
what

lo que no me gusta es su actitud what I don't like is his attitude

loco

loco, a
['loko, a] *adj*
1. mad, crazy

* *Es un loco. No teman, lo llevaremos al manicomio de donde se ha escapado...* He's mad. Don't worry, we'll take him to the mental hospital he escaped from... *

2. Idiom
loco de remate as mad as a hatter

...loco

está loco por ella
he's crazy about her

► **locura**
[lo'kura] *n f*
madness

fue una locura hacer eso it was madness to do that

Es un loco. No teman, lo llevaremos al manicomio de donde se ha escapado ...

lograr

lograr
[lo'ɣrar] *v t*
1. to get, to achieve

2. Idiom
lograr hacer to manage to do

lotería

lotería
[lote'ria] *n f*
lottery

lucir

lucir
[lu'θir]
I. *v i*
to shine

II. *v t*
to show off, to wear

luchar

luchar
[lu'tʃar] *v i*
to fight, to struggle

...luchar

Luchan violentamente.

* *Luchan violentamente.* They are fighting fiercely. *

luego

luego
['lweɣo] *adv*
1. next, (and) then

primero comí, luego fui a pasear first I had lunch, and then I went for a walk

...luego

2. later
te lo diré luego I'll tell you later

3. Idiom
¡hasta luego! see you later!

desde luego of course

lugar

lugar
[lu'ɣar] *n m*
1. place, spot

...lugar

¡qué lugar más agradable! what a nice place!

2. room, space
no hay lugar para más cosas aquí there's no room for any more things in here

3. Idiom
tener lugar to take place

dar lugar a to give rise to

en primer lugar in the first place

en lugar de instead of

luna

luna
['luna] *n f*
1. moon

2. Idiom
claro de luna moonlight

luna de miel honeymoon

* *Está en la luna.* He's got his head in the clouds *

...luna

Está en la luna.

lunes

lunes
['lunes] *n m*
Monday

el lunes pasado last Monday

luz

luz
[luθ] *n f*
light

* *Hay luz en la*

...luz

Hay luz en la cabaña.

*cabaña.*There is a light in the hut. *

llama

llama
['ʎama] *n f*
llama

* *¿Qué hay en las alforjas de las llamas?* What is in the saddlebags on the llamas? *

...llama

¿Qué hay en las alforjas de las llamas?

llama

llama
['ʎama] *n f*
1. flame

2. Idiom
estallar en llamas to burst into flames

el avión estalló en llamas y cayó a plomo a la tierra the plane burst into flames and plummeted down to the earth

llamar

llamar, llamarse
[ʎamar, se]
I. *v t*
1. to call

alguien te llama someone is calling you

2. to phone
llámame a las seis phone me at six

II. *v i*
to knock at the door
llaman a la puerta there's someone knocking at the door

III. *v pr*
to be called, to be named

¿cómo te llamas? what's your name?

► **llamada**
[ʎa'maða] *n f*
(phone) call, knock

llamada interurbana long-distance call

llanura

llanura
[ʎa'nura] *n f*
plain

llave

llave
[ʎaβe] *n f*
key

* No, lo siento... No consigo abrir con esta llave... No, I'm sorry... I can't get the door open with this key... *

...llave

No, lo siento... No consigo abrir con esta llave...

llegar

llegar
[ʎe'ɣar] *v i*
1. to arrive (at/in), to get to, to reach

al llegar a la estación, vimos a mi primo on arriving at the station, we saw my cousin

llegamos a la cima a las dos we reached the top at two o'clock

2. Idiom
llegar a ser to become

llegó a ser muy famoso he became very famous

ese dinero no te llegará that money won't be enough

► **llegada**
[ʎe'ɣaða] *n f*
arrival

llegadas y salidas arrivals and departures

llenar

llenar, llenarse
[ʎe'nar, se]
I. *v t*
to fill up

voy a llenar el depósito I'm going to fill up the tank

II. *v pr*
to fill up

► **lleno, a**
['ʎeno, a] *adj*
full

llevar

llevar, llevarse
[ʎe'βar, se]
I. *v t*
1. to wear

¡qué traje más bonito llevas! that's a nice suit you're wearing!

2. to carry
pesa demasiado; no lo puedo llevar it's too heavy for me to carry

3. to take
¿me puedes llevar en tu coche hasta la esquina? can you take me to the corner in your car?

4. Idiom
¿cuánto tiempo llevas estudiando inglés? how long have you been learning English?

II. *v pr*
1. to take (away)

llévatelo si quieres take it if you like

...llevar

2. Idiom
llevarse bien to get on (well)

llorar

llorar
[ʎo'rar] *v i & v t*
to cry over

* *No llore...* Don't cry... *

No llore...

llover

llover
[ʎo'βer] *v impers*
to rain

* *Llueve a cántaros.* It's pouring with rain. *

► **lluvia**
['ʎuβja] *n f*
rain

Llueve a cántaros.

M M M M

maceta

maceta
[ma'θeta] *n f*
(flower) pot

tengo que comprar una maceta para esta planta I must buy a pot for this plant

madera

madera
[ma'ðera] *n f*
wood

madre

La niña encuentra a su madre...
¡Mamá! ¡Miarca!

madre
['maðre] *n f*
mother

* *La niña encuentra a su madre...* The little girl has found her mother...
¡Mamá! Mummy!
¡Miarca! Miarka! *

madrugar

madrugar
[maðru'ɣar] *v i*
to get up early

mañana tenemos que madrugar we have to get up early tomorrow

▶ **madrugada**
[maðru'ɣaða] *n f*
early morning, daybreak

maestro

maestro, a
[ma'estro, a]
I. *n*
master *m*,
mistress *f*,
schoolteacher *m f*

el maestro del pueblo the village schoolteacher

II. *adj*
1. masterly
2. master, main

la llave maestra the master key

3. Idiom
una obra maestra a masterpiece

Aquí puede ver usted a mi admirable hijo Abdallah, inmortalizado en esta obra maestra...

* *Aquí puede ver usted a mi admirable hijo Abdallah, inmortalizado en esta obra maestra...* Here's my admirable son Abdullah, immortalized in this masterpiece... *

maíz

maíz
[ma'ɪθ] *n m*
maize (*Am*: corn)

maíz en la mazorca corn on the cob

mal

mal
[mal]
I. *adj*
→ MALO

...mal

¡Caramba! ¡Me ha salido mal!

II. *n m*
evil, wrong

el bien y el mal good and evil

III. *adv*
1. badly

lo has hecho muy mal you've done it very badly

2. bad
sabe mal it tastes bad

3. Idiom
salir mal to go wrong, to come unstuck

* ¡Caramba! ¡Me ha salido mal! Damn! I've come unstuck! *

sentirse mal to feel ill

sentar mal
→ SENTAR

maleta

¡Una maleta llena de bombas!... ¡Detengan a ese hombre!...

maleta
[ma'leta] *n f*
(suit)case

* ¡Una maleta llena de bombas!... ¡Detengan a ese hombre!... A case full of bombs!... Arrest that man!... *

malo

malo, mal, mala
[malo, mal, mala] *adj*
1. bad

¡mala suerte! bad luck!

2. naughty
un niño muy malo a very naughty child

3. ill
hoy está malo he's ill today

4. Idiom

lo malo es que... the trouble is...

tener mala cara to be off-colour/to be under the weather

mamá

mamá
[ma'ma] *n f*
mummy

manchar

manchar
[man'tʃar] *v t*
to stain

no te manches la ropa don't stain your clothes

▶ **mancha**
['mantʃa] *n f*
stain

una mancha de aceite an oil stain

mandar

mandar
[man'dar]
I. *v t*
1. to order

el sargento manda a los soldados que presenten armas the sergeant is ordering the soldiers to present arms

2. to send
* Alguien manda un mensaje. Someone is sending a message. *

Alguien manda un mensaje.

...mandar

3. Idiom
mandar hacer algo to have/to get something done

mandaron pintar la casa they had the house painted

II. *v i*
to be in charge

¡soy yo quien manda aquí! I'm in charge here!

manera

manera
[ma'nera]
I. *n f*
1. way, manner, fashion

hazlo de esta manera do it (in) this way

2. Idiom
no hay manera it's hopeless

de todas maneras anyway, anyhow

¡Quiero jugar, de manera que juego! ¡Ab--- dallah!

II. *conj*
de manera que so (that)

* ¡Quiero jugar, de manera que juego! I want to play, so I'll play! ¡Abdallah! Abdullah! *

mano

mano
['mano] *n f*
1. hand

2. Idiom
de segunda mano second-hand

* ¡Vaya! ¡Una avería!... Nunca más compraré un coche de segunda mano... Damn! A breakdown!... I'll never buy a second-hand car again... *

...mano

a mano derecha on the right

manta

manta
['manta] *n f*
blanket

¡Vaya! ¡Una avería!... Nunca más compraré un coche de segunda mano...

mantequilla

mantequilla
[mante'kiʎa] *n f*
butter

manzana

manzana
[man'θana] *n f*
1. apple

2. block (of houses)
demos una vuelta a la manzana let's go for a walk round the block

mañana

Una mañana...

...mañana

mañana
[ma'ɲana]
I. *n f*
morning

* *Una mañana...* One morning... *

II. *n m*
future

el mañana es incierto the future is uncertain

III. *adv*
tomorrow

¡*hasta mañana!* see you tomorrow

pasado mañana the day after tomorrow

mañana por la mañana/por la noche tomorrow morning/night

mañana por la tarde tomorrow afternoon/evening

mapa

mapa
['mapa] *n m*
map

un mapa de España a map of Spain

máquina

máquina
['makina] *n f*
machine

una máquina de coser a sewing-machine

mar

mar
[mar] *n m & f*
1. sea

el Mar mediterráneo the Mediterranean Sea

en alta mar on the high seas

2. Idiom
la mar de a lot of, lots of, ever so many

está la mar de contenta she's ever so happy

maravilla

maravilla
[mara'βiʎa] *n f*
1. wonder, marvel

2. Idiom
de maravilla marvellous(ly)

habla español de maravilla he speaks Spanish marvellously

▶ **maravilloso, a**
[maraβi'ʎoso, a] *adj*
marvellous

...maravilla

Un palacio maravilloso...

* *Un palacio maravilloso...* A marvellous palace... *

marca

marca
['marka] *n f*
1. mark

2. make
¿qué marca de coche es? what make of car is it?

marcha

marcha
['martʃa] *n f*
1. march

2. Idiom
puso el coche en marcha atrás he put the car in reverse (gear)

puso el coche en marcha he started the car

le va la marcha he's with it

marcharse

Tintín se marcha.

marcharse
[mar'tʃarse] *v pr*
to go (away), to leave

* *Tintín se marcha.* Tintin is leaving. *

margen

margen
['marxen] *n m*
border, margin

deja margen en la hoja leave a margin on the paper

marido

marido
[ma'riðo] *n m*
husband

marisco

marisco
[ma'risko] *n m*
shellfish, seafood

marrón

marrón
[ma'ron] *adj & n m*
brown

siempre lleva zapatos marrones he always wears brown shoes

martes

martes
['martes] *n m*
Tuesday

el martes que viene next Tuesday

marzo

marzo
['marθo] *n m*
March

más

más
[mas] *adv*
1. more

¿quieres más té? do you want (any) more tea?

no quiero más pastel de momento I don't want any more cake for the moment

no quiero más I don't want any more

2. more, *adj* + er

él es más listo que yo he is cleverer than I am

ella es más inteligente que su amiga she is more intelligent than her friend

3. the most,
the *adj* + est
el río más largo del mundo the longest river in the world

la chica más her-

...más

mosa que conozco the most beautiful girl I know

4. Idiom
eso está de más that's unnecessary

a más de apart from

no más only, just, simply

* *¡Abdallah! No haces más que tonterías...* Abdullah! You're just being stupid...
¡Hiii! Ha ha! *

¡Abdallah! No haces más que tonterías...

¡ HIII !

¡qué casa más bonita! what a pretty house!

por más que however much/hard

por más que lo intentáramos, no pudimos levantarlo however much we tried, we were not able to lift it

es más furthermore

no necesito su regalo; es más, me niego a aceptarlo I don't need his present;

furthermore, I refuse to accept it

a lo más at the most

le echaría cincuenta años a lo más I'd say he's fifty at the most

mata

mata
['mata] *n f*
bush

matar

matar
[ma'tar] *v t*
to kill

* *¡Lo has matado!* You've killed him!
Pam Bang *

...matar

¡lo has matado!

PAM

materno

materno, a
[ma'terno, a] *adj*
maternal

abuelo materno maternal grandfather/ grandfather on your mother's side

matrimonio

matrimonio
[matri'monjo] *n m*
1. marriage

2. married couple

3. Idiom
una cama de matrimonio a double bed

mayo

mayo
['maλo] *n m*
May

mayor

mayor
[ma'λor] *adj*
1. bigger, biggest, larger, largest, greater, greatest

...mayor

la mayor ciudad de la región the biggest town in the area

2. grown up

3. older, oldest, elder, eldest
es mayor que yo he's older than me

mi hermana mayor my elder sister

es la mayor de la familia she's the eldest of the family

me

me
[me] *pron*
1. (to) me

he hit me me pegó

dímelo tell it to me

2. (to) myself
me hice daño I injured myself

3. Idiom
* *¡Capitán! ¡Por fin! ¡Me alegro mucho de verlo!* Captain! At last! I'm very pleased to see you! *

mecánico

mecánico
[me'kaniko]
I. *adj*
f mecánica [me'kanika]
mechanical

II. *n m*
mechanic

el mecánico repara el coche the mechanic is repairing the car

▶ **mecánica**
[me'kanika] *n f*
mechanics

medianoche

medianoche
[meðja'notʃe] *n f*
midnight

la fiesta no empezó hasta pasada la medianoche the party did not begin until past midnight

medicina

El médico está preocupado.

¡Ninguna reacción! Tiene el pulso tranquilo... pero es mejor hospitalizarlo... ¡Llame una ambulancia!

medicina
[meði'θina] *n f*
medicine

tómate la medicina take your medicine

▶ **médico, a**
['mediko, a] *n*
doctor

* *El médico está preocupado.* The doctor is worried. *¡Ninguna reacción! Tiene el pulso tranquilo... pero es me-* jor hospitalizarlo... *¡Llame una ambulancia!* No reaction! His pulse is steady... but it's better if we get him into hospital... Call an ambulance! *

medio

medio
['meðjo]
I. *adj*
f media ['meðja]

1. half

media hora half an hour

2. middle, mid, halfway
a media mañana in the middle of the morning

a medio camino in mid journey/halfway there

3. Idiom
a medias partly, not entirely

...medio

1. half

media hora half an hour

2. middle, mid, halfway
a media mañana in the middle of the morning

a medio camino in mid journey/halfway there

3. Idiom
a medias partly, not entirely

satisfecho a medias not entirely satisfied

II. *n m*
1. means

el medio de hacerlo the means to do it

2. media
los medios de comunicación the mass media

3. environment, atmosphere

...medio

el medio ambiente the environment

4. Idiom
en medio de in the middle of

en medio del océano in the middle of the ocean

▶ **media**
['meðja] *n f*
1. average

2. stocking

▶ **a mediados de**
[a me'djados de] *prep*
in the middle of/in mid

a mediados de julio in mid July

mediodía

mediodía
[meðjo'ðia] *n m*
midday, noon

mejor

mejor
[me'xɔr]
I. *adj*
better

ésta es mejor que aquélla this one is better than that one

II. *adv*
1. better

tú lo harás mejor que yo you'll do it better than me

2. Idiom
a lo mejor probably, maybe

a lo mejor no viene he probably won't come

melocotón

melocotón
[meloko'ton] *n m*
peach

melón

melón
[me'lon] *n m*
melon

memoria

memoria
[me'morja] *n f*
1. memory

tienes mala/poca memoria you have a bad memory

...memoria

* *¿Así que ha perdido la memoria? A ver si la recobra...* So you've lost your memory? Let's see if you get it back... *

la memoria del ordenador the memory of the computer

2. Idiom
aprender de memoria to learn by heart

¿ Así que ha perdido la memoria? A ver si la recobra...

menor

menor
[me'nor] *adj*
1. smaller, less, lesser

ése es menor que el mío that one is smaller than mine

2. least, slightest
sin la menor dificultad without the least difficulty

no tengo la menor idea I haven't the slightest idea

3. younger, youngest
ella es la menor de las tres hermanas she is the youngest of the three sisters

menos

menos
['menos]
I. *adj*
less, fewer, least, fewest

...menos

haz menos ruido make less noise

II. *adv*
1. less, least

ella es la menos inteligente de las tres she is the least intelligent of the three

2. Idiom
echar de menos to miss

* *¡Hola, Milú! ¡Cuánto te he echado de menos!...* Hello, Snowy. I've really missed you!... *¡Mi querido Tintín!* My dear Tintin!*

eso es lo de menos that's the least of it

¡menos mal! just as well! thank goodness!

al menos, por lo menos at least

III. *prep*
except

¡Hola Milú! Cuánto te he echado de menos...

¡Mi querido Tintín!

todos menos tu hermano vinieron a la fiesta everyone except your brother came to the party

mentir

mentir
[men'tir] *v i*
to lie

¡mientes! you're lying!

...mentir

► **mentira**
[men'tira] *n f*
1. lie

2. Idiom
parece mentira it's incredible

menú

menú
[me'nu] *n m*
menu

...menú

el menú del día today's menu

menudo

menudo, a
[me'nuðo, a] *adj*
1. small, fine

lluvia menuda fine rain

2. Idiom
a menudo often

...menudo

¡menudo lío! what a mess!

¡menudo coche! what a fantastic car!

¡menuda vida te pegas! what a life/time you have!

mercado

mercado
[mer'kado] *n m*
market

...mercado

* *¡Qué pánico en el mercado!* What a panic at the market! *

merendar

merendar
[meren'dar]
I. *v i*
to have a snack

¿has merendado ya? have you had your snack yet?

¡Qué pánico en el mercado!

...merendar

II. *v t*
to have as a snack

merendamos huevos con beicon we had egg and bacon as a snack

► **merienda**
[me'rjenda] *n f*
snack

mes

mes
[mes] *n m*
month

el mes que viene
next month

mesa

mesa
['mesa] *n f*
table

...mesa

Este barco es mío...¿ Puede usted explicarme qué hace sobre esta mesa?

* *Este barco es mío... ¿Puede usted explicarme qué hace sobre esta mesa?* This boat is mine... Could you tell me what it's doing on this table? *

meseta

meseta
[me'seta] *n f*
plateau

mesón

mesón
[me'son] *n m*
hotel

* *Me gustaría dormir en este mesón... ¿Le quedan habitaciones?* I'd like to sleep in this hotel... Have you any rooms left? *Naturalmente.* Of course. *

...mesón

Me gustaría dormir en este mesón... ¿Le quedan habitaciones?

Naturalmente.

mestizo

mestizo, a
[mes'tiθo, a] *adj & n*
half-caste

meta

meta
['meta] *n f*
goal, aim

su meta es llegar a ser un artista his goal is to become an artist

meter

meter, meterse
[me'ter, se]
I. *v t*
1. to put

métalo en la caja put it in the box

2. Idiom
meter la pata to put one's foot in it

II. *v pr*
1. to go in, to get in, to enter, to slip in

Me meteré en esta casa antes de que me vean...

* *Me meteré en esta casa antes de que me vean...* I'll slip into this house before they see me... *

2. Idiom
meterse con alguien to tease someone

meterse en los asuntos ajenos to interfere in other people's business

metro

metro
['metro] *n m*
metre

metro

metro
['metro] *n m*
underground

mí

mí
[mi] *pron pers*
1. (to) me, myself

dámelo a mí give it to me

2. Idiom
por mí as far as I'm concerned

por mí, se lo puede llevar as far as I'm concerned, you can take it

mi

mi, mis
[mi, mis] *adj*
my

mis padres my parents

mía

mía
→ MÍO

miedo

El gorila tiene miedo de Milú.

...miedo

miedo
['mjeðo] *n m*
1. fear

2. Idiom
tener miedo de to be afraid of

* El gorila tiene miedo de Milú. The gorilla is afraid of Snowy. *

miel

miel
[mjel] *n f*
honey

mientras

mientras
['mjentras]
I. *conj*
1. while

suelo escuchar las noticias mientras

...mientras

me afeito I usually listen to the news while I'm shaving

2. while, whereas
él es vago, mientras que su hermana es todo lo contrario he is lazy, whereas his sister is quite the opposite

II. *adv*
meanwhile,
in the meantime

voy a lavar los

platos; tú lee mientras (tanto) I'll wash up; you read in the meantime

miércoles

miércoles
['mjerkoles] *n m*
Wednesday

militar

Son cinco militares.

...militar

militar
[mili'tar]
I. *adj*
military

II. *n m*
soldier,
military man

* ¡Estupendo! Marvellous!
¡Fantástico! Fantastic!
¡Formidable! Splendid!
Son cinco militares. There are five military men. *

mimar

mimar
[mi'mar] *v t*
to spoil,
to make a fuss of

minuto

minuto
[mi'nuto] *n m*
minute

mío

mío, mía, míos, mías
['mǐo, a, os, as]
I. *adj pos*
my, of mine

un amigo mío one of my friends/a friend of mine

II. *pron pos*
mine

ese bolso es mío that bag is mine

mirador

mirador
[mira'ðor] *n m*
vantage point,
look-out

mirar

mirar, mirarse
[mi'rar, se]
I. *v t*
to look at

mira mi coche nue-

...mirar

vo look at my new car

II. *v i*
1. to look

* ¡Mire!... ¡El avión está allí! Look! The plane's down there! *

2. Idiom
mirar de reojo to look out of the corner of one's eye

III. *v pr*
to look at oneself

...mirar

a la Castafiore le gusta mirarse en el espejo Castafiore likes to look at herself in the mirror

▶ **mirada**
[mi'rada] *n f*
look, glance

déjame echar una mirada let me have a look

misa

misa
['misa] *n f*
mass

miserable

miserable
[mise'raβle] *adj*
mean, miserable,
wretched

mismo

mismo, a
['mizmo, a] *adj*
1. same

* Mi querido colega, debo decirte que pienso lo mismo que tú. My dear colleague, I must confess that I feel the same way as you.
Yo aún diría más: pienso lo mismo que tú. To be precise: I feel the same way as you. *

...mismo

2. Idiom
me da lo mismo it's all the same to me

3. ...self, ...selves
yo mismo lo hice I did it myself

él mismo he himself

4. very, same
en ese mismo momento at that very moment

Mi querido colega, debo decirte que pienso lo mismo que tú.

Yo aún diría más: pienso lo mismo que tú.

DESPA DEL RECT

misterio

misterio
[mis'terjo] *n m*
mystery

mitad

mitad
[mi'tad] *n f*
half

la mitad para mí, la mitad para ti half for me, half for you

moda

moda
['moda] *n f*
1. fashion, style

está de moda it's in fashion

2. Idiom
está pasado de moda it's out of fashion/old-fashioned

moderno

moderno, a
[mo'derno, a] *adj*
modern

* *En un edificio moderno siempre hay...* In a modern building there is always...
...una escalera exterior. ...an outside flight of steps. *

...moderno

¡En un edificio moderno siempre hay...

...una escalera exterior.

modo

modo
['modo]
I. *n m*
1. way, manner·

2. Idiom
de todos modos anyway, anyhow

en cierto modo to a certain extent

II. *prep*
a modo de by way of

III. *conj*
de modo que so (that)

mojar

mojar, mojarse
[mo'xar, se]
I. *v t*
to (make) wet, to soak

II. *v pr*
to get wet/soaked/drenched

* *¡Cómo se mojan!* They're getting drenched! *

¡Cómo se mojan!

molestar

molestar
[moles'tar] *v t*
I. *v t*
to bother, to trouble

no molestes a tu padre ahora don't bother your father now

II. *v pr*
to bother, to put oneself out

no se moleste por nosotros don't put yourself out on our account

molino

molino
[mo'lino] *n m*
mill

un molino de viento a windmill

momento

¡Rápido, abran la puerta! ¡Pueden morir de un momento a otro!

momento
[mo'mento] *n m*
1. moment

un momento, por favor just a moment, please

2. Idiom
* *¡Rápido, abran la puerta! ¡Pueden morir de un momento a otro!* Quick! Open the door! They may die any minute now! *

...momento

por el momento/de momento for the moment

no necesito ayuda de momento I don't need any help for the moment

de un momento a otro any time/minute (now)

moneda

moneda
[mo'neða] *n f*
1. currency

¿cuál es la moneda de Suiza? what is the currency in Switzerland?

2. coin, piece
una moneda de oro a gold coin

▶ **monedero**
[mone'ðero] *n m*
purse

mono

mono, a
['mono, a]
I. *n*
monkey

* *Dos monos traviesos...* Two mischievous monkeys... *

II. *adj*
pretty, nice

¡qué mono! isn't it pretty!

Dos monos traviesos...

montaña

montaña
[mon'taɲa] *n f*
1. mountain

2. Idiom
hace de todo una montaña he makes mountains out of molehills

monumento

monumento
[monu'mento] *n m*
1. monument,

Se esconde detrás del monumento.

...monumento

memorial

* *Al general Olivaro*
To General Olivaro
Se esconde detrás del monumento. He is hiding behind the monument. *

2. Idiom
visitar los monumentos de una ciudad to see the sights of a town, to go sightseeing in a town

morder

...morder

morder
[mor'ðer] *v i & v t*
to bite

* *¡Te voy a morder!* I'm going to bite you! *

moreno

moreno, a
[mo'reno, a]
I. *adj*
1. dark(-haired)

un chico moreno a dark-haired boy

2. brown, sun-tanned
¡qué morena estás! aren't you brown!

II. *n f*
brunette

se enamoró de una morena he fell in love with a brunette

morirse

morirse
[mo'rirse] *v pr*
1. to die

se murió de repente de un ataque al corazón he died suddenly of a heart attack

...morirse

Están muertos de miedo.

...morirse

2. Idiom
me muero de hambre I'm starving

* *¡Manos... arriba!*
Hands... up!
Están muertos de miedo. They're half dead with fright. *

moro

moro, a
['moro, a]

...moro

¡Vaya! ¡Pero...no es un moro... es Tintín!...

I. adj
Moorish

II. n
Moor

* *¡Vaya! ¡Pero... no es un moro... es Tintín!...* Well, I'm blowed! But... it isn't a Moor... it's Tintin! *

mostrar

mostrar
[mos'trar] v t
to show

motivo

motivo
[mo'tiβo] n m
1. motive, reason, cause

lo hizo sin motivo he did it for no reason at all

...motivo

2. Idiom
con motivo de on the occasion of

motocicleta

motocicleta, moto
[motoθi'kleta, 'moto] n f
motorbike

* *¡Menos mal que he encontrado esta moto! Tintín por*

...motocicleta

¡Menos mal que he encontrado esta moto, Tintín por poco me atrapa!...

poco me atrapa.
Thank goodness I found this motorbike! Tintin almost caught me. *

mover

mover, moverse
[mo'βer, se]
I. v t
to move

no nos moverán we

...mover

¡No se muevan!

...mover

shall not be moved

las hojas se movían al viento the leaves were moving in the wind

II. v pr
to move (oneself)

¡venga! ¡muévete! tenemos prisa come on! move! we're in a hurry

* *¡No se muevan!* Don't move! *

▶ **movimiento**
[moβi'mjento] n m
1. movement

2. Idiom
un movimiento sísmico an earth tremor

muchacho

muchacho, a
[mut'ʃatʃo, a] n
boy m,
girl f

mucho

mucho
['mutʃo]
I. adj
f mucha ['mutʃa]
1. a lot of, lots of, much, many

...mucho

no tengo mucho dinero I haven't much money

2. very
hace mucho calor it's very hot

3. Idiom
hace mucho (tiempo) for a long time, a long time ago

hace mucho que no lo veo I haven't seen him for a long time

la vi hace mucho tiempo I saw her a long time ago

muchas veces (very) often

II. adv
1. (very) much, a lot, a great deal

éste es mucho más grande que el mío this one is far bigger than mine

no fuma mucho he

...mucho

doesn't smoke very much

2. Idiom
por mucho que however much

por mucho que lo intentes, no lo levantarás however much you try, you won't be able to pick it up

III. *pron*
a lot, much

tengo mucho que hacer I have a lot to do

mueble

mueble
['mweβle] *n m*
piece of furniture

muebles furniture

muerte

muerte
['mwerte] *n f*
death

mujer

mujer
[mu'xer] *n f*
woman

mula

mula
['mula] *n f*
mule

es testaruda como una mula she is as stubborn as a mule

multa

multa
['multa] *n f*
fine

me han puesto una multa por tener el coche mal aparcado I got a parking fine

mundo

mundo
['mundo] *n m*
world

...mundo

* *Al ir hacia el Nuevo Mundo, mi antepasado tuvo que luchar contra numerosos piratas... zzzum...* On his journey to the New World, my ancestor had to fight numerous pirates... swish... *

...mundo

Al ir hacia el Nuevo Mundo, mi antepasado tuvo que luchar contra numerosos piratas... zzzum...

muñeca

muñeca
[mu'ɲeka] *n f*
1. doll

la niña está jugando con la muñeca the little girl is playing with the doll

2. wrist
lleva un reloj de oro en la muñeca he is wearing a gold watch on his wrist

museo

museo
[mu'seo] *n m*
museum

* *Museo etnográfico* Ethnographic Museum
Entra en el museo. He is going into the museum.*

Entra en el museo.

música

música
['musika] *n f*
music

música ambiental piped music

* *¿De dónde viene esta música?* Where is this music coming from? *¡Guau! ¡Guau!* Bow-wow! *

▶ **músico, a**
['musiko, a] *n*
musician

muy

muy
[mwi] *adv*
1. very

* *¡Estoy muy contento!* I'm very happy! *

2. Idiom
Muy señor mío, le escribo... Dear Sir, I am writing...

muy de noche very late at night

es muy hombre he is a real man

nacer

nacer
[na'θer] *v i*
to be born

nació en Málaga she was born in Malaga

▶ **nacimiento**
[naθi'mjento] *n m*
birth

ciego de nacimiento blind from birth

nacionalidad

nacionalidad
[naθjonali'ðað] *n f*
nationality

tengo (la) nacionalidad española I have Spanish nationality

nada

nada
['naða]
I. *pron indet*

...nada

1. nothing

no es nada it's nothing

este asunto no tiene nada que ver contigo this matter has nothing to do with you

nada de particular nothing special

2. Idiom
¡gracias! – de nada thank you! – not at all/you're welcome

II. *adv*
1. not at all

no es nada fácil it isn't at all easy

2. Idiom
nada más llegar, nos fuimos a dormir just as soon as we arrived, we went to bed

¡nada! ¡nada! no! no!

nadar

nadar
[na'dar] *v i*
to swim

▶ **nadador, a**
[naða'ðor, a] *n*
swimmer

* *Pluf* Splash
Tintín es un buen nadador. Tintin is a good swimmer. *

...nadar

Tintín es un buen nadador.

nadie

nadie
['naðje] *pron indet*
1. nobody, no-one

nadie lo sabe nobody knows

2. not anybody, not anyone
no veo a nadie I can't see anyone

naipe

naipe
['naĩpe] *n m*
(playing) card

una baraja de naipes a pack of cards

hay que barajar los naipes antes de empezar la partida you must shuffle the cards before beginning the game

naranja

Hace caer las naranjas.

...naranja

naranja
[na'ranxa] *n f*
orange

* *Hace caer las naranjas.* He has knocked the oranges all over the place. *

nariz

nariz
[na'riθ] *n f*
nose

...nariz

Así se le pasará el dolor de la nariz...

* *Así se le pasará el dolor de la nariz...* That'll make the pain in your nose go... *

▶ **narices**
[na'riθes] *n f pl*
nostrils

nata

nata
['nata] *n f*
1. cream

2. Idiom
la flor y nata de the cream of, the pick of

natural

natural
[natu'ral]
I. *adj*
1. natural

...natural

2. at room temperature, unchilled
agua mineral natural unchilled mineral water

II. *n*
native, inhabitant

▶ **naturaleza**
[natura'leθa] *n f*
Nature

* *¡Qué hermosa es la naturaleza!* How beautiful Nature is! *

...natural

¡Qué hermosa es la naturaleza!

Navidad

Navidad
[naβi'ðað] *n f*
Christmas

pasaremos el día de Navidad en casa de mi tía we're spending Christmas Day at my aunt's

¡feliz Navidad! happy Christmas!

necesitar

necesitar
[neθesi'tar] *v t*
to need

* *¡El capitán necesita ayuda!* The Captain needs help! *

▶ **necesario, a**
[neθe'sarjo, a] *adj*
necessary

es necesario que seas puntual it is necessary for you to be punctual

¡El capitán necesita ayuda!

necesidad

necesidad
[neθesi'ðað] *n f*
necessity

no hay necesidad de quedar aquí there is no need for us to stay here

necio

necio, a
['neθjo, a] *adj*
silly, foolish

¡no seas necio! don't be silly!

negocio

negocio
[ne'ɣoθjo] *n m*
business

...negocio

hombre de negocios business man

negro

negro, a
['neɣro, a] *adj*
1. black

2. Idiom
poner negro to make angry

...negro

¡Rayos y centellas! ¡Abdallah me ha puesto un petardo en el sillón! ¡Este niño me pone negro, mil millones de demonios!

* *¡Rayos y centellas! ¡Abdallah me ha puesto un petardo en el sillón! ¡Este niño me pone negro, mil millones de demonios!* Thundering typhoons! Abdullah put a banger on my chair! That boy makes me angry, billions of blue blistering barnacles! *

nene

nene, a
['nene, a] n
baby, child

nervioso

nervioso, a
[ner'βjoso, a] adj
1. nervous

2. highly-strung, excitable

...nervioso

3. Idiom
ponerse nervioso to get worked up

¡no te pongas nervioso! calm down!

neutro

neutro, a
['neŭtro, a] adj
neutral

nevar

nevar
[ne'βar] v impers
to snow

* *Nieva...* It is snowing... *

nevera

nevera
[ne'βera] n f
refrigerator, fridge

Nieva...

ni

ni
[ni] conj
1. not... either... or/ neither... nor

no le gustan ni las espinacas ni el hígado he doesn't like (either) spinach or liver/he likes neither spinach nor liver

2. Idiom
ni idea I've no idea

▶ **ni siquiera**
[nisikjera] adv

...ni

not even

ni siquiera me ha llamado he hasn't even rung me

nido

nido
['niðo] n m
nest

* *¡Estaba seguro!... Aquí están las*

...nido

¡Estaba seguro!... Aquí están las joyas, en el nido de la urraca...

Grrrr

¡Ladrón!

joyas, en el nido de la urraca... Just as I thought!... Here are the jewels, in the magpie's nest...
Grrr Caw caw
¡Ladrón! Thief! *

nieto

nieto, a
['njeto, a] n
grandson m,

...nieto

granddaughter f

nietos grandchildren

nieve

nieve
['njeβe] n f
snow

ninguno

ninguno, a, ningún
[nin'ɣuno, a, nin'ɣun]
I. adj indet
no, not any, not a

no es ningún tonto he's no fool

II. pron indet
1. none, not any

no me queda ninguno I have none left/I haven't any left

2. nobody, no-one, not anybody, not anyone

niño

Los niños van a recibir a Tintín.

¡Tintín!...

niño, a
['niɲo, a] n
(little) boy m, (little) girl f, child

* *Los niños van a recibir a Tintín.* The children are running to meet Tintin.
¡Tintín!... Tintin!... *

▶ **niñez**
[ni'ɲeθ] n f
childhood

no

No, gracias. las bebidas alcohólicas no me gustan.

¿Prefiere gaseosa?

no
[no] adv
1. no

* *No, gracias. Las bebidas alcohólicas no me gustan.* No, thank you. I don't like alcoholic drinks.
¿Prefiere gaseosa? Would you prefer some lemonade? *

2. not
no voy I'm not going

noche

noche
['notʃe] n f
1. night

¡Estoy tan cansado que me voy a dormir enseguida! ¡Buenas noches, Milú!

* *¡Estoy tan cansado que me voy a dormir enseguida! ¡Buenas noches, Milú!* I'm so tired that I'm going straight to bed. Good night, Snowy! *

pasamos la noche en el tren we spent the night in the train

2. evening
buenas noches ¿llegamos tarde? good evening, are we late?

3. Idiom
hacerse de noche to get dark

nochebuena

nochebuena
[notʃe'bwena] n f
Christmas Eve

nochevieja

nochevieja
[notʃe'βjexa] n f
New Year's Eve

nombre

nombre
['nombre] n m
name

¿cuál es su nombre? what's your name?

* *En nombre de la ley, quedan detenidos... ¡Manos arriba!* In the name of the law, you're under arrest!... Hands up! *

...nombre

En nombre de la ley, quedan detenidos...¡Manos arriba!

normal

normal
[nor'mal] adj
normal

es perfectamente normal it's quite normal

norte

norte
['norte] n m
north

...norte

¡Mil millones de demonios! ¿No puede usted echarnos una mano en vez de pasear este estúpido péndulo?

No, hacia el norte no, siempre al oeste.

* *¡Mil millones de demonios! ¿No puede usted echarnos una mano en vez de pasear este estúpido péndulo?* Billions of blue blistering barnacles! Can't you help us instead of wandering around with that stupid pendulum? *No, hacia el norte no; siempre al oeste.* No, not north; due west. *

nos

nos
[nos] pron
1. (to) us

nos explicaron los sucesos they explained what had happened to us

2. (to) ourselves
tenemos que protegernos del frío we must protect ourselves from the cold

nosotros

nosotros, as
[no'sotros, as] pron pers
we, us, ourselves

llegaste después de nosotros you arrived after us

nota

nota
['nota] n f
1. note, footnote

...nota

toma nota take note

2. mark
siempre saca buenas notas en inglés he always gets good marks for English

3. note (música)
entona la nota give us the note

▶ **notar**
[no'tar] v t
to note, to notice

noticia

¡Milú! Estoy contento porque he tenido noticias de Tchang, ¡va a venir a vernos!

...noticia

noticia(s)
[no'tiθja(s)] *n f*
news

una noticia a piece of news

* *¡Milú! Estoy contento porque he tenido noticias de Tchang, ¡va a venir a vernos!* Snowy! I'm happy because I've got news from Chang. He's coming to see us! *

novedad

novedad
[noβe'ðað] *n f*
1. novelty

2. Idiom
las últimas novedades the latest fashions

3. news, new development, change
el día ha transcurrido sin novedad there has been no change today

novela

novela
[no'βela] *n f*
novel

una novela policiaca a detective story

noviembre

noviembre
[no'βjembre] *n m*
November

novio

novio, a
['noβjo, a] *n*
1. fiancé *m*, fiancée *f*

2. bridegroom *m*, bride *f*

3. boyfriend *m*, girlfriend *f*

4. Idiom
los novios the newly-weds, the fiancés

viaje de novios honeymoon

nube

nube
['nuβe] *n f*
1. cloud

no hay nubes en el cielo there isn't a cloud in the sky

2. Idiom
poner a alguien por las nubes to praise someone to the skies

▶ **nublado, a**
[nu'βlaðo, a] *adj*
cloudy

nuclear

nuclear
[nukle'ar] *adj*
nuclear

la energía nuclear nuclear energy

nudo

nudo
['nuðo] *n m*
knot

nuestros

nuestro, a, os, as
['nwestro, a, os, as]
I. *adj pos*
our, of ours

* *¡Bienvenido a nuestra casa, señor! Nuestro amo saldrá a recibirle enseguida!* Welcome to our home, sir! Our master will be with you right away! *

II. *pron pos*
ours

estas maletas son nuestras these cases are ours

nuevo

nuevo, a
['nweβo, a] *adj*
1. new

no hay nada nuevo bajo el sol there's nothing new under the sun

...nuevo

2. Idiom
de nuevo again

¡ya te has equivocado de nuevo! you've made a mistake again

¿qué hay de nuevo? what's new?

nuez

nuez
[nweθ] *n f*
nut, walnut

número

número
['numero] *n m*
number

números pares e impares odd and even numbers

nunca

nunca
['nunka] *adv*
1. never

Milú no dejará nunca a Tintín Snowy will never abandon Tintin

2. Idiom
nunca más, nunca jamás never again

* *¿Qué? ¿¿¿Volver a la luna??? ¡¡¡Nunca jamás!!! ¡Déme más bien algo de*

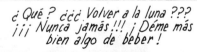

beber! What? Go back to the moon??? Never again!!! I'd rather you gave me a drink! *

ñoño

ñoño, a
['ɲoɲo, ɑ] *adj*
silly, insipid

obedecer

obedecer
[oβeðe'θer] *v i & v t*
to obey

el soldado debe obedecer a sus superiores the soldier must obey his superiors

▶ **obediente**
[oβe'ðjente] *adj*
obedient

los perros son muy obedientes dogs are very obedient

objeto

objeto
[oβ'xeto] *n m*
1. object

2. Idiom
con objeto de with the object/aim of, so as to, in order to

levantó la tapa con objeto de examinar el contenido he lifted the lid in order to examine the contents

obra

obra
['oβra] *n f*
1. work

una obra de arte a work of art

2. play
una obra (de teatro) de Shakespeare a play by Shakespeare

3. (road) works *pl*

4. Idiom
* *Están haciendo*

Están haciendo obras.

...obra

obras. They are working on the road. *

estamos en obras we have the workmen in

obrero

obrero, a
[o'βrero, a] *n*
worker, workman *m*,
(woman) worker *f*

obscuro

obscuro, a
(spelt oscuro nowadays)
[os'kuro, a] *adj*
1. dark

Es un lugar muy obscuro...

* *Es un lugar muy o(b)scuro...* It's a very dark place... *

azul o(b)scuro dark blue

2. Idiom
a o(b)scuras in the dark

observar

observar
[oβser'βar] *v t*
to observe,
to watch

obstáculo

obstáculo
[oβs'takulo] *n m*
obstacle

...obstáculo

* *¿Lo ve, Tintín? ¡Hemos vencido todos los obstáculos!* You see, Tintin? We've surmounted all the obstacles! *

...obstáculo

¿Lo ve, Tintín?
¡Hemos vencido todos
los obstáculos!

obtener

obtener
[oβte'ner] *v t*
to obtain

*obtuvo una beca
para estudiar en el
extranjero* he obtained
a grant to study abroad

ocasión

ocasión
[oka'sjon] *n f*
1. occasion

...ocasión

en varias ocasiones
on various occasions

2. Idiom
de ocasión second-
hand

occidente

occidente
[okθi'ðente] *n m*
west

---

océano

océano
[o'θeano] *n m*
ocean

* *En las profundi-
dades del océano...*
In the depths of the o-
cean... *

octubre

octubre
[ok'tuβre] *n m*
October

En las profundidades del océano...

...octubre

*nació el doce de
octubre de 1800* he
was born on the twelfth of
October 1800

ocupar

ocupar, ocuparse
[oku'par, se]
I. *v t*
to occupy,
to take up

...ocupar

*estos trastos ocu-
pan demasiado sitio*
this junk takes up too
much room

II. *v pr*
to look after

* *Riiing* Riiing
*Se ocupa de la
casa.* He looks after the
house. *

...ocupar

RIIING RIIING

Se ocupa de la casa.

ocurrir

ocurrir, ocurrirse
[oku'rir, se]
I. *v impers*
to happen, to occur

* *¿Qué ocurre?*
What's happening *

II. *v pr*
to occur, to think of

*se me ocurre una
idea* an idea has
occurred to me

no se me ocurre

¿Qué ocurre?

nada I can't think of
anything

oeste

oeste
[o'este] *n m*
1. west

*al oeste del pueblo
se levanta una
antigua iglesia* to the
west of the village there is

...oeste

an ancient church

2. Idiom
*las películas del
oeste* westerns

oficina

oficina
[ofi'θina] *n f*
office

* *¿El capitán Haddock y Tintín? Hágalos entrar en mi oficina. Los estaba esperando.* Captain Haddock and Tintin? Send them into my office. I was expecting them. *

oficio

oficio
[o'fiθjo] *n m*
job, profession

ofrecer

ofrecer
[ofre'θer] *v t*
to offer, to give

* *¡Te ofrezco este reloj!* I'd like to give you this clock! *

...ofrecer

oído

oído
[o'ido] *n m*
1. ear

todo le entra por un oído y sale por el otro with him, everything goes in one ear and out the other

2. hearing
el catarro me ha afectado el oído the cold has affected my hearing

oír

oír
[o'ir] *v i & v t*
to hear,
to listen to

* *Clingg* Clink
Oyen un ruido extraño. They hear a strange noise. *

¡oye!/¡oiga! listen to this!

Oyen un ruido extraño.

¡ojalá!

¡ojalá!
[oxa'la]
I. *interj*
let's hope so!, I do hope so!

II. *conj*
ojalá (que) I wish, if only, let's hope

¡ojalá dejara de llover! if only it would stop raining!

* *¡Ojalá no sea una bomba!* Let's hope it isn't a bomb! *

ojo

ojo
['oxo] *n m*
1. eye

tiene los ojos azules she has blue eyes

2. Idiom
¡vete con ojo!, ¡ojo! be careful!

ola

ola
['ola] *n f*
wave

* *La ola los arrastra...* The wave is carrying them away... *

¡olé!

¡olé!
[o'le] *interj*
bravo! well·done!

La ola los arrastra...

oler

oler
[o'ler] *v i & v t*
to smell

la comida huele bien the food smells good

▶ **olor**
[o'lor] *n m*
smell

* *¡Dios mío!... ¡Qué olor más penetrante!... Es cloroformo... Tengo sueño... pero... no de-*

...oler

bo... dormir... Good heavens!... What a pungent smell!... It's chloroform... I feel sleepy... but... I mustn't... sleep... *

oliva

oliva
[o'liβa] *n f*
olive

aceite de oliva olive oil

...oliva

▶ **olivo**
[o'liβo] *n m*
olive tree

los olivos están en flor the olive trees are in bloom

olvidar

olvidar, olvidarse
[olβi'ðar, se] *v t & v pr*
to forget

...olvidar

* *¡Mire! Es la prueba de que Tornasol ha venido aquí, se ha olvidado el paraguás...* Look! This is proof that Calculus has been here, he forgot his umbrella... *

▶ **olvido**
[ol'βiðo] *n m*
1. omission
2. forgetfulness

¡Mire! Es la prueba de que Tornasol ha venido aquí, se ha olvidado el paraguas...

opinar

opinar
[opi'nar] *v i*
to think

¿qué opina usted de la decisión? what do you think of the decision?

▶ **opinión**
[opi'njon] *n f*
opinion

en mi opinión in my opinion

oponer

¡Si es así, no iré a la luna, me opongo rotundamente!

oponer, oponerse
[opo'ner, se]
I. *v t*
to oppose

II. *v pr*
to object,
to be opposed

* *¡Si es así, no iré a la luna, me opongo rotundamente!* If that's the case, I'm not going to the moon; I'm flatly opposed to the idea! *

oportunidad

oportunidad
[oportuni'dad] *n f*
opportunity, chance

no he tenido la oportunidad de ir I haven't had the chance to go

igualdad de oportunidades equality of opportunity

▶ **oportunidades**
[oportuni'dades] *n f pl*
bargains

optimista

optimista
[opti'mista]
I. *adj*
optimistic

II. *n*
optimist

orden

orden
['orðen]

...orden

I. *n m*
order

orden alfabético alphabetical order

II. *n f*
order

las órdenes del general the General's orders

una orden religiosa a religious order

oreja

oreja
[o'rexa] *n f*
ear

* *¡Grrr!* Grrr!
Milú levanta las orejas. Snowy pricks up his ears. *

orgulloso

orgulloso, a
[orɣu'λoso, a] *adj*
proud

¡GRRR!

Milú levanta las orejas.

...orgulloso

Tintín está muy orgulloso de Milú Tintin is very proud of Snowy

origen

origen
[o'rixen] *n m*
1. origin, cause

los orígenes de la guerra the causes of the war

...origen

2. Idiom
dar origen a to give rise to

orilla

orilla
[o'riλa] *n f*
bank, side, shore

* *Paseando por la orilla del mar...* Walking along the seashore... *

...orilla

Paseando por la orilla del mar...

oro

oro
['oro] *n m*
gold

no es oro todo lo que reluce all that glitters is not gold

orquesta

orquesta
[or'kesta] *n f*
orchestra

...orquesta

* *Nuestra orquesta va a interpretar el concierto...*Our orchestra is going to perform the concerto...
¡Chis! Shush!
Pero... But... *

os

os
[os] *pron*
1. (to) you

...os

os voy a dar un poco de dinero I'm going to give you a little money

2. (to) your-selves

oscuro

oscuro, a
→ OBSCURO

oso

¡Vaya! ¡Ahora llegan los osos padres!...

...oso

oso
['oso] *n m*
bear

* *¡Vaya! ¡Ahora llegan los osos padres!...* Well, well, well! Now the mother and father bears are arriving!... *

otoño

otoño
[o'toɲo] *n m*
autumn

otro

otro, a
['otro, a]
I. *adj indet*
(an)other,
some other

otro día another day/some other day

II. *pron indet*
1. (an)other (one), some other (one) (some) others *pl*

2. Idiom
¡otra! encore!

oveja

oveja
[o'βexa] *n f*
sheep

contar ovejas to count sheep

oyente

oyente
[o'ʎente] *n*
listener, hearer

...oyente

* *Queridos oyentes, a continuación van a escuchar a Bianca Castafiore... ¡Ah! Me río...* Dear listeners, next you are going to hear Bianca Castafiore... Oh! I laugh... *

paciencia

paciencia
[pa'θjenθja] *n f*
patience

* **¡Mil diablos! ¡Monos estúpidos! ¡Se me acaba la paciencia!** Blistering barnacles! Stupid monkeys! My patience is running out! *

▶ **paciente**
[pa'θjente] *adj & n*
patient

padecer

padecer
[pade'θer] *v i & v t*
to suffer

padece asma he suffers from asthma

▶ **padecimiento**
[paðeθimiento] *n m*
suffering

padre

padre
['padre] *n m*
father

mi padre aparenta menos años de los que tiene my father looks younger than he is

▶ **padres**
['padres] *n m pl*
parents

mis padres están preocupados por mi hermano my parents

...padre

are worried about my brother

pagar

pagar
[pa'ɣar] *v i & v t*
to pay

déjame pagar esto let me pay for this

¿has pagado? have you paid?

...pagar

¡me las pagarás! you'll pay for this!

página

página
['paxina] *n f*
page

al pie de la página at the bottom of the page

país

país
[païs] *n m*
country

* **Como te lo digo, Tchang, las costumbres de mi país son muy diferentes de las vuestras.** As I was saying, Chang, the customs in my country are very different to yours.
¡Ja! ¡Ja! ¡Qué divertidos sois en tu país! Ha! Ha! You're so funny in your country! *

paisaje

paisaje
[païsaxe] *n m*
countryside, landscape

el cuadro representa un paisaje the painting is a landscape

P

paja

paja
['paxa] *n f*
straw

beber con una paja
to drink through a straw

pájaro

pájaro
['paxaro] *n m*
1. bird

...pájaro

* *¿Qué va a hacer
este pájaro?* What is
this bird going to do? *

el pájaro carpintero
the woodpecker

2. Idiom
*más vale pájaro en
mano que cien vo-
lando* a bird in the hand
is worth two in the bush

¿Qué va a hacer este pájaro?

palabra

palabra
[pa'laβra] *n f*
word

*no entiendo el signi-
ficado de esta pala-
bra* I don't understand
the meaning of this word

*ha cumplido con su
palabra* he has kept his
word

palacio

palacio
[pa'laθjo] *n m*
1. palace

*van a renovar el
palacio* they are going to
renovate the palace

2. Idiom
*las cosas de palacio
van despacio* it all
takes time

paladar

paladar
[pala'ðar] *n m*
palate

paliza

paliza
[pali'θa] *n f*
beating

*le pegaron una
buena paliza* they
gave him a good beating

palma

palma
['palma] *n f*
1. palm *(de la mano)*

2. Idiom
dar palmas to clap, to
applaud

3. palm, palm tree,
palm leaf

4. Idiom
llevarse la palma to
win, to triumph

▶ **palmada**
[pal'maða] *n f*
1. slap, pat

* *¡Ah! ¡Mis queridos
amigos, qué conten-
to estoy de verles!...*
Ah! My dear friends, how
happy I am to see you!...
*Tintín les da una
palmada en la es-
palda.* Tintin gives them
a slap on the back. *

2. Idiom
dar palmadas to clap

Tintín les da una palmada en la espalda.

palmera

palmera
[pal'mera] *n f*
palm tree

* *Descansaremos a
la sombra de esas
palmeras.* We'll rest in
the shade of those palm
trees. *

Descansaremos a la sombra de esas palmeras.

palo

palo
['palo] *n m*
1. stick, club

2. blow, beating
* *¡Y otro palo!* And
another blow! *

¡Y otro palo!

paloma

paloma
[pa'loma] n f
dove, pigeon

paloma mensajera
carrier pigeon

pampa

pampa
['pampa] n f
pampas, prairie

pan

pan
[pan] n m
bread

pan integral brown
bread

▶ **panadería**
[pana ðe'ria] n f
bakery, baker's

*hay una panadería
a la vuelta de la
esquina* there's a
baker's just round the
corner

pandilla

pandilla
[pan'ðiλa] n f
group, gang

* *¡Sois unos male-
ducados!* You're very
bad-mannered!
*Una pandilla de
niños rodea al
capitán.* A group of
children are gathering
round the Captain. *

Una pandilla de niños rodea al capitán.

pánico

pánico
['paniko] n m
panic

*¡no se dejen llevar
por el pánico!* don't
panic!

preso del pánico in a
panic

pantalón

pantalón
[panta'lon] n m
1. a pair of trousers

2. Idiom
*pantalones vaque-
ros* jeans

pantalla

pantalla
[pan'taλa] n f
1. screen

*está limpiando la
pantalla del ordena-
dor* he is wiping the
screen of the computer

2. lampshade

pantano

pantano
[pan'tano] n m
1. marsh(land)

2. reservoir
*debido a la escasez
de lluvias, los pan-
tanos están casi
vacíos* owing to the lack
of rain, the reservoirs are
almost empty

pantorrilla

pantorrilla
[panto'řiλa] n f
calf *(de la pierna)*

*me duelen las pan-
torrillas* my calves ache

pañuelo

pañuelo
[pa'ɲwelo] n m
1. handkerchief,
hanky

...pañuelo

*Se han puesto un
pañuelo en la cabeza.*

* *Se han puesto un
pañuelo en la cabe-
za.* They have put hand-
kerchiefs on their heads. *

2. (head)scarf

papá

papá
[pa'pa] n m
dad, daddy

papel

papel
[pa'pel] n m
1. paper

* *¡No me impor-
tan estos papeles!*
I couldn't care less about
these papers! *

2. rôle, part
*desempeñar un pa-
pel* to play a part

hacer el papel de to
play the part of

par

par
[par] n m
pair

* ¡Caramba! ¡Vaya par de botas! Y parecen casi nuevas... Y el hombre está durmiendo... ¡Es una ocasión formidable! Well! What a pair of boots! And they look almost new... And the man's sleeping... It's a tremendous opportunity! *

para

para
['para]
I. prep
1. for

* No pretenderá hacerme creer que todas estas botellas son para usted... Ya sabe que aquí el alcohol está prohibido... You don't expect me to believe that all these bottles are for you... You know that alcohol is forbidden here... *

...para

esto lo quiero para el sábado I want this for Saturday

2. (in order) to
lo hice para ayudarle I did it (in order) to help you

II. conj
so (that),
in order that

te doy esta foto para que no me olvides I'm giving you this photo so you won't forget me

parada

parada
[pa'rada] n f
stop

bajamos en la próxima parada we get off at the next stop

▶ **parado, a**
[parado, a] adj
1. unemployed

2. Idiom
quedarse parado to be left speechless, to be shocked

parador

parador
[para'dor] n m
state-owned hotel

paraguas

paraguas
[pa'raɣwas] n m
umbrella

* Lleva un paraguas. He is carrying an umbrella. *

...paraguas

Lleva un paraguas.

paraíso

paraíso
[para'iso] n m
paradise

ave del paraíso bird of paradise

parecer

parecer, parecerse
[pare'θer, se]
I. v i
1. to look (like), to seem (like)

parece un castillo it looks like a castle

* ¿Qué... qué... qué quiere usted, Tintín? What... what... what do you want, Tintin?
Sólo una pequeña conversación... Parece usted muy preocupado, señor Wagner... Just a little conversation... You seem very worried, Mr Wagner... *

2. to think
¿qué le parece? what do you think?

II. v pr
to resemble,
to look like (each other)

se parecen mucho they look a lot like each other

se parece mucho a su hermano he looks a lot like his brother

III. n m
1. opinion, view

a mi parecer in my opinion

2. Idiom
al parecer seemingly, apparently

pared

pared
[pa'reð] n f
1. wall

* *La pared está rota.*
The wall is damaged. *

2. Idiom
estar cara a la pared to be stood in the corner

La pared está rota.

pareja

pareja
[pa'rexa] n f
pair, couple

pariente

pariente
[pa'rjente] n m
relative, relation

* *¿De modo que usted conoce a Tchang?* So you know

...pariente

Chang?
¡Oh sí! Es pariente mío. Si quieren, les acompaño a su casa... Oh yes! He's a relation of mine. If you wish, I'll take you to his home... *

párpado

párpado
['parpaðo] n m
eyelid

parque

parque
['parke] n m
park

* *¡Rápido! ¡Qué no salga del parque!* Quick! He mustn't get out of the park!
¡Guau! Bow-wow! *

párrafo

párrafo
['paɾafo] n m
paragraph

este párrafo no tiene ni pies ni cabeza this paragraph is completely confused

parte

parte
['parte] n f
1. part

...parte

el cuento tiene dos partes the story has two parts

2. Idiom
de parte de from, on behalf of

* *Este perro viene de parte de Tintín... Debe de haberle ocurrido algo... ¡Vamos a buscarlo!* This dog has come on behalf of Tintin... Something must have happened

to him... Let's go and find him! *

¿de parte de quién? who's calling?

salúdale de mi parte give him my regards

por todas partes everywhere

en ninguna parte nowhere

tomar parte in to take part in

participar

...participar

participar
[parti'θipar] *v i*
to participate,
to take part

* *Mire... ¿Sabe quiénes son?* Look... Do you know who they are? *Sí, han participado en el espectáculo...* Yes, they took part in the show... *

partida

partida
[par'tida] *n f*
1. game

vamos a echar una partida de ajedrez let's have a game of chess

2. certificate
partida de matrimonio marriage certificate

partida de nacimiento birth certificate

3. departure

partidario

partidario, a
[parti'darjo, a] *adj & n*
1. partisan,
supporter

* *Muera Alcázar* Death to Alcazar
A las Dopicos To las Dopicos
Los partidarios del general Tapioca se manifiestan General Tapioca's supporters are demonstrating. *

2. Idiom
ser partidario de to be in favour of

Los partidarios del general Tapioca se manifiestan.

partido

partido
[par'tido] *n m*
1. game, match

¿viste el partido de fútbol ayer? did you see the football match yesterday?

2. party *(político)*

3. Idiom
sacar partido de to profit from

es un buen partido he's a good catch/he's very eligible

partir

partir
[par'tir]
I. *v t*
to divide, to split, to crack open

partió la nuez he cracked the nut open

II. *v i*
1. to start,
to set off,
to set out, to leave

usted ha partido de un supuesto falso you've started from a false assumption

2. Idiom
a partir de as from, starting from

el decreto tendrá validez a partir del lunes que viene the decree will come into force as from next Monday

pasajero

Los pasajeros bajan del avión.

pasajero, a
[pasa'xero, a] *n*
passenger

* *Los pasajeros bajan del avión.* The passengers are getting off the plane. *

pasaporte

pasaporte
[pasa'porte] *n m*
passport

pasar

pasar, pasarse
[pa'sar, se]
I. *v t*
1. to pass

¿me pasas la sal, por favor? would you pass me the salt, please?

Buenos días. Le traigo el loro que...
¡Ah sí! ¡Pase!

2. to spend
¿dónde pasas el verano? where do you spend the summer?

3. Idiom
pasar por alto to miss, to skip

II. *v i*
1. to pass through, to go through

pasamos por Lérida camino de Huesca we passed through Lérida on the way to Huesca

2. to go in,
to come in, to enter

* *Buenos días. Le traigo el loro que...* Good morning. I've brought you the parrot that... *¡Ah sí! ¡Pase!* Oh yes! Come in! *

III. *v impers*
1. to happen,
to go on
¿qué pasa? what's going on?

2. Idiom
pase lo que pase whatever happens

IV. *v pr*
1. to spend

me he pasado el día en la playa I've spent the day on the beach

2. to go too far
¡no te pases! don't go too far!

...pasar

▶ **pasado, a**
[pa'sado, a]
I. *adj*
past, last

II. *n m*
past

Pascua

Pascua
['paskwa] *n f*
1. Easter

...Pascua

2. Christmas
¡felices Pascuas!
merry Christmas!

pasear

pasear, pasearse
[pase'ar, se]
I. *v t*
to take for a walk

* *¡Eureka!* Eureka!
Pasean a los perros. They are taking the

...pasear

Pasean a los perros.

dogs for a walk. *

II. *v i & v pr*
to go for a walk

fuimos a pasearnos por el bosque we went for a walk in the woods

▶ **paseo**
[pa'seo] *n m*
1. walk, stroll, ride, drive

* *Aquel día...* That day...

Hemos dado un buen paseo. We've had a good walk. *

2. Idiom
enviar/mandar a paseo to send packing

...pasear

Aquel día...

Hemos dado un buen paseo.

pasillo

pasillo
[pa'siʎo] *n m*
passage, corridor

* *Al final del pasillo a la derecha, puerta catorce.* At the end of the passage on the right, door fourteen. *

paso

paso
['paso] *n m*

...paso

Al final del pasillo a la derecha, puerta catorce.

1. step

dar un paso to take a step

2. passage, passing
el paso del tiempo the passage of time

3. passage, way through, crossing
paso a nivel level crossing

paso de peatones

zebra crossing/pedestrian crossing

4. pace, gait

5. Idiom
andar a paso ligero to walk briskly

de paso in passing

estar de paso to be passing through

pasta

pasta
['pasta] *n f*
1. paste

2. pastry

pastas

pastas
['pastas] *n f pl*
1. pasta

2. cakes

pastel

pastel
[pas'tel] *n m*
cake

▶ **pastelería**
[pastele'ria] *n f*
1. cake shop

2. pastry-making

pastilla

pastilla
[pas'tiʎa] *n f*
1. tablet, pastille

pastillas para la tos throat tablets

2. Idiom
ir a toda pastilla to go flat out, to belt along

pastor

pastor, a
[pas'tor, a] *n*
shepherd *m*,
shepherdess *f*

el pastor ha perdido dos ovejas the shepherd has lost two sheep

pata

pata
['pata] *n f*
1. leg

la pata de la mesa the table leg

* *¡Milú! ¿¿¿Has bebido???* Snowy? Have you been drinking?
¡Mira! ¡Sé andar sobre las dos patas delanteras! Look! I can walk on my two front legs! *

...pata

2. Idiom
meter la pata to put one's foot in it

patas arriba in a mess, in disorder, upside down

andar a la pata coja to play hopscotch

¡qué mala pata! what bad luck!

patada

patada
[pa'tada] *n f*
1. kick

* *¡Y hala!* Take that!
Le da una patada.
He is kicking him. *

2. Idiom
echar a patadas
to kick somebody out

Le da una patada.

patata

patata
[pa'tata] *n f*
1. potato

2. Idiom
patatas fritas chips
(*Am*: French fries), crisps
(*en bolsa*) (*Am*: potato chips)

patente

patente
[pa'tente] *adj*
obvious

paterno

paterno, a
[pa'terno, a] *adj*
paternal

mi abuela paterna
my paternal grand-mother/my grandmother on my father's side

patinar

patinar
[pati'nar] *v i*
1. to skate

* *Aprende a patinar.*
He is learning to skate. *

2. to skid
el coche patinó sobre el hielo the car skidded on the ice

Aprende a patinar.

patio

patio
['patjo] *n m*
yard, courtyard

los niños juegan en el patio the children are playing in the yard

pato

pato, a
['pato, a] *n*
duck

...pato

▶ **patoso, a**
[pa'toso, a] *adj*
clumsy

patria

patria
['patrja] *n f*
native country, homeland

...patria

▶ **patriota**
[patrj'ota] *n*
patriot

pavo

pavo, a
['paβo, a] *n*
1. turkey

2. Idiom
pavo real peacock

payaso

payaso
[pa'jaso, a] *n m*
1. clown

2. Idiom
hacer el payaso
to clown around

paz

paz
[paθ] *n f*
1. peace

2. Idiom
* *¡Déjeme en paz! ¡Soy un desgra-ciado!* Leave me alone! I'm a poor soul!
¡Ande! Tómese esto, que le ento-nará... Come on! Take this; it'll make you feel better... *

peaje

peaje
[pe'axe] *n m*
1. toll

2. Idiom
una autopista de peaje a toll-paying motorway

peatón

peatón
[pea'ton] *n m*
pedestrian

...peatón

▶**peatonal**
[peato'nal] *adj*
pedestrian

pecho

pecho
['petʃo] *n m*
chest, breast

pedalear

Tintín pedalea a toda velocidad.

...pedalear

pedalear
[pedale'ar] *v i*
to pedal

* *¡Stop!* Stop!
Tintín pedalea a toda velocidad. Tintin is pedalling at full speed. *

pedazo

pedazo
[pe'daθo] *n m*
1. piece

...pedazo

un pedazo de pan a piece of bread

2. Idiom
hacerse pedazos to break into pieces, to fall to pieces

pedir

pedir
[pe'dir] *v t*
1. to ask (for)

...pedir

me pidió ayuda he asked me for help

nos pidieron que les ayudáramos they asked us to help them

2. Idiom
a pedir de boca just as one wants

* *¡Nos ha salido a pedir de boca!* It's turned out just as we wanted! *

pegar

pegar, pegarse
[pe'ɣar, se]
I. *v t*
1. to stick, to glue

pegó el sello en el sobre he stuck the stamp on the envelope

2. to hit, to strike

II. *v pr*
to hit each other, to fight

*¡Ya te tengo!... ¡Toma!... ¡Vas a

Se pegan en la calle.

ver!...* I've got you!... Take that!... You wait!...
Se pegan en la calle. They are fighting in the street. *

peinar

Carmen es la que me peina Carmen is the one who does my hair

II. *v pr*
to comb/do one's hair

me voy a peinar I'm going to comb my hair

peinar

peinar, peinarse
[pei̯'nar, se]
I. *v t*
to comb/do someone's hair

...peinar

▶**peine**
['pei̯ne] *n m*
comb

pelar

pelar
[pe'lar] *v t*
1. to peel

voy a pelar las patatas I'm going to peel the potatoes

2. Idiom
hace un frío que pela it's freezing cold

pelear

pelear, pelearse
[pele'ar, se] v i & v pr
1. to fight

¡No os peleéis! Stop fighting! *

2. to argue, to quarrel

¡No os peleéis!

película

película
[pe'likula] n f
film

* *Van a ver una película al cine.* They are going to the cinema to see a film. *

Van a ver una película al cine.

peligro

peligro
[pe'liɣro] n m
danger

...peligro

* *Su vida corre peligro...* His life is in danger... *

pelo

pelo
['pelo] n m
1. hair

tienes un pelo en la americana there's a hair on your jacket

2. Idiom

Su vida corre peligro...

...pelo

tomarle el pelo a alguien to make a fool of somebody, to pull somebody's leg

no tiene pelos en la lengua he's very outspoken

pelota

pelota
[pe'lɔta] n f
ball

peluquería

peluquería
[peluke'řia] n f
hairdresser's

* *¡Esto no es una peluquería y yo no soy peluquero! Ya estoy harto de cortarles el pelo sin parar... si es que se le puede llamar pelo...* This is not a hairdresser's and I'm not a hairdresser! I'm sick of cutting your hair nonstop... if this can be called hair... *

...peluquería

¡Esto no es una peluquería y yo no soy peluquero! Ya estoy harto de cortarles el pelo sin parar... si es que a esto se le puede llamar pelo...

pellizcar

pellizcar
[peλiθ'kar] v t
to pinch

si vuelves a pellizarme, gritaré if you pinch me again, I'll shout

pena

pena
['pena] n f
1. grief, sadness, sorrow

2. Idiom
no vale la pena it isn't worth it

dais pena you're pathetic

3. shame, pity
¡qué pena! what a shame!

pendiente

¡Ah! Me río de verme tan bella en este espejo...

Lleva pendientes azules.

pendiente
[pen'djente]
I. n m
earring

* *¡Ah! Me río de verme tan bella en este espejo...* Oh! I laugh to see myself so beautiful in this mirror...
Lleva pendientes azules. She is wearing blue earrings. *

II. n f
slope, hill

...pendiente

* *¡Capitán, no corra tanto!* Captain, don't run so fast!
¡La pendiente es empinada!... It's a steep slope!... *

III. *adj*
1. hanging

2. Idiom
estar pendiente to be hanging, to hang, to depend on

estamos pendientes de lo que diga él everything depends on what he says

península

península
[pe'ninsula] *n f*
péninsula

pensar

pensar
[pen'sar] *v i & v t*
to think

* *... Cómo habrá sabido este señor que estoy en China si no he comunicado a nadie mi llegada...* ... How could this man have known I'm in China if I didn't tell anybody about my arrival...
¿En qué piensas? ¿Estás hablando solo? What are you thinking about? Are you talking to yourself? *

...pensar

peón

peón
[pe'on] *n m*
unskilled workman/labourer

peón de albañil building labourer

peor

peor
[pe'or] *adj & adv*
worse, worst

...peor

el tiempo es peor que ayer the weather is worse than yesterday

es uno de mis peores enemigos he's one of my worst enemies

* *¡Esto cada vez es peor! ¡Ahora Tintín se ha escapado!... Pero ¡perseguidle, imbéciles!* This is getting worse and worse! Now Tintín has got away!... Go after him, you fools! *

pequeño

pequeño, a
[pe'keno, a] *adj*
small, little

un chico pequeño a little boy

percha

percha
['pertʃa] *n f*
1. coat hanger

...percha

2. perch
el loro se balanceaba en la percha the parrot rocked to and fro on the perch

perder

perder, perderse
[per'der, se]
I. *v t*
1. to lose

...perder

* *¿Ha perdido algo, capitán?* Have you lost something, Captain? *

2. to miss
¡corre! vamos a perder el autobús hurry up! we'll miss the bus

II. *v pr*
to lose one's way, to get lost

me perdí en el bosque I got lost in the wood

III. *v i*
to lose

nuestro equipo perdió our team lost

perdonar

perdonar
[perðo'nar] *v t & v i*
1. to forgive, to pardon

...perdonar

2. Idiom
¡perdone! excuse me! *(para introducir una pregunta)*, sorry! *(para pedir disculpas)*

▶ **¡perdón!**
[per'don] *interj*
1. excuse me!

2. sorry!

perezoso

perezoso, a
[pere'θoso, a] *adj*
lazy

▶ **pereza**
[pere'θa] *n f*
1. laziness

2. Idiom
me da pereza I can't be bothered

perfecto

perfecto, a
[per'fekto, a] *adj*
perfect

perfume

perfume
[per'fume] *n m*
scent, perfume

periodista

periodista
[perjo'ðista] *n*
journalist

una periodista desea verle there's a journalist to see you

▶ **periódico**
[pe'rjodiko] *n m*
(news)paper

*Tintín lee el periódico. Tintin is reading the paper. *

perjudicar

perjudicar
[perxuði'kar] *v t*
to damage,
to harm

fumar perjudica los pulmones smoking damages the lungs

▶ **perjuicio**
[per'xwiθjo] *n m*
damage,
harm

* El incendio está apagado, pero ha habido muchos perjuicios... ¡Qué mala suerte! The fire's out, but there's a lot of damage... What bad luck! *

permanecer

permanecer
[permane'θer] *v i*
to stay, to remain

permaneció inmóvil he remained motionless

permaneceremos cinco días en Madrid we'll stay in Madrid for five days

▶ **permanente**
[perma'nente]
I. *adj*
permanent

en ese país, había una tensión permanente que condujo a la guerra civil in that country, there was a permanent tension which led to the civil war

II. *n f*
perm

* ¡Tengo las manos llenas de ampollas! ¿No está contento? ¿Quería usted una permanente? My hands are covered in

...permanecer

blisters! Aren't you satisfied? What did you want, a perm? *

permiso

permiso
[per'miso] *n m*
permission, permit

* ¿Quién le ha dado permiso para entrar aquí? Who gave you

...permiso

permission to come in here?
Bueno, ya salgo... No dispare... All right, I'm coming out... Don't shoot... *

▶ **permitir**
[permi'tir] *v t*
1. to allow, to permit

2. Idiom
¿me permite? may I? do you mind?

P

pero

perro

persona

pero
['pero] *conj*
1. but

está bien, pero todavía no basta it's all right, but not good enough yet

2. Idiom
¡no pongas peros! no buts!

perro, a
['peʀo] *n*
dog *m*,
bitch *f*

* *He decidido emprender este viaje a África para cazar leones. Nosotros, los perros, somos muy valientes...* I've decided to make this journey to Africa to hunt lions. We dogs are very brave... *

persona
[per'sona] *n f*
1. person

2. Idiom
es buena persona he's a good bloke/sort

en persona in person

* *¡Viva Tintín!* Hurray for Tintin!
¡Viva Milú! Hurray for Snowy!
¡Viva Tintín! Hurray for Tintin!

...persona

¡Mirad! Es Tintín en persona... Look! It's Tintin in person... *

▶ **personaje**
[perso'naxe] *n m*
personage, celebrity, character

un personaje importante a celebrity

personal

persuadir

...pesadilla

...pesado

personal
[perso'nal]
I. *n m*
staff, personnel

II. *adj*
personal

este asunto es personal this matter is personal

persuadir
[perswa'ðir] *v t*
to persuade

no se dejará persuadir she won't allow herself to be persuaded

pesadilla

pesadilla
[pesa'ðiʎa] *n f*
nightmare

Tintín tiene una pesadilla.

* *Tintín tiene una pesadilla.* Tintin is having a nightmare. *

pesado

pesado, a
[pe'saðo, a] *adj*
1. heavy

* *¡Es muy pesado!* It's very heavy! *

2. tiresome
es una persona muy pesada he's a very tiresome person

▶ **pesadez**
[pesa'ðeθ] *n f*
1. heaviness

2. tediousness

141

...pesado

¡ Es muy pesado !

pesar

pesar
[pe'sar]
I. v t
to weigh

pésame esta fruta
weigh this fruit for me

II. v i
to be sorry

¡te pesará! you'll be
sorry!

▶ **a pesar de,
pese a**

[ape'sarde, 'pesea]
prep
1. in spite of,
despite

*a pesar de su edad,
escaló la montaña* in
spite of his age, he
climbed the mountain

2. although
*a pesar de encon-
trarse mal, vino a la
reunión* although she
felt ill, she came to the
meeting

pescar

pescar
[pes'kar] *v i & v t*
1. to fish, to catch

*pescaron una enor-
me ballena* they caught
an enormous whale

2. to catch, to hear
*no he pescado lo
que has dicho* I didn't
catch what you said

▶ **pesca**
['peska] *n f*
fishing

▶ **pescado**
[pes'kado] *n m*
fish

▶ **pescador, a**
[peska'dor, a]
I. *adj*
fishing

un pueblo pescador
a fishing village

II. *n*
fisherman *m*,
fisherwoman *f*

...pescar

* ¿Llevarles a la Isla
Negra? ¡Ni hablar!
¡Yo soy pescador,
señor, y no acróba-
ta! Take you to Black
Island? Nothing doing! I'm
a fisherman, sir, not an
acrobat! *

peseta

peseta
[pe'seta] *n f*
peseta

pesimista

pesimista
[pesi'mista] *n*
pessimist

pésimo

pésimo, a
['pesimo] *adj*
terrible,
extremely bad

*los resultados son
pésimos* the results are
terrible

pestaña

pestaña
[pes'taɲa] *n f*
eyelash

petición

petición
[peti'θjon] *n f*
request, petition

*una petición por la
paz* a petition for peace

*un programa a
petición de radio-
yentes* a listeners'
request programme

petróleo

petróleo
[pe'troleo] *n m*
oil, petroleum

*una lámpara de
petróleo* an oil lamp

* ¡Petróleo! Milú,
hemos encontrado
petróleo... ¡Es una
verdadera lluvia de
petróleo! Oil! Snowy,
we've found oil... It's
actually raining oil!
Pero, sale del
suelo... Yo no sabía

¡ Petróleo! Milú, hemos
encontrado petróleo...
¡ Es una verdadera lluvia
de petróleo !

Pero, sale del
suelo... Yo no
sabía que el
petróleo se
encontrara
bajo tierra...

que el petróleo se
encontrara bajo
tierra... But, it's spurting
from the earth... I didn't
know oil could be found
underground. *

pez

pez
[peθ] *n m*
fish

...pez

¡ Está lleno de peces voladores !...

...pez

* *¡Está lleno de pe-ces voladores!...* It's full of flying fish!... *

picar

picar
['pikar]
I. *v t*
to sting

me ha picado un mosquito I've been stung by a mosquito

...picar

II. *v i*
to itch

me pica la nariz my nose itches

pícaro

pícaro, a
['pikaro, a]
I. *adj*
villainous
II. *n*
villain

pie

pie
[pje] *n m*
1. foot

subimos a pie we went up on foot

2. Idiom
dar pie a to give rise to

piedra

¡Cuidado con las piedras!

...piedra

piedra
['pjedra] *n f*
1. stone, rock

* *¡Cuidado con las piedras!* Mind the rocks! *

2. Idiom
a tiro de piedra within a stone's throw

piel

piel
[pjel] *n f*
1. skin

tiene la piel muy sensible she has very sensitive skin

2. fur
* *Milú lleva un abri-go de piel.* Snowy is wearing a fur coat. *

Milú lleva un abrigo de piel.

pierna

pierna
['pjerna] *n f*
leg

el escalador se ha roto la pierna the climber has broken his leg

pila

pila
['pila] *n f*
1. pile

...pila

* *La pila de libros se ha venido abajo...* The pile of books has collapsed... *

2. battery

3. Idiom
nombre de pila first name, Christian name

...pila

La pila de libros se ha venido abajo...

pillar

pillar, pillarse
[pi'λar, se] *v t*
1. to pillage, to plunder

2. to catch
¡cómo te pille,...! if I catch you,...!

la puerta le ha pillado la cola a Milú Snowy got his tail caught in the door

* *¡El capitán ha pillado la escarla-*

¡El capitán ha pillado la escarlatina! Eso es contagioso, ¿no?

tina! Eso es con-tagioso, ¿no? The Captain's caught scarlet fever! That's contagious, isn't it? *

3. Idiom
* *Esos dos... Los han pillado con las manos en la masa...* Those two... They caught them red-handed... *

...pillar

Esos dos... Los han pillado con las manos en la masa...

pimienta

pimienta
[pi'mjenta] *n f*
pepper

pinchar

**pinchar,
pincharse**
[pin'tʃar, se]
I. *v t*
1. to puncture,
to prick

...pinchar

El neumático se ha pinchado.

...pinchar

2. to give an injec-
tion

3. to prod,
to encourage
*pínchale para que
se compre coche*
prod him to make him buy
himself a car

II. *v i*
1. to prick

2. to get a flat tyre

III. *v pr*

1. to prick oneself

2. to burst,
to go flat
* *El neumático se
ha pinchado.* The tyre
has burst. *

▶ **pinchazo**
[pin'tʃaθo] *n m*
1. prick

2. flat tyre, puncture

pino

pino
['pino] *n m*
pine (tree)

pintar

pintar, pintarse
[pin'tar, se]
I. *v t*
to paint

*mandó pintar la
casa de azul* he had

...pintar

El capitán está lleno de pintura.

...pintar

the house painted blue

II. *v pr*
to put make-up on,
to make up

se pinta la cara she
puts make-up on her face

▶ **pintor, a**
[pin'tor, a] *n*
painter, artist

▶ **pintura**
[pin'tura] *n f*

1. paint

* *El capitán está
lleno de pintura.* The
Captain is covered in
paint. *

2. painting
una pintura al óleo
an oil painting

pintoresco

Es un pueblo muy pintoresco ¿no le parece?

...pintoresco

pintoresco, a
[pinto'resko, a] *adj*
picturesque

* *Es un lugar muy pintoresco, ¿no le parece?* It's a very picturesque place, don't you think? *

piña

piña
['piɲa] *n f*

...piña

1. pineapple

2. pine cone

3. blow
¡vaya piña que le ha dado! what a blow he struck him!

pisar

¡He pisado...

... un cangrejo!...

pisar
[pi'sar] *v t*
to step on,
to tread on

* *¡He pisado...* I've stepped on...
... un cangrejo!... ... a crab!... *

▶ **pisada**
[pi'sada] *n f*
1. footstep

2. Idiom

seguir las pisadas de alguien to follow in somebody's footsteps

3. footprint
* *Estas pisadas son gigantescas... ¿De quién serán?* These footprints are gigantic... Whose can they be? *Grrrr* Grrrr *

...pisar

Estas pisadas son gigantescas... ¿ De quién serán?

GRRRR GRRRR

piscina

piscina
[pis'θina] *n f*
swimming-pool

prefiero nadar en la piscina antes que en el mar I prefer to swim in the swimming-pool rather than in the sea

piso

piso
['piso] *n m*
1. floor, storey

* *¡Ánimo! Tenemos que subir al tercer piso...* Come on! We have to go up to the third floor... *

2. flat
(*Am*: apartment)

...piso

¡Ánimo! Tenemos que subir al tercer piso...

pito

pito
['pito] *n m*
1. whistle

2. Idiom
entre pitos y flautas what with one thing and another

pizarra

pizarra
[pi'θaɾa] *n f*

...pizarra

¡A ver! ¡Mirad la pizarra! ¿ Quién puede darme el resultado?

2 + 2

1. blackboard

* *¡A ver! ¡Mirad la pizarra! ¿Quién puede darme el resultado?* Now then! Look at the blackboard! Who can give me the result? *

2. slate

plan

plan
[plan] *n m*
1. plan, scheme

2. programme

3. Idiom
en plan de divertirse
out for a good time

plan de estudios
curriculum

planeta

planeta
[pla'neta] *n m*
planet

plano

plano
['plano]
I. *adj*
f plana ['plana]
flat

II. *n m*
1. plane

2. Idiom
en el primer plano in
the foreground

...planta

2. floor, storey
*vivimos en la sexta
planta* we live on the
sixth floor

la planta baja the
ground floor

planta

planta
['planta] *n f*
1. plant

riega las plantas
water the plants

plantar

plantar
[plan'tar] *v t*
to plant

* *He plantado una
nueva especie de
rosas... Se trata de
una creación perso-
nal, de la que estoy
bastante satisfe-
cho... Pero ¡chis!,
¡es un secreto!*
I've planted a new species
of rose... it's a creation of
my own, and I'm fairly
satisfied with it... But

...plantar

hush!; it's a secret!
¡De acuerdo! All right! *

plantear

plantear
[plante'ar] *v t*
to raise

*plantea problemas
sin resolver ninguno*
he raises problems without
solving any of them

plantilla

plantilla
[plan'tiʎa] *n f*
staff, personnel

*la plantilla de la
fábrica* the staff of the
factory

plástico

plástico
['plastiko] *n m*
plastic

plata

plata
['plata] *n f*
silver

un anillo de plata a
silver ring

* *Oro, plata, perlas
preciosas... El teso-
ro de los incas está
bien escondido... Y
nadie se lo llevará.*
Gold, silver, precious
pearls... The Inca treasure
is well hidden... And
nobody will take it. *

...plata

plátano

plátano
['platano] *n m*
banana

plato

plato
['plato] *n m*
1. plate

2. dish, course
de primer plato

...plato

comimos judías we
had beans for our first
course

▶ **platillo**
[pla'tiʎo] *n m*
saucer

playa

playa
['plaja] *n f*
beach

plaza

plaza
['plaθa] *n f*
1. square

2. Idiom
ir a la plaza to go
shopping (at the market)

plaza de toros
bullring

3. seat

4. post, position,
job

plazo

plazo
['plaθo] *n m*
period

en un plazo de seis meses within a period of six months

pleito

pleito
['pleito] *n m*
lawsuit, case, trial

...pleito

* *Aquel día...* That day...
El pleito de Tintín se ha terminado. Los japoneses lo han condenado a muerte... Tintin's trial is over. The Japanese have sentenced him to death... *

pluma

pluma
['pluma] *n f*
1. feather

duerme en un colchón de plumas he sleeps on a feather bed

2. pen
pluma estilográfica fountain pen

población

población
[poβla'θjon] *n f*
1. population

la población ha aumentado the population has increased

2. village, town
la montaña está sembrada de poblaciones the mountains are studded with villages

pobre

pobre
['pobre] *adj*
poor

* *¡Pobre gente! ¡Es inhumano dejarles vivir en estas condiciones!* Poor people! It's inhuman to allow them to live in these conditions! *Ha sido muy amable con ellos.* You were very kind to them. *

▶ **pobreza**
[po'βreθa] *n f*
poverty

▶ **pobremente**
[poβre'mente] *adv*
poorly

poco

poco
['poko]
I. *adj*
f poca ['poka]
little, not much

recibimos poca ayuda de los demás we receive little help from others

II. *n m*
a little, a bit of

un poco de queso a little cheese/a bit of cheese

III. *adv*
1. little, not (very) much, only a little

trabaja poco he doesn't work very much

2. Idiom
* *Por poco se cae.* He almost fell over. *

poco a poco little by little, gradually

...poco

Por poco se cae.

poder

poder
[po'ðer]
I. *vt & vi*
1. to be able to, can

el capitán no puede caminar the Captain can't walk

2. Idiom
puede ser maybe, perhaps

puede que llueva it may rain

¿puedes (con eso)? can you manage (that)?

¿se puede? can I come in?

* *¡Estoy cansadísimo! ¡No puedo más!* I'm exhausted! I can't go on! *

II. *n m*
power

el poder legislativo the legislative power

el poder del motor the power of the engine

▶ **poderoso, a**
[poðe'roso, a] *adj*
powerful

poema

poema
[po'ema] *n m*
poem

he leído muchos poemas de Antonio Machado I have read a lot of Antonio Machado's poems

▶ **poesía**
[poe'sia] *n f*
poetry

▶ **poeta**
[po'eta] *n m*
poet

un poeta del siglo veinte a twentieth-century poet

▶ **poético, a**
[po'etiko] *adj*
poetic

una imagen poética a poetic image

policía

policía
[poli'θia]
I. *n*
policeman *m*, policewoman *f*

* ... ¡Vaya!... ¡Policías! ... Drat!... Policemen! *

II. *n f*
police

voy a llamar a la policía I'm going to call the police

política

política
[po'litika] *n f*
politics

polvo

polvo
['polβo] *n m*
1. dust

los muebles están llenos de polvo the

...polvo

furniture is covered in dust

2. powder

3. Idiom
estoy hecho polvo I'm shattered/exhausted

pollo

pollo
['poλo] *n m*
chicken

...pollo

* ¡Qué rico debe de estar este pollo! I bet this chicken's tasty! Crrr Crrr *

poncho

poncho
['pontʃo] *n m*
poncho

* Lleva un poncho. He's wearing a poncho. *

...poncho

Lleva un poncho.

poner

poner, ponerse
[po'ner, se]
I. *v t*
1. to put, to place

* Más telegramas de felicitaciones, señor... ¿Los pongo sobre la mesa con los otros, o prefiere que los ponga en otro sitio? More telegrams of congratulation, sir... Shall I put them on the table with the others, or do you want me

to put them somewhere else? *

2. to lay, to set
pon la mesa, por favor lay the table, please

II. *v pr*
1. to stand (up)

se puso al lado de la puerta he stood beside the door

me pondré de pie I'll stand up

2. to put on
se puso el traje he put his suit on

3. to go, to get
se puso colorada she went red

¡se pone tan nervioso! he gets so worked up!

4. Idiom
ponerse a to begin to

el sol se pone por el oeste the sun sets in the west

popular

popular
[popu'lar] *adj*
popular

tocan un tema muy popular they are playing a very popular number

por

por
[por] *prep*
1. by

...por

escrito por él written by him

por correo by post

2. through
por el túnel through the tunnel

3. for
lo hará por ella he'll do it for her

por amor al arte for the love of it

por miedo a for fear of

4. Idiom
queda por hacer it's still to be done

por eso/por esa razón/por consiguiente so/for this reason/that's why

por la tarde in the afternoon/evening

* Por la noche... At night...
Ya hemos llegado. Pasaremos la noche en ese antiguo

sepulcro y mañana por la mañana nos marcharemos. We're here. We'll spend the night in that ancient tomb and tomorrow morning we'll set off. *

▶ **por qué**
[porˈke] *adv interr*
why

* No te asustes, pequeña... ¿Por qué lloras? ¿Te has perdido? Don't be afraid,

...por

little one... Why are you crying? Are you lost? *

el profesor no sabe por qué los alumnos se ríen de él the teacher does not know why the pupils laugh at him

porque

porque
[porˈke] *conj*
because

te defiendo porque te quiero I stand up for you because I love you

portarse

portarse
[porˈtarse] *v pr*
to behave

portería

portería
[porteˈrʎa] *n f*
1. porter's lodge, caretaker's office

2. goal

▶ **portero, a**
[porˈtero, a] *n*
1. porter, caretaker

* Y eso es todo... Espero haberle sido útil. Y si puede hacer algo por este

loro... And that's all... I hope I've been of some use to you; and if you can do anything for this parrot...
Ya lo miraré... Es usted una portera excelente... ¡Adiós! I'll look into it... You're an excellent caretaker... Goodbye! *

2. goalkeeper, goalie

...portería

poseer

poseer
[poseˈer] *v t*
to possess, to own

poseen muchas tierras they own a lot of land

posibilidad

posibilidad
[posiβiliˈðað] *n f*
possibility, chance

...posibilidad

existe la posibilidad de guerra there is a chance of war

▶ **posible**
[poˈsiβle] *adj*
1. possible

* ¡Dios mío!... ¡Wolff!... ¡No es posible! Good gracious!... Wolff!... It's not possible! ¿Qué ha hecho? ¿Qué ha pasado? What's he done? What's happened? *

2. Idiom
haremos lo posible por conseguirlo we'll do everything we can to achieve it

¡será posible! well I never!

postal

postal
[pos'tal]
I. adj
postal

servicio postal postal service

II. n f
postcard

mándame una postal send me a postcard

postre

postre
['postre] n m
sweet, dessert

pozo

pozo
['poθo] n m
well

practicar

practicar
[prakti'kar] v i & v t
to practise

práctico

práctico, a
['praktiko, a] adj
practical, handy

* Lo ve usted? Resulta muy práctico. Son patines con

...práctico

motor incorporado. ¿Qué le parece? Es ingenioso, ¿verdad? You see? It's very handy. It's a pair of skates with a built-in engine. What do you think? It's ingenious, isn't it? *

prado

prado
['prado] n m
meadow, field

las vacas están en el prado the cows are in the meadow

▶ **pradera**
[pra'dera] n f
meadow, grassland

precio

precio
['preθjo] n m
price

¿me puede decir el precio de este vestido? can you tell me the price of this dress?

precioso

precioso, a
[pre'θjoso, a] adj
1. precious,

...precioso

valuable

metales preciosos
precious metals

2. lovely, beautiful
* Mientras tanto...
Meanwhile...
Papá, mira, he encontrado unas tijeras preciosas... ¿Te gustan? Daddy, look, I've found a lovely pair of scissors... Do you like them?
¡Oh! ¡sí! ¡mucho! Oh! Yes! Very much! *

preciso

preciso, a
[pre'θiso, a] adj
1. precise, exact

2. necessary

3. Idiom
es preciso que duermas you must sleep

▶ **precisamente**
[preθisa'mente] adv
exactly, just

no eres precisamente un experto you're

not exactly an expert

preferir

preferir
[prefe'rir] v t
to prefer

prefiero gaseosa a agua mineral I prefer lemonade to mineral water

prefiero quedarme

...preferir

aquí antes que ir al cine I prefer to stay here rather than go to the cinema

▶ **preferencia**
[prefe'renθja] n f
preference

▶ **preferentemente**
[preferente'mente] adv
preferably

▶ **preferido, a**
[prefe'rido] adj
favourite

pregunta

pregunta
[pre'ɣunta] n f
question

* ¿Alguna pregunta más? Any more questions? *

hacer una pregunta
to ask a question

▶ **preguntar, preguntarse**
[preɣun'tar, se]
I. v i & v t
to ask

...pregunta

II. *v pr*
to wonder

premio

premio
['premjo] *n m*
prize

*el premio Nóbel de
la paz* the Nobel Peace
Prize

...premio

el premio gordo first
prize

prenda

prenda (de vestir)
['prenda] *n f*
article of clothing

*siempre lleva unas
prendas preciosas*
she always wears lovely
clothes

prensa

prensa
['prensa] *n f*
1. press

una prensa de uvas
a wine press

*el libro está en
prensa* the book is in
press

2. press,
newspapers
*una conferencia/
rueda de prensa* a
press conference

Tintín lee la prensa

* *Rrrring* Rrrring
Tintín lee la prensa.
Tintin is reading the
paper. *

*tiene muy buena
prensa* she gets a very
good press

preocupar

**preocupar,
preocuparse**
[preoku'par, se]
I. *v t*
to worry

*no le preocupa en lo
más mínimo* he isn't
the least worried about it

II. *v pr*
to worry

no te preocupes don't
worry

preparar

**preparar,
prepararse**
[prepa'rar, se]
I. *v t*
to prepare,
to make

*voy a preparar la
cena* I'm going to make
supper

II. *v pr*
to get ready,
to prepare (one-
self)

*Prepárate a pasar la
noche en esta cama,
Milú... Te la he impro-
visado con la tela del
paracaídas.*

* *Prepárate a pasar
la noche en esta ca-
ma, Milú... Te la he
improvisado con la
tela del paracaídas.*
Get ready to spend the
night in this bed, Snowy...
I've made it up for you with
the parachute material. *

presa

presa
['presa] *n f*
1. capture, loot,
prey

un ave de presa a
bird of prey

2. dam
*hay un lago artificial
detrás de esta presa*
there is an artificial lake
behind this dam

prescindir

prescindir
[presθin'dir] *v i*
to do without

*no podemos pres-
cindir de su ayuda*
we cannot do without their
help

presencia

*Señora Yamilah, voy a señalar a
una de las personas que presencian
el espectáculo, al azar...*
Vale.

presencia
[pre'senθja] *n f*
presence

en presencia de in the
presence of

▶ **presenciar**
[presen'θjar] *v t*
to witness, to see,
to watch

* *Señora Yamilah,
voy a señalar a una
de las personas que
presencian el es-*

pectáculo, al azar...
Mrs Yamilah, I'm going to
point to one of the people
watching the show, at
random...
Vale. All right. *

presentar

presentar
[presen'tar] *v t*
to present,
to introduce

preso

preso, a
['preso, a]
I. adj
under arrest, caught

* *Ahora estás preso... Al menor gesto...* Now you're caught... One move from you and... *

II. n
prisoner

prestar

prestar, prestarse
[pres'tar, se]
I. v t
1. to lend

¿me prestas un boli? can you lend me a pen?

2. Idiom
prestar atención to pay attention

II. v pr
to lend oneself to

la situación se presta a muchas interpretaciones the situation lends itself to many interpretations

presumido

presumido, a
[presu'miðo, a] adj
conceited

presumir

presumir
[presu'mir] v i
1. to be conceited, to boast

2. Idiom
* *Esta noche, Milú, te llevo a cazar un leopardo...* Tonight, Snowy, I'll take you on a leopard hunt...
Presume de listo, pero ya verá, ya... He thinks he's clever, but he'll see... *

...presumir

presupuesto

presupuesto
[presu'pwesto] n m
budget

pretender

pretender
[preten'der] v t
to try, to mean, to intend

* *¿Y usted pretende atravesar este río así? ¡Es una locura!*

...pretender

And you mean to cross this river like that? It's madness! *

pretexto

pretexto
[pre'testo] n m
pretext, excuse

bajo ningún pretexto under no pretext

primavera

primavera
[prima'βera] n f
spring

en (la) primavera in (the) spring

primero

primero, primer, a
[pri'mer, o, a]
I. adj num & n
1. first

...primero

la primera vez the first time

llegó el primero he was first

viajar en primera to travel first class

2. Idiom
a primeros de siglo at the beginning of the century

II. adv
first(ly)

primero, vamos a repasar lo que hemos hecho first, let's revise what we've done

primo

primo, a
['primo. a] n
cousin

princesa

princesa
[prin'θesa] n f
princess

príncipe

príncipe
['prinθipe] n m
prince

el Príncipe Azul Prince Charming

principio

principio
[prin'θipjo] n m
1. beginning

volvamos al principio let's go back to the beginning

2. Idiom
el principio de muchos males the thin end of the wedge

3. principle
* *Nuestro método de investigación se*

...principio

basa en un principio fundamental: no llamar la atención... Our method of inquiry is based on a fundamental principle: don't attract attention...
Yo aún diría más: no llamar la atención... To be precise: don't attract attention... *

4. Idiom
sin principios unprincipled

prisa

prisa
['prisa] n f
1. hurry, haste

2. Idiom
¡date prisa! hurry up!

* *Pero bueno, ¿qué pasa?* Hey, what's going on?
¡Date prisa, Milú! Hurry up, Snowy!
¡Guau! Bow-wow! *

lo siento pero tengo prisa I'm afraid I'm in a hurry

...prisa

¡de prisa! move!

probar

probar, probarse
[pro'βar, se]
I. v t
1. to prove

esto no prueba nada this doesn't prove anything

2. to try (on)

...probar

pruébalo try it (on)

3. to try, taste
* *¿Esto se come?... ¿Es bueno? ¿Puedo probarlo?* Is this edible?... Is it nice? May I try it?
Sí, señor, sí. Yes, sir, yes. *

II. v pr
to try on

voy a probarme este vestido I'm going to try this dress on

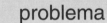

problema

problema
[pro'βlema] n m
problem

espero que no surjan problemas I hope no problems arise

producir

producir, producirse
[proðu'θir, se]

...producir

I. v t
to produce

España produce mucho vino Spain produces a lot of wine

II. v pr
to happen, to take place, to arise

se produjeron varios cambios several changes took place

profundidad

profundidad
[profundi'ðað] n f
depth

* *A cien metros de profundidad...* A hundred metres down... *

▶ **profundo, a**
[pro'funðo, a] adj
deep

estos peces se encuentran en aguas muy profundas these fish are found in very deep waters

A cien metros de profundidad...

programa

programa
[pro'ɣrama] n m
programme

* *En el programa de hoy, la divina Bianca Castafiore, considerada como la mejor cantante del mundo...* In today's programme, the divine Bianca Castafiore, considered to be the best female singer in the world... *

P

...programa

▶ **programar**
[proɣra'mar] *v t*
to programme

*el vídeo está pro-
gramado para apa-
garse a las diez* the
video is programmed to
turn itself off at ten o'clock

progresar

progresar
[proɣre'sar] *v i*
to progress

▶ **progreso**
[pro'ɣreso] *n m*
progress, advance

*los progresos tecno-
lógicos* the advances in
technology

prohibir

prohibir
[proï'βir] *v t*
1. to prohibit,
to forbid

* *Está prohibido
beber alcohol en el
cohete, pero me da
igual...* It is forbidden to
drink alcohol in the rocket,
but I don't care... *

2. Idiom
se prohibe fumar no
smoking

prójimo

prójimo
['proximo] *n m*
neighbour,
fellow creature

promesa

promesa
[pro'mesa] *n f*
promise

*cumplir una pro-
mesa* to keep a promise

...promesa

*faltar a una prome-
sa* to break a promise

▶ **prometer**
[prome'ter] *v t*
to promise

* *¡Pssst! Estoy aquí,
señores...* Psst! I'm
here, gentlemen...
*¿Lo ve? Había pro-
metido que ven-
dría...* You see? He
promised to come... *

pronto

pronto
['pronto]
I. *adv*
1. early, soon

*es demasiado pron-
to para saberlo* it's
too soon/early to know

2. Idiom
de pronto suddenly

* *¡Hasta pronto!* See
you soon! *

*lo más pronto posi-
ble* as soon as possible

...pronto

*tan pronto como
lleguemos...* as soon
as we arrive...

II. *adj*
prompt
*una respuesta pron-
ta* a prompt reply

pronunciar

pronunciar
[pronun'θjar] *v t*
to pronounce

propina

propina
[pro'pina] *n f*
tip

* *Plac* Plip
*Lo siento, no acepto
esta clase de
propina...* I'm sorry, I
don't accept tips like
this...
*¡Caramba! Le he
dado una moneda
falsa.* Wow! I gave him a
dud coin. *

proponer

**proponer,
proponerse**
[propo'ner, se]
I. *v t*
to propose,
to suggest

* *Mi querido Tintín...
Mire, lo he pensado
bien y le propongo
una solución amisto-
sa... Sí, sí, con toda
sinceridad, puede
usted creerme...* My
dear Tintin... Look, I've
thought it over properly
and I propose a friendly

...proponer

Mi querido Tintín...
Mire, lo he pensado
bien y le propongo
una solución amisto-
sa... Sí, sí, con toda
sinceridad, puede
usted creerme...

¿Ah sí?...

solution... Yes, yes, quite
sincerely, you can believe
me...
¿Ah sí?... Can I?... *

II. *v pr*
to plan, to intend

proteger

proteger
[prote'xer] *v t*
to protect

provincia

provincia
[pro'βinθja] *n f*
province

próximo

próximo, a
['proksimo, a] *adj*
next, near

la próxima parada
the next stop

proyecto

proyecto
[pro'jecto] *n m*
project, plan

cambiar de proyecto
to change one's plans

prudencia

prudencia
[pru'denθja] *n f*
care, prudence

...prudencia

▶ **prudente**
[pru'dente] *adj*
prudent, careful

*sé prudente con la
bebida; tienes que
conducir* be careful with
the drink; you have to drive

publicidad

publicidad
[publiθi'ðað] *n f*
1. publicity

...publicidad

2. advertising
*una agencia de
publicidad* an advertis-
ing agency

público

público
['publiko]
I. *adj*
f **pública** ['publika]
1. public

...público

2. Idiom
hacer público to
publicize

II. *n m*
public, audience

*el museo se abrirá
al público a las diez*
the museum will be open
to the public at ten o'clock

pueblo

pueblo
['pweβlo] *n m*
1. town, village

* *Kiltoch es un
pueblo encantador.*
Kiltoch is a charming
village. *

2. people, nation
el pueblo español the
Spanish people

Kiltoch es un pueblo encantador.

puente

PAM
PAM

Tintín salta del puente

puente
['pwente] *n m*
bridge

* *Pam* Bang
*Tintín salta del puen-
te.* Tintin has jumped off
the bridge. *

puerta

puerta
['pwerta] *n f*
door

...puerta

RRRRRING

Llama a la puerta

una puerta giratoria
a revolving door

* *Rrrring* Rrrring
Llama a la puerta.
He's ringing at the door. *

puerto

puerto
['pwerto] *n m*
1. port, harbour
(*Am*: harbor)

...puerto

En el puerto de Akureyri...

* *En el puerto de Akureyri...* In the port of Akureyri... *

2. (mountain) pass
el puerto está cerrado a causa de la nieve the pass is closed because of the snow

pues

pues
[pwes]
I. *adv*
well

pues no lo sé well, I don't know

II. *conj*
for, since, as

no pude ir, pues no sabía cómo llegar I couldn't go as I didn't know how to get there

puesta

puesta
['pwesta] *n f*
1. putting, placing

2. Idiom
puesta del sol sunset

puesta en escena staging

la puesta en libertad de los presos the release of the prisoners

puesto

puesto
['pwesto] *n m*
1. place, position

2. post, job

3. (market) stall

puesto que

puesto que
['pwestoque] *conj*
since, as

pulsera

pulsera
[pul'sera] *n f*
bracelet

¡ Esta pulsera de oro es magnífica! Y además encuentro que me va muy bien... Voy a ver qué me dicen los amigos...

* *¡Esta pulsera de oro es magnífica! Y además encuentro que me va muy bien... Voy a ver qué me dicen los amigos...* This gold bracelet is magnificent! What's more, it's just my size... I'm going to see what my friends say... *

punta

punta
['punta] *n f*
1. end, tip

lo tengo en la punta de la lengua it's on the tip of my tongue

2. Idiom
sacar punta al lápiz to sharpen one's pencil

punto

punto
['punto] *n m*
1. point

hay varios puntos para discutir there are several points to discuss

otro punto de vista another point of view

2. dot

3. knitting

puñado

puñado
[pu'nado] *n m*
handful

puñetazo

puñetazo
[puɲe'taθo] *n m*
punch

* *Tintín le da un puñetazo.* Tintin is punching him. *

...puñetazo

Tintín le da un puñetazo.

puño

puño
['puɲo] *n m*
1. fist

2. cuff
los puños de la camisa the shirtcuffs

3. handle
el paraguas tenía el puño de plata the umbrella had a silver handle

puro

puro
['puro]
I. *n m*
cigar

II. *adj*
f pura ['pura]
1. pure

2. Idiom
es la pura verdad it's the plain/solemn truth

que

El día que los gitanos llegaron a Moulinsart...

...que

que
[ke] *pron rel*
1. who, whom, which, that

el hombre que vimos ayer es mi tío the man (that/who) we saw yesterday is my uncle

la carta que mandé no llegó the letter (that/which) I sent did not arrive

aquel hombre, que es médico, vive solo that man, who is a doctor, lives on his own

aquel hombre, a quien saludamos ayer, es muy conocido that man, whom we said hello to yesterday, is very well-known

el castillo, que domina el pueblo, *es del siglo XIII* the castle, which dominates the town, is thirteenth-century

2. Idiom

tengo mucho que hacer I have a lot to do

* *El día que los gitanos llegaron a Moulinsart...* The day (that/when) the gipsies arrived at Marlinspike... *

▶**el que, la que, los que, las que**
pron
1. he who, those who, the one(s) that

los que lleguen tarde no podrán entrar those who arrive late won't be allowed in

2. who(m), which, that

la silla en la que estás sentado está rota the chair (which/that) you are sitting on is broken

el hombre con el que hablamos no es de aquí the man (whom/that we spoke to is not from here/the man to whom we spoke is not from here

...que

el asunto del que te hablo es muy importante the matter (which/that) I am talking to you about is very important

la dirección a la que has escrito es incorrecta the address (which/that) you wrote to is wrong

* *Pam Pam Pam* Knock Knock Knock
Cierra el armario en el que esconde el

whisky. He is closing the cupboard in which he hides the whisky. *

el pueblo por el que pasamos era muy poco atractivo the town through which we passed was very unattractive

▶ **lo que** → LO

Cierra el armario en el que esconde el whisky.

que

que
[ke] *conj*
1. that

dijo que no venía he said (that) he wasn't coming

2. than
el profesor es más delgado que el capitán the Professor is thinner than the Captain

3. because
no viene, que no le

gustan las fiesta he's not coming because he doesn't like parties

4. Idiom
dile que pase tell him to come in

qué

qué
[ke]
I. *pron interr & adj interr*
what, which

¿qué es eso? what's that?

¿qué cuadro te gusta? which picture do you like?

II. *pron & adj*
what, which

no sé qué día vienen I don't know what day they are coming

III. *adj excl*
what a, what

¡qué día más bonito! what a lovely day!

¡qué zapatos más monos! what lovely shoes!

quebrar

quebrar
[ke'βrar] *v t*
to break

quedar

quedar, quedarse
[ke'ðar, se]
I. *v i*
1. to be left

* *¡Nos queda poco tiempo para llegar*

...quedar

¡Nos queda poco tiempo para llegar antes que Tintín!

...quedar

antes que Tintín! We haven't much time left to get there before Tintin. *

2. to arrange to meet
he quedado con él a las dos I've arranged to meet him at two

II. *v pr*
1. to stay, to remain

¡quédate aquí! stay here!

2. Idiom
te lo puedes quedar you can keep it

queja

queja
['kexa] *n f*
complaint

▶ **quejarse**
[ke'xarse] *v i*
to complain

...queja

¡Me quejaré a mi padre!

* *¡Me quejaré a mi padre!* I'll complain to my father! *

▶ **quejido**
[ke'xido] *n m*
moan, groan

quemadura

quemadura
[kema'ðura] *n f*
burn

...quemadura

▶ **quemar, quemarse**
[ke'mar, se]
v i, v t & v pr
to burn

* *¡Perfecto! Las ataduras se queman...* Perfect! The rope's burning...
Voy a llevar a un muchacho a su hospital... Es muy peligroso... I'm going to bring a boy to your hospital... He's very dangerous... *

...quemadura

querer

querer
[ke'rer] *v i & v t*
1. to want, to wish

¿quiere algo más?
do you want anything
else?

2. to love
te quiero mucho
I love you very much

▶ **querido, a**
[ke'rido, a] *adj*
dear, beloved

querida Marta dear
Marta

queso

queso
['keso] *n m*
cheese

queso de bola Dutch
cheese

quien

quien, quienes
[kien, 'kienes] *pron rel*
who, whom

...quien

*los amigos con
quienes fui de
excursión* the friends
with whom I went on the
excursion

* *Así que este es el
joven de quien me
ha hablado el jefe...*
So this is the young man
(who) the boss spoke to
me about...
*Venga conmigo,
señor...* Come this way,
sir...
¡Muy bien! Very good! *

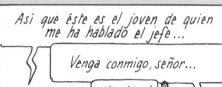

quién

quién
[kien] *pron interr*
who

¿quién es? who is she?

quieto

quieto, a
['kieto, a] *adj*
still

¡estate quieto! keep
still!

química

química
['kimika] *n f*
chemistry

quinta

quinta
['kinta] *n f*
1. country house,
villa

2. call-up (*para el
servicio militar*)

quitar

quitar, quitarse
[ki'tar, se] *v t & v pr*
1. to take away

2. to remove,
to take off
* *Hay que quitarse
los zapatos en la
mezquita.* You must
take your shoes off in the
mosque. *

quitasol

quitasol
[kita'sol] *n m*
parasol

quizás

quizás
[ki'θas] *adv*
perhaps, maybe

quizás no venga
perhaps he won't come

rabia

rabia
[ˈraβja] *n f*
1. rabies

* *¡Salga del taxi! ¡Este perro tiene la rabia!* Out of the taxi! This dog's got rabies! *

2. fury, rage

3. Idiom
me da rabia eso that makes my blood boil

rábano

rábano
[ˈraβano] *n m*
radish

rabo

rabo
[ˈraβo] *n m*
tail

Milú menea el rabo Snowy is wagging his tail

radiador

radiador
[raðjaˈðor] *n m*
radiator

pon los radiadores turn the radiators on

radio

radio
[ˈraðjo]
I. *n m*
radius

...radio

en un radio de diez kilómetros alrededor del pueblo within a radius of ten kilometres round the town

II. *n f*
radio

* *¡Estoy salvado! ¡Una radio!...* I'm saved! A radio!...*

...radio

raíz

raíz
[raˈiθ] *n f*
1. root

2. Idiom
echar raíces to take root

a raíz de as a result of

a raíz de su discusión, se pelearon as a result of their argument, they fought

rama

rama
[ˈrama] *n f*
1. branch

2. Idiom
andar por las ramas to beat about the bush

ramo

ramo
[ˈramo] *n m*
bunch (of flowers),

...ramo

...ramo

bouquet

* *¡Qué ramo más bonito! ¡Gracias profesor!* What a lovely bunch of flowers! Thank you, Professor! *Smak* Smack *

rana

rana
['rana] *n f*
frog

rancho

rancho
['rantʃo] *n m*
ranch

* *¡Este es el rancho que buscamos, Tintín!* This is the ranch we are looking for, Tintin! *

rápido

rápido, a
['rapiðo] *adj*
fast, rapid

¡Éste es el rancho que buscamos, Tintín!

...rápido

el avión es más rápido que el tren the plane is faster than the train

raro

raro, a
['raro, a] *adj*
1. rare, uncommon

esta especie es muy rara this species is very rare

...raro

2. strange, odd
¡qué bicho más raro! what a strange animal!

rascacielos

rascacielos
['raska'θjelos] *n m inv*
skyscraper

rastro

rastro
['rastro] *n m*
track, trail, scent

* *¡Miren! Me parece que Milú ha encontrado una pista... Sí... ¡Ha olfateado el rastro de Tchang!* Look! I think Snowy has picked up the trail... Yes... He's caught scent of Chang! *

¡Miren! Me parece que Milú ha encontrado una pista... Sí... ¡Ha olfateado el rastro de Tchang!

rata

rata
['rata] *n f*
rat

* *¡Cuántas ratas! ¿De dónde vendrán? Parecen aterrorizadas...* What a lot of rats! Where can they have come from? They look terrified... *

...rata

¡Cuántas ratas! ¿De dónde vendrán? Parecen aterrorizadas...

rato

rato
['rato] *n m*
1. while, spell

siéntate un rato sit down for a while

2. Idiom
a ratos now and then

¡hasta otro rato! see you again! (*Am*: so long!)

matar/pasar el rato to pass the time

ratón

ratón
['raton] *n m*
mouse
pl mice

* *¿Logrará cazar al ratón?* Will he manage to catch the mouse? *

los ratones tienen miedo del gato the mice are afraid of the cat

...ratón

¿ Logrará cazar al ratón ?

raya

raya
['r̄aja] *n f*
1. line

2. stripe

3. Idiom
se hace la raya a la izquierda he parts his hair on the left

una camisa a rayas a striped shirt

pasarse de la raya to go too far

rayo

El rayo devasta la habitación.

rayo
['r̄aλo] *n m*
1. ray, beam

un rayo de sol a ray of sunshine

2. (flash of) lightning
* *El rayo devasta la habitación.* The lightning is devastating the room. *

razón

razón
['r̄a'θon] *n f*
1. reason

¿cuál es la razón de esto? what is the reason for this?

2. Idiom
tener razón to be right

no tener razón to be wrong

sin razón for no reason at all

reaccionar

reaccionar
['r̄eakθjo'nar] *v i*
to react

* *¡Rataplán! ¡Rataplán!* Tarum-tum-tum! Tarum-tum-tum!
¡Tampoco reacciona! Still no reaction!
No sé qué hacer... I don't know what to do...*

▶ **reacción**
['r̄eak'θjon] *n f*
reaction

real

real
['r̄e'al] *adj*
1. real

2. royal
el palacio real the royal palace

realidad

realidad
['r̄eali'ðað] *n f*
reality

enfrentémonos a la realidad let's face reality

rebaja

rebaja
['r̄e'βaxa] *n f*
1. discount,

...rebaja

reduction, reduced price

2. Idiom
las rebajas the sales

rebanada

rebanada
['r̄eβa'naða] *n f*
slice

rebelarse

...rebelarse

rebelarse
[ťeβe'larse] *v pr*
to rebel

▶ **rebelde**
[ťe'βelðe] *adj & n*
rebel

* *Los rebeldes han volado el oleoducto.* The rebels have blown up the pipeline. *

recado

recado
[ťe'kaðo] *n m*
message, errand

¿quiere dejar algún recado? do you want to leave a message?

* *¿Puede dar un recado al profesor?* Can you give the Professor a message? *¿El profesor Tornasol? Debe estar en su habitación: su llave no está aquí...*

¿ Puede dar un recado al profesor ?

¿ El profesor Tornasol ? Debe estar en su habitación : su llave no está aquí...

...recado

Professor Calculus? He must be in his room: his key isn't here... *

receta

receta
[ťe'θeta] *n f*
1. recipe
2. prescription

recibidor

recibidor
[ťeθiβi'ðor] *n m*
entrance hall

están hablando en el recibidor they are talking in the entrance hall

recién

recién
[ťe'θjen] *adv*
1. recently, newly, just

...recién

una casa recién construida a newly-built house

2. Idiom
recién pintado wet paint

recién casado newly-wed, just married

un huevo recién puesto a new-laid egg

▶ **reciente**
[ťe'θjente] *adj*
recent

los sucesos recientes recent events

recitar

recitar
[ťeθi'tar] *v t*
to recite

recitó una poesía de Lorca she recited a poem by Lorca

recoger

recoger
[ťeco'xer] *v t*
to pick up,

* *¿No puedes recoger las naranjas?* Can't you pick the oranges up? *¡Aaaay!* Ow! *

...recoger

¿ No puedes recoger las naranjas?

¡Aaaay!

recompensa

recompensa
[ťekom'pensa] *n f*
reward

recordar

recordar
[ťekor'ðar]
I. *v i & v t*
to remember, to recall, to recollect

...recordar

* *Recuerda los buenos ratos que hemos pasado con Tchang. ¡Cuando pienso que ha desaparecido...!* Remember the good times we've had with Chang. To think he's disappeared...! *

II. *v t*
to remind, to recall

esta voz me recuerda a alguien this voice reminds me of someone

Recuerda los buenos ratos que hemos pasado con Tchang. ¡ Cuando pienso que ha desaparecido...!

recorrer

recorrer
[r̄eko'r̄er] *v t*
to go over, to cover

Mientras tanto...
Meanwhile...
Hemos recorrido toda la región y no los hemos encontrado. We've gone over the whole area and haven't found them. *

▶ **recorrido**
[r̄eko'r̄iðo] *n m*
run, journey, route

el recorrido turístico promete ser interesante the tourist route should be interesting

recortar

recortar
[r̄ekor'tar] *v t*
to cut out, to trim

* *¡El capitán Haddock y la señora*

...recortar

Castafiore!... Voy a recortar las fotos de esta revista. Captain Haddock and Signora Castafiore!... I'm going to cut out the photos in this magazine. *

▶ **recortable**
[r̄ekor'table] *n m*
cut out

▶ **recorte**
[re'korte] *n m*
cutting

rectángulo

rectángulo
[r̄ek'tangulo] *n m*
rectangle

recto

recto
['r̄ekto]
I. *adj*
f recta ['r̄ekta]
straight

una línea recta a straight line

...recto

II. *adv*
straight on

siga recto go straight on

recuerdo

recuerdo
[r̄e'kwerðo] *n m*
1. memory, recollection

...recuerdo

2. souvenir, keepsake
me trajo un recuerdo de Mallorca he brought me a souvenir from Majorca

3. Idiom
dale recuerdos de mi parte give him my regards

* «...*Así pues, he aceptado y llegaré en el avión de las 19h30. Espero con gran impaciencia el momento de verle... Muchos recuerdos, Tchang.» Tchang viene a Europa, ¡fantástico!...* «...So I've accepted and I'll be arriving on the 19.30 plane. I can't wait to see you... All the best, Chang.» Chang's coming to Europe. Fantastic!... *

redondo

redondo, a
[re'ðondo] *adj*
round

referirse

referirse
[r̄efe'rirse] *v pr*
to refer

el texto se refiere a la guerra the text refers to the war

reflejar

reflejar
[r̄efle'xar] *v t*
to reflect

la obra refleja las costumbres de la época the work reflects the customs of the period

▶ **reflejo**
[r̄e'flexo] *n m*
reflection

reflexionar

reflexionar
[r̄efleksjo'nar] *v i*
to reflect, to think

* *Tendría que reflexionar un poco...* I'll have to think a little... *

▶ **reflexión**
[r̄eflek'sjon] *n f*
reflection, meditation

refrán

refrán
[r̄e'fran] *n m*
proverb, saying

¿cómo dice el refrán? how does the saying go?

refresco

refresco
[r̄e'fresko] *n m*
refreshment, drink

...refresco

* *¡Profesor! ¡Tintín! ¿Les apetece un refresco?* Professor! Tintin! Do you fancy a drink?
El cielo se está despejando... The sky's clearing... *

refugiarse

refugiarse
[ˈrefuˈxiarse] *v i*
to shelter,

...refugiarse

to take shelter

▶ **refugio**
[ˈreˈfuxio] *n m*
shelter, refuge

regalar

regalar
[ˈreˈɣalar] *v t*
to give (*as a present*)

...regalar

▶ **regalo**
[ˈreˈɣalo] *n m*
present

regar

regar
[ˈreˈɣar] *v i & v t*
to water

está regando las plantas he's watering the plants

* *¿Quién riega?...*

...regar

¿Se piensan acaso que soy una flor...? Who's throwing water about?... What do they think I am? A flower?... *

regresar

regresar
[ˈreɣreˈsar] *v i*
to return,
to go back

regresamos el miér-

...regresar

coles we're going back on Wednesday

▶ **regreso**
[ˈreˈɣreso] *n m*
return

el viaje de regreso the return journey

reina

reina
[ˈreina] *n f*
queen

reír

...reír

reír, reírse
[ˈreˈir, se] *v i & v pr*
1. to laugh

no te rías de mí don't laugh at me

* *¡Ja! ¡Ja! Déjeme que me ría... Así que quiere usted ir a la luna... ¡Qué bromista es usted!... ¡Y lo dice como si fuera la cosa más natural del mundo!* Ha ha! Excuse me laugh-

ing... So you want to go to the moon... What a joker you are!... And you say it as if it were the most natural thing in the world! *

2. Idiom
reírse a carcajadas to roar with laughter

reja

reja
[ˈrexa] *n f*
grating, grid, bars

le metieron entre rejas they put him behind bars

relámpago

relámpago
[ˈreˈlampaɣo] *n m*
(flash of) lightning

...relámpago

Un relámpago...

* *Crac* Crack
Un relámpago... A flash of lightning... *

relatar

relatar
[ˈrelaˈtar] *v t*
to relate, to tell

relató los sucesos she told us what had happened

relieve

relieve
[ṝe'ljeβe] *n m*
1. relief

el relieve de la Península the relief of the Peninsula

2. Idiom
poner de relieve to emphasize, to point out

religión

religión
[ṝeli'xjon] *n f*
religion

* *Son novicios probablemente... Juegan con cometas... ¿De qué religión deben de ser?* They're probably novices... They're playing with kites... I wonder what religion they belong to. *

Son novicios probablemente... juegan con cometas... ¿De qué religión deben de ser?

reloj

reloj
[ṝe'lox] *n m*
1. clock

el reloj marca las cinco the clock says five o'clock

2. watch
mi reloj siempre adelanta my watch is always fast

remar

remar
[ṝe'mar] *v i*
to row

* *Han remado hasta Tintín.* They have rowed up to Tintin. *

▶ **remo**
[ṝe'mo] *n m*
1. oar

2. Idiom
conducir un bote a remo to row a boat

...remar

Han remado hasta Tintín.

remedio

remedio
[ṝe'meðjo] *n m*
1. remedy, cure

2. Idiom
no tener más remedio que to have no alternative but to

no tuvimos más remedio que volver a casa we had no alternative but to return home

remordimiento

remordimiento
[ṝemorði'mjento] *n m*
remorse, pangs of conscience

* *En el cohete...* In the rocket...
Vamos a morir todos... por mi culpa... Los remordimientos me agobian... We're all going to die... it's all my fault... I'm overcome with remorse... *

En el cohete...

Vamos a morir todos... por mi culpa... Los remordimientos me agobian...

---

renunciar

renunciar
[ṝenun'θjar] *v i & v t*
to renounce, to give up, to drop

tuvo que renunciar a sus proyectos he had to give up his plans

reñir

reñir
[ṝe'ɲir]
I. *v i*

...reñir

to argue, to fight

ha reñido con la novia he's had a fight with his girlfriend

II. *v t*
to tell off, to scold

su padre le riñó por llegar tarde his father told him off for being late

reparar

reparar
[ṝepa'rar]
I. *v t*
to repair, to mend, to fix

hay que reparar el tejado we must repair the roof

II. *v i*
to notice, to observe

no había reparado en la hora I hadn't noticed the time

repartir

repartir
[ṝepar'tir] *v t*
to distribute, to hand out

reparte las hojas hand out the paper

▶ **reparto**
[ṝepar'to] *n m*
delivery

sólo hay un reparto de cartas por día there is only one delivery of letters per day

repasar

repasar
[ṝepa'sar] *v i & v t*
to revise, to check, to go over

vamos a repasarlo otra vez let's go over it again

▶ **repaso**
[ṝe'paso] *n m*
revision, check

(de) repente

(de) repente
[(de) ˈreˈpente] *adv*
suddenly

* *Pof Pof* Plump Plump
De repente, el profesor llegó como un bólido y los hizo caer. Suddenly, the Professor fell like a thunderbolt and knocked them over. *

De repente, el profesor llegó como un bólido y los hizo caer.

repetir

repetir
[ˈrepeˈtir] *v t*
1. to repeat

* *¿Puede repetirlo? No estoy muy seguro de haber entendido bien...* Could you repeat that? I'm not sure I've fully understood... *

2. to have a second helping

---

reportaje

reportaje
[ˈreporˈtaxe] *n m*
report, news item

* *En este reportaje exclusivo, están viendo ustedes a los más extraordinarios acróbatas aéreos: la pareja inseparable Hernández y Fernández realiza ante nuestros ojos un peligroso rizo...* In this exclusive report, you are

watching the most extraordinary aerial acrobats: the inseparable pair Thompson and Thomson are dangerously looping the loop before our very eyes... *

reportero

reportero, a
[ˈreporˈtero, a] *n*
reporter

representar

representar
[ˈrepresenˈtar] *v t*
1. to stand for,
to represent,
to show, to depict

el cuadro representa una escena rural the painting depicts a country scene

2. to perform,
to act, to play
representar un papel to play a part

3. to mean

---

reproche

reproche
[ˈreproˈtʃe] *n m*
reproach, reproof

resbalar

resbalar
[ˈresβaˈlar] *v i*
to slip

* *¡Cuidado! Yo también he resbalado...* Be careful! I slipped, too... *

...resbalar

resfriarse

resfriarse
[ˈresˈfriarse] *v pr*
to catch (a) cold

abrígate, si no, te resfriarás wrap up, otherwise you'll catch cold

▶ **resfriado**
[ˈresˈfriado] *n m*
cold

medicamentos contra el resfriado medicines for colds

resistir

resistir
[ˈresisˈtir] *v i & v t*
to resist,
to withstand,
to bear

no puedo resistir el frío I can't bear the cold

resolver

resolver
[ˈresolˈβer] *v t*
to solve, to resolve

...resolver

resolvimos el problema sin dificultad we solved the problem without any trouble

* **Gracias a este péndulo, resolveremos el enigma de la desaparición de nuestros amigos.** Thanks to this pendulum, we'll solve the enigma of the disappearance of our friends. *

Gracias a este péndulo, resolveremos el enigma de la desaparición de nuestros amigos.

respecto

respecto
[r̄es'pekto] *adv*
Idiom

a ese respecto on that score

al respecto about the matter under discussion

(con) respecto a/de with regard to

respetar

respetar
[r̄espe'tar] *v t*
to respect

los niños deben respetar a los ancianos children should respect elderly people

▶ **respeto**
[r̄es'peto] *n m*
respect

el respeto a los derechos humanos respect for human rights

respirar

respirar
[r̄espi'rar] *v i & v t*
to breathe (in)

respira hondo breathe in deeply

* **¡Pobre Milú! Dígame, doctor, está vivo, ¿verdad? Por favor, doctor, su corazón late, ¿no?** Poor Snowy! Tell me, doctor, he's alive, isn't he? Please, doctor, his heart's beating, isn't it? **Tranquilícese, lo oi-**

¡Pobre Milú! Dígame doctor, está vivo, ¿verdad? Por favor, doctor, su corazón late ¿no?

Tranquilícese, lo oigo respirar.

go respirar. Don't worry, I can hear him breathing. *

restar

restar
[r̄es'tar] *v t*
to take away, to subtract

▶ **resta**
[r̄es'ta] *n f*
subtraction

restaurante

restaurante
[r̄estaŭ'rante] *n m*
restaurant

* **En el restaurante...** In the restaurant... *

restaurar

restaurar
[r̄estaŭ'rar] *v t*
to restore

En el restaurante...

resultar

resultar
[r̄esul'tar] *v t*
1. to prove to be, to turn out to be, to be

resulta difícil calcularlo it is difficult to calculate

* **Como pueden ver, este mecanismo resulta muy eficaz...** As you can see, this device proves to be very effective... *

Como pueden ver, este mecanismo resulta muy eficaz...

2. Idiom
resulta que... it seems that...

▶ **resultado**
[r̄esul'taðo] *n m*
result

resumir

resumir
[r̄esu'mir] *v t*
to summarize, to sum up

...resumir

▶ **resumen**
[re'sumen] *n m*
summary

retrasar

retrasar, retrasarse
[r̄etra'sar, se]
I. *v t*
to delay, to postpone

...retrasar

retrasaron la fecha de la boda they postponed the wedding day

II. v i & v pr
to be late,
to be slow

mi reloj retrasa my watch is slow

* Se ha retrasado... He's late... *

▶ **retraso**
[ṝe'traso] n m
delay, lateness, slowness

Se ha retrasado...

retratar

retratar
[ṝetra'tar] v t
1. to paint a picture of

2. to photograph

▶ **retrato**
[ṝe'trato] n m
1. portrait

2. photograph

retroceder

retroceder
[ṝetroθe'ðer] v i
to go back,
to retreat

reunir

reunir, reunirse
[ṝeǔ'nir, se]
I. v t
1. to join together

...reunir

2. Idiom
reunir fondos to raise money

II. v pr
to meet,
to gather together

nos reuniremos en casa de mi hermana we'll meet in my sister's house

▶ **reunión**
[ṝeǔ'njon] n f
meeting

¡ La reunión queda terminada !
Yo estoy de acuerdo.
Yo también...

* ¡La reunión queda terminada! The meeting's over!
Yo estoy de acuerdo. I agree.
Yo también... So do I... *

revés

revés
[ṝe'βes] n m
1. reverse side, other side

...revés

2. Idiom
al revés the wrong way round

te has puesto el jersey al revés you've put your jersey on the wrong way round

revista

revista
[ṝe'βista] n f
magazine

...revista

¿¿ Cómo ?? ¿¿ Que me voy a casar con Bianca Castafiore ?? ¡ Esta revista no escribe más que tonterías !

*¿¿Cómo?? ¿¿Que me voy a casar con Bianca Castafiore?? ¡Esta revista no escribe más que tonterías! What?? I'm marrying Bianca Castafiore?? This magazine's full of nonsense! *

rey

rey
[ṝeǐ] n m
king

* Soy el rey de este mundo... I'm the king of this world... *

rezar

rezar
[ṝe'θar] v i & v t
to pray

Soy el rey de este mundo...

rico

rico, a
['r̄iko, a] adj
1. rich

los ricos no suelen ser humildes the rich are not usually humble

2. delicious
¡qué tarta más rica! what a delicious cake!

ridículo

ridículo, a
['r̄i'ðikulo, a] adj
ridiculous

hacer el ridículo to act ridiculous

rincón

rincón
[r̄in'kon] n m
corner (*of a room, house*)

...rincón

sentado en el rincón sitting in the corner

riña

riña
['r̄iɲa] n f
quarrel, fight

una riña callejera a street fight

río

...río

río
['r̄io] n m
river

* *¿No podíamos atravesar el río de otra manera?* Couldn't we cross the river some other way? *

riqueza

riqueza
[r̄i'keθa] n f

...riqueza

1. wealth, riches

2. richness

risa

risa
['r̄isa] n f
1. laugh, laughter

hubo risas there was laughter

2. Idiom

...risa

dar risa to amuse, to be funny

* *¡Ja! ¡Ja! ¡Ja! Esto da mucha risa, capitán... Es usted formidable por la radio; debería ser reportero...* Ha ha! This is really funny, Captain... You're incredible on the radio; you ought to be a reporter... *

mondarse de risa to split one's sides with laughing

ritmo

ritmo
['r̄itmo] n m
rhythm, rate

ritmo de crecimiento rate of growth

rizado

rizado, a
[r̄i'θaðo, a] adj
curly

...rizado

pelo rizado curly hair

▶ **rizar**
[r̄i'θar] v t
to curl

robar

robar
[r̄o'βar] v t
to rob, to steal

...robar

¡Me ha robado usted el monedero! ¡Devuélvamelo inmediatamente!

no sólo robaron un banco; también robaron un coche not only did they rob a bank; they also stole a car

* *¡Me ha robado usted el monedero! ¡Devuélvamelo inmediatamente!* You stole my purse! Give it back to me at once! *

roble

roble
['r̄oβle] n m
oak (tree)

robo

robo
['r̄oβo] n m
robbery, theft

¡esto es un robo! this is daylight robbery!

roca

roca
['ᵬoka] n f
rock

* ¿Has visto? ¡Bastaba con apartar esta roca para dejar libre este pasadizo subterráneo! Do you see that? All you have to do is pull this rock away to get into this underground tunnel. *

rodar

rodar
['ᵬo'ðar]
I. v i & v t
to roll, to wheel

la pelota de golf rodó suavemente hacia el hoyo the golf ball rolled gently towards the hole

II. v t
to shoot (a film)

* ¡Silencio! Quiet! ¡Acción! Action!

Están rodando una película.

...rodar

¿Listos?... ¡Motor! Ready?... Go! Están rodando una película. They are shooting a film. *

rodear

rodear
['ᵬoðe'ar] v t
to surround

la policía rodeó el

...rodear

banco the police surrounded the bank

le rodeó el cuello con los brazos y le estampó dos sonoros besos she put her arms around his neck and gave him two loud kisses

▶ **rodeo**
['ᵬo'ðeo] n m
detour,
roundabout way

rodilla

rodilla
['ᵬoðiλa] n f
knee

* ¡Ay! ¡Me he hecho daño en las rodillas! ¡¿Para qué sirven todos estos hilos que hay por el suelo?! Ow! I've hurt my knees! What are all these wires on the floor for?! *

rogar

rogar
['ᵬo'ɣar] v t
to beg

le rogué (que) me disculpara I begged him to excuse me

rojo

rojo, a
['ᵬoxo, a] adj
1. red

...rojo

2. Idiom
la atmósfera está al rojo vivo the atmosphere is electric

romper

romper, romperse
['ᵬom'per, se]
I. v t
1. to break

* Cling Clink

...romper

Ha roto un vaso. He's broken a glass. *

2. to tear

II. v pr
to break, to tear

se rompe con facilidad it breaks/tears easily

Ha roto un vaso.

ropa

ropa
['ropa] n f
clothes, washing

¿*dónde dejo la ropa sucia?* where shall I leave the dirty clothes?

rosa

rosa
['rosa]
I. n f

...rosa

rose

* *¡Rosas blancas!... ¡Oh! profesor ¿cómo lo ha adivinado? Son las que más me gustan... Mire, capitán...* White roses!... Oh Professor! How did you guess? They're my favourites... Look, Captain... *Ejem... Ejem...* Ahem... Ahem... *

II. *adj*
pink

la *Pantera Rosa* the Pink Panther

rostro

rostro
['rostro] n m
face

* *¡Buaaa buaaa buaaa!* Boo-hoo-hoo! *Se cubre el rostro con las manos.* She is

...rostro

Se cubre el rostro con las manos

...rostro

covering her face with her hands. *

rótulo

rótulo
['rotulo] n m
1. sign, notice

* *Hay muchos rótulos luminosos.* There are lots of illuminated signs. *

...rótulo

Hay muchos rótulos luminosos.

2. heading, inscription

rozar

rozar
[ro'θar] v t
to rub (against)

el respaldo del sillón ha rozado la pared the back of the chair has rubbed against the wall

rubio

Tintín es rubio.

rubio, a
['ruβjo, a] *adj*
blond(e), fair-haired

* *Tintín es rubio.* Tintin is fair-haired. *

rueda

rueda
['rweða] n f
wheel

una rueda de recambio a spare wheel

ruego

ruego
['rweɣo] n m
request

ruido

ruido
['rwiðo] n m
noise

¡*cuánto ruido de fondo!* what a lot of background noise!

ruina

En el castillo en ruinas...

ruina
['rwina] n f
ruin

* *En el castillo en ruinas...* In the castle in ruins/In the ruined castle... *

rumor

rumor
[ru'mor] n m
1. murmur

...rumor

2. rumour

rural

rural
[ru'ral] *adj*
rural, country

una escena rural a country scene

sábado

sábado
['saβaðo] n m
1. Saturday

2. Idiom
hacer sábado to have
a good clean-up

sábana

sábana
['saβana] n f
sheet

* *Tengo que mover
esta viga como sea.
A ver si con estas
sábanas anuda-
das...* I've got to move
this beam somehow. Let's
see if with these sheets
knotted together... *

saber

...saber

saber
[sa'βer] v i & v t
to know

* *Estoy furioso. ¿Sa-
bes lo que pienso de
todo esto?* I'm furious.
Do you know what I think
about all this?
*No, no lo sé, pero
yo también estoy
furioso...* No, I don't,
but I'm also furious... *

saborear

saborear
[saβore'ar] v t
to taste, to savour

▶ **sabor**
[sa'βor] n m
taste

un sabor a pescado
a taste of fish/a fishy taste

sacar

sacar
[sa'kar] v t
1. to take out,
to get out

* *Milú, pero ¿por
qué te empeñas en
sacar este sombrero
del agua?* Snowy, why
are you determined to get
this hat out of the water? *

2. Idiom
sacar entradas to get
tickets

sacar fotos to take
photos

sacerdote

sacerdote
[saθer'ðote] n m
priest

saco

saco
['sako] n m
bag, sack

* ¡Un saco! A sack! *

sacudir

sacudir
[saku'ðir] v t
to shake

sacude el mantel por favor shake the tablecloth, please

...sacudir

Hubo una sacudida violenta...

▶ **sacudida**
[saku'ðiða] n f
shaking, jerk, jolt

* Hubo una sacudida violenta... There was a violent jolt... *

sal

sal
[sal] n m
salt

sala

sala
['sala] n f
room

sala de estar living room

salado

salado, a
[sa'laðo, a] adj
salty, salted

cacahuetes salados salted peanuts

salida

salida
[sa'liða] n f
1. exit, way out

* A la salida de la

...salida

A la salida de la ópera...

ópera... On their way out of the opera... *

2. departure
el avión tiene la salida prevista para las cuatro the plane is due to leave at four

salir

salir
[sa'lir] v i
1. to go out,

...salir

to leave

salió de la habitación he went out of the room

salimos de Madrid a las nueve we left Madrid at nine

2. Idiom
¡sal a la calle! step outside!

salir bien/mal to go well/badly

salón

salón
[sa'lon] n m
lounge,
living room

* Estará usted mejor con el teléfono en el salón, capitán. You'll be better with the telephone in the lounge, Captain.
Gracias, Tintín, muchas gracias. Thank you, Tintin, thank you very much. *

Estará usted mejor con el teléfono en el salón, capitán.
Gracias, Tintín, muchas gracias...

saltar

saltar
[sal'tar] v i
1. to jump, leap

* ¡Tintín, no saltes! Eso está muy alto... ¡Es peligroso!... Tintin, don't jump! It's very high... It's dangerous!... ¡Ven, Milú! Come on, Snowy! *

2. to skip
has saltado una página entera you've skipped a whole page

...saltar

3. Idiom
eso salta a la vista that's obvious

► **salto**
['salto] *n m*
1. jump, leap, bound

2. Idiom
de repente dio un salto he suddenly leapt

salto de agua waterfall

* ¡Hola! Estoy detrás del salto de agua... ¿No me oyen?... ¡Capitán!... ¡Zorrino! Hey! I'm behind the waterfall... Can't you hear me?... ¡Captain!... Zorrino! *

llevo una semana comiendo a salto de mata I've been eating irregularly for a week

salud

salud
[sa'luð] *n f*
health

gozar de buena salud to enjoy good health

saludar

saludar
[salu'ðar] *v i & v t*
to say hello,

...saludar

to greet

salúdale de mi parte say hello to him for me/give him my regards

► **saludo**
[sa'luðo] *n m*
1. greeting

saludos de Tintín greetings/regards from Tintin

2. salute

salvación

salvación
[salβa'θjon] *n f*
salvation, rescue

la salvación de los náufragos the rescue of the shipwrecked

salvaje

salvaje
[sal'βaxe] *adj & n*
savage, wild

salvar

salvar
[sal'βar] *v t*
1. to save, to rescue

* ¿Por qué me has salvado la vida?... No sabes siquiera quién soy... Why have you saved my life?... You don't even know who I am... *

2. to cross, to jump over

...salvar

salvamos el arroyo we jumped over the stream

san

san → SANTO, A

sandía

sandía
[san'ðia] *n f*
watermelon

sangre

sangre
['sangre] *n f*
1. blood

2. Idiom
tener sangre fría to keep calm/cool

...sangre

* Tranquilícese; hay que tener sangre fría... Voy a intentar aterrizar... Calm down; we must keep cool... I'm going to try and land... ¡Déme un paracaídas inmediatamente! ¡Que vamos a estrellar! Give me a parachute at once! We're going to crash! *

le mató a sangre fría he killed him in cold blood

sano

sano, a
['sano, a] *adj*
healthy

es muy sano porque practica muchos deportes he is very healthy because he does a lot of sports

el clima de la montaña es más sano que el de la ciudad the climate in the mountains is healthier than in the city

santo

santo, san, a
['santo, san, a]
I. *adj*
holy

II. *n m*
1. saint

San Antonio Saint Anthony

Santa María Saint Mary

2. saint's day

sardina

sardina
[sar'ðina] *n f*
sardine

una lata de sardinas a tin of sardines

satélite

satélite
[sa'telite] *n m*
satellite

la luna es el satélite de la tierra the moon is the earth's satellite

satisfacer

satisfacer
[satisfa'θer] *v t*
to satisfy, to meet

satisfacer las necesidades de alguien to meet somebody's needs

se

se
[se] *pron*
1. (to)him/her/them/you

...se

se lo daré I'll give it to him/her/them/you

2. *no traducible*
* *¡Adiós!...* Goodbye!...
Los detectives se van. The detectives are leaving. *

3. (to)himself, herself, themselves, yourself, yourselves

4. Idiom
aquí se habla inglés English is spoken here

...se

Los detectives se van.

secano

secano
[se'kano] *n m*
unirrigated land

secar

secar
[se'kar] *v t*
to dry (off/up)

* *Está completamente mojado, se va a resfriar.* You're

...secar

wet through; you'll catch cold.
¡Qué va! ¡El sol me secará! No, I won't! The sun will dry me off! *

voy a secar los platos I'll dry the plates

▶ **secador**
[seka'dor] *n m*
hair dryer

▶ **secamente**
[seka'mente] *adv*
drily

▶ **seco, a**
['seko, a] *adj*
dry

un clima seco a dry climate

secretario

secretario, a
[sekre'tarjo, a] *n*
secretary

secreto

secreto
[se'kreto]
I. *adj*
f secreta [se'kreta]
secret

un túnel secreto a secret passage

II. *n m*
secret

un secreto de estado a state secret

sed

sed
[seð] *n f*
1. thirst

2. Idiom
tener sed to be thirsty

seda

seda
['seða] *n f*
silk

...seda

un gusano de seda a silk worm

sediento

sediento, a
[se'ðjento, a] *adj*
thirsty

* *En el desierto...* In the desert...
Tintín está sediento... Tintin is thirsty... *

...sediento

En el desierto...

Tintín está sediento...

las sedientas plantas se marchitan the thirsty plants are withering away

segar

segar
[se'ɣar] *v i & v t*
to cut, to harvest

están segando la hierba they are cutting the grass

▶ **segador**
[seɣa'ðor, a] *n m*
harvester (*person*)

▶ **segadora**
[seɣa'ðora] *n f*
harvester (*person, machine*)

(en) seguida

(en) seguida
[(en)se'ɣiða] *adv*
immediately, right away

voy en seguida I'll be right there

seguir

seguir
[se'ɣir]
I. *v t*

...seguir

¡Siga ese coche! ¡No hay tiempo que perder!

to follow

* *¡Siga ese coche! ¡No hay tiempo que perder!* Follow that car! There's no time to lose! *

II. *v i* .
to go on, to continue

siguió hablando he went on talking

sigue haciendo frío it continues to be cold

según

según
[se'ɣun]
I. *prep*
according to

según el profesor,... according to the Professor,...

II. *adv*
as, depending on whether

según llueva o no depending on whether it rains or not

según subes, notas más el frío as you go up, you notice the cold more

seguro

seguro, a
[se'ɣuro, a] *adj*
sure, certain

estoy seguro I'm sure/certain

selva

En la selva virgen ...

selva
['selβa] *n f*
forest

* *En la selva virgen...* In the virgin forest... *

sello

sello
['seλo] *n m*
stamp

...sello

hace colección de sellos he collects stamps

▶ **sellar**
[se'λar] *v t*
to stamp

el policía no me selló el pasaporte the policeman didn't stamp my passport

semáforo

semáforo
[se'maforo] *n m*
(traffic) lights

saltó el semáforo he jumped the lights

semana

semana
[se'mana] *n f*
1. week

...semana

2. Idiom
¿qué haces los fines de semana? what do you do at the weekend?

sembrar

sembrar
[sem'brar] *v t*
to sow

semilla

semilla
[se'miλa] *n f*
seed

sencillez

sencillez
[senθi'λeθ] *n f*
simplicity

▶ **sencillo, a**
[sen'θiλo, a] *adj*
simple

...sencillez

Es un problema sencillo, Tintín, muy sencillo ...

Sí, sí, eso es... Yo aún diría más : es un problema sencillo, muy sencillo...

Nada complicado, vaya ...

* *Es un problema sencillo, Tintín, muy sencillo...* It's a simple problem, Tintin, very simple...
Sí, sí, eso es... Yo aún diría más: es un problema sencillo, muy sencillo... Yes, yes, that's right... To be precise: it's a simple problem, very simple...
Nada complicado, vaya... Not at all complicated, at any rate... *

sensible

sensible
[sen'siβle] *adj*
sensitive

sentar

sentar, sentarse
[sen'tar, se]
I. *v t*
to seat

II. *v i*
to agree with, to suit

...sentar

no me sentó bien la comida the lunch didn't agree with me

* *¡Mire su melena!*
Look at his hair!
¡Ja! ¡Ja! ¡Este peinado te sienta muy bien! Ha ha! The hair-do suits you! *

III. *v pr*
to sit (down)

el gatito se sentó en sus rodillas the kitten sat on his lap

sentido

sentido
[sen'tiðo] *n m*
1. sense, meaning

no tiene sentido it doesn't make any sense

no tiene ni pizca de sentido común he hasn't an ounce of common sense

2. Idiom
* *Ha perdido el sentido.* He has lost consciousness. *

...sentido

Ha perdido el sentido.

sentimiento

sentimiento
[senti'mjento] *n m*
feeling, sentiment

un sentimiento de alegría a feeling of joy

sentir

sentir, sentirse
[sen'tir, se]
I. *v t*
1. to feel

...sentir

siente la música profundamente he feels music deeply

2. to be sorry
lo siento mucho I'm very sorry

II. *v pr*
to feel

* *¡Hip!... me siento... ¡hip!... raro... ¡hip!* Hic!... I feel... hic!... funny... hic! *

señal

señal
[se'ɲal] *n f*
1. sign

hacer una señal to make a sign

2. signal, tone
señal de marcar dialling tone

3. deposit
dejo cinco mil pesetas como (paga y) señal I'll leave five thousand pesetas as a deposit

...señal

▶**señalar, señalarse**
[seɲa'lar, se]
I. *v t*
1. to mark (*con una pluma*)

2. to point out
me señaló la iglesia en el horizonte he pointed out the church on the horizon to me

II. *v pr*
to distinguish oneself

señor

señor, a
[se'ɲor, a] *n*
gentleman, man, Mr *m*, lady, Mrs *f*

* *Rring* Rring
¿Diga? Buenos días, señora Marín... No, el señor no está. Hello? Good morning, Mrs Marin... No, the gentleman isn't in. *

señoras y señores ladies and gentleman
Sr. Marín Mr Marin
Sra. Marín Mrs Marin

septiembre

septiembre
[seβ'tjemβre] *n m*
September

septiembre es un mes cálido y agradable September is a warm, pleasant month

sequía

sequía
[se'kia] *n f*
drought, dry weather

ser

ser
[ser]
I *v i*
1. to be

Juan es médico Juan is a doctor

...ser

¡No quiero que los maten, son mis amigos!

soy de Toledo I'm from Toledo

2 y 2 son 4 2 and 2 are 4

* **¡No quiero que los maten, son mis amigos!** I don't want you to kill them; they're my friends! *

2. Idiom
es de madera it's made of wood

a no ser que unless

II. *n m*

ser humano human being

sereno

sereno, a
[se'reno, a] *adj*
calm, quiet

* **¡Qué noche más serena! Después de esta ruda jornada vamos a dormir profundamente, Milú...**

...sereno

¡Qué noche más serena! Después de esta ruda jornada vamos a dormir profundamente, Milú...

...sereno

What a quiet night! After such a rough day we're going to sleep tight, Snowy... *

seriedad

seriedad
[serje'ðað]
seriousness, gravity

▶ **serio, a**
['serjo, a] *adj*

...seriedad

1. serious, grave

éste es un asunto muy serio this is a very serious business

2. Idiom
¿lo dices en serio? are you serious?

lo encuentro difícil tomarlo en serio I find it difficult to take him seriously

serpiente

serpiente
[ser'pjente] *n f*
snake

una serpiente venenosa a poisonous snake

* **¡Vaya, Zorrino! esta serpiente por poco te ahoga...** Good heavens, Zorrino! This snake almost suffocated you...
Gracias Tintín, sin ti, era hombre muerto... Thank you Tintin; without you, I'd have been a dead man... *

¡Vaya, Zorrino! esta serpiente por poco te ahoga...

Gracias Tintín, sin ti, era hombre muerto...

servicio

servicio
[ser'βiθjo] *n m*
service

▶ **servicios**
[ser'βiθjos] *n m pl*
toilets *pl*

servilleta

servilleta
[serβi'ʎeta] *n f*
serviette

servir

servir, servirse
[ser'βir, se]
I. *vi & vt*
to serve

* **Este aparato sirve simplemente para ir por debajo del agua.** This machine simply serves to go under water in. *

II. *v pr*
1. to help oneself

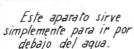

Este aparato sirve simplemente para ir por debajo del agua.

sírvase usted mismo help yourself

2. to make use of

sesión

sesión
[se'sjon] *n f*
session, performance

severo

severo, a
[se'βero, a] *adj*
strict, severe, hard

un profesor severo a strict teacher

si

si
[si] *conj*
if

...si

si te esfuerzas mu-
cho, ganarás el
premio if you try hard,
you'll win the prize

sí

sí
[si]
I. adv
1. yes

* ¿Cómo?... ¿Que
viene la Castafiore?

...sí

Néstor, ¡haga mi
maleta inmedia-
tamente! What?...
Bianca Castafiore's com-
ing? Nestor, pack my case
at once!
Sí, señor. Yes, sir. *

2. Idiom
¡claro que sí! of course!

II. pron
himself, herself,
themselves

está contenta de sí
she's pleased with herself

sidra

sidra
[ˈsiðra] n f
cider

siempre

siempre
[ˈsjempre] adv
always

Hernández y Fer-
nández siempre di-
cen lo mismo Thomp-
son and Thomson always
say the same thing

sierra

sierra
[ˈsjeɾa] n f
1. saw (para serrar)

2. mountain range

siesta

siesta
[ˈsjesta] n f
siesta

...siesta

echar una siesta to
have a siesta

siglo

siglo
[ˈsiɣlo] n m
century

en el siglo dieci-
nueve in the nineteenth
century

significar

significar
[siɣnifiˈkar] v t
to mean, to signify

* *Haw hawaaaw* Haw
hawaaaw
¿Qué significa este
alboroto? What does
this growl mean *

siguiente

siguiente
[siˈɣjente] adj
following, next

...siguiente

¡el siguiente! next!

al día siguiente the
next/following day

a la mañana
siguiente the next/
following morning

silencio

silencio
[siˈlenθjo] n m
silence

* ...toplasmas ...plas-
mas ...asmas ...toplasm
...plasm ...asm
¡Silencio, ahí arriba!
¡Callaos! Silence, up
there! Be quiet!
Capitán, no hay
nadie, es el eco.
Captain, there's no-one
there; it's the echo. *

...silencio

silla

silla
[ˈsiʎa] n f
chair

sentado en una silla
sitting on a chair

* *Crac* Snap
La silla se ha roto.
The chair has broken. *

La silla se ha roto.

sillón

sillón
[siˈʎon] n m
armchair

simpático

simpático, a
[simˈpatiko, a] adj
nice, pleasant

¡qué simpática es!
isn't she nice!

sin

sin
[sin] *prep*
1. without

sin azúcar without sugar

2. Idiom
está todavía sin arreglar it hasn't been mended yet

sin cesar/parar non-stop

sin embargo
→ EMBARGO

sincero

sincero, a
[sin'θero, a] *adj*
sincere

sé sincero y di lo que piensas be sincere and say what you think

sino

sino
[si'no] *conj*
but

...sino

no es blanco sino negro it's not white but black

no sólo... sino también not only... but also

siquiera

siquiera
[si'kjera] *adv*
1. at least

deja siquiera en paz a los demás at least

...siquiera

...siquiera

leave other people alone

2. Idiom
* *Te voy a matar, Tintín, y ni siquiera te darás cuenta.* I'm going to kill you Tintin, and you won't know anything about it. *

sitio

sitio
['sitjo] *n m*

1. place, spot

* *¡Qué sitio más siniestro!* What a sinister place! *

2. Idiom
en algún sitio somewhere

en ningún sitio nowhere

en cualquier sitio anywhere

situar

situar
[si'twar] *v t*
to place, to situate

sobra

sobra
['sobra] *n f*
1. excess

2. Idiom
de sobra(s) plenty of, more than enough

...sobra

tenemos tiempo de sobras we've got plenty of time

▶ **sobras**
['sobras] *n f pl*
leftovers *pl*

* *Esto no son más que huesos de pájaros y otros animales...* These are just bones of birds and other animals...
¡Yo me contentaré con estas sobras! I'll

...sobra

be satisfied with these leftovers! *

▶ **sobrar**
[so'βrar] *v i*
to be left over, to be spare

esto sobra this is spare

sobra mucho there's a lot left over

sobre

sobre
['soβre] *n m*
envelope

sobre

sobre
['soβre] *prep*
1. on (top of)

* *¡Guau!* Bow-wow!
Se ha sentado sobre Milú. He sat on Snowy. *

...sobre

Se ha sentado sobre Milú.

...sobre

2. about
sobre las tres about three o'clock

un libro sobre Méjico a book about Mexico

sobrenatural

sobrenatural
[soβrenatuˈral] *adj*
1. supernatural

...sobrenatural

2. Idiom
las ciencias sobre-naturales the occult sciences

sobresalir

sobresalir
[soβresaˈlir] *v i*
to stand out, to jut out

sobresale entre los demás alumnos he

...sobresalir

stands out above the other pupils

► **sobresaliente**
[soβresaˈliente] *adj*
excellent, outstanding

sobrino

sobrino, a
[soˈβrino, a] *n*
nephew *m*, niece *f*

sociedad

sociedad
[soθjeˈðað] *n f*
society

socio

socio, a
[ˈsoθjo, a] *n*
member

¿quiere hacerse socio del club? do you want to become a member of the club?

socorrer

socorrer
[sokoˈřer] *v t*
to help

► **socorro**
[soˈkořo] *n m*
help

* *¡Socorro!* Help! *

► **socorrismo**
[sokoˈřismo] *n m*
life-saving

...socorrer

sofocante

sofocante
[sofoˈkante] *adj*
stifling, suffocating

hace un calor sofo-cante it's stifling.

sol

sol
[sol] *n m*
sun

...sol

* *Un eclipse de sol...* An eclipse of the sun... *

solemne

solemne
[soˈlemne] *adj*
solemn

un acto solemne a solemn act

Un eclipse de sol...

soler

soler
[soˈler] *v i*
1. to be in the habit of, to usually do something

* *Suelo levantarme tarde...* I usually get up late...
¿De veras? Really? *

2. Idiom
solía levantarme temprano I used to get up early

...soler

Suelo levantarme tarde...

¿De veras?

solo

solo, a
[ˈsolo, a] *adj*
1. single, sole

2. Idiom
una sola vez just once

3. alone, on one's own, lonely
* *¡Ja! ¡Ja! Ha venido solo... ¡Mejor!... ¡Esta es la mía...* Ha ha! He's come on his own... All the better!... Just what I was waiting for... *

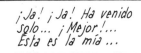

¡Ja! ¡Ja! Ha venido solo... ¡Mejor!... Esta es la mía...

sólo

sólo
[ˈsolo] *adv*
only

sólo estuvo un momento he was only here for a moment

soltar

soltar
[solˈtar] *v t*
1. to untie

* *Ya casi estoy... Le voy a desatar...* I'm almost there... I'm going to untie you...
Demasiado tarde, muchachos, soy yo quien os voy a soltar... Too late, boys; I'm the one who's going to untie you. *

...soltar

**2. to set free,
to release, to let go**
¡suéltame! let me go!

soltero

soltero, a
[sol'tero, a]
I. adj
unmarried, single

II. n
bachelor m
unmarried woman f

sombra

sombra
['somβra] n f
1. shade

2. shadow

▶ **sombrío, a**
[som'βrío, a] adj
dark, sombre

sombrero

El viento se ha llevado el sombrero.

sombrero
[som'βrero] n m
hat

* ¡Milú, corre! ¡Coge el sombrero! Snowy, quick! Get the hat!
El viento se ha llevado el sombrero. The wind has carried the hat away. *

sombrilla

sombrilla
[som'βriλa] n f
parasol, sunshade

sonar

sonar
[so'nar]
I. v i & v t
1. to ring, to sound

* ¡Rrrring! ¡El teléfono suena! Rrrring!

...sonar

The phone's ringing! *

2. Idiom
este nombre me suena this name rings a bell

II. v pr
to blow one's nose

suénate (las narices) blow your nose

▶ **sonido**
[so'niðo] n m
sound

sonoro

sonoro, a
[so'noro, a] adj
sonorous, ringing

una voz sonora a ringing voice

sonreír

sonreír
[sonre'ir] v i
to smile

* ¡Ale! No tengas

...sonreír

miedo... ¿Por qué estás tan asustada? ¡Vale! Sonríe un poco... Hey! Don't be afraid... Why are you so frightened? OK! Smile a bit...
Kilikilikili kilikilikili *

▶ **sonriente**
[son'rjente] adj
smiling

una cara sonriente a smiling face

...sonreír

▶ **sonrisa**
[son'risa] *n f*
smile

una sonrisa forzada
a forced smile

soñar

soñar
[so'ɲar] *v t*
1. to dream

* *El capitán sueña...*
The Captain is dreaming...

...soñar

El capitán sueña...

¡AH! ME RÍO...

¡Ah! Me río...! Oh!
I laugh...! *

2. Idiom
¡ni soñarlo! not on your
life!

sopa

sopa
['sopa] *n f*
1. soup

sopa de legumbres
vegetable soup

...sopa

¡Estoy hecho una sopa!

2. Idiom
* *¡Estoy hecho una sopa!* I'm sopping wet! *

soplar

soplar
[so'plar] *v i*
to blow

* *Bang* Bang
El viento sopla muy fuerte... The wind is blowing very hard... *

...soplar

BANG

El viento sopla muy fuerte...

soportal

soportal
[sopor'tal] *n m*
porch

espérame en el soportal wait for me in the porch

▶ **soportales**
[sopor'tales] *n m pl*
arcade

soportar

soportar
[sopor'tar] *v t*
1. to support

2. to put up with, to stand, to bear
no lo soporto I can't stand him

sordo

sordo, a
['sorðo, a] *adj*
1. deaf

...sordo

¡Pero bueno, es usted sordo o ¿qué?!

* *Pero bueno, ¿es usted sordo o qué?* Look here, are you deaf or what? *

2. Idiom
más sordo que una tapia as deaf as a post

sorprender

sorprender
[sorpren'ðer]
I. *v t*
to surprise,
to take by surprise

la lluvia nos sorprendió the rain took us by surprise

II. *v pr*
to be surprised

se sorprendió she was surprised

sorpresa

sorpresa
[sor'presa] *n f*
surprise

* *¡Tintín! ¡Usted por aquí! ¡Qué sorpresa!* Tintin! What are you doing here! What a surprise! *

▶ **sorprendente**
[sorpre'dente] *adj*
surprising

¡Tintín! ¡Usted por aquí! ¡Qué sorpresa!

RRR RRR RRR

soso

soso, a
['soso, a] *adj*
tasteless, dull, wet

sospechar

sospechar
[sospe'tʃar]
I. *v i*
to suspect

* *El general Alcázar sospecha de us-*

...sospechar

El general Alcázar sospecha de usted... ¡Queda usted detenido!

¿Yo? ¿Detenido?

...sospechar

ted... ¡Queda usted detenido! General Alcazar suspects you... You're under arrest! *¿Yo? ¿Detenido?* Me? Under arrest? *

II. *v t*
to suspect

▶ **sospechoso, a**
[sospet'ʃoso, a]
I. *adj*
suspicious

II. *n*
suspect

sótano

sótano
['sotano] *n m*
basement

* *¡Mire! ¡Lo habían encerrado en el sótano!* Look! They've

...sótano

locked him up in the basement! *

su

su, sus
[su, sus] *adj*
1. his, her, their

el niño juega con su tren the little boy is playing with his train

...su

2. your
cojan ustedes sus pasaportes take your passports

suave

suave
[sw'aβe] *adj*
smooth, soft

¡qué música más suave! what soft music!

subdesarrollado

subdesarrollado, a
[suβðesaꞧo'ʎaðo, a] *adj*
underdeveloped

subir

subir
[su'βir]
I. *v t*
to raise, to lift up,
to bring up,
to take up

...subir

sube esa carga take that load up

subimos la montaña we went up the mountain

II. *v i*
to go up,
to come up

la gasolina ha subido petrol's gone up

submarino

...submarino

submarino, a
[suβma'rino, a]
adj & n m
submarine

* *Nunca adivinarán que he logrado escaparme gracias a este submarino...* They'll never guess I managed to escape thanks to this submarine... *

subrayar

subrayar
[suβꞧa'jar] *v t*
to underline

subrayar el título de la redacción underline the title of the composition

suceder

suceder
[suθe'ðer]
I. *v i*
to happen

¿qué ha sucedido? what's happened?

II. *v i & v t*
to succeed,
to follow, to inherit

suceder al trono to succeed to the throne

suciedad

Milú está sucio.

S

...suciedad

suciedad
[suθjeˈðað] *n f*
dirt, filth

▶ **sucio, a**
[ˈsuθjo, a] *adj*
dirty, filthy

* *Milú está sucio.*
Snowy is dirty. *

una jugada sucia a
dirty trick

sueldo

sueldo
[swelˈðo] *n m*
salary

suelo

suelo
[ˈswelo] *n m*
1. ground, soil,
earth

suelo fértil fertile soil

* *El capitán se ha
caído al suelo.* The

...suelo

El capitán se ha caído al suelo.

Captain has fallen to the
ground. *

2. floor
*el suelo de esta
habitación está res-
baladizo* the floor of this
room is slippery

suelto

suelto, a
[ˈswelto, a]
I. *adj*

...suelto

1. free, loose

*un bloc de hojas
sueltas* a loose-leaf pad

2. isolated,
separate
dos poesías sueltas
two separate poems

II. *n m*
(small/loose) chan-
ge

no tengo suelto I have
no small change

sueño

sueño
[ˈsweɲo] *n m*
1. dream

*mi sueño es casar-
me con un millona-
rio* my dream is to marry
a millionaire

2. sleep
*necesito ocho horas
de sueño* I need eight
hours' sleep

* *Después de la tor-
menta de arena...*
After the sandstorm...

Después de la tormenta de arena...
¡Mira cómo duerme Tintín! Pobrecillo, se caía de sueño...
Rrron

*¡Mira cómo duerme
Tintín! Pobrecillo, se
caía de sueño...*
Look, Tintin's fast asleep!
Poor little thing, he could
hardly keep his eyes
open...
Rrron Zzzz *

suerte

suerte
[ˈswerte] *n f*
(good) luck

...suerte

¡suerte! good luck!

* *¡Qué mala suerte!
Justo cuando esta-
ba a punto de cap-
turar a Tintín, me
caí al suelo...* What
bad luck! Just when I was
about to capture Tintin, I
fell over...
*Yo también me caí
al suelo cuando iba
a capturar a Tintín...
¡Qué mala suerte!* I
also fell over when I was
about to capture Tintin...
What bad luck! *

...suerte

¡Qué mala suerte! Justo cuando estaba a punto de capturar a Tintín, me caí al suelo...
Yo también me caí al suelo cuando iba a capturar a Tintín... ¡Qué mala suerte!

sugerir

sugerir
[suxeˈrir] *v t*
to suggest

▶ **sugerencia**
[suxeˈrenθja] *n f*
suggestion

sujetar

sujetar
[suxeˈtar] *v t*
1. to hold, to fasten

*le sujetaron los pies
y las manos* they held
his feet and hands

2. to keep hold of
sujeta al niño keep
hold of the baby

3. to hold in place
*la grapa sujeta las
hojas* the staple's
holding the sheets of
paper in place

sumar

sumar
[suˈmar] *v i & v t*
to add up

sumiso

sumiso, a
[suˈmiso, a] *adj*
submissive,
docile, obedient

superar

superar
[supe'rər] v t
1. to surpass

2. to overcome
superamos las dificultades we overcame the difficulties

superior

superior
[supe'rjor] adj
upper, higher, advanced

supermercado

supermercado
[supermer'kaðo] n m
supermarket

suprimir

suprimir
[supri'mir] v t
to suppress,
to abolish, to cancel

* *¿Por qué nos paramos?* Why have we stopped?

...suprimir

¡El tren con destino a Hou Kou queda suprimido! The train to Hou Kou has been cancelled! *

sur

sur
[sur] n m
south

al sur de Madrid south of Madrid

surtidor

surtidor
[surti'ðor] n m
jet, fountain

* *Se ha caído en el estanque del surtidor.* He's fallen into the bowl of the fountain. *

suspender

suspender
[suspen'ðer] v t
1. to suspend,

Se ha caído en el estanque del surtidor.

...suspender

to adjourn,
to postpone

se suspende la sesión the session is adjourned

2. to fail
he suspendido mates I've failed maths

suspirar

suspirar
[suspi'rar] v i
to sigh

susto

susto
['susto] n m
fright

* *El capitán se ha llevado un buen susto.* The Captain got quite a fright. *

...susto

El capitán se ha llevado un buen susto

suyo

suyo, a, os, as
['suǰo, a, os, as]
I. adj pos
1. his, her, their, of his, of hers, of theirs

Tintín está con un amigo suyo Tintin is with a friend of his

2. your, of yours
Tornasol, creo que este paraguas es suyo Calculus, I think this umbrella is yours

II. pron pos
1. his, hers, theirs

es la cartera de Tintín; es la suya this is Tintin's wallet; it's his

2. yours
¿este sombrero es suyo? is this hat yours?

3. Idiom
salirse con la suya to get one's own way

tabaco

tabaco
[ta'βako] *n m*
1. tobacco

2. cigarettes

tal

tal
[tal]
I. *adj*
1. such

...tal

tal cosa such a thing

* *¡Mire, capitán!...
¿Qué puede ser?*
Look, Captain!... What can
it be?
*¡Caramba! Jamás
había visto tal cosa
antes...* Good gracious!
I've never seen such a
thing before... *

2. a certain,
someone called
un tal López someone
called Lopez

II. *adv*
1. so, in such a way

2. Idiom
*pasó tal como te he
explicado* it happened
just as I've explained to
you

hola ¿qué tal? hello,
how are things?

III. *conj*
con tal (de) que
provided that, on condition
that

...tal

* *Te dejo la vida con
tal que me digas
dónde se encuentra
la estatua...* I'll spare
your life provided that you
tell me where the statue
is...
¡Nunca! Never! *

taller

taller
[ta'ʎer] *n m*
workshop, studio

tamaño

tamaño
[ta'maɲo] *n m*
size

* *No te imaginabas
que existieran ani-
males de este tama-*

...tamaño

...tamaño

ño... You didn't imagine that there were animals this size... *

también

también
[tam'bjen] *adv*
also, too, as well

yo también me too

tambor

tambor
[tam'bor] *n m*
drum

tampoco

tampoco
[tam'poko] *adv*
nor, neither, either

* *Yo no veo a nadie...* I can't see anyone...
Yo tampoco... Me neither... *

tan

tan
[tan] *adv*
so, as

es tan alto como yo he's as tall as I am

* *¡Mil millones de demonios!* Billions of blue blistering barnacles!
¡No hable usted tan fuerte; va a provocar un alud! Don't speak so loud; you'll cause a landslide! *

tanto

tanto, a
['tanto]
I. *adj*
as/so much *sing*, as/so many *pl*

no comas tanto arroz don't eat so much rice

II. *adv*
1. so much, so hard

no trabajes tanto don't work so hard

...tanto

ha llovido tanto que el campo está inundado it has rained so hard that the countryside is flooded

2. Idiom
tanto mejor/peor so much the better/the worse

* *¡Tanto peor! ¡Tú lo habrás querido!* So much the worse! You asked for it! *

por (lo) tanto so, consequently, therefore

tapa

tapa
['tapa] *n f*
lid, cover, top

tapar

tapar
[ta'par] *v t*
1. to cover up, to fill in

* *Pero ¿qué hacen?* But what are you doing?
Tapamos el agujero que hemos hecho... La gente es tan distraída que podría caerse dentro... We're filling in the hole... People are so busy thinking about other things that they might fall in... *

...tapar

2. to put the lid on

3. to hide,
to blot out
el árbol tapa el sol
the tree blots out the sunlight

tapia

tapia
['tapja] *n f*
wall

taquilla

taquilla
[ta'kiʎa] *n f*
ticket office

tardar

tardar
[tar'ðar] *v i*
to take (time)

* *Rring* Rring
¿Vas a contestar al

...tardar

teléfono? Are you going to answer the phone?
¡Hombre! Yo estoy durmiendo... ¿Por qué no vas tú? Hey! I'm sleeping... Why don't you go?
¡Cuánto tardan en contestar! What a time they take to answer! *

tarde

tarde
['tarðe]
I. *n f*
afternoon,
evening

por la tarde in the afternoon/evening

* *¡Buenas tardes, Chiquito! ¿Pasa algo?* Good evening, Chiquito! Is anything wrong?
Buenas tardes, señor. No, nada... Es

el gato... Good evening, sir. No, nothing... It's the cat... *

II. *adv*
1. late

un poco más tarde a little later

se hace tarde
it's getting late

2. Idiom
tarde o temprano sooner or later

tarjeta

tarjeta
[tar'xeta] *n f*
card

tarjeta de crédito
credit card

taxi

taxi
['ta(k)si] *n m*
taxi

* *¡Taxi! ¿Está libre?*

...taxi

Taxi! Are you free?
Sí, señor. Yes, sir. *

▶ **taxista**
[ta(k)'sista] *n*
taxi-driver

taza

taza
['taθa] *n f*
cup

...taza

dos tazas de té two cups of tea

te

te
[te] *pron*
1. (to) you

2. *no traducible*
* *¡Por fin!* At last!
Menos mal!... Te das cuenta... sin ti, no sé qué habría pasa-

...te

...te

do... Thank goodness!... Fancy that... without you, I don't know what would have happened... *

3. (to) yourself
hazte una taza de té make yourself a cup of tea

té

té
[te] *n m*
tea

teatro

teatro
[te'atro] *n m*
1. theatre

2. Idiom
una obra de teatro a play

tebeo

tebeo
[te'beo] *n m*
comic

...tebeo

lee muchos tebeos he reads a lot of comics

techo

techo
['tetʃo] *n m*
ceiling

* *¡El techo se derrumba!...* The ceiling's falling in!... *

...techo

tejado

tejado
[te'xaðo] *n m*
roof

hay un gato en el tejado there's a cat on the roof

tejido

tejido
[te'xiðo] *n m*
1. fabric

...tejido

2. Idiom
una fábrica de tejidos a textile factory

telefonear

telefonear
[telefone'ar] *v i & v t*
to telephone, to phone

* *¡No me telefonee más, demonios! ¡Es-*

...telefonear

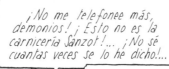

to no es la carnicería Sanzot!... ¡No sé cuántas veces se lo he dicho!... Don't phone me any more, blistering barnacles! This is not Mr Cutts the butcher!... I don't know how many times I've told you!...
Rrrring Rrrring! *

▶ **teléfono**
[te'lefono] *n m*
telephone, phone

telegrama

telegrama
[tele'grama] *n m*
telegram

televisión

televisión
[teleβi'sjon] *n f*
television

la vi en (la) televisión I saw her on television

tema

tema
['tema] *n m*
subject, theme

el tema de la película the subject of the film

temblar

temblar
[tem'blar] *v i*
to tremble, to shake

...temblar

* *¡Cielos! ¡Un gorila!* Heavens! A gorilla! *Milú tiembla de miedo.* Snowy is trembling with fright! *

temer

temer
[te'mer] *v t*
to be afraid

teme que no vuelva he's afraid she won't come back

...temer

...temer

* ¡Ay! Zorrino, temo que Tintín haya desaparecido para siempre... Oh! Zorrino, I'm afraid Tintin has disappeared for ever... *

▶ **temor**
[te'mor] *n m*
fear, dread

no lo dijo por temor a herir sus sentimientos he didn't say it for fear of hurting her feelings

tempestad

En medio de la tempestad.

tempestad
[tempes'taθ] *n f*
storm

* *En medio de la tempestad.* In the middle of the storm. *

templado

templado, a
[tem'plaθo, a] *adj*
1. lukewarm

...templado

agua templada lukewarm water

2. mild
el país goza de un clima templado the country has a mild climate

temporada

temporada
[tempo'raθa] *n f*
1. season, period

...temporada

temporada de exámenes examination period

2. time, spell
* *¿Qué le parece nuestra temporada en el Tibet?* What do you think of our spell in Tibet?
Ha sido una idea excelente... Me encanta este paisaje. It was an excellent idea... I love this countryside. *

...temporada

temprano

temprano
[tem'prano] *adv*
early

nos levantamos temprano we got up early

tenedor

tenedor
[tene'θor] *n m*
fork

tener

tener
[te'ner] *v t*
1. to have

tengo mucho trabajo I have a lot of work

2. Idiom
tener que to have to, must

* *Tengo que advertir al Sr. Cantonneau que su vida corre peligro.* I must warn Mr Cantonneau that his life is in danger. *

terminar

terminar, terminarse
[termi'nar, se]
I. *v i & v pr*
to finish, to end

terminó por decir que... he ended by saying that...

II. *v t*
to finish, to end

termina lo que estabas diciendo finish what you were saying

término

término
['termino] *n m*
1. finish, end

2. boundary, limit

ternera

ternera
[ter'nera] *n f*
veal

ternura

ternura
[ter'nura] *n f*
tenderness

necesita mucha ternura he needs a lot of tenderness

terraza

terraza
[te'rraθa] *n f*
terrace

terremoto

...terremoto

terremoto
[teˈre'moto] *n m*
earthquake

* *¡Señor! ¡Un terremoto!* Heavens! An earthquake! *

terreno

terreno
[teˈreno] *n m*
1. terrain, land

...terreno

terreno accidentado rugged terrain

2. field, sphere
en el terreno de la física in the field of physics

tesoro

tesoro
[te'soro] *n m*
treasure

...tesoro

* *En vez de cavar, deberían buscar el tesoro...* Instead of digging, you should be looking for the treasure... *

testarudo

testarudo, a
[testa'ruðo, a] *adj*
stubborn,
pig-headed

nunca hace caso de los consejos de los demás; es muy testarudo he never takes any notice of other people's advice; he's very stubborn

testigo

testigo
[tes'tiɣo] *n m*
witness

* *He sido testigo del accidente, lo he visto todo. Esos bandidos le han echado al lago deliberadamente.* I witnessed the accident; I saw it all. Those scoundrels threw him into the lake deliberately.
Yo también he asistido al accidente. I was also a witness to the accident. *

texto

texto
['te(k)sto] *n m*
text

un libro de texto a textbook

ti

ti
[ti] *pron pers*
you

esto es para ti this is for you

tibio

tibio, a
['tiβjo, a] *adj*
lukewarm

tiempo

tiempo
['tjempo] *n m*
1. time

al mismo tiempo at the same time

...tiempo

2. weather
* *¡Qué buen tiempo hace para cuidar del jardín! ¿Verdad?* What fine weather we're having to look after the garden, don't you think?
Sí, capitán... Aprovecho el buen tiempo para podar los rosales... Yes, Captain... I'm taking advantage of the fine weather to prune the rose bushes... *

3. Idiom
hace tiempo for a long time/for some time

hace tiempo que no viene por aquí he hasn't been round here for a long time

andando el tiempo as time goes by

tienda

tienda
['tjenða] n f
1. shop, store

2. tent

...tierno

2. fresh
pan tierno fresh bread

tierno

tierno, a
['tjerno, a] adj
1. tender, soft

tierra

tierra
['tjeʈa] n f
1. earth, soil

* *¡Oh! Mi collar se ha roto y se han caído todas las perlas...*

...tierra

¡Oh! Mi collar se ha roto y se han caído todas las perlas... Ahora estarán sucias de tierra.

Ahora estarán sucias de tierra. Oh! My necklace has broken and all the pearls have fallen off... Now they've got earth all over them. *

2. country, land
ha vuelto a su tierra natal he's gone back to his native land

tijeras

tijeras
[ti'xeras] n f pl
scissors pl

timbre

timbre
['timbre] n m
1. bell

* *Rrrring* Rrrring
Tintín toca el timbre.
Tintin is ringing the bell. *

...timbre

RRRRING
21

Tintín toca el timbre.

2. timbre
su voz tiene un timbre nasal his voice has a nasal timbre

tímido

tímido, a
['timiðo, a] adj
shy, timid

tinta

tinta
['tinta] n f
1. ink

2. Idiom
saber algo de buena tinta to know something on good authority

tío

tío, a
['tío, a] n
uncle m, aunt f

▶ **tíos**
['tíos] n m pl
uncle and aunt

típico

típico, a
['tipiko, a] adj
1. typical, characteristic

2. regional, quaint, traditional
* *Nos hemos vestido con el traje típico para poder desenmascarar a este individuo.* We dressed up in the regional costume in order to expose this individual.
Yo aún diría más...
To be precise... *

Nos hemos vestido con el traje típico para poder desenmascarar a este individuo.

Yo aún diría más...

tirar

tirar
[ti'rar]
I. v t
to throw,
to throw away

tíralo throw it away

II. v i
1. to pull

tira de la cuerda pull the rope

2. to shoot
¡no tiren! don't shoot!

...tirar

3. Idiom
vamos tirando we're managing/jogging along

tiritar

tiritar
[tiri'tar] *v i*
to shiver

tiro

tiro
['tiro] *n m*
1. throw

2. shot
* *¿Han oído?... Parece como si hubiera sido un tiro...* Did you hear that?... It sounded like a shot... *Pam* Bang *

¿Han oído?... Parece como si hubiera sido un tiro...

PAM

título

título
['titulo] *n m*
1. title

el título del libro the title of the book

2. degree, diploma
tiene el título de abogado he has a degree in law

toalla

toalla
[to'aʎa] *n f*
towel

tocar

tocar
[to'kar] *v t*
1. to touch

se ruega no tocar please do not touch

2. to play

...tocar

Aquel día...

Ya estoy harto de tocar el piano...

* *Aquel día...* That day...
Ya estoy harto de tocar el piano... I'm fed up with playing the piano... *

todavía

todavía
[toða'βia] *adv*
still, yet

...todavía

¿todavía está en la cama? is he still in bed?

todavía no lo he hecho I haven't done it yet

todo

todo, a
['toðo, a]
I. *adj*
all

* *Senhor de Oliveira, tengo que ir a casa del profesor Smith imperativamente... ¿Puede usted ayudarme?* Senhor de Oliveira, it's essential that I get to Professor Smith's house... Can you help me?
¡No hay cosa más

...todo

Senhor de Oliveira, tengo que ir a casa del profesor Smith imperativamente... ¿Puede usted ayudarme?

¡No hay cosa más fácil! Voy a su casa todas las mañanas. Puede acompañarme cuando quiera...

fácil! Voy a su casa todas las mañanas. Puede acompañarme cuando quiera... That's as easy as ABC! I go to his house every morning. You can come with me whenever you want... *

II. *pron*
all·

lo han vendido todo they've sold it all

todos están de acuerdo they all agree

III. *adv*
1. all

el suelo está todo mojado the ground is all wet

2. Idiom
ante todo first of all

del todo completely

IV. *n m*
whole

forma un todo it forms a whole

▶**todo el que, todos los que**
anyone/everyone who

todos los que quieran pueden irse anyone who wants to may leave

▶**todo lo que**
all/everything (that)

todo lo que dijo es mentira all that he said is a pack of lies

▶**todo lo... que**
quite as... as

la habitación no está todo lo preparada que debiera the room isn't quite as ready as it might be

tomate

tomate
[to'mate] n m
tomato

salsa de tomate
tomato sauce

tomar

tomar
[to'mar] v t
1. to take

2. to have

...tomar

voy a tomar un café
I'm going to have a coffee

3. Idiom
tomar el sol to sun-
bathe

tono

tono
['tono] n m
tone, pitch

tontería

tontería
[tonte'ria] n f
1. stupidity,
stupid act

2. Idiom
hacer tonterías to do
stupid things, to be stupid

* *¡Abdallah! ¡No
hagas tonterías!...
¡Ven aquí!* Abdullah!
Don't be stupid!... Come
here! *

▶**tonto, a**
['tonto, a] adj
1. stupid, silly

2. Idiom
no hagas el tonto
don't be silly

*escribe a tontas y
locas* he writes just any
old how

torear

torear
[tore'ar] v i & v t
1. to fight bulls

2. to cope with
someone
lo has toreado bien
you coped with him well

▶**torero**
[to'rero] n m
bullfighter,
toreador

▶**toro**
['toro] n m
bull

tormenta

tormenta
[tor'menta] n f
storm

* *¡Menuda tormenta!*
What a storm!
¡Estoy calado! I'm
soaked to the skin! *

torpe

torpe
['torpe] adj
awkward

...torpe

movimientos torpes
awkward movements

▶**torpeza**
[tor'peθa] n f
awkwardness,
clumsiness

torre

torre
['tore] n f
1. tower

...torre

* *Tampoco están en
lo alto de la torre... El
péndulo indicaba
que debían de estar
en un lugar ele-
vado...* They're not right
up in the tower either...
The pendulum indicated
that they must be some-
where high up... *

2. house (*in Catalonia
and Aragon*)
*se han comprado
una torre* they've
bought themselves a
house

torrente

torrente
[to'rente] n m
stream, torrent

* *¿Cómo salimos de
este torrente?* How do
we get out of this
stream? *

torta

torta
['torta] n f
1. cake

2. blow,
punch

tortilla

tortilla
[tor'tiλa] n f
1. omelette

...tortilla

una tortilla de pata-tas a potato omelette

2. *Am:* maize pancake

tos

tos
[tos] *n f*
cough

la tos no le deja

...tos

dormir he can't get to sleep with that cough

▶ **toser**
[to'ser] *v i*
to cough

tostada

tostada
[tos'taða] *n f*
piece of toast

...tostada

una tostada con mermelada de naranja a piece of toast and marmalade

▶ **tostar**
[tos'tar] *v t*
1. to toast

2. to tan
tostado por el sol sun-tanned

trabajar

trabajar
[traβa'xar] *v i & v t*
to work

trabaja demasiado he works too hard

▶ **trabajo**
[tra'βaxo] *n m*
1. work, labour, job

está sin trabajo he has no work

estoy buscando un trabajo I'm looking for a job

2. effort, trouble
tomarse el trabajo de to take the trouble to

traducir

traducir
['tradu'θir] *v i & v t*
to translate

* *Buenos días, señores. Les puedo*

...traducir

servir de guía y traducir lo que no entiendan. Good morning, gentlemen. I can act as your guide and translate what you don't understand. *

▶ **traductor, a**
[traduk'tor] *n*
translator

traer

traer
[tra'er] *v t*
to bring, to fetch

¿podrías traerme mis zapatillas? could you fetch/bring me my slippers?

tráfico

tráfico
['trafiko] *n m*
1. traffic

el tráfico en las carreteras de circunvalación es muy denso the traffic on the bypasses is very heavy

* *Y al día siguiente...* And the following day...
¿De dónde sale este vaquero? Where has this cowboy come from?

¡No se quede ahí plantado! ¡Oiga, que no estamos en el campo, aquí hay mucho tráfico! ¡Vamos! ¡Circule! Don't just stand there! Hey, we're not in the country! There's a lot of traffic here! Come on! Move along! *

2. trade, traffic, trafficking
el tráfico de narcóticos drug trafficking

...tráfico

tragar

tragar
[tra'ɣar] *v i & v t*
to swallow

le duele la garganta al tragar los alimentos his throat hurts when he swallows food

▶ **trago**
['traɣo] *n m*
1. drink, swig

2. Idiom
de un trago in one gulp

* *El capitán se lo bebió de un trago.* The Captain drank it in one gulp. *

...tragar

El capitán se lo bebió de un trago.

traje

traje
['traxe] *n m*
suit

nunca lleva traje
he never wears a suit

* *El traje de baño es inútil...*
Our bathing suits are useless...
puesto que aquí no hay agua... as there's no water here... *

trampa

trampa
['trampa] *n f*
trap

tranquilo

tranquilo, a
[tran'kilo, a] *adj*
quiet, calm

un barrio tranquilo a quiet area

transeúnte

transeúnte
[transe'ŭnte] *n*
passer-by

un grupo de transeúntes comentaba el accidente a group of passers-by commented on the accident

transformar

transformar
[transfor'mar] *v t*
to transform, to change

transportar

transportar
[transpor'tar] *v t*
to transport, to carry

...transportar

▶ **transporte**
[trans'porte] *n m*
transport
(*Am*: transportation)

tras

tras
[tras] *prep*
1. behind

* *Estaré en mayor seguridad tras esta puerta.* I'll be safer

...tras

...tras

behind this door. *

2. after
tras asistir a la conferencia, fuimos a cenar after attending the lecture, we went for supper

trasladar

trasladar, trasladarse
[trasla'ðar, se]

...trasladar

I. *v t*
to transfer, to move

II. *v pr*
to move

nos trasladamos we are moving

▶ **traslado**
[tras'laðo] *n m*
move, removal, transfer

tratar

El yeti fue muy bueno conmigo. Me trató siempre con cariño, me parece que me quería mucho...

tratar
[tra'tar]
I. *v t*
to treat

* *El yeti fue muy bueno conmigo. Me trató siempre con cariño; me parece que me quería mucho...* The yeti was very good to me. He always treated me affectionately; I think he was very fond of me... *

II. *v i*
1. to deal with, to be about

la película trata de la vida de un político the film is about the life of a politician

2. to have dealings/ contact with
trata con toda clase de personas he has contact with all sorts of people

...tratar

III. *v impers*
to be about,
to be a ques-
tion of

se trata del dinero que me debes it's about the money you owe me

se trata de ahorrar mucho it's a question of saving up

través

(a) través de
[a tra'βes de] *prep*
1. across, over

el puente está si-tuado a través del río the bridge stretches ac-ross the river

2. through
a través de la venta-na through the window

lo supe a través de mi hermano I heard about it through my brother

travesura

travesura
[traβe'sura] *n f*
prank

son travesuras de niños they're just childish pranks

► **travieso, a**
[tra'βjeso, a] *adj*
naughty

tren

tren
[tren] *n m*
train

siempre viajo en tren I always travel by train

* *Si toda esta gente sube al tren, irá abarrotado.* If all these people get on the train, it'll be packed. *

Si toda esta gente sube al tren, irá abarrotado.

trigo

trigo
['triɣo] *n m*
wheat

trimestre

trimestre
[tri'mestre] *n m*
term

el primer trimestre del curso univer-sitario empieza en octubre the first term of the university year begins in October

...trimestre

...triste

triste
['triste] *adj*
sad

* *Sin Tintín estoy triste.* I'm sad without Tintin. *

Sin Tintín estoy triste.

► **tristeza**
[tris'teθa] *n f*
sadness

triunfo

triunfo
[tri'umfo] *n m*
triumph

tronco

?
La flecha fue a clavarse en el tronco.

...tronco

tronco
['tronko] *n m*
(tree) trunk, log

* *La flecha fue a clavarse en el tron-co.* The arrow landed in the tree trunk. *

tropa

tropa
['tropa] *n f*
troop

trotar

trotar
[tro'tar] *v i*
to trot

el caballo trotaba alegremente por el prado the horse trotted gaily around the field

► **trote**
[trote] *n m*
trot

ir al trote to trot

trozo

trozo
['troθo] *n n m*
piece

un trozo de carne a piece of meat

trueno

trueno
['trweno] *n m*
thunder,
thunderclap

...trueno

se oyó a lo lejos un trueno estruendoso there was a loud thunder-clap in the distance

tú

tú
[tu] *pron pers*
you

tú, ¿qué vas a ha-cer? what are you going to do?

tu

tu, tus
[tu, tus] *adj pos*
your

¿dónde está tu co-che? where's your car?

* *¡Ya está! ¡Ya tie-nes tu cola curada!* There you are! Your tail's better!
¡Estupendo! ¡Hasta puedo bailar! Great! I can even dance! *

...tu

tubo

tubo
['tuβo] *n m*
tube, pipe

túnel

túnel
['tunel] *n m*
tunnel

* *¡Por fin hemos salido del túnel!* At

...túnel

last we're out of the tunnel! *

ya han hecho el túnel de la Mancha they have made the Channel Tunnel

---

tupido

tupido, a
[tu'piðo, a] *adj*
thick, dense

turismo

turismo
[tu'rismo] *n m*
1. tourism

2. Idiom
están haciendo turismo they're travelling around

▶ **turista**
[tu'rista] *n*
tourist

los turistas sacan muchas fotos tourists take a lot of photos

turno

turno
['turno] *n m*
1. turn, shift

todavía no ha llegado tu turno it isn't your turn yet

turno de noche night shift

2. Idiom
farmacia de turno all-night chemist's

turrón

turrón
[tu'ron] *n m*
nougat

por Navidad comemos turrón at Christmas time we eat nougat

tuyo

tuyo, a, os, as
['tuǰo, a, os, as]
I. *adj pos*
your, of yours

un amigo tuyo a friend of yours

una camisa tuya a shirt of yours

II. *pron pos*
yours

* *Si me atreviera... ¡Tengo ganas de*

...tuyo

bailar contigo! ¡Dame la mano! If I dared... I feel like dancing with you! Give me your hand!
¡No! ¡Dame la tuya! ¡Venga, bailemos! No! Give me yours! Come on, let's dance! *

U V U V U

u

u
[u] *conj*
or *used instead of "o"
before the vowel "o"*

siete u ocho seven or
eight

último

último, a
['ultimo, a] *adj*
1. last

...último

la última vez the last
time

2. Idiom
por último lastly

umbral

umbral
[um'bral] *n m*
threshold, doorway

* *Esperan en el
umbral...* They are
waiting in the doorway... *

...umbral

Esperan en el umbral...

un

un, a, unos, as
[un, 'una, os, as]
art indet
a, some

un chico a boy

unos chicos some
boys

un ala a wing

*a unos cinco kilóme-
tros de aquí* some five
kilometres from here

...un

No me queda
más que una
botella de
whisky...

▶ **un, uno, a**
[un, 'uno, a]
adj & pron num
one

* *No me queda
más que una bo-
tella de whisky...*
I've only got one bottle
of whisky left... *

▶ **uno**
pron indet
one

uno nunca sabe

lo que va a pasar
one never knows what
is going to happen

▶ **uno, a, os, as**
pron indet
one *sing*, some *pl*

*unos están de
acuerdo, y otros
no* some agree and
others don't

▶ **cada uno, a**
['cada 'uno, a]
each one,

every one

▶ **unos(as) cuantos(as),
unos(as) pocos(as),**
['uno(as) 'kuantos(as)]
a few

▶ **uno(s) a otro(s),**
['unos a 'otros]
una(s) a otra(s)
['una(s) a 'otra(s)]
each other,
one another

único

único, a
['uniko, a] *adj*
1. only, sole

*lo único que quiero
es paz* the only thing I
want is peace

2. unique
* *¿Cuánto es?* How
much is it?
*Lo vendo bastante
caro porque se trata
de una pieza única.
Este barco data de
una época remota...*

...único

¿Cuánto es?

Lo vendo bastante caro porque se trata de una pieza única. Este barco data de una época remota...

I'm charging quite a lot because it's a unique item. This boat dates from remote times... *

universidad

universidad
[uniβersi'ðað] *n f*
university

uña

uña
['uɲa] *n f*
1. (finger/toe) nail

2. claw
el gato tiene que afilarse las uñas the cat has to sharpen its claws

urgente

urgente
[ur'xente] *adj*
urgent

usar

usar
[u'sar]
I. *v t*
to use, to employ

apenas uso el coche I hardly use the car

II. *v pr*
to be in use,
to be in fashion,
to be worn

el jubón ya no se usa the doublet is no longer worn

▶ **uso**
['uso] *n m*
use

de uso corriente in everyday use

▶ **usado, a**
[u'sado, a] *adj*
1. used

2. worn out

usted

usted, es
[us'teð, es] *pron pers*
you

* *Tiene usted unas amistades algo indeseables, caballero.* You have some rather undesirable friends, sir.
¡A usted no le conozco, pero sepa que no permitiré que hable mal del profesor Tornasol! I don't know you, but let me tell you I won't allow you

to run Professor Calculus down. *

útil

útil
['util] *adj*
useful

si le puedo ser útil en algo,... if I can help you at all,...

Tiene usted unas amistades algo indeseables, caballero.

¡A usted no le conozco, pero sepa que no permitiré que hable mal del profesor Tornasol!

...útil

▶ **utilidad**
[utili'ðað] *n f*
usefulness, utility

uva

uva
['uβa] *n f*
grape

un racimo de uva a bunch of grapes

vaca

vaca
['baka] *n f*
cow

vaca lechera dairy cow, milk cow

vacaciones

vacaciones
[baka'θjones] *n f pl*
holiday(s)

* *Me encanta ir de vacaciones a la montaña, ¿a ti no?* I love going on holiday in the mountains, don't you? *

Me encanta ir de vacaciones a la montaña, ¿a ti no?

vaciar

vaciar
[ba'θjar] *v t*
to empty

la policía vació el local the police cleared the premises

▶ **vacío, a**
[ba'θio, a] *adj*
empty

una botella vacía an empty bottle

vacilar

vacilar
[baθi'lar] *v i*
1. to wobble,
to totter

al dar con la pared, vaciló pero no cayó when he bumped into the wall, he tottered but did not fall

2. to hesitate
no vaciles; decídete ya don't hesitate; decide now

vago

vago, a
['baɣo, a] *adj*
1. vague

una vaga sensación de vértigo a vague feeling of dizziness

2. lazy
un alumno vago a lazy pupil

vagón

vagón
[baˈɣon] *n m*
(railway) carriage, coach, wagon

* *¡Ya está! ¡Ya he desenganchado el vagón!* That's it! I've unhooked the carriage! *¡Bravo!* Bravo! *

valer

valer, valerse
[baˈler, se]
I. *v i*
1. to be worth, to cost

no vale la pena it isn't worth it

¿cuánto vale? how much does it cost?/how much is it?

2. to be useful
esta tela vale para hacer cortinas this material is useful for making curtains

II. *v pr*
valerse de to make use of

se valió de un enchufe para conseguir el puesto he made use of a connection to get the job

▶ **vale**
[ˈbale] *interj*
(all) right, OK

valiente

valiente
[baˈljente] *adj*
brave

* *Debes ser valiente, Milú... No será muy largo.* You must be brave, Snowy... It won't be very long. *

valor

valor
[baˈlor] *n m*
1. value, worth

esta moneda es falsa; no tiene valor alguno it's a fake coin; it has no value

2. bravery, courage
armarse de valor to pluck up courage

valla

valla
[ˈbaʎa] *n f*
fence

valle

valle
[ˈbaʎe] *n m*
valley

un valle profundo a deep valley

vanidad

vanidad
[baniˈðað] *n f*
vanity

vaquero

vaquero
[baˈkero] *n m*
cowboy

▶ **vaqueros**
[baˈkeros] *n m pl*
jeans

variado

variado, a
[baˈrjaðo, a] *adj*
varied, assorted

fruta variada assorted fruit

▶ **variedad**
[barjeˈðað] *n f*
variety

* *Aquella noche hubo un espectáculo de variedades.* That night there was a variety show. *

Aquella noche hubo un espectáculo de variedades.

varios

varios, as
[ˈbarjos, as] *adj pl*
several, a number of

lo vimos varias veces we saw him several times

varón

varón
[baˈron] *adj & n m*
male, man, boy

...varón

tiene tres hijos, todos varones he has three children, all boys

vaso

vaso
['baso] *n m*
glass

un vaso para vino a wine glass

vecino

vecino, a
[be'θino, a]
I. *adj*
neighbouring

II. *n*
neighbour

vejez

vejez
[be'xeθ] *n f*
old age

...vejez

se murió de vejez he died of old age

vela

vela
['bela] *n f*
1. sail

2. Idiom
* *¡Mil millones de demonios! ¿Qué hace este barco de vela por estos para-*

...vela

¡Mil millones de demonios! ¿Qué hace este barco de vela por estos parajes?

...vela

jes? Billions of blue blistering barnacles! What's this sailing boat doing around here? *

3. candle

velocidad

velocidad
[beloθi'ðað] *n f*
speed

* *Piipp* Whizz

...velocidad

Corre a toda velocidad... No podré alcanzarlo...

veloz

veloz
[be'loθ] *adj*
rapid, fast, quick

una veloz carrera a quick sprint

vencedor

vencedor, a
[benθe'ðor, a]
I. *adj*
winning, victorious

II. *n*
winner, victor

▶ **vencer**
[ben'θer]
I. *v i*
to win

II. *v t*
to beat

vendedor

Es inútil insistir, caballeros, no lo quiero vender.

vendedor, a
[bende'ðor, a] *n*
seller, vendor, salesman *m*, salesgirl, saleswoman *f*

un vendedor de periódicos a newspaper vendor

▶ **vender**
[ben'der] *v i & v t*
to sell

Corre a toda velocidad... No podré alcanzarlo... He's running at full speed... I won't be able to catch him up... *

* *Es inútil insistir, caballeros, no lo quiero vender.* It's no use insisting, gentlemen; I don't want to sell it. *

vendimia

vendimia
[ben'dimja] *n f*
grape harvest, wine harvest

veneno

veneno
[be'neno] *n m*
poison

venganza

venganza
[ben'ganθa] *n f*
revenge, vengeance

▶ **vengar, vengarse**
[ben'gar, se]

...venganza

I. *v t*
to avenge

II. *v pr*
to take revenge

* *¡Rayos y truenos! ¡Me vengaré, miserables, y ese día, no os escaparéis...* Thundering typhoons! I'll take revenge, you wretches, and when that day comes, you won't get away... *

venir

venir
[be'nir] *v i*
1. to come

ven a verme come and see me

* *¡Ya vengo!... ¡Qué impaciencia!* I'm coming!... Such impatience! *

2. Idiom
me viene bien it's just right for me/it suits me

el mes que viene next month

venta

venta
['benta] *n f*
sale

ventaja

ventaja
[ben'taxa] *n f*
advantage

¿qué ventaja tiene esto? what's the advantage of this?

ventana

ventana
[ben'tana] *n f*
window

* *¡Lástima! Ya no los alcanzamos...* What a pity! We can't get them now...
La ventana da a la carretera. The window gives onto the road. *

▶ **ventanilla**
[benta'niʎa] *n f*
window

La ventana da a la carretera.

¿puedo sentarme cerca de la ventanilla? may I sit by the window?

ver

ver
[ber] *v t*
1. to see

¿ha visto a Milú? have you seen Snowy?

2. to watch
los niños están viendo la televisión the children are watching television

veranear

veranear
[berane'ar] *v i*
to spend the summer (holidays)

veranean en Cataluña they spend the summer in Catalonia

▶ **veraneante**
[berane'ante] *n*
holidaymaker

▶ **veraneo**
[bera'neo] *n m*
summer holidays

vamos de veraneo a la montaña we are going to the mountains for the summer holidays

▶ **verano**
[be'rano] *n m*
summer

de veras

(de) veras
[de'beras] *adv*
really

* *¡Dios mío! Lo siento de veras, Tintín...* Oh dear! I'm really sorry, Tintin...
Ya puede estar contento... Y ahora, ¿qué hacemos? I hope you're satisfied... Now what do we do? *

verdad

verdad
[ber'ðað] *n f*
1. truth

2. Idiom
es verdad it's true

¿verdad? isn't it?/don't we?/mustn't they?, etc

fuiste solo, ¿verdad? you went on your own, didn't you?

▶ **verdadero, a**
[ßerða'ðero, a] *adj*
true, genuine

verde

verde
['berðe] *adj*
green

* *El profesor lleva un abrigo verde.* The

...verde

El profesor lleva un abrigo verde.

Professor is wearing a green coat. *

verdura

verdura
[ßer'ðura] *n f*
greens
(green vegetables)

los niños deben comer verdura children must eat greens

vergüenza

¡Milú! ¡Me das vergüenza!

vergüenza
[ber'ɣwenθa] *n f*
1. shame, shamefulness

2. Idiom
dar vergüenza to make someone feel ashamed

* *¡Milú! ¡Me das vergüenza!* Snowy! I'm ashamed of you! *

verificar

verificar, se
[berifi'kar, se] *v t*
to check, to verify

hemos verificado el resultado we've checked the result

verso

verso
['berso] *n m*
verse

vestido

vestido
[bes'tiðo] *n m*
1. dress, clothing

2. dress, frock

▶ **vestir, vestirse**
[bes'tir, se]
I. *v t*
1. to dress,
to get dressed

viste a la niña get the girl dressed

...vestido

2. to wear,
to dress in
* *¡Irma!* Irma!
¿Mande señora?
Yes, ma'am?
Irma viste siempre de negro Irma always wears black/dresses in black. *

II. *v pr*
to dress (oneself),
to get dressed

Irma viste siempre de negro.

vez

vez
[beθ] *n f*
1. time

tres veces al día
three times a day

2. Idiom
una vez once

dos veces twice

a veces, algunas veces sometimes

de vez en cuando
from time to time

muchas veces (very) often

lo he visto muchas veces I have often seen it

en vez de instead of

¿por qué no me ayudas en vez de ver la televisión? why don't you help me instead of watching television?

tal vez perhaps

tal vez no venga
perhaps he won't come

cada vez más → *más*

cada vez menos → *menos*

por última vez last

¿cuándo esquiaste por última vez? when did you last ski?

vía

vía
[ˈbía] n f
track, line

* *Estos bandidos me han atado sólidamente a la vía férrea. Por más que lo intento, no consigo desatarme...* These bandits have tied me firmly to the track. However hard I try, I can't unfasten myself... *

viajar

...viajar

viajar
[bjaˈxar] v i
to travel

▶ **viaje**
[ˈbjaxe] n m
journey, trip

* *Adiós, Tintín. ¡Buen viaje y que le vaya bien!* Goodbye, Tintin. Have a good journey and I hope everything goes well! *Es un joven reportero que va a hacer un viaje por África...* He's a young reporter who's going on a trip round Africa... *

está de viaje he's away on a trip

víbora

víbora
[ˈbiβora] n f
viper

víctima

víctima
[ˈbiktima] n f
victim, casualty

* *¡Qué suerte! No ha habido ninguna víctima.* That was lucky! There are no casualties. *

victoria

...victoria

victoria
[bik'torja] n f
victory

* ¡Bravo! ¡Es una
victoria bien mereci-
da!... ¡Un aplauso pa-
ra los campeones!
Bravo! It's a well-deserved
victory!... Three cheers for
the champions! *

vid

vid
[bið] n f
vine

vida

vida
['biða] n f
life

llevamos una vida
ajetreada we lead a
hectic life

vidrio

vidrio
['biðrjo] n m
glass

vidrio de color stained
glass

viejo

...viejo

viejo, a
['bjexo, a] adj
old

* Bienvenidos a
nuestro monasterio.
Pero... ¿qué lleva
en las manos?
Welcome to our monas-
tery. But... what have you
got in your hands?
Unos zapatos vie-
jos... A pair of old
shoes... *

viento

Soplaba un viento violento.

viento
['bjento] n m
wind

* ¡Eh! Ooh!
Soplaba un viento
violento. There was a
wild wind. *

vientre

vientre
['bjentre] n m
stomach

...vientre

me duele el
vientre I have
stomach ache

viernes

viernes
['bjernes] n m
Friday

los viernes co-
memos pescado
we eat fish on Friday

vigilar

vigilar
[bixi'lar] v t
to watch,
to keep an eye on

* ¡Vigile los tejados!
Watch the roofs!
¡Bien jefe! Yes, boss! *

▶**vigilante**
[bixi'lante] n m
watchman, guard,
warder, warden

vigilante nocturno
night watchman

...vigilar

villancico

villancico
[biʎan'θiko] n m
carol

cantaron villancicos
ante el belén they
sang carols round the crib

vinagre

vinagre
[bi'naɣre] n m
vinegar

vino

vino
['bino] n m
wine

vino tinto red wine

vino rosado/clarete
rosé wine

viña

viña
['biɲa] n f
vineyard

violencia

violencia
[bio'lenθja] n f
violence

ha habido un au-
mento de la violen-
cia callejera there has
been an increase in street
violence

violín

...virgen

violín
[bjo'lin] *n m*
violin

toca el violín en la orquesta she plays violin in the orchestra

virgen

virgen
['birxen] *adj & n f*
virgin

* *En la selva virgen...* In the virgin forest... *

visita

visita
[bi'sita] *n f*
visit

hacer una visita to pay a visit

▶ **visitar**
[bisi'tar] *v t*
to visit

* *Desearíamos visitar el templo...* We'd like to visit the temple... *

víspera

víspera
['bispera] *n f*
eve, day before, evening before

la víspera de Navidad Christmas Eve

vista

vista
['bista] *n f*
1. (eye)sight

...vista

tiene buena vista he has good eyesight

tener una vista de lince to have keen eyesight, to be eagle eyed

2. Idiom
hacer la vista gorda to turn a blind eye

¡hasta la vista! see you again!/so long!

3. view
* *Esta vista del mar es magnífica...* This

view of the sea is magnificent... *

4. Idiom
en vista de esto in view of this

un piso con vistas al mar a flat overlooking the sea

▶ **vistazo**
[bis'taθo] *n m*
glance, look

echar un vistazo to have a look

...vista

Esta vista del mar es magnífica...

vivienda

vivienda
[bi'βjenða] *n f*
housing, accommodation, house

vivir

vivir
[bi'βir] *v i*
to live

...vivir

¡Alabado sea Dios!
¡Está vivo!

vivimos aquí desde el año pasado we've been living here since last year

▶ **vivo, a**
['biβo, a] *adj*
1. living, live, alive

* **¡Alabado sea Dios! ¡Está vivo!** God be praised! He's alive! *

2. lively

3. sharp, clever

volar

volar
[bo'lar]
I. *v t*
to blow up

II. *v i*
to fly

III. *v pr*
to fly away,
to get blown away

* **¡La tienda se nos vuela!...** The tent is getting blown away!... *

¡La tienda se nos vuela!...

volcar

volcar, volcarse
[bol'kar, se]
I. *v t*
to upset,
to overturn

II. *v pr*
to fall, to tip over

* **¿Podrá evitar que se vuelquen las botellas?** Will he be able to stop the bottles from tipping over? *

¿Podrá evitar que se vuelquen las botellas?

volumen

volumen
[bo'lumen] *n m*
volume

ha puesto la radio a todo volumen he's put the radio on at full volume

▶ **voluminoso, a**
[bolumi'noso, a] *adj*
voluminous, bulky

voluntad

voluntad
[bolun'tað] *n f*
will, willpower

tiene mucha voluntad he has a great deal of willpower

▶ **voluntario, a**
[bolun'tarjo, a]
I. *adj*
voluntary

II. *n*
volunteer

volver

volver
[bol'βer]
I. *v i*
1. to go back,
to come back,
to return

* **¡Milú, volvamos a Moulinsart!** Snowy, let's go back to Marlinspike! *

2. Idiom
volveré a llamar I'll call back

¡Milú, volvamos a Moulinsart!

II. *v t*
1. to turn over,
to turn inside out

2. Idiom
me volvió la espalda he turned his back on me

III. *v pr*
1. to turn round

2. to become,
to turn

vosotros

...Y vosotros ¿por qué no me ayudáis a buscar la botella?

Es inútil, señor, el yeti se la ha llevado.

...vosotros

vosotros, as
[bo'sotros, as] *pron pers*
you

* *...Y vosotros, ¿por qué no me ayudáis a buscar la botella?*
...And you, why don't you help me to look for the bottle?
Es inútil, señor; el yeti se la ha llevado.
It's no use, sir; the yeti has taken it. *

votar

votar
[bo'tar] *v i & v t*
to vote

voten por el mejor candidato vote for the best candidate

▶ **voto**
['boto] *n m*
1. vote

2. vow
el voto de pobreza
the vow of poverty

voz

voz
[boθ] *n f*
1. voice

hablar en voz alta to talk in a loud voice

2. shout, cry

3. Idiom
dar voces to shout

* *¡Aaaaaaaay!*
Ooooooooow!
¡Oooooooh! Oooooooh!
¿Quién da estas voces? Who's shouting? *

¿ Quién da estas voces ?

vuelo

vuelo
['bwelo] *n m*
1. flight

* *Los pasajeros del vuelo 802 desembarcan...* The passengers on flight 802 are disembarking... *

2. Idiom
alzar/levantar el vuelo to take flight

vuelta

vuelta
['bwelta] *n f*
1. walk, stroll

* *¡Vamos a dar una vuelta por la ciudad!*
Let's go for a walk around the city!
¡Con mucho gusto!
With pleasure! *

2. return journey
la vuelta será más rápida the return journey will be quicker

...vuelta

3. change
quédese con la vuelta keep the change

4. Idiom
un billete de ida y vuelta a return ticket

vuestro

vuestro, a, os, as
['bwestro, a, os, as]
I. *adj pos*
your, of yours

...vuestro

* *¡Dejad vuestros caballos aquí! Y tú, estate al tanto...* Leave your horses here! And you, keep an eye on things...
Pero, ¿qué están preparando? What are they up to? *

II. *pron pos*
yours

mi casa es más pequeña que la vuestra my house is smaller than yours

vulgar

vulgar
[bul'ɣar] *adj*
vulgar, common

W X Y Z

windsurf

windsurf
[win'sərf] *n m*
windsurfing

xenófobo

xenófobo, a
[se'nofoβo, a]
I. *adj*
xenophobic

II. *n*
xenophobe

xilófono

xilófono
[si'lofono] *n m*
xylophone

y

y
[i] *conj*
and

indios y vaqueros
cowboys and Indians

ya

Ya no llueve.

...ya

ya
[ĵ(dʒ)a]
I. *adv*
1. already

ya lo he hecho I've
already done it

2. now
vamos a hacerlo ya
let's do it now

3. Idiom
ya no no longer, not any
longer, no more, not any
more

* *Ya no llueve.* It's not
raining any more. *

¡ya está! that's it!

¡ya lo sé! I know that!

II. *conj*
ya que since, as

*no puede salir ya
que esta enferma*
she can't go out since
she's ill

yema

yema
[ĵ(dʒ)ema] *n f*
1. yolk

la yema del huevo
the yolk of the egg

2. fingertip

3. bud, shoot
*las yemas apare-
cidas en las ramas
de los árboles* the
shoots on the boughs of
the trees

yeso

yeso
[ĵ(dʒ)eso] *n m*
plaster

*le quitarán el yeso
de la pierna el
viernes*
they'll take the plaster off
his leg on Friday

yo

yo
[ĵ(dʒ)o] *pron pers*
I, me

yo creo que sí I think
so

soy yo it's me

zaguán

zaguán
[θa'ɣwan] *n m*
entrance, hall

...zaguán

Si no le importa, esperaré al capitán en el zaguán.

* **Si no le importa, esperaré al capitán en el zaguán.** If you don't mind, I'll wait for the Captain in the hall! *

zambullirse

zambullirse
[θambu'ʎirse] v pr
to dive, to plunge

* **Tintín se ha zambullido.** Tintin has dived into the water. *

...zambullirse

Tintín se ha zambullido.

zanahoria

zanahoria
[θana'orja] n f
carrot

zanahorias ralladas
grated carrots

zapato

zapato
[θa'pato] n m
shoe

...zapato

¡Rayos y truenos! No sé qué pasa... No consigo ponerme los zapatos...

CRAC

* **¡Rayos y truenos! No sé qué pasa... No consigo ponerme los zapatos...** Thundering typhoons! What's going on?... I can't get my shoes on... *Crac* Snap *

▶ **zapatilla**
[θapa'tiʎa] n f
slipper

zarzuela

zarzuela
[θar'θwela] n f
operetta, zarzuela

zona

zona
['θona] n f
zone, area

* **Es una zona prohibida.** It's a prohibited area. *

...zona

Es una zona prohibida.

zoo

zoo
['θoo] n m
zoo

vamos con los niños al zoo let's take the children to the zoo

zorro

zorro
[θo'ro] n
fox

zumbar

zumbar
[θum'bar] v i
to buzz, to hum, to drone

▶ **zumbido**
[θum'biðo] n m
buzz(ing), hum(ming), drone, whirring

oímos el zumbido del helicóptero por encima de nuestras cabezas we heard the helicopter whirring above our heads

zumo

zumo
['θumo] n m
juice

zumo de melocotón peach juice

zurcir

zurcir
[θur'θir] v t
to darn

se sentó a zurcir calcetines she sat down to darn socks

zurdo

zurdo, a
['θurðo, a] adj
left-handed

GRAMÁTICA INGLESA

ABREVIATURAS

S = sujeto
Aux = verbo auxiliar (*have, do*) o auxiliar modal (*must, should*)
V = forma base del verbo (infinitivo sin *to*)
PP = participio pasado
Adj = adjetivo
Sust = sustantivo
CV = complemento (objeto) verbal
Ø = indica que no hay palabra en este lugar en la frase

EL VERBO

FORMAS

La forma afirmativa

Be* y *have got
I am, you are, he/she/it is, we/you/they are. I/you have got, he/she/it has got, we/you/they have got.

• S + *be* + Adj/Sust
He is happy.
Es feliz.
Tintin is a reporter.
Tintín es reportero.
• S + *have got* + Sust
He has got a camera.
Tiene una máquina de fotografiar.

S + *have* + PP
He has seen that film.
Ha visto esa película.
She has taken her umbrella.
Ha cogido el paraguas.

S + Aux + V (+ *ing*)
• S + Aux + V + *ing*
He is playing in the garden.
Está jugando en el jardín.

• S + Aux + V
He can swim very well.
Sabe nadar muy bien.
• S + Ø + V
They get up at seven o'clock every morning.
Se levantan cada mañana a las siete.

La forma interrogativa

Be* y *have got
• *Be* + S + Adj/Sust
Is he happy?
¿Es feliz?
• *Have* + S + *got* + Sust
Has Tintin got a camera?
¿Tiene máquina de fotografiar Tintín?

***Have* + S + PP**
Have you finished the work?
¿Has terminado el trabajo?

Aux + S + V
• *Be* + S + V + *ing*
Are they playing football?
¿Están jugando al fútbol?
• Aux + S + V
Can you swim?
¿Sabes nadar?
• La forma interrogativa de las estructuras del tipo S + Ø + V se construye con el verbo auxiliar *do* (tercer persona singular *does*, pasado *did*).
Do they get up at seven o'clock?
¿Se levantan a las siete?
Did they get up at seven o'clock?
¿Se levantaron (levantaban) a las siete?

La forma negativa

Be* y *have got
• S + *be* + *not*
I am not, you are not (you aren't), he/she/it is not (he/she/it isn't), we/you/they are not (we/you/they aren't)
Captain Haddock is not a reporter.
El capitán Haddock no es reportero.

• S + *have not, has not* (**haven't, hasn't**) + *got*
Snowy hasn't got a camera.
Snowy no tiene máquina de fotografiar.

S + *have not, has not* (haven't, hasn't) + PP
He hasn't taken his umbrella.
No ha cogido el paraguas.

S + Aux + *not* + V (+ *ing*)
• S + Aux + *not* + V + *ing*
Abdallah isn't playing in the garden.
Abdallah no está jugando en el jardín.
• S + Aux + *not* + V
He can't (cannot) swim very well.
No sabe nadar muy bien.
• La forma negativa de las estructuras del tipo S + Ø + V se construye con el verbo auxiliar do (tercer persona singular *does*, pasado *did*).
They don't get up at seven o'clock.
No se levantan a las siete.

TIEMPO Y ASPECTO

Cuando se hace referencia en inglés a una acción o situación que se está desarrollando en el momento presente, o sea, cuando se describe el aspecto durativo de una acción o situación, se emplea la forma progresiva del verbo (p. ej. *I'm playing*) y no la forma simple (*play*). Esta norma rige para todos los tiempos del verbo, y no sólo el presente (p. ej. *I was playing*, frente a *I played*).

La forma simple

El presente simple
• Todas las personas emplean la forma base del verbo, menos la tercera singular, que agrega -*s* a la forma base:

*I give, you give, he give**s**.*
Doy, das, da.

Para *to be* y *to have*, ver arriba.
El presente simple en inglés se emplea para describir acciones o situaciones habituales; por lo tanto, se acompaña a menudo por los adverbios de frecuencia, como *always*, *never*, *often*, *usually*.
*Captain Haddock **lives** in Marlinspike.*
El capitán Haddock vive en Moulinsart.

El pasado simple

• V + *ed* para todas las personas en el caso de los verbos regulares. Se emplea este tiempo para hacer referencia a acciones o situaciones habituales en el pasado. También se usa para hablar de acciones concluidas o situaciones que han cambiado.
*When he was a child, Brian liv**ed** in London.*
Cuando era niño, Brian vivía en Londres.
• Las formas interrogativa y negativa son iguales que las del presente, pero se emplea *did* en vez de *do*:
*Did you play football yesterday? No, I **didn't**; I played tennis.*
¿Jugaste al fútbol ayer? No, jugué al tenis.

La forma progresiva (formas en *ing*)

El presente progresivo

• Se forma con *be* + V + *ing*.
Describe una acción o situación que está en vías de desarrollo:
*What **are** you **doing**? I'm **having** a bath.*
¿Qué haces? Estoy tomando un baño.
• Esta forma verbal se emplea también para hablar del futuro:
*I'm **going** to London tomorrow.*
Mañana me voy a Londres.

El pasado progresivo

• Se forma con el pasado de *be* + V + *ing* y describe una acción o situación que estaba en vías de desarrollo en el pasado. Dicha acción o situación constituye el trasfondo de otras acciones de mayor importancia.
*I **was having** a bath when the telephone rang.*
Tomaba un baño cuando sonó el teléfono.
*What **were** you **doing** at eight o'clock yesterday?*

• Para las formas interrogativa y negativa, ver "Formas" (arriba).

Have + PP

El pretérito perfecto: *Have* + PP
• Se emplea este tiempo verbal en inglés para hablar de una acción o situación sin hacer referencia al momento preciso de su desarrollo, y cuando dicha acción o situación sigue rigiendo en el presente:
*I'**ve already read** this book.*
Ya he leído este libro.
*I can't open the door. I'**ve lost** the key.*
No puedo abrir la puerta. He perdido la llave.
• Se emplea el pretérito perfecto con *since* o *for*, y no el presente, para indicar el tiempo durante el cual se ha prolongado una acción:
*He'**s worked** in this factory since 1965.*
Trabaja en esta fábrica desde 1965.
*I'**ve known** him for three years.*
Hace tres años que lo conozco.

El pretérito pluscuamperfecto: *Had* + PP
El pluscuamperfecto sitúa una acción anterior a otra en el pasado:
*When I **had had** a shower, I dressed.*
Cuando me había duchado, me vestí.

El pretérito perfecto y el pretérito pluscuamperfecto: forma progresiva:
Have + *been* + V + *ing*
Had + *been* + V + *ing*
• Aunque tanto la forma simple como la forma progresiva pueden emplearse para describir acciones o estados que siguen rigiendo, se prefiere la forma progresiva cuando se trata de hechos de naturaleza no permanente:
*He'**s been standing** on the corner all day.*
Se ha estado en la esquina todo el día.
Compárense:
*The castle **has stood** on the hill for nine centuries.*
El castillo se ha elevado sobre la colina durante nueve siglos.
• La forma progresiva de estos tiempos verbales se emplea también para hacer referencia a las causas de un estado determinado, o para hacer hincapié en la intensidad o repetición de una acción:
*He'**s sweating** - he'**s been running**.*
Está sudando. Ha estado corriendo.
*I'**ve been writing** letters all morning.*
Llevo toda la mañana escribiendo cartas.

LOS VERBOS MODALES

Estos verbos se emplean para hacer referencia a hechos de carácter dudoso; no se usan para describir hechos que sabemos se han producido con toda seguridad. Se trata de verbos invariables (a excepción de have to), que no llevan una -s en la tercera persona singular del presente. Para la forma interrogativa y negativa, véase "Formas" (arriba).

Obligación = *must/have to* + V

*You **must visit** your grandparents.*
Debes visitar a tus abuelos.
*He **has to work** hard at the factory.*
Tiene que trabajar mucho en la fábrica.
• A diferencia de *must*, que se emplea para hablar de obligaciones que uno mismo se impone, *have to* hace referencia a obligaciones que proceden de otra persona o una institución ajena. *Must* sólo existe en el presente; su infinitivo es *have to* (Tendré que... = *I'll have to...*) y la forma de pasado es *had to* (tuve/tenía que... = *I had to*).
• La prohibición se expresa a través de *mustn't* + V
*You **mustn't eat** that: it's poisonous.*
No debes comer eso: es venenoso.
• La ausencia de obligación se expresa con *needn't* (o *don't need to*), *haven't got to* (o *don't have to*):
*We **needn't leave** yet. There's plenty of time.*
No hace falta que nos vayamos todavía. Tenemos mucho tiempo.

Consejo y recomendación = *should* + V o *ought to* + V

*If you are tired, you **should go** to bed.*
Si estás cansado, deberías acostarte.
• Las formas de pasado son *should* + *have* + PP y *ought to* + *have* + PP, y se utilizan para expresar un reproche:
*You **should have told** me before.*
Deberías habérmelo dicho antes.

Capacidad = *can* + V

*He **can swim** very well.*
Sabe nadar muy bien.
• En el pasado se emplea *could*, y en el

condicional *could* o *would be able to*. La forma de infinitivo es *be able to* (PP *been able to*).

Permiso = *may/can* + V

*When you've finished eating, you **may/can leave**.*
Cuando hayais acabado de comer, podéis iros.
• El pasado de *may* es *might*. La forma de infinitivo para expresar permiso es *be allowed to*:
*I don't think I'll **be allowed to play** football tomorrow.*
No creo que me dejen jugar al fútbol mañana.

Futuridad = *will* + V

*We'll **be** in London next week.*
La semana que viene estaremos en Londres.
• La forma negativa de will es *won't*.
• El futuro se expresa también con *be going to*, sobre todo cuando se trata de la intención del sujeto o de una acción premeditada. Compárense:
*We've no coffee. Don't worry; I'**ll get** some.* (reaccion)
No tenemos café. No te preocupes; ya compraré.
*We've no coffee. Don't worry; I'**m going to** get some.* (premeditado : ya sabía yo que no teníamos café)
No tenemos café. No te preocupes; ya compraré.
• El futuro se expresa también con el presente progresivo cuando se trata de un suceso planeado de antemano con seguridad, y que se considera prácticamente irreversible.
*I'**m seeing** Tintin tomorrow.*
Mañana voy a ver a Tintín.

Condicionalidad = *would* + V

*If I could, I **would go** with you.*
Si pudiese, iría con usted.
• Pasado: *would + have + PP*
*If I had been able to, I **would have gone** with you.*
Si hubiese podido, habría ido con usted.

Sugerencias, ofrecimientos = *shall* + V

Shall we go?
¿Vámonos?
Shall I make you some tea?
¿Le hago un poco de té?

Peticiones = *will/can/could* + V

*Will/Can/Could you **open** the window?*
¿Quieres/Puedes/Podrías abrir la ventana?

Probabilidad = *must/may/ might/could* + V

*He **must be working**.*
Debe de estar trabajando/Estará trabajando.
*It **may/might/could rain**.*
Puede que llueva.

Pasado: *must/may/might/ could + have + PP*

*He **must have got lost**.*
Debe de haberse perdido.
*He **may have got lost**.*
Puede que se haya perdido.

EL GERUNDIO

Aparte de su uso en la formación de las formas progresivas del verbo, el gerundio (la forma verbal que termina en *ing*) desempeña también en inglés una función sustantiva y adjetiva:
Smoking is bad for you. (función sustantiva, sujeto)
Fumar es perjudicial.
I don't like smoking. (función sustantiva, complemento)
No me gusta fumar/que la gente fume.
a smoking cigarette (función adjetiva)
un cigarrillo encendido/humeante
She is fond of smoking. (objeto de preposición)
Es aficionada a fumar.

LA VOZ PASIVA

La voz pasiva es de uso muy frecuente en inglés, y corresponde a menudo a la pasiva refleja (se vende, se ve, etc) en español.
Se forma con los diferentes tiempos del verbo *be* + PP.
• El complemento agente se introduce por *by*, pero no se expresa siempre. Compárense:
*The cathedral **was built by** Wren.*
La catedral fue construida por Wren.
*The house **was** blown down (by the wind).*
La casa fue derribada (por el viento).
• Si un verbo se acompaña por preposición, dicha preposición aparecerá en la voz pasiva:
*The children were **well looked after**.*
Los niños fueron bien cuidados.
• Cuando hay dos complementos verbales, el complemento indirecto de un verbo en la voz activa puede aparecer como sujeto de una frase en la voz pasiva:
*Somebody gave him a present → He **was given** a present.*
Alguien le dio un regalo → Le dieron un regalo.
• Las frases en la voz pasiva pueden construirse con un verbo modal:
*He **must be driven** to hospital.*
Hay que llevarlo al hospital.

EL SUSTANTIVO

Los sustantivos en inglés pueden ser contables o no contables. Si son contables, poseen una forma de plural: *a house → two houses*. Los no contables suelen ser invariables, es decir, no tienen forma de plural: *butter, milk, music, happiness*. Estos no pueden ir precedidos del artículo indeterminado.
Hay sustantivos que pertenecen a ambas categorías: *paper*, papel, *a paper*, un periódico, *work*, trabajo, *a work*, una obra.

El plural

• El plural de los sustantivos en inglés se forma agregando una *s* al singular, o *es* si el sustantivo termina en *s*, *ss*, *sh*, *ch*, *tch*, *x*, y a veces *o*: *cat-s, house-s, bus-es, kiss-es, dish-es, peach-es, patch-es, box-es, tomato-es*.
f final cambia a *ves*: *knife → knives, thief → thieves*.
y final cambia a *ies* despues de una consonante: *city → cities, ferry → ferries*.
• Los siguientes sustantivos tienen una forma de plural irregular:
child → children, man → men, foot → feet.

Para otras formas irregulares, véase un buen diccionario.

El género

Para referirnos a las personas en inglés, empleamos *he* (masculino) y *she* (femenino). Plural: *they* (masculino/ femenino).
El pronombre correspondiente a los objetos es *it*, forma que también se emplea a veces para hablar de los bebés. En ocasiones se emplea el femenino *she* para hablar de coches, motocicletas, barcos y navíos, etc, y también de países:
*He loves Spain – **her** culture, **her** history, etc.*
Ama a España – su cultura, su historia, ...

LOS ARTÍCULOS

El artículo determinado *the*

El artículo determinado se omite con los sustantivos plurales contables y los sustantivos singulares no contables, vayan o no acompañados de adjetivos, cuando la referencia es genérica:
I like Spanish literature.
Disfruto con la literatura española. (= toda en general)
Houses are expensive.
Las casas están caras. (= todas en general)

El artículo indeterminado *a, an*, y el adjetivo indefinido *some*

• Se emplea la forma *an* delante de vocal o *h* muda: *an apple, an hour, an honest man* (pero *a hotel*).
• Se emplea el artículo indeterminado para hablar de los oficios y profesiones:
*He's **an** architect; she's **a** doctor.*
El es arquitecto; ella es médica.
• No se emplea el artículo indeterminado

ante los sustantivos no contables:
It is of great importance.
Tiene una gran importancia.
• La forma *some* se utiliza con los sustantivos singulares no contables y los sustantivos plurales contables para expresar una cantidad o número indefinido:
*Would you like **some** more lemonade y some more sweets?*
¿Quieres algo más de gaseosa y unos cuantos caramelos más?

Los demostrativos

• Singular: *this*, éste, a, o ; *that*, ese, a, o/ aquél, aquella, o; plural: *these*, estos, as, *those*, esos, as/aquellos, as.
***This** car is better than **that** one.*
Este coche es mejor que aquél.
*Don't do **that**.*
No hagas eso.

Cuantificadores

• Con los sustantivos contables:
too many = demasiados, as
a lot of, lots of, plenty of, many = muchos, as
some, a few = unos cuantos, unas cuantas, algunos, as
some more = unos cuantos más, unas cuantas más
• Con los sustantivos no contables:
too much = demasiado, a
a lot of, lots of, much = mucho, a
some = algo de, un poco de
some more = algo más de
a little = un poco de
• Obsérvese que *much* y *many* se emplean sobre todo en las frases afirmativas o interrogativas.
• *Any* se emplea sobre todo en las frases interrogativas o negativas:
*Did you buy **any** vegetables?*
¿Compraste legumbres?
*I haven't got **any** money.*
No tengo dinero.
En las frases afirmativas, *any* significa cualquiera, cualesquiera :
*Come **any** day.*
Ven cualquier día.
• *Some* suele emplearse en las frases afirmativas. Se usa en las frases interro-

gativas cuando se espera la respuesta *yes:*
*Would you like **some** tea?*
¿Quieres un poco de té?

Los posesivos

Los adjetivos posesivos, que son invariables, son : *my*, mi(s) ; *your*, tu(s), vuestro, a, os, as, su(s) (de usted(es)) ; *his*, su de él ; *her*, su de ella ; *its*, su (de él/ ella/o) ; *our*, nuestro, a, os, as ; *their*, su de ellos, as.
His se emplea para sujetos masculinos, *her* para sujetos femeninos, y *its* hace referencia a los otros sujetos (animales, objetos):
*John and **his** dog.*
John y su perro.
*Mary has lost **her** watch.*
Mary ha perdido su reloj.
Obsérvese el uso del posesivo en inglés cuando se hace referencia a partes del cuerpo o a prendas de vestir:
*He put **his** hand in **his** pocket.*
Se metió la mano en el bolsillo.
*The cat hurt **its** foot.*
El gato se hizo daño en la pata.

El caso posesivo

• Para expresar relaciones del tipo de el coche de mi padre y los juguetes de los niños, se emplea el caso posesivo en inglés:
my father's car, the children's toys.
Obsérvese que el primero de los dos sustantivos es el poseedor, y se marca con *'s*. En el caso de los sustantivos plurales que terminan en *-s*, se agrega sólo el apóstrofe:
The girls' father.
El padre de las chicas.
• Aunque esta construcción se utiliza principalmente cuando el poseedor es un ser viviente, también hay expresiones de tiempo que usan el caso posesivo :
today's date la fecha de hoy ; *an hour's journey* un viaje de una hora.

El adjetivo calificativo

El adjetivo en inglés es siempre invariable y se coloca delante del sustantivo : *three big houses* tres casas grandes.

Formación

• Algunos adjetivos se forman a partir del sustantivo mediante el sufijo *-ful* :
use → *useful* (útil), *help* → *helpful* (servicial).

Algunos adjetivos negativos terminan en *-less* :
careless descuidado, *worthless* sin valor.

Hay también adjetivos negativos con el prefijo *un-* : *unhappy* infeliz, *untidy* desordenado, *unfair* injusto.

• Los adjetivos compuestos
Estos adjetivos se forman de dos maneras principales:
Adj + V + *ed*
A fair-haired boy
Un chico rubio
Adj + V + *ing*
A good-looking woman
Una mujer guapa

La comparación de adjetivos

• El comparativo
– A los adjetivos cortos se les agrega la terminación *-er* :
He's taller and fatter than me.
El es más alto y gordo que yo.
Obsérvese la duplicación de la consonante final de *fat*.
Los adjetivos terminados en *-y* cambian la *-y* por *i*:
pretty → *prettier*, *dirty* → *dirtier*.
– Los adjetivos largos forman el comparativo con *more*:
This book is more interesting than that one.
Este libro es más interesante que aquél.
– Hay algunas formas comparativas irregulares :
good → *better*, *bad* → *worse*, *far* → *further/farther*, *old* → *elder/older*, *much/many* → *more*, *little* → *less*.
– Para indicar parecido entre dos entidades, empleamos la construcción *as* + Adj + *as*. La forma negativa es *not as/so* + Adj + *as* o *less* + Adj + *than*.
He is as clever as his brother.
El es tan inteligente como su hermano.
He isn't as/so clever as his brother.
El no es tan inteligente como su hermano.
He is less clever than his brother.
El es menos inteligente que su hermano.

• El superlativo
– A los adjetivos cortos se les agrega la terminación *-est* :
He's the tallest and fattest boy in the class.

Obsérvese el uso de *in* en la frase inglesa.
– Los adjetivos largos forman el superlativo con *most* :
the most beautiful landscape in the world
el paisaje más hermoso del mundo
Para modificaciones ortográficas al sufijar *-est*, véase el comparativo.
– Hay algunos superlativos irregulares:
good → *best*, *bad* → *worst*, *far* → *farthest/furthest*, *old* → *oldest/eldest*, *much/many* → *most*, *little* → *least*.

El pronombre

El sustituto *one*
One (plural: *ones*) se emplea a menudo para evitar la repetición de un sustantivo:
The red pen and the blue one
El bolígrafo rojo y el azul
A big box and two small ones
Una caja grande y dos pequeñas.

Los pronombres personales
• Los pronombres personales sujeto son:
I, you, he, she, it, we, you, they.
• Los pronombres personales complemento son:
me, you, him, her, it, us, you, them.
Cuando el complemento directo es un sustantivo y el indirecto un pronombre, éste se suele colocar delante del directo:
I gave him a present.
Le di un regalo.
Si hay dos pronombres, el directo suele preceder al indirecto, que se introduce con *to* :
I gave it to him.
Se lo di.

Los pronombres posesivos
Mine, yours, his, hers, ours, theirs.
A excepción de *mine*, tienen la forma del adjetivo posesivo (véase) + s.
This book is his and that one is hers.
Este libro es suyo (de él) y ése es suyo (de ella).

Los pronombres reflexivos
Myself, yourself, himself, herself, itself, ourselves, yourselves, themselves.
En comparación con el español, los pronombres reflexivos se emplean relativamente poco en inglés.
Did yoy enjoy yourselves?
¿Lo pasasteis bien?

Los pronombres indefinidos
• Las normas sobre el uso de *some* y *any* como adjetivos rigen también en su función pronominal (véase el sustantivo, los cuantificadores). Los compuestos *somebody, anybody*, etc, que a continuación se detallan, también se rigen por estas normas.
somebody/someone, alguien, *something*, algo, *somewhere*, en alguna parte
anybody/anyone, anything, anywhere
I can't find my purse anywhere.
No encuentro el monedero en ninguna parte.
• Las formas negativas absolutas de *some* y sus compuestos son *no, nobody/no-one, nothing y nowhere*, y se emplean solos o delante del verbo:
Where are you going? Nowhere.
¿Adónde vas? A ninguna parte.
No-one knows.
Nadie lo sabe.
Obsérvese la forma *everybody/everyone* = todo el mundo (*every* = cada).

Los pronombres interrogativos

Para las personas:
who, who(m), whose
• *Who* es la forma de sujeto:
Who are you?
¿Quién eres?
• *Who(m)* es la forma de complemento:
Who(m) are you calling?
¿A quién llamas?
• *Whose*, que funciona tanto de adjetivo como pronombre, es el posesivo:
Whose book is this?/Whose is this book?
¿De quién es este libro?

Para las cosas:
what (pronombre y adjetivo)
What's going on?
¿Qué pasa?
What day can you come?
¿Qué día puede venir?
Cuando se trata de una elección entre dos o tres posibilidades, la pregunta se formula con *which* (pronombre y adjetivo ; para personas y cosas) :
Which day can you come, Tuesday or Wednesday?
¿Qué día puede venir, el martes o el miércoles?